THE ROUGH GUIDE TO
MYANMAR (BURMA)

ROUGH GUIDES

this second editio
Stuart Butler,

Contents

Introduction to
Myanmar (Burma)

Until recently the least-known nation in Southeast Asia, Myanmar is finally getting the attention it deserves. For half a century, the country languished in self-imposed obscurity under the rule of its despotic and enigmatic military rulers, little visited and even less understood. All that is now changing, and with breathtaking speed. Following recent economic and political upheavals, the national landscape is being transformed in ways that were unimaginable even a few years ago, and visitors have begun flocking to Myanmar in unprecedented numbers.

Ironically, it's precisely these decades of suffocating political isolation, combined with economic stagnation, that have helped preserve much of Myanmar's magically **time-warped character** into the twenty-first century (albeit at a terrible human cost). The old Burma immortalized by Kipling and Orwell is still very much in evidence today: this remains a land of a thousand gilded pagodas, of ramshackle towns and rustic villages populated with innumerable red-robed monks and locals dressed in flowing, sarong-like longyi, their faces smeared in colourful swirls of traditional *thanaka*. It's a place in which life still revolves around the temple and the teahouse, and where the corporate chains and global brands that have gobbled up many other parts of Asia remain notably conspicuous by their absence.

It's also a uniquely diverse nation. Physically, Myanmar encompasses **landscapes** ranging from the fertile plains of the majestic Ayeyarwady River to the jungle-covered highlands of Shan State, and from the jagged, snowy Himalayan peaks bounding the northern edge of the country down to the emerald confetti of tropical islands dotting the Andaman Sea in the far south. **Culturally**, too, it's a bewilderingly eclectic place, sandwiched between Bangladesh, India, China and Thailand – all of which have exerted their own distinctive influence on Burmese architecture, culture, cuisine and much more. Myanmar's position at one of Asia's great cultural watersheds also accounts for its extraordinary **ethnic diversity**, with well over a hundred minority peoples who continue to follow their

ABOVE A FISHERMAN ON INLE LAKE; NUNS' SANDALS OUTSIDE A TEMPLE

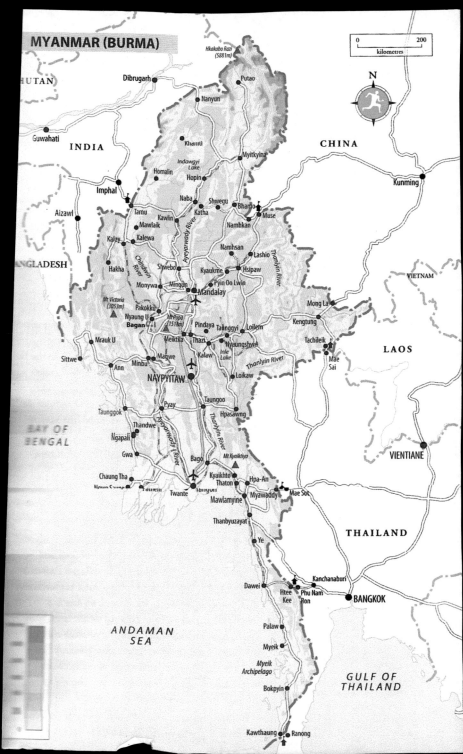

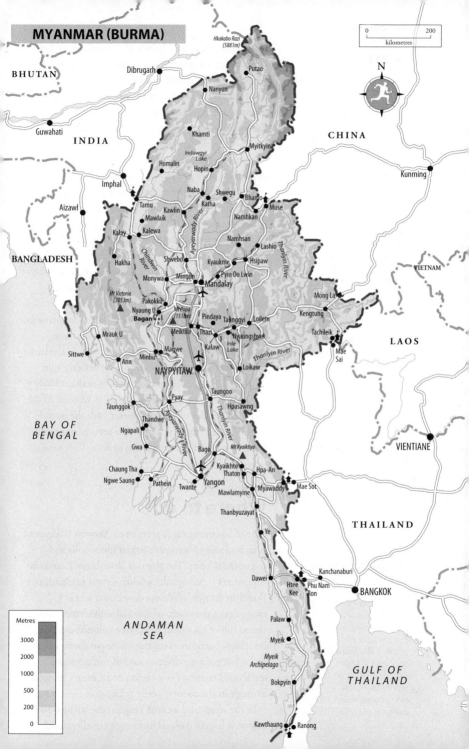

traditional culture and beliefs, from the long-necked ladies of the Kayan (Padaung) tribe to the warlike Wa, whose fierce reputation endures to this day.

For the visitor, it's these images of old Burma – the spectacular temples of Bagan; the great golden stupa of Yangon's Shwedagon Pagoda at sunset; traditional leg-rowed boats drifting across Inle Lake – that provide the touchstone of the Burmese experience. The winds of change, however, are blowing steadily through the country following the recent stunningly swift and remarkably peaceful transition to democracy, followed by the election in 2015 of a new NLD government led by Nobel laureate **Aung San Suu Kyi**. The new NLD administration may have so far disappointed, amid rising levels of ethnic and religious tension, heightened press censorship and a range of other muddles and abuses, although the fact that the country has a democratic government at all stands as a monument to the many thousands of unheralded Burmese who sacrificed their liberty, and often their lives, in the battle for freedom during the five decades of military rule.

Given the tragic recent past, what is perhaps likely to linger most in the memory is the sheer warmth of the Burmese people, starved of contact with the outside world for so many years, and who remain among the friendliest and most welcoming in Asia. Visit now, before it all changes.

Where to go

One of Southeast Asia's great cities, **Yangon** (Rangoon) is far and away Myanmar's largest metropolis and commercial heart. The glorious Shwedagon Pagoda is Myanmar's – perhaps the world's – most extraordinary Buddhist temple, while the downtown area is a magnificent showpiece of colonial architecture, with streets full of memorably decaying colonial-era buildings, hectic markets, miniature pavement cafés and a fascinatingly diverse range of multicultural attractions ranging from Hindu and Chinese temples through to the country's only synagogue.

To the south and west of Yangon, the fertile **Delta region** is largely ignored by foreign travellers, with

BURMESE CHIC

Want to dress up like a Burmese? Just don a longyi, and slap on some *thanaka*. The **longyi** is a sarong-like garment worn by both men and women in most parts of the country. Patterns vary by gender, as does the style of folding. You may notice certain colour-related traits – green, for example, is strongly associated with education and thus *de rigueur* with students, while those working in the service industry often opt for sky blue. Longyis are extremely comfortable in hot weather and can be picked up in any local market for as little as a couple of dollars.

Then there's **thanaka**, a bright yellow paint that many of the country's women and children (and a fair few men as well) plaster on their faces – often in elaborate patterns. Made from ground tree bark, *thanaka* is usually applied in the morning and serves as an all-purpose sunblock, insect repellent, perfume, skincare product and adornment. *Thanaka* powder is widely available in shops countrywide: just mix with a little water to form a paste and daub away.

most of those who do visit hurrying straight to the idyllic beach at **Ngwe Saung**. North of here, in Rakhine State, is the perhaps even more stunning beach resort of **Ngapali**, while in the far north of the state is far-flung **Mrauk U**, a sleepy backwater dotted with magnificent temples dating back to its glory days as one of Myanmar's richest and most cosmopolitan cities. North of Mrauk U, remote **Chin State** is one of Myanmar's final frontiers, only recently opened to foreigners and still seeing barely a trickle of adventurous travellers lured by the chance of climbing soaring **Mount Victoria** and meeting the state's famous women with facial tattoos.

South of Yangon (and also accessible overland from Thailand), **southeastern Myanmar** offers a relatively untouristy but rewarding destination. **Bago** boasts a dazzling crop of golden stupas and giant Buddha statues, while further south is the so-called **Golden Rock** at Kyaiktiyo, a gravity-defying giant golden boulder balanced on the edge of a cliff – one of the country's most jaw-dropping sights. South of here, the absorbing former British capital of **Mawlamyine** is a lovely place to kick back for a few days, and it's also the starting point for enjoyable boat trips along the Thanlyin River to **Hpa-An**, which is

MYANMAR OR BURMA?

Burma was renamed Myanmar by the country's military rulers in 1989 – a move widely resisted by opposition groups, including Aung San Suu Kyi's National League for Democracy (NLD). Following the return to democracy, Myanmar is nowadays increasingly used as the nation's default name (including even by the NLD themselves), although it's fine to use Burma if you prefer. We've used Myanmar throughout the book, except when referring to the historical colonial era, and "Burmese" to describe the food and the language. For more on the naming debate, see Contexts (p.380).

surrounded by beautiful, cave-studded karst countryside. In the far south of the country is the wonderfully unspoilt **Tanintharyi Region**, with the gorgeous white-sand beaches of the undeveloped **Myeik Archipelago** the main draw.

North of Yangon, the wide-open plains of **central Myanmar** are, for most visitors, simply a region to be traversed en route between Yangon and Bagan or Mandalay. In reality, the provincial towns of **Taungoo** and **Meiktila** offer an enjoyable taste of traditional Burmese life away from the tourist hordes, while the sprawling remains of the great Pyu city of Thayekhittaya (Sri Ksetra) can be seen just outside the similarly engaging, low-key Ayeyarwady town of **Pyay**. Further north is the country's outlandish modern capital, **Naypyitaw**, a surreal monument to the former ruling generals' megalomaniac ambitions, with its vast (but eerily deserted) multi-lane highways and government buildings.

North of here is Myanmar's most spectacular attraction, **Bagan**, nestled beside the Ayeyarwady River and surrounded by sweeping plains covered in an astonishing profusion of ancient temples. This is unquestionably one of Asia's greatest spectacles and demands at least a few days of cycling among and delving inside the myriad monuments, with perhaps a side-trip to the quirky, *nat*-infested **Mount Popa** as well.

The southern half of Shan State epitomizes the appeal of the hilly **east** of the country. Laidback **Nyaungshwe** is the major tourist hub, close to the northern end of spectacular **Inle Lake** with its stilt villages and colourful markets. A great way of reaching the lake is to hike there from **Kalaw**, a lofty town with its own appealing ambience, on a beautiful two- or three-day trek among the hills through ethnic-minority villages.

Mandalay, Myanmar's second city, doesn't quite live up to the promise of its evocative name, but compensates for its manic traffic and faceless concrete architecture with an impressive palace and a fine crop of pagodas – including those lining beautiful Mandalay Hill, with its sweeping sunset city views. You'll find a memorable array of attractions dotted around the fringes of the city, including the former royal capitals of **Inwa** and **Amarapura** (the latter with its iconic U Bein teak footbridge), the stupa-studded hills of **Sagaing**, and the monumental (although unfinished) stupa at **Mingun**, accessible via a breezy boat trip up the Ayeyarwady.

West of Mandalay, it's possible to take a day-trip to the remarkable, skyscraper-sized Buddha statue at Maha Bodhi Tataung, near the town of **Monywa**. Striking off northeast of Mandalay, quaint colonial **Pyin Oo Lwin** retains a decidedly British feel, while further northeast the towns of **Kyaukme** and **Hsipaw** offer good trekking and the chance to stay in traditional ethnic-minority villages in the surrounding hills.

Author picks

Our authors made their way across every (accessible) corner of Myanmar for this second edition of the Guide. Aside from the major sights, here are some of their personal favourites.

Big Buddhas Big is definitely best when it comes to Buddhist merit-making, as exemplified by the supersized Buddhas of Yangon (p.78) and Bago (p.142) or the stupendous, sky-high statue at Maha Bodhi Tataung, near Monywa (p.343).

Cycling Four wheels are good but two wheels are even better (p.31). Cycling offers a brilliant way of seeing the countryside, whether you're exploring the spectacular temples of Bagan (p.223), freewheeling around the shores of Inle Lake (see box, p.251) or heading through the hills around Kalaw (p.242).

Teahouses Teahouses (see box, p.37) are an integral part of daily Burmese life – as much a social institution as a place to drink and eat. Tea is served Burmese style (sweet, milky and with a kick) and usually accompanied by bite-sized snacks ranging from curried mutton puffs to sticky-rice confections.

Markets Local markets are at the heart of traditional Burmese life, complete with huge stacks of fruit and vegetables, piles of colourful longyi and vast vats of rice, and ranging in size and style from the urban mercantile mazes of Yangon's Theingyi Zei (p.68) and Mandalay's Zegyo (p.287) through to the colourful ethnic-minority markets (p.241) of Inle Lake.

Remnants of colonialism Myriad relics of British colonial rule can be seen dotted across Myanmar, from the quaint hill stations of Pyin Oo Lwin (p.314) and Kalaw (p.238) through to the lakeside villas of Kengtung (p.270) and the great municipal monuments of downtown Yangon (p.59).

Nat ceremonies Don't miss the chance to catch one of Myanmar's raucous *nat* (spirit) ceremonies (p.386). Khayone Cave (Mawlamyine) has daily *nat*-driven séances (p.165), while Taungbyone's *nat pwè* (see box, p.298) is a magnet for energetic *nat kadaw* (see box, p.49).

> Our author recommendations don't end here. We've flagged up our favourite places – a perfectly sited hotel, an atmospheric café, a special restaurant – throughout the Guide, highlighted with the ★ symbol.

FROM TOP CYCLISTS IN BAGAN; TEA-MAKING, BURMESE STYLE; A *NAT KADAW* PREPARES FOR TAUNGBYONE *NAT PWÈ*

BETEL JUICE

Spend much time in Myanmar and you won't fail to notice two curious features of the country: the wretched state of many locals' teeth, and the odd red blotches peppering streets across the land. These are both related to the chewing of **betel** (*ku-nya*), a popular pastime with male and female, young and old. Betel is made using areca nuts mixed together with tobacco and other (optional) ingredients, folded up inside a leaf and pasted together with slaked lime. Users experience a slight rush, similar to that of coffee or a cigarette. Addiction can develop quickly and repeated use can lead to oral cancer, while permanently stained, vampire-like red teeth are virtually guaranteed.

One or two parcels are unlikely to damage your health, however, and some travellers are keen to see what all the fuss is about; the tastiest is said to come from the Kalaw area (see box, p.244). Parcels are sold in packs from roadside stalls all over Myanmar, usually costing just K100 or so. If you're chewing, remember to spit out the first few times your mouth fills with saliva, since the slaked lime can (ultimately) destroy your liver.

Much of the country **further north** remains closed to foreigners. The easiest way to strike into the heart of the region is to catch a slow boat up the Ayeyarwady north from Mandalay to George Orwell's erstwhile home at **Katha** and beyond to **Bhamo** – both places where the lack of tourists makes it easy to get a sense of the traditional rhythms of Burmese life. Further north still, there's superb trekking and cycling around unspoiled **Indawgyi Lake**, while within hailing distance of China the remote town of **Myitkyina** is an offbeat melting pot of Kachin, Chinese and Indian cultures. Keep going until you reach the topmost tip of the country and you'll find the small town of **Putao**, which is the starting point for tours and treks into a fascinating region of wildlife-rich subtropical rainforest nestled in the shadow of vast, snowbound Himalayan peaks.

When to go

Myanmar boasts a **tropical climate**, with the year divided between the **dry months** from November to April, and the **rainy season** from May to October. Temperatures remain consistently warm year-round, rising noticeably from February onwards and reaching a peak in April/May and the onset of the rains. The main tourist season runs from November to February, when the country enjoys a winning combination of azure-blue skies and relatively cool temperatures. **November** is a good month to visit – both temperatures and visitor numbers are still quite low, and much of the country remains a lush green from the rains. **December** and **January** see Western tour groups arriving en masse, with accommodation at its most scarce; if Chinese New Year falls in January, things can get particularly busy with domestic travellers and those from neighbouring countries added to the mix.

RIGHT RICE PADDIES NEAR KENGTUNG

AVERAGE MONTHLY TEMPERATURES AND MONTHLY RAINFALL

	Jan	Feb	March	April	May	June	July	Aug	Sept	Oct	Nov	Dec
YANGON												
Max/min (°C)	32/18	35/19	36/22	37/24	33/25	30/24	30/24	30/24	31/24	32/24	32/22	31/19
Rainfall (mm)	5	3	7	15	301	545	557	603	368	204	61	8
MANDALAY												
Max/min (°C)	29/13	32/15	35/20	38/24	37/26	34/26	34/26	32/25	32/25	32/24	30/19	28/15
Rainfall (mm)	5	2	1	39	134	153	87	113	153	129	35	7
MYITKYINA												
Max/min (°C)	24/10	27/12	30/16	33/20	33/22	31/24	30/24	30/24	31/23	30/21	27/16	25/12
Rainfall (mm)	8	18	27	48	156	536	512	412	283	158	27	9

As long as you don't mind getting hot or wet, it's perfectly feasible to visit Myanmar outside the main season; New Year aside, you'll get to see the country at its most refreshingly tourist-free. The country starts to sizzle in **March**, and by **April** temperatures are at their year-round high – all the more excuse for Thingyan, a huge water festival that occurs around this time (be prepared to get very, very wet, whether you want to or not). Those arriving after Thingyan may get the same kind of feeling, since **May** sees the sudden onset of the rainy season – be aware that during the monsoon some places are inaccessible and transport services may not run. Things only get wetter in **June**, and conditions stay that way through the months of **July** and **August**. **September** is already usually dry enough to make for pleasant travel, and **October** even more so.

Large as Myanmar is, this month-by-month advice generally applies across the board. Temperatures do tend to be slightly lower the further north you head, and the sheltered positions of Mandalay and Bagan help them escape the worst of the rainy season, though this also makes them bake more in hotter months. If the heat's getting too much for you, head up to loftier, cooler climes on the Shan plateau, such as Kalaw or Pyin Oo Lwin.

20

things not to miss

It's impossible to see everything that Myanmar has to offer in one trip – and we don't suggest you try. What follows, in no particular order, is a selective and subjective taste of the country's highlights, from impressive Buddhist monuments to spectacular journeys. All entries have a page reference to take you straight into the Guide, where you can find out more. Coloured numbers refer to chapters in the Guide section.

1

1 BAGAN
Page 200
One of the great wonders of Asia – and the world – with (literally) thousands of majestic temples rising from the central plains.

2 TAUNG KALAT AND MOUNT POPA
Page 228
Dramatic volcanic plug covered in shrines dedicated to Myanmar's bizarre *nat* spirits.

3 COLONIAL ARCHITECTURE, YANGON
Box, page 63
They may have seen better days, but Yangon's colonial-era buildings and streetscapes remain among Asia's most impressive colonial-era relics.

4 MANDALAY'S ROYAL CAPITALS
Pages 299–306
Explore the former royal capitals dotting the margins of modern Mandalay: the backcountry lanes of rustic Inwa, the stupa-swathed slopes of Sagaing and lakeside Amarapura, home to the emblematic U Bein teak bridge.

5 ETHNIC-MINORITY GROUPS

Pages 381–388

Myanmar is home to an extraordinary tapestry of diverse ethnic groups, best appreciated during a trek or tour around the eastern towns of Kalaw, Kengtung or Loikaw.

6 SHOPPING

Page 45

Myanmar's markets and shops serve up plenty of unusual souvenirs, including beautiful parasols, lacquerware, wood ornaments and all sorts of traditional textiles.

7 SHWE OO MIN CAVE

Page 246

Spectacular cave filled with an extraordinary quantity of gilded Buddha statues, wedged into a cliff-face high above the pretty town of Pindaya.

8 HPA-AN

Page 151

Watch the sunrise from a mountaintop monastery and disturb squeaking clouds of bats in holy caves outside laidback Hpa-An.

9 BOAT TRIPS ON THE AYEYARWADY

Box, page 222 & box, page 334

Head upstream from Bagan to Mandalay or foray into the far north along Myanmar's most important river, jumping ship at remote villages as you go.

10 HIKING AROUND KALAW
Box, page 243

Trek among ethnic-minority villages amid the stunning scenery around Kalaw, up to Pindaya or east on the memorable trek to Inle Lake.

11 MOHINGA
Page 35

This hearty fish broth – flavoured with lemongrass, lime, chilli and coriander – is Myanmar's essential power-breakfast.

12 GOKTEIK VIADUCT
Box, page 320

Enjoy the view on the slow trip across this latticework railway viaduct, Myanmar's highest bridge.

13 KYAIKTIYO
Page 148

Join thousands of pilgrims at the precarious Golden Rock, a giant gilded boulder held steady by a few strands of the Buddha's hair.

14 YANGON STREET LIFE
Box, page 93

Traditional and modern Myanmar collide in downtown Yangon, with roving food hawkers and impromptu pavement cafés set up amid the bustling streets.

15 NGAPALI BEACH
Page 113

Legendary beach in deepest Rakhine, with smooth white sands, stylish resorts and super-fresh seafood.

17

Itineraries

Myanmar is a large country, and you could spend months here and still not see everything. You'll realistically need a couple of weeks just to properly see the "big four" sights of Yangon, Inle Lake, Mandalay and Bagan, and more like a month to begin really scratching the surface of this big and bafflingly diverse nation.

THE GRAND TOUR

Myanmar's default itinerary focuses mainly on the country's "big four", with perhaps a visit to the Golden Rock as an optional side-trip from Yangon. You could visit all the following in two weeks, at a push, although you might want to spend a little longer, especially if you include Kyaiktiyo.

❶ **Yangon** The country's largest city, home to the stupendous Shwedagon Pagoda as well as one of Asia's most perfectly preserved colonial centres, along with a fascinatingly eclectic mix of cultures and people. **See p.56**

❷ **Kyaiktiyo (Golden Rock)** Join local pilgrims on a night-time walk up Mount Kyaiktiyo to the golden, gravity-defying rock that's outlandishly balanced upon its summit. **See p.148**

❸ **Kalaw** Appealing old colonial hill station offering a refreshingly crisp climate and great trekking, including the memorable two- or three-day hike down to Inle Lake. **See p.238**

❹ **Inle Lake** Take a boat trip around Inle Lake with its beautiful backdrop of misty mountains, stilted villages, floating gardens and leg-rowing Intha fishermen. **See p.258**

❺ **Mandalay** Explore the absorbing pagodas and former royal palace of Myanmar's second city, and then head out to see the fascinating

array of former royal capitals – Amarapura, Inwa and Sagaing – nearby. **See p.276**

❻ **Bagan** One of Asia's great sights, with a surreal profusion of ancient temples rising from the central plains, best appreciated at sunrise or sunset from a perch high on one of the pagodas themselves. **See p.200**

ETHNIC MINORITIES

Few countries in the world can rival Myanmar's incredibly diverse tapestry of ethnic-minority peoples, many sharing links with groups in neighbouring Thailand, China and India and each boasting their own distinctive style of dress, culture and traditional beliefs. Count on around three weeks to cover all the places here, especially if you want to do some trekking along the way.

❶ **Hpa-An** The startling limestone karst scenery around Hpa-An is home to the Kayin, who are resplendent in their distinctive striped longyi. **See p.151**

❷ **Mrauk U** A boat trip from Mrauk U offers a rare glimpse of traditional Chin culture, including the chance to see some of the famous women with facial tattoos. **See box, p.124**

❸ **Myitkyina** Catch the colourful Kachin National Day celebrations way up north in multicultural Myitkyina. **See box, p.346**

ABOVE ARTWORK ON DISPLAY, BOGYOKE MARKET, YANGON; BOAT, NEAR NYAUNGSHWE

❹ Kyaukme and Hsipaw Two laidback towns offering an enjoyable taste of Shan culture. Alternatively, head for the tea-swathed hills to the north, where Shan-dominated valleys give way to tea-growing hills tended by the Palaung, crisscrossed with great trekking routes. **See p.321 & p.324**

❺ Inle Lake Myanmar's most visible minority groups can be found around Inle Lake, including Shan, Danu, red-turbaned Pa-O, the lake-loving Intha and a smattering of the famous long-necked Kayan (Padaung) ladies. **See p.258**

❻ Kengtung This remote and still largely untouristy Shan State town is surrounded by a bewildering patchwork of Akha, Lahu, Loi and other villages – it's easily visited en route to or from northern Thailand. **See p.270**

ROADS LESS TRAVELLED

Myanmar is a big country – certainly big enough to absorb the burgeoning number of tourists descending on it. Huge swathes of the country still see few, if any, tourists. Count on at least three weeks to cover all the places here.

❶ Tanintharyi Region Head down to Myanmar's deep south, with its abundant white-sand beaches and idyllic islands. **See p.169**

❷ Pyay An enjoyable stopover on the slow road from Yangon to Mandalay, with ancient Pyu ruins, the towering Shwesandaw Pagoda and one of central Myanmar's best night markets. **See p.192**

❸ Meiktila This little-visited crossroads town has a beautiful lakeside setting, a clutch of quirky temples and stand-out street food. **See p.189**

❹ Loikaw Only recently opened to foreigners, the enjoyably low-key capital of Kayah State is a great place to kick back for a few days, with rewarding day-trips to time-warped local villages in the unspoiled surrounding countryside. **See p.266**

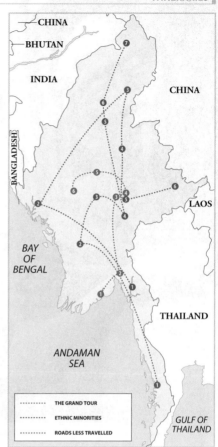

❺ Katha Inspiration for the town of Kyauktada in Orwell's novel *Burmese Days*, Katha's backstreets are dotted with atmospheric colonial buildings – the 1924 tennis club still hosts matches today. **See p.337**

❻ Indawgyi Lake Kayak across or bike around Myanmar's biggest lake to seldom-visited villages and Shwe Myitzu, a golden pagoda that seems to float above the water. **See p.351**

❼ Putao Discover Kachin State's wild side in the thickly forested Himalayan foothills outside this remote far northern town. **See p.353**

BUDDHIST MONK WITH CHEROOT

Basics

Getting there

Travelling to Myanmar used to be a question of flying into Yangon or catching one of the few international flights to Mandalay. Then, in 2013, four of the five border crossings between Myanmar and Thailand opened fully to independent foreign travellers. Now, there are lots of interesting possibilities for entering Myanmar overland, especially in the south of the country.

Even so, most visitors continue to arrive at **Yangon International Airport**, which has been radically modernized and enlarged over the past few years. The least expensive way to get here is to travel through a regional hub. Bangkok and Singapore are the best options, with regular low-cost flights to both Yangon and **Mandalay International Airport**. Flight prices are slightly higher during the winter peak season (December to February) and over the Thingyan Water Festival, or Burmese New Year (see p.42), which falls in April each year.

As well as an increasing number of routes in and out of the country, **visa restrictions** have recently been greatly eased up and today visas can be obtained from a Myanmar embassy in your home country or online.

Flights from the UK and Ireland

At the time of research there were no direct flights from the UK and Ireland to Myanmar. The most convenient (and frequently the cheapest) indirect flights transit through **Bangkok** (11hr 30min), **Kuala Lumpur** (12hr 30min) and **Singapore** (12hr 50min), with daily flights from each of these cities directly to Yangon, as well as from Bangkok direct to Mandalay (see p.24). Air China (ⓦairchina.com), Cathay Pacific (ⓦcathaypacific.com), Emirates (ⓦemirates.com) and Qatar Airways (ⓦqatar airways.com) also operate daily flights from London to their airport hubs, with several direct flights on to Yangon each week.

Other airlines that fly to Bangkok or Singapore with a stop en route from London include Air France (ⓦairfrance.com), Jet Airways (ⓦjet airways.com), KLM (ⓦklm.com) and Lufthansa (ⓦlufthansa.com). If you're travelling to Myanmar from another UK airport or from the Republic of Ireland, you will need to fly to London Heathrow or another hub city first. From the UK, the lowest available return fares to Yangon, changing planes in Bangkok, Kuala Lumpur or Singapore, start at around £500.

Flights from the US and Canada

When flying to Myanmar from US and Canadian cities on the **east coast**, your route might see you transiting through Europe or via Asia – the latter is often more direct, as well as slightly cheaper. There are regular flights from New York, Chicago and Toronto to Beijing on Air China (ⓦairchina .com), Hong Kong on Cathay Pacific (ⓦcathay pacific.com), Seoul on Asiana (ⓦflyasiana.com) and Korean Air (ⓦkoreanair.com), and Tokyo on All Nippon Airlines (ⓦana.co.jp) and Japan Airlines (ⓦjal.com), with direct flights from all of these cities to Yangon. Emirates (ⓦemirates.com) fly from New York, Boston, Houston and a number of other east coast cities to Dubai, where you can then catch one of their daily flights to Yangon. Boston, Chicago, Montreal, New York and several other destinations are also served by daily flights to Doha on Qatar Airways (ⓦqatarairways.com), from where you can take one of the five weekly flights to Yangon. Return fares with Emirates and Qatar start from $1300 (Can$1420), and flight times are all upwards of 20hr.

The major Asian airports are also the most convenient transit points between the **west coast** and Myanmar. There are flights from Los Angeles, San Francisco, Seattle and Vancouver to Beijing, Hong Kong, Seoul, Tokyo and Taipei (the latter on China Airlines (ⓦchina-airlines.com), with direct flights from all of these Asian hubs to Yangon. Return tickets start at around $1100 (Can$1200), and the shortest flights take around 18hr, including

---

A BETTER KIND OF TRAVEL

At Rough Guides we are passionately committed to travel. We believe it helps us understand the world we live in and the people we share it with – and of course tourism is vital to many developing economies. But the scale of modern tourism has also damaged some places irreparably, and climate change is accelerated by most forms of transport, especially flying. All Rough Guides' flights are carbon-offset, and every year we donate money to a variety of environmental charities.

time spent in transit. Airlines flying from the west coast include China Airlines, China Eastern (Ⓦfly chinaeastern.com), Singapore Airlines (Ⓦsingapore air.com) and Cathay Pacific.

Flights from Australia, New Zealand and South Africa

When travelling to Myanmar from the southern hemisphere, **Bangkok**, **Singapore** and **Kuala Lumpur** are the most convenient places to transfer onto a flight to Yangon. From Australia, Kuala Lumpur is typically the cheapest destination of the three, with direct flights from Adelaide, Brisbane, Sydney, Melbourne and Perth starting from just Aus\$300 return, thanks to the presence of **budget carriers** (including Jetstar (Ⓦjetstar .com), Scoot (Ⓦflyscoot.com) and AirAsia (Ⓦairasia.com) on various routes, along with full-price airlines. There are also daily direct flights from Brisbane, Melbourne, Perth and Sydney to Singapore (from Aus\$350) and Bangkok (from Aus\$500).

Thai Airways (Ⓦthaiairways.com) operates several direct flights from Auckland (from NZ\$1700) and Johannesburg (from ZAR8500) to Bangkok each week, Singapore Airlines (Ⓦsingaporeairlines .com) flies direct to Singapore from Auckland and Christchurch (from NZ\$1650) and Johannesburg (ZAR9250). Malaysia Airlines (Ⓦmalaysiaairlines .com) also operates daily flights from Auckland (from NZ\$1385) to Kuala Lumpur. All prices are for return airfares.

Flights from Southeast Asia

Flights between **Bangkok** and **Yangon** (1hr) start at \$70 return, with the cheaper airlines often flying out of Don Mueang International Airport (DMK) rather than the larger Suvarnabhumi Airport (BKK), which is preferred by standard-price carriers. Ensure that you leave enough time between connections if you're flying into one airport and out of the other – it can take over an hour to drive between the two. Airlines flying between Bangkok and Yangon include Bangkok Airways (Ⓦbangkokair.com), Thai Airways (Ⓦthaiairways.com) and Myanmar Airways International (Ⓦmaiair.com) out of Suvarnabhumi, and Nok Air (Ⓦnokair.com) and AirAsia (Ⓦairasia .com) out of Don Mueang.

The longer flight from **Singapore** to Yangon (3hr) is well served by budget airlines, with Jetstar Asia (Ⓦjetstar.com) and Tigerair (Ⓦtigerair.com) operating daily services between the two cities.

Return airfares start from around \$200. Full-price carriers, including Golden Myanmar Airlines (Ⓦgmairlines.com), SilkAir (Ⓦsilkair.com) and Singapore Airlines (Ⓦsingaporeair.com), also operate daily flights, with airfares from around \$250 return.

Airlines that fly directly to Yangon from cities around Southeast Asia include AirAsia and Malaysia Airlines (Ⓦmalaysiaairlines.com) from **Kuala Lumpur** and Vietnam Airlines (Ⓦvietnamairlines .com) from **Hanoi** and **Ho Chi Minh City**. Air Bagan (Ⓦairbagan.com) fly between Yangon and **Chiang Mai** several times per week, and Asian Wings Airlines (Ⓦasianwingsairlines.com) fly between Chiang Mai and Mandalay.

Regional airports

Mandalay International Airport is served by an increasing number of direct international flights. At the time of research, there were non-stop flights to Mandalay from Bangkok Suvarnabhumi (daily; 2hr; around \$200), Bangkok Don Mueang (daily; 2hr; around \$150), Chiang Mai (daily; 1hr 30min; \$170) and Singapore (2 weekly; 3hr 25min; \$360), as well as Kunming in Yunnan, China, and Gaya in Bihar, India.

In addition, Bangkok Airlines (Ⓦbangkokair.com) operates five flights each week between Bangkok Suvarnabhumi and **Naypyitaw**'s recently expanded airport (2hr 30min; \$245), and there are also occasional charter flights from further afield.

Overland from Thailand

Of the five border crossings between Myanmar and **Thailand**, four were fully opened to independent travellers at the time of research. **Ranong–Kawthaung** (see box, p.177) and **Phu Nam Ron–Htee Kee** (see box, p.172) in Tanintharyi Region, **Mae Sot–Myawaddy** (see box, p.158) in Kayin State and **Mae Sai–Tachileik** (see box, p.275) in southern Shan State are all now open to travellers with valid Myanmar visas. The fifth checkpoint, **Three Pagodas Pass** between Sangkhlaburi in Thailand and Payathonzu, is not open to foreign tourists.

Visas on arrival are no longer available to tourists at any border (or airport), but Myanmar e-visas (visas applied for online) are valid for entry into Myanmar via all of the open crossing points except for the **Phu Nam Ron–Htee Kee border**.

If you plan to cross at Mae Sai–Tachileik, note that it is not possible to travel overland further into Myanmar beyond Kengtung without a special permit. There is, however, an airport in Tachileik with flights to Mandalay, Yangon and Heho (for Inle Lake) that you can visit without a permit. Travellers planning to use the Phu Nam Ron–Htee Kee crossing should also note that the road on the Myanmar side of the border is largely impassable during the rainy season, when it's best to enter the country elsewhere.

Overland from China

The **Myanmar–China** border crossing between Muse in northern Shan State and Ruili in China's Yunnan province (see box, p.331) is nominally open to foreigners, but it's necessary to hold a permit and to be part of an officially sanctioned tour in order to either enter or leave Myanmar.

Overland from India, Laos and Bangladesh

The crossing between **Moreh** in India and Tamu in Sagaing Division is open to foreigners, but a border crossing permit is required and this takes at least a month to be issued. You will also need to leave Myanmar again via the same crossing, unless you have your own transport. However, the good news is that you no longer need a permit to travel around much of the rest of Sagaing division or Manipur.

There are no official border crossings along Myanmar's short borders with **Bangladesh**, and currently all areas close to this border are closed to foreigners and considered dangerous. There are also no official border crossing points with **Laos**, but there were persistent rumours of a new border crossing in the works at the time of research – check with the travel agencies in Yangon for the latest.

INTERNATIONAL AGENTS AND OPERATORS

Operators specializing in cycling tours are covered under "Getting around" (see p.31).

Asian Pacific Adventures US ☎ 1 800 825 1680, ⓦ asianpacific adventures.com. Offers several group and private tours of Myanmar, the most interesting of which focus on ethnic minority regions in Chin and Shan states and river cruises along the Ayeyarwady River.

Backroads US ☎ 1 800 462 2848, ⓦ backroads.com. Short cycling tours around Myanmar's main tourist sights.

Belmond UK ☎ 0845 217 0799, US ☎ 1 800 524 2420; ⓦ voyagesinmyanmar.com. Formerly known as Orient Express Travel, Belmond operates high-end cruises on its two boats, *Road to Mandalay* and *Orcaella*, along several Ayeyarwady itineraries.

Exodus UK ☎ 0203 131 7053, ⓦ exodus.co.uk. Offers a small selection of two-week trips around the usual suspects of Yangon, Mandalay, Inle Lake and Bagan, along with a more interesting (and challenging) trekking trip that will see you ascend Mount Victoria in Chin State.

Exotissimo Thailand ☎ 02 633 9060, ⓦ exotissimo.com. Bangkok-based company with offices in Yangon and Mandalay, offering a good selection of tours countrywide lasting from a couple of days to a month. There are family-friendly tours, as well as more adventurous trips to newly opened areas such as the jade mines around Mogok, plus overland journeys from Mandalay to Yunnan, Chiang Mai to Kengtung and Yangon to Phuket.

Explore UK ☎ 01252 883 704, US ☎ 1 800 715 1746, Canada ☎ 1 888 216 3401, Australia ☎ 1300 439 756, New Zealand ☎ 0800 269 263; ⓦ explore.com. Big range of small-group and tailor-made trips around Myanmar, ranging from nine to 21 days, with a flexible approach and reasonable mid-range prices.

InsideBurma Tours UK ☎ 0117 370 9759, ⓦ insideburmatours .com. Reliable outfit that really knows Myanmar well. They offer tailored tours and a selection of off-the-peg group itineraries; the latter include a family holiday, off-the-beaten-track tours and an interesting "Kipling's Burma" option, which weaves together aspects of colonial heritage and local culture.

North South Travel UK ☎ 01245 608291, ⓦ northsouthtravel .co.uk. Friendly travel agency offering discounted fares worldwide. Profits are used to support projects in the developing world, especially those that promote sustainable tourism.

Panoramic Journeys UK ☎ 01608 676821, ⓦ panoramic journeys.com. This operator has a focus on ethical travel. Tours are often arranged to coincide with festivals, and there are also several trekking trips and occasional forays off the beaten track. Private tours also available.

Regent Holidays UK ☎ 020 381 16184, ⓦ regent-holidays.co.uk. Specializing in offbeat tours, this operator has a range of itineraries that include trips on Myanmar's railways plus cruises along the Ayeyarwady and through the Myeik Archipelago.

STA Travel UK ☎ 0333 321 0099, US ☎ 1 800 781 4040, Australia ☎ 134 782, New Zealand ☎ 0800 474 400, South Africa ☎ 086 1781781; ⓦ statravel.co.uk. Worldwide specialists in independent travel, also able to provide student IDs, travel insurance and a range of other services. Good discounts for under-26s.

Steppes Travel UK ☎ 01285 601 767, ⓦ steppestravel.co.uk. UK-based tour operator offering a range of tailored private tours around Myanmar.

Trailfinders UK ☎ 0207 368 1200, Ireland ☎ 01 677 7888; ⓦ trailfinders.com. One of the best-informed and most efficient agents for independent travellers.

Travel CUTs Canada ☎ 1 800 667 2887, ⓦ travelcuts.com. Canadian youth and student travel firm.

USIT Ireland ☎ 01 602 1906, ⓦ usit.ie. Ireland's main student and youth travel specialists.

Wild Frontiers UK ☎ 020 8741 7390, ⓦ wildfrontierstravel.com. A small range of standard Myanmar journeys with an emphasis on sustainable travel, and one or two more adventurous options.

MYANMAR-BASED AGENTS AND OPERATORS

There are lots of tour operators based in Yangon and Mandalay, and a few more in Bagan, around Inle Lake and in some of the other tourist hotspots. Most offer a fairly standard set of tours, tailored itineraries and car and driver hire. The following operators are all highly recommended.

Ayarwaddy Legend Travels & Tours ☎ 01 252 007, 🌐 ayarwaddylegend.com. As well as the full range of standard tours around Myanmar, this operator runs exciting treks into Chin State.

Khiri Travel ☎ 01 375 577, 🌐 khiri.com. This is one of the more adventurous tour companies, with kayaking trips and a variety of cultural immersion options.

Myanmar Delight Travels & Tours ☎ 09 5165 1833, 🌐 myanmardelight.com. Offers exciting trekking opportunities in the far north and east, as well as bicycle trips and cultural tours.

Myanmar Good News Travel ☎ 09 511 6256, 🌐 myanmargoodnewstravel.com. High-end private tours that can be customized to your budget and interests. Also rents excellent cars and good drivers. The owner, William, is endlessly helpful.

Pegu Travels ☎ 01 371 937, 🌐 pegutravels.com. One of the best tour companies out there, with a highly knowledgeable team that can put together almost any kind of trip. Also runs the highly informative travel information website Go Myanmar (🌐 go-myanmar.com).

SST Tours ☎ 09 5125 5536, 🌐 ssttourism.com. An eco-tourism operator running fabulous birding trips to remote parts of the country, as well as tours that mix the classic tourist sights with a wildlife-watching twist.

Tango Tour & Trek ☎ 09 7310 9637, 🌐 tangotours.webs.com. Offers a variety of standard and tailor-made tours tours throughout the country.

Visas

All foreign nationals, apart from citizens of a few Southeast Asian countries, require a visa in order to visit Myanmar. Although a visa-on-arrival system does exist, it applies only to business visitors or conference guests who are able to provide documents such as letters of invitation.

You can apply for a visa at your nearest Myanmar embassy or consulate, although it's generally easiest to apply online for a tourist e-visa at 🌐 evisa .moip.gov.mm. In order to apply, your passport must be valid for at least six months from your proposed date of arrival. Tourist visas typically last for 28 days from the date of entry, which must be within three months of issue, cost $50 and are usually issued within a couple of days. E-visas are valid at Yangon, Mandalay and Naypyitaw international airports and at all land crossings apart from

the Phu Nam Ron–Htee Kee and Three Pagodas Pass border crossings with Thailand.

Tourist visas cannot be extended, but it is possible to overstay them by up to as much as ninety days (at a cost of $3 per day, payable on departure at the airport). The only possible hitch is that guesthouses occasionally express concern about expired visas.

MYANMAR EMBASSIES OVERSEAS

Australia 22 Arkana St, Yarralumla, ACT 2600, Canberra ☎ 02 6273 3811, 🌐 mecanberra.com.au.

Canada 336 Island Park Drive, Ottawa, Ontario K1Y 0A7 ☎ 613 232 9990, 🌐 meottawa.org.

China 6 Dong Zhi Men Wai St, Chao Yang District, Beijing 100600 ☎ 010 6532 0351, 🌐 myanmarembassy.com; Consulate-general, 99 Ying Bin Lu, Guan Du Qu, Kunming, Yunnan Province ☎ 0871 6816 2804, 🌐 mcgkunming.org.

South Africa 210 Leyds St, Arcadia, Pretoria ☎ 027 12341 2556, 🌐 myanmarembassysa.com.

Thailand 132 S Sathorn Rd, Khwaeng Khlong Toei Nuea, Sathon, Bangkok 10120 ☎ 022 337 250, 🌐 myanmarembassybkk.com.

UK 19A Charles St, London W1J 5DX ☎ 020 7148 0740, 🌐 londonmyanmarembassy.com.

US 2300 S St. N.W. Washington D.C. 20008 ☎ 202 332 3344, 🌐 mewashingtondc.com.

Getting around

Getting around Myanmar can take as much or – at least travelling between major cities – as little time as you like. At one end of the scale, it's possible to zip around the major destinations by plane, while at the other you can join the locals on bumpy trains and unhurried river-boats. Somewhere in the middle lies Myanmar's surprisingly modern bus network, its speedy air-conditioned coaches providing a winning combination of quick(ish) journeys and reasonable ticket prices.

By plane

In addition to state-owned **Myanmar National Airlines** (🌐 flymna.com), which has long had a poor reputation for the condition of its aircraft (though standards have improved somewhat over the past few years), an array of **private airlines** – among them Air KBZ (🌐 airkbz.com), Air Mandalay (🌐 airmandalay.com), Air Bagan (🌐 airbagan.com), Apex Airlines (🌐 apexairline.com), Asian Wings

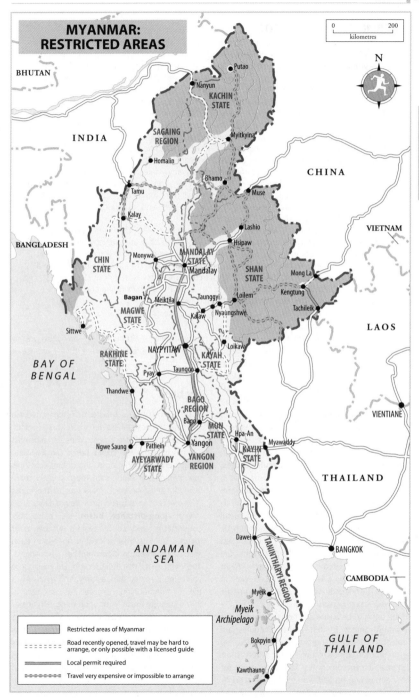

MYANMAR: RESTRICTED AREAS

BHUTAN

0   200
kilometres

N

Putao

Nanyun

KACHIN STATE

INDIA

SAGAING REGION

Homalin

Myitkyina

CHINA

Bhamo

Tamu

Muse

Kalay

Lashio

VIETNAM

BANGLADESH

Monywa

CHIN STATE

MANDALAY STATE

Hsipaw

Mandalay

SHAN STATE

Mong La

Bagan   Meiktila

Taunggyi

Loilem

Kengtung

MAGWE STATE

Kalaw

Nyaungshwe

Tachileik

Sittwe

RAKHINE STATE

NAYPYITAW

KAYAH STATE

Loikaw

LAOS

BAY OF BENGAL

Pyay

Taungoo

Thandwe

BAGO REGION

Bago

MON STATE

Hpa-An

Myawaddy

VIENTIANE

Ngwe Saung   Pathein

Yangon

AYEYARWADY STATE

YANGON REGION

KAYIN STATE

THAILAND

ANDAMAN SEA

Dawei

TANINTHARYI REGION

BANGKOK

CAMBODIA

Myeik

Myeik Archipelago

Bokpyin

GULF OF THAILAND

Kawthaung

     Restricted areas of Myanmar

- - - - - - Road recently opened, travel may be hard to arrange, or only possible with a licensed guide

━━━━━ Local permit required

◦━◦━◦━◦ Travel very expensive or impossible to arrange

> ## PERMITS: GO OR NO-GO?
>
> While Myanmar has opened up enormously to foreign visitors in the past few years and independent travel has become straightforward in much of the country, you will quickly run into **travel restrictions** if you want to explore the country's remote mountainous fringes. In some areas – such as large parts of Shan and Kachin states – foreigners' access is limited as a result of government conflict with ethnic minority groups, while other areas are cut off to protect dubious business interests – among them drug-dealing hotspots as well as jade and gem mines (although since 2015 even many of these mining areas have opened up to permit-free independent travel). Many of these regions are either completely closed to foreign visitors or require permits that may take several weeks to obtain.
>
> Myanmar's no-go zones are in constant flux – parts of Rakhine State, for example, have closed and reopened repeatedly over the last few years – and these closures and requirements can change without warning. Currently, anywhere in the vicinity of the Bangladesh border is a closed military region, and to try and visit would be foolhardy. Our map (see p.27) shows regions where travel was restricted at the time of research, but for the latest information you should contact Myanmar Tours and Travels (MTT; ⓦmyanmartourism.org) or get in touch with an authorized tour operator.
>
> Make sure to plan well in advance if you would like to visit a restricted area. **Permits** for many restricted areas take at least a month to arrange, with a private tour operator approved by MTT (these are listed under "Services" on the MTT website) making the application on your behalf. You will be required to book onto an **official tour** or – at the bare minimum – hire a guide to make sure you don't misbehave. Permit **costs** themselves are nominal, but the strings attached to the permit (often requiring you to be accompanied by a guide and driver, or to join a group) drive up the price of visiting off-limits regions.

(ⓦasianwingsair.com), Golden Myanmar Airlines (ⓦgmairlines.com) and Yangon Airways (ⓦyangonair.com) – run services on domestic routes and have offices in major towns and cities.

Given the long journey times overland, travelling by plane can be an attractive choice if you're not on a tight budget (one-way airfares from Yangon to Mandalay start from $100), and in a few cases, such as visiting Kengtung, air travel is the only option as overland routes are closed to foreigners. Many services fly on **circular routes**, stopping at several airports on the way, and it may therefore be easier to make a journey one way rather than the other.

Besides Yangon and Mandalay, the most useful regional airports for visitors are **Bagan** (Nyaung U), **Heho** (for Inle Lake, Kalaw and Pindaya) and **Thandwe** (Ngapali Beach). Note that flights are always heavily booked over the Thingyan Water Festival, when you will need to book well in advance. The luggage weight limit on domestic flights is 20kg per person.

One thing to be aware of when travelling by air within Myanmar is that flight schedules are subject to change at short notice, and delays are very common. If you're only flying a very short distance, it can sometimes be just as quick (or slow depending on how you look at it) to go by road. Some domestic airlines still do not sell tickets online – although they may allow you to make an online reservation and then pay once in the country.

By bus

Buses are usually much faster than trains, and are generally the best way to get around on a budget. There are many different bus companies and most are privately owned. Taking buses can be quite tiring, however, since most long-distance services run through the night, stop roughly every three hours for toilet or food breaks (not all the buses have toilets on board), and arrive before dawn.

Most **long-distance buses** are reasonably comfortable, and an increasing number offer luxuries such as small television screens in each seat, complimentary toothbrushes and snacks, and even seats that fully recline. Do make sure you bring warm clothes, as they tend to crank up the air-conditioning, as well as earplugs if Burmese pop music isn't your thing. On major routes, it's often possible to take a slightly faster and more comfortable "VIP" or "**express**" bus service for a small additional fee. **Ordinary buses** also run segments of longer routes, such as Taungoo to Mandalay (rather than the full Yangon to Mandalay trip); these are usually in worse condition but are cheaper for shorter trips, as on long-distance buses you will pay the fare for the full journey even if you get on or off part-way through. You'll also find smaller, 32-seat buses – these should be avoided if possible for long trips, as they tend to be jam-packed with luggage. As for **prices**, the 9hr trip between Yangon and Mandalay costs around K32,000 on an express bus, compared to K17,000 by ordinary bus. Note that on express buses, large items of luggage are stowed in compartments underneath the coach, while on ordinary buses bags are stored anywhere the owner can find space.

Some bus routes are **off limits** to foreigners (such as Bhamo to Mandalay). If in doubt about your route, check with local guesthouse staff at either end of the journey, as they are often the most clued up on the local situation.

It's a good idea to **book** a day or two ahead for busy routes (such as Bagan to Nyaungshwe), ones where only a few buses run (such as Ngwe Saung to Yangon) or where you're joining a bus part-way through its route (in Kalaw, for example). Guest-houses can often help book tickets for a small fee (usually K2000–3000), or you can buy them either from bus stations (which in some cases are outside of town), from in-town bus company offices or from local travel agents. Tickets booked privately often include **transfers** to and from the bus station, which is particularly convenient when the station is out of town.

Note that all of Myanmar's bus services **close down** for a week or more over the Thingyan Water Festival; make sure that you have alternative arrangements – typically by plane or train – if you need to travel over that period. Finally, prepare for **delays**, particularly if travelling during Myanmar's rainy season (June to October) each year.

By train

The **railway system** in Myanmar is antiquated, slow and generally uncomfortable. The entire network, which dates from the days of British Burma, is narrow gauge, and although frequent repairs have been made (thankfully), train journeys in Myanmar are often comically bouncy and the timing is unpre-dictable in the extreme. On most routes buses are faster and more reliable – it is not uncommon for express trains to be delayed by several hours, and local trains are usually even worse.

All that said, there are reasons why you might want to take a train at least once during your trip. One is that on a few routes, such as from Mandalay up to Naba, Katha and Myitkyina, road transport is

closed to foreigners. Another is for the experience itself: many routes run through areas of great beauty, for example the rickety Gokteik Viaduct between Pyin Oo Lwin and Kyaukme (see box, p.320). Trains also offer more opportunities than buses to interact with local people.

Routes and train types

The country's most important line (and one of the few stretches of double track) runs between Yangon and Mandalay via Naypyitaw, and this line has the most modern rolling stock. Additional **major lines** run from Myitkyina in the far north to Mandalay, and south of Yangon as far as Mawla-myine. **Branch lines** connect towns to the east and west of the main railroad to the network. Myanmar's railways are currently being extended in several directions, with **new track** being laid to Bhamo in the northeast, Kengtung in the east, Myeik in the south and Pathein in the southwest.

A range of services operates on each of the major lines. Where possible, it's worth opting for the slightly faster "**express**" services, as these trains are given priority over slower **local** services, and are thus less likely to be delayed – tickets for the various classes cost the same, regardless of the train type.

Train classes and sleepers

All trains have **upper-** and **ordinary-class** carriages. Upper class has reservable reclining seats (which can be more of a curse than a blessing if the mechanism is broken), while ordinary class has hard seats that cannot be reserved – you may end up standing if the train is crowded. Some trains also have **first-class** carriages, which actually fall between upper and ordinary class in price and comfort, with seating usually on a padded wooden bench. **Upper-class sleeper carriages**, available between Yangon and Mandalay, Yangon and Bagan, and on some Mandalay to Myitkyina services, offer two- and four-berth lockable compartments with bedclothes provided. **Special sleepers** are available between Yangon and Mandalay, with self-contained compartments sleeping up to four passengers, a private toilet and sitting area as well as a private entrance. For the moment only the Yangon to Mandalay trains have air-conditioning – on all other trains, open windows are the order of the day.

Express trains may have restaurant cars, and on all trains food vendors either come on board or carry out transactions through the windows at stops. Whatever the class of train, the bathrooms on board all services are basic and often unclean.

Fares and bookings

In April 2014, Myanmar Railways ended a system that saw foreign travellers charged substantially higher **ticket prices** than local people, and required them to pay in dollars. Now everyone pays the same price, denominated in kyat. By way of example, ticket prices between Yangon and Mandalay are as follows: ordinary class K4650; upper class K9300; upper-class sleeper K12,700. You will require your passport to buy train tickets.

It's almost mandatory to **book** sleeper berths well in advance (these tickets can be booked up to two weeks before you travel), and a good idea to book ahead even if you're planning to travel by upper class (generally tickets go on sale three days in advance for upper class and a day in advance for ordinary tickets). However, at inter-mediate stops between major stations, tickets may only go on sale shortly before the train arrives. Foreigners are usually dealt with separately from local passengers, and you will find that station staff often invite you into their offices while they write out your ticket. Even so, don't rush up moments before a train leaves and hope to have time to buy a ticket – it can still take around half an hour to buy a ticket.

It's possible to buy tickets before you travel through a handful of Yangon **travel agents**, including Pegu Travels (ⓦ pegutravels.com), Exotic Myanmar Travels & Tours (ⓦ exoticmyanmartravel .com) and Myanmar Tour East (ⓦ myanmartoureast .com). Once you're in the country, you'll need to head to the station yourself to buy a ticket direct from the booking office.

For the latest **information** on travelling by train in Myanmar (and timetables for the most popular services), The Man in Seat 61 (ⓦ seat61.com/Burma .htm) is the most comprehensive and reliable online resource.

By ferry

Myanmar offers some of Asia's great river journeys and travelling by boat is, in places, an excellent alternative to buses and trains. Boats connect some of the country's major destinations, most notably Mandalay and Bagan, and can be a good way to experience local life. The most popular routes are concentrated on the upper reaches of the **Ayeyar-wady River**, but there are also interesting trips on the **Thanlyin** and **Chindwin rivers**, as well as from Sittwe to Mrauk U. Several sea routes link places that are difficult to reach overland, with ferries plying the waters between Sittwe to Taunggok.

Inland Water Transit or **IWT** (ⓦ www.iwt.gov.mm /en), a government-run service, used to operate slow two-storey ferries that ran daily services along the Ayeyarwady River between Mandalay and Bhamo, and Mandalay and Nyaung U (for Bagan) from October to April and an irregular service from May to September. However, at the time of research the company had cut seventy percent of its services and was in imminent danger of ceasing operations altogether for financial reasons. It's worth checking in port towns if the IWT ferries are still running, but if not then the routes they once covered have, in many cases, been taken over by private operators running cargo ships and ferries along the backwa-ters of Myanmar.

Boats are often stacked high with cargo, leaving some covered deck space and a few cabins for passengers, with most locals setting up camp on deck for the duration of their voyage. Bring something comfortable to sit on and sleep under – if you're planning to travel on deck, take a mat and a blanket. Simple meals are sometimes available on board, and vendors swarm onto the ship at each stop.

Privately run "**fast boats**" – usually long, thin motorboats carrying anywhere between thirty and eighty passengers – cover some Ayeyarwady routes, as well as the beautiful trip down the Thanlyin from Mawlamyine to Hpa-An, the journey down the Tanintharyi coast and the river voyage from Sittwe to Mrauk U. The comfort levels of the boats can vary wildly. Some vessels offer spacious seats and air-conditioning, while on others you'll have to make do with cramped wooden benches and a tarpaulin roof.

Upmarket **river cruises** along the Ayeyarwady (and, less commonly, the Chindwin) have also long been popular in Myanmar. The majority of cruises are between **Mandalay** and **Bagan**, while a few also continue north up the river all the way to **Bhamo**. In addition, an increasing number of cruises are now being offered along the Ayeyar-wady south of Mandalay, with some longer cruises ending in (or starting from) **Yangon**. Cruises can last from just a few days to over two weeks and offer a memorable and often very luxurious way to see the country, although as you'd expect they don't come cheap, with daily rates for a twin cabin on most boats starting from around $300–400.

As with most forms of transport in Myanmar, journeys by boat can take far longer than adver-tised, particularly during the dry season (December to May) when water levels are low and the vessels – particularly the large, heavy IWT ferries – can get stuck on sand banks. **Fares** for boat journeys are quoted throughout the Guide.

LUXURY RIVER CRUISES

Amara ⓦ amaragroup.net. Offers scheduled trips from Mandalay to Bhamo aboard a pair of beautiful small teak boats with just 5–7 cabins; also available to charter.

Belmond ⓦ voyagesinmyanmar.com. 2- to 4-night cruises between Mandalay and Bagan aboard the large and lavish *Road to Mandalay* riverboat, and from Mandalay up to Bhamo on the old-style *Orcaella*.

Pandaw 1947 ⓦ pandaw1947.com. 5- to 10-night cruises north up the Ayeyarwady as far as Bhamo and all the way down to Yangon on a luxurious sixteen-berth vessel built in 1947 to the same design as the original Irrawaddy Flotilla Company's steamers.

Princess Pahnwar ⓦ iglucruise.com. 16-night cruises between Bagan, Mandalay and Yangon.

Sanctuary Ananda ⓦ sanctuaryretreats.com. One of the most luxurious boats on the river, offering 3- to 11-night cruises from Mandalay north to Bhamo and south to Yangon.

The Strand Cruise ⓦ thestrandcruise.com. Cruises between Bagan and Mandalay on board a ship run by the same team as the famous *Strand Hotel* in Yangon (see p.65), with plenty of luxurious, colonial-style character.

By car

As yet, self-drive holidays are not really a realistic prospect in Myanmar – current laws require that foreign drivers get permission from two different government departments and have a local driver on board at all times. Red tape aside, at the time of writing no international car rental companies had a presence in Myanmar, although this will surely change. Fortunately, it's relatively easy to arrange a **car and driver** (from around $40 per day) through your accommodation or a tour operator – it's best to work through the latter if you want anything more complicated than a day-trip. Straightforward as it may be to find a man with a car, do take care to specify exactly what is included. Useful questions to ask include how much mileage or petrol will be included, who will pay for the driver's food and accommodation and whether you are expected to tip or not in addition to the daily rate.

By bike and motorcycle

Cycling is a brilliant way to explore parts of Myanmar, and bicycle tours of Bagan and Mandalay are a particular highlight for many visitors. Bikes are widely available to rent for around K2000 per day.

But you certainly aren't limited to short bicycle excursions, and an increasing number of saddle-hardy travellers are cycling all over the country – the mountainous frontier areas in particular are especially rewarding for cyclists. Several tour operators are now organizing multi-day bicycle tours of the country (see below).

In some parts of the country it is also possible to rent a **motorcycle**, typically for K8000–40,000 a day plus fuel, depending on bike quality and size. Note that motorcycles have been banned in central Yangon since 2003 when, rumour has it, a motorcyclist almost knocked over a senior general. Petrol can be bought at filling stations or, more commonly in the countryside, from stalls set up along the roadside selling one-litre bottles. Safety helmets may be provided, although not always – be aware that you can be fined for riding without one. Before renting a motorbike, check that your travel insurance covers you for such activities (see box, p.49).

There are numerous **hazards** for cyclists and motorcyclists: traffic can be very heavy in the cities, while in rural areas the roads are often in poor condition. Adding to these dangers is the fact that most cars are right-hand drive imports from Japan or Thailand even though Myanmar drives on the right (see p.388), meaning that cars have large blind spots.

Motorbike touring is relatively new in Myanmar. Mandalay Motorbike Rental (ⓦ www.mandalay motorbike.com) organizes group motorcycle tours as well as rentals, and Southeast Asian motorbiking site GT Rider (ⓦ gt-rider.com) also has some basic information on riding in the country.

CYCLING TOUR OPERATORS

Grasshopper Adventures UK ☎ 020 8123 8144, US ☎ 1 818 921 7101, Australia ☎ 03 9016 3172; ⓦ grasshopperadventures.com. Specializing in cycling tours, Grasshopper organizes half-day tours around Bagan and Mandalay, as well as longer trips (6–13 days) around Inle Lake, Bagan and Mandalay.

Myanmar Cycling Tours Myanmar ⓦ www.myanmarcycling tours.com. The local branch of Indochina Bike Tours, this Yangon-based company organizes everything from half-day cycling tours of Yangon and Mandalay to 18-day countrywide fly-and-cycle tours.

Spice Roads Thailand ☎ 66 2 381 7490, ⓦ spiceroads.com. Southeast Asian cycling specialists, Spice Roads offer several multi-day bike tours of Myanmar, including a great 14-day trip from Bangkok to Yangon.

Veloasia US ☎ 1 415 731 4377, ⓦ veloasia.com. Organizing small-group trips on a single 12-day itinerary that takes in the "Big Four" sights, this firm also customizes cycling trips for couples and families.

Shared taxis, vans and pick-ups

Although not as common as in some Southeast Asian countries, **shared taxis** and **shared vans** are available on some routes, from Mandalay to Pyin Oo Lwin and Hsipaw, for example. Prices are typically around fifty percent more than a seat on an air-conditioned bus, and you will generally pay the full fare regardless of where you get on or off. They will usually drop you wherever you like, however, which saves on transfer costs in towns where the bus station is inconveniently located. Vehicles can be arranged either through accommodation or at shared-taxi stands in town centres.

In addition to these routes between towns, which are primarily used by locals, there are a handful of services aimed specifically at foreigners. These are typically round trips, such as to Mount Popa from Bagan.

Local transport

Local transport in Myanmar is provided by a colourful mix of public buses, taxis, pick-ups, tuk-tuks, motorbike taxis and cycle rickshaws. **Public buses** run only in the largest cities, including Yangon and Mandalay, and are very cheap. Unless you read Burmese, it can be a challenge to work out the routes, and consequently we have not covered them in detail in the Guide, but if you aren't in a rush, riding on the buses is certainly an experience. The same can be said of **pick-ups** or *lain-ka* – adapted pick-up trucks with seating in the covered back portion – which cover set routes and pick up and drop people off on the way. They usually depart when full, which may include passengers riding on the roof. If you want the most comfortable seats, in the cabin, then you can pay a little extra; a seat in the back (or on the roof) will seldom set you back more than K600.

Taxis are available in large towns and cities, and range from 1970s Toyotas to occasional new left-hand-drive Chinese imports. There are no meters, but drivers tend not to overcharge as outrageously as in many other Southeast Asian countries. Expect to pay around K1500–2000 for a trip across town of a reasonable length, such as from a bus station on the edge of town to a central hotel. Burmese-style **tuk-tuks** (*thoun-bein*) – motorbikes with roofed flat-bed trailers attached behind them, with rows of wooden benches for seats – replace taxis in smaller towns and villages, and often work out slightly cheaper, starting at K500–1000 for a short ride. **Cycle rickshaws** (*saiq-ka*), also known as trishaws,

are still in use in many towns, although these are being edged out by **motorbike taxis** (on which the passenger rides pillion). The latter are much faster and normally around the same price (starting from K500 per trip).

Most of these forms of transport can also be hired (with driver) for a day, and can be arranged direct, through accommodation or via travel agents; you'll need to bargain to get a good price. Motorbike taxis may not work out much more expensive than renting a self-drive motorcycle, while groups can often get a good deal on a pick-up or tuk-tuk for the day.

Finally, in small towns, **horse-drawn carriages** are used as a key form of transportation, and also ferry tourists around in a number of places, notably Bagan, Inwa and Pyin Oo Lwin. The horses are not always well looked after, however, and the lack of suspension on bumpy Burmese roads makes them uncomfortable for longer trips.

Accommodation

Accommodation in Myanmar is significantly more expensive than in other countries in the region, and although prices have gradually begun to fall over the past few years as supply slowly catches up with demand, the cost of your room is still likely to be far and away your biggest daily expense. In many places, you're unlikely to find a reasonable en-suite room for less than $20–25, while in some areas, particularly on the coast, even very ordinary rooms in a mid-range hotel can go for over $100. On the plus side, the country's burgeoning number of hostels means that those on a shoestring budget can now find dorm beds in most major tourist centres for under $10 a night – which is particularly useful for solo travellers.

Be aware that not all guesthouses are **licensed to accept foreign guests**, so some places (particularly small guesthouses in remote towns that don't see many foreigners) may be forced to turn you away even if they have space. **Homestays** are technically illegal for the same reason, unless arranged as part of an official trek. Places licensed to take foreigners should in theory meet certain minimum standards, and although a fair number of basic and grubby old-style guesthouses and hotels survive, most places are reasonably well equipped and generally

ACCOMMODATION PRICES

Rates quoted throughout the Guide are for the cost of the **cheapest double room** in high season (November to February), excluding peak-period spikes such as over Christmas and New Year and during the Thingyan Water Festival. Different places give room rates in either dollars or kyat (or sometimes both), and we've quoted prices throughout in the currency used by the establishment itself.

Rates at most places include all relevant **taxes and service charges**, although some top-end places quote pre-tax rates and then add on an additional fee – typically a ten percent service charge and a ten percent government tax. If in doubt, check when you book or check in.

Breakfast is normally included (see p.34), and all places listed have **free wi-fi** unless specifically stated otherwise. Single room rates, where available, are normally around two-thirds to three-quarters of the price of a double room.

clean, even at the budget end of the scale. **Air-conditioning** is provided in the majority of places (including most budget options) except for destinations up in the hills (Kalaw, for example), where it's not generally needed. Some places give you the option of taking a room with or without a/c (usually costing around $5–7 per night extra if you opt to have it turned on). Many places offer the option of taking a room with either **twin** or **double beds** – those with double beds are often a bit cheaper. **Hot water** is also the norm except in the very cheapest places, while free **wi-fi** is provided pretty much everywhere, although it's often erratic. National power shortages can be a problem in some more remote destinations, with **electricity** only available for set periods (typically 6am–6pm, although in some places electrical cuts may happen in the middle of the night). Most, but not all, mid- and top-end places have their own generators – and therefore 24-hour electricity. In budget places you'll have to do without electricity during outage hours.

Booking accommodation

Where you stay will depend a lot on where you are. In larger tourist centres (Yangon, Mandalay,

Bagan) there's plenty of accommodation and you can afford to pick and choose (assuming you reserve ahead). In smaller and/or less touristed places there may be only a handful of options, if that. Given all this, it pays to **reserve in advance**. Most places are now available to **book online** on one of the major booking websites (most commonly Booking.com and/or Agoda). It might also be worth a look at Airbnb, although most of the places advertised on the website are just conventional guesthouses and hotels.

If you're arriving somewhere as a walk-in guest it's often worth **bargaining**, especially in budget guesthouses (although you may even have some joy at mid-range places), particularly in low season or if you're staying several days.

Budget accommodation

Budget accommodation aimed at foreign visitors is mainly in **family-run guesthouses** or **smaller hotels**. Rooms typically cost between $15 and $30 per night for a double room. At the lower end of this price range, you'll probably be sharing a bathroom (possibly with cold water only), while some cheap rooms lack air-conditioning and can be pretty shabby. For around $20–25 per night, you can usually find somewhere reasonably clean and comfortable with an en-suite bathroom and hot water.

Mid-range and expensive accommodation

Most **mid-range accommodation** ($50–100 per night) is in functional concrete-box hotels. Rooms tend to be larger and with a few extra trimmings (perhaps a fridge, safe, satellite TV and writing desk), and there might be an in-house restaurant and

TOP FIVE BUDGET GUESTHOUSES

Chan Myaye Guest House, Yangon
See p.88
Motherland Inn II, Yangon See p.88
Galaxy Motel, Hpa-An See p.156
Myanmar Beauty Guesthouse, Taungoo See p.184
Ostello Bello Bagan, New Bagan See p.225

24-hour reception – although, all things considered, you may find yourself paying $50–70 per night for a room not appreciably better than one costing $30.

Rates at **top-end accommodation** are no bargain either. A few places offer genuinely stylish and enjoyable lodgings for as little as $100 per night, though you can easily pay double that, and rates at the very best establishments typically run into the hundreds of dollars. There's a real paucity of good upmarket **city hotels**. Most of the big international chains have yet to arrive in Myanmar – you won't find a single Hilton, Sheraton or Marriott in the entire country, for example – although Yangon boasts a trio of fine old colonial establishments. Many upmarket hotels out in rural areas like Bagan are attractively presented and professionally run, although most follow an identikit resort-style template, usually with bungalow-style rooms with wooden floors and furniture (plus a few Burmese artefacts for decorative effect) set among lush gardens. There's also usually a swimming pool and a spa.

Food and drink

As Myanmar is sandwiched between gastronomic big-hitters India, Thailand and China, Burmese food is one of Asia's least-known cuisines. While its food does absorb influences from its better-known culinary neighbours, it remains unique in many respects: Burmese cooks use fewer spices than their Indian counterparts; Thai cuisine's chilli and coconut milk are notably absent; and pulses and beans are used with an abandon that would be foreign to most Chinese chefs. As with elsewhere in Asia, much of daily life in Myanmar revolves around food and mealtimes, and the phrase "Sa pi bi la?" or "Have you eaten?" is a common greeting.

Meals

Most Burmese people eat **breakfast** early in the morning, often stopping for a bowl of noodles or a fried snack at a teahouse. Although many hotels in Myanmar do include breakfast in their room rates, it's worth forgoing what is usually a fairly depressing offering of white bread, fried eggs and instant coffee, and venturing out to a nearby market or teashop for something tastier. Bigger places may lay out a more interesting buffet spread, sometimes featuring Burmese dishes, although disappointingly few places offer *mohinga*, the delicious fish-based broth eaten by many Burmese themselves at the start of the day (see opposite).

One of the Eight Buddhist Precepts (see box, p.35) states that good Buddhists ought to eat only after sunrise and before noon, and **lunch** in Myanmar is consequently taken rather earlier than is common in the West (although for all except the most devout, this precept is conveniently forgotten around dinnertime). Most people tuck into their lunchtime noodles or curry between 11am and 1pm. Make sure to eat your **evening meal** early too, as many restaurants will be closed by 9pm.

A wide variety of snacks and salads fill the gaps between meals, and there's usually some kind of deep-fried treat available if you're ever in danger of running low on calories. Cakes and sweets are often flavoured with coconut and palm sugar and eaten between meals rather than as a dessert, and it's common to just have a lump of *t'änyeq* (jaggery, or unrefined palm sugar) at the end of a meal.

Burmese food

A brief look around any market in Myanmar will reveal the **key ingredients** of Burmese cuisine: onions and shallots, rice and *ngapi* – a pungent fermented fish paste that vendors often stick incense sticks into to take the edge off the smell. If you are at all interested in food, it's well worth seeking out **wet markets** on your travels (see box, p.38). These colourful, messy markets reveal the huge range of exotic ingredients that go into Burmese cooking, and are often a focus of local life.

In Burmese cooking it's considered important to **balance flavours**, with sour, spicy, bitter and salty tastes combined in each meal; this is generally done across a series of dishes rather than on a single plate. For example, a mild curry might be accompanied by bitter leaves, dried chilli and a salty condiment such as *ngapi*.

TOP FIVE BURMESE RESTAURANTS

999 Shan Noodle Shop, Yangon See p.91
Lucky Seven, Yangon See p.92
San Ma Tu, Hpa-An See p.156
Esso Restaurant, Maungmagan See p.172
Shan Ma Ma, Mandalay See p.296

Noodles

A typical local breakfast is **noodle soup**, such as the delicious and surprisingly sweet national dish **mohinga** (catfish soup with rice vermicelli, onions, lemongrass, garlic, chilli and lime, with some cooks adding things like boiled egg, courgette fritters and fried bean crackers). Alternatives include *oùn-nó k'auq-s'wèh* (coconut chicken soup with noodles, raw onions, coriander and chilli) and Shan noodles or *Shan k'auq-s'wèh* (rice noodles in a thin savoury broth, topped with minced chicken or pork, spring onions and ground peanuts, served with pickled vegetables). Another tasty Shan noodle dish is *mi-shay*, thin rice noodles topped with minced chicken or pork, coriander, deep-fried shallots and soy sauce, which is served with clear soup and pickles.

Salads and snacks

Salads are a common snack, although they may not resemble salad as you know it – the Burmese term, *ăthouq*, simply means "mixed" – and they are usually cold dishes built around a single central ingredient with raw onions, gram flour, chilli and coriander in a savoury dressing. Common *ăthouq* are *nàn-gyì thouq* (thick rice noodle salad), *kayan-jin-dhì thouq* (tomato salad) and *myin-kwa-yuet thouq* (pennywort salad). Another more commonly seen salad on most tourist restaurant menus is

papaya salad, and it's likely you'll quickly become a fan. It's also worth trying *samusa thouq* (samosa salad), a delicious dish of chopped-up samosas served with the same toppings.

Burmese **tea-leaf salad** (*lahpet thouq*) and ginger salad (*jin thouq*) are also worth trying, particularly the former, which is something of a national favourite. Fermented tea leaves (see box, p.324) are topped with vegetable oil, fried garlic and crisp broad beans, crushed dried shrimp and occasionally chopped tomato and whole green chilli. The end result is not unlike Italian pesto with a kick of caffeine, which makes it a popular afternoon pick-me-up with Myanmar's students.

Many other common Burmese **snacks** are deep-fried, ranging from familiar things like home-made potato crisps flavoured with dried chilli, to deep-fried insects sold in paper cones. In teahouses across the land you will have the chance to breakfast on greasy-but-delicious *cha kway* (Chinese-style doughnuts), best dipped in tea or coffee; French toast (*chit-u bamoq gyaw*), served with sugar; as well as **samosa** and various Indian-influenced breads (most commonly paratha – called *palata* in Myanmar – naan and puri), served with mild vegetable-based curries.

Curries

Curry and rice, or *t'ămìn hin*, is the quintessential Burmese meal, best sampled at lunchtime when the food is fresh – the curries are usually cooked in the morning and left in pots all day. Although many good restaurants still attract crowds of evening diners, you may prefer to eat dinner in Chinese restaurants or teahouses where the food is cooked to order. A meat, fish or prawn curry (*hìn*) in a thin gravy will be accompanied by a hearty bowl of rice (*t'ămìn*), a clear **soup** (usually peppery *hin gyo* or sour *chinyay hin*) and dishes of fried vegetables. A great deal of oil is added to

BUDDHISM AND FOOD IN BURMA

Happily, it's possible to be considered a devout Buddhist in Myanmar even if you only practise the **Eight Precepts** (which include bans on intoxicating drinks, dancing and eating after noon, among other good things) for two days a month. In daily life, however, Burmese Buddhists are more likely to abstain from eating **beef** than from drinking **alcohol**, the former being considered taboo as cows are highly respected. That said, beef curries are still available in some Myanmar restaurants, but chicken, pork and fish are far more common.

Many Burmese people will be temporarily **vegetarian** at various points during the year, particularly during **Buddhist Lent**, which usually falls between July and October. Outside of this period meat is eaten freely, in apparent violation of yet another precept – to refrain from taking life – the thinking being that as long as one doesn't kill the animal oneself, it's a-okay to eat it.

VEGETARIAN FOOD IN MYANMAR

Despite the fact that many people in Myanmar are Buddhists, most are enthusiastic omnivores rather than strict vegetarians (see box, p.35). There are plenty of **vegetarian** options out there for travellers, but at times – typically when faced with a meat-only curry spread – it might not feel like it.

One of the first things to learn is "*theq-thaq-luq*", a Burmese phrase meaning "without living things" that is widely used to describe vegetarian food. In many instances, it's possible to point at a dish and ask for it served *theq-thaq-luq*. Although this approach doesn't guarantee that the chef will hold back on the fish sauce or bone stock, it will produce the same dish served without obvious meat or fish.

For true vegetarian food, you may need to be slightly conservative in regard to what and where you eat. **Curries** (even the egg ones) are often prepared with either *ngapi* fish paste or meat-based stock, and are best avoided if that concerns you. In Burmese curry restaurants you can fill up instead on lightly flavoured **side dishes and salads**, as these are often served *theq-thaq-luq* to begin with. Vegetable and tofu dishes in Chinese restaurants are generally vegetarian-friendly, and Indian and Western restaurants often serve a range of vegetarian dishes.

Vegan travellers will face similar challenges, although – thanks to the lack of dairy products used in Burmese cooking – the vast majority of Burmese dishes are dairy-free to begin with.

Burmese curries, supposedly to keep bacteria out, but like locals you can skim the oil off. At the best restaurants, the meal will also include a selection of up to a dozen small **side dishes**, including *balachaung*, a spicy mix of crisp deep-fried shallots, garlic, chilli and dried prawns, plus fresh vegetables and herbs with a dip (usually *ngapi-ye*, a watery fish sauce). Chinese green tea will usually be thrown in, and sometimes you'll get a **dessert** such as tasty *lahpet thouq* (tea-leaf salad; see p.324) or jaggery.

While many people now use a fork and spoon to eat curry and rice in restaurants, traditionally the Burmese eat with their **hands**. In some places you will see people using their right hands to massage lumps out of the steamed rice, before ladling gravy onto the same plate and mixing it through with their fingers. When it's satisfactorily mixed, a small handful will be gathered in a pinching motion and pushed into the mouth using the thumb, with the diner taking bites of the meat and vegetables in between. Often, the quantity of rice seems ridiculous when compared to the small bowls of curry that are dished up, but these quantities make sense when eating with your hands – the gravy goes a lot

further. People generally eat with their right hands, although the taboo against eating with the left hand is not as strong here as it is in India. Chinese-style spoons are used to serve from common dishes and for eating soup.

Regional cuisine

Thanks perhaps to the ubiquitous Shan noodles and *mi-shay*, **Shan cooking** has a higher profile inside Myanmar than the cuisine of many other ethnic minorities. While some dishes are similar to their Bamar counterparts, the Shan versions are often less oily and feature more fresh ingredients, often being served with a small dish of *mon-nyin jin* (pickled vegetables). Shan **tofu soup** (*tohu ngwe*) is a popular breakfast dish – the tofu is actually a gram flour paste, cooked with rice vermicelli and topped with coriander and chilli to serve. Shan-style **buffet meals** are common in Mandalay (perhaps more so than in Shan State itself), with big colourful spreads served all day – best eaten in the morning or at lunchtime.

Further north, the traditional food from **Kachin State** is also lighter than most Burmese cuisine, with many steamed dishes and some interesting salads, including *amedha thouq*, which comprises pounded dried beef flavoured with chilli and herbs, and *shat jam*, a dish of rice, diced vegetables, ground meat and herbs mixed together. Other cooked dishes include *chekachin*, a dish of chicken steamed with herbs in a banana leaf, and *sipa* – steamed vegetables with herbs topped with a vaguely sesame-flavoured sauce.

TOP FIVE FOOD AND DRINK

Shan buffets See above
Teahouses See box opposite
Mohinga See p.35
Night markets See box, p.38
Lahpet thouq (tea-leaf salad) See p.324

International food

While people in Myanmar take great pride in their cuisine, if you ask someone for a restaurant recommendation then there's a good chance that they will suggest a place serving **Chinese food**. This is partly because they worry that foreign stomachs can't cope with local cuisine, but also because most people rarely go to more formal restaurants, so when they do they eat Chinese as a treat. Most towns will have at least a couple of Chinese restaurants, typically with large menus covering unadventurous basics such as sweet and sour chicken; dishes start at around K1500 for vegetables or K2000 for meat. **Indian restaurants** are also popular in larger urban areas, particularly in Yangon, which had a very large Indian population during the British colonial era. In many such restaurants, Indian curries and dhal are served Burmese-style, accompanied by side dishes and fresh vegetables.

In the far south and in tourist hotspots across the country, you'll find that **Thai dishes** make an appearance on many menus, thanks to the availability of similar ingredients in both countries, and the thousands of Burmese people who have brought a taste for Thai flavours home with them from living abroad. **Western food** of wildly varying quality is available in the main tourist destinations, with Italian cuisine being particularly popular.

Drink

Tap water isn't safe to drink in Myanmar; bottled water is available throughout the country for around K300 for a small bottle. Many businesses and homes will have large earthenware jars outside, which are provided – along with a common cup – for thirsty passers-by as a way of accruing good karma. The water ranges from clean, UV-treated water to stuff straight from the village well – it might be useful in a pinch, but drink it at your own risk.

Tea and coffee

In many restaurants, free jugs of **green tea** (*lahpet-ye-gyàn* or *ye-nwè-gyàn*) and cups are left on each table, with customers often rinsing their cups out with a little of the tea before drinking from them. **Black tea** (*lahpet-ye*) is served with lavish quantities of condensed milk. Burmese tea-drinkers are often quite specific about how they take their tea, ordering it *paw kya* (strong and not too sweet), *cho hseint* (milky and sweet) or *paw hseint* (milky and not too sweet) – drinking black tea without sugar is not an option.

A request for **coffee** (*kaw-p'í*) will get you a cup of hot water and a packet of coffee mix (pre-mixed instant coffee, creamer and sugar) for you to stir in yourself – keep in mind that almost all Western visitors find it utterly vile. If you want to try the good home-grown coffee or are just desperate for a change from coffee mix, ask for Burmese coffee (*Bamar kaw-p'í*), which will get you a cup of black coffee, served with sugar and lime on the side – unusual, but delicious.

A hot drink in a teahouse will cost around K300, far less than it would set you back in one of the Western-style coffee shops that are popping up in Myanmar's larger cities and the main tourist hotspots, where an **espresso** will typically cost around K800–1000.

TEAHOUSES

Wherever you are in the country, a trip to a Burmese **teahouse** is a great way to experience local life. These institutions are hugely popular places to meet friends, family and business acquaintances, with tables and low plastic chairs often spilling out onto the pavements. Most open early in the morning and serve up hot drinks and inexpensive meals all day – only closing when the last customers ebb away in the evening. The busiest times are usually early mornings and later in the evening, when many show live Premier League football matches.

Each teahouse has its own **specialities** and, given the rarity of English menus, your best bet is often to point and order. Common dishes include *mohinga*, Shan noodles, and deep-fried snacks, with prices starting at just K100–200 for a snack or K500 for a bowl of noodles.

When you sit down in a teahouse a tea-boy will bring a selection of snacks to your table unasked. When you come to leave – air kissing for your waiter's attention (see box, p.44) – you will only pay for what you've eaten. Noodle dishes and salads are generally only made to order.

STREET FOOD AND MARKETS

Street food isn't as abundant in Myanmar as elsewhere in Southeast Asia, but there are still plenty of street eats available – particularly in **Yangon**, where vendors sling entire stalls from shoulder yokes and set up shop in side streets across the city centre (see box, p.93). Outside Yangon the situation varies, though some towns offer a good variety of food stalls.

Markets – both wet markets, selling fresh food, and night markets – are perhaps a better bet for informal dining, and an excellent place to try authentic local dishes, from Shan tofu soup (see p.36) in markets across Shan State, to *bein moun* – rice flour pancakes smeared with jaggery syrup and shreds of coconut – in Hpa-An. **Night markets** are particularly popular with foreign visitors, and most towns host one of some kind. An hour or two before it starts to get dark, vendors usually start to set up a few tables and chairs as well as a small mobile kitchen somewhere in the centre of town. Typically, you'll see a vast array of uncooked offerings displayed on a table, and you can then take your pick and choose to have it boiled, fried or steamed. Seafood, pigs' innards and chicken feet are all popular night-time delicacies. Note that food hygiene isn't always a priority in these sorts of places, so make sure you dine with care.

Whether in a market or on the street, most stalls will specialize in a small selection of dishes or drinks, with noodle dishes, curry and rice combos and barbecued skewers being particularly common.

Alcohol

Burma's only home-grown alcoholic drink is *t'àn-ye* – **toddy** or palm wine (see box, p.165), which is usually only available in low-key village toddy bars not far from where it's made, thanks to the drink's incredibly short shelf life (it turns to vinegar in a matter of hours). Although there are few places resembling Western bars or pubs outside of Yangon and Mandalay, most towns will have a couple of **beer stations** that can be identified by their obvious signs and predominantly male clientele. These places usually serve draught beer (around K500 for a glass) as well as bottles (from K1000–1500 for 640ml), with the former usually restricted to the most popular brew, **Myanmar Beer** (produced by a government joint venture). Other local beers include Dagon, Double Strong (around nine percent alcohol), and ABC Stout. Adventurous drinkers may want to try Myanmar Beer's Spirulina Beer, made with nutritional algae from Sagaing Region, which reputedly has an anti-ageing effect. Imported beers such as Tiger and Singha are also occasionally available on draught.

Mid-range and upmarket restaurants will often have a list of imported **wine**. There are even a couple of **vineyards** making wine in Shan State: look out for Red Mountain (see box, p.256) and Aythaya. Fruit wines are produced around Pyin Oo Lwin from plums and other fruit.

Locally distilled **spirits** are widely available and popular as a cost-effective alternative to beer, with a large bottle of whisky starting at K1200. Grand Royal Whisky and Mandalay Rum are both common brands. Imported spirits are only available in the larger cities and hotel bars.

Cold drinks

Due to Myanmar's unreliable electricity supply, refrigeration is not widespread and providing cold drinks is a specialist business. Ice factories deliver clear slabs of ice to cold-drink stores each morning, and the stores then use it to cool drinks and make ice cream. Although Myanmar's fruit is excellent, fruit shakes and smoothies aren't as widespread here as elsewhere in Southeast Asia, and the drinks owe more to South Asia, with **falooda** (milk, ice and flavouring mixed together with jelly cubes, tapioca pearls and vermicelli) and various **lassi**-type drinks being particularly popular. Strawberry **pyo-yeh** (*p'yaw-ye* meaning juice) is a delicious drink to try if you're in Myanmar during strawberry season (Feb–April) – the crushed berries are mixed with sweetened milk and yogurt then poured over chunks of ice. **Sugar-cane juice** is another popular beverage – look for the hand-operated presses outside stalls or shops.

Health

The quality of healthcare in Myanmar is generally fairly abysmal. Routine advice and treatment are available in Yangon and Mandalay, but elsewhere the hospitals often lack even basic supplies. Minor injuries and ailments can be dealt with by pharmacists, but if you are

seriously ill it's best to contact your embassy for help. As always, it is important to travel with insurance that covers medical care and emergency evacuation – international-quality care is expensive and in certain situations you may need to be moved to Thailand or Singapore for treatment.

Vaccinations and prophylaxis

Besides ensuring that any routine **immunizations** are up to date, your doctor may recommend that you be vaccinated against hepatitis A and typhoid before travelling to Myanmar, as well as taking malaria prophylactics while in the country. Immunization against hepatitis B, cholera, Japanese encephalitis and rabies is often also suggested.

Malaria is a risk throughout Myanmar, except for in Yangon and Mandalay and areas above 1000m elevation. The strain of malaria found along Myanmar's eastern borders from Kachin State to Tanintharyi is resistant to chloroquine and proguanil (Malarone), and doctors may recommend that you take mefloquine or doxycycline instead, but preventing insect bites is important regardless of your anti-malarial regimen (see below).

Hepatitis A is a viral infection spread by contaminated food and water, whereas the rarer **hepatitis B** is spread through unprotected sexual contact, unscreened blood transfusions and dirty needles. Both diseases cause inflammation of the liver, with symptoms including lethargy, fever and pains in the upper abdomen, and lead to yellowing of the eyes and skin if left untreated.

Typhoid and **cholera** are infections spread by food and water that have been contaminated by bacteria from another infected person, typically in localized epidemics. Typhoid fever is the more common of the two, with symptoms usually appearing up to three weeks after exposure. They start with extreme fatigue, fever and headaches, with some people also suffering from constipation or diarrhoea. Travellers have a lower risk of contracting cholera, which begins with a sudden but painless onset of watery diarrhoea, later combined with vomiting, nausea and muscle cramps. Rapid and severe dehydration, rather than the infection itself, is the main danger, and patients should be treated with constant oral rehydration solutions.

Japanese encephalitis and **rabies** are both zoonoses – animal diseases that can spread to humans. Those living and working in rural areas in close proximity to farm animals are at particular risk of contracting Japanese encephalitis from mosquitoes that have bitten infected livestock. Rabies spreads to humans through the saliva of infected mammals, typically from feral dogs, as well as monkeys and bats, although all mammals are at risk. Both Japanese encephalitis and rabies can be fatal.

A yellow fever vaccination certificate is only required to enter Myanmar if you are travelling from a region where the disease is endemic (i.e. parts of Africa or South America) or if you have been in airport transit in such an area for more than twelve hours. For more information visit ⓦwho.int/media centre/factsheets/fs100/en.

Diarrhoea

The most common health hazard for visitors to Myanmar is **travellers' diarrhoea**, usually a mild form while your stomach gets used to the unfamiliar food and drink. In more serious cases, diarrhoea is accompanied by stomach cramps and vomiting, indicating **food poisoning**. In both cases, get plenty of rest, drink lots of water and use **oral rehydration salts** (ORS) to replace lost fluids – this is particularly important when treating young children. Take a few sachets of ORS with you, or make your own by mixing half a teaspoon of salt and three of sugar to a litre of bottled water.

While you're suffering from diarrhoea, avoid spicy and greasy foods, milk, coffee and most fruit in favour of plain rice, bananas and clear, bland soup. If symptoms persist, or if you notice blood and mucus in your stools, consult a doctor as you may have **dysentery**, which requires medication to cure.

To avoid upset stomachs, eat at places that look busy and clean, and stick – as far as possible – to fresh, thoroughly cooked food and only eat fruit that you have peeled yourself. Drink **boiled or bottled water** and hot drinks, and avoid untreated tap water. Ice is generally made with treated water in dedicated ice factories, but may not be transported or handled hygienically – travellers with sensitive stomachs may want to avoid ice cream and ice cubes in drinks.

Insect bites

Mosquitoes are not only responsible for spreading malaria and Japanese encephalitis (see opposite) – they also transmit **dengue fever**, for which there is no vaccination or cure. The symptoms of dengue fever include a high fever and severe headache, joint and muscle pain as well as a rash, nausea and vomiting. There is no specific treatment for the virus, save for resting and taking paracetamol – do not take aspirin, as this will increase the likelihood of haemorrhaging.

Because of the risks, in addition to taking malaria prophylactics, it is important to try and avoid insect bites while you are travelling. Whereas malaria is spread by a mosquito that bites between dusk and dawn, the dengue-carrying mosquito typically bites during the daytime and at any time of year – don't let your guard down in dry season – with occasional concentrated outbreaks.

Prevent mosquito bites by wearing **light-coloured clothes** that cover your arms and legs. Cover any exposed skin with an insect repellent containing a high percentage of **DEET** – around 30 percent. Use mosquito nets or screens when sleeping, and spray any holes in the netting with your insect repellent before going to sleep.

Heat problems

Most places in Myanmar are hot year-round. For visitors from cooler climates, it can take some time to adjust to the temperatures, especially when you are frequently walking outdoors. The most common heat-related complaint is **dehydration**, which should be dealt with immediately to avoid developing into **heat exhaustion**. Symptoms include weakness, headaches, vomiting and nausea, and a weak and rapid pulse. Dilute ORS in a litre of water, try to get out of the heat, and rest with the legs elevated until the symptoms abate. The same measures can be taken to reduce swelling of the feet and ankles, another common irritation in this climate.

Heatstroke is a more serious medical problem. Symptoms include a sudden increase in body temperature, weakness, confusion, loss of coordination, fitting and – eventually, if left untreated – death. If you or anyone in your party is showing symptoms of heatstroke, seek medical help immediately, get out of the heat and apply cold, wet cloths and ice to the patient's body.

Hospitals, clinics and pharmacies

In Yangon there are several international-standard **medical centres** (see p.97), and large towns will often have several private medical centres that are used by wealthier locals. Conditions in these clinics are variable but generally better than those in

public hospitals, which are best avoided where possible. Whichever type of hospital you use, you will typically be required to pay upfront in US dollars before receiving treatment.

Outside the main cities, **local pharmacies** are a good place to seek help for medical problems, and you'll often see queues of people waiting outside the better ones. In the major tourist destinations pharmacists will often speak English. Be aware that there are considerable problems with fake and **out-of-date drugs** in Myanmar – if you take regular medication, ensure that you bring enough with you to last for your entire stay, and avoid buying over-the-counter drugs wherever possible.

MEDICAL RESOURCES

Canadian Society for International Health ☎ 613 241 5785, ⊛ csih.org. Extensive list of travel health centres.

CDC ☎ 1 800 232 4636, ⊛ wwwnc.cdc.gov/travel. Official US government travel health site.

International Society of Travel Medicine ☎ 1 404 373 8282, ⊛ istm.org. A comprehensive list of travel health clinics in the US.

London Hospital for Tropical Diseases ⊛ www.thehtd.org. The UK government's latest travel advice, as well as travel health information.

MASTA (Medical Advisory Service for Travellers Abroad) ⊛ masta-travel-health.com. Information on UK travel clinics and health advice for travellers.

The Travel Doctor (TMVC) ⊛ traveldoctor.com.au. Lists travel clinics in Australia.

The media

Not surprisingly, Myanmar's media was kept in an iron-fisted grip under the country's military regime. Strict censorship was introduced following the military coup of 1962 and relaxed only in 2012, although controls remain tight to this day – the country was ranked a modest 131 out of 180 in the 2017 worldwide Press Freedom Index produced by Reporters Without Borders (although even this is a massive improvement on its 2010 position, when it ranked 174 out of 178 countries surveyed, above other Southeast Asian nations including Malaysia, Singapore and Brunei).

The 2012 reforms allowed at least a modicum of press freedom, including the private ownership of daily newspapers and the lifting of pre-publication censorship, leading to the increasingly wide spread of newspapers and magazines you'll see laid out on the pavements of Yangon and other cities. Online, international news and exiled Burmese websites were unblocked (along with YouTube).

Following the National League for Democracy's (NLD) sweeping electoral victory in 2015, it was widely expected that most remaining press restraints would be swept away. As it turned out, the NLD government did nothing of the sort, but has retained many of the junta's old powers and even ramped up their enforcement, regularly jailing – often on the flimsiest pretexts – those who criticize Aung San Suu Kyi or other government officials.

Newspapers and magazines

There are four state-owned **daily newspapers**: three in Burmese plus the rather Orwellian English-language *New Light of Myanmar* (Ⓦwww.moi.gov .mm/npe/nlm). The only major privately owned English-language paper is the *Myanmar Times* (Ⓦmmtimes.com), founded in 2000 by Sonny Swe and Australian Ross Dunkley and now published five times per week. Granted special privilieges under the military regime, the paper was often criticized as an upmarket propaganda tool given a touch of Western-style window-dressing (although this didn't prevent Sonny Swe from being sent to prison for eight years in 2004). Post-independence, the paper transformed briefly into one of the finest in the region, until a disastrous change of management led to nose-diving journalistic standards, the loss of most of its staff and a great deal of shameless kowtowing to assorted vested interests. Whether it survives this latest setback remains to be seen.

For the time being, Myanmar's top English-language journalism is to be found in the hard-hitting *Frontier* magazine (published weekly; Ⓦfrontiermyanmar.net), established by Myanmar Times co-founder Sonny Swe, which has taken up the investigative slack left by the collapse of his former paper and covers a wide range of controversial national issues.

NEWS WEBSITES

Burma News International Ⓦ bnionline.net. News aggregator focusing on stories relating to the country's ethnic minorities.
Burma Times Ⓦ burmatimes.net. Online news portal highlighting the plight of the Rakhine Rohingya (see p.121).
Democratic Voice of Burma Ⓦ english.dvb.no. Hard-hitting coverage of controversial news countrywide.

Independent Mon News Agency Ⓦ monnews.org. Focusing on Mon-related news and issues.
The Irrawaddy Ⓦ irrawaddy.org. Website of the now defunct magazine, with a mix of breaking news and op-ed columns on national issues.
Shan Herald Agency for News (S.H.A.N.) Ⓦ english.panglong .org. Shan-related news and opinion.

Television and radio

The state-run **Myanmar Radio and TV** (MRTV) broadcasts in various languages including English and is as exciting as you'd expect, as is the state-run, English-language Myanmar International TV. Many rooms now come with a TV, although only upmarket places generally offer international satellite channels. **Radio** stations include the state-run Radio Myanmar and the most populist Yangon City FM (89.0FM).

Festivals and events

Myanmar's busy festival calendar still revolves almost exclusively around religious festivals marking the cycles of the Buddhist calendar (see box, p.42). Each of the twelve months of the Buddhist lunar calendar has its own associated festival, although with the exception of the big three festivals – Thingyan, Thadingyut and Tazaungdaing – these are likely to pass largely unnoticed by casual visitors.

As well as the major national festivals, many towns have their own **pagoda festival** (*paya pwè*), a kind of Burmese equivalent of a country fair, with impromptu day and night markets and food stalls mushrooming around the pagoda, accompanied by performances of traditional dance, drama, comedy and music. Notable pagoda festivals are held at the Ananda Paya and Shwezigon Pagoda in Bagan; at the Shwedagon and Botataung pagodas in Yangon; at the Mahamuni Pagoda (Mandalay); at Kyaiktiyo (the Golden Rock); and at the Shittaung Paya (Mrauk U), Shwesandaw Pagoda (Twante) and Shwemawdaw Pagoda (Bago).

The second major type of traditional Burmese festival is the **nat pwè**. This is a more raucous version of the homely pagoda festival, dedicated to the country's revered *nat* spirits (see p.386) and featuring copious drinking, dancing and music, as

THE BURMESE BUDDHIST CALENDAR

The **Burmese Buddhist calendar**, like the Western calendar, has twelve months, consisting alternately of 29 and 30 days (each equivalent to a lunar month), totalling 354 days. Leap years (of either 384 or 385 days, featuring a second Waso month) are inserted roughly every four years in order to keep lunar and solar cycles in sync. The twelve months (corresponding, extremely roughly, to the Western January, February and so on) are: Pyatho, Tabodwe, Tabaung, Tagu, Kason, Nayon, Waso, Wagaung, Tawthalin, Thadingyut, Tazaungmone and Nadaw).

well as appearances by Myanmar's colourful *nat kadaw* (see box, p.49). Major *nat pwè* festivals are held at Mount Popa and at a number of places around Mandalay including Mingun, Taungbyone and Amarapura (p.298).

Festival **dates** are set according to the Buddhist lunar calendar, typically shifting by a week or two year on year (with the exception of the Thingyan Festival, which has now been given fixed dates). **Public holidays** are listed under "Travel essentials" (see p.51).

FESTIVAL CALENDAR

The following is a short list of countrywide festivals or local festivals of national significance; other local festivals are covered throughout the Guide.

Naga New Year Northwest Myanmar; Jan 15. A unique festival in Myanmar's remote Naga tribal districts, during which all Naga tribes converge to celebrate the harvest and welcome in the new year with dancing and singing. A rare and remarkable glimpse into a vanishing world, to which some operators (see p.25) run tours.

Shwedagon Pagoda Festival Yangon; two weeks in Feb/March. Myanmar's largest pagoda festival, during which pilgrims descend on the great pagoda from all over the country to make offerings, accompanied by *pwè* dancing and theatre, robe-weaving competitions and more.

Thingyan Water Festival Countrywide; April 13–16. The mother of all national festivals, for which the entire country more or less shuts down for the duration. In theory, the festival is a celebration of the Burmese New Year and a time to observe and reaffirm one's Buddhist beliefs. In reality, it's more like an enormous water fight, with children and hormonal teenagers taking to the streets and dousing one another (and anyone else nearby, foreigners especially) with huge buckets of water, and special streetside platforms erected from which revellers hose down passing motorists, accompanied by deafening music.

Thadingyut Festival of Lights Countrywide; three days in Oct. After Thingyan, the second-biggest national festival, celebrating the end of Buddhist Lent and the descent of the Buddha from heaven after preaching to the gods. Events are held at pagodas across Myanmar (particularly in Yangon and at Inle Lake), along with food stalls galore and performances of traditional drama and dance, while locals fill their houses with lanterns and candles.

Taunggyi Fire-Balloon Festival Inle Lake; one week in Oct or Nov. A local offshoot of the Tazaungdaing Festival (see above), during which Inle Lake's Pa-O community release hundreds of giant paper balloons, often designed in the shape of animals such as ducks, dragons and elephants, amid a great barrage of fireworks (see box, p.264).

Tazaungdaing (aka Tazaungmone) Festival of Lights Countrywide; Nov. Held on the full-moon night of the Buddhist month of Tazaungmone and celebrating the end of the rainy season. Streets, homes and pagodas are brilliantly illuminated and offerings are made to monasteries, with triangular wooden frames erected around towns and along roadsides to which devotees pin banknotes and attach other gifts to be handed over to local monks. In some places (particularly Taunggyi) hot-air balloons illuminated with candles are released, while special robe-weaving competitions (the biggest at Yangon's Shwedagon Pagoda) are also held at shrines countrywide, with young women attempting to weave a new monastic robe in the course of a single night.

Outdoor activities and sports

With its wide-open spaces, lakes, hills, mountains and thousands of kilometres of coast, Myanmar is a potential gold mine of adventure tourism. It remains largely unexploited, although a few places in the hills lure visitors with well-developed trekking networks, and there's a decent selection of other outdoor activities available, from cycling to scuba-diving.

Trekking, rock-climbing and mountaineering

The most popular outdoor activity in Myanmar is undoubtedly **trekking**, which offers the chance to experience the country's superb landscapes while interacting with local people, particularly minority ethnic groups. The hike from Kalaw to Inle Lake (see box, p.243) remains enduringly popular, though there are numerous other possibilities for trekking around Kalaw, Pindaya and Inle Lake, hikes among

CHINLONE

Somewhere between sport and dancing, **chinlone** is one of Myanmar's most distinctive pastimes. A non-competitive sport, *chinlone* is traditionally played by six or so people standing in a circle and kicking a rattan ball between themselves. The basic aim of the game is to stop the ball from touching the ground for as long as possible, although additional kudos is attached to the skill and style with which the ball is kept aloft – over 200 types of kick are recognized using five different parts of the foot, plus knees. A popular, competitive variant of the game, akin to Malaysian *sepak tawkraw* (kick volleyball), is also often played, with a net between opposing players/teams and rules similar to volleyball, except that the ball is kicked rather than punched.

the hill tribes around Kengtung (see box, p.272), and treks into the tea-swathed hills and villages of northern Shan State from Kyaukme (see box, p.321) and Hsipaw (see box, p.327). In the far north, challenging treks up into the high Himalaya can be arranged from Putao (see p.354), while the ascent of Mount Victoria in Chin State (see box, p.136) offers a real taste of Myanmar well off the beaten track. Unlike trekking, Myanmar's enormous potential for **rock-climbing** and **mountaineering** remains almost totally untapped. The Technical Climbing Club of Myanmar (find them on Facebook) is attempting to develop rock-climbing in the country and establish bolted routes.

Cycling

Cycling is another rewarding activity – much of the country is predominantly flat, although potholed roads and heavy traffic can prove challenging. Biking around Bagan is one of Myanmar's classic experiences (see p.223), while the Inle Lake area (see box, p.251) also offers some great riding opportunities, with a growing number of operators offering tours (sometimes combined with trekking). Cycling also offers a convenient way of exploring Mandalay and its surroundings, so long as you don't mind the frequently heavy traffic. A few tour operators run multi-day bike tours and longer cross-country journeys if you don't fancy going it alone (see p.31).

Diving and watersports

There's very little **diving** compared to other nearby countries. There are basic dive centres at Ngapali (see box, p.116) and Ngwe Saung (see box, p.110), although serious divers head to the spectacular Myeik Archipelago in the far south, where you can also arrange snorkelling, kayaking and sailing trips (see box, p.175). Some **watersports**, though nothing very sophisticated, are available at Ngapali and Chaung Tha (see box, p.109), where you can also set up **fishing** trips, including deep-sea fishing.

Sport

Myanmar isn't an especially sporty country. **Football** is the most popular game and Premier League (and other European) games are widely broadcast. The country also boasts its own modest professional league, the Myanmar National League (MNL), established in 2009 with eight teams representing individual regions. The two biggest are Yangon United and Mandalay's Yadanarbon FC, who between them have won every MNL title since its inception. Other leading teams include Shan United (formerly Kanbawza FC; based in Taunggyi), Zayar Shwe Myay (Monywa), Ayeyawady United (Pathein) and Naypyitaw FC.

Golf is also modestly popular, although courses are relatively few. The best is probably the Gary Player-designed Pun Hlaing Golf Club in Yangon, and there are also courses at Mandalay, Bago, Bagan, Ngapali, Pyin Oo Lwin, Kalaw and Taunggyi.

Indigenous sports include **lethwei**, a Burmese martial art similar to Thai kick boxing featuring a mix of punching, kicking, head-butts and blows with the elbows and knees. Fights are held regularly around the country during pagoda festivals.

Culture and etiquette

In common with the people of other Southeast Asian Buddhist countries, the Burmese are profoundly polite people, with a gentle, ceremonious culture and customs rooted in the country's Buddhist beliefs.

Burmese manners and social interactions are rooted in the notion of **āna**, a multifaceted concept defined by the *Myanmar–English Dictionary* as "a tendency to be embarrassed by feelings of respect, delicacy; to be restrained by fear of offending". For the Burmese, *āna* applies particularly to the business of dealing with strangers, when the risk of causing accidental offence or embarrassment is greatest – hence the sometimes exquisite levels of politeness you will encounter anywhere from a local teahouse to a five-star hotel.

Compared to some of their less scrupulous cousins in neighbouring countries such as India and Thailand, it's worth noting that most of the Burmese you'll have dealings with during your travels – taxi and rickshaw drivers, shop and guest-house owners, and so on – are still refreshingly honest. Tourist **scams** are rare and you'll generally be offered a fair price for whatever you're looking for. There's still some scope for **bargaining** in shops and perhaps when haggling over transport costs, but bear in mind that the cut-throat haggling that's more or less obligatory in some other Asian countries doesn't apply here, and given how impoverished most Burmese are it's worth reminding yourself what a difference even a handful of kyat can make to a local cycle-rickshaw-driver or market-stall owner.

The Burmese **dress** modestly. In some ethnic minority villages it's still the norm to wear traditional dress, and even in cities many men and women still wear longyi (see box, p.7), although Western-style clothes are increasingly common. People will be too polite to say anything, but they may be offended by the sight of tourists wearing revealing clothes, including shorts cut above the knee, and – particularly for women – tops that are tight or show the shoulders.

Physical **demonstrations of affection** (particularly holding hands) are common between friends of the same sex and family members, but not between men and women. Couples will rarely even hold hands in public, although they can often be seen sitting very close together in parks under the shelter of a protective umbrella.

You should also avoid touching another person's head (considered the most sacred part of the body), and when sitting try to avoid pointing your feet (which are considered impure) at anyone. Always use your right hand when shaking hands or passing something to someone (the left hand is traditionally used for toilet ablutions). If invited inside a Burmese **house**, remove your shoes before going inside.

Greetings

There's no equivalent in Myanmar to the prayer-like **greetings** employed in other nearby Buddhist countries (such as the Thai *wai*, Cambodian *sampeah* or the Sri Lankan *ayubowan*). Men will shake hands on meeting; women meeting one another or a woman meeting a man will content themselves with a smile and a *mingalaba*. Men should not try to shake hands with women.

The standard Burmese greeting is the rather formal *mingalaba* (meaning roughly "blessings upon you"), although this only entered the language in the post-colonial period as a replacement for the colonial "Good morning/good afternoon". Given that there's no clear equivalent of "hello" in Burmese, foreign visitors have adopted *mingalaba* as an easy, all-purpose greeting, and the phrase has been embraced with gusto by the Burmese as a way of addressing foreigners.

Burmese speakers themselves rarely use *mingalaba*, preferring more informal greetings, typically *nei kaun la* ("how are you?") or just "hello". You might also hear *htamin sa pi bi la* – literally, "have you eaten rice?".

WHAT'S IN A NAME?

Burmese names are traditionally of two syllables only, although three-, four- and even five-syllable names are becoming increasingly popular. Two-syllable names are also sometimes turned into three by repeating one of the constituent parts – Ma Ma Lay, for example. There are no family surnames in Burmese, nor can names be shortened or divided – a man named Tin Moe, for example, can't be called "Tin" or "Mr Moe". Women do not change their names upon marriage and there are no family names. Tin Moe, for example, might have a wife called Mi Khaing, a son called Than Tut and a daughter named Mya Aye. Some Burmese (particularly those working with foreigners) also adopt alternative Western first names, using both their Burmese and Western monikers in parallel.

Prefixes are usually added to names, except when talking to close friends or small children. "U" (signifying "Mr" or "uncle") is used in formal situations or when addressing an older man, and "Ko" or "Maung" (meaning "brother") is preferred when addressing someone younger or of one's own age. The female equivalents are "Daw" ("Mrs" or "aunty") and "Ma" (sister).

Astrology also plays a major role, with children often given a name reflecting the day of the week on which they were born – a child born on a Thursday, for example, would traditionally be given one name starting with a P, B or M. In addition, the Burmese commonly change their names to reflect changing circumstances – Aung San, for example, was born Htein Lin, but changed his name to Aung San (meaning "victory") when embarking upon his revolutionary career.

Traditional naming systems have been increasingly modified by **Western influences** with the incorporation of maternal, paternal and other names, although still not in any particularly consistent fashion – as demonstrated by Aung San Suu Kyi herself, who was named after her father (Aung San), grandmother (Suu) and mother (Khin Kyi), giving her a name which translates (loosely) as "a bright collection of strange victories".

Temple etiquette

Dress conservatively when visiting **temples** (some travellers carry a longyi for such situations) and make sure you take shoes and socks off before entering. Inside, try not to point your feet at any Buddha images – locals tend to sit with their legs tucked beneath themselves. It's traditional to walk around stupas in a clockwise direction, although no one will particularly mind if you go in the opposite direction.

Shopping

Myanmar isn't quite the shopper's paradise of neighbouring Thailand and India, but it still has plenty of affordable traditional souvenirs and crafts worth looking out for. The best places to shop are Yangon (Bogyoke Market in particular), Mandalay and Bagan; elsewhere, pickings can be thin on the ground.

Bargaining is generally the order of the day, except in more upmarket shops or places with clearly marked prices – although you could always try your luck. Note that the **export of antiques** is prohibited, although exactly what constitutes an

antique is not entirely clear. If in doubt, ask the shop you're buying from if they can supply you with an export licence.

Traditional artefacts

Lacquerware is perhaps the most emblematic of all Burmese crafts: lacquerware vessels are still used in many homes and a lacquered bowl or plate makes a beautiful, if pricey, souvenir. Lacquerware is available all over the country, although Bagan offers the best selection and lowest prices, as well as the chance to visit local workshops and see pieces being made.

Another iconic Burmese collectible is the colourful, beautifully decorated **umbrellas** carried by the country's monks and nuns (see box, p.106). Pathein remains the main production centre for traditional cotton umbrellas, while silk parasols (originally from Bagan and Mandalay) can also be found here and elsewhere.

Carvings in sandalwood, stone, marble and other materials are also widespread. Buddha images are ubiquitous, although there are also more unusual statuettes to be found depicting *nats*, mythical beasts and other creatures. Mandalay, particularly the area near the Mahamuni Paya, is a major stone-carving centre.

LUCK BIRDS

Travelling around Myanmar, you'll sooner or later notice the cages set up by roadsides and around towns (particularly outside temples) stuffed full of frantically fluttering and chirruping birds. These are so-called **luck birds**, the unfortunate victims of a popular Buddhist practice whereby birds are captured by local villagers and farmers to be purchased and set free by those seeking to acquire merit by saving a life. The act of buying and freeing a caged bird may appear selfless and spiritually fulfilling, but the practice is far from humane. Many birds die (or are fatally injured) in captivity, while numerous endangered species are threatened by the luck bird trade – common-or-garden species cost a dollar or so, but this rises significantly for larger and more exotic captives. Lucky for seller and buyer, perhaps, but certainly not for the birds themselves.

Traditional Burmese **puppets** also make fun souvenirs. Many are made in Mandalay, where you'll find the biggest selection and best prices. **Sand paintings** are a particular speciality of Bagan, and are sold by local artists and hawkers at all the major temples. Many feature copies of Bagan's ancient temple murals, although you'll also find pieces in a more contemporary style. The detail and workmanship are often superb, and prices are a snip, with smaller pieces going for just a few dollars. They're also easily transportable since you can roll them up without destroying them.

Look out, too, for the **pyit taing daung** (or *pyit taing htaung*). One of Myanmar's most distinctive traditional toys, these odd-looking dolls resemble a papier-mâché Easter egg with an oversized smiley face painted on it. They're also weighted inside, meaning that however much you bash them, they never fall down, rather like the Western Weeble – hence their name meaning "up whatever thrown".

Clothes, textiles and jewellery

Beautiful cotton and, especially, silk **fabrics and textiles** are widely available. Mandalay is again the main centre of production, although many of the country's ethnic minorities also produce their own distinctive weavings. A **longyi** (see box, p.7) makes a practical and portable souvenir, available either in inexpensive, functional cotton or more lavish silk. In addition, skirts, scarves, shirts and fabric shoulder bags can all make good buys.

Myanmar has an extraordinary wealth of natural minerals and precious stones. **Jade** (most of it from the far north of the country) is very much in evidence, from simple traditional bangles through to chintzy statuettes and other bric-a-brac – although note that buying jade is fraught with ethical complications (see box, p.352). There's also plenty of gold and silver **jewellery**, as well as precious stones including rubies and sapphires.

Fakes are not unknown, though – buy from a reputable dealer or risk being ripped off.

Travelling with children

Few Westerners travel with children in Myanmar, but if you do you'll be guaranteed a very warm welcome, with locals going out of their way to make a fuss of your kids and help in any way they can.

Having said that, although you can be guaranteed plenty of social interaction, specific kids' attractions are pretty thin on the ground, given that most of the country's major draws are essentially cultural. The generally long journeys involved in getting from A to B are a further drawback, while parents of fussy eaters may also struggle, especially outside major tourist centres. Travelling with **babies and toddlers** is a real challenge. You'll struggle to find formula milk, nappies or baby food (although discreet breast-feeding is perfectly acceptable), and you'll also need to be aware of the potentially serious effects of heat, sunstroke, dehydration and the risk of malaria (and other diseases) (see p.38). And be aware that, should anything go wrong, medical facilities in the country are rudimentary at best.

Activities

Older kids may enjoy exploring the ruins of Bagan by **bike** or in a **horse-drawn carriage** (especially if you can dress it up in suitably Indiana Jones style) and might enjoy a **boat trip** on Inle Lake, and possibly a **day trek** through local villages. The **beaches** are another possible draw, although there's not a lot in terms of specific child-friendly activities apart from a few watersports (for older kids who are also confident swimmers).

RESPONSIBLE TRAVEL

The question of whether or not it was right to visit Myanmar was for many years an emotive issue. In 1995, Aung San Suu Kyi's National League for Democracy (NLD) called for an international **tourist boycott** of the country, arguing that foreign visitors were putting money directly into the pockets of the regime. Many foreigners respected this call to stay away. Others continued to visit, saying that with care it was possible to minimize the money given to the regime and to ensure that foreign cash still reached local communities – and also arguing that plunging the country into complete isolation simply caused further hardship for the long-suffering Burmese. Following tentative reforms, in 2010 the NLD softened its stance, saying that it opposed only package and cruise tourism, and in May 2012 it dropped its boycott entirely.

With the NLD now in power, it's safe to say that the ethical dilemma has reduced significantly, if not entirely vanished. Nevertheless, despite the advent of **democracy** (or at least something reasonably close) in 2015, the former ruling military elite and their business cronies still control large swathes of the economy, including numerous hotels (many built using forced labour on stolen land), as well as banks and airlines. Take a flight, withdraw money from an ATM or stay at one of many of the country's upmarket hotels and you'll be putting money, however indirectly, into their bank accounts.

It's not an ideal situation, although now not much different from that in, say, neighbouring Cambodia, Laos and Thailand, whose often repressive rulers and associated cronies also derive significant income from tourism. It's also worth remembering that crony companies employ thousands of ordinary Burmese, untainted by the old regime, whose livelihoods depend upon their continued employment – indeed, post-democracy some crony companies have been praised for being model employers, paying above-average wages as well as contributing significant amounts of tax to NLD government coffers.

As such, the best policy is to follow the usual **ground rules of ethical tourism** in Asia. Staying in local guesthouses, eating in local restaurants and hiring local guides helps keep your money in the communities you're visiting, while spreading your money around rather than spending it all in one place (when shopping, for example) is also helpful, and travelling by bus or local boat is better than flying or taking a tourist cruise. Bear in mind, too, that the vast majority of visitors to Myanmar confine themselves to Yangon, Mandalay, Inle Lake and Bagan. Visiting one or two more off-the-beaten-track destinations not only offers you the chance to escape the coach-party hordes but also brings money into parts of the country that have yet to enjoy the fruits of the recent tourism boom.

In Mandalay, kids may enjoy the **puppet performances** at Mandalay Marionettes or the Minta Theater, as well as the dances of the Moustache Brothers (though the satire at the latter will likely go over children's heads). Sporty youngsters will also get a kick out of just hanging out with the locals, maybe joining in an impromptu football match or trying a spot of **chinlone** (see box, p.43) – locals will be delighted to take them under their wing.

Travel essentials

Addresses

The words "road" and "street" are used interchangeably throughout Myanmar. In some towns streets are clearly signed, whereas in other places signage can be nonexistent. As elsewhere in Asia, directions are usually given in relation to local landmarks rather than using street names and house numbers.

Costs

Accommodation (see p.32) is likely to be your main cost in Myanmar, with even the cheapest rooms costing around $15–25 and upmarket lodgings going for $150 or considerably more. **Food** is much more affordable – you can get a meal on the streets or in local cafés for just a couple of dollars, with mains in more touristy places costing around $3–5 (although equally some top-end places charge prices on a par with Europe or North America). **Bus** and **train** tickets are also relatively (if not exceptionally) cheap – an express bus from Yangon to Bagan, for example, costs around $15–20. **Flying** is obviously much pricier but not prohibitively

EMERGENCY NUMBERS
Police ☎ 199
Ambulance ☎ 192
Fire ☎ 191

expensive, especially when you consider the time-saving involved – Yangon to Bagan, for example, will cost somewhere in the region of $70–100. Hiring your own car and driver is expensive (at least $60/day, often significantly more), as are packaged trips, especially cruises – more upmarket river trips can cost thousands of dollars. **Admission fees** aren't too punitive – the week-long ticket covering the whole of Bagan costs a relatively modest $25 (compared to $37 for a one-day ticket to Angkor, for example). Government museums typically charge a K5000 entrance fee.

All things considered, if you're travelling around Myanmar as a couple you might conceivably be able to get by on a **daily budget** of $15–20/£12–16/€14–19 per person (maybe even less), although $25/£20/€23 per day is a more realistic target. For $40/£32/€37 per person per day you can be pretty comfortable. Equally, it's perfectly easy to spend $200/£160/€185 per day if you're staying and eating in top-end hotels and travelling with a car and driver. Travelling on your own obviously bumps costs up considerably, given that you'll have no one to split pricey accommodation rates with.

Upmarket restaurants and hotels may add a ten percent service charge. Elsewhere, **tipping** in local restaurants, teahouses, taxis and so on isn't really expected (although of course is always appreciated). Caretakers and guardians will expect a tip for unlocking a temple, museum or other monument for you.

Crime and personal safety

Despite decades of military oppression, often grinding poverty and a string of local insurgencies, Myanmar remains an extremely safe place for foreign visitors. Violent crime against tourists is extremely rare, and even petty theft is relatively uncommon, although obviously it pays not to leave valuables lying around or rooms unlocked. If you are unlucky enough to suffer a theft you'll need to report it to the **police** to get a statement for your insurance claim. Taking a Burmese-speaking companion to translate is pretty much essential – ask at your accommodation. Major tourist centres have dedicated tourist police, although even so it's worth taking a Burmese-speaker with you if possible.

Realistically, the biggest dangers to travellers in Myanmar are entirely prosaic. **Health risks** (see p.38) shouldn't be underestimated, while **traffic** can also be a menace, particularly in Mandalay. On top of this, there's a real possibility of injuring yourself by falling into a **pothole** or a gap in the pavement after dark, so it's best to pack a torch.

There's also a slight risk of becoming accidentally caught up in **political or ethnic violence**. Tensions are likely to be particularly high during elections (avoid large crowds and rallies), while there are also sporadic outbreaks of religious and ethnic unrest – for instance the ongoing tensions in Rakhine State between the Burmese and the Rohingya (see p.121), or sporadic clashes between Buddhists and Muslims (something that appears to be getting worse under the new NLD government). There are also ongoing clashes in various parts of the country between the army and various ethnic resistance groups, including (at the time of research) northern Shan State and parts of Kachin State; obviously the situation is in constant flux and it pays to check the latest situation if travelling to remote areas. The government generally closes off any area where there's even a hint of danger, however, both to keep tourists safe and to stop them witnessing things the military doesn't want outsiders to see.

ROUGH GUIDES TRAVEL INSURANCE
Rough Guides has teamed up with WorldNomads.com to offer great travel insurance deals. Policies are available to residents of over 150 countries, with cover for a wide range of adventure sports, 24hr emergency assistance, high levels of medical and evacuation cover and a stream of travel safety information. Roughguides.com users can take advantage of their policies online 24/7, from anywhere in the world – even if you're already travelling. And since plans often change when you're on the road, you can extend your policy and even claim online. Roughguides.com users who buy travel insurance with WorldNomads.com can also leave a positive footprint and donate to a community development project. For more information, go to ⊚ roughguides.com/travel-insurance.

MYANMAR'S GAY SHAMANS

Despite being widely ignored or villified by conservative Burmese, gay men (as well as transgendered women and male transvestites) in Myanmar have found an unlikely niche in one of the country's most traditional religious settings through their role as **nat kadaw**. A kind of Burmese shaman, *nat kadaw* (literally "nat wives") serve as mediums for the country's revered pantheon of *nats* (see p.386), entering trances during which the spirit of any one of the various *nats* takes possession of their bodies.

Nat kadaw were traditionally women, with the profession being passed down from mother to daughter, but over the past thirty years gay men have increasingly taken their places. Male *nat kadaw* will dress either as a man or woman depending on the identity of the *nat* currently possessing them – and even when identifying with a male *nat*, they will typically wear sumptuous clothing, with considerable quantities of make-up. The fact that such overt gender bending is generally accepted most likely derives from the nature of **nat pwè** themselves (see p.41). These are typically raucous, carnivalesque affairs, during which large quantities of booze are consumed and things are done that would not be considered entirely respectable in more workaday settings (*nat kadaw* themselves typically drink and smoke their way into a state of high intoxication in order to best communicate with the spirits of the *nats*).

The **Taungbyone Nat Pwè** (see box, p.298) is particularly well known in this respect. Although not in any sense a specifically gay festival, the *pwè* nowadays attracts large numbers of LGBT locals and travellers alike – and the *nat kadaw* are particularly flamboyant.

Customs regulations

Arriving in Myanmar, you're allowed to bring in **duty free** up to two litres of liquor, 150ml of perfume and four hundred cigarettes (or fifty cigars). You have to declare hard currency over $2000 or equivalent and fill in an FED (Foreign Exchange Declaration) form. The **export of antiques** is prohibited (see p.45).

Electricity

Myanmar mains electricity runs at 230 volts. Most **sockets** take two round-pin plugs, and UK-style sockets with three square pins are occasionally found in upmarket hotels. Adaptors are cheap and readily available. **Power cuts** are a way of life; in many smaller towns electricity is cut off for a fixed number of hours every day, and outages are still common across the country, even in Yangon. Avoid leaving gadgets plugged in during a power cut, as there may be a surge when the supply is restored. Note that many air-conditioning units are fitted with special boxes to protect against power surges; there's often a delay of five minutes between turning the unit on and it actually beginning to work.

Insurance

It's essential to take out **insurance** before travelling, to cover against theft, loss and illness or injury. A typical travel insurance policy usually provides cover for loss of baggage, tickets and – up to a certain limit – money, as well as cancellation or early curtailment of your journey. Most of them exclude so-called dangerous sports unless an extra premium is paid: in Myanmar this might mean scuba diving, trekking, rock-climbing and mountain expeditions. Many policies can be chopped and changed to exclude coverage you don't need – for example, sickness and accident benefits can often be excluded or included at will. When securing baggage cover, make sure that the per-article limit – typically under £500 – will cover your most valuable possession. If you need to make a claim, you should keep receipts for medicines and medical treatment, and in the event you have anything stolen, you must obtain an official statement from the police. Finally, ensure that your insurance cover will still be valid if you're planning on visiting any areas that your home government is currently advising against visiting (including, at the time of research, parts of Rakhine and Shan states).

Internet and wi-fi

Until recently, Myanmar had one of the world's lowest internet penetration rates. Internet access wasn't available anywhere until 2000, and remained severely limited (and heavily censored) until 2011, although recent reforms mean that the country is now as wired as most other places in the region. Free **wi-fi** is now available at virtually every hotel and guesthouse (although connections are often hit and miss), as well as a fair number of restaurants and other establishments. **Internet cafés** are becoming increasingly hard to find; the few surviving places typically charge around K500 per hour.

The formerly stifling levels of internet **censorship** have also been radically scaled back since 2012, allowing unrestricted access to international news sites, dissident bloggers and the like. You probably won't be aware that there's any censorship at all unless you go surfing online for porn, poker or Myanmar brides.

Laundry

Not surprisingly, you won't find any laundrettes in Myanmar. Upmarket (and some mid-range) hotels generally have a laundry service, usually pricey, while budget guesthouses may be able to wash clothes (or farm them out to someone who does). Alternatively, just look out for a convenient back-street laundry. These should be able to turn washing around overnight, charging in the region of K500 per item.

LGBT travellers

Homosexuality is technically illegal in Myanmar and punishable by fines or imprisonment – anything up to life in theory under the country's archaic penal code, which dates back to colonial times. Actual arrests are rare, however, and LGBT communities are gaining more recognition and acceptance following the return to democracy, while Aung San Suu Kyi herself had called for the decriminalisation of homosexuality (even if her ruling NLD party has yet to do anything about it). See ⓦen.wikipedia.org/wiki/LGBT_rights_in_Burma for more detailed background on the general cultural and political situation, and ⓦutopia-asia.com/tipsburm.htm for practical information.

There's a discreet LGBT scene in Yangon – the city hosted its first **Gay Pride** event in 2012, followed in 2014 by its first (unofficial) gay marriage and first LGBT film festival (which has run each year since then at the Institut Francaise, organized by the city's &Proud group, who also organize other LGBT-oriented cultural events in the city – check ⓦfacebook.com/andPROUD for further information. There's also a regular LGBT club night, Fab (ⓦfacebook.com/EventsYG), currently held at the Muse Bar on Ahlone Rd.

Outside Yangon (and indeed even in most parts of Yangon itself), however, the LGBT scene remains largely undercover, with rigidly conservative attitudes to homosexuality still the norm, informed by traditional Buddhist beliefs and the idea that all LGBT relations are simply some kind of perversion indulged in only by foreigners. As such, **discretion** is naturally advised – you're unlikely to encounter any problems unless you very clearly call attention to yourself. Note that it's culturally acceptable for Burmese friends of the same sex to hold hands in public, although this is no indication of their sexual orientation.

Maps

The best country maps of Myanmar currently available are the ones published by Reise Know-How (1:1,500,000) and by Freytag & Berndt (1:1,200,000), although neither is generally available in Myanmar itself. The local fold-up maps of major tourist towns around the country produced for the Ministry of Tourism by DPS Maps (ⓦdpsmap.com) are also useful. They're sometimes handed out free by hotels, and are also widely available from local hawkers for $1–2.

Meditation

Myanmar is a good place to study or practise meditation. Some centres will only take foreigners who commit to staying for several weeks, but there are also courses available in Yangon (see p.87) and at Sagaing near Mandalay (see p.292). A special **meditation visa**, valid for three months, is available for people staying at a recognized meditation centre.

Money

Myanmar's currency is the **kyat** (pronounced something like "chat"), usually abbreviated as K or Ks (or, officially, as MMK). Notes are available in denominations of K1, K5, K10, K20, K50, K100, K200, K500, K1000, K5000 and K10,000, although the lowest value you're likely to encounter is the K100 note. There are no coins. The **US dollar** (again, notes only) is widely used alongside the kyat as a secondary currency to pay for more expensive items and services such as hotel rooms.

In the past, dollars were specifically needed to pay for things like train tickets, entrance tickets to certain sights and other items, although now it's possible to pay for just about everything in kyat.

EXCHANGE RATES
At the time of research, the **exchange rate** was roughly K1370 to $1, K1700 to £1 and K1150 to €1.

Note, however, that many touristy places (including hotels, restaurants, shops and tour operators) quote prices and prefer payment in dollars, and some more upmarket hotels and operators may insist on payment in dollars (it's certainly easier than counting out huge wads of kyat), although this is becoming increasingly rare. If you do pay in local currency at such places where kyat are preferred, the kyat price may be calculated at a disadvantageous exchange rate (sometimes as low as $1=K1000), making it slightly cheaper to pay with dollars – keep some low-denomination notes handy for such occasions. Change may be given in either dollars or kyat.

Changing money

At one time the official exchange rate for kyat was kept artificially low and most people changed money on the black market, but today banks and official moneychangers offer a realistic rate. Avoid changing money on the street, however good the rate you're offered, as scams are common. Kyat can't be exchanged overseas – be sure to change all your leftover currency before leaving the country.

Dollars are the easiest overseas notes to exchange, although you should also be able to change euros, pounds and other major currencies. Note that you won't be able to exchange US dollars issued before 2006. High-value notes (particularly $100 bills) also attract the best exchange rates.

It's imperative (this can't be stressed enough) that any notes that you intend to use in Myanmar are in **pristine condition** (ideally, ask if your home bank can get you mint-condition notes). Banknotes that are creased, torn or marked in any way – however minor – may not be accepted in payment, or you'll be forced to sell them at a reduced rate if exchanging for kyat. Similarly, in the (slightly unlikely) event that you end up having to buy dollars in Myanmar, reject any note not in perfect condition.

ATMs and credit cards

ATMs have mushroomed across the country in recent years, while more and more places have begun to accept credit cards. Western Union and MoneyGram services are also now available. There are now a fair number of **ATMs** in all major towns and tourist centres; most accept both Visa and MasterCard (exceptions are noted in the Guide), although it's still worth bringing a decent stash of dollars (ATMs dispense only kyat) as a backup. Note, too, that ATMs typically charge a $5 withdrawal fee (on top of whatever your bank at home might charge you). **Credit cards** are now generally accepted in all top-end and some mid-range hotels, plus some more upmarket shops and restaurants.

Opening hours and public holidays

Standard **business hours** are Monday to Friday 9am to 5pm; **banks** typically open Monday to Friday 9am to 3pm, although some close earlier and currency exchange counters may not open until 11am. Major **temples** may stay open 24 hours a day (especially during festivals and holidays), and will certainly be open (at minimum) from around 6am to 9pm. Opening times for **restaurants**, **teahouses**, **bars** and **shops** are given throughout the Guide.

PUBLIC HOLIDAYS

Several holidays (marked *) are based upon the lunar calendar and therefore change date each year.

January 4 Independence Day
February 12 Union Day
March 2 Peasants' Day
March/April* Tabaung full moon
March 27 Armed Forces Day
April 13–16 Thingyan Water Festival
April 17 New Year
May 1 Labour Day
May* Kasong full moon
July 19 Martyrs' Day
July* Waso full moon (beginning of Buddhist "Lent")
October* Thadingyut full moon (end of Buddhist "Lent")
November* Tazaungmone full moon
November/December* National Day
December/January* Kayin New Year
December 25 Christmas Day

Phones

Most guesthouses will let you make calls **within Myanmar** from a phone at reception (check the cost first), and staff are often happy to make the call for you if you're worried that the phone will be answered by a non-English-speaker. Calls made from the in-room IDD phones found in some top-end hotels always come with a massive mark-up. It's possible to call **internationally** using a

VOIP (Voice Over Internet Protocol) service such as Skype or Voipfone, although erratic connections can make this a very hit-and-miss business. Otherwise you'll need to use public call centres (try asking at the post office), although international calls are expensive.

By far the cheapest way of making both local and international calls is by getting hold of a **local SIM card**. This used to be a difficult and expensive business until 2014, when the government began issuing licences to foreign mobile companies, and local SIMs can now be picked up from phone (and other) shops all over the country for just a few dollars – you may need to show your passport if buying from one of the phone companies' own offices. There are currently three operators: Telenor (W telenor.com .mm), Ooredoo (W ooredoo.com.mm) and MPT (Myanmar Post & Telecommunications; W mpt .com.mm), with top-up cards widely available and usually sold in values of K1000, K3000, K5000 and K10,000. Telenor and Ooredoo have the most modern 3G networks, although MPT has more extensive coverage in rural areas. Note that all users are now required to **register** their SIM card; you will need to provide your name, address and passport number, plus a scan or picture of the photo page from your passport. Registrations can be submitted online on your phone provider's website – failure to do so may result in your service being disrupted or blocked. Mobile phone numbers start with 09, though the exact number of digits varies.

To **call home from Myanmar**, dial the international access code (W 00), then the country code (UK W 44; US & Canada W 1; Ireland W 353; Australia W 61; New Zealand W 64; South Africa W 27), then the area code and subscriber number. Note that the initial zero is omitted from the area code when dialling the UK, Ireland, Australia and New Zealand from abroad.

To **call Myanmar from abroad**, dial the international access code and the country code for Myanmar (W 95), then the area code, minus the initial zero, and the subscriber number.

Photography

Most Burmese love having their photo taken, but it's polite to ask before shoving a lens in someone's face and, assuming you're using a digital camera, to show them the picture afterwards. To ask "Is it okay if I take a photo?" in Burmese, say *"Daq-poun yaiq-teh, ya-deh naw?"*. Don't photograph anything resembling a military installation, and it's probably best to avoid snapping police and soldiers as well. There are usually no restrictions on taking photographs in temples.

The best photographic conditions can usually be found early in the morning, around 6–8am. Not only is the light at its best, but this is one of the busiest times of the day around local markets and also a good time to photograph popular temples and other attractions before hordes of tourists arrive.

Post

The postal service in Myanmar isn't known for its efficiency; sending postcards is cheap, although they don't always reach their destinations. **Post offices** are typically open Monday to Friday 9.30am to 4.30pm and sometimes on Saturday mornings, and many have an EMS (Express Mail Service) counter offering faster and more reliable international delivery.

Time

Myanmar time is 6hr 30min ahead of GMT (5hr 30min ahead of British Summer Time), 11hr 30min ahead of US Eastern Standard Time, 14hr 30min ahead of US Western Standard Time, and 3hr 30min behind Australian Eastern Standard Time. There are no daylight-saving time changes in Myanmar.

Tourist information

The government-run **Myanmar Travels & Tours** (MTT; W myanmartourism.org) maintains tourist offices in Yangon and Mandalay, but in general the best sources of travel information are generally local travel agents or the staff at your guesthouse or hotel. There are no Myanmar tourist information offices abroad, although embassies and consulates may be able to help with information about which areas are currently restricted or off limits.

MYANMAR ONLINE

Good online news resources are listed in "The Media" section (see p.41).

W **burmalibrary.org** Handy links to thousands of Myanmar-related websites and publications.

W **go-myanmar.com** Far and away the best online resource for travellers to Myanmar, crammed with practical information, detailed accommodation and eating listings and a wealth of other information.

Ⓦ **myanmartourism.org** Official tourism website with general background information, although note that the list of places that are off limits or require permits is usually utterly out of date.

Ⓦ **seat61.com/Burma** This excellent website covers all things railway-related in Myanmar.

Ⓦ **tourismtransparency.org** Good background on responsible travel in Myanmar, although the site isn't regularly updated and is now becoming rather out of date.

Travellers with disabilities

Myanmar is poorly set up for travellers with disabilities, although with a bit of determination and pre-planning you can still enjoy much that the country has to offer. Getting around is the first challenge. Public **transport** by bus or train is a total non-starter for disabled travellers, meaning that you'll have to contact a local or foreign tour operator (see p.25) to arrange for suitable transport by private vehicle. The various domestic airlines should be able to take care of you, however, given appropriate notice of any special

requirements. Specially adapted **accommodation** is also virtually nonexistent, although given that most accommodation outside Yangon and Mandalay is typically laid out in one-storey bungalow-style buildings, accessibility, at least, shouldn't be a major obstacle.

In terms of **sights**, many of the major ones in Yangon and Mandalay are relatively accessible, although the densely crowded pavements of downtown will present serious difficulties. Burmese temples are typically set at the top of long flights of steps, although some of the biggest (including the Shwedagon in Yangon) have lifts, making them relatively accessible. Many of Bagan's temples are also fairly easy to visit, often with fewer steps (and, in any case, it's often the exteriors of these temples and the surrounding landscape that provide the main draw). **River cruises** should also be possible on dedicated tourist boats (but not public ferries), though this does not really extend to Inle Lake, where vessels are small, narrow and difficult to negotiate at the best of times.

Yangon
and around

SHWEDAGON PAGODA

1

Yangon and around

Myanmar's largest city, Yangon, still sometimes referred to by its old colonial name of Rangoon, is a city of startling contradictions. Decades of economic and cultural isolation are still very much in evidence, exemplified by the old downtown district with its endless streets of decaying colonial buildings, erratic electricity and sardine-packed rustbucket buses. The international chains and logos which are steadily consuming many other cities in the region are conspicuous by their almost complete absence, and the fabric of downtown city life – a dense honeycomb of pavement cafés, ramshackle markets and soaring stupas – looks, in places, strangely untouched by the modern world.

And yet the winds of change are already gusting through the city, with streams of late-model Japanese cars flooding the city streets, along with a rapidly growing number of swanky hotels, formica-clad local fast-food joints, illuminated billboards and shops flogging the latest smartphones, tablets and other digital accessories. All of which gives the strange impression of a city divided in time: at once thoroughly modern but also several decades out of date – which is perhaps the essence of the place's peculiar appeal.

For visitors, Yangon is very much a city of two halves. The old colonial city – or **downtown Yangon**, as it's often described – remains far and away the most absorbing area in this rapidly expanding megalopolis, a fascinating urban landscape of picturesquely decaying colonial architecture dotted with gilded Buddhist pagodas, Hindu and Chinese temples, mosques and markets. North of here stretch the endless suburbs of **modern Yangon**, a largely featureless urban sprawl dotted with a sequence of florid Buddhist shrines and the sylvan Inya and Kandawgyi lakes. Pride of place goes to the stupendous **Shwedagon Pagoda**, one of the world's most spectacular Buddhist temples, while it's also worth searching out some of the other pagodas and supersized Buddha statues that dot the area.

Brief history

A relative newcomer by Burmese standards, Yangon is a largely colonial creation, although its roots run deep into early Burmese history. A fishing village named **Dagon** was established here in the early eleventh century by the Mon, then the dominant power in Lower Burma, although it remained a relative backwater despite the presence of the revered Shwedagon Pagoda. In 1755, King Alaungpaya, founder of the Konbaung dynasty (see p.364), seized control of Dagon, renaming it **Yangon** and diverting trade here from nearby Thanlyin, previously the major port hereabouts. The British captured Yangon during the First Anglo-Burmese War (1824–26), but returned it to the Burmese in 1827 following the conclusion of hostilities.

Yangon's sudden and unexpected rise to national pre-eminence occurred following the **Second Anglo-Burmese War** of 1852, during which the British recaptured the city (along with the rest of Lower Burma). The formerly modest town was selected as the site of the new capital of British Burma thanks to its location at the meeting point of the

COLONIAL ARCHITECTURE, YANGON

Highlights

❶ Sule Pagoda Landmark temple in the dead centre of Yangon, its soaring golden spire featuring in many of downtown's most memorable views. **See p.59**

❷ Colonial architecture Despite rapid development, downtown Yangon remains one of Asia's finest showpieces of British colonial urban planning, with streets full of majestically time-warped architecture in various states of atmospheric decay. **See box, p.63**

❸ Bogyoke Market Enjoyable British-era bazaar, home to dozens of shops piled high with gems, jade, handicrafts, slippers and more. **See p.67**

❹ Shwedagon Pagoda Myanmar's greatest temple, its unforgettable gilded stupa rising high above the city and packed with colourful shrines busy at all times of day and night. **See p.72**

❺ Ferry ride to Dalah Take the short ferry ride over the river to Dalah for memorable views of the Yangon waterfront and for a startlingly abrupt change of scenery, offering a glimpse of authentic rural Burmese life just ten minutes from downtown. **See p.83**

❻ Street food Eat your way around the city pavements, crammed with food stalls dishing up everything from exotic tropical fruits to deep-fried snakes. **See box, p.93**

HIGHLIGHTS ARE MARKED ON THE MAP ON P.60

1

Indian Ocean and Ayeyarwady River, navigable for almost 1600km into the heart of the country. The antique Mon riverside settlement was razed and a grandiose new urban design laid out, based on the gridiron plan created by army engineer Alexander Fraser.

British rule

Following the conquest of Upper Burma in the Third Anglo-Burmese War of 1885, colonial **Rangoon** (as it was known by the British) became the undisputed economic and commercial heart of Burma. Grandiose new buildings were raised in the fashionable Neoclassical and Indo-Saracenic styles, new hospitals, schools and colleges established, parks laid out, a railway constructed and Inya and Kandawgyi lakes created to provide water for the new city. There was also substantial immigration to the new city from other parts of the British Empire, notably India, giving the city a pronounced subcontinental flavour which endures (in places) to this day.

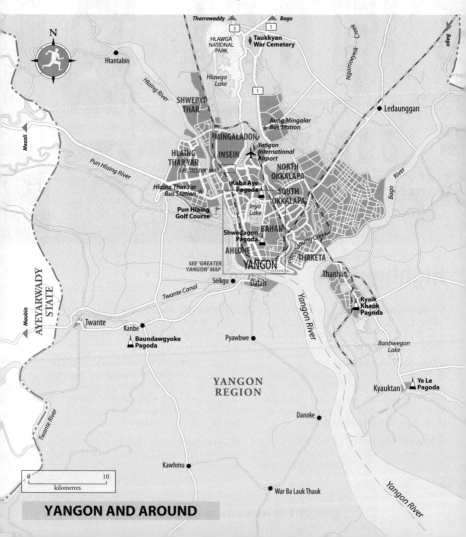

YANGON AND AROUND

Following World War I, Rangoon became the heart of the Burmese **independence movement**, led by students from the British-created Rangoon University and culminating in a series of national strikes (in 1920, 1936 and 1938). The British were finally ousted during **World War II**, during which the city fell under Japanese occupation (from 1942 to 1945), before being retaken by the Allies in 1945, after suffering heavy damage.

Independence

Rangoon became the capital of the new Union of Burma upon **independence** in 1948. The city continued to expand exponentially outwards, with new suburbs mushrooming to the north of the old colonial centre. At the same time, the city's demographic make-up changed substantially, with many Burmese of Indian descent, plus the city's once sizeable Jewish community and other ethnic groups, leaving following independence and later during Ne Win's isolationist rule of the 1960s. Many of the city's old colonial street names were changed, while in 1989 the country's military rulers changed the city's name from Rangoon back to **Yangon**, although the change was not recognized by many local and international organizations, and the old name continues sporadically in circulation right up to the present.

Yangon became a major hotbed of **pro-democracy protests**, particularly during the popular uprisings of 1974, 1988 and 2007. Further carnage ensued in 2008, when **Cyclone Nargis** devastated Yangon's industrial infrastructure – although human casualties were mercifully few. The city suffered a significant symbolic blow in 2005 with the founding of a new Burmese capital at Naypyitaw, but despite being stripped of capital-city status and losing a few ministerial privileges en route, Yangon remains very much the economic, cultural and political heart of the country, with a current population of over five million spreading over an area of over sixty square kilometres.

Downtown Yangon

The old colonial-era city – or **downtown Yangon** as it's now generally known – remains the heart of modern Yangon and far and away its most absorbing district. Laid out by the British in the 1850s, downtown comprises a geometrical gridiron of streets, almost 5km wide and 1km deep, although the original design has proved hopelessly insufficient to deal with the sheer weight of twenty-first-century vehicular and pedestrian traffic, and regularly descends into gridlock, on both the roads and pavements.

Rapid development notwithstanding, downtown remains one of Asia's great colonial-era cityscapes, with streets full of Neoclassical public buildings in various states of monsoon-stained, tropical-overload decay. Superimposed on the old-world fabric, the bustling street life of Yangon continues unabated, with roads and pavements crammed full of more food stalls, touts, shoppers and red-robed monks than you'd believe possible – this is very much a place where it pays to go slow and savour the detail. It's also the place where you'll get the best sense of Yangon's rich multicultural heritage, with a dense confusion of *thanaka*-smeared Burmese, bearded Muslims, dark-skinned Tamils and pale Chinese, all navigating their way between innumerable street-side stalls and pavement cafés.

Sule Pagoda

ဆူးလေဘုရား • Sule Pagoda Rd • Daily 5am–9pm • K3000

Rising out of the very heart of downtown Yangon, the **Sule Pagoda** is the most visible of all Burmese temples, its soaring golden stupa providing the old colonial city with

GREATER YANGON

Insein (2km)

Aung Mingalar Bus Terminal & Airport (9km)

Hlaing Thar Yar Bus Terminal (4km)

Yaegu

MAYANGONE

HIGHLIGHTS

1 Sule Pagoda
2 Colonial architecture
3 Bogyoke Market
4 Shwedagon Pagoda
5 Ferry ride to Dalah
6 Street food

DRINKING & NIGHTLIFE
GTR Club 2
The Vibe 1

0 ———— 1
kilometre

HLAING

Mahapasana Guha

GAN DA MAR ROAD

Kaba Aye Pagoda

Myanmar Gems Museum

PA RAMI ROAD

Parami

PARAMI ROAD

EATING
Le Planteur 2
L'Opera 1
Shan Yoe Yar 3

Kamaryut

THE WAING BU TAR YONE ROAD

PYAY ROAD

HLAING STATION ROAD

Inya Lake

KANBE ROAD

N

BAYINT NAUNG ROAD

Hledan Market

University of Yangon

Sedona Hotel

YANKIN TOWNSHIP

Hledan

UNIVERSITY AVENUE

INYA MYAING ROAD

E
US Embassy

2
Aung San Suu Kyi's House

U RACE COURSE RD

Tamwe

NA NATTAW ROAD

KAMAYUT TOWNSHIP

PYAY ROAD

INYA ROAD

Kokine Swimming Club

E RACE COURSE ROAD

HANTHAWADDY ROAD

Junction Square

DHAMMAZEDI ROAD

KAN BANZA ST

BAHAN TOWNSHIP

KYEE MYIN DAING TOWNSHIP

Kyee Myin Daing

SAN CHAUNG TOWNSHIP

GOLDEN VALLEY

Drug Elimination Museum

U WISARA RD

Chauk Htat Gyi Pagoda

KABA AYE PAGODA ROAD

SHWEGONDAING ROAD

Nga Htat Gyi Pagoda

SEE 'MIDTOWN YANGON' MAP

TAMWE TOWNSHIP

KYEE MYIN DAING KANNAR ROAD

BAGAYA ROAD

Martyrs' Mausoleum

NAT MAUK ROAD

Hlaing River

SHINSAW PU ROAD

PYAY ROAD

People's Park & Square

4 Shwedagon Pagoda

Kandawgyi Lake

Karaweik Palace

Pan Hlaing

BARO ROAD

Maha Wizaya Pagoda

KAN YEIK THAR RD

Ahlone Road

AHLONE ROAD

KHA YAE PIN RD

DAGON TOWNSHIP

ZIWAKA ST

Yangon Zoological Gardens

ZOOLOGICAL GARDEN ST

MYA YAR GONE ST

Pazundaung

Shan Road

National Museum

U WISARA ROAD

Dargah of Bahadur Shah Zafar

MIN KAUNG ST

U GYO ROAD

UPPER PANSODAN ST

MINGALAR TAUNG NYUNT TOWNSHIP

Thanlyin (10km)

Htwe Oo Myanmar Traditional Puppet Theatre

Pyay Road

Phaya Lan

Aung San Stadium

Yangon Central Railway Station

Pazundaung Creek

AHLONE TOWNSHIP

3

LANMADAW TOWNSHIP

LAN THIT ST

PHONG GYI ST

LANMADAW ST

Lanmadaw

SHWEDAGON PAGODA RD

BOGYOKE

ANAWRAHTA

AUNG SAN ROAD

Sule Pagoda

ANAWRAHTA ROAD

2

PANSODAN ST

PAZUNDAUNG TOWNSHIP

MAHABANDOOLA ROAD

2

Kheng Hock Keong Temple

6

1

KYAUKTADA TOWNSHIP

Botataung Pagoda

MERCHANT ROAD

BOTATAUNG TOWNSHIP

Lan Thit Jetty

STRAND RD

Yangon River

SEE 'DOWNTOWN YANGON' MAP

STRAND ROAD

5 Pansodan St Jetty

ACCOMMODATION
Inya Lake Hotel 1
Motherland Inn II 2

Dalah (500m)

its defining landmark, towards which all streets seem to converge. Placed at the centre of the British gridplan in the 1850s, the pagoda remains very much at the centre of downtown life, both physically and culturally (all distances to other parts of the nation are still measured from the pagoda, like a Burmese version of London's Charing Cross). The pagoda is particularly beautiful when illuminated at night, although it looks rather incongruous by day, marooned within a busy roundabout, surrounded by a constant swirl of traffic and with a string of small shops inserted into its base.

According to local tradition, the pagoda was built during the lifetime of the Buddha himself, although the more likely, albeit prosaic, explanation is that it dates back to the Mon era in the tenth century, or thereabouts. The 43m-high stupa was enlarged to its present size by Queen Shinsawbu (ruled 1453–72) and is said to enshrine one of the Buddha's hairs, given (it's said) by the Buddha himself to the brothers Tapissa and Balika, two itinerant merchants from Myanmar. More recently, the Sule Pagoda served as an important rallying point for pro-democracy activists during both the 1988 uprising and the 2007 Saffron Revolution – and was the scene of a brutal massacre during the latter, when the military opened fire on unarmed protestors, killing nine people.

Four staircases lead up to the pagoda from each of the cardinal points, with four matching shrines attached to the base of the stupa at the top of each flight of stairs, all topped with flamboyant gilded roofs. The stupa itself sits on an octagonal base (following the standard Burmese design) but is unusual in that both the bell and spire of the stupa continue the octagonal shape, rather than following the circular pattern adopted by virtually all other Burmese stupas.

Early evening is particularly busy and atmospheric, while you'll also see many people praying in the direction of the stupa in the streets outside as they pass.

Mahabandoola Garden

မဟာဗန္ဓုလပန်းခြံ • Between Sule Pagoda Rd and Mahabandoola Garden St • Daily 6am–6pm • Free

Providing a blissful square of open green space amid the super-compacted streets of downtown Yangon, **Mahabandoola Garden** is at once a peaceful city park and also a shrine to Burmese nationalism. Formerly known as Fytche Square (in honour of Albert Fytche, Chief Commissioner of British Burma), the park was later renamed after the legendary General Mahabandoola (or Maha Bandula), leader of Burmese forces during the First Anglo-Burmese War (see p.366), and is also home to the soaring Independence Monument, commemorating Burmese independence in 1948. The garden itself, dotted with little bonsai-like topiary trees and a fancy modern fountain, is a popular spot for locals practising *t'ai chi* before and after work, and is a nice place to stretch your legs after the cramped downtown pavements; it also offers good views of the neighbouring City Hall and Sule Pagoda. A line of palmists ply their trade outside the railings along the garden's west side.

Around Mahabandoola Garden

Yangon's finest array of **colonial architecture** lies clustered in the area immediately to the east of Mahabandoola Garden and down Pansodan Street. Flanking the northern side of Mahabandoola Garden is the imposing **City Hall** (1924), its Neoclassical outlines jazzed up with a riot of ersatz-oriental decorative motifs including pagoda-topped roofs, chintzy stone latticework and a pair of dragons suspended over the main entrance, with a peacock between.

The large, faintly French-looking building opposite was originally the **Rowe & Co. Department Store** (built 1910), the "Harrods of the East", which survived here until being nationalized by the army in 1964. It now houses a branch of the AYA Bank. One of the few major downtown landmarks to have been thoroughly restored, it offers a good example of what these superb old buildings could look like, given sufficient time, love and money.

On the other side of Mahabandoola Road, a pair of distinctively spiky spires top the **Immanuel Baptist Church** of 1952 (the original church, commissioned by an American missionary in 1885, was destroyed during World War II), while sprawling beyond down the east side of Mahabandoola Garden is the former **Supreme Court** building (1911) in generic Neoclassical style with cream details, topped by a giant red-brick clocktower.

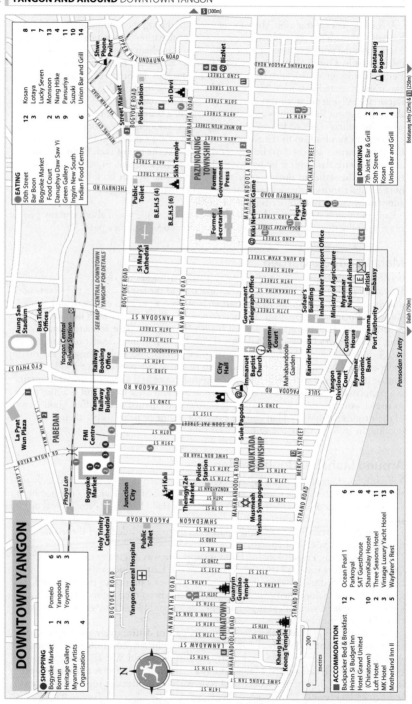

DOWNTOWN YANGON

▲ 5 (300m)

● **SHOPPING**
Bogyoke Market	1
Bontun	3
Heritage Gallery	2
Myanmar Artists Organisation	4
Pomelo	6
Yangoods	5
Yoyomay	3

● **EATING**
50th Street	8
Bar Boon	1
Bogyoke Market	7
Food Court	13
Danuphyu Daw Saw Yi	4
Green Gallery	11
Ingyin New South	10
Indian Food Centre	14
Kosan	12
Lotaya	3
Lucky Seven	7
Monsoon	5
Nang Htike	9
Pansuriya	6
Suzuki	
Union Bar and Grill	6

■ **DRINKING**
7th Joint Bar & Grill	2
50th Street	1
Kosan	
Union Bar and Grill	4

■ **ACCOMMODATION**
Backpacker Bed & Breakfast	12
Hnin Si Budget Inn	7
Hotel Grand United (Chinatown)	10
Loft Hotel	2
MK Hotel	3
Motherland Inn II	5
Ocean Pearl 1	6
Parkroyal	1
SAT Guesthouse	8
ShannKalay Hostel	4
Three Seasons Hotel	11
Vintage Luxury Yacht Hotel	13
Wayfarer's Rest	9

SEE MAP "CENTRAL DOWNTOWN YANGON" FOR DETAILS

Botataung Jetty (25m) & 11 (250m) ▶
Botataung Pagoda ▲
Dalah (750m) ▶
Pansodan St Jetty

N

0   200
metres

Pansodan Street

ပန်းဆိုးတန်းလမ်း

The southern end of **Pansodan Street** was once the city's most prestigious address, and today the street is still lined with a veritable beauty parade of fine old colonial edifices. The following account is ordered from north to south.

Government Telegraph Office and around

Starting from the junction with Mahabandoola Road, the first major building is the **Government Telegraph Office** – a red-brick colossus with paired white Ionic columns above its entrance, although the whole thing's looking a bit run-down, with a crumbling upper storey and a radio mast plonked unceremoniously on the roof.

Past here, the road continues along the back of the Supreme Court, the pavement below usually dotted with pavement **booksellers** seated behind piles of dog-eared old books and magazines. At the southern end of the block a few buildings have been impressively restored and converted into a cluster of upmarket restaurants and shops, including the fine *Rangoon Tea House* (see p.93).

Sofaer's Building and Rander House

On the east side of Pansodan Street at the junction with Merchant Street is the chintzy **Sofaer's Building**, built in 1906 by the Baghdad-born, Rangoon-educated Jewish brothers Isaac and Meyer Sofaer. This was once the epicentre of city life, home to the city's Reuters telegram office and shops selling German beer, Scottish whisky, Egyptian cigarettes and English sweets. The ground floor has now been taken over and largely renovated by the KBZ Bank and the excellent *Gekko* restaurant (see p.92) – the latter with original Manchester-manufactured floor tiles and Lanarkshire steel beams preserved *in situ* – although the upper two floors could use some TLC.

Opposite stands **Rander House** of 1936 (now home to the Internal Revenue Department), commissioned by a consortium of Indian traders from the town of Rander in Gujarat, although the building's eye-catching Art Deco design gives no hint of its subcontinental origins.

Southern Pansodan Street

Further down Pansodan Street (on the left) is the large and rather plain **Inland Water Transport office** (1933), its corniche decorated with seashells. This was formerly the headquarters of the Irrawaddy Flotilla Company, a Scottish-owned enterprise which

---

YANGON'S COLONIAL HERITAGE

Downtown Yangon boasts one of the world's greatest collections of **colonial architecture**, and is the last major city in Myanmar to preserve its original nineteenth-century core at least partially intact, with (in places, at least) entire streets still lined with their original buildings. Decades of neglect have taken a serious toll, however, with historic buildings subdivided into shops, flats or just abandoned to squatters, as well as being disfigured with adverts, satellite dishes, radio masts and mass air-conditioning units. Many structures are now in an advanced state of disrepair, while other landmark buildings once occupied by various ministries have all been left empty since the government upped sticks and moved to Naypyitaw in 2005.

The scale of the preservation required is immense (the cost of restoring the landmark Secretariat building alone has been estimated at $100m-plus, for example), while the urgent need for land and new buildings in downtown means that many colonial-era structures face an uncertain future. The establishment in 2012 of the **Yangon Heritage Trust** (w yangonheritagetrust.org) by influential authors and historian Dr Thant Myint-U is a major step in the right direction, with the aim of establishing a citywide plan for the conservation of historically significant buildings, although how much can be saved in this rapidly developing city remains to be seen. The trust also runs excellent downtown **walking tours** (see p.87).

1

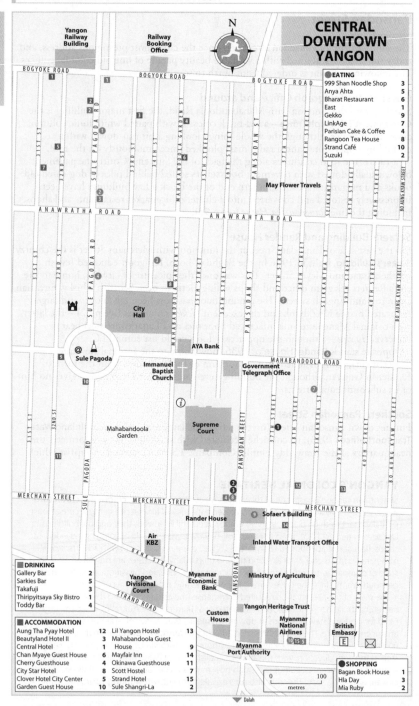

CENTRAL DOWNTOWN YANGON

Yangon Railway Building

Railway Booking Office

N

BOGYOKE ROAD

BOGYOKE ROAD

BOGYOKE ROAD

May Flower Travels

ANAWRATHA ROAD

ANAWRAHTA ROAD

City Hall

AYA Bank

MAHABANDOOLA ROAD

Sule Pagoda

Immanuel Baptist Church

Government Telegraph Office

Mahabandoola Garden

Supreme Court

MERCHANT STREET

MERCHANT STREET

MERCHANT STREET

Rander House

Sofaer's Building

Air KBZ

Inland Water Transport Office

Yangon Divisional Court

Myanmar Economic Bank

Ministry of Agriculture

Custom House

Yangon Heritage Trust

Myanma Port Authority

Myanmar National Airlines

British Embassy

Dalah

31ST ST · 32ND ST · SULE PAGODA RD · 33RD ST · 34TH ST · MAHABANDOOLA GARDEN ST · 35TH STREET · 36TH STREET · PANSODAN ST · 37TH STREET · 38TH STREET · SEIKKANTHA STREET · 39TH STREET · 40TH STREET · BO AUNG KYAW STREET

BANK STREET · STRAND ROAD

0 · 100 · metres

EATING
999 Shan Noodle Shop	3
Anya Ahta	5
Bharat Restaurant	6
East	1
Gekko	9
LinkAge	7
Parisian Cake & Coffee	4
Rangoon Tea House	8
Strand Café	10
Suzuki	2

DRINKING
Gallery Bar	2
Sarkies Bar	5
Takafuji	3
Thiripyitsaya Sky Bistro	1
Toddy Bar	4

ACCOMMODATION
Aung Tha Pyay Hotel	12	Lil Yangon Hostel	13
Beautyland Hotel II	3	Mahabandoola Guest	
Central Hotel	1	House	9
Chan Myaye Guest House	6	Mayfair Inn	14
Cherry Guesthouse	4	Okinawa Guesthouse	11
City Star Hotel	8	Scott Hostel	7
Clover Hotel City Center	5	Strand Hotel	15
Garden Guest House	10	Sule Shangri-La	2

SHOPPING
Bagan Book House	1
Hla Day	3
Mia Ruby	2

during the 1920s operated the world's largest fleet of river boats, with over six hundred vessels carrying some nine million passengers a year.

Next door, the **Ministry of Agriculture and Irrigation** was originally home to Grindlay's Bank, one of the largest in British India (and also housed the National Museum from 1970 to 1996). The building's banking origins can be seen in the very solid-looking vaulted doors which protect the entrance, while a quirky facade of green semicircles, topped with lion heads, rises above.

Diagonally opposite the Ministry of Agriculture is the fortress-like **Myanmar Economic Bank**, with its rather severe Art Deco styling and distinctive hexagonal corner tower. One of the last architectural hurrahs of Rangoon under British rule, the building was constructed in 1939–41 as the Burma HQ of the Chartered Bank of India, Australia and China (later Standard Chartered) and considered one of the most modern buildings in Asia of its time, complete with steel-framed, reinforced-concrete construction, underground parking and a huge banking hall.

Further south, at the end of the street, stands the imposing **Myanma Port Authority** building with its landmark tower and huge arched windows, with roundels decorated with ships and anchors between.

Strand Road

At the bottom end of Pansodan Street, a left turn along Strand Road leads to the *Strand Hotel* (see below). Alternatively, heading right brings you to the neat red-brick **Custom House**, complete with clock and cupola. Past here is the huge **Yangon Divisional Court**, originally the office of the British Accountant General and the place where all government taxes were collected on products ranging from salt through to teak and opium. The building is now slowly emerging from a massive restoration project, its facade decorated with freshly cleaned six-pointed stars and fleurs-de-lys.

The Strand Hotel

စတ္ဒရန်းဟိုတယ် · 92 Strand Rd · ☎ 01 243377, ⓦ hotelthestrand.com

Downtown Yangon's address of choice for the rich and famous is the **Strand Hotel**, looking like a staid elderly duchess amid the disreputable hubbub of Yangon's historic, but run-down, waterfront Strand Road. Opened in 1901, the *Strand* was the brainchild of Aviet and Tigran Sarkies, two of the four entrepreneurial, Armenian-descended Sarkies brothers, who established a string of luxury hotels throughout Southeast Asia including the *Raffles* in Singapore and the *Eastern & Oriental* in Penang. The whites-only hotel (Burmese were not admitted until 1945) was described as "the finest hostelry east of the Suez" by John Murray in his *Handbook for Travellers,* and guests included Rudyard Kipling, Somerset Maugham and Lord Mountbatten. It fell into disrepair following independence but reopened in 1993 after extensive renovations, and is today one of the city's most exclusive places to stay (see p.90).

The Secretariat

ဝန်ကြီးများ:ရုံး: · Between Mahabandoola, Anawrahta, Bo Aung Kyaw and Theinbyu roads · Closed to the public except once a year on Martyrs' Day (July 19)

The most impressive of all Yangon's colonial monuments is the gargantuan **Secretariat** (also known as the Ministers' Building), a vast red-brick Neoclassical structure occupying an entire city block, sprawling over sixteen acres and with 37,000 square metres of floor space – roughly two-thirds the size of the Paris Louvre. Completed in 1902 (with the east and west wings added three years later), this is the most famous and historically significant colonial building in Yangon: the former seat of British administrative power in Burma; the spot where Aung San and

1

six cabinet ministers were assassinated on 19 July 1947; and also the place where the country's independence ceremony was conducted the following year. It later served as the national parliament building until the 1962 coup, since when it has been off limits. The entire building is currently wrapped in scaffolding pending a decision about its future and, hopefully, restoration – a massive task, likely to cost at least $100m and to be "potentially one of the largest historic restoration projects in the world", as Al Jazeera described it.

St Mary's Catholic Cathedral and around

စိန်မေရီကက်သလစ်ဘုရားရှိခိုးကျောင်း • Junction of Bogyoke Aung San and Bo Aung Kyaw roads • Daily 8.30am–noon & 2–6pm • Free (no photography)

The imposing **St Mary's Catholic Cathedral**, immediately north of the Secretariat, is the city's principal Catholic place of worship and the country's largest church. Designed by Dutch architect Jos Cuypers (son of Pierre Cuypers, creator of Amsterdam's Central Station and Rijksmuseum), the building was finished in 1899 in a neo-Gothic style not dissimilar to that of the rival Holy Trinity Anglican cathedral across the city (see p.68), topped with a pair of spiky steeples and with an impressively vaulted white-brick interior decorated with colourful red and blue trimmings.

On the south side of the cathedral is the impressive **B.E.H.S. (6) Botahtaung** of 1860 – just two of a number of old colonial-era B.E.H.S. (Basic Education High Schools) which still dot the city. Formerly known as St Paul's English High School, this was once one of the most elite schools in Yangon. East of the cathedral, on Theinbyu Road, the all-girls **B.E.H.S. (4) Botahtaung** (formerly St Mary's Convent School) is another fine old colonial memento still in use today. A fine **Sikh temple** flanks the southern side of the school, while across the road is the former **Government Press** – yet another handsome red-brick Neoclassical edifice, now sadly derelict.

Sri Devi Temple

Anawrahta Rd, between 50th & 51st sts • Daily 6–11.30am & 4.30–8.30pm • Free

Dedicated to the Hindu mother goddess Devi, the **Sri Devi Temple** provides spiritual succour to the many Indian-descended Yangonites living in the subcontinental enclave around the eastern end of Anawrahta Road (the modern-day descendants of Yangon's once omnipresent Indian community who settled in the city during the era of British rule). The temple features the usual multicoloured *gopuram* plus red-and-white-striped walls and an inner shrine manned by a couple of a resident Brahmins.

Botataung Pagoda

ဗိုလ်တထောင်ဘုရား • Strand Rd (foreign entrance on east side) • Daily 6am–9pm • K6000

Tucked away on the far eastern side of downtown is the **Botataung Pagoda**, the second of colonial Yangon's two major Buddhist pagodas – the name (literally "1000 officers") refers to the soldiers of the king who are said to have formed a guard of honour to celebrate the arrival here of precious Buddhist relics from India. The current complex dates from the Mon era, around the same time as the Shwedagon Pagoda, although it was largely obliterated by a stray RAF bomb in 1943 (they were aiming for the nearby Yangon wharves). Reconstruction work started on January 4, 1948 – the first day of Burmese independence. During rebuilding, a previously unknown relic chamber was uncovered containing an extraordinary treasure-trove of seven hundred items including precious stones, jewellery, gold, silver and brass statues and – most importantly – a pure gold stupa-shaped reliquary containing two tiny body relics ("each the size of a mustard seed", as it was reported) and what is believed to be a hair relic of the Buddha.

The stupa

The temple's highlight is the 39m-high gilded **stupa**, particularly its hollow **interior** (a result of post-war rebuilding – the original stupa was solid). At the centre of the stupa, a spectacularly embellished shrine contains the Buddha's hair relic, along with other items from the excavated chamber; peering through the glass, you can just about make out an enormous well descending into the depths of the stupa to the right of the shrine. From the shrine, a corridor zigzags around the inside of the stupa, with walls and ceilings covered in intricate gilded panels and pious locals wedged into the angles of the corridor, meditating or praying while facing the hair relic at the stupa's core.

Around the stupa

The terrace surrounding the stupa is surrounded by a cluster of slightly ramshackle-looking shrines. Starting at the southeast corner of the courtyard, an elaborate covered bridge leads over a small rectangular pond to Botataung's cluster of **nat shrines** including an image of the pagoda's white-turbaned *nat* guardian, or Bo Bo Gyi ("great grandfather"), with a shrine to Shin Upagot (see p.386) beside. Continuing clockwise, halls along the **western side** of the terrace contain several fine gilded Buddhas plus accompanying monks and *nats*, as well as a typical Myanmar-style temple-cum-fairground attraction, comprising a revolving table with several alms bowls on it, into which visitors attempt to throw folded-up banknotes.

At the southern edge of the temple complex, a large **bronze Buddha** dating from 2008 sits on top of a writhing mass of hooded snakes in a pavilion facing the river, with attractive views over the water.

Bogyoke Market and around

ဗိုလ်ချုပ်အောင်ဆန်းဈေး • Bogyoke Aung San Rd • Tues–Sun 10am–5pm • ⓦ bogyokemarket.com

Bookending the northern side of downtown Yangon is the city's principal tourist honeypot, **Bogyoke Market** – or Bogyoke Aung San Market, as it's officially known – home to Myanmar's most diverse and foreigner-friendly collection of souvenir shops, jewellery-wallahs and other consumerist collectibles. Built in 1926, this colonial-era Burmese bazaar was formerly called Scott Market after the then municipal commissioner. The market was renamed Bogyoke ("General") Aung San Market after the country's beloved independence leader in 1948 (with "Bogyoke" being pronounced "Boh-cho").

The modern market is an attractive and atmospheric place, albeit a million miles away from the ramshackle chaos of your average Myanmar bazaar, and also hosts the best collection of craft and souvenir shops (see p.96) under a single roof in the country. The most upmarket and touristy shops are the streetside places under the arcade fronting Bogyoke Road, many of them stuffed with huge quantities of Myanmar jade (including some spectacularly tasteless statues and assorted bric-a-brac aimed at visiting Chinese) plus considerable quantities of lacquerware, paintings and textiles. The main alleyway through the centre of the covered market is lined with dozens of jewellers selling gold, silver, rubies, emeralds and yet more jade, fashioned into bangles, pendants and necklaces, plus a few touristy souvenir places. Shops get gradually more downmarket as you move away from the central alleyway.

There's a handy **short cut** around the back of Bogyoke Market, where a small footbridge near the *Lotaya* restaurant crosses the railway lines – useful if you're heading north of the tracks.

East along Bogyoke Road

East of Bogyoke Market, **Bogyoke Road** is usually busy with pavement hawkers selling an entertaining medley of stuff ranging from old coins and colonial-era bric-a-brac through to tropical fruit and Aung San Suu Kyi T-shirts. At the end of the block, you

1

can't fail to see the fine old **Yangon Railway Building** at the junction with Sule Pagoda Road, another of the city's colonial landmarks currently under restoration.

Holy Trinity Cathedral

Corner of Bogyoke Aung San and Shwedagon Pagoda roads • Daily 10am–5pm • Free

The **Holy Trinity Cathedral** is one of the largest of the many colonial-era churches which still dot Yangon, and Myanmar's principal Anglican cathedral. The foundation stone was laid by the Viceroy of India, Lord Dufferin, in 1886, although a lack of funds meant that it took eight years to complete, didn't acquire its spire until 1913 and had the indignity of being converted by the Japanese into a brewery during World War II. Designed by Madras-based architect Robert Chisholm in High Gothic style, the cathedral's soaring spire and strident red-painted, white-trimmed brick exterior are hard to miss, even if it does looks more like a giant piece of Lego than a place of worship. The whitewashed interior beneath a dark wooden roof is contrastingly plain, bar some fine stained-glass windows. A moving little Forces Chapel commemorates the many British and Commonwealth soldiers who died in the Burma Campaign of 1942–45, while in the southwest corner of the grounds stands a memorial to the troops of many different Commonwealth countries killed in the vicious World War II battles at Kohima and elsewhere.

Yangon General Hospital

West of the cathedral, the rambling buildings of the **Yangon General Hospital** of 1899 are another of the city's British-era landmarks and scene of a particularly vicious massacre on August 10, 1988, when soldiers fired into the hospital, killing injured patients (who were assumed to have taken part in anti-government protests) along with doctors and nurses. Two weeks later, Aung San Suu Kyi made her first ever public speech in the hospital grounds.

Sri Kali

Anawrahta Rd • Daily 6–11.30am & 4–8pm • Free

Originally constructed by Tamil immigrants in 1871, the colourful **Sri Kali temple** is where the area's sizeable local Indian population come to pay their respects to the fearsome mother goddess Kali, whose black image sits in the temple's inner shrine, surrounded by shrines to Shiva, Ganesh, Laxmi and Karthik. Shiva and Parvati sit in a subsidiary shrine outside, with Shiva's bull Nandi carefully looking on.

Theingyi Zei Market

သိမ်ကြီးဈေး • In the block between Anawrahta and Mahabandoola roads, bounded by 25th St to the west and Kon Zay Dan St to the east • Daily 8am–5pm

A world away from the clean, calm and carefully manicured Bogyoke Market, **Theingyi Zei** is what a proper Burmese bazaar looks like, filling almost an entire city block with a chaotic crush of stalls, shoppers, sacks, boxes, bicycles, piles of rubbish and the occasional rat. The market's rather curious name (zei means "market", while theingyi means "great ordination hall") derives from its location on the site of a former pagoda, although it was originally known as the Surati Bara Bazaar – the "Great Surat Bazaar" – after the town in Gujarat from where many of Rangoon's Indian population originally arrived, and who first purchased the land from the British in 1854.

The market is divided between two parallel buildings separated by one of Yangon's biggest and busiest vegetable markets, which runs along 26th Street between Anawrahta and Mahabandoola roads. The western of the two buildings is insanely crowded, especially on its Mahabandoola Road side, usually rammed with crazed bargain-hunters and stuffed with huge quantities of cheap clothes piled up on the quaint wooden stalls (most of which appear to date back to colonial times, with an unusual design resembling large, two-storey cupboards). The eastern building is only fractionally less chock-a-block, although things become a little calmer as you head north, and the market acquires a distinctly Indian flavour as you approach Anawrahta Road and the Sri Kali temple, with shops full of sacks of spices, pulses, dried herbs, and mysterious bits of culinary and medicinal herb and root.

Musmeah Yeshua Synagogue

26th St • Mon–Sat 9.30am–2.30pm • Free

The self-effacing **Musmeah Yeshua Synagogue** is easily missed in one of downtown Yangon's busiest districts. The synagogue was constructed between 1893 and 1896 to replace an earlier building of 1854 and served colonial Rangoon's thriving community of Sephardic Jews from Baghdad and India (such as the Sofaer brothers; see p.63). Before World War II the city was home to as many as 2500 Jews, although most left either during the wartime Japanese occupation or later, following Ne Win's military coup of 1962. The synagogue lost its last rabbi in 1969; Yangon's current Jewish population now numbers fewer than twenty and much of the synagogue congregation comes from overseas visitors. The interior is one of Yangon's most beautifully preserved period pieces, with a gold-railed *bimah* (the platform from which the Torah is read) flanked by a pair of *menorah* lamps, a finely decorated ceiling and high arches supporting a pair of wooden balconies – for women – on either side.

Chinatown

တရုတ်တန်း

Yangon's bustling **Chinatown** (roughly the area south of Anawrahta Road between Shwedagon Pagoda Road and Lanmadaw Street) is the major home for the city's Chinese-descended inhabitants, and one of the liveliest and most enjoyable parts of downtown.

Guanyin Gumiao Temple

Mahabandoola Rd • Free • Daily 24hr

At the heart of Chinatown, the imposing **Guanyin Gumiao Temple** (aka the Guangdong Guanyin Temple) is dedicated to Guanyin (the Chinese version of Avalokitesvara, the Bodhisattva of compassion), attracting a mainly Cantonese crowd. The original temple was built in 1823, and destroyed by a fire in 1855 before rising back up out of the ashes in 1864. The tiled interior is less impressive than the Kheng Hock Keong (see below), but still a fine sight, with red tables laden with incense pots, flower vases, and assorted fairy-lit shrines.

Kheng Hock Keong Temple

ခိန့်ဟုတ်ဗုဒ္ဓဘာသာဘုရားကျောင်း • Strand Rd, between 18th and Sinn O Dan sts • Free • Daily 24hr

The flamboyant **Kheng Hock Keong** Chinese temple ("Temple in Celebration of Good Fortune") is the city's largest and most impressive – a wooden temple was first erected here in 1861, replaced by the current brick structure in 1903. Standing close to the waterfront and docks, the temple is dedicated to the sea goddess Mazu and maintained by the local Hokkien clan association, attracting mainly Hokkien and Hakka worshippers. The central altar enshrines an image of Mazu within an intricate riot of gold decoration, flanked on her left by Guan Gong, god of war, and on her right by Bao Sheng Da Di, god of medicine.

1

Midtown Yangon

The suburbs of **midtown Yangon** immediately north of the old colonial centre are home to some of the city's leading attractions. Pride of place goes to the stunning **Shwedagon Pagoda**, Myanmar's greatest Buddhist place of worship, while there are further supersized Buddhas nearby at the **Chauk Htat Gyi** and **Nga Htat Gyi** pagodas, as well as the pick'n'mix attractions at the city's sporadically entertaining **National Museum** and the **Aung San Museum**, set in the former Burmese leader's time-warped family home.

National Museum of Myanmar

အမျိုးသား ပြတိုက် • Pyay Rd • Tues–Sun 9.30am–4.30pm (last entry 4pm) • K5000 (including free audioguide) • No photography

Yangon's **National Museum of Myanmar** is a bit of a mixed bag. There are some outstanding artefacts here, although the badly lit rooms and erratic signage don't help (the free audioguide fills in some of the gaps), while parts of the five-storey museum's huge exhibition space are rather lacking in actual exhibits. Explore selectively, however, and it's worth at least an hour or two of your time.

Ground floor

The ground floor focuses on exhibits from **Mandalay (Yadanabon)**. The undoubted highlight, and the museum's most celebrated exhibit, is the splendid **Lion Throne**, in a room all of its own. Made for King Bodawpaya in 1816, this was originally one of nine similar thrones, models of which can also be seen here, but it is the only one to survive, despite being carted off to India in 1902 (it was returned by Lord Mountbatten after Independence in 1948).

The adjacent **Yadanabon gallery** showcases the artistry of Mandalay's court, with cabinets full of extravagant and finely worked artefacts including toy-sized wooden models of the Mandalay Royal Palace and assorted clothes and palanquins, although the randomness of the exhibits and lack of signage make the overall effect feel rather like browsing a superior handicrafts shop.

First floor

Top of the bill on the first floor is the magnificent, solid-gold **Royal Regalia**, comprising the royal helmet, fan, sash and sandals plus assorted betel containers, caskets, goblets, urns and an entertaining, vaguely Dalí-esque crayfish-shaped pitcher.

The grindingly dull **Natural History** gallery has the inevitable dishes of prehistoric bones and Stone Age tools – a clump of fossilized poo is about as exciting as it gets – while the **Bronze Age Axes and Spearheads** gallery is as yawn-worthy as you'd suspect. Fractionally more absorbing is the **Burial Urns and Stone Carvings** gallery, with exhibits from Sri Ksetra (Thayekhittaya; see p.193), Hanlin (see p.341) and Beikthano (see p.196), featuring some delicate metalwork and statuettes.

Second floor

The second floor is the most enjoyable in the museum, displaying a rich selection of distinctively Burmese craftsmanship at its extravagant best. The **Traditional Folk Art** gallery holds a wide range of crafts, from beautiful glass mosaic work and spectacular lacquerware through to fun and colourful toys and dolls, animal figurines, and wooden carts, plus a pumpkin-shaped alms bowl and a pair of ingenious chairs with antler horns for legs.

Equally fine is the **Performing Arts Gallery** – home to an excellent array of musical instruments, although it's frustrating that you can't hear what any of them actually sound like. These include several quaint *mi-gyaung*, a crocodile-shaped, three-string zither (the strings are plucked with a plectrum), enormous Shan pot drums and

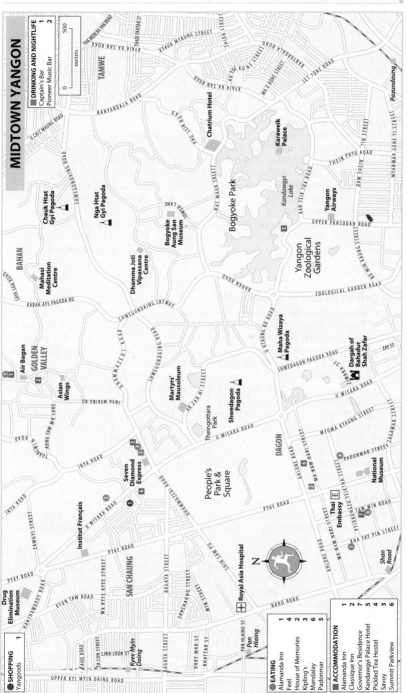

SHOPPING
Yangoods 1

DRINKING AND NIGHTLIFE
Captain's Bar 1
Pioneer Music Bar 2

metres
0 500

TAMWE

Chatrium Hotel

Karaweik
Palace

Chauk Htat
Gyi Pagoda

Nga Htat
Gyi Pagoda

Bogyoke Park

Kandawgyi
Lake

BAHAN

Bogyoke
Aung San
Museum

Yangon
Airways

Mahasi
Meditation
Centre

Dhamma Joti
Vipassana
Centre

Yangon
Zoological
Gardens

Pazundaung

Air Bagan

GOLDEN
VALLEY

Asian
Wings

Martyrs'
Mausoleum

Shwedagon
Pagoda

Maha Wizaya
Pagoda

Dargah of
Bahadur
Shah Zafar

Theingottara
Park

DAGON

Institut Français

Seven
Diamond
Express

People's
Park &
Square

Padonmar

National
Museum

Thai
Embassy

Drug
Elimination
Museum

SAN CHAUNG

Royal Asia Hospital

Shan
Road

Pan
Hlaing

N

Kyee Myin
Daing

EATING
Alamanda Inn 1
Feel 4
House of Memories 2
Kipling's 3
Mandalay 6
Padonmar 5

ACCOMMODATION
Alamanda Inn 1
Classique Inn 2
Governor's Residence .. 7
Kandawgyi Palace Hotel 5
Pickled Tea Hostel 4
Savoy 3
Summit Parkview 6

1

a spectacular glass-mosaic xylophone in the shape of the *pancharupa*, one of Myanmar's many mythical beasts, made from a combination of five other animals. There are also two complete drum ensembles comprising gongs, bamboo clapper, oboe, "timing bell", a "drum circle" (a kind of traditional Burmese drum kit, with the performer sitting inside a ring of drums), and a big drum hung from a *pancharupa* stand. Other exhibits include some fabulous marionettes and assorted masks worn by actors during performances of the Yama Zatdaw, the Burmese version of the Ramayana.

Third and fourth floors

The dull **third floor** is mainly occupied by a large **Art Gallery** featuring an endless succession of watercolours and oil paintings by assorted national painters, with the emphasis on chintzy landscapes and chocolate-box scenes of Burmese rural life.

Few visitors see the museum all the way through to its bitter end on the deserted **fourth floor**. The **Buddha Images Gallery** houses numerous statues from the second century BC through to the eighteenth century – all impressive enough, although none is especially memorable.

Also on this floor, the **National Races Gallery** showcases the crafts and cultures of the nation's ethnic minorities, although most of the stuff here looks like unlabelled bric-a-brac – and exhibits like the "big bamboo spoon" are unlikely to set the pulse racing.

Dargah of Bahadur Shah Zafar

Ziwaka St • No fixed opening hours but usually open daily 8am–8pm • Donation

One of Yangon's most interesting curiosities is the *dargah* (shrine) of the last Mughal emperor of India, **Bahadur Shah Zafar**, or Bahadur Shah II (1775–1862). The poetry-loving, largely powerless emperor became the reluctant figurehead of the Indian Mutiny of 1857, during which many of his family were killed, including two of his own sons (the full and fascinating story of the emperor's role in the uprising is brilliantly told in William Dalrymple's *The Last Mughal*). Having surrendered to the British, Bahadur was exiled to Rangoon, where he lived out the rest of his days before being buried in an unmarked grave which was only rediscovered in 1991. The tomb of the last Mughal emperor now lies in a crypt below ground, with three further tombs (including that of his wife Zinat, in the middle) above – each a simple rectangular block draped in copious green silks and scattered with rose petals. The emperor is still regarded as a Sufi saint by many Burmese Muslims, who come here to seek blessings at his shrine.

Shwedagon Pagoda

ေရႊတိဂုံေစတီေတာ် • Shwedagon Pagoda Rd • Daily 4am–10pm • K8000 • ⓦ shwedagonpagoda.com • Allow 2–3hr for a visit, best towards sunset (although this is when the pagoda is also at its busiest) • Guides can normally be found for hire at the top of the southern stairs

Myanmar's greatest temple, and one of the world's most majestic Buddha monuments, the **Shwedagon Pagoda** towers above Yangon like some kind of supersized spiritual beacon – a magically shimmering outline by day, a spectacular blaze of gold after dusk, when the lights come on. The pagoda is the most revered in Myanmar, said to enshrine eight strands of hair of the historical Buddha, Gautama, along with further relics of his three predecessors (see box, p.74): the staff of Kakusandha, the water bottle of Konagamana, and a fragment of Kassapa's robe. The pagoda remains not only the holiest shrine in Myanmar but also a potent symbol of national identity and a major rallying point for the pro-democracy movement since colonial times. It remains magical at any time of the day or night, but is particularly beautiful around sunset, when locals come to pray and the great gilded stupa seems almost to catch fire in the last of the day's light.

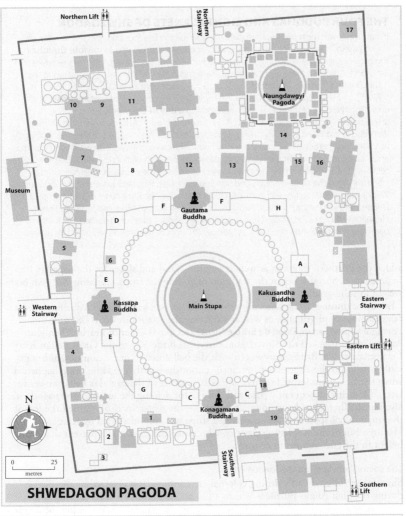

SHWEDAGON PAGODA

KEYS

1	Solid jade Buddha	9	Chanthargyi Buddha	17	Dhammazedi Inscription	
2	Sun–Moon Buddha	10	Shinsawbu Buddha	18	Child-clutching Brahma statue	
3	Commemorative column	11	Photo gallery	19	Replica of the Shwedagon	
4	Rakhaing Tazaung	12	Sacred Hair Relic Washing Well			
5	Buddha's Tooth replica	13	Mahabodhi Pagoda			
6	King Okkalapa statue	14	Shin Izzagona Buddha			
7	Bell of King Singu	15	Pyidawpyan Buddha			
8	Wish-fulfilling Place	16	King Tharyarwady's Bell			

PLANETARY POSTS

A	Monday
B	Tuesday
C	Wednesday
D	Rahu
E	Thursday
F	Friday
G	Saturday
H	Sunday

Brief history

According to local legend, the Shwedagon dates back to around 588 BC, making it the oldest stupa in Myanmar, if not the world – although more likely it was originally built by the Mon between the sixth and tenth centuries. Mon king Binnya U of Bago (ruled 1348–84) had the stupa raised to a height of 18m, but the temple only really started taking shape a century later under **Queen Shinsawbu** (reigned 1453–72), who had the height of the stupa doubled to 40m and also laid out the terrace around the stupa and

1

THE FOUR BUDDHAS AND EIGHT PLANETS OF SHWEDAGON

In common with most Burmese temples, the Shwedagon has four principal shrines attached to the base of the stupa at each of the cardinal points and dedicated to the **four Buddhas** of the current *kalpa*. These include the historical Buddha, Gautama, along with his predecessors Kakusandha, Konagamana and Kassapa (a few temples have a fifth shrine, dedicated to the future Buddha Maitreya, the last of the Buddhas of the present *kalpa*).

Also found here (and at other Burmese temples) is a sequence of "**planetary posts**" encircling the base of the stupa, each representing **a day of the week**, along with its associated heavenly body and animal (although one curiosity of Burmese astrology is that Wednesday is divided into two, giving eight "days" in total). Astrology is still taken very seriously in Myanmar – particular importance is attached to the day of the week on which one is born, and locals come to pray at the relevant planetary shrine, each with its own little Buddha image set on a plinth, which worshippers wash reverently during the course of their devotions.

Starting from the southern stairs and heading clockwise, the pagoda's planetary posts are: Wednesday a.m. (Mercury; elephant with tusks); Saturday (Saturn; a *naga*, or snake); Thursday (Jupiter; rat); Wednesday p.m., or "Rahu" as it's known in Burmese (the moon, ascending; elephant without tusks); Friday (Venus; guinea pig); Sunday (the sun; a *garuda*, the mythical bird-mount of the Hindu god Vishnu); Monday (the moon; tiger); and Tuesday (Mars; lion).

added the northern stairway, as well as assigning land and slaves for the pagoda's maintenance. She also began the tradition of gilding the stupa, donating her own body weight in solid gold.

By the beginning of the sixteenth century the pagoda had become Myanmar's most famous place of pilgrimage, as well as attracting the attentions (in 1608) of the Portuguese adventurer **Filipe de Brito e Nicote** (see p.84), ruler of nearby Thanlyin, whose troops attacked the Shwedagon, carrying off the 325-tonne Great Bell of King Dhammazedi. De Brito's plan was to melt the bell down to make cannons, although sadly it fell into the Bago River in transit (curiously, exactly the same thing happened when the British attempted to make off with another of the pagoda's bells two centuries later). De Brito subsequently paid with his life for defiling the temple. The pagoda was also repeatedly rocked by various earthquakes – the worst, in 1768, caused the top of the stupa to collapse. A new and enlarged stupa was commissioned by King Hsinbyushin of the Konbaung dynasty, who raised the stupa to its present shape and height in the late eighteenth century.

The colonial era and independence

Shwedagon suffered badly during colonial-era conflicts. It was seized by the British during the First Anglo-Burmese War in 1824 and held for two years (during which it was fortified and suffered the inevitable pillaging and vandalism, including the digging of a tunnel into the depths of the stupa in an attempt to discover if it could be used as a gunpowder magazine). It was reoccupied and refortified during the Second Anglo-Burmese War in 1852, although this time the British retained control of it until 1929.

The pagoda played a leading symbolic role in many of Myanmar's twentieth-century political upheavals. Burmese students met at the pagoda in 1920 to plan protests against the colonial University Act – a monument (see opposite) now marks the spot – while protesting students also camped out on the pagoda's terrace during the second university students' strike of 1936, followed by a similar strike-camp of protesting oil workers in 1938 during the so-called "1300 Revolution" (see p.368). General Aung San addressed a mass meeting at the stupa in 1946 demanding independence from Britain, while during the pro-democracy uprising of 1988 his daughter Aung San Suu Kyi spoke to another huge gathering at the pagoda, which was also a focal point of the 2007 Saffron Revolution, with huge demonstrations and protest marches featuring as many as twenty thousand monks and nuns.

The stairways

Four majestic covered **stairways** (*zaungdan*) lead up from street level to the pagoda above. Those at the north, south and west are guarded at the bottom by pairs of enormous chinthe, although these impressive guardian figures failed to prevent the destruction of the western stairway by fire in 1931, nor the British from badly damaging the eastern stairs when they attacked the temple during the Second Anglo-Burmese War. There are lifts on the north and south sides, although it's much more fun to walk. The **southern stairway** (with 104 steps) is perhaps the most impressive, its roof supported by rich red columns and lined with shops selling assorted religious artefacts – Buddha images, miniature paper umbrellas, incense sticks, flowers, religious tomes, and so on. Further shops line the almost equally impressive **eastern stairway** (118 steps), decorated with gilded columns with fancy woodwork. The chintzy, almost rococo-looking **northern stairs** (128 steps) look like something out of the interior of a French chateau. The **western stairs** are the longest (166 steps), and contrastingly plain, with white walls, golden columns, and an escalator down the middle.

The stupa

The stupa is 99m high, the entire gargantuan structure gilded using the metal from almost 22,000 gold bars. It's the iconic example of the classic Burmese stupa and has served as the prototype for hundreds of other stupas across the country (see p.390). The entire structure sits on a square white base encircled with a mass of colourful statues positioned at ground level, including dragons, chinthe, sphinxes and assorted figures ranging from gods and kings through to loin-clothed ascetics and dancing girls wringing out their hair – as well as a string of **planetary posts** (see box opposite).

Rising up from its square platform, the first section of the stupa proper comprises three octagonal **terraces** (*paccaya*), ringed with 64 mini-stupas (eight on each of the eight sides) – only monks are allowed to ascend these terraces. Above rises the huge bell and spire, crowned with a **hti** (umbrella) said to be set with 5448 diamonds, 2317 rubies and 1065 golden bells, along with sapphires and other gems, the whole thing topped with a single 76-carat diamond designed to catch the first and last rays of the sun every dawn and dusk.

Around the terrace

The **terrace** surrounding the stupa is scarcely less eye-popping than the stupa itself, ringed with a veritable forest of shrines and pavilions topped with spiky golden roofs, like dozens of Buddhist antennae pointing towards heaven.

Between the southern and western staircases

Arriving at the top of the southern stairs you come out onto the terrace opposite the ornate shrine housing an image of the **Konagamana Buddha** (signed "Kawnagammana"), one of the four Buddhas of the present *kalpa* (see box opposite) which sit at the stupa's cardinal points. All four were commissioned by King Singu (reigned 1776–82) using a five-metal alloy containing gold, silver, copper, iron and lead – a particularly auspicious metal (derived from the ancient Hindu tradition of *panchaloha*) favoured for sacred icons – although the Kassapa image (on the west side of the stupa) was subsequently damaged by fire and replaced.

Turning left and heading clockwise around the terrace brings you to the Chinese Merited Association pavilion housing a single **solid jade Buddha**, made in 1999 with 324kg of jade from Kachin in northern Myanmar and inlaid with 2.5kg of gold, 91 rubies and nine diamonds. Just behind here is the so-called **Sun–Moon Buddha**, flanked with images of a peacock and a hare (symbolizing the sun and moon respectively), while immediately behind that image stands a small square **Commemorative column** inscribed in Burmese, English, French and Russian and honouring the student leaders of the 1920 revolt (see p.368).

1

Continuing around the terrace, the florid **Rakhaing Tazaung** (or Arakan Pavilion) was commissioned by a pair of wealthy Rakhine merchant brothers and houses a large reclining Buddha almost 10m long, plus miniature paintings-cum-sculptures showing the founding of the Kyaiktiyo temple.

Between the western and northern staircases

A **Kassapa Buddha** image (see box, p.74) stands in a shrine opposite the top of the western stairs. Just past the western staircase, a shiny-bright shrine with dazzling glass mosaic pillars houses a replica of the **Buddha's Tooth** (a copy of the original, held in Kandy's Temple of the Tooth in Sri Lanka). Opposite, on the base of the stupa, is a small golden statue of **King Okkalapa**, the ruler who is said to have helped establish the original Shwedagon Pagoda back in 588 BC, while behind the Buddha's Tooth pavilion a **museum** houses items gifted to the pagoda over the years.

Continuing around the terrace, a pavilion on the northwest side of the stupa holds the gargantuan bronze **Bell of King Singu** (also known as the Maha Ganda Bell), commissioned by King Singu in 1778, weighing almost 25 tonnes and standing over 3m tall. An attempt by the British to steal the bell backfired when the boat carrying it sank in the Yangon River; it was subsequently rescued and restored by the Burmese.

The large area of open terrace directly in front of the bell pavilion is known variously as the "**Auspicious Ground**" or "**Wish-fulfilling Place**" and is said to be particularly favourable for the granting of boons – hence the locals who can usually be found praying here. Behind here is the huge seated **Chanthargyi Buddha**, the temple's largest, and the small gilded **Shinsawbu Buddha** (to the left of the Chanthargyi Buddha), donated by Queen Shinsawbu (see p.73) herself. A small **photo gallery** next to the Chanthargyi Buddha has some interesting shots of the pagoda including close-ups of details (including the extravagant *hti*) impossible to see with the naked eye.

Further around is the eye-catching **Sacred Hair Relic Washing Well** (signed "Hsandawtwin" [Hair Relic Well]), an odd-looking green and blue shrine with glass mosaic inlay, built in 1879 over the site of the spring in which the Buddha's eight hairs are said to have been washed before being enshrined in the pagoda.

Between the northern and eastern staircases

The terrace on the northern side of the stupa is much larger than on the other sides, covered in a dense and disorienting maze of shrines. Facing the northern stairs, the shrine at the base of the stupa houses an image of the historical Buddha, **Gautama**. Diagonally opposite is the unusual **Mahabodhi Pagoda**, a garish parody of the great Mahabodhi Stupa at Bodhgaya in North India, looking as incongruous amid the surrounding Burmese architecture as a panda at a bishop's convention. Past here, and dominating the northeast corner of the terrace, is the brilliantly gilded **Naungdawgyi** ("Elder Brother") **Pagoda**, like a miniature of the main stupa, said to mark the spot where the eight hair relics were first stored.

A further sequence of revered images can be found close to the Mahabodhi Pagoda. These include the **Shin Izzagona Buddha** (signed "Shin Issa Gawna's Buddha Image" and flanked by images of holy men) and – opposite – the small, golden **Pyidawpyan Buddha** (signed "Pyidaw Pyan Returned Buddha Image"), given back to the Shwedagon after having been removed to England in colonial times, and now protected by stout bars. Next door is **King Tharyarwady's Bell** (aka the Maha Tithaddha Gandha), cast in 1841 and even more massive than King Singu's Bell, with a weight of 42 tonnes, a height of 2.6m and a diameter (at its mouth) of 3.3m.

Tucked away at the far northeast corner of the platform is the celebrated **Dhammazedi Inscription**, erected by King Dhammazedi in 1485 and cataloguing the history of the pagoda in three languages (Burmese, Mon and Pali) on a trio of huge stone slabs.

Between the eastern and southern staircases
An image of the third of the four present-era Buddhas, **Kakusandha**, occupies the shrine opposite the top of the eastern stairs. Almost back at the southern staircase, set against the base of the stupa just past the Tuesday Planetary Post, is the **Child-clutching Brahma** (signed "Child holding Brahma Image"), showing the Indian god holding an infant and popular with devotees hoping to have children of their own. Directly opposite, a glass case holds a solid-gold miniature **Replica of the Shwedagon**.

Maha Wizaya Pagoda

မဟာဝိဇယစေတီ • Corner of Shwe Dagon Pagoda and U Htaung Bo roads • Daily 6am–9pm • Free

Built in 1980, the **Maha Wizaya Pagoda** was officially constructed to commemorate the unification of all Theravada orders in Burma, although unofficially it stands as a monument to its creator, military ruler Ne Win (not to mention the king and queen of Nepal, who also contributed various Buddhist relics). Sitting virtually in the shadow of the Shwedagon, from the outside the Maha Wizaya Pagoda looks like a modest miniature sister of its huge neighbour. Inside the hollow stupa it's a completely different story, with a bizarre interior done up to look like a miniature forest with a night sky above, decorated with myriad symbolic animals and other objects.

Martyrs' Mausoleum

အာဇာနည်ဗိမာန် • Ar Zar St (entrance roughly opposite the bottom of the Shwedagon Pagoda's northern staircase) • Tues–Sun 8am–5pm • K3000

The striking **Martyrs' Mausoleum**, immediately north of the Shwedagon Pagoda, is a vaguely Soviet-looking mausoleum-cum-monument shaped rather like a skateboarding ramp, painted bright red and sporting the five-pointed star which also appears on the national flag, symbolizing the union of Myanmar. The graves of General Aung San and the eight cabinet ministers assassinated alongside him in 1947 at the city's Secretariat (see p.65) are laid out along the front of the mausoleum, alongside the remains of Khin Kyit (Aung San's spouse), Queen Supayalat (wife of Burma's last king, Thibaw), and former UN Secretary-General U Thant.

The original mausoleum was largely destroyed in a 1983 bomb blast carried out by North Korean agents in an attempt to assassinate South Korean president Chun Doo-hwan during a visit to the memorial – the president escaped, but 21 others were killed in the explosion. The monument was subsequently rebuilt but kept closed to the public until 2013 for fear that it would serve as a rallying point for pro-democracy campaigners thanks to its association with General Aung San and his family.

You can get a reasonable view of the mausoleum without actually going through the gates, and there's nothing much to see inside apart from assorted pictorial displays (in Burmese only) of General Aung San dotted around the grounds surrounding the memorial – although the views of the monument framed against the Shwedagon spires behind are impressive.

Yangon Zoological Gardens

ရန်ကုန် တိရိစ္ဆာန် ဥယျာဉ် • There are three entrances to the gardens: the Southern Gate, at the junction of Zoological Garden and Bo Min Khaung roads; the Northern Gate (off Lake Rd); and the Museum Gate (at the junction of Upper Pansodan and Bo Min Khaung roads) • Daily 7am–6pm • K3000

Yangon's old-fashioned **Zoological Gardens** (opened in 1906) aren't exactly state of the art but, equally, aren't as bad as some Asian zoos. The fact that many of the animals formerly held here have now been moved to the new zoo in Naypyitaw (see p.188) means that overcrowding isn't a problem, although the handful of tigers which remain are still confined within wretchedly small pens, and the monkey cages are pretty

1

medieval too. Visitors are also allowed to feed some of the animals (including elephants, bears, hippos and monkeys) with selected foods bought next to the pens in question (sugar cane for the elephants, for example). Needless to say, such unregulated feeding runs contrary to all good zoological and veterinary practice, although it does at least save the zoo the cost and bother of feeding the animals itself.

Kandawgyi Lake

ကန်တော်ကြီး

Much of the area immediately east of the Shwedagon Pagoda and north of Yangon Zoo is occupied by the attractive **Kandawgyi Lake**, a crinkly-edged expanse of water wrapped up in attractively landscaped gardens and surrounded by some of the city's prime real estate. The "Great Royal Lake" (as the name translates) was created by the British using water channelled from Inya Lake – it's around 8km in circumference, but not much more than 1m deep at any point. The best views of the water are from Khan Yeik Thar Road on its southern side, either from an attractive (although badly maintained) lakeside boardwalk or from the adjacent public road.

Karaweik Palace

ကရဝိက်နန်းတော်

Impossible to miss on the east side of the lake is the striking **Karaweik Palace**, a chintzy pagoda-style hall built in 1974 and set on a pair of barges pointing out into the water, each with the head of an enormous karaweik (a mythical bird famous for its melodious song) on its prow. The design echoes the *pyigyimun*, or royal barge, commonly used for ceremonial purposes by Burmese monarchs of the past. It's a nice place to watch the sun set over Shwedagon, while the lavish interior now houses a restaurant staging a touristy nightly dinner buffet-cum-cultural show (see p.96).

Bogyoke Aung San Museum

ဗိုလ်ချုပ် အောင်ဆန်း ပြတိုက် • 25 Bogyoke Museum Lane • Tues–Sun 9.30am–4.30pm • K5000

The rewarding **Bogyoke Aung San Museum** has a double significance, occupying the building which was both the last residence of General Aung San, father of independent Burma, and also the first home of the mother of contemporary Myanmar, Aung San Suu Kyi. It was here that General Aung San lived from 1945 until his assassination in 1947, and where his daughter (born 1945) also spent the first two years of her life. The museum was until recently open for just one day each year due to its connections with Aung San Suu Kyi, but is now accessible six days a week, attracting a regular stream of visitors ranging from dutiful school parties to elderly Burmese paying their respects.

The fine old house itself is full of period character, somewhere between a traditional Burmese teak mansion and a miniature French chateau, complete with sweeping staircase, shady veranda and a whimsical circular turret. Inside, the time-warped wood-panelled rooms have been left atmospherically empty bar a few simple but well-chosen exhibits – assorted photographs, some pieces of original furniture and Aung San's iconic trenchcoat (a gift from Indian leader Jawaharlal Nehru) – which offer a moving memorial to Myanmar's charismatic lost leader.

Chauk Htat Gyi Pagoda

ခြောက်ထပ်ကြီးဘုရား • Shwegondaing Rd • Daily 6am–8pm • Free

Even in a land of big Buddhas, the giant reclining figure at the **Chauk Htat Gyi Pagoda** (also spelt "Kyauk Htat Gyi") is an unquestionable show-stopper: almost 66m long, with a 7.3m-long face, 2.7m-worth of nose, and 50cm-high eyes.

The figure was begun in 1959 but not completed until 1974, replacing an earlier giant seated Buddha on the same site which was demolished in 1957 (there's a photo of it, labelled "Wingaba, Rangoon", in front of the reclining image). The name of the pagoda, meaning "Six-storey Pagoda", refers to this impressively huge and now-vanished seated statue – the present reclining figure being more of a three- or four-storey affair.

Housed within a huge corrugated-iron shed propped up on glass mosaic columns, the Buddha has a delicate, rather feminine-looking face complete with blue eye shadow and supersized eyelashes (each 33cm long). A stylish little bindi, diamond-encrusted crown, delicate pink fingernails and golden robes decorated with glass mosaics complete the look, while the soles of the image's huge feet are covered in auspicious golden markings. A gilded statue of the ubiquitous Shin Upagot (see p.386) sits in a small shrine at the far end of the hall, near the Buddha's feet.

Nga Htat Gyi Pagoda

ငါးထပ်ကြီးဘုရား• Shwegondaing Rd (turn right out of the Chauk Htat Gyi Pagoda, head down Shwegone Rd for 100m then go left through the arch signed "Nat Htat Gyi Pagoda" and down this side road for 100m, then head up the covered staircase on your right) • Free

The **Nga Htat Gyi Pagoda** ("Five-storey Pagoda") is home to another of Yangon's supersized Buddhas – not quite the equal of the nearby Chauk Htat Gyi in size at a mere 9m high, although the super-intricate, hyperactive decoration makes the Chauk Htat Gyi Buddha look positively boring in comparison. Seated in the earth-witness mudra, the figure – one of the country's most flamboyant images – brushes the ground lightly with enormous pink fingernails and sports riotously decorated golden robes plus a jewel-encrusted crown, the whole thing set against a magnificent wooden backdrop, with a sequence of planetary posts (see box, p.74) around the base.

Drug Elimination Museum

မူးယစ်ဆေးဝါးပပျောက်ရေး အထိမ်းအမှတ်ပြတိုက် • Hanthawaddy Rd (if coming by taxi and your driver doesn't know the museum, ask him to head to the nearby Junction Square shopping mall, from where it's a 5min walk) • Tues–Sun 9am–4pm • $3, camera $5

The **Drug Elimination Museum** is unquestionably one of Yangon's wackier attractions, looking like some kind of monstrous Stalinist carbuncle amid the upmarket streets off Pyay Road. Opened in 2001, the museum is a grandiose monument of the era of the generals, commemorating the junta's heroic efforts to fight the evils of heroin, opium and other illegal substances, with many photos of former generalissimo Than Shwe on view – and conveniently skating over the extent to which the military themselves used the drug trade to their own political and financial advantage.

The museum is spread over three spacious floors complete with life-size dioramas and other diverse exhibits ranging from the pickled organs of expired junkies through to a small plane – not to mention the bodies of various museum staff, who can often be found blissfully asleep among the exhibits. Clunky displays of state propaganda showcase local drug-eradication programmes, crop-substitution activities and pictures of happy rebel ethnic groups "returning to the legal fold" under the loving encouragement of the beneficent Tatmadaw (Burmese armed forces). Elsewhere, a dimly lit room invites you to experience the horrors of drug addiction at first hand, with lurid photos of skeletal addicts and a soundtrack featuring random snippets of music and disembodied voices, while another exhibit allows you to "set fire" to a pile of seized drugs. There's also a small collection of real drugs on display – although the section intended to contain a sample of heroin is suspiciously empty.

Northern Yangon

1

The featureless suburbs of **northern Yangon** straggle all the way up to the airport and beyond. None is of any particular interest, although they are dotted with a few further Buddhist monuments including the fanciful **Kaba Aye Pagoda** and the grand **Lawka Chantha Abhaya Labha Muni Buddha** statue, the latter easily combined with a trip to the suburb of Insein on the city's popular **Circle Line** railway. Kabe Aye Pagoda, **Inya Lake** and the **Myanma Gems Museum** can easily be seen together as a single day-trip; a taxi out from downtown should cost around K4000–5000.

Inya Lake and around

အင်းယားကန်

Centrepiece of northern Yangon is the extensive **Inya Lake** (formerly Lake Victoria), created by the British in 1883 to provide water for the city. It's now one of the city's favourite pleasure-spots, with attractive (and free) lakeside walkways along its eastern and western sides, usually busy with couples smooching under umbrellas.

The area around the lake is home to some of Yangon's premier real estate, particularly along **University Avenue**, on the south side of the lake. Here, at no. 54, you'll find the **house of Aung San Suu Kyi**, where Myanmar's most famous dissident was kept under house arrest for fifteen years, although there's not much to see apart from the large walled compound topped with metal spikes, razor wire, a couple of National League for Democracy flags and a photo of General Aung San over the main gate.

Myanma Gems Museum

မြန်မာကျောက်မျက်ရတနာပြတိုက် • Third floor, 66 Kaba Aye Pagoda Rd • Tues–Sun 9.30am–4pm • $5 • No photography

If you want to fully understand Myanmar's incredible mineral wealth, the government-run **Myanma Gems Museum** offers a good introduction (shame about the rip-off entry fee). Start off with the fun illuminated map which helps you locate where everything comes from at the press of a button, then explore the miniature royal regalia (modelled after that in the National Museum), along with myriad other gems and artefacts, some of considerable beauty, others veering into tat.

Kaba Aye Pagoda

ကမ္ဘာအေးစေတီ • Kaba Aye Pagoda Rd • 9km north of downtown • Daily 6am–9pm • Free

The cartoonish **Kabe Aye Pagoda** (meaning "World Peace Pagoda" and pronounced *k'bah AY* with the stress on the last syllable, pronounced like the letter "A") is one of the first great landmarks of independent Myanmar, commissioned by U Nu – the first prime minister of independent Myanmar – and completed in 1952 in time for the Sixth Buddhist Synod of 1954 (celebrating the 2500th anniversary of the Buddha's enlightenment).

Shop-lined stairs (which also house a number of palmists) lead up to the unusual stupa (measuring precisely 34m high and 34m around the base). The odd, chintzy-looking pagoda comprises a relatively small stupa-spire above and a circular shrine below, with (unusually) five entrances rather than the customary four in order to accommodate an additional shrine to the future Buddha Maitreya (see box, p.74). Inside, five large seated Buddhas face each of the five doors, with statues of the 28 previous Buddhas seated around the huge central column. At the very centre of the pagoda, a small shrine, protected by bank-vault-style doors, houses a further, splendidly costumed, silver Buddha and numerous other precious artefacts donated to the temple.

1

Mahapasana Guha

မဟာပါသာဏလှိုင်ဂူ သိမ်တော်ကြီး • Kaba Aye Pagoda Rd • Daily 6am–9pm • Free

Built at the same time as the adjacent Kaba Aye Pagoda, the **Mahapasana Guha** ("Great Stone Cave") was constructed to host meetings of the Sixth Buddhist Synod in 1954, during which 2500 monks descended on the cave to recite the entire Tripitaka in Pali. The Mahapasana Guha is a modern remake of the Sattapannin Cave in India, where the First Buddhist Synod was held shortly after the Buddha's death. From the outside it resembles a huge rocky hillock; inside, the "cave" is actually just a huge conference hall, capable of holding up to ten thousand people, supported on six enormous pillars and with a single small illuminated Buddha flashing crazily on a shelf at the far end.

Insein

အင်းစိန်

Several of northern Yangon's most interesting attractions are clustered in the northern suburb of **Insein** – home of the city's notorious Insein Prison – and easily visited in combination with a partial circumnavigation of the city's Circle Line (see box opposite).

Kyauk Daw Kyi Pagoda

ကျောက်တော်ကြီးဘုရား • Min Dhamma Rd • Daily 6am–9pm • Free

Insein's major attraction is the **Kyauk Daw Kyi Pagoda** (pronounced "Chow *daw* gee", with the final syllable said like the letter "g"), home to the revered **Lawka Chantha Abhaya Labha Muni Buddha**, an 11m-high seated Buddha carved from a single gigantic piece of marble discovered near Mandalay in 1999. The military, always keen to deflect attention from their repressive regime by spectacular acts of religious merit-making, commissioned the statue and had the 500-tonne image conveyed with great ceremony to Yangon by barge and a specially constructed railway track; murals showing the transfer and arrival of the image can be seen over the two sets of staircases leading up to the statue, with assorted generals very much to the fore. The image is fine enough, although not as impressive as others in Yangon, while the glass case it's encased in makes it frustratingly difficult to see.

Hsin Hpyu Daw Elephant Park

ဆင်ဖြူတော်ဥယျာဉ် • Min Dhamma Rd (turn left out of the Kyauk Daw Kyi Pagoda and walk down the road for about 3min; the park – no sign – is on the opposite side of the road) • Daily 9am–5pm • Free

A companion piece to the nearby Kyauk Daw Kyi Pagoda, and offering further subtle propaganda on behalf of the ruling military, the **Hsin Hpyu Daw Elephant Park** is home to a trio of rare white elephants (plus a normal grey elephant) discovered in Rakhine State and brought to Yangon in 2001–2. White elephants are traditionally regarded as a symbol of good fortune and prosperity in Myanmar and the junta has been keen to collect as many as possible – further specimens can be found at the Uppatasanti Pagoda in Naypyitaw (see p.186).

Despite the name, white elephants are actually albinos and not really white at all, but rather a pale reddish-brown (or pink when wet). Their colour may be regarded as lucky for their military owners, but has proved less so for the poor elephants themselves, who now find themselves miserably chained up for the greater part of every day in a small pavilion.

THE CIRCLE LINE

A popular excursion with many visitors, the **Circle Line** – or the **Yangon Circular Railway** as it's officially known – describes a huge loop around the city, running for 46km and stopping at 39 stations on the way. Admittedly, it's not the world's most exciting rail journey, although the train's slow, ambling pace, with glimpses of house backs, gardens and trackside life en route, is pleasant enough, and makes a change from yet more pagodas. The complete circuit takes around three hours, which is probably a bit long for most tastes. A good plan is to ride the train as far as Insein (1hr) then hop off to explore local attractions (see opposite).

PRACTICALITIES

Circle Line trains leave Yangon Central Railway Station from platforms 6 and 7 (on the far side of the main station relative to the main entrance, although right in front of you if you come in via the small back entrance off the Pansodan Road bridge from the south. There's also an office on platform 6/7 from where you can buy tickets, costing just K200. There are currently nineteen services daily (eleven travelling clockwise, eight anticlockwise), running between 6am and 6.10pm – it's a good idea to check latest times the day before travel. Note that if you're not completing the full circuit you'll need to produce your passport when buying a train ticket back to central Yangon, which also involves the sort of form-filling normally associated with visa applications – an entertaining or maddening insight into Burmese bureaucracy, depending on whether you're about to miss your train or not.

Arlein Ngar Sint Pagoda

အာလိန်ငါးဆင့်ဘုရား• Lanthit Rd • Daily 6am–9pm • Free

A short walk from Insein station, the **Arlein Ngar Sint Pagoda** is well worth a look, and easily combined with a visit to the Kyauk Daw Kyi Pagoda. This is without doubt one of Yangon's kookiest temples, particularly the strange central shrine, topped with what looks like a large pineapple and surrounded by a miniature maze arranged around dozens of little golden pavilions. A large, green, rather Chinese-looking pagoda-tower stands behind, guarded by pairs of horses, tigers and elephants.

Around Yangon

Despite the city's size, it's surprisingly easy to get out of Yangon (assuming you don't head north through the endless suburban sprawl). The quickest escape is by hopping on the ferry south over the Yangon River to **Dalah**, from where you can continue to the pottery and temple town of **Twante**, with perhaps a visit to the weird **Snake Temple** en route. Heading southeast, the oil-based boom town of **Thanlyin** is home to another fine temple, while the gorgeous **Ye Le Pagoda**, memorably located on an island in the middle of a lake, is also close by.

Dalah

ဒလ • Ferry $2 one-way • Boats depart every 20min from the Pansodan St Jetty (at the end of Pansodan St); the crossing takes 10min

On the far side of the Yangon (Hlaing) River, the tumbledown little village of **DALAH** offers a truly surreal contrast between the crowded streets of downtown on the one side and the rural landscapes of the Burmese Delta (see p.100) on the other. The ten-minute ferry ride is an experience in itself, usually packed with both passengers and hawkers and offering fine views of Yangon's waterfront. You'll probably be approached on the boat itself with offers of onward tours or transport to Twante. There's not much to Dalah itself, although the flyblown little market and dusty streets offer an interesting snapshot of rural life, seemingly a million miles away from the densely packed buildings of the city rising just over the river.

1

Twante

တွံတေး • Horribly crowded and uncomfortable pick-ups (K1000; 1hr) run between Dalah and Twante, leaving when full; alternatively, a motorbike taxi will cost in the region of K4000 one-way, or a taxi will cost around K6000–8000 one-way

For an instant taste of small-town rural life in the Burmese Delta, within an hour of downtown Yangon, **TWANTE** is the place to go. Twante is known within Myanmar for its cotton-weaving and, especially, as a major **pottery centre**, with workshops scattered all over town, including the well-known Oh-Bo Pottery Sheds – most workshops are happy for visitors to drop in and have a look around at their pottery wheels, kilns and great stacks of bowls. The town's other main attraction is the fine **Shwesandaw Pagoda**, centred on a 76m-high Shwedagon-style stupa.

Baungdawgyoke Pagoda (Snake Temple)

ဗောင်းတော်ချုပ် • 6km east of Twante • Daily 8am–8pm • Free

Local motorbike taxi drivers in both Twante and Dalah will probably try to get you on the back of their bike for a trip to the **Baungdawgyoke Pagoda**, commonly described as the **"Snake Temple"**, just east of Twante. An interesting alternative to your usual Burmese pagoda, the temple comprises a small shrine in the middle of a square lake, connected to the shore by four long wooden walkways. The real surprise is inside, however, where a couple of dozen huge (but harmless) Burmese pythons roam, sliding around Buddhas and dangling from windows. The snakes are cared for by the temple's nuns, who consider them holy – not so surprisingly, given that they're one of the world's five largest snake species, with an average length approaching 4m.

Thanlyin and around

သန်လျင်မြို့ • 15km southeast of Yangon

Southeast of Yangon, across the confluence of the Yangon and Bago rivers, the city of **THANLYIN** (formerly known as "Syriam") has been one of Myanmar's principal ports for centuries, pre-dating the much younger city over the water. The town first rose to prominence in the fifteenth century and was controlled successively by the kingdoms of Hanthawaddy and Taungoo before (in 1599) falling to a Rakhine attack led by Portuguese soldier-of-fortune **Filipe de Brito e Nicote**. Appointed the city's new governor, De Brito subsequently declared independence from his Rakhine masters, ruling over Thanlyin until he was overthrown by soldiers from Taungoo in 1613. De Brito was executed by impalement, a gruesome punishment reserved for those who had defiled Buddhist shrines.

The imposing **Kyaik Khauk Pagoda**, on a small hill on the southern side of town, has fine views over the Yangon River. The impressive stupa is thought to date back to around 1300 and is claimed to enshrine two Buddha hair relics.

Ye Le Pagoda

ရေလယ်ဘုရား • Kyauktan, 15km south of Thanlyin • Daily 6am–8pm • $2, boat crossing $5

South of Thanlyin in the town of **KYAUKTAN** is the superb **Ye Le Pagoda**, built on an island in Hmaw Wun Creek and appearing to float miraculously in the water. The pagoda's elaborate collection of shrines includes structures dedicated to Shin Upagot, a moustachioed, white-turbaned Bo Bo Gyi, and a marble Buddha seated on an extra-ordinarily detailed golden Lion Throne-style affair, while you can also buy food to offer to the catfish that splash around the temple. Unfortunately, the fees levied on foreigners for entrance and the thirty-second boat crossing to the temple are a complete rip-off.

Taukkyan War Cemetery

ထောက်ကြံ့စစ်သင်္ချိုင်း • Bago Rd, Taukkyan, 15km north of Yangon airport (take any bus heading towards Bago) • Daily 8am–5pm • Free

North of Yangon, in the town of **TAUKKYAN**, the immaculately maintained **Taukkyan**

1

War Cemetery (the largest of three such sites in Myanmar) provides a moving and sombre monument to the many thousands of Allied and Commonwealth soldiers (including large numbers from India and Africa) who lost their lives fighting the Japanese in Burma and Assam during World War II. There are 6374 named soldiers buried here, with a further 867 graves containing unidentified bodies, as well as the cemetery's Rangoon Memorial, inscribed with the names of 27,000 further soldiers whose bodies were never recovered.

ARRIVAL AND DEPARTURE   YANGON

BY PLANE

Yangon International Airport (☏ 01 533 0316, ⓦ yangonairport.aero) is around 15km north of downtown Yangon, with separate domestic and international terminals around 500m apart. You'll find a handful of ATMs as you exit the building, plus several moneychangers all offering very similar rates.

Transport to/from the city A taxi to downtown costs a fixed K8000 if booked through the taxi counter in the international terminal, or K8000 at the domestic terminal. You may be able to negotiate a slightly cheaper fare with one of the freelance drivers outside the terminals, but check the latest official fares before doing so. The journey to downtown usually takes around 40min, although it can be considerably longer during rush hours. There's no direct bus between the airport and downtown, although it's possible, albeit tricky, to do the journey using a combination of buses. First you need to walk or take a taxi from the airport south to Pyay Rd (1.7km from the international terminal, 1.2km from the domestic terminal) then catch a #37 bus (colour-coded blue) to Myinigone (on Pyay Rd a little south of the Drug Elimination Museum), then catch bus #61 (blue) which will take you to downtown. It's time-consuming, although the buses won't cost more than K300 each.

Tickets Plane tickets can be booked through many travel agents around town including the reliable Dana Moe and May Flower Travels & Tours (see p.87).

Destinations Dawei (1–2 daily; 1hr); Heho, for Inle Lake (6–7 daily, plus additional services via Mandalay and/or Nyaung U; 45min); Kawthaung (1–2 daily via Mawlamyine and/or Dawei; 2–3hr); Lashio (4 weekly, plus additional services via Heho, Tachileik and Mandalay; 1hr 45min); Mandalay (around 10 daily; 1hr); Mawlamyine (1 weekly; 40min); Myeik (1 daily; 1hr 30min); Myitkyina (1–2 daily, plus additional services via Mandalay, Heho and Nyaung U; 2hr 15min); Naypyitaw (5 daily; 45min); Nyaung U, for Bagan (10 daily; 1hr 20min); Thandwe, for Ngapali (3–4 daily; 50min); Sittwe (2–3 daily, plus additional services via Thandwe; 1hr 20min); Tachileik (1–2 daily, plus additional services via Heho and/or Lashio; 1hr 40min).

BY BUS

Bus stations Most buses to and from Yangon arrive at/depart from one of the city's two enormous bus stations:

Hlaing Thar Yar terminal, in the northwest of the city, which is the starting point for buses to the Delta; and Aung Mingalar terminal in the city's north, which is where most other services depart.

Transport to/from the city Both terminals are around 20km from the centre – the journey to either can take anything from 40min to over an hour depending on traffic, so allow plenty of time. Most companies also require you to check in for your bus half an hour beforehand. Given how large both terminals are, make sure your taxi driver takes you to the relevant bus office. Failing this, you'll have to put yourself in the hands of one of the touts working the terminals, who will expect a tip in return for walking you to your bus. A taxi to either terminal from downtown should cost around K8000; arriving in Yangon, you'll have to bargain hard to get a reasonable fare since the cab drivers who work the terminal are (by Yangon standards) an unusually rapacious and pushy bunch – you might be asked K12,000 or more for the ride downtown. You can reach the bus station by bus from Sule Pagoda by catching bus 7 (colour-coded red) and then changing at Zawana to bus 18 (red) – although check the latest information at your guesthouse since it's possible a direct service will have started by the time you read this.

Tickets Most bus companies have offices on Kun Chan Rd, near the Aung San Stadium, although everything is signed in Burmese and hardly any English is spoken. It's much easier to book bus tickets either through your hotel or through one of the numerous travel agencies which dot the city – although note that hotels/travel agents might not sell tickets for all bus companies (or even be aware of all the services available), so shop around if you can't find a service that suits. The tourist office at 122 Mahabandoola Rd (see p.86) can also help book bus tickets.

Aung Mingalar destinations Bagan (10 daily; 10hr); Bago (8 daily; 2hr); Dawei (11 daily; 12hr); Hpa-An (6 daily; 8hr); Hsipaw (1 daily; 16hr); Kalaw (6 daily; 10hr); Kinpun for Kyaiktiyo (15 daily; 5hr); Mandalay (18 daily; 8–10hr); Mawlamyine (10 daily; 8hr); Naypyitaw (10 daily; 6hr); Ngapali (2 daily; 16–18hr); Pyay (6 daily; 6hr); Shwenyaung, for Inle Lake (6 daily; 12hr); Taungoo (4 daily; 5hr); Thaton (3 daily; 7–8hr).

Hlaing Thar Yar destinations Chaung Tha (2 daily; 6hr); Ngwe Saung (2 daily; 6hr); Pathein (4 daily; 4hr).

1

BY TRAIN

Yangon Central Railway Station is just north of downtown. The entrance is on the north side of the station, although there's a short cut entering via the back of the station next to platforms 6 and 7 (for the Circle Line) from the flyover at the top of Pansodan St.

Tickets and information Advance tickets can't be bought at the station itself but must be booked at the antiquated (and easily missed) Myanma Railways Booking Office on Bogyoke Rd (daily 7am–3pm). Staff here don't speak much English, however, and information is hard to obtain, so you might want to visit the information office at the station itself (daily 9.30am–4pm; turn right as you go in through the main entrance) and work out which train you want before heading to the booking office.

Destinations Bagan (1 daily; 17hr); Bago (3 daily; 2hr); Dawei (1 daily; 23hr); Kyaikhto, for Kyaiktiyo (3 daily; 4hr 30min); Mandalay (3 daily; 15hr); Mawlamyine (3 daily; 9hr); Naypyitaw (3 daily; 10hr); Pyay (1 daily; 8hr 30min); Shwenyaung (1 daily; 27hr); Taungoo (3 daily; 6hr 30min); Thanbyuzayat (1 daily; 12hr 15min); Thaton (3 daily; 7–8hr); Thazi (3 daily; 12hr).

GETTING AROUND

Despite its size, Yangon is reasonably easy to get around. **Downtown** is relatively compact, making it possible to walk between most of the major sights, although narrow pavements and dense crowds can make for painfully slow going in the very centre. **Outside the centre**, distances between attractions are significantly longer, although there are plenty of inexpensive taxis available. Note that motorbikes and tuk-tuks have been banned from the city centre, meaning that traffic in the city, while often dense, is relatively orderly by Burmese standards.

By taxi The easiest way to get around Yangon is by catching one of the city's plentiful taxis (mostly white Toyota Corollas; all clearly identified by the "TAXI" sign on their roofs). None are metered, so you'll have to agree a fare before setting off – most drivers speak at least a little English. Count on around K1500–2000 for short trips, rising to K3000–5000 for longer journeys between downtown and northern parts of the city, and K6000/8000 to the airport and bus stations respectively. It's usually straightforward to flag a cab down on the street, or get your guesthouse to order one (although you might pay over the odds for this). Note that most cabbies won't turn on their vehicle's air-conditioning unless you ask them to, and you might be charged extra for it.

By train The city's famous Circle Line (see box, p.83) is worth taking just for the fun of the ride, and also offers a cheap and convenient way of reaching Insein (see p.82).

By bus Yangon's bus service has recently been given a major upgrade, with some new vehicles added to the network – although services are still numbered and signed using Burmese numerals only, so it's best to do a bit of homework before trying to catch one. There's a complete route network map at ⓦ ygnbuses.com (Burmese only).

By cycle rickshaw Cycle rickshaws are still fairly common throughout the city and, although not particularly fast, offer a pleasant respite from slogging along crowded downtown streets as well as the chance to experience a quintessential but rapidly vanishing slice of old Asian life. Count on around K1000–1500 for a short journey around downtown.

INFORMATION

Tourist office The official Directorate of Hotels & Tourism office (daily 8.30am–5.30pm; ☎ 01 252859) is on the eastern side of Mahabandoola Gardens at 122 Mahabandoola Rd. Staff here are helpful and informative, and can also help book bus tickets.

Online ⓦ yangonite.com, ⓦ yangonlife.com.mm and ⓦ myanmore.com/yangon all have good listings of upcoming events around the city, plus plenty of reviews, articles and other info, while the excellent ⓦ go-myanmar.com website also has plenty of general information about the city.

CABBIES OF CONSCIENCE

For an interesting alternative to your average Yangon taxi, consider hiring one of the cabs run by the **Golden Harp Taxi Service** (☎ 09 450 019 186), established in 2010 by three former political prisoners – Shell, Bobo and Talky (their prison nicknames) – looking to earn a living after regaining their freedom. The taxi service now offers former prisoners of conscience the micro-finance needed to establish themselves as city cab drivers, while visitors using their services get the opportunity to meet some of those involved at the sharp end of the pro-democracy struggles of recent years.

WALKING TOURS IN DOWNTOWN YANGON

The pioneering **Yangon Heritage Trust** (YHT; ☎01 240544, ⊛yangonheritagetrust.org) runs pricey but excellent walking tours of downtown ($30 per person, with proceeds going to support YHT's invaluable conservation work). There are three different walks (morning and afternoon every Wed, Sat & Sun), each lasting around 2hr 30min and departing from the YHT office on the 1st floor of 22–24 Pansodan St.

Alternatively, the handy little **iDiscover Yangon City Walks** phone app features a series of informative self-guided walks exploring assorted areas of Downtown Yangon, picking out dozens of absorbing off-the-beaten-track historic buildings and other attractions along the way ($1.99 per walk to download, with all profits going to support the local Hla Day social enterprise). You may also be able to pick up free printed copies of the walking maps from the Hla Day shop (see p.97) – although they lack the background information included in the app.

TRAVEL AGENTS AND TOUR OPERATORS

There are plenty of travel agents around town, and many guesthouses can also arrange bus and plane tickets, as well as taxis and simple sightseeing tours.

AIR TICKETS

Most travel agents can arrange plane tickets, although the two following places are particularly well set up for organizing air travel.

Danna Moe Air Ticket Centre Bogyoke Rd (next to Central Hotel) ☎01 383655, ✉myanmardanamoe @gmail.com.

May Flower Travels and Tours 240 Pansodan Rd ☎01 377495, ⊛mayflower-travels.com.

BUS AND OTHER TRAVEL ARRANGEMENTS

Global Myanmar Glory 256/257 Mahabandoola Garden St (next door to Chan Myaye Guesthouse) ☎09 797 211 264.

MS Myanmar Travels & Tours Botataung Pagoda Rd (just south of the Hninn Si guesthouse) ☎01 397880.

Myanmar Delta 33rd St (next door to Beautyland II Hotel) ☎01 386938.

TOUR OPERATORS

Most of the tour operators listed below are located in suburbs away from the centre, but you can book tours via their websites or on the phone.

Good News Travels ☎09 595 116 256, ⊛myanmargoodnewstravel.com

Myanmar Delight ☎01 651833, ⊛myanmar delight.com

Myanmar Shalom ☎01 252814, ⊛myanmar shalom.com

Pegu Travels ☎09 5137 1937, ⊛pegutravels.com

Santa Maria Travels & Tours ☎01 537191, ⊛myanmartravels.net

Seven Diamond Express ☎01 500712, ⊛sevendiamondtravels.com

ACTIVITIES

Golf Around 15km northwest of the centre, the Pun Hlaing Golf Club (☎01 684020, ⊛punhlainggolfestate.com) is probably the best course in Myanmar, with eighteen immaculate holes laid out to a Gary Player design.

Meditation The well-regarded Mahasi Meditation Centre, 16 Thathana Yeiktha Rd (☎01 549290, ⊛mahasi.org.mm) runs courses in Vipassana meditation for committed meditators. At least two weeks' advance notice is required, and there's a minimum ten-day stay (although for full benefit the centre recommends courses lasting six to twelve weeks). Alternatively, the Dahmma Joti Vipassana Centre, near the Chauk Htat Gyi Pagoda on Nga Htat Gyi Pagoda Rd (☎01 549290, ⊛joti .dhamma.org; donation), offers ten-day courses. Courses at both centres are free, although donations towards costs are welcomed.

Swimming Some of the city's larger hotels sometimes open their pools to non-guests depending on occupancy levels, usually for a charge of $15–20. Places worth trying include the *Parkroyal* (see p.90), the *Inya Lake Hotel* (see p.91), the *Sedona Hotel* (Kaba Aye Pagoda Rd; ☎01 860 5377, ⊛sedonahotels.com.sg/yangon) and the fine, palm-studded pool at the *Chatrium Hotel* (40 Nat Mauk Rd, north side of Kandawgyi Lake; ☎01 544 500, ⊛chatrium.com). The pools at the city-centre *Sule Shangri-La* (see p.90) and at the beautiful colonial *Savoy* (see p.91) and *Governor's Residence* (see p.90) hotels are usually shut to outsiders, but you could always try your luck, especially during low season. For something cheaper, try the attractive colonial-era Kokine Swimming Club (up near Inya Lake at 23 Sayar San Rd, Bahan; ☎01 542749; K10,000), with two 30m outdoor pools set among peaceful gardens.

1

ACCOMMODATION

As you'd expect, there's a good spread of accommodation in Yangon, from backpacker guesthouses to five-star palaces – although few bargains. The overall shortage of accommodation means that places can get booked solid days or weeks in advance; reserve as far ahead as you can whenever possible. The **downtown** area is where you'll find almost all the city's **budget** accommodation (including a burgeoning number of **hostel** dorm beds), as well as many **mid-range** places, although very few upmarket options. Staying here has the obvious benefit of putting you right in the thick of things, although pressure of space means that rooms are generally small (if not positively microscopic), while cheaper places often lack windows and are located up many flights of stairs. Most of the city's more **upmarket** options are found scattered around the city's modern **suburbs** north of downtown; the majority are cast in the generic international five-star mould and singularly lacking in character, although there are a few honourable exceptions including a trio of fine old colonial piles: the *Strand*, *Savoy* and *Governor's Residence*. All the places listed have a/c, free wi-fi and include breakfast in their rates unless otherwise stated.

DOWNTOWN

BUDGET

Backpacker Bed & Breakfast 2nd floor, 38 Shwe Bon Thar Rd ☎09 263 728 438, ⓦbackpackerbnyangon .com; map p.62. Smart new hostel on attractive Shwe Bon Thar Rd just east of the centre, offering deluxe dorm accommodation at super-competitive rates. The four-bed a/c dorms come with cosy curtained wooden bunks, each with their own reading light and socket, plus in-dorm bathroom and lockers. There is also a decent selection of private doubles (although most are windowless), plus larger and smarter superior rooms with window for a modest $5 surcharge. Dorms $12, doubles $28

Beautyland Hotel II 188/192 33rd St ☎01 240054, ⓔbeautylandtwo@gmail.com; map p.64. Pleasantly old-fashioned, homely and peaceful guesthouse (despite the very central location). The whole place feels a fraction less cramped than other central budget options (although not all rooms have windows), and there's a nice first-floor lounge and breakfast restaurant. $30

★**Chan Myaye Guest House** 256 Mahabandoola Garden St ☎01 382022, ⓦchanmyaeguesthouse.com; map p.64. Excellent guesthouse right in the thick of the downtown action with professional service and competitive rates. Cheaper rooms are poky, with bunk beds, shared bathroom and no windows; the slightly more expensive en-suite rooms ($5 extra) are relatively spacious, and some even have windows. There are also two state-of-the-art dorms with individually curtained beds, all with a/c units, reading lights and sockets. Staying here will keep you fit too, with rooms are spread between the fourth and eighth floors – and no lift. Dorms $10, doubles $25

Cherry Guesthouse 278/300 Mahabandoola Garden St ☎01 255946 or ☎09 534 0623, ⓔcherry .gesthouse@gmail.com; map p.64. One of central downtown's most reliable budget options, on the fourth and fifth floors of a characteristically tall and skinny downtown building with the bonus of an (oversubscribed) lift. Rooms are all en suite, although they're as small as you'd expect in such a central location, while cheaper ones lack windows. Good single rates ($18) too. $27

Garden Guest House 441–445 Mahabandoola St ☎01 253779; map p.64. You'll not get more central than this long-running budget stalwart, right next to Sule Pagoda. Rooms resemble wooden boxes and are shabby but bearable; all are en suite (although with cold water only in cheaper rooms) and rates are as low as almost anywhere, although the general air of dinginess and uninterested service doesn't exactly warm the soul. $18

Hninn Si Budget Inn 213–15 Botataung Pagoda Rd ☎01 299941, ⓦhninnsibudgetinn.com; map p.62. Neat, clean and quiet little guesthouse (entrance upstairs on the first floor next to some seriously impressive plumbing and crazy wiring). Rooms share a clean and spacious bathroom, and are boxy and mostly windowless, but good value at the price. $22

Mahabandoola Guest House 453/459 Mahabandoola Rd ☎01 248104; map p.64. Very basic, but as cheap as it gets in Yangon (and with singles for just $6) – the memorably decrepit staircase is almost a museum piece in its own right. Accommodation is in tiny cubicle rooms (with a/c) – shabby but reasonably clean, and all sharing a grubby bathroom. No breakfast. $12

Mayfair Inn 57 38th St ☎01 253454, ⓔmayfair-inn @myanmar.com.mm or ⓔmaytinmg@gmail.com; map p.94. Long-running guesthouse in a quiet side street in the heart of Yangon's finest colonial district. Scores highly for its homely atmosphere, peaceful location and spacious – if rather sterile – tiled rooms (all en suite; hot water $5 extra), although service can be haphazard and there's no breakfast. $25

★**Motherland Inn II** 433 Lower Pazundaung Rd ☎01 291343, ⓦmyanmarmotherlandinn.com; map p.60 and map.62. One of Yangon's best budget options – if you don't mind the inconvenient location a 20min walk (or short taxi ride) from the centre of downtown. Rooms are unusually large, bright and peaceful (cheaper ones come with fan only and shared bathroom), and there's a well-equipped internet café, free airport pick-up for international arrivals (plus free morning and afternoon airport bus shuttles), and an excellent range of travel services. Rates include an excellent breakfast, either Western or Burmese. $25

YANGON HOSTELS

There's a growing number of modern and well-equipped **hostels** in Yangon – although prices are such that if you're travelling in a couple the cost of two dorm beds might not work out any cheaper than taking a private room. As well as the places below there are also dorm beds at *Backpacker Bed & Breakfast* (see p.88), *Chan Myaye Guest House* (see p.88) and *ShannKalay Hostel* (see below).

Lil Yangon Hostel 102 39th St ☎ 09 791 677 731, ⓦ littleyangonhostel.com; map p.64. Not the fanciest of the many hostels to have opened recently in Yangon, but a reliable and relatively inexpensive choice, with assorted eight-bed dorms (the cheapest without windows; all beds with individual curtains, reading light, charger and locker) and nice modern shared bathrooms, plus café and kitchen. Dorms $13

Pickled Tea Hostel 11 Myaynigone Zay St ☎ 09 250 903 363, ⓦ pickledteahostel.com; map p.71. Upmarket hostel in a quiet side street northwest of Shwedagon Pagoda, offering exceptionally well-equipped and spacious accommodation in a mix of four- and six-bed dorms. Dorms $16

Scott Hostel 198 31st St ☎ 01 246802, ⓦ scotthostelyangon.com; map p.64. The stylish entrance and lobby café make this place look more like a boutique hotel than a hostel, and the six-bed dorms are also pretty much state of the art, with sturdy curtains and keycard lockers. Dorms $15

Wayfarer's Rest 640 Mahabandoola Rd ☎ 09 779 922 075, ⓔ wayfarerrest@gmail.com; map p.62. In the heart of Chinatown, this top-notch new hostel is one of the city's best budget bargains at present, with a lovely eight-bed dorm featuring curtained teakwood bunks and quality mattresses, plus individual lights and sockets. Dorms $12

Ocean Pearl 1 215 Botataung Pagoda Rd ☎ 01 296637, ⓦ oceanpearlinn.com; map p.62. Long-running guesthouse, a decade or two past its best, although rooms (all en suite; a few with windows) are bigger than average and kept spotlessly clean. Rates include free airport pick-up (8.30am–6pm) and twice-daily drop-offs – a major bonus. $23

Okinawa Guesthouse 64 32nd St ☎ 01 374318; map p.64. Unusual-looking place with a distinct touch of Japanese style in its minimalist wooden rooms with hardly any furniture and mattresses on the floor under big mosquito nets. It's a characterful, if not especially comfortable, option, with very gloomy lighting, and pricier than it should be. They run a second place, the *Okinawa Guesthouse 2*, just down the road, with similar rooms at similar rates. $25

SAT Guesthouse 93 Lanmadaw St ☎ 01 251001, ⓦ sathostelyangon.com; map p.62. Peaceful small hotel west of downtown (although conveniently close to Chinatown), offering a bit more space to swing a cat than more central places. Rooms (some without windows) all share well-equipped modern bathrooms, and are neat, clean and a decent size, albeit a bit bare. It's a bit expensive at the published rates, although prices are sometimes discounted on agoda.com or booking.com. $32

ShannKalay Hostel 3rd floor, 166 49th St ☎ 01 397627, ⓦ shannkalay.com; map p.62. Easy-to-miss little hostel on the quiet eastern side of downtown offering some of the cheapest beds in the city and one of Yangon's prettiest reception areas, stuffed with Burmese artefacts and old photos. Rooms (with shared bathroom only) are

simple windowless boxes – basic, but OK at the price (and with single rates from just $15). Only sardines, however, will feel entirely comfortable in the cramped four-bed dorm. Dorms $9, doubles $20

Three Seasons Hotel 83–85 52nd St ☎ 01 901 0066, ⓔ threeseasonshotel7@gmail.com; map p.62. Enjoyably time-warped guesthouse (not a hotel, whatever the name says) in a wood-panelled house full of old-fashioned character and slightly battered charm. Rooms are relatively basic and rather past their best, and rates a bit higher than they could be, but for old-world atmosphere it's hard to beat. $30

MID-RANGE AND EXPENSIVE

★**Aung Tha Pyay Hotel** 38th St ☎ 01 378663, ⓦ aungthapyayhotel.com; map p.64. Downtown's best mid-range option, in an attractive old colonial building, dated but comfortable and very competitively priced. Rooms are bigger than in many other similar hotels and well equipped with tea- and coffee-making facilities, fridge and flatscreen TV, while the location on a very central but relatively quiet side street is good too. $45

Central Hotel 335–37 Bogyoke Rd ☎ 01 241001, ⓦ centralhotelyangon.com; map p.64. Long-running three-star (popular with visiting Chinese), dowdy and dated but in a brilliant location and reasonably priced. Rooms are frumpy and well past their best, but also bigger than average and well equipped with tea- and coffee-making facilities, flatscreen TV and minibar. $60

City Star Hotel (formerly the Orchid Hotel City Hall) 169 Mahabandoola Garden St ☎ 01 370920, ⓦ citystar hotelyangon.com; map p.64. Humdrum hotel, although in a great position right in the thick of the downtown action. Rooms are dated and bland but unusually spacious for the location, and there are nice views from higher floors. $60

Clover Hotel City Center 217 32nd St ☎01 377720, ⓦcloverhotelsgroup.com; map p.64. Tucked away behind the *Sule Shangri-La Hotel*, this small hotel makes the most of a very cramped location, with eight floors of slightly capsule-like but surprisingly chic rooms, with pure-white minimalist decor and mod cons including TV, safe and fridge – although the staff might well be the grumpiest in Yangon. $48

Hotel Grand United (Chinatown) 621 Mahabandoola Rd, at the corner of Bo Ywe St (reception on 4th floor) ☎01 372256, ⓦhotelgrandunited.com; map p.62. Reliable mid-range option in the middle of Chinatown – slightly better (albeit a bit pricier) than other choices in this category, with small but neatly furnished modern rooms equipped with minibar, tea- and coffee-making facilities and flatscreen TV; superior rooms ($10 extra) have good bird's-eye views of the streets below. $65

Loft Hotel 33 Yaw Min Gyi St ☎01 372299, ⓦtheloftyangon.com; map p.62. This funky boutique hotel is one of the most stylish downtown accommodation options, with loft-style decor featuring lots of hardwood floors and brick walls, with splashes of white and red. Rooms are stylishly kitted out with arty black-and-white photographs of Burmese scenes and cool contemporary furniture, and well equipped with writing desks and big flatscreen TVs. $175

MK Hotel 1 Wut Kyaung St ☎01 297274, ⓦmkhotelyangon.com; map p.62. Above-average mid-range option at a competitive price. Rooms are well equipped with an eclectic mishmash of furniture plus fridge, kettle and writing desk. Less dated and drab than many other places in this price range, complemented by friendly, efficient service. $45

Parkroyal 33 Alan Pya Phaya Rd ☎01 250388, ⓦparkroyalhotels.com; map p.62. Swanky, albeit profoundly bland, five-star in a conveniently central location and with a host of facilities including pool, spa, gym, sauna and a trio of restaurants (international, Chinese, Japanese). Rooms are kitted out in generic five-star plush style – comfortable if characterless – and rates are often good value. $200

Strand Hotel 92 Strand Rd ☎01 243377, ⓦhotelthestrand.com; map p.64. Yangon's finest old colonial pile (see p.65), still going strong after a century in business and with plenty of atmosphere, although overzealous restorations have robbed the place of some of its old-world character, and parts of the hotel don't look very different to any of the city's modern five-star hotels. The 31 huge, high-ceilinged suites are nicely furnished, although the faux-colonial decor borders on bland

– disappointing, especially given the massive price tag. Facilities include a pair of overpriced restaurants, a popular bar (see p.95) and a spa – but no pool. $620

Sule Shangri-La 223 Sule Pagoda Rd ☎01 242828, ⓦshangri-la.com; map p.64. Swanky five-star in a prime central location between Sule Pagoda and Bogyoke Market. Accommodation is in spacious if rather unexciting rooms with all the usual mod cons, and facilities include two good if pricey restaurants, the pleasant *Gallery Bar* (see p.95), and an upstairs outdoor pool, all backed up by the city's smoothest service. $220

Vintage Luxury Yacht Hotel 6 Bothataung Jetty ☎01 901 0555, ⓦvintageluxuryhotel.com; map p.62. Wacky concept hotel set in a retired cruise ship moored near the Botataung Pagoda. The nautical 1920s theme includes staff dressed up in sailors' uniforms and rooms (with great river views for $15 extra) decorated in cod-colonial style, complete with dark wood furnishings, fake antique telephones, and minibars concealed in a ship's barrel. Facilities include two restaurants, a bar and a spa. Hokey, but fun. $129

OUT OF THE CENTRE

★**Alamanda Inn** 60b Shwe Taung Gyar Rd ☎01 534513, ⓦhotel-alamanda.com; map p.71. This place is a real find, occupying a homely colonial-style villa set amid lush gardens in the exclusive Golden Valley area – all very peaceful, and feeling a long way from the hubbub of the city centre. The spacious, old-fashioned rooms are nicely kitted out with colonial-style furniture and the occasional artwork – a little worn around the edges but full of character and charm. There's also a good restaurant in the garden out the front. A taxi from here to Sule Pagoda costs around K3000. $90

Classique Inn 53b Shwe Taung Kyar St (Golden Valley Rd) ☎01 525557, ⓦclassique-inn.com; map p.71. Guesthouse-style accommodation in an attractive modern villa in the smart Golden Valley suburb, with eleven stylishly furnished rooms with wooden floors and crisp white linen (plus another three in the adjacent family house). A taxi from here to Sule Pagoda costs around K3000. $70

Governor's Residence 35 Taw Win Rd ☎01 229860, ⓦbelmond.com/governors-residence-yangon; map p.71. An oasis of calm in one of Yangon's most superior suburbs, occupying a lovely old 1920s two-storey mansion with wrap-around wooden balconies, gorgeous gardens and plenty of period charm. The 49 spacious suite-size rooms are attractively decorated in colonial style with teak and silk furnishings, while facilities include a pair of good (though pricey) restaurants (see p.94) plus a spa and a big fan-shaped garden pool. Rates are seriously steep, although special offers and low-season discounts can sometimes reduce prices by a third or more. $550

Inya Lake Hotel 37 Kaba Aye Pagoda Rd ☎01 966 2866, ⓦinyalakehotel.com; map p.60. Huge grounds and a fine setting on Inya Lake make this place feel more like a country resort than an uptown hotel – an impression unfortunately spoilt by the ugly, vaguely submarine-shaped hotel building itself, resembling a badly converted multistorey car park. Rooms are arranged along possibly Myanmar's longest corridor (complete with squeaky parquet), functionally furnished in bland and dated international generic with all the mod cons. Surprisingly few rooms have lake views, although there's a nice waterside bar and a large lakeside pool. $150

Kandawgyi Palace Hotel Kan Yeik Tha Rd ☎01 249255, ⓦkandawgyipalace-hotel.com; map p.71. This long-running tour-party favourite (owned by notorious military crony Tay Za) isn't very politically correct but is also one of Yangon's best upmarket options, in an attractive location by Kandawgyi Lake. Built around the old Rangoon Rowing Club of 1934, the hotel's handsome traditional architecture, palm-filled gardens and the Shwedagon views are a pleasure. Rooms are full of attractive Burmese touches, and the excellent facilities include good Japanese,

Chinese and international restaurants plus a beautiful waterfront pool and spa. $200

★**Savoy** 129 Dhammazedi Rd ☎01 526289, ⓦsavoy -myanmar.com; map p.71. The third of Yangon's trio of old colonial hotels: less grand than the *Strand*, less luxurious than the *Governor's Residence*, but with more genuine old-world character than either (and at half the price, to boot). Unassuming from the outside, the interior has heaps of charm, with a pair of fine restaurants (see p.94), the cosy *Captain's Bar* (see p.95), plus a spa, a neat little garden pool with loungers, and gorgeous rooms, beautifully furnished with faux-colonial wooden and rattan furnishing. $290

Summit Parkview 350 Ahlone Rd ☎01 211888, ⓦsummityview.com; map p.71. Run-of-the-mill four-star in a rather shabby concrete block attempting (and failing) to hide behind fancy wooden pagoda-style porticoes. Rooms are spacious and well furnished, if bland; some at the front have fine views of the Shwedagon. It's very handy for the Shwedagon and National Museum, and there are several passable restaurants nearby. Facilities include pool and gym. $150

EATING

Yangon's eating scene is still recovering from the country's long years of isolation, with a surprising lack of Western-style cafés and restaurants for a place with a population now approaching that of Singapore's – you'll search in vain for a *McDonald's* or a *Starbucks* (although the country did acquire its first *KFC* in 2015). As you'd expect, most of the best food on offer is Burmese, although you'll also find cheap Chinese, Indian and plenty of other Asian fare, alongside a modest number of more upmarket places serving international cuisine. The city's **street food** is a major draw (if you don't mind the sometimes dodgy hygiene), and many Yangonites still eat on the streets, perched on tiny plastic chairs amid the endless pavement cafés which mushroom throughout downtown from late afternoon onwards, while locals and foreigners alike flock to the lively food stalls and beer stations of **Chinatown**, stretching along 19th Street and (increasingly) spilling out into the streets beyond.

DOWNTOWN

50th Street 50th St ☎01 397060, ⓦ50thstreetyangon .com; map p.62. Formerly Yangon's expat haven of choice, the US-style 50th Street pub-cum-restaurant is no longer quite the livewire venue it once was – not helped by the authorities' grotesque decision in 2015 to sentence former Kiwi manager Philip Blackwood to two and a half years in notorious Insein jail for publishing a promotional poster showing the Buddha wearing headphones. Religious controversy apart, it's still a pleasant place for passable, if significantly overpriced, Western fare including pizzas, burgers and burritos alongside standard fish 'n' chips and pie of the day (mains K1100–1500). Good spot for a drink too (see p.95). Daily 9am–midnight.

★**999 Shan Noodle Shop** 130B 34th St ☎01 389363; map p.64. Shoebox café serving up superb Shan noodles (sticky, flat-rice and wheat) at rock-bottom prices (mains K1500–3000) in a range of soups, salads and stir-fries. Gets packed at lunchtime, so expect to share a table. No alcohol. Daily 6am–7pm.

Anya Ahta 37th St; map p.64. Innovative remake of a traditional beer station, looking halfway between a drinking den and an art gallery and attracting a mainly local crowd plus occasional tourists thanks to its cheap draught beer and short but excellent selection of traditional Burmese snacks and mains (K1000–3000). Food includes assorted salads (tea-leaf, paratha, pickled green mango) alongside traditional pork sausages, *seik tha lon kyaw* (goat meat and flour-fried meatballs) and a tasty "lad's chicken curry". Daily 8am–10pm.

Bar Boon FMI Centre, Bogyoke Rd ☎09 960 245 731; map p.62. Hip modern "Dutch Deli & Espressobar" overlooking busy Bogyoke Rd and serving up quality Illy coffee (from K3000) along with assorted baguettes, salads and sandwiches (K6500–8000). Daily 8am–9pm.

Bharat Restaurant Mahabandoola St, at the corner of Seikkantha Rd; map p.64. No-frills local restaurant offering an authentic taste of India in the middle of downtown Yangon. Food includes South Indian thali-style set meals (veg K2500, meat K3500, including free refills)

1

alongside lighter meals and snacks including a good masala dosa and classic subcontinental sweets like *Mysore pak* and *gulab jamun*. Daily 6.30am–8.30pm.

★ **Bogyoke Market Food Court** West side of Bogyoke Market, behind Bambi Hot and Cold Drink; map p.62. A great place to refuel during a shopping expedition into Bogyoke Market, this little covered courtyard of colourful cafés looks like a real slice of Burmese life, with the various resident chefs dishing up simple fried noodles, rice dishes and curries (around K2000–3000). Most places have English menus, although few show prices – check before you order. It's also a good place for an iced coffee or fresh juice, with unusual beverages including freshly squeezed avocado, plum and black seaweed. Tues–Sun 10am–5pm.

Danuphyu Daw Saw Yi 175–177 29th St ☎ 01 248977; map p.62. Neat little no-frills restaurant popular both with locals and tourists. There's no menu – food is laid out behind the counter and the helpful staff will talk you through what's available, which might include anything from simple chicken and veg dishes through to butterfish and lobster. Food is good, although prices are above average – expect to spend around K4000–5000 for a main course plus rice, soup and veg side dish. Daily 10am–9pm.

East East Hotel, 234–240 Sule Pagoda Rd ☎ 09 7313 5311; map p.64. Modern hotel restaurant alongside Sule Pagoda Rd – zero atmosphere, but a comfortable retreat from the streets. The wide-ranging menu (mains $5–6) features plenty of Asian classics – *pad thai*, nasi goreng, various Malaysian and Chinese options – as well as pasta, burgers, salads and soups, and they also do a decent Myanmar curry. Daily 11am–9pm.

Gekko 535 Merchant St, between 37th and Pansodan sts ☎ 01 386986; map p.64. Cool restaurant in a lovingly restored section of the old Sofaer Building (see p.63), serving up top-quality Japanese food at top-dollar prices. Food features a range of sushi, sashimi, yakitori, teppanyaki and other Far Eastern classics, served up in either "small plate" (K3000–8000) or "large plate" (K10,000–16,000) portions. Daily 11am–11pm.

Green Gallery 52nd St ☎ 09 3131 5131, ⓦ facebook .com/yangongreengallery; map p.62. This rustic little shoebox-sized café is the unlikely venue for some of Yangon's finest Thai food, with a short but sweet menu of excellent and authentic salads, soups and flavour-filled curries (mains K4000–6000). Seating is at a premium, so arrive early or expect to wait. Mon–Sat noon–3pm & 6–9pm.

Ingyin New South Indian Food Centre Corner Bo Soon Pat and Anawrahta roads; map p.62. Lively little place dishing up good, cheap South Indian food. Choose from veg, chicken, mutton, prawn, fish and crab curries served with puri or chapati. They also do a good dosa, although you might wish to steer clear of the "Mutton

Fighting Ball", which is just a fancy name for goats' testicles. Mains K1500–3000 (or K5000 for prawn and crab dishes) – and they'll keep on topping up your plate until you can eat no more. Daily 5am–10pm.

Kosan 108 19th St ☎ 01 503232, ⓦ facebook.com /kosan.myanmar; map p.62. One of the liveliest of 19th St's bustling restaurants, and also one of the few serving food other than Burmese or Chinese, with an eclectic selection of mains (K2500–3000) including taco rice, jerk pork, fried chicken wings and German sausage. Or just come for a drink (see p.95). Daily 4pm–midnight.

LinkAge 1st floor, 141 Seikkantha St ☎ 09 451 933 034; map p.64. Brave the treacherously steep stairs to reach this cosy little restaurant, serving up good authentic Burmese food including lots of Myanmar-style fish and seafood curries, salads and soups – the pickled mango with roasted peanut salad is a treat. Most mains K4000–8000. Tues–Sun 11am–2pm & 6–10pm.

Lotaya Bogyoke Market (turn right out of the principal exit at the back of the main market building); map p.62. This unpretentious little café provides a useful pit stop behind Bogyoke Market, dishing up above-average Shan noodles, with assorted Thai and Chinese dishes thrown in for good measure (mains K3000–4000). Tues–Sun 9am–5pm.

★ **Lucky Seven** 130 49 St ☎ 01 292382; map p.62. One of the few remaining traditional teahouses left in downtown Yangon, packed most hours of the day with a lively local crowd enjoying tea, noodles and buns. The big picture menu is full of good things (mains K1000–1500) – an excellent breakfast *mohinga*, noodles and dumplings galore, Indian-style curries with puris or parathas, spare ribs and tasty samosa salads. Seating is either inside or on the pretty little outdoor terrace smothered in plants. Daily 6am–5.30pm.

Monsoon 85–87 Theinbyu Rd ☎ 01 295224; map p.62. Upmarket restaurant in a high-ceilinged old colonial building with fans twirling overhead. There's a good selection of Western food available, but it's the restaurant's Southeast Asian cuisine that really hogs the limelight, with oodles of Thai, Lao, Vietnamese and Cambodian dishes plus excellent Burmese food – try the Ayeyarwady butterfish, or the "Bachelor's curry" with chicken and gourd (most mains K7000). Good drinks list too, with half-price cocktails during happy hour (daily 5–7pm). Daily noon–2.30pm & 6–10.30pm.

Nang Htike Bogyoke Rd, between 46th and 47th sts; map p.62. No-frills restaurant serving up decent Shan noodles (K1000–1500), plus various other noodle and rice dishes, with seating either in the cramped interior or on the pavement outside. Handy if you're staying in the area, but not worth a special trip otherwise. Daily 7am–11pm.

★ **Pansuriya** 102 Bogalayzay ☎ 09 778 949 170; map p.62. In a lovely airy colonial building with walls covered in artworks and photos, *Pansuriya* has bags of

YANGON STREET FOOD

Large parts of downtown Yangon often resemble an enormous outdoor café, especially after dark, when every available piece of pavement seems to fill up with **food stalls** and crowds of locals perched around low-slung tables on tiny child-sized plastic chairs. Burmese curries and noodles are ubiquitous, while *kyay-oh* is another local favourite, with diners seated around vats of bubbling water in which they cook their own slivers of meat and vegetables. Also worth seeking out is the local *samusa thote* – slices of samosa served in a minty salad. Food stalls are often interleaved with market stalls piled high with vegetables and colourful tropical fruit, plus mobile vendors sitting behind enormous mangling machines selling glasses of freshly crushed cane sugar – a popular local beverage.

One major caveat applies, however: **hygiene**. A study in early 2014 revealed that over a third of food tested from Yangon street stalls contained *Staphylococcus aureus* and *Bacillus cereus* bacteria, both of which can lead to food poisoning (and a quarter of the samples contained these bacteria in dangerously high levels). Choosing busy stalls where food appears to be hot and freshly prepared may help reduce risks, as does patronizing stalls where vendors use plastic gloves rather than scooping food up with their bare hands. The major underlying factors – utensils washed in dirty water and poor food hygiene and storage – are more difficult to spot, however. You may prefer to save your street food sampling for the end of your trip, meaning that if you do get ill, it at least won't wreck your holiday.

WHERE TO EAT

The most popular street-food experience among tourists is on **19th Street** in Chinatown where you can snack to your heart's content on everything from pig's ears and glutinous sausages to chicken wings, crunchy tofu and lots of seafood. Most of the pavement venues here are actually extensions of the various cafés lining the road rather than proper food stalls, although the grub is excellent and the beer's cheap and plentiful (unlike the city's traditional food stalls, which only serve tea and soft drinks). The cafés here now spill out into Mahabandoola Road, which is lined with further food stalls and market stands offering up some of the city's more outlandish foodstuffs – including deep-fried locusts and snakes, severed duck heads and assorted pieces of pig.

Elsewhere in the city, **Anawrahta Road** is arguably the king of food streets, particularly around the junction with Sule Pagoda Road. The sections of Anawrahta Road around the Sri Devi and Sri Kali temples also boast stalls selling Indian nibbles including the inevitable samosas and other deep-fried snacks, as well as shops loaded with traditional Indian sweets, including *rasmalai, jalebi* and *gulab jamun*. A few places (such as *Shwe Bali*, on Anawrahta Road just west of Sule Pagoda) also sell delicious lassis, while elsewhere you might find another classic subcontinental cocktail, *falooda* – a kind of fluorescent milky concoction loaded with bits of fruit and jelly.

---

old-world atmosphere backed up by some of the best Burmese food in downtown, including a great range of salads, soups and noodle dishes (K3000), plus great Myanmar curries served thali-style on huge white plates. Daily 8am–10pm.

Parisian Cake & Coffee 132 Sule Pagoda Rd ⊕01 387298; map p.64. A smart modern makeover may have robbed *Parisian* of its erstwhile enjoyably ramshackle atmosphere, but it still provides a handy downtown pit stop, with passable coffee and colourful cakes served out of big glass cases. Daily 9am–7pm.

★**Rangoon Tea House** 77 Pansodan St ⊕09 979 078 681; map p.64. Innovative venue in a chic refurbished colonial building on historic Pasodan St. The decor is modern, but the nostalgic menu is an unashamed paean to colonial Rangoon's grass-roots culinary traditions, serving

up a wildly eclectic selection of local dishes ranging from Indian, Burmese and Chinese street snacks – egg parathas, crispy wontons, samosa salads – through to assorted mains ($5–10) stretching from birianis to Burmese salads, plus feisty glasses of authentically strong and sweet teahouse tea and a good drinks list. Also home to the cool little *Toddy Bar* upstairs (see p.95). Daily 8am–10pm.

Shan Yoe Yar 169 War Tan St ⊕09 250 566 695; map p.60. Top-notch Shan cuisine in a handsome traditional teak house on the edge of downtown. The menu features all sorts of authentic and unusual dishes – banana-bud pork curry, beef salad with bitter sauce, stir-fried catfish with quince – with heaps of authentic soups and salads to accompany. Not cheap (mains K6500–15,000), but worth it for a unique taste of northeastern Myanmar. No English sign, although it's hard to miss. Daily 6am–10pm.

1

Strand Café 92 Strand Rd ☎01 243377, ⓦhotelthe strand.com; map p.64. The more affordable of the two restaurants in Yangon's most famous colonial hotel (see p.65), serving up a range of European and Asian light meals – although most people visit for the sumptuous afternoon teas (served either European- or Burmese-style, from 2.30pm to 5pm; $22). Daily 6.30am–11pm.

Suzuki 182 Sule Pagoda Rd ☎01 392686; also 149 Bogalayzay St ☎01 380 826; map p.62 & p.64. A popular backpacker hangout, this long, skinny café squeezed in along Sule Pagoda Rd serves up a good selection of authentic Thai and Chinese food (mains K2500–4000) at bargain prices, with cheapish beer thrown in for good measure. There's also a second branch on Bogalayzay St, serving the same menu. Both daily 8am–10pm.

Union Bar and Grill 42 Strand Rd, at the corner of 42nd St ☎09 3101 8272, ⓦunionyangon.com; map p.62. This buzzing bistro adds some welcome pizzazz to Yangon's moribund Strand Rd. The funky interior has plenty of urban chic (the clientele just as much as the decor) while the mainly Western menu serves up good pizza, pasta, burgers, sandwiches and fish and chips (most mains K10,000–17,000) plus more expensive steaks. Daily 10am–midnight.

OUT OF THE CENTRE

Alamanda Inn 60b Shwe Taung Gyar Rd ☎01 534513, ⓦhotel-alamanda.com; map p.71. Idyllic restaurant attached to one of Yangon's most appealing small hotels (see p.90), set beneath a sweeping pavilion in the garden in front. The mainly French menu (mains $9–14) features classics like pork filet mignon and steak tartare alongside salads and baguettes ($6–8), and there are also a few Burmese dishes and an incongruous but possibly welcome selection of tagines and couscous dishes. Daily 7am–9.30pm.

★Feel 124 Pyidaungzu Yeiktha St ☎09 7320 8132; map p.71. Plenty of Yangonites vote this the city's best place to sample Burmese food, as proven by the dawn-to-dusk hordes of diners who descend on the place. The restaurant proper occupies an attractive bamboo-lined, jungle hut-style construction, with customers spilling out on to the streetside tables outside, lined with additional cooking stations and merging with the adjacent *Taste Za-Lone* teahouse – an enjoyably manic slice of traditional Myanmar life. Food is laid out in a big buffet spread at the back of the restaurant – the helpful, English-speaking staff will explain what's on offer, typically including all sorts of Burmese veg and meat curries. Expect to pay around K6000 for one dish plus vegetables, soup and rice. The main restaurant closes at 8pm, although food is served at the streetside tables until 11pm. Daily 6am–8pm.

House of Memories 290 U Wisara Rd (on a small side road just past the Edo Zushi restaurant) ☎01 534242, ⓦhouseofmemoriesmyanmar.com; map p.71. A real taste of colonial Yangon, set in a chintzy old half-timbered house (once home to the office of General Aung San) and with an interior last updated in around 1930. There's good Myanmar food – including chicken *chet* curry, beef yoghurt curry with raisins, and prawn and coconut curry (mains K7500–9000) – plus some Thai and Chinese options, and a pianist tinkles the ivories every Fri and Sat evening. Popular with tour groups, so worth reserving. Daily 11am–11pm.

Kipling's Savoy Hotel, 129 Dhammazedi Rd ☎01 526289; map p.71. Appealing colonial-style restaurant in the lovely old *Savoy Hotel* (see p.91) with plenty of white linen and wickerwork chairs, plus views of nearby Shwedagon and seating either inside or on the pool-facing terrace. The resident German chef rustles up a mix of Burmese and other Asian dishes (mains $16–25), backed up by a good drinks list and wine selection. Daily 6–11pm.

Le Planteur 80 University Ave ☎01 541230, ⓦleplanteur.net; map p.60. Generally considered Yangon's top foodie destination, this beautiful fine-dining garden restaurant next to Inya Lake majors in exquisite modern European cuisine. The main restaurant is pricey, even by European standards (mains $26–57; six-course set menus $65/87, vegetarian $49), although there's less expensive food available in the more casual bistro (mains $12–20), plus opulent afternoon teas ($22) and a superbly stocked wine bar. Daily 11.30am–11.30pm.

L'Opera 62d U Htun Nyein St ☎01 665516, ⓦoperayangon.com; map p.60. Idyllic little backstreet restaurant, with the Italian owner and chef providing Yangon's best Italian food either in the attractive a/c dining room or on a gorgeous lakeside terrace outside. The menu features a mix of pasta, plus meat and fish mains (K26,000–36,000) along with cheaper pizzas (K12,000–17,000). It's also a nice spot to have just a drink. Reservations recommended. Daily 11am–2pm & 6–10.30pm.

Mandalay Governor's Residence, 35 Taw Win Rd ☎01 229860; map p.71. Set on the ground floor and terrace of the beautiful *Governor's Residence* hotel (see p.91), this is one of the city's most alluring, romantic and expensive places to eat, serving up quality international dishes ranging from filet mignon to Chilean sea bass, along with the signature Ngapali lobster. Mains from $25. Noon–2.30pm & 6–10.30pm.

Padonmar 105/107 Kha Yae Bin Rd ☎01 538895, ⓦmyanmar-restaurantpadonmar.com; map p.71. Another of Yangon's engagingly time-warped restaurants, set in an atmospheric old colonial house and serving a huge selection of Myanmar and Thai food (mains K6000–1000) including traditional dishes like banana-bud salad, pork curry with pickled mangoes and so on, plus Myanmar set menus (around K6000). Handy for the National Museum, but can get busy with tour parties so worth booking ahead. Daily 11am–11pm.

DRINKING AND NIGHTLIFE

There's a distinct lack of Western-style **pubs** and **bars** in Yangon, and although there are a fair number of local cafés-cum-beer stations they tend to get packed, and aren't always the nicest places for a quiet tipple. If you want to drink with off-duty Yangonites the best plan is to head out to **19th Street** in Chinatown, lined with cafés and food stalls all serving up cheap beer, and with a permanent party atmosphere. Yangon's nightlife is getting livelier, but still has a long way to go before it's anything close to that of somewhere like Bangkok. Check ⊛ myanmore.com and ⊛ yangonite.com for events listings. With a few exceptions, **nightclubs** in Yangon tend to involve little dancing; many have nightly "fashion shows" (in which fully clothed young women walk up and down on a stage) or karaoke. You may encounter sexpat-oriented prostitution in some places, but it's low-key compared to many other large cities in Southeast Asia.

BARS

7th Joint Bar & Grill Mahabandoola Rd, near the corner of 47th St (around the side of the YKKO restaurant) ☎ 09 260 600 552; map p.62. Lively reggae bar-cum-restaurant with a party atmosphere most evenings and regular live music. Drinks are reasonably priced (a big bottle of Myanmar beer costs K4000) and there's also a decent menu of grilled meats (including the inevitable jerk chicken) and burgers. Daily 5pm–1am.

50th Street 50th St ☎ 01 397060, ⊛ 50thstreetyangon .com; map p.62. This cool US-style bar makes a nice change from the Burmese norm, with a big if rather pricey drinks list (half price during the Mon–Fri 6–8pm happy hour, plus various weekend deals), pool table and regular live music. A big bottle of Myanmar Beer costs K5000. Decent but expensive food, too (see p.91). Daily 9am–midnight.

Captain's Bar Savoy Hotel, 129 Dhammazedi Rd ☎ 01 526289; map p.71. Yangon's nicest colonial-style bar, in its most characterful old hotel, with an extensive drinks list and live piano music on Mon, Wed and Fri (7–9pm). Daily 10am–1am.

Gallery Bar Sule Shangri-La Hotel, 223 Sule Pagoda Rd ☎ 01 242828; map p.64. A pleasant retreat in the heart of Yangon – lacking any particular character besides the usual five-star bland, admittedly, but does the job after a hard day pounding pavements and pagodas, with a pool table, live sports on TV and a daily two-for-one happy hour (7–8pm), during which drinks become reasonably affordable (two large glasses of beer for $4, for example). They also offer a short selection of Asian-style tapas ($6–15) if you're in for the long haul. There's a small upstairs pool bar if the *Gallery* doesn't appeal. Daily 1pm–1am.

Kosan 108 19th St ☎ 01 503232; map p.62. This popular little Chinatown restaurant (see p.92) is also a good place for a drink, serving up inexpensive beer (big bottle of Myanmar for K1900) alongside cheap mojitos and caipirinhos (K900) and other cocktails (K2000). Daily 4pm–midnight.

Sarkies Bar Strand Hotel, 92 Strand Rd; map p.64. Renovations have robbed the old *Strand Hotel* bar of much of its musty old colonial character, but it remains a pleasant, if slightly anonymous, place for a drink. It can be somnolent verging on moribund some evenings, except during the weekly two-for-one happy hour (Fri 5–9pm), a popular social event among local expats – although even then drinks remain pricey, with a small glass of beer costing around K2500. Daily 9am–midnight.

Takafuji 176 Sule Pagoda Rd ☎ 09 7303 6638; map p.64. Lively little place, with seating either in the small interior or on the pavement outside, attracting an eclectic mix of local boozers and foreign travellers. It's nominally a restaurant (with Chinese and Burmese mains for K3500–4000), but most people come for the beer, with a big bottle of Myanmar costing K2000. Daily 9am–11pm.

Thiripyitsaya Sky Bistro 20th floor, Sakura Tower, corner of Sule Paya and Bogyoke roads ☎ 01 255277; map p.64. This bistro bar atop the Sakura Tower has all the atmosphere of an airport lounge but compensates with fine city views through wraparound floor-to-ceiling windows, with the Shwedagon Pagoda magnificently floodlit after dark. Prices are predictably steep, with a minimum spend of K7000 per person after 7pm, although the 5–7pm happy hour keep prices sensible, with two draught beers for K3000 and discounted cocktails. Daily 10am–10pm.

Toddy Bar Upstairs inside the Rangoon Tea House, 77 Pansodan St ☎ 09 979 078 681; map p.64. Stylish little bolthole on the upper floor of the enjoyable *Rangoon Tea House* (see p.93), serving up a great selection of Asian-style cocktails, alongside a good range of wines and beers. Daily 8am–10pm.

Union Bar and Grill 42 Strand Rd ☎ 09 3101 8272, ⊛ unionyangon.com and ⊛ facebook.com /UnionBarAndGrill; map p.64. This busy modern restaurant (see p.94) is also a decent place for a drink, especially during daily happy hour (5am–7pm), when cocktails are $4. At other times a big bottle of Myanmar will set you back around K5000. Regular live music and other events – check their Facebook page for forthcoming events. Daily 10am–midnight.

NIGHTCLUBS

GTR Club 37 Kaba Aye Pagoda Rd, in the Inya Lake Hotel complex ☎ 09 513 5061, ⊛ facebook.com /GTRClub; map p.60. Aimed mainly at well-heeled locals, this is one of the most fashionable clubs in the city, playing mostly electro house. Entry is free, but drinks are pricey. Daily 9pm–3am.

Pioneer Music Bar Yangon International Hotel Compound, 330 Ahlone Rd ☎09 510 8635; map p.71. Long-running Yangon nightlife institution offering fun, no-frills clubbing with a cheesy but enjoyable soundtrack, reasonably priced drinks and lots of lasers and working girls. Free entry. Daily 10pm–3am.

The Vibe Kan Yeit Thar St ☎09 975 553 230; map p.60. Cool bar-lounge-cum-club, popular with expats and serving up a decent selection of drinks, tunes and shisha. Daily 11am–1am.

ENTERTAINMENT

CULTURAL SHOWS

Htwe Oo Myanmar Traditional Puppet Theatre 12 Yama St, Ahlone ☎09 512 7271, ⦿htweoomyanmar.com. A more unusual (and a lot less touristy) alternative to the Karaweik Palace show listed below, featuring displays of traditional Burmese puppetry in the owner's front room. Enquire ahead to check when the next show is scheduled and to reserve a place.

Karaweik Palace Kandawgyi Lake ☎01 295744, ⦿karaweikpalace.com. Traditional cultural variety shows (usually comprising a mix of dancing, music and puppetry) staged every evening at the landmark Karaweik

Palace ($30 including buffet dinner). Touristy and pricey, but fun and with expert performers – although the food won't win any awards. Daily 6.30–8.30pm.

CINEMA

Yangon is a cinema-crazy city, with dozens of movie theatres screening Hollywood blockbusters (with English subtitles) along with the latest Bollywood offerings. The Nay Pyi Taw Cinema and the Shae Saung Cinema, either side of the *East* hotel and restaurant on Sule Pagoda Rd, are both modern and central. Tickets cost K1000–1800 downstairs, K2500–4000 upstairs.

SHOPPING

Bagan Book House 100 37th St ☎01 377227; map p.64. On a street full of secondhand booksellers, this shoebox shop is a treasure-trove of Myanmar-related titles, including some rare older publications (including colonial-era volumes) you're unlikely to find elsewhere. Daily 9am–7pm.

Bogyoke Market Bogyoke Rd; map p.62. Yangon's pre-eminent market and shopping attraction (see p.67), stuffed full of artefacts from every corner of the country, including heaps of jade and jewellery, antique curios, contemporary artefacts and more run-of-the-mill items. It's also worth browsing the stalls of the pavement hawkers outside, stretching east along Bogyoke Rd almost to the junction with Sule Pagoda Rd and selling everything from old coins and

banknotes through to contemporary paintings. These stalls are also a great place to pick up Aung San Suu Kyi memorabilia including T-shirts and mugs emblazoned with the Burmese icon's ubiquitous portrait – images of which were banned until just a few years ago. Tues–Sun 10am–5pm.

Bontun 149 Central Arcade (near the rear entrance to the main market building), Bogyoke Market ☎01 384573; map p.62. Established in 1936, this quaint little shop usually has a good range of unusual Burmese artefacts, curios and colonial bric-a-brac for sale – anything from old coins and banknotes to antique wooden *nat* statuettes. Tues–Sun 9.30am–5pm.

Heritage Gallery Bogyoke Market (around the east side of the market's upstairs front floor, next to

YANGON FESTIVALS

As well as all the usual national events (see p.41), Yangon hosts a number of its own annual festivals.

Yangon Photo Festival Institut Français, 340 Pyay Rd ☎01 536900, ⦿yangonphoto.com. Exhibitions and talks by leading international photographers. Two weeks in Feb/March.

Shwedagon Pagoda Festival Myanmar's largest pagoda festival, during which pilgrims descend on the great pagoda from all over the country to make offerings, accompanied by *pwè* dancing and theatre, weaving competitions and more. Two weeks in Feb/March.

Murugu Festival Colourful Hindu festival featuring processions and acts of ritual self-mortification in honour of the God Murugan, centred on downtown's Sri Kali and Sri Devi temples. March/April.

Shwesandaw Pagoda Festival Annual pagoda festival at the main temple in Twante, coinciding with Burmese New Year. April.

Tazaungdaing (Robe-Weaving) Festival Shwedagon, Botataung and other pagodas host robe-weaving contexts, during which young women attempt to weave a perfect Buddha's robe in the course of a single night. One night in November. See p.42.

Yoyomay) ☎01 10527, ✉nostalgia.arts@gmail.com; map p.62. Beautiful Burmese artefacts featuring some particularly gorgeous lacquerware (including antique pieces) along with other traditional bric-a-brac and collectibles. Daily 9.30am–4.30pm.

★**Hla Day** 81 Pansodan St ☎09 452 241 465, ⓦhladaymyanmar.org; map p.64. The city's most enjoyable souvenir shop, bursting with a colourful array of work by local artists and artisans – anything from beautiful traditional textiles through to funky souvenirs made out of recycled plastics. Daily 10am–9.30pm.

Mia Ruby 79 Pansodan St ☎09 457 183 424, ⓦmiaruby.co; map p.64. Shoebox boutique jewellers selling hand-cut rubies, sapphires, spinels and other precious stones, and featuring a beautiful selection of rings, earrings, pendants and bracelets, with all pieces designed and made in Myanmar. All stones are sourced exclusively from non-military mines according to best social and environmental practice, offering gems without guilt and the chance to put money into an industry long tainted by its intimate connections with the military and their cronies. Mon–Sat 9.30am–5.30pm.

Myanmar Artists Organisation East side of Bogyoke Market ☎09 420 027 304; map p.62. One of several impromptu galleries along the east side of Bogyoke

Market, showcasing a diverse and affordable range of work by local artists. Tues–Sun 9.30am–5pm.

Pomelo 2nd floor, 89 Theinbyu Rd ☎09 506 2655, ⓦpomeloformyanmar.org; map p.62. Fun little boutique supporting local social projects. The shop's signature brightly painted papier-mâché animals make a nice souvenir, and there are also lots of colourful stuffed toys, Pathein parasols and other miscellanea, along with some lovely, if pricey, fabrics. Daily 9.30am–9.30pm.

Yangoods Bogyoke Market ☎09 973 780 501; map p.62. Also 62 Shan Kone St, northwest of the Shwedagon Pagoda ☎09 261 076 370; map p.71; ⓦyangoods.com. Quirky bric-a-brac and homeware – calendars, pictures, bags, cushions, coasters and so on – featuring colourful designs from old colonial prints and posters. Bogyoke Market Tues–Sun 9am–5pm; Shan Kone St daily 11am–8pm.

★**Yoyamay** Bogyoke Market (around the east side of the market's upstairs front floor, next to Heritage Gallery) ☎09 450 029 481, ⓦyoyamay.com; map p.62. This unusual "ethnographic textile gallery" specializes in traditional Chin, Kayin and Naga fabrics made into bags, cushion covers, table runners, decorative hangings and so on. Superlative quality, although with prices to match. They also have a little pop-up stall downstairs next to the market's food stalls. Tues–Sun 9am–5pm.

DIRECTORY

Banks There are now hundreds of ATMs scattered all over Yangon; most accept both Visa and MasterCard. Changing money is also straightforward, with many banks having Forex desks, while some travel agents double as licensed moneychangers. In central downtown there are a number of licensed moneychangers around the front of Bogyoke Market and another handy Forex desk in the AGD Bank opposite the western side of Mahabandoola Gardens. In eastern downtown, try Swan Htet Yee, a few doors south of the *Hninn Si Guesthouse*, or Farmer Phoyarzar moneychanger opposite the *Eastern Hotel* on Bo Myat Htun St.

Embassies Australia, 88 Strand Rd (☎01 251810, ⓦburma.embassy.gov.au); China, 1 Pyidaungsu Yeiktha Rd (☎01 221280, ⓦmm.china-embassy.org); New Zealand, 43c Inya Myaing Rd (☎01 230 6046, ⓦmfat.govt .nz); Republic of Ireland, c/o Embassy of Ireland, 12th Floor, 208 Wireless Rd, Lumpini, Bangkok (☎+66 2 016 1360, ⓦdfa.ie/irish-embassy/thailand/); South Africa, c/o South African Embassy, 12th Floor, M Thai Tower, All Seasons Place, 87 Wireless Road, Lumpini, Bangkok, Thailand (☎+66 2 659 2900, ⓦdirco.gov.za/bangkok); Thailand, 94 Pyay Rd (Mon–Fri 9am–noon & 1–5pm; ☎01 222784; ⓦwww.thaiembassy.org/yangon/en); UK, 80 Strand Rd (Mon–Thurs 8am–4.30pm, Fri 8am–1pm; ☎01 370865, ⓦgov.uk/government/world/organisations /british-embassy-rangoon); US, 110 University Ave (Mon–Fri 8am–4.30pm; ☎01 536509, ⓦmm.usembassy.gov).

Hospitals and health clinics Standards of healthcare are abysmally low in Myanmar. The city's main hospital, the Yangon General on Bogyoke Rd, is one of the best in the country, but still worth avoiding if possible. In an emergency you're better off contacting either the Myanmar branch of International SOS, *Inya Lake Hotel*, 37 Kaba Aye Pagoda Rd (open 24hr; ☎01 657922, ⓦinternationalsos .com), or the private Asia Royal Hospital (14 Baho St; ☎01 538055, ⓦasiaroyalhospital.com).

Internet There aren't many internet cafés left in Yangon; most charge around K400/hr. Try the trio of small internet cafés inserted into the base of the Sule Pagoda on the northwest side of Sule Pagoda roundabout, or Ki Ki Network Game (daily 9am–8pm) on Mahabandoola Rd between 41st and 42nd streets. In eastern downtown, try the well-equipped BizNet (8am–midnight), just south of the *Hninn Si Guesthouse*.

Laundry There are no self-service laundrettes in Yangon, although virtually all guesthouses and hotels provide some sort of laundry service.

Pharmacies AA Pharmacy, 146 Sule Pagoda Rd, near the junction with Anawrahta Rd (daily 8am–8.30pm; ☎01 242651); City Care Pharmacy (daily 9am–9pm), basement of the FMI Centre (Parkson Building; go in between the escalators) on Bogyoke Rd.

Post office The main post office is at the corner of Strand Rd and Bo Aung Kyaw St (Mon–Fri 9.30am–4.30pm).

The Delta and western Myanmar

MRAUK U

The Delta and western Myanmar

West of Yangon stretches Myanmar's Delta region, an endless swathe of pancake-flat, emerald-green paddy fields irrigated by the waters of the Ayeyarwady and its innumerable tributaries, which empty through mangrove-fringed creeks into the waters of the Andaman Sea. Lying just a few metres above sea level, the Delta's rich alluvial soils are among Myanmar's most agriculturally productive, while its rivers provide much of the country's fishing catch. Up the west coast, the land dries out and steep mountains begin to form a natural barrier between the ocean and the Bamar heartland. Here you'll find some of the best beaches in the country, plus the fascinating but troubled city of Sittwe. To the north lie the remarkable fortified temples of Mrauk U and the wild Chin State – which is only now opening to foreigners.

Much of the Delta was devastated in 2008 when **Cyclone Nargis** (see p.376) ripped through the densely populated flatlands, leaving around 130,000 people dead and at least a million homeless, although surprisingly little physical evidence of the cyclone's destructive passage now remains.

Most of the region remains firmly off the tourist trail despite its economic importance, with hardly any foreign visitors getting past the region's enjoyable capital, **Pathein**, and its two nearby beach resorts – the cheerful, local-leaning village of **Chaung Tha** and the more upmarket and foreigner-friendly **Ngwe Saung**.

Further north up the coast, remote **Rakhine State** (also spelled "Rakhaing") was formerly the independent kingdom of **Arakan** (see box, p.120) and preserves a strong sense of its own identity, culture and history quite separate from the rest of the country. As with the Delta, the state remains largely unexplored by foreigners save for a pair of headline attractions: the seductive beach of **Ngapali** and the remarkable temple-town of **Mrauk U** (which is reachable by boat via the absorbing but unsettled city of **Sittwe**).

Northeast of Mrauk U lies the huge **Chin State**, which recently opened up for the first time in decades to independent tourists. Remote, mountainous, forested and little known, the largely Christian Chin State is a world away from the Bamar mainstream. The Chin people who call the state's steep valleys home are best known for their (now obsolete) custom of tattooing spiderweb-like patterns onto the faces of women, but there's more than just ethnographical interest here. Mount Victoria (Nat Ma Taung) is Myanmar's highest mountain south of the Himalayas, and there are untold possibilities for adventure tourism.

CHIN WOMAN

Highlights

❶ Pathein Capital of the Delta, with a breezy riverfront and plenty of colourful temples – and even more colourful parasols. **See p.103**

❷ Ngwe Saung An enjoyable beach on the west coast, still unspoiled despite its accessibility and clutch of places to stay and eat. **See p.109**

❸ Ngapali One of the top beach boltholes, with idyllic sands and the sense of being a long way from anywhere else. **See p.113**

❹ Shittaung Paya A magical grotto of medieval Burmese art, packed with spectacular sculptures and carvings. **See p.127**

❺ Htukkanthein Paya Perhaps the most iconic of all Mrauk U temples, with its fortress-like exterior and richly decorated subterranean corridors within. **See p.128**

❻ Chin State Go where few have gone before in the newly opened Chin State, a land of soaring mountains that are home to the last of the tattooed ladies. **See p.135**

❼ Mount Victoria Hike above the clouds to the summit of Mount Victoria (Nat Ma Taung), where you'll find breathtaking views and exotic birdlife. **See p.136**

HIGHLIGHTS ARE MARKED ON THE MAP ON P.102

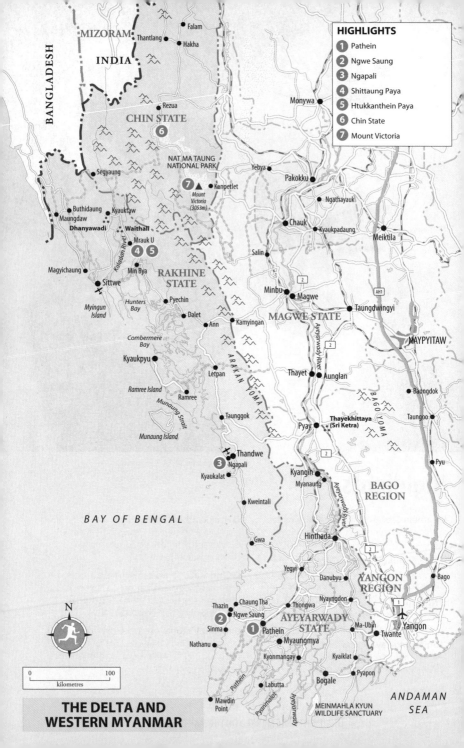

HIGHLIGHTS

1. Pathein
2. Ngwe Saung
3. Ngapali
4. Shittaung Paya
5. Htukkanthein Paya
6. Chin State
7. Mount Victoria

BANGLADESH

INDIA

MIZORAM

Falam
Thantlang
Hakha

CHIN STATE
6

Rezua

Segyaung

NAT MA TAUNG
NATIONAL PARK

7 ▲ Kanpetlet
Mount
Victoria
(3053m)

Yebya
Pakokku

Monywa

Buthidaung
Maungdaw
Dhanyawadi
Kyauktaw
Waithali
Mrauk U
4 5

Ngathayauk

Chauk
Kyaukpadaung

Meiktila

Magyichaung
Sittwe
Min Bya

RAKHINE
STATE

Salin

Myingun
Island

Hunters
Bay

Pyechin

Dalet
Ann
Kamyingan

Minbu
Magwe

MAGWE STATE

Taungdwingyi

AH1

MAYPYITAW

Combermere
Bay

Kyaukpyu

Ramree Island

Letpan

Thayet
Aunglan

ARAKAN YOMA

Ramree

Munaung Strait

Taunggok

BAGO YOMA

Baungdok

Taungoo

Munaung Island

Pyay
Thayekhittaya
(Sri Ketra)

Thandwe
3 Ngapali
Kyaukalat

Kyangin
Myanaung

Pyu

BAGO
REGION

BAY OF BENGAL

Kweintali

Gwa

Hinthada

Yegyi

Danubyu
Nyaungdon

Bago

YANGON
REGION

Thazin
Chaung Tha
2 Ngwe Saung
Sinma
1 Pathein

Thongwa

Myaungmya

Ma-Ubin

AYEYARWADY
STATE

Twante

Yangon

Nathanu

Kyonmangay

Kyaiklat

Bogale
Pyapon

Mawdin
Point

Labutta

MEINMAHLA KYUN
WILDLIFE SANCTUARY

ANDAMAN
SEA

N

0   100
kilometres

THE DELTA AND
WESTERN MYANMAR

Pathein

ပုသိမ်

The largest settlement in the Delta, breezy **PATHEIN** is one of Myanmar's more enjoyable provincial capitals. Although most foreign visitors pass straight through, it's well worth an overnight stop for the colourful array of temples – including the landmark **Shwemokhtaw Pagoda** – and the chance to visit the workshops, where the city's famous brightly coloured cotton and silk **umbrellas** are made.

Historically, Pathein was part of the **Mon kingdom**, although the modern city now has few ethnic Mon residents; the majority today are Bamar and Kayin, though there are also sizeable Karen and Rakhine minorities. The city has long been an important port, enjoying close links with India – its name is said to derive from the Burmese word for Parsi, *"Pathi"*, due to the large number of Arab and Indian traders who once lived here. It was also a major centre of **British** rule (during which it was known as Bassein), when a fort was built and a garrison established in 1826 following the First Anglo-Burmese War.

Modern Pathein is the sixth-largest city in Myanmar, with a population of around 286,000, and is still (despite lying slightly inland, up the broad Pathein – or Bassein – River) the most important port in the country after Yangon, serving as the main conduit for the Delta's huge rice exports. Even so, Pathein still feels like a small, slow rural town.

Shwemokhtaw Pagoda

ရွှေမှော်တော်စေတီ • Main entrance from Pagoda Rd • Daily 6am–9pm • Free

Pathein's main sight is the **Shwemokhtaw Pagoda**, squeezed tightly into the very centre of town between Pagoda, Merchant and Panchan streets. Local legend claims that it was built at the request of a Muslim princess named Onmadandi, who challenged each of her three Buddhist suitors to build her a stupa in order to discover who could furnish her with the most impressive erection. Fables aside, dull historical fact suggests that what you see now is largely the work of Bagan's King Alaungsithu (in 1115) and the Mon King Samodogossa (in 1263), who raised the stupa to something approaching its current height of 47m. The crowning *hti* is said to be made of 6kg of solid gold, set on tiers of silver and bronze and encrusted with over 1600 diamonds and rubies – although you can't really see any of this from the ground.

Inside, you'll find one of Myanmar's more architecturally harmonious temple complexes, and while the stupa itself isn't particularly huge, it compensates with its elegantly slender outline. Surrounding the stupa you'll find eight shrines, dedicated to the various Burmese **days of the week**, plus a ninth shrine representing the ruling astrological sign, Ketu. Each one is equipped with its own Buddha seated on a tiny circular garden plinth, complete with a tap for watering.

On the south side of the pagoda, a shrine houses the revered **Thiho-shin Phondawpyi** Buddha image, said to have been made in ancient Sri Lanka and then set adrift on a raft, after which it floated over to Pathein. Make sure you also look

---

TRAVEL RESTRICTIONS

Most of this region is fully open to foreign visitors (including all towns and cities featured in this Guide). Exceptions include the far north of **Rakhine State**, close to the border with Bangladesh (see p.27), which is now a military area and completely closed to tourism. Although Chin State has opened up considerably in the past couple of years, there are still areas here that are closed and/or need permits.

2

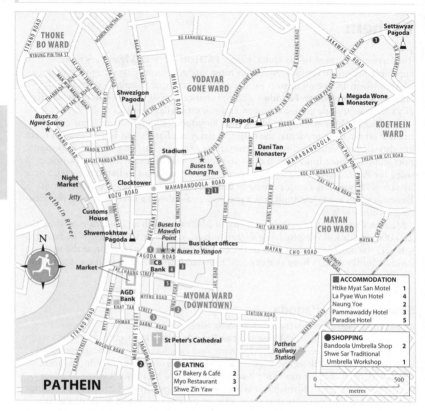

out for an image of a frog eating a snake – you can pour nine cups of water over the frog and make a wish. On the opposite, northwest, side of the terrace is a shrine to **Shin Upagot** (see p.386), set in the middle of a small pond. Close by are a couple of small *nat* shrines, with an image of the elephant-headed Hindu god Ganesh (incorporated into the Burmese *nat* pantheon under the name of Maha Peinne) between.

The northern entrance frames excellent views of the Shwezigon Pagoda's giant seated Buddha.

Shwezigon Pagoda

ရွှေစည်းခုံ · Kozu Rd · Daily 24hr · Free

Due north of the Shwemokhtaw, the **Shwezigon Pagoda** is hard to miss thanks to its huge, open-air seated Buddha. The rest of the temple comprises a fairly cursory and haphazard collection of shrines, including a series of decaying sculptures in rusty cages (among them a procession of monks, Brahma mounted upon a *hamsa* and the ubiquitous Shin Upagot) as well as further assorted *nats*.

The market and riverfront

Pathein's **market** is spread over two blocks. The newer southern block is relatively humdrum, with lots of stalls selling cheap clothes. The older northern block

> **MAWDIN POINT**
>
> At the very southwestern tip of the country, Mawdin Point (also known as Maw Tin) is the spot at which **Buddhism** is said to have first arrived in Myanmar – most likely brought here by traders from India. Today, the area's Phaung Daw U and Mawtinsoun pagodas are highly significant pilgrimage sites for the Burmese. The most colourful time to visit is during the huge **Mawdin Zun Payar** festival between late February and early March each year, although the site is generally busy at any time of year.
>
> From Pathein there are buses (5–6hr) and boats (6–8hr) to Mawdin Point. A huge naval base means that foreign visitors are sometimes asked for a permit. Local Pathein guide and schoolteacher Soe Moe Aung (🌐 traveltopathein.me) can organize permits and transport for $30 per day.

looks fairly sedate from the outside, but is typically congested and borderline chaotic within, with old-fashioned wooden stalls like enormous, two-storey cupboards.

North and south of here, **Strand Road** runs along the breezy Pathein River waterfront. Facing the river just north of the market is the attractive colonial **Customs House**. The area along Strand Road north of here is home to the city's busy **night market**, where the local seafood is served up in all manner of creative ways.

Dani Tan Monastery

ဓနိတန်းဘုန်းကြီးကျောင်း • Mahabandoola Rd • Daily dawn–dusk

It's difficult to miss the modern **Dani Tan Monastery** (aka Tikekyi), as the roof of its main hall is topped with outlandish models of the Shwedagon and Golden Rock at Mount Kyaiktiyo, appearing (at least from certain angles) to float miraculously in midair.

28 Pagoda

၂၈ဆူဘုရား • 28 Pagoda Rd • Daily dawn–dusk

Directly behind the Dani Tan monastery, the long, low **28 Pagoda** is contrastingly self-effacing. The rustic-looking shrine is named after the 28 standing Buddhas, with 28 further Buddhas sitting in niches behind them – the standing figures are posed in the characteristic Mandalay style with hands holding the hems of the outer robe open around the knees, as though about to step through a puddle. The building is usually kept locked, although you can get a decent view in through the windows even if you can't locate a keyholder to open it for you.

Eastern monasteries

The area east of the centre along Mahabandoola Road is dotted with further temples and monasteries – none is of any particular antiquity, although the various clusters of often colourful and quirky buildings make an attractive backdrop to a walk out to the Shwe Sar Traditional Umbrella Workshop (see p.107), which is also in this part of town. Most attractive is the large **Megada Wone Monastery** near the end of 28 Pagoda Street, while further east (and just around the corner from Shwe Sar) is the **Settawyar Pagoda**, one of the largest in town.

ARRIVAL AND DEPARTURE   PATHEIN

By bus There's no central bus station in Pathein – different services arrive and depart in various places around town (see map, p.104). Clapped-out minibuses run to Ngwe Saung and Chaung Tha, and comfortable express buses go to Yangon. Bus ticket offices can be found on Pagoda Rd.

Destinations Chaung Tha (6 daily; 2hr); Ngwe Saung (3 daily; 2hr); Yangon (4 daily; 4hr).
By boat The IWT Yangon to Pathein ferry was not running at the time of writing, but it's worth asking around in case it's restarted.

GETTING AROUND

Pathein is a very walkable city and everywhere of interest is within a 15min walk away from the centre. There are still plenty of motorbike taxis and cycle rickshaws – a ride across town on a motorbike taxi won't cost any more than around K2000.

ACCOMMODATION

Accommodation in Pathein is generally good value, but very few of the cheapest include breakfast in their rates.

Htike Myat San Motel 8 Mahabandoola Rd ☎042 22742, ✉htikemyatsan@gmail.com. Run by a friendly Chinese family, this hotel has small, clean and rather institutional rooms. The cheaper ($20) rooms share cold-water bathrooms. Opt for a room at the back to avoid the worst of the road noise. Unusually for Pathein, rates include breakfast on the breezy rooftop, which offers views of the quirky Dani Tan Monastery. $35

La Pyae Wun Hotel 30 Mingyi Rd ☎042 24669. This comfortable hotel seems as though it's stuck in a time warp, though this gives it more character than most other places in Pathein. The decent-sized rooms come with a/c, TVs and fridges. Top-floor rooms (same price) are brighter and quieter, but have cold water only. $30

Naung Yoe 7A Mahabandoola Rd ☎042 25179. Newly constructed and currently the top choice in Pathein, the *Naung Yoe* has smart rooms with desks, big TVs and comfy beds. Get a room at the back of the hotel to avoid the road noise. $40

Pammawaddy Hotel 14a Mingyi Rd ☎042 21165. This is a functional, concrete hotel with zero atmosphere, but it's pleasant enough, with a/c rooms equipped with TVs, fridges and hot water. $25

Paradise Hotel 14 Zay Chaung Rd ☎042 25055. This family-run hotel is set in a compound just back from the road, which makes it quieter than most other places, and the small, dark-blue rooms are very good value. Even the cheapest rooms have attached bathrooms – the only difference between them and the most expensive rooms is that you get a fan rather than a/c. $15

EATING

Eating options in Pathein are strictly limited. As well as the places listed here, the **night market** on Strand Road offers a bewildering variety of seafood, though it's rather crammed in alongside the road and not the most relaxing place to eat. A number of other restaurants can be found beside the **waterfront**, but they mainly serve as local drinking dives.

PATHEIN PARASOLS

Pathein is famous for its colourful **umbrellas**, perhaps Myanmar's most iconic handicraft – you'll often see both monks and nuns carrying them and looking absurdly picturesque, as though dressed up specially for some Burmese photoshoot. Umbrellas have always served as a symbol of distinction in Burmese life. They once formed part of the royal regalia, while an architectural umbrella (*hti*) crowns the top of the spire of all the country's most important stupas, often richly decorated with precious stones.

Strictly speaking, the items made in Pathein are **parasols** rather than umbrellas, since they're designed to protect against the sun rather than the rain (although they're also claimed to be waterproof – not that you'll want to test this theory if you buy one yourself). There are two styles of umbrella: the traditional Pathein-style **cotton hti**, and the rather Chinese-looking Mandalay/Bagan-style **silk umbrella**. Umbrellas take around a week to make. Handles, stems and spokes are crafted from bamboo, with intricate geometrical and floral designs hand-painted on the top. An extract from the *tae* fruit (persimmon) is used to waterproof the umbrellas, and also boiled to create the glue that holds them together. Umbrellas come in a wide range of colours – rich reds and intense oranges are perhaps the most traditional, although many other colours can also be found. Monks traditionally carry dark-red umbrellas (pink for nuns), with no decoration on the underside.

There are a number of workshops in Pathein around the **28 Pagoda** – owners are always pleased to see visitors and happy to explain the umbrella-making process, and prices for umbrellas bought straight from the maker are a snip compared to what you'll pay elsewhere.

G7 Bakery & Café 28 Min Gyi Rd ☎042 25467. This place brings a dash of big-city class to little old Pathein. This calm and cool café serves a very good array of cakes, milkshakes, proper coffee, savoury snacks and light meals of the fried rice variety. Cakes around K800, light meals K2000–2500. Daily 9am–9.30pm.

Myo Restaurant Bwat Kyi Tan Rd. This scruffy local drinking hole doesn't look like much but serves up a big selection of surprisingly good (if rather oily) meat and seafood mains in the usual Chinese-y style (most mains around K2000), plus cheap beer and Premier League footie on the TV. Daily 10am–11pm.

Shwe Zin Yaw Pagoda Rd. Cheery local café with a short English menu, offering a range of so-so dishes (K1500–2000) including citrus, pennywort and grilled prawn salads, Malay soup and various curries including duck, goat's liver, mutton, catfish and sardine – although don't expect all of this to be available at the same time. Daily 7am–9pm.

2

SHOPPING

Bandoola Umbrella Shop Merchant St. A charmingly antiquated shop, and a good place to pick up a cut-price Pathein-style silk umbrella, which sell here for as little as K2000–2500. Daily 8am–8pm.

Shwe Sar Traditional Umbrella Workshop 653 Tawyakyaung Rd ☎09 961 565 166, ✉myanmar hteeshwesar@gmail.com. This is Pathein's best-known umbrella workshop, run by the same family for more than a century – some of their earlier work can now be seen in museums around the country. They make a mix of silk and cotton umbrellas, created using top-quality traditional ingredients including persimmon glue and bamboo from the Rakhine mountain. The smallest umbrellas cost just K2000, rising to K70,000 for the largest – way less than you'll pay for the same umbrella elsewhere in the country. Daily 8am–6pm.

DIRECTORY

Banks The CB and AGD banks have ATMs; there's also a moneychanger at the AGD Bank.

Chaung Tha

ချောင်းသာ

If you're looking for a picture-postcard tropical beach with deserted sands, unspoiled coastal scenery and nothing to break the silence save the sound of a distant cocktail being discreetly mixed, then **CHAUNG THA** definitely isn't the place to come. The beach is none too clean, and despite its considerable size fills up quickly (at weekends especially) with vast hordes of visiting Yangonites playing football and *chinlone*, splashing around in inner tubes, and consuming astonishing quantities of grilled seafood and beer. Opportunities for peaceful swimming, sunbathing and contemplation of the waves are strictly limited, but as a place to observe Myanmar's middle classes at play, there's probably nowhere better, and if you take Chaung Tha for what it is – a kind of miniature Burmese Bognor Regis, with a determinedly bucket-and-spade ambience – you might find the place surprisingly enjoyable.

It's situated on a promontory between the Bay of Bengal and the Chaung Tha River. The main beach road runs roughly northwest to southeast for about 2.5km, passing a burgeoning straggle of restaurants and hotels before terminating in Chaung Tha **village**, where you'll find the biggest concentration of guesthouses, cafés and souvenir shops, catering to a determinedly local crowd and always lively after dark. The **beach** itself is extremely wide, dotted with barbecue stalls, plastic chairs and parasols at its far end. As you head away from the village it becomes quieter and emptier, and you'll pass a lumpy-looking pagoda built on top of a small limestone outcrop.

White Sand Island

သဲဖြူကျွန်း • Boats to the island leave from the jetty in the village every hour or so (15–20min; K3000)

To escape the crowds your best bet is to head out to the tiny speck of land known as **White Sand Island** (Thel Phyu), which is good for swimming and snorkelling (you can rent snorkelling gear from Mr George; see opposite), although there are no facilities, and not much shade either.

ARRIVAL AND DEPARTURE   CHAUNG THA

Arriving at the beginning of the main road through Chaung Tha, you'll almost immediately pass the *Belle Resort* and *Shwe Ya Minn* (on the right and left respectively). The bus/minibus "station" (an open space in the middle of a small square of shops) is about another 750m down the road.

By bus It's best to buy bus tickets at least a day in advance, particularly in peak season. Tickets can be bought at the bus station or possibly through your hotel.
Destinations Pathein (6 daily; 2hr); Yangon (2–4 daily; 6hr).
By motorbike taxi It's possible to travel directly from Chaung Tha to Ngwe Saung by motorbike (2hr; K20,000), a fun if bumpy ride through the wild and hilly coastal hinterlands, with three short ferry crossings en route.

Ask at any of the tour company offices (see box opposite) or your hotel.
By boat Travelling to Ngwe Saung, a more comfortable (but considerably more expensive) alternative to motorbike taxi is to charter a boat (2hr; K100,000–150,000 for up to five people), though be prepared to wade ashore like a shipwrecked sailor with your bags held high.

ACCOMMODATION

There are loads of places to stay in Chaung Tha, but most are drab and poor value. Weekends can get insanely busy; things are slightly quieter, and rates more negotiable, during the week. As with other places along the coast, the government **electricity** supply operates only from 6pm to 6am. More upmarket places have their own generators, but even then additional power may only be available from around 1pm to 4pm. Most places slash rates or close entirely during the rainy season.

Amazing Chaung Tha Resort Main Rd ☎ 09 777 123 700 ⓦ amazingchaungtharesort.com. A well-run hotel with homely rooms with big, draping curtains, slightly old-fashioned furniture and beds covered in flowers. The very helpful staff are as much of a highlight as the rooms themselves. There's a pool that's watched over by dolphin statues (or maybe they're whales?) and far too many fairy lights stretched out around the gardens. $80
Belle Resort Main Rd ☎ 042 42112, ⓦ belleresorts .com. Chaung Tha's most appealing place to stay, rather

more stylish than pretty much everywhere else in the village and at a very competitive price, with attractive bungalows set around peaceful gardens overlooking the sea, plus a spa and smallish pool. $70
Hill Garden Hotel North of the village ☎ 09 4957 6072. A peaceful retreat from the beachside hubbub, set amid fields a 10min bike ride north from the village. There are rustic wooden cabanas, which come with either a shared bathroom (cold water only; $40) or en-suite hot water bathroom ($55 with a/c). There's a small, and for

---

MEINMAHLA KYUN WILDLIFE SANCTUARY

For a truly off-beat adventure in Myanmar's Delta region you can't do better than the **Meinmahla Kyun Wildlife Sanctuary**. A visit to this reserve, which isn't far from the town of Bogale southeast of Pathein, combines wildlife-watching, boating and the opportunity to get a glimpse of intensely rural Delta life. The sanctuary was formed in 1986 in a joint partnership with Fauna and Flora International (ⓦ fauna-flora.org) and the Myanmar government, and is focused on preserving a swampy region of mangroves and forest which is home to estuarine crocodiles, otters and even rare Irrawaddy dolphins – as well as hundreds of species of birds.

Very few international tourists visit the park and facilities are still basic. You don't need a permit to go, but you do need to get permission from the sanctuary headquarters in Bogale, which is based inside the Forest Department building on Strand Road. To make a visit worthwhile, you should plan on spending at least one night in the reserve (making for a 3–4 day round trip from Pathein). Conservation NGO FREDA (☎ 01 243827, ⓔ fredamyanmar@gmail .com) have a guesthouse intended for sanctuary staff, but tourists are normally welcome to stay. To get to the sanctuary from Bogale, you will need to rent a small boat for around K50,000 (plus fuel) from the waterfront in Bogale or via the sanctuary staff. Make sure you take food and water with you.

CHAUNG THA ACTIVITIES AND EXCURSIONS

There's a small selection of tours and activities to keep you occupied in Chaung Tha, including various thrills-and-spills-style **watersports**, aimed mainly at visiting Burmese. More interesting are local river and sea **boat trips**, perhaps in combination with a spot of snorkelling at the small coral reef just offshore.

TOUR OPERATORS

Mr George Main Rd near Shwe Hin Tha hotel, towards the northwest end of the beach ☎ 09 4973 4562, ✉ mrgeorgeprince292@gmail.com. Chaung Tha's long-serving Mr Fixit. Services include bus ticket sales, bike (K3000/day) and motorbike (K10,000/day) rental; snorkelling equipment rental (K3000/day) and a small book exchange. Also arranges tours and activities including snorkelling from the shore (K1500pp), mangrove, river and fishing-village boat trips (K30,000 for up to 5 people); all-day sea-fishing trips (K150,000 for up to 5 people); and cooking classes (K15,000/person), starting with a 7am visit to a market followed by four

hours of cooking and eating. Open daily from 7am–10pm. **Shwe Ya Minn Hotel** Main Rd ☎ 042 42126. Runs a wide range of boat trips featuring fishing, snorkelling and river, mangrove and village tours. Half-day tours cost K25,000–30,000 for a boat seating up to 5 people. **Water Sport Entertainment** c/o the Lai Lai, Golden Beach and New Chaung Tha hotels. Provides splashtastic entertainment to Chaung Tha's Burmese visitors, including jet skiing, banana boating and various other activities involving being dunked in the waves on various kinds of inflatables – it's wildly popular with locals.

Chaung Tha quiet, beach nearby, and bikes are available for K2000/day. **$15**
Shwe Ya Minn Main Rd ☎ 042 42126. Chaung Tha's only real budget guesthouse for foreign visitors, which fortunately is pretty good. Rooms (a/c K10,000

extra) are small and simple but perfectly comfortable, with decent mosquito nets, and there's also a good breakfast included in the price. The professional staff can arrange a wide range of boat trips and excursions. **K35,000**

EATING

As you'd expect, Chaung Tha majors in seafood, with a string of restaurants down the road with identical signs and near identical menus (although hardly any of them ever have prices on – check before you order). Food isn't particularly cheap (it's around K5000–7000 for a whole fish), but ingredients are fresh and portions consistently huge.

★Pasta Fresca 30 Khine Shwe War St; turn inland off Main Rd down the track past the Alliance Resort and follow the signs ☎ 09 422 445 138. A very unexpected find in determinedly local Chaung Tha, this little garden restaurant is run by a charming Italian mother-and-son team with excellent, authentic pizza and home-made pasta at bargain prices (most mains K5500). Daily noon–2pm & 7–10pm.
Shwe Pyae Aung Main Rd ☎ 09 4972 1897. One of the string of identikit seafood restaurants along the main road,

serving up well-prepared fish, prawns, crab, squid, octopus, oysters and abalone, plus a few meat dishes. Daily 10am–11pm.
Shwe Ya Minn Shwe Ya Minn Hotel, Main Rd ☎ 042 42126. Chaung Tha's best-looking restaurant, with smooth service, cheap beer and well-prepared versions of all the usual seafood dishes, plus one of the village's biggest selections of meat and veg curries, noodles and so on (mains K4000–5000). Daily 7am–11pm.

DIRECTORY

Banks There are a couple of ATMs outside some of the bigger hotels.

Ngwe Saung

ငွေဆောင်

NGWE SAUNG ("Silver Beach"; pronounced, approximately, "Nway Song") sees far more foreign visitors than nearby Chaung Tha, and for good reason. The fine swathe of wide, golden sand here stretches north and south of the small village for kilometre after kilometre. The beach is backed by a series of mainly upmarket resorts (plus a couple of

NGWE SAUNG TOURS AND ACTIVITIES

There's plenty to keep you busy in Ngwe Saung should you tire of the beach. Bikes and motorbikes for rent aren't as easy to find as in some other places in Myanmar, but there are a couple of places in the village and some hotels also rent them. Pretty much every hotel offers the same combinations of tours listed here, though you'll normally pay more booking through them rather than going direct to the operators.

TOUR OPERATORS

Micheal Kyaw Village Opposite the Golden Myanmar Restaurant ☎ 09 250 118 008. Offers bike rental (K5000p/d), motorbike rental (from K10,000p/d), tours and boat trips to Bird Island for snorkelling (K25,000) and full-day fishing trips (K150,000).

WSE Company Village Royal Flower restaurant ☎ 09 454 545 505. Full range of local tours, including snorkelling boat tours to Bird Island and Lover's Island ($35 plus meals for overnight trip). Book through the *Royal Flower* restaurant.

WATERSPORTS

Myanmar Dive Centre Next to the Golden Myanmar Restaurant ☎ 09 977 441 611, ✉ myanmardivecenter@gmail.com. Managed by a PADI dive master with many years of experience, this place offers a Discover Scuba Diving course (from $60) and dive excursions to a variety of sites in the waters off Ngwe Saung (from $100).

Ngwe Saung Yacht Club Watersports Center 6km south of the village ☎ 042 40100, ⊕ ngwesaungyachtclub.com. With kitesurfing (6hr for up to four; $200), stand-up paddleboarding (3hr; $90), surfing (3hr; $90), bodyboarding (3hr; $50) and windsurfing lessons (6hr; $140), as well as boat hire and more, this professional centre offers plenty of fun.

good budget places), hidden at discreet intervals among the endless palms. Ongoing development is steadily changing the face of the area (and not generally for the better), while road improvements mean the journey from Yangon can now be made in less than five hours – putting the beach firmly on the map both of foreign tourists and wealthy Burmese fleeing the congested capital. For now, at least, Ngwe Saung retains its somnolent atmosphere and feeling of a place where the clock is stuck permanently at four o'clock on a Sunday afternoon.

Towards the northern end of the beach, compact Ngwe Saung village is as lively as things ever get hereabouts, stuffed with a good collection of restaurants, handicrafts shops and stalls piled high with huge mounds of dried fish and – unfortunately – coral and shell souvenirs. The coast **north of the village** has been mainly gobbled up by a collection of generally lacklustre resorts enclosed within fortress-like walls, though the peaceful beach **south of the village** remains attractive with its endless swathe of sand, and it's often deserted entirely.

Quietist and least developed of all is the beach around **Lover's Island** (offshore roughly opposite *Shwe Hin Tha* hotel, about 4km south of the village), which you can wade out to at low tide. There's a bit of snorkelling around here – you may be able to rent equipment from *Shwe Hin Tha* hotel (see p.112).

Thazin and Sinma

သာဇင်/ဆင်းမ • Count on around K10,000 for the trip to Thazin by motorcycle taxi, and slightly more to Sinma

Local excursions offered by Ngwe Saung's tour operators (see box above) are to a couple of fishing villages just along the coast. The village of **THAZIN** (the first village you reach on the way to Chaung Tha, around half an hour away by motorbike) offers the chance to see locals fishing off the beach using enormous nets. If you arrive before about 8am, the local fleet of night-fishing boats returns to shore, hauling in that day's catch of tiger prawns, barracuda, squid, tuna and mackerel. However, during the monsoon season, the fishing fleets are often grounded due to high seas.

Slightly further away (around 45min by motorbike, with one ferry crossing en route), **SINMA** village is another good place to see the morning's catch being landed, as well as vast quantities of fish drying on the beach.

Bird Island
ငှက်ဥယျာဉ်ကျွန်း
The trip out to **Bird Island**, about one hour offshore, makes for an interesting half- or full-day excursion. Despite the name, the island is best for snorkelling rather than birdwatching, with plenty of colourful fish and live coral, and the boat ride out through the crashing waves is also fun. Trips through a tour operator cost around $75 for a boat seating five or more, though you might be able to negotiate a good per-person rate (from as little as $25) from a boatman on the beach.

ARRIVAL AND DEPARTURE   NGWE SAUNG

Ngwe Saung lies at the end of a twisty road from Pathein, which winds its way through hills that only a few years ago were blanketed in lush rainforest – unfortunately, they've now been almost totally logged.

By bus Old and cramped minibuses make the journey from Pathein to Ngwe Saung, and there are also comfortable express buses direct from Yangon's Hlaing Thar Yar bus terminal. Buses tend to drop off passengers all along the main road before terminating by the junction between the village and the beach strip.
Destinations Pathein (3 daily; 2hr); Yangon (3 daily; 6hr).
By motorbike taxi and boat It's possible to get to

Ngwe Saung directly from Chaung Tha overland by motorbike taxi (K20,000), which involves a fun, if bumpy, 2hr ride with three small ferry crossings en route. Alternatively, you can hire a boat (K120,000–150,000) seating five-plus people – a great way to arrive if you can get a group together to share the cost. Transfers by boat and motorbike can be organized through local tour operators (see box, p.110).

GETTING AROUND

The beach area is very spread out – it's at least 6km from the village to the *Ngwe Saung Yacht Club*, for example. Some guesthouses and hotels have **bikes** for rent (K3000/day), though **motorbikes** (K10,000/day) can also be rented from tour operators. A few **motorbike taxis** and **rickshaws** tend to meet arriving buses, but other than this, transport is thin on the ground.

ACCOMMODATION

Hotels and guesthouses are strung out along the beach. Most are located **south of the village**, although there's a further cluster of large and more upmarket resorts **north of the village**, too. Pretty much all Ngwe Saung's restaurants and shops are concentrated **in the village** itself, which also boasts a few places to stay if you want to be in the thick of things and don't mind being a walk or bike ride away from the sand. Note that the majority of places are closed May–September, and that the government **electricity** supply only runs (erratically at best) from 6pm–6am. More upmarket places have their own generators, but in budget establishments expect to be powerless during the day.

IN THE VILLAGE
Hotel Lux 40 Myoma Rd ☏042 40252, ⊛www .hotellux.com.mm. Attractive mid-range resort in the middle of the village, set in a modern white-and-cream building backing onto the beach. It has a smallish pool, which sits right above the sand. Rooms are spacious and attractively furnished – oddly, they become cheaper the higher up the building you go. Those at the top are very good value. There are also a few fancier suite-sized bungalows ($140) almost on the beach, with private verandas overlooking the ocean. **$70**

NORTH OF THE VILLAGE
Aureum Palace Myoma Rd, 1.5km north of the village

☏042 40218. This is one of Ngwe Saung's best-looking resorts, right through from its thatched lobby to the immaculately manicured gardens and attractive swathe of sand beyond. Accommodation is in a cluster of spacious wooden villas (from $169), plus there are cheaper rooms in a two-storey block behind – nice enough, but lacking the wow factor you might expect at this price. Facilities include a spa, a nice restaurant and decent-sized pool. **$140**

SOUTH OF THE VILLAGE
★**Emerald Sea Resort** 2.5km south of the village ☏042 40247, ⊛emeraldseahotel.com. One of Ngwe Saung's most attractive and affordable resorts, set around a pleasingly landscaped, palm-studded lawn backing onto

2

2

the beach. The thatched chalets ($125) are spacious and attractively furnished with traditional artworks and textiles (some also have outdoor showers). There are also some slightly cheaper rooms at the back, which have quirky temple-style staircases. Also look out for the large pool, very affordable spa and pavilion restaurant. Easily one of the better-value places to stay. **$100**

Eskala 1km south of the village ☎042 40341, ⊚eskalahotels.com. Upmarket resort with a minimalist style – and a pavilion lobby that's so large it could swallow up several smaller hotels. The best of the rooms are in stylish cream and wood bungalows ($145) spread around spacious beachfront gardens, but there are also some slightly cheaper and less appealing rooms at the back of the property. There's also a spa and a lovely, big pool. It's more popular with well-to-do Yangonites than foreign tourists. **$110**

Myanmar Treasure Resort 250m south of the village ☎042 40224, ⊚myanmartreasureresorts .com. This village-style resort is one of Ngwe Saung's most upscale options, with lush gardens and buildings almost buried under huge thatched roofs. Rooms come with wooden furniture, four-poster beds and big bathrooms with mirrors worthy of a film star. Facilities include a big pool, spa and games room (which has pool and table tennis). **$125**

★**Ngwe Saung Yacht Club & Resort** 6.5km south of the village ☎042 40100, ⊚ngwesaungyachtclub .com. Way down beyond Lover's Island and on its own vast beach with no other hotels around, *Ngwe Saung Yacht Club* is a large, upmarket and very slickly run resort with a variety of accommodation options, including pre-erected tents for backpackers ($30 per person), plain but

well-kitted-out budget rooms ($50) and beautiful deluxe rooms ($120) with a nautical flavour. There's a very good in-house restaurant, spa and infinity pool, and there are also lots of watersports on offer (see box, p.110). **$50**

Palm Beach Resort 2km south of the village ☎042 40233, ⊚palmbeachngwesaung@gmail.com. Peaceful, village-style beach resort, with thatched chalets arranged around magnolia-shaded walkways. Rooms are furnished with benches, desks and four-poster beds, as well as well-equipped bathrooms (sea-view rooms come with a $20 surcharge). Facilities include a spa and T-shaped infinity pool, with a cute bar and restaurant spreading out around it. **$140**

Shwe Hin Tha 4km south of the village ☎042 40340. This is Ngwe Saung's most popular budget option, based towards the southern end of the beach with Lover's Island rising out of the waters opposite. Choose between the rather plain bungalows ($55) right on the beachfront (with a/c, hot water, TV and fridge) or the cheaper and more characterful – but less comfortable – wooden cabanas behind (with wall fan and cold water only; $33). Also has an attractive beachfront restaurant. Cabanas **$33**

Silver Coast Beach Hotel 4.5km south of the village ☎042 40324, ⊚htoo.maw@mptmail.net.mm. Close to Lover's Island at the sleepy southern end of the beach, this place has an atmosphere worthy of Robinson Crusoe, with little to disturb the peace apart from the occasional falling coconut. The simple but large and comfortable bungalows come with sea views and big verandas to enjoy them from. There are also some good-value economy rooms (table fans and cold water only; $30) in a little building at the back – they're plain but spacious and adequately furnished. Simple attached restaurant. **$40**

EATING

Just like in neighbouring Chaung Tha, the restaurants in Ngwe Saung major in **seafood**, offering largely generic menus featuring the same dishes prepared in pseudo-Chinese style (sweet and sour, hot and spicy, and so on), along with a couple of Burmese curry-style variations. What's actually available will depend on what the local fishermen have recently hauled in – you could ask to have a look in the kitchen to see what's in stock, and to check how fresh it is.

Golden Myanmar Restaurant In the village ☎042 40241. This entertaining local restaurant is usually one of the village's most enjoyable places to hang out over a meal or a beer, offering an array of decent food as well as cheery service. The menu features a good range of seafood and meat dishes (mains around K5000), plus cheaper options such as noodles and salads. Daily 7am–10pm.

Royal Flower In the village ☎042 40309. This is without doubt one of the village's most popular hangouts among visiting Westerners, thanks to its cooler-than-average decor and ambience. Mains (mostly K5000) feature all the old seafood and meat favourites served in

generic Chinese style, with a pinch of Thai inspiration. There's also a handful of pizza and pasta dishes available on the menu. The staff are very welcoming, although the occasional live music acts can play havoc with your digestion. Daily 7am–10pm.

Ume 3km south of the village, next to the main road between the Silver View and Yamonnar Oo resorts. One of the few independent restaurants based outside the village, this friendly little place dishes up a short menu of simple Japanese dishes (mains K5000–7000), plus a couple of assorted light meals and snacks accompanied by nightly fire dancing displays at 7.30pm. Daily 10am–10pm.

DIRECTORY

Banks There are ATMs outside some of the bigger resort hotels, but they're often out of order so it's safer to bring all the cash you might need with you.

Swimming pools Hotels in Ngwe Saung tend to charge exorbitant rates for non-guests to use their pools. The most affordable is the medium-sized pool at the *Bay of Bengal*

Resort (K5000/day), though the lovely pool at the *Eskala* resort (K7000/3hr) is another possibility. *Myanmar Treasure Resort* charges an eye-watering $10/hr, while the *Aureum Palace* comes in at a whopping $15/day – but you do at least get a fruit juice thrown in.

Ngapali and around

ငပလီ

Asked to vote for their favourite Burmese beach, nine out of ten travellers will most likely plump for **NGAPALI**. Named, according to folklore, by a homesick Italian in memory of his native city, Ngapali (pronounced "Napoli") has just about everything you'd expect of the perfect tropical getaway: kilometres of idyllic and fairly undeveloped beach, with powder-fine white sands backdropped by swaying palms and fringed with a discreet line of upmarket resorts. The perfect bolthole, it feels a long way from anywhere but is easily accessible via a short flight from Yangon (although reaching it overland remains a real slog). The only downside is the exorbitant cost of accommodation here, even by skyrocketing Myanmar standards – expect up to double the cost of similar places down the coast in Ngwe Saung.

"Ngapali" is a rather loose umbrella term used to cover several former fishing villages, now all but linked up into a long necklace of hotels and resorts. At the north end of the beach, the area around the airport is home to a burgeoning number of large resorts, while south of here the villages of **Lin Thar** and **Mya Pyin** (aka "Myabin") are where you'll find most of Ngapali's other hotels.

South of Mya Pyin (just past the *Pleasant View Resort*), the larger village of **Gyeiktaw** (aka Jade Taw) remains determinedly local, with lots of little thatched huts and a pervasive smell of drying seafood – there's a lively fish market here that's best in the early morning (around 6–7am). The next village south is **Lon Tha**. A small hilltop temple here offers superb views over the area.

There's nothing much to distract you from the beach here, although there are a few tours and water-based activities on offer (see box, p.116). For something more cultural, check out Ngapali Art Gallery (ⓦngapaliartgallery.com) and Htein Lin Thar Art Gallery, next door to one another at the northern end of Lin Thar village, which both display and sell locally produced art.

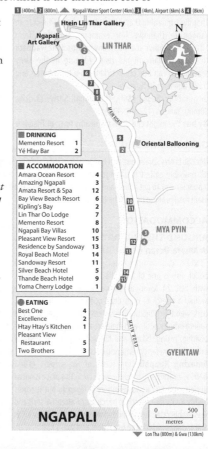

1 (400m), **2** (800m), ▲ Ngapali Water Sport Center (4km), **3** (4km), Airport (6km) & **4** (8km)

Htein Lin Thar Gallery

Ngapali Art Gallery

LIN THAR

MAIN ROAD

Oriental Ballooning

MYA PYIN

MAIN ROAD

GYEIKTAW

■ DRINKING	
Memento Resort	1
Yé Hlay Bar	2

■ ACCOMMODATION	
Amara Ocean Resort	4
Amazing Ngapali	3
Amata Resort & Spa	12
Bay View Beach Resort	6
Kipling's Bay	2
Lin Thar Oo Lodge	7
Memento Resort	8
Ngapali Bay Villas	10
Pleasant View Resort	15
Residence by Sandoway	13
Royal Beach Motel	14
Sandoway Resort	11
Silver Beach Hotel	5
Thande Beach Hotel	9
Yoma Cherry Lodge	1

● EATING	
Best One	4
Excellence	2
Htay Htay's Kitchen	1
Pleasant View Restaurant	5
Two Brothers	3

NGAPALI

0   500
metres

▼ Lon Tha (800m) & Gwa (130km)

2

2

FLOATING ABOVE NGAPALI

From sea level Ngapali looks beautiful, but see it from above and it will take your breath away. Oriental Ballooning offer hour-long sunrise **hot air-balloon flights** ($380 per person; ☎043 42166, ⓦorientalballooning.com), which will have you drifting with the breeze above the mist-dappled rivers, forests and pagoda-topped hills of the countryside. Although it's not as iconic a place to take to the skies as Bagan, the scenery is just as good – and as there are far fewer people choosing to balloon here, there's every chance you'll have the basket virtually to yourself. Oriental Ballooning have a booking office in Ngapali.

ARRIVAL AND DEPARTURE   NGAPALI

By plane Domestic flights arrive at Thandwe Airport at the northern end of Ngapali's beach. The hotels stretch from just outside the airport all the way down the coast to the *Pleasant View Resort*, around 10km south, and most provide free airport transfers – check when you book. There are regular flights to Thandwe Airport with FMI, Golden Myanmar, KBZ, Yangon Air, Air Mandalay, Mann Yadanarpon and Myanmar Airlines. Most stop at Thandwe as part of longer circular routes, including Yangon–Thandwe–Sittwe and Nyaung U–Heho–Thandwe, meaning that although you can fly direct from Yangon to Thandwe (for example), travelling from Sittwe to Thandwe you might have to go all the way back to Yangon. Many flights cease running in the rainy season. You can buy plane tickets from most hotels and travel agencies in Ngapali.

Destinations Bagan (daily; 1hr 20min); Sittwe (3 daily; 40min); Yangon (12 daily; 40min).

By bus You might end up in the nearby town of Thandwe (see p.118) if you're approaching by bus, from where it's a short ride by tuk-tuk (around K7000) or pick-up (K500) to Ngapali. There are services direct to Ngapali from Yangon via Pyay and there's also a nightly one (12hr) from Pyay to Thandwe – these pick up and drop off passengers at hotels along the beach, and some hotels also sell bus tickets. There are sometimes additional services to Yangon, travelling down the coast via Gwa, which can be slightly quicker depending on the latest road conditions.

Destinations Pyay (daily; 12hr); Sittwe (daily; 12hr); Yangon via Pyay (daily; 18hr); Yangon via Gwa (daily; 16hr).

By boat Boats run from Sittwe (see p.123) to the small town of Taunggok, around 80km north of Thandwe, from where pick-ups (4hr) run on to Thandwe. You'll most likely have to either spend the night in Taunggok (as pick-ups tend to run in the mornings) or splash out on a taxi to Ngapali, assuming you can find one. There are a couple of basic guesthouses in Taunggok – the *Khant Guesthouse* is probably preferable to the *Royal*.

GETTING AROUND

Ngapali is very spread out, and transport is in short supply. Occasional **tuk-tuks** and **pick-up** trucks ply the main road, but it's probably easiest to arrange something through your accommodation. **Bicycles** (from K500p/h or K3000p/d) are a popular way to get about, and there are many places (hotels, restaurants and travel agencies) that rent them along the main road running behind the beach.

ACCOMMODATION

AROUND THE AIRPORT

★**Amara Ocean Resort** 3km north of airport ☎01 556117, ⓦamaragroup.net. Well away from the hoi polloi, this is one of Ngapali's more exclusive addresses, with just 24 luxurious bungalows scattered discreetly around a stretch of drop-dead gorgeous beach. The cool, dark-wood architecture is very easy on the eye (as is the superb infinity pool), and there are ample opportunities for boating, hiking, biking and birdwatching in the unlikely event that you fancy venturing outside. **$290**

Amazing Ngapali 1km south of the airport ☎043 42011, ⓦamazingngapaliresort.com. This place is not as designer-perfect as some others in Ngapali, but it scores highly for its fine stretch of beach, ultra-attentive staff and reasonable rates. Accommodation is in rather chintzy villas and facilities include the usual pool and spa. **$180**

LIN THAR VILLAGE

Bay View Beach Resort Main Rd, south of the village ☎043 42299, ⓦbayview-myanmar.com. One of Ngapali's better-value options, with accommodation in spacious bungalows crisply furnished in a cool, contemporary style. The real attraction is the gorgeously styled gardens, filled with flowers and vines dangling down from the room balconies. Facilities include the in-house *Catch* restaurant and the attractive (but expensive) *Sunset Bar* on the beach. There's also a big pool, plenty of loungers on the beach, plus a spa and a billiards and darts room. Guests also get free access to bikes, and kayaking and catamaran trips can be arranged. **$199**

★**Kipling's Bay** Aye Pyar Ye Lan ☎09 250 756 636, ⓔpaivi.lehtiranta@gmail.com. Utterly different to anything else in Ngapali, the Finnish-owned, ten-room

Kipling's Bay is mostly based in an old, stilted Burmese house, though some rooms are in a newer replica block. The rooms are thoughtfully decorated with seashells and other flotsam and jetsam from the beach, and the traditional design means they are dark and cool enough not to need a/c. The breakfast is unusually good, and it's a two-minute walk from the village centre down a quiet lane to the beach (it's a working fishermen's beach but the swimming and lazing are just fine). **$45**

Lin Thar Oo Lodge South of the village ☎043 42426, ⊚lintharoo-ngapali.com. This popular family-owned beachfront place has appealing wooden cottages ($110) with a front-row seat on the beach. The rooms are a little gloomy, but there are terraces to lounge about on. Avoid the garden-facing rooms (which actually just face another building) as they are so close to the noisy road you might as well sleep inside a moving car. **$90**

Memento Resort Main Rd ☎09 250 880 852, ⊜ngapalimementoresort@gmail.com. This is a rare sort-of budget option, with a good location on a prime stretch of beach and helpful, professional staff. The four budget rooms at the back ($50) are basic but comfortable enough (with floor fans and cold water only), and there are also various more expensive rooms along the resort's extensive beachfront (from $60), which offer some of the cheapest sea views in Ngapali. The pleasant stilted restaurant right over the beach makes a nice spot for breakfast or a sundowner – and it's a lot cheaper than at the other hotels along the seafront. **$50**

Silver Beach Hotel Main Rd ☎043 42266, ⊚silverbeachngapali.com. This peaceful, old-fashioned place has simple but tidy bamboo-thatch rooms set in expansive grounds. The cheapest rooms are in a modern block set back towards the road a little. It's a good price for Ngapali, but the staff aren't the most effervescent group. **$90**

Thande Beach Hotel Main Rd ☎043 42278, ⊚thandehotel.com. One of Ngapali's best-value places, set amid lush and gorgeously manicured palm-studded gardens. The rooms are attractively kitted out with antique-repro wooden furniture, and there's a decent-sized pool plus a spa. Sea-view surcharges are less crippling than at other places, though some of the cheaper rooms suffer from road noise. **$100**

★Yoma Cherry Lodge ☎043 42239, ⊚yomacherry lodge.com. Right in the heart of the village, overlooking a lovely beach frequented by few tourists, the UK-owned *Yoma Cherry Lodge* simply oozes class. Its fifteen contemporary-chic rooms have exposed wooden beams and wood or slate terraces, and there's plenty of stunning photo art adorning the walls. The gardens are also dreamy, with tranquil ponds full of fish, palm trees poking through the boardwalks and orchids and other tropical flowers everywhere. To round it all off, the

service is excellent and there's a bar-restaurant hanging out over the sands. **$115**

MYA PYIN VILLAGE

Amata Resort & Spa On the hotel strip ☎043 42177, ⊚amataresort.com. Ngapali's most original-looking resort, from the stunning wooden lobby (topped by a kind of abstract boat) through to the cute two-storey villas, set amid dense trees, constructed in a mix of wood and concrete and topped with bits of thatch and curiously shaped pitched roofs sticking out at quirky angles. Inside, big windows illuminate stylish rooms decorated with colourful fabrics and artworks. Facilities include an excellent spa and a rather undernourished pool. Fancier rooms with sea views come with a massive mark-up. **$185**

Ngapali Bay Villas North of the village ☎043 42301, ⊚ngapalibay.com. This super-chic resort looks like something straight out of a designer magazine. Rooms come with huge picture windows and giant mosquito nets cascading from the high wooden ceilings, while bathrooms feature roll-top baths and gilded washbasins – and special sea-view windows from *inside* the showers. Some rooms also have their own plunge pools. There are also beautiful gardens, a well-equipped spa, medium-sized pool and upmarket restaurant, and guests also have their own numbered loungers on the beach – so there'll be no squabbling with towel-droppers. Closed May–Sept. **$285**

Pleasant View Resort On the hotel strip ☎043 42224, ⊚pvrngapali.com. This is one of Ngapali's better-value resorts and, with its quasi-industrial design, most inventive. Rooms in the two-storey block at the back get a bit too much road noise for our liking, but the attractive bungalows ($160) at the front are right on the beach – so only the lapping of waves will disturb your sleep. The attractive *Pleasant View Restaurant* (see p.116) is right next door. **$130**

Residence by Sandoway On the hotel strip ☎043 42240, ⊚sandowayresort.com. Squeezed between the buildings of the *Amata Resort*, this easily missed little outpost of the *Sandoway Resort* has just fourteen beautiful rooms in a very quiet location close to the waves – the six beachfront rooms ($70 extra) are as close to the sand as you'll get in Ngapali, and guests can use all the *Sandoway Resort* facilities, a 200m stroll up the beach. Good value. **$140**

Royal Beach Motel Southern end of the hotel strip ☎043 42411, ⊚royalbeachngapali.com. One of the few budget options in Ngapali, the *Royal Beach* has basic rooms in what look like converted wooden sheds, although they do at least have attached bathrooms (cold water only). There are also some more expensive wood and brick cabanas (from $90) in a mishmash two-storey block on the beach. **$60**

NGAPALI ACTIVITIES

Various **watersports** can be arranged through Ngapali Water Sport Center (see below), and you can also generally arrange snorkelling through some of the hotels for around K35,000 per boat for a half day. The best area is thought to be around Pearl Island, at the southern end of the beach, which has a good array of fish but hardly any coral. Some hotels can arrange other activities like kayaking, boating and fishing, while local sailors also offer trips out to sea and hang out on the stretch of beach between the *Memento* and *Thande* hotels. You'll also find various **massage shacks** here (around K8000/hr), but there's very little privacy.

OPERATOR

Ngapali Water Sport Center Airport Rd ☎ 09 4957 7070, ⓦ ngapaliwatersport.com. Arranges diving trips (from $119 plus $25 equipment rental), as well as snorkelling, kayaking, fishing and local tours.

★ **Sandoway Resort** On the hotel strip ☎ 043 42233, ⓦ sandowayresort.com. One of Ngapali's longest-running places, open fifteen years but still looking minty fresh. The resort feels like a miniature self-contained village, full of twists and turns amid the densely tree-studded grounds. There's a range of attractively furnished rooms (as usual, sea-view rooms come with a hefty surcharge, and there are no in-room TVs), while the superb facilities include one of the biggest and nicest pools in Ngapali, as well as an attractive library, spa and beachfront restaurant. There is also a superb little in-house cinema. To top it all off, you'll struggle to find a more perfect stretch of beach than the one out front. Closed May–Oct. **$200**

EATING

There's plenty of **seafood** in Ngapali and it's generally pretty good, but if you want more local Burmese dishes, then prepare for something very bland and lacklustre because most places are catering purely to a tourist market. There are plenty of **restaurants** along the main road, which are mostly small, family-run affairs without much to distinguish one from another. For something a bit different, you could try the cluster of impromptu beach-bar shacks and little wooden cafés strung out on the beach between the *Memento Resort* and *Thande* hotel, which are particularly pretty after dark.

Best One Mya Pyin ☎ 043 42042. There's a fairly classic selection of seafood available here, but it's cooked with a little more attention to detail than elsewhere and served with more panache. If you need a break from rice, opt for the tuna steak with home-made chips. Mains K4000–5000. Daily 9am–9.30pm.

Excellence Lin Thar ☎ 043 42249. This is a big, attractive wooden pavilion restaurant with friendly service and a typical Ngapali menu focusing on fish – mainly Burmese-style, but with a few Thai dishes and token Western options (mains around K3000). The set three-course fish menus (K7000) are guaranteed crowd-pleasers. Daily 7am–10pm.

Htay Htay's Kitchen Lin Thar ☎ 043 42081. A bit more stylish than other places hereabouts, this place comes complete with romantically moody lighting and flowers on tables. The seafood-leaning menu features the usual Thai and Chinese dishes, along with a good selection of Burmese options ranging from smoked fish soup to fishball salad with lemon leaves and assorted coconut-flavoured curries. Mains K4000–5000. Daily 8am–10pm.

Pleasant View Restaurant Mya Pyin ☎ 043 42224, ⓦ pvrngapali.com. Ngapali's most appealing restaurant is set on a little rocky islet just offshore, and is connected to the beach by a short wooden bridge – sometimes, getting here involves wading through a few centimetres of water when the tide is coming in, though a free boat is provided when the water gets too high. Food is a bit pricey (most mains K5500–8000) but generally good, featuring a mix of Burmese, Thai, Chinese and Western dishes (fish and seafood only). Daily 9am–9pm.

Two Brothers Mya Pyin, opposite the Amata Resort ☎ 09 4965 3655. Cute little rattan-roofed restaurant with friendly service and a menu bursting with assorted seafood, including lobster, crab, oyster, squid, prawns, octopus and other fruits of the waves. Mains are generally K4000–5000, though there are some more expensive seafood options. Daily 6am–9pm.

DRINKING

Memento Resort Main Rd. The breezy little outlet here (raised on stilts over the beach) is a pleasant spot for a drink – and a lot cheaper than many other places along the sand. Daily 8am–10pm.

Yé Hlay Bar Aureum Palace Hotel, Main Rd. Cute bar in an old wooden boat right next to the sand. The drinks list features cocktails only, for a pricey K7000, but you can get two-for-one deals during the daily 5–7pm happy hour. Daily 2–10pm.

FROM TOP NGAPALI BEACH (P.113); MRAUK U FERRY (P.133) >

Banks There are several ATM kiosks along the road beside the beach and inside the lobbies of the bigger hotels, and there's also a currency exchange desk at the airport.
Pharmacy Main Road, opposite the *Sandoway Resort*.

Swimming pools Non-guests can use the lovely, serpentine pool at the *Aureum Palace* hotel for free if they take a meal in the hotel restaurant; alternatively, the big pool at the *Bay View Beach Resort* costs $10/day for non-residents.

Thandwe

သဲတွဲ

Around 10km inland from Ngapali, the town of **THANDWE** provides a low-key but enjoyable reminder of Burmese life beyond the beach – and sees quite a few visitors from the resorts looking for a slice of the "real" Myanmar. It has a long history, as Minbin himself (see p.363) served as governor for a decade before launching his bid for power, and the British (who called it **Sandoway**) also established a garrison here. It's now the largest town in southern Rakhine, although there's nowhere for foreigners to stay and food is limited to the usual noodle and curry stalls around the market.

Thandwe's intensely atmospheric **market**, housed (bizarrely) in the old colonial jail, is worth a look, and there are also three temples, each said to enshrine a body part of the Buddha. Just over 1.5km northwest of the market, the **Nandaw Paya** is said to have one of the Enlightened One's ribs, while to the east of the market the **Sandaw Paya** has a hair and the **Andaw Paya** a tooth.

South to Gwa

The beautiful swathe of coastline south of Ngapali is open to foreigners, but remains largely unexplored. A few adventurous travellers village-hop up and down the coast, stopping off in Kanthaya and Gwa (which have basic accommodation) en route.

Gwa is the biggest town along the way and there are frequent buses to and from Thandwe and Yangon. The main beach is very wide and could be beautiful, but currently it's a working fishing beach and so somewhat marred by rubbish. A better option is to take a ferry (K1000) to the other side of the river, where a string of almost untouched beaches stretches down along the peninsula. Ask around in Gwa and you should be able to find a motorbike (K10,000 per day) that you can use to explore the peninsula's beaches beyond. Just remember to take food and water with you, as there are no facilities of any sort on any of the beaches there.

A half-hour (20km) motorbike ride north of Gwa is the beach of **Zak Hone**, which is close to the village of Nyaung Kyaung. It's a long, wide bend of pure white sand, backed by hundreds of palm trees and with one tiny fishing village next to it. A little further north of Zak Hone is **Kanthaya**, which was once earmarked for tourist development. A big hotel was built here to host the hordes of tourists the military government of the time hoped would come, but they never arrived and now just a shell remains. The beach itself is more developed than at Zak Hone, but you'll still probably be the only tourist here. There are a couple of beach shack restaurants and very simple guesthouses – though not all are licensed to accept foreigners.

Sittwe

စစ်တွေ

Capital of Rakhine State and gateway to Mrauk U, the remote town of **SITTWE** is one of western Myanmar's most absorbing – and disquieting – destinations. Landing here (or arriving after the arduous bus journey), you'll feel a long way from the rest of Myanmar and that's because, to all intents and purposes, you are. For decades Sittwe

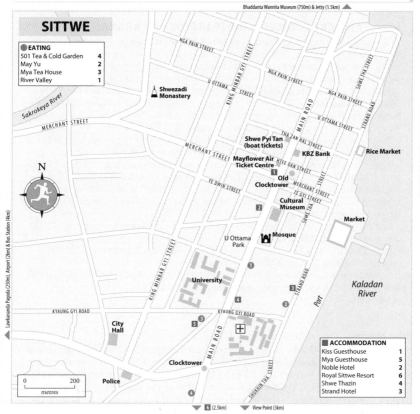

Bhaddanta Wannita Museum (750m) & Jetty (1.5km)

SITTWE

EATING

501 Tea & Cold Garden	4
May Yu	2
Mya Tea House	3
River Valley	1

Shwezadi Monastery

Shwe Pyi Tan (boat tickets)

Mayflower Air Ticket Centre

KBZ Bank

Rice Market

Old Clocktower

Cultural Museum

Market

U Ottama Park

Mosque

University

Kaladan River

City Hall

Clocktower

Police

Lawkananda Pagoda (250m), Airport (2km) & Bus Station (4km)

ACCOMMODATION

Kiss Guesthouse	1
Mya Guesthouse	5
Noble Hotel	2
Royal Sittwe Resort	6
Shwe Thazin	4
Strand Hotel	3

6 (2.5km) View Point (3km)

2

has been cut off from mainstream Burmese life, and the town immediately feels less developed and somehow a little different to many others in Myanmar.

Sittwe occupies a superb natural setting, at the point where the Kaladan River and other inland waterways drain into the Bay of Bengal, with views of endless water (or, at low tide, mud flats) and distant hills in every direction, while the battered traces of old colonial architecture, *thanaka*-smeared Rakhine and lively market make the town one of Myanmar's more personable provincial capitals.

That, at least, is the surface. Less savoury is the town's recent history as the major flashpoint for clashes between the Rakhine and the town's **Rohingya Muslims** (see box, p.121), who once made up half the town's population but have now been driven out of their homes and forced into refugee camps in the surrounding countryside – ethnic cleansing, by any other name. The character of the town has now significantly changed, and little evidence of the Rohingya's centuries-long presence in Sittwe now survives, save for the beautiful old Friday Mosque (see p.121), currently fenced off and watched over by armed police. The town wears a largely peaceful air following the upheavals of 2012–13, although an undercurrent of tension persists, with further riots erupting in early 2014 against locally based Western NGOs, whom the local population saw as pro-Rohingya, and the current troubles in the countryside north of here towards the border with Bangladesh (which is just 100km away as the crow flies). Even in periods of calm, you will almost certainly be confronted by locals spouting vicious racist nonsense concerning the brutalized Rohingya minority, which leaves a very sour taste.

2

KINGS AND CROCODILES: A BRIEF HISTORY OF ARAKAN

The history of the kingdom of **Arakan** (modern-day **Rakhine State**) is claimed to date back nearly five thousand years, and the Rakhine preserve a genealogy of 227 native kings lasting until the Konbaung conquest in 1784. At its height, it covered large parts of what is now modern Myanmar and Bangladesh, stretching from the mouth of the Ganges to the Ayeyarwady. According to tradition, the first Rakhine kingdom emerged around the northern town of **Dhanyawadi** in about 3400 BC, lasting until the founding of Waithali in 327 AD – the Buddha himself is alleged to have visited the kingdom, with the famous Mahamuni Buddha image (see p.289) being cast at around the same time.

The capital subsequently shifted to **Waithali** (aka Vesali), which grew prosperous on trade with India and China. In around 818 a new dynasty arose on the Laymro River, ushering in the **Lemro** period. The final Rakhine kingdom was founded in 1429 by Min Saw Mon at **Mrauk U** – the golden age of Rakhine history (see p.362 & p.363). Mrauk U was conquered by the Konbaung dynasty in 1784, and then passed to the British in 1826 following the First Anglo-Burmese War, after which the capital was transferred to Sittwe, where it remains to this day.

Rakhine saw fierce fighting during World War II, including the Arakan Campaign of 1942–43 and the notorious **Battle of Ramree Island**, during which almost a thousand Japanese soldiers are said to have been eaten by crocodiles – listed by the *Guinness Book of World Records* as the "Worst Crocodile Disaster In The World".

Arakan became part of the newly independent Union of Burma in 1948, although the 1950s saw increasing calls for a restoration of Arakanese independence, and nationalist feelings remain high.

Brief history

Formerly known as **Akyab**, Sittwe ("Sit-way" according to Burmese pronunciation, or "Sigh-tway" in Rakhine) is a largely colonial creation. Originally a small fishing settlement, the town was occupied by the British during the First Anglo-Burmese War, and then chosen as the administrative capital of the annexed kingdom of Arakan (modern Rakhine State) in preference to the historic capital of Mrauk U. Sittwe grew exponentially during the years that followed, developing into an important port and major colonial centre, with direct steamers plying the route between here and Kolkata (Calcutta). If the current troubles in Rakhine state don't get in the way, then the city's maritime importance may well be revived, following the joint Myanmar–India construction of a massive, modern port complex in 2016 to facilitate trade between India's northeastern states, as well as direct large-scale shipping between Sittwe and Kolkata.

Sittwe also has a long tradition of radical Buddhism, most notably as the birthplace of radical monk **U Ottama**, a leading figure in the colonial-era independence movement, and the city's monks also played a leading role in the so-called Saffron Revolution (see p.376). Religious belligerence has also shown an uglier face in recent years during repeated clashes between the city's Rakhine population and the increasingly brutalized **Rohingya** minority (see box opposite).

Strand Road

ကမ်းနားလမ်း

Sittwe's most interesting street, **Strand Road** runs along the east side of the centre, and is dotted with some of the town's best surviving colonial architecture including a couple of fine old wooden garden villas down near the *May Yu* restaurant (see p.124).

The street's major landmark is the historic **market** building, which is stuffed with both fresh and preserved marine creatures, including eye-catching bundles of enormous air-dried fish tied by their tails. Further north along the road, a second building provides a home for local rice dealers, with huge piles of sacks laid out.

Unfortunately, the construction of the new port (not open to the public) means the sea views that once gave a lovely backdrop to parts of Strand Road are now no more, and the road has lost some of its former appeal.

Main Road

လမ်းမကြီး

Heading a block inland from the market brings you out on **Main Road** close to the old **colonial clocktower** – a chintzy, falling-to-bits Victorian relic set on top of a large pylon.

A short walk south, just past the Cultural Museum (see p.122), is the town's main **mosque**, now a fitting symbol of Sittwe's oppressed Muslim minority, its entrance blocked off with barbed-wire-festooned crash barriers and guarded by gun-toting

---

ROHINGYA REPRESSION IN RAKHINE

One of the world's most persecuted minorities (according to the UN), the **Rohingya Muslims** of Myanmar are currently facing a titanic battle not just for basic political rights, but for their very survival. Around 800,000 Rohingya live in Rakhine State, with a further million spread across Bangladesh, Pakistan, Thailand and Saudi Arabia. Most Burmese regard them, bizarrely, as illegal immigrants (even though they have been in the country since at least colonial times, possibly much longer), and insist they should all be sent back to Bangladesh, which doesn't want them – and in which the vast majority of Rohingya have never set foot. They are also **stateless**, having been stripped of their citizenship in 1982. Despite their large numbers, the Rohingya ethnicity was not even recognized in the national census of 2014.

Tensions between the Burmese and Rohingya have simmered for decades – particularly since the withdrawal of the British – and the government has routinely discriminated against the Rohingya. As well as being stripped of citizenship, the Rohingya have also been forbidden from travelling even locally without permission, or from having more than two children. Forced labour, extortion, arbitrary taxation, land seizures and chronic food shortages have also been common facts of life.

In 2012, things got even worse with the outbreak of major riots throughout Rakhine State, following the rape and murder of a Buddhist woman and the retaliatory killing of ten. Dozens, perhaps hundreds, of Rohingya were killed, and thousands were displaced. Today, more than 100,000 continue to languish in **camps** in Myanmar, along with many thousands more similarly detained in Bangladesh, and in areas around the Myanmar–Thai border. Efforts by international organizations to ease the plight of those living in the camps have been strongly resisted – the Buddhist clergy have been particularly noisy in condemning organizations working with them.

In 2015, thousands of Rohingya in Myanmar and Bangladesh attempted to escape increasing violence and persecution by heading in (often unseaworthy) **boats** to various Southeast Asian countries. However, hundreds died and thousands had to be rescued at sea. In October 2016, Myanmar border police camps were attacked by unknown assailants and nine police were left dead. The military responded with an extreme crackdown, which by early 2017 had driven thousands more Rohingya into refugee camps on the Myanmar–Bangladesh border. UN and Amnesty International reports (all denied by the Myanmar government) speak of numerous cases of police and military-committed extrajudicial killings, rapes and the burning of villages.

Myanmar's desire to ethnically cleanse itself of the Rohingya appears to permeate all levels of society. Members of the National League for Democracy, while loudly protesting their own lack of political freedom, have been equally dismissive of the Rohingya's plight, and even Aung San Suu Kyi – the one figure in Myanmar with the moral authority to possibly shift entrenched attitudes – has, by and large, remained silent. In an interview with the BBC in April 2017, she asserted: "I don't think there is ethnic cleansing going on; I think ethnic cleansing is too strong an expression to use for what is happening".

soldiers. It's difficult to see much of the mosque now, as it's shielded by high walls and being rapidly reclaimed by the prolific tropical vegetation, although you can catch a few glimpses of the florid colonial-era building, its Neoclassical ground floor complete with incongruous Doric columns topped with a flamboyant mass of diminutive domes and miniature minarets.

A further block south, the trees opposite the *Shwe Thazin* hotel (see p.124) are home to an enormous colony of **fruit bats**, hanging spookily from the trees in big black clusters by day, then waking at dusk and swirling above the streets before setting off to hunt through the night.

Cultural Museum

ယဉ်ကျေးမှုပြတိုက် • Main Rd • Tues–Sun 10am–4pm • $5

Sittwe's lacklustre **Cultural Museum** serves to fill an hour – just. Ground-floor exhibits focus on Rakhine culture and crafts, and provide an introduction to the moves of Rakhine wrestling. Rakhine history (see box, p.120) takes over on the **first floor**. Most impressive is the 3m-tall Anandacandra Pillar, commissioned by King Anandacandra in 729 and recording the achievements of the previous 37 Rakhine monarchs in faded Sanskrit – the only surviving historical record of the entire Wethali (Vesali) period.

Bhaddanta Wannita Museum

ဘဒ္ဒန္တဝဏ္ဏိတတိုပြတိုက် • Main Rd, 1.5km north of the centre • No fixed opening hours, although there's likely to be someone around to let you in • Free; donations appreciated

Housed in a fine old colonial mansion north of the centre, the Maha Kuthala Kyaung Tawgyi monastery is home to the **Bhaddanta Wannita Museum**, showcasing (if that's the right word) the great heaps of bric-a-brac collected by the late Venerable U Bhaddanta Wannita. The museum's dusty display cases are stuffed full of coins, notes, Buddhas, pipes, bits of coral and a couple of golfing trophies. Nothing's actually labelled, and – although most of it is just the rambling collection of a man who clearly couldn't bear to throw anything out – the overall effect is interesting. Resident monks often hang around wanting to practise their English.

Lawkananda Pagoda

လောကနန္ဒာဘုရား • Airport Rd • Daily 6am–9pm • Free

A short walk southwest of the centre is the imposing **Lawkananda Pagoda**, Sittwe's principal temple. The huge Shwedagon-style pagoda (the gift of military ruler Than Shwe in 1997) sits on a vast, empty terrace covered in jazzy blue and white tiles, with four faux-antique stone doorways leading into the opulent interior, which is painted in wall-to-wall gold and red with numerous gilded pillars supporting the domed ceiling.

From the west side of the terrace, steps lead down to a small octagonal pavilion topped with a many-tiered gilded roof, like a very fancy hat. This is home to the exquisite **Sakyamuni Buddha**, a 45cm-high bronze Buddha said to be more than two thousand years old. The statue is seated in the earth-witness pose, holding a star-shaped *dharmachakra* ("wheel of dharma") and clad in a robe and hat covered with more than a thousand finely carved mini-Buddhas.

View Point

ရှုခင်းသာ • K2000 by tuk-tuk

The best place to appreciate Sittwe's superb natural setting is at the beautiful **View Point** (or just "The Point"), 3km south of town along the peaceful waterfront road. There's also a small café here (daily 6am–9pm), which is a great place for a beer while watching the sunset over the waves. The viewpoint is a pleasant 45-minute walk from town or a short tuk-tuk ride.

ARRIVAL AND DEPARTURE   SITTWE

BY PLANE

Sitte Airport is 2.5km west of town (K3000 by tuk-tuk). The best local source of air tickets and other flight info is the Rainbow Air Ticket Centre on Main Rd, opposite the KBZ Bank. Thandwe (for Ngapali's beach) is just 40min away by air. Although airlines typically travel a circular Yangon–Thandwe–Sittwe route, there are a few direct Sittwe–Thandwe flights.

Destinations Thandwe (1–2 daily; 45min); Yangon (6 daily; 1hr 20min).

BY BUS

Foreigners were previously banned from taking the road out of Sittwe, due to the large number of military bases along the route. The road was opened to foreigners in 2013, but may conceivably close once more in the event of trouble. Check the situation locally and book tickets at least a day ahead. Reaching Sittwe by bus remains a hard slog. The closest jumping-off point is Magwe, although direct buses also run from as far afield as Meiktila and Mandalay; all of these services go via Mrauk U. The road running from Mrauk U to Sittwe has recently been upgraded, and the previously rough and long bus ride has been reduced to four hours (or three in a private vehicle). It's likely that as road improvements continue, journey times from the rest of Myanmar will drop. The bus station is 4km west of town, around K3000 by tuk-tuk from the centre.

Destinations Magwe (daily; 15hr); Mandalay (daily; 30hr); Meiktila (daily; 26hr); Mrauk U (3–4 daily; 4hr); Yangon (daily; 30hr).

BY BOAT

TO MRAUK U

There is at least one ferry daily to Mrauk U, run by different operators on different days – all boats depart at 7am from the jetty at the end of Main Rd, around 2km north of the centre (K2000 by tuk-tuk).

IWT ferry The slowest option is the government boat (Tues & Fri; 6hr 30min–7hr 30min; K7000). Tickets for this can be bought at the jetty from 6am on the morning of departure. The boat can get pretty packed, so arrive in good time. You'll have to pay an extra K1000 for a seat – usually a deckchair.

Aung Kyaw Moe boat Faster is the thrice-weekly Aung Kyaw Moe boat (Mon, Thurs & Sat; 4–5hr; K10,000); either buy your ticket when you turn up, or in advance from their office at the jetty.

Shwe Pyi Tan Quickest of all is the Shwe Pyi Tan boat (Wed, Fri & Sun; 2hr 30min; K25,000) – twice as fast and twice as expensive. Tickets are available from the Shwe Pyi Tan office (☏ 09 4967 4569) just north of KBZ Bank on Main Rd – there's no English sign, although the big banner of a boat over the door rather gives it away.

Private boats You could also arrange a private boat (up to four people; 5–6hr; K170,000 return) and leave the same day, so long as you arrive by about 2.30pm. Make sure you agree on how many days they'll wait for you in Mrauk U. Ask directly at the port, with your hotel or with guides.

TO TAUNGGOK

The ferry to Taunggok leaves from the jetty at 6.30am on Tues, Wed and Sun, arriving in Taunggok at around 4pm. Tickets (K45,000) can be bought from the Shwe Pyi Tan office (see above).

GETTING AROUND

Central Sittwe is pretty compact, although you'll need transport when travelling to and from the airport or boat jetty, and out to the View Point. There are plenty of Rakhine-style **tuk-tuks** (a kind of pick-up truck attached to a motorbike) cruising the streets, and you may also be able to rent a **bicycle** from the *Shwe Thazin* hotel (see p.124).

ACCOMMODATION

There are plenty of places to stay in Sittwe, but many of the cheapest aren't licensed to accept foreigners – and the mid-range options are a fairly dreary collection of identical, shoddily constructed business hotels.

Kiss Guesthouse 145 Main Rd (opposite the old clocktower) ☏ 09 451 165 896. Probably the best budget hotel in town, with basic but clean and comfy tiled rooms with attached bathrooms (cold water only). Rooms close to the road are a bit noisy. The manager speaks brilliant English and can help with onward travel connections. $25

Mya Guesthouse 51/6 Bowdhi St ☏ 043 23315. Sittwe's best-known budget guesthouse has simple rooms with a/c and attached cold-water bathrooms. Single rooms are very inexpensive at just $20. While this place is

somewhat let down by its indifferent staff, it's otherwise a good deal. $30

Noble Hotel 45 Main Rd ☏ 043 23558, ✉ anw.noble @gmail.com. This is a reasonably smart, mid-range hotel that's right in the heart of town. Unusually for Sittwe, a little creativity has been shown in the styling here, with bold wallpaper patterns throughout. Rooms come with a/c, TVs, minibars and safes. $50

Royal Sittwe Resort 3km south of town ☏ 043 23478, ⊕ royalsittweresort.asia. Sittwe's most upmarket option – although the workaday resort-style complex hardly sets the pulse racing. The old-fashioned and rather plain rooms aren't particularly good value, and the restaurant is humdrum, although the fine location overlooking the Bay of Bengal partly compensates. Free transfers from airport/boat jetty included. $95

Shwe Thazin 250 Main Rd ☎043 23579, ⓦshwe thazinhotel.com. Central Sittwe's most popular option with passing travellers, the *Shwe Thazin* has small but comfortable and well-furnished rooms at reasonable prices, plus decent service and a good breakfast buffet. $45

Strand Hotel 9 Strand Rd ☎043 22881. On paper this is the best hotel in town, and its $60 bungalows are peaceful, clean and polished. That said, the standard rooms here leave much to be desired, with big patches of mould on the walls despite the hotel only being a couple of years old. The location, opposite the new port but at the quieter end of the street, is great. $50

EATING

501 Tea & Cold Garden Main Rd. This is an attractive local garden restaurant with friendly service and well-prepared versions of all the usual Chinese and seafood dishes (mains K1500–4000). It's a nice place for a beer, even if you choose not to eat. The sign is in Burmese only. Daily 8am–10pm.

May Yu Strand Rd, opposite the new port. A pleasant seafront restaurant (although the new port construction opposite blocks out the waves) in a cheery wooden building painted blue outside and pink within, with a nice terrace in front. Food includes a smallish selection of local seafood plus all the usual Chinese staples (mains K1500–4000). Daily 8am–10pm.

Mya Tea House Next to the Mya Guesthouse. This is a friendly garden teahouse, dishing up simple, inexpensive meals including big bowls of nourishing *mohinga* (K500). Daily 6am–7pm.

River Valley 5 Main Rd ☎043 23234. Convivial, foreigner-friendly restaurant with seating in a pleasant garden illuminated with fairy lights after dark. Serves a long list of mainstream but well-prepared Chinese dishes (mains K3500–5000), as well as a few local specialities like a chicken curry served in an unusually tangy sauce. Make sure you also order one of the delicious fruit juices. Daily 7.30am–10pm.

DIRECTORY

Banks There's an ATM and moneychanger at the big branch of KBZ on Main Rd (but not at the smaller KBZ on Strand Rd).

Mrauk U and around

 မြောက်ဦးမြို့

Hidden upriver amid the watery labyrinths of the Kaladan River, the remote and decidedly rustic town of **MRAUK U** was once the last and greatest capital of the kingdom of **Arakan** (see p.120 & pp.362–363), its 49 kings ruling for 350 years over an empire stretching, at its apogee, from the Ayeyarwady to the mouth of the Ganges and controlling large areas of what is now Myanmar and Bangladesh. Mrauk U also served as a unique medieval melting pot of foreign influences. Its Buddhist rulers adopted Islamic titles and customs influenced by the nearby Sultanate of Bengal, while the city also faced off Portuguese incursions and later served as a major pan-Asian trading base.

The conquest and sack of the city at the hands of the Konbaung dynasty in 1784 brought Mrauk U's glory days to an end, while the British decision to move the provincial capital to Sittwe in 1826 further hastened its decline. Lasting mementoes of Mrauk U's glory days survive, however, in the shape of a unique collection of remarkable fortified **temples** – among Asia's weirdest Buddhist monuments.

MRAUK U: "MONKEY EGG"

One popular theory holds that the **name** Mrauk U is a corruption of *myauk u*, meaning "Monkey Egg", said to have been offered to the Buddha by a monkey as a sign of his devotion. It's pronounced "Mrow-Oo" by the Rakhine, or as a rather feline-sounding "Meow-Oo" by the Burmese.

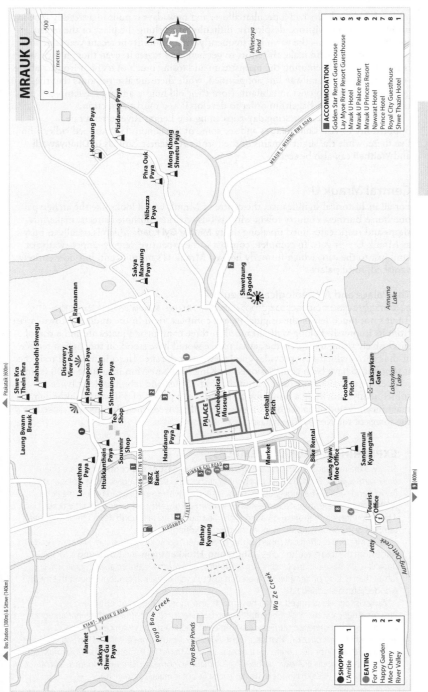

MRAUK U

ACCOMMODATION
Golden Star Resort Guesthouse	5
Lay Myoe River Resort Guesthouse	6
Mrauk U Hotel	3
Mrauk U Palace Resort	4
Mrauk U Princess Resort	9
Nawarat Hotel	2
Prince Hotel	7
Royal City Guesthouse	8
Shwe Thazin Hotel	1

SHOPPING
L'Amitie	1

EATING
For You	3
Happy Garden	2
Moe Cherry	1
River Valley	4

2

2

Mrauk U has always had a peculiar allure, and nowadays it pulls in a steadily growing number of foreign visitors, despite the difficulty of reaching the place or the recent troubles in Rakhine – the town has frequently been off-limits in recent years due to local unrest. Few who make the effort to get here ever regret it, even though the town is now increasingly entering the mainstream and losing much of its final-frontier allure – a new airport and railway line are planned, while there are also rumours that the government plans to evict inhabitants from their old houses among the temples (as happened in Old Bagan) in order to develop it as a tourist attraction.

Around Mrauk U, interesting day-trips along the Lemro River offer a rare opportunity to visit **Chin villages** and see some of the famous last tattooed ladies who live there, while the slight remains of the former Arakanese capitals of **Dhanyawadi** and **Waithali** can also be seen.

Central Mrauk U

For all its historical significance, the centre of Mrauk U still looks like the archetypal one-horse Burmese country town, with its busy market, potholed streets, makeshift shops and rustic cafés lined up along dusty **Minbar Gyi Road**, which is usually as busy as Mrauk U ever gets. In complete contrast is the expansive, largely empty swathe of land just to the east, which formerly housed Mrauk U's magnificent, but now entirely vanished, royal **palace**.

The Palace and Archeological Museum

နန်းတော်နှင့် / ရှေးဟောင်းသုတေသနပြိတိုက် • **Palace** Daily 24hr • Free • **Museum** Tues–Sun 9.30am–4.30pm • $5

There's not much left of the original **Palace** complex, right in the middle of town, apart from its impressively long walls arranged in three concentric squares around a trio of successively rising terraces – the actual palace would have stood on the highest terrace at the centre, which now provides good views over the site. The original royal residence is thought to have been commissioned by King Min Saw Mon in around 1430 (some sources say it wasn't constructed until the mid-1500s) and rebuilt at least twice subsequently, providing a home for 49 kings over a period of 350 years – although the magnificent wooden palace building itself was destroyed when the city was sacked by the forces of the Konbaung dynasty in 1784.

EXPLORING MRAUK U'S TEMPLES

The two main groups of temples are to the **north** and **east of the centre**; most are open daily 7am–5.30pm (although actual opening and closing times of individual temples are very flexible and seem to be largely up to the gatekeeper), with entry covered by a single ticket (K5000). Tourists are stopped as they arrive in town off the ferry or bus and sold the ticket, but if you slip through they are also issued at the Shittaung Paya (although ticket checks at other temples were virtually nonexistent at the time of writing).

While Mrauk U is often described as the "new Bagan", comparisons are somewhat misleading. Aside from the "big three" temples – **Shittaung**, **Htukkanthein** and **Kothaung** – Mrauk U doesn't really have Bagan's landmark monuments and must-see sights, and in some ways rather than ticking off temples it's more fun just to cycle or walk at random among the thickly wooded, stupa-studded hills.

Many visitors are surprised at just how much, and, more to the point, just how unsympathetically, many of the temples have been restored. The Htukkanthein has an ugly cement roof and there are numerous examples of Buddha statues with cement ears amateurishly stuck back on. That said, most visitors do actually prefer Mrauk U to Bagan.

Easily the best introduction to ancient Arakan and Mrauk U is Pamela Gutman's *Burma's Lost Kingdoms: splendours of Arakan*, although it's difficult to come by. *Famous Monuments of Mrauk U* by Myar Aung (K5000) is widely available locally, but is mainly gibberish.

On the western side of the complex, the government **Archeological Museum** has a mediocre collection of assorted finds from around the site, plus some artefacts from the previous Arakanese capital of Waithali (see p.132) just down the road.

Haridaung Paya
ဟာရိတောင်ဘုရား
On a small, steep hill just north of the Palace area, the tiny **Haridaung Paya** is little more than a simple gold-painted stupa but offers one of Mrauk U's finest views, with dozens of stupas crowning the hills all around and glimpses of water between the trees. It's not signed: look out for the white steps (which can get appallingly hot under bare feet) next to the road, from where it's a few minutes' walk to the top.

Market
Mrauk U's little tree-studded **market** is an appropriately rustic affair, with the usual stalls full of fruit, vegetables and herbs alongside piles of traditional Rakhine-style pointed bamboo hats, heaps of *chinlone* balls, anchors, enormous saws and a surprising quantity of pharmacies, including one alleyway stuffed entirely with little shops selling either pills or beer. The west side of the market is where you'll find the town's tailors, lined up at a row of tables behind heaps of cloth and old-fashioned sewing machines.

Northern group
Mrauk U's **Northern group** of temples is the undoubted highlight of the ancient city, centred on the landmark **Shittaung** and **Htukkanthein** temples. Both are classic examples of the city's unique style of fortified temple, set upon impregnably high bases with thick, almost windowless walls. The design offers an apt reflection of medieval Arakan's turbulent history, during which the city was attacked on numerous occasions – the temples themselves possibly served as refuges for the embattled population. Later and more decorative monuments such as the nearby **Ratanapon** and **Laung Bwann Brauk** offer a notable contrast in style.

Shittaung Paya
ရှစ်သောင်းဘုရား: • Entry covered by main temple ticket
The usual starting point for tours of Mrauk U is the landmark **Shittaung Paya**, built by the founder of Mrauk U, King Minbin, in 1535 to celebrate his reconquest of "the twelve towns of the Ganges" (roughly half of modern Bangladesh) – the name refers to the 80,000 (*shittaung*) images said to be housed here. The temple is set on a huge fortified terrace and surrounded by numerous small stupas in Mrauk U's distinctive style, topped not by the usual spire but with a truncated finial vaguely resembling a stone mushroom. Some faint reliefs can also be seen in places around the outer walls (including a couple of vaguely erotic scenes on the southern side). Unfortunately the exterior is now a complete mess following the addition of a modern prayer hall and stairway in the mid-twentieth century, and in 2003 (following the discovery of cracks in the main stupa) the Archeology Department decided to encase the temple's upper terrace in eyesore concrete in order to stop water leaking into the temple below.

The Shittaung Pillar
At the bottom of the steps up to the temple stands the **Shittaung Pillar** (set inside in a green barred shelter), with inscriptions in badly eroded Sanskrit recording the genealogy of the Arakan kings. The three sides (the fourth is blank) are thought to have each been carved two hundred years apart, in the sixth, eighth and tenth centuries respectively.

2

The prayer hall and central shrine

At the top of the stairs, entry is via a small vestibule where tickets are issued and guidebooks sold (walking straight through the vestibule and exiting via the rear door brings you out right next to the Andaw Thein). Turn left into the colourful modern **prayer hall**, with gilded Buddhas stacked up around the walls and bright ceiling paintings overhead. An elaborate stone door directly ahead of you (as you enter the hall) leads into a **central shrine** with a large gilded Buddha, its body patterned with squares of gold leaf applied by worshippers.

The corridors

Shittaung's real highlight, however, is the pair of marvellously atmospheric corridors reached via doors in the far left corner of the prayer hall. The **inner corridor**, walled with roughly hewn sandstone and lined with dozens of Buddhas, coils round on itself before reaching a dead end, with tiny openings in the walls offering glimpses of the main prayer hall and outer corridor.

Even more impressive is the **outer corridor**, however, more than 100m long and lined with a spectacularly intricate stone frieze decorated with more than a thousand sculptures. The frieze is divided into six levels, alternately projecting and recessed, with faded paint covering many surfaces. Carvings depict the usual Jataka scenes and miscellaneous mythical monsters along with figures from Rakhine life (musicians, dancers, soldiers). Larger projecting sculptures include King Minbin himself (in the southwest corner), Indra mounted on his three-headed elephant Erawan, and Brahma astride his *hamsa*.

Htukkanthein Paya

ထုက္ကန္သိမ် · Daily 7am–5.30pm · Entry covered by main temple ticket

The **Htukkanthein** (or "Dukkanthein") **Paya** is the most memorable of all Mrauk U's temples, and the perfect example of the town's distinctive architectural style: a huge mass of brick and stone virtually unrelieved by any kind of decoration and looking more like a fortress, high-security prison or nuclear bomb shelter than anything remotely religious. The temple's defensive qualities are enhanced by its setting on a high, almost sheer-sided, terrace, with just a single entrance – even the tiny square windows look like embrasures for cannons rather than sources of light.

Built in 1571 by King Min Phalaung, the U-shaped temple itself is linked to a small rectangular shrine at the back and topped with five "mushroom" stupas in a quincunx pattern (or almost). Most of the interior is occupied by a remarkable **corridor**, which loops around on itself twice and connects two interior chambers before climbing up to the barn-like rooftop shrine. Lining the corridor are 179 seated Buddha images in niches, each flanked by carved male and female figures said to represent the donors who financed construction of the temple. The figures are famous for modelling all 64 of medieval Mrauk U's **traditional hairstyles**, most of which seem to involve big topknot and turban-style arrangements – not a million miles away from the mushroom-shaped caps on the stupas outside.

Like a number of Mrauk U temples, this one suffers from some poorly executed renovation work, carried out by the former military government using big dollops of cement.

Lemyethna Paya

လေးမျက်နှာဘုရား· Daily 7am–5.30pm · Entry covered by main temple ticket

Next to the road just past the Htukkanthein, the small **Lemyethna Paya** was built in 1430 by King Min Saw Mon. Outside, it's another of Mrauk U's characteristically impregnable constructions: a windowless bunker topped with a stupa with cut-off spire. Four entrances lead into the circular interior, with eight seated Buddhas placed around the central octagonal pillar beneath a vaulted ceiling.

Andaw Thein

အံတော်သိမ်ဘုရား: • Immediately north of Shittaung Paya • Daily 7am–5.30pm • Entry covered by main temple ticket • Exit the rear side of Shittaung's antechamber leading to the main prayer hall

The **Andaw Thein** was originally built as an ordination hall (*thein*) in 1521 by King Thazata, and subsequently expanded into a temple by King Raza II to house a tooth relic (*andaw*) of the Buddha brought back from a visit to Sri Lanka in around 1600. Fourteen stupas (each hollow, and with a small seated Buddha inside) are arranged around three sides of the octagonal **main shrine**, built in the usual bunker style and topped with further stupas. Two concentric corridors penetrate the inside, lined with niched Buddha statues.

Attached to the shrine is a rectangular **prayer hall** still boasting a fine stone doorway on its eastern side, although the original roof has gone, now replaced with a corrugated-iron shelter.

Ratanapon Paya

ရတနာပုံ ဘုရား: • Open access 24hr • Entry covered by main temple ticket

Immediately past Andaw Thein is the **Ratanapon** (aka "Yadanpon") **Paya**. Built in 1612 by King Min Khamaung (or possibly his wife), this is one of Mrauk U's later and less militaristic-looking monuments, centred on an unusually tall (if rather bottom-heavy) stupa. A necklace of seventeen mini-stupas encloses the main stupa, set on an octagonal terrace decorated with a few lion sculptures, now badly eroded. The temple's name translates as "Pile of Jewels", referring, it's said, to the precious stones enshrined in the central stupa, although none has ever been found despite the best efforts of bounty hunters – and a direct hit from a Japanese bomb in World War II also failed to reveal any buried treasure (the damage has since been restored).

Mahabodhi Shwegu

မဟာဗောဓိရွှေဂူ • Daily 7am–5.30pm • Entry covered by main temple ticket • Go north along the road from the Ratanapon towards the Laung Bwann Brauk, and just before you reach the latter you'll see a covered well on your right – follow the steep path up the hill behind this to reach the temple

Dating from the latter half of the fifteenth century, the tiny **Mahabodhi Shwegu** is one of Mrauk U's more unusual monuments, with a quaint little octagonal domed shrine connected to a narrow antechamber. Its main interest, however, is the intricate, albeit very eroded, carvings decorating the antechamber walls and the throne of the central Buddha image. These include representations of the Buddhist heaven and hell along with some erotic images – although you'll have to look very closely to make anything out.

Laung Bwann Brauk

လောင်ပွန်းပြောက်ဘုရား: • Daily 24hr • Entry covered by main temple ticket

Laung Bwann Brauk temple is characterized by its fractionally tilted outline (more obvious from some angles than others), as the stupa has crumpled slightly under its own weight. The base of the octagonal stupa is ringed with elaborately carved niches, some still containing Buddha images (or what's left of them), while the front of the terrace is decorated with unusual flower-shaped glazed tiles, although many are now sadly crumbling into dust.

Just north of here on the other side of the road stands the diminutive **Shwe Kra Thein Phra**: a pretty little stupa raised high on a finely carved six-tier base.

Pitakataik

ပိဋကတ်တိုက် • Daily 7am–5.30pm • Entry covered by main temple ticket

Mrauk U's smallest and prettiest monument, the quaint **Pitakataik** is the only one of the city's original 48 libraries to have survived – although it looks far too small to have stored more than a handful of books. The building was commissioned by King Min Phalaung in 1591 to house a set of the Buddhist Tripitaka, and is unusual in being constructed of solid stone rather than the usual brick. It's elaborately decorated with abstract geometrical shapes, a fancy door and a spiky zigzag roof in four tiers, which is now sagging slightly under its own weight. The tiny vaulted interior is contrastingly bare.

2 Eastern group

Mrauk U's **eastern group** of monuments is rather more scattered and low-key than the northern group, barring the massive **Kothaung Paya**, one of the town's stand-out sights. Many date from the kingdom's middle years and include a trio of fine stupas – at the **Mong Khong Shwetu**, **Sakyaman Aung** and **Ratanaman** temples – exemplifying Mrauk U's later and lighter architectural style.

Phra Ouk and Mong Khong Shwetu

ဘုရား အုပ် / မင်းခေါင်ရွှေတု • Daily 24hr • Entry covered by main temple ticket

Set atop a small hillock next to the road, the pint-sized **Phra Ouk Paya** is said to have been erected as a talisman by King Phalaung in 1571 when warned of external threats against his kingdom. The building comprises an unusually shaped, angular brick stupa-shrine, with a disproportionately large stone doorway (probably a later addition) and a chain of Buddhas set in niches around the base, looking out in all directions over the surrounding countryside, perhaps in order to face off approaching invaders.

The **Mong Khong Shwetu Paya** (1629) on the opposite side of the road is a good example of Mrauk U's later style, with a tall and elegant sandstone stupa (although parts of the stonework are beginning to sag with age) topped with a distinctive star-shaped finial and finely carved double niches arranged around each of its four sides.

Pizidaung Paya

ပိစိတောင်ဘုရား • Daily 24hr • Entry covered by main temple ticket

The **Pizidaung Paya** is said to contain a testicle (*pizi*) relic of the Buddha – although this sounds suspiciously like another Burmese cock-and-bull story, and the site's main attraction is its gorgeous view of the nearby Kothaung Paya. There's not much left of the temple itself, situated on a hillock right next to the road junction but surprisingly easy to miss. Much of the shrine has collapsed, leaving one Buddha sitting lone and proud at the top of the hill, with four more Buddhas seated in the remains of the ambulatory below, also now open to the sky.

Kothaung Paya

ကိုးသောင်းဘုရား • Daily 7am–5.30pm • Entry covered by main temple ticket

Built between 1554 and 1556, the gigantic **Kothaung Paya** is the result of a piece of shameless one-upmanship by King Dikkha, who ordered a building large enough to store 90,000 (*kothaung*) Buddha images – just that little bit bigger than his father King Minbin's landmark temple, which could hold just 80,000 (*shittaung*). Dikkha's vainglory did him little good: he reigned for just three years and his vast temple fell rapidly to pieces (its marshy location causing the foundations to subside) and had to be meticulously put back together again in a massive restoration programme starting in 1997.

Even by Mrauk U's outlandish standards it's a singularly strange structure, looking like some kind of huge Buddhist bomb shelter, its stepped sides stacked with hundreds of mini-stupas. There's nothing else like it in Myanmar, although it does bear a certain (probably fortuitous) resemblance to the great stupa-mountain of Borobudur in Java.

Entry is from the east, and there are often groups of nuns and monks gathered outside waiting for alms from passing tourists. Inside the walls (which are sandstone on the outside, and faced with brick within), most of the temple is actually open, split on two levels with corridors, now largely roofless, around each level and a large stupa on the higher section. The **outer corridor** (on the lower level) is particularly fine, its walls intricately carved with thousands of identikit miniature mosaic-style Buddhas interspersed with larger Buddhas seated on plinths. The **inner corridor** (on the upper level) is more fragmentary, lined with hundreds of small, seated Buddhas, while two quaint ogre guards flank the entrance to the corridor on the northern side opposite the stupa.

Sakya Manaung Paya

သကျမာန်အောင်ဘုရား• Daily 24hr • Entry covered by main temple ticket

The **Sakya Manaung Paya** was built at the same time as the similar Mong Khong Shwetu Paya nearby. Two huge, brightly painted ogres stand guard over the entrance, facing outwards, while behind them two more supersized figures stand praying towards the temple – the statues are revered in their own right, with squares of gold leaf applied to their bases (although some people content themselves with offering strips of gold-coloured adhesive tape rather than the real thing).

The **main stupa** is a classic example of the later Mrauk U style, set inside a ring of eleven mini-stupas and rising from a quasi-octagonal, zigzagging base which has now expanded to many levels, making up almost half the height of the entire structure. Elaborate two-storey niches decorate the stupa's four faces, with *makara*-like finials at the corners of the three main base terraces.

Ratanaman

ရတနာမာန်• Daily 24hr • Entry covered by main temple ticket

Halfway between the northern and eastern groups, the **Ratanaman** is another elegant, late-period stupa set on a many-tiered octagonal base. Eight colourful little figures representing the days of the week (see box, p.74) stand around the base of the stupa, along with a modern prayer hall and a pair of old brick shrines. At the time of research, major restoration work was under way here.

South of the centre

The area south of the centre is relatively devoid of ancient monuments, although you can still see the modest remains of the old **Laksaykan Gate**, leading through to the gorgeous **Laksaykan Lake**.

Sandamuni Kyaungtaik

စန္ဒာမုနိကျောင်းတိုက်• Daily 24hr • Free; donations welcome • Approaching from the town centre, turn off the road running south from the bike rental shop through a yellow arch (signed, but in Burmese only) and continue to the end of the road, before turning left up the steps at the sign saying "Sanda Muhni Phara Gri Kyang Tak"

The extensive **Sandamuni Kyaungtaik monastery** (aka the Bandoola Kyaung) complex spreads up a grassy hillside just west of the gently rippling waters of Laksaykan Lake. It's best known as the home of the **Sandamuni Buddha**, which is said to date from as far back as 308 BC. The image had once been covered with a thick layer of cement – possibly to hide it from marauding British troops in the 1850s – and was then somehow forgotten about until one of the eyes suddenly dropped out in 1988, revealing the original statue hidden deep within.

There's also a small museum here – the metal table-top on the right as you enter is actually an original copper roof tile from the old Mrauk U palace, which is one of the few pieces of the royal residence that escaped being looted when the city was sacked in 1784.

2

CHIN VILLAGE TRIPS

If you don't have time to go and explore recently opened Chin State (see p.135) proper, then a day-trip from Mrauk U along the sylvan Lemro River to a series of nearby **Chin villages** (none of which is actually in Chin State) will give you a little hint of what you're missing higher up in those tantalizing mountains. There are a number of villages along the river where you can meet people from this large ethnic minority group, who are best known for the practice of tattooing the faces of their womenfolk. The practice was outlawed during the 1960s, although in most villages you'll see at least one or two older women with the markings – though every year there are fewer left. Local stories suggest that this painful procedure (using a mix of soot and buffalo liver) was intended to make girls less attractive to raiders, but more likely it was as a mark of identity for the various Chin tribes.

The **tattooed ladies** are used to attracting attention: some of them produce handicrafts for sale, while others charge a small fee to be photographed. Many visitors find the experience uncomfortably voyeuristic, although money from tourism helps fund community projects such as schools and water pumps (you may be asked for a donation) and provides much-needed income to one of Myanmar's most impoverished ethnic groups. Day-trips to the villages typically cost $80 for a boat seating up to four people (including guide), and the price includes lunch. Fees for photography in the villages are negotiable. Trips can be booked a day in advance via any hotel or tour company office in town.

Shwetaung Pagoda

ရွှေတောင်ဘုရား • Daily 24hr • Entry covered by main temple ticket

It's worth climbing the hill up to the **Shwetaung Pagoda** not for the temple itself (which is just an average-sized, bog-standard stupa) but for what is probably the definitive view of Mrauk U – particularly memorable at dusk and around dawn, with the mysterious outlines of myriad stupas emerging from the early-morning mists in every direction, and flashes of water between.

To **reach the temple**, head 100m down the side road that runs south off the main road between the centre and the *Prince Hotel*, looking for a pink archway (leading to a small monastery complex) on your left. Turn left off the road, go up to the arch (but not through it) and turn left again along the wide dirt track immediately in front of the archway skirting the monastery boundary wall. Follow this for around 20m, just past the end of the wall, and you'll see a small, steep path on your right snaking its way up the hill. Follow this to reach the temple at the top – a brisk ten-minute walk.

North to Dhanyawadi and Waithali

The remains of two more of ancient Arakan's former capitals – **Dhanyawadi** (former home of the revered Mahamuni Buddha) and **Waithali** – can be visited close to Mrauk U. To get to them, you can either hire a tuk-tuk and driver for the day, or opt for a more organized tour of the sites arranged through your hotel or a tour company.

Waithali

ဝေသာလီမြို့

Hidden among rolling hills some 9km north of Mrauk U are the remains of the ancient city of **WAITHALI** (also spelled "Wethali" and often referred to by its Pali name, "**Vesali**"), founded in the fourth century and capital of Arakan (see box, p.120) from around 327 to 794. According to the Anandacandra pillar (see p.122), its subjects practised Mahayana Buddhism, although its monarchs considered themselves descendants of the Hindu god, Shiva – a characteristically Arakanese syncretism.

Much of the former city has now fallen into ruin, although you can still make out the remains of a few temples and fragments of the city's brick walls and the palace within. The main attraction is the **Great Waithali Payagyi**, a huge seated Buddha image more than 5m tall and said to be made from a single piece of stone. One of Myanmar's oldest Buddhas, it was (according to legend) a gift of the chief queen of King Maha Taing Candra, who founded the city in 327 AD – although the original features have been altered somewhat by modern restorations.

Dhanyawadi

ဓညဝတီ

Around 40km northwest of Mrauk U are the remains of the first of Arakan's four capitals, **DHANYAWADI**. As at Waithali, the ruins of the old city are fragmentary and the site is best known nowadays as the original home of the enormously revered **Mahamuni Buddha** statue (see p.289). Ancient Arakanese chronicles claim, perhaps a little ambitiously, that the Buddha himself visited the city in 554 BC, during which a statue – the Mahamuni – was made. Worshipped for centuries by Rakhine's monarchs, the statue was regarded as a symbol and protector of the country – although it couldn't prevent the sack of Mrauk U in 1784, after which the Mahamuni was carried off by King Bodawpaya to Mandalay, where it remains to this day.

The modernized temple in which the image was once housed survives, however, along with three ancient Buddhas which still attract many worshippers, particularly the 1.5m-high central image, known as "Mahamuni's Brother". There's also a small **museum** here, with some fragments of stone carvings and inscriptions found around the site.

2

ARRIVAL AND DEPARTURE

MRAUK U AND AROUND

By bus Foreigners are now allowed by road to Mrauk U, but aside from those travelling between here and Sittwe, few people brave the long journeys to other parts of the country.

Destinations Magwe (daily; 10hr); Mandalay (1–2 daily; 24hr); Sittwe (3–4 daily; 4hr); Yangon (1–2 daily; 24hr).

By boat Most visitors still come by boat from Sittwe (see p.123). Services dock at the jetty close to the town centre, which is within walking distance of most accommodation. A tuk-tuk to outlying hotels will cost K1000–2000. Leaving Mrauk U, there is currently one boat daily back to Sittwe. The fastest is the *Shwe Pyin Tan* (Mon, Thurs & Sat; 2hr 30min; K25,000; buy tickets in advance from the *Hay Mar* restaurant by the jetty); slightly slower is the *Aung Kyaw Moe*

(Tues, Fri & Sun; 4–5hr; K10,000; tickets available in advance from their office near the jetty, or you can buy them as you board the boat); the slow government boat (Wed & Sat; 6hr 30min–7hr 30min; $6 or K7000, plus K1000 for a seat) fills in one of the remaining days. All boats leave at 7am. You can also charter a boat from Sittwe (see p.123).

By car Increasing numbers of foreign tourists travelling between Sittwe and Mrauk U choose to take the boat one-way and then hire a private car to get back again (2.5hr). This is easily organized through most hotels in and around Mrauk U (less so from Sittwe) and costs K90,000–100,000. The driver can drop you straight at the airport.

GETTING AROUND

Although there was plenty of road reconstruction taking place at the time of writing, the roads in Mrauk U remain some of the worst in Myanmar – more pothole than actual road in many places – and just riding a bike can be a bit of a rattle, while even a kilometre in a tuk-tuk can turn into a bone-shatteringly bad trip.

By bike Although the town centre is very compact, heading out to the temples is best done by bike. Than Tun Bicycle Rental (closed Sun), which is based between the town centre and the jetty, has loads of gearless bikes available to rent for K3000/day. Alternatively, you can try asking about bike rental at your guesthouse.

By tuk-tuk Rakhine-style tuk-tuks look quite a bit like motorbikes with mini pick-up style attachments bolted to the back, and crowds of them park up beside the jetty to meet all incoming ferries. They charge around K2000 for a trip to the centre of the village.

INFORMATION AND TOURS

Tourist information The tourist office (signed "Regional Guides Society"; ☎ 09 421 720 168, ✉ rgs.mrauku@gmail.com) is opposite the ferry jetty, although it's not often manned. If you want to arrange a local guide to show you round the temples it's best to call or email in advance.

Tours Tours (to local Chin villages and elsewhere) can be arranged through most guesthouses and hotels, or try Aung Zang ("Mr Fix-It"; ☎ 09 421 722 241, ✉ aungzanmrauku2015@gmail.com), who can usually be found hanging out at the *Lay Myoe River Resort Guesthouse* (see below).

ACCOMMODATION

Electricity supplies to Mrauk U can be temperamental – most upmarket places have their own generators, while budget options will leave you in the dark.

Golden Star Resort Guesthouse 116 Minbar Gyi Rd ☎ 09 2507 6538. This is a friendly and competitively priced guesthouse (with singles for just $13). The whole place feels a bit makeshift and tumbledown, but the communal garden is pleasant. They can be a bit reluctant to rent the cheaper rooms to foreigners. **$15**

Lay Myoe River Resort Guesthouse Minbar Gyi Rd ☎ 09 253 770 556. One of Mrauk U's cheapest accommodation options, with simple boxy rooms with fans and attached bathrooms (cold water only). It's basic but reasonably clean, and comes at a very fair price. **$15**

Mrauk U Hotel Yangon–Sittwe Rd ☎ 09 977 990 036. First impressions are of a large, moribund hotel, so it comes as a surprise that the rooms are some of the best around with good mattresses, blue sashes on the beds and bright bathrooms. The lack of wi-fi is a drag. **$50**

Mrauk U Palace Resort Alodawpyi St ☎ 09 853 2277, ⊛ mraukupalaceresort.com. A palace it most certainly isn't, but it is a good-value, clean, reliable but rather unexciting mid-range hotel. Rooms are in individual bungalows arranged around a garden, which needs a few more years to grow in. **$30**

Mrauk U Princess Resort Riverfront ☎ 09 850 0556, ⊛ mraukuprincess.com. The town's only upmarket option at present – attractive enough, but overpriced in the absence of any competition. Accommodation is in 33 rather stern-looking black-wood "village houses" lined up next to a gorgeous lotus pond, which has a swimming pool plonked in the middle of it. But considering the price, it's not all that. **$266**

Nawarat Hotel Yangon–Sittwe Rd ☎ 043 50203. Offers functional chalets a few minutes' walk from the main northern group of temples. It hardly lights a fire of excitement, but it's comfortable enough. If you pay $13 more, you can have a quieter room at the back of the gardens. **$55**

Prince Hotel Myaung Bwe Rd ☎ 09 260 701 079, ⊛ mraukuprince.com. In a pleasant rural setting a 10min walk from town. The rooms here are only so-so, but the family who run this place make up for any discomfort – you'll barely have time to put your bags down before they're plying you with tea and snacks. The $40 rooms contain a double bed and bunk beds, making them a good bet for young families. They also have six-bed dorms ($15), which are probably the cheapest beds in town. **$30**

Royal City Guesthouse Near the ferry dock ☎ 043 50257. This place is spread across both sides of the road, conveniently close to the town and ferry dock. The cheaper rooms (fans and cold water only) on the reception side of the road are one of Mrauk U's better deals – neat, tiled and clean, with writing desks. The handful of fancier bungalows opposite (with a/c, hot water and TVs; $40) are spacious and nicely furnished, although right next to the road. Don't rely on their wi-fi working. **$30**

★Shwe Thazin Hotel Yangon–Sittwe Rd ☎ 09 265 923 233. Mrauk U's best mid-range option by a long way, with attractive stone-and-wood chalets decorated with fancy traditional carvings, which give the impression of sleeping inside a temple. Pretty gardens and excellent staff round out the deal. **$65**

EATING

For You Minbar Gyi Rd. A decent lunch stop in town, serving up a short menu of tasty fried rice, noodles and soups (most featuring either chicken or pork) for around K3000. Daily 8am–8pm.

Happy Garden Minbar Gyi Rd. Cheery little local café-cum-bar set in a cute little wooden building on stilts (although the "garden" below is just a sandy space under a large awning). The inexpensive mains (K2000–4000) include no-frills noodles and fried rice dishes, plus grilled fish and the usual Chinese staples. Daily 7am–11pm.

Moe Cherry Northeast corner of the palace complex ☎ 09 421 733 711. Deservedly popular with visiting foreigners, the Myanmar curries (around K4000) here are nicely cooked and served with a decent selection of vegetable side dishes, plus soup. Daily 7am–10pm.

River Valley Near the ferry dock. An offshoot of the popular Sittwe restaurant, set on a pleasant terrace hung with multicoloured lanterns and serving up an identical menu (mains K3500–5000) to its sister, with a big and competent (if unremarkable) selection of Chinese-style seafood and meat dishes. Daily 7.30am–10pm.

SHOPPING

L'Amitie Just north of the Shittaung Paya
✉ artsmtmu@yahoo.com. This art gallery is the base
of the father-and-son painting team of Shwe Maung
Tha (who has had his work shown overseas) and Khine
Minn Tun – one of them can usually be found around
this place. Daily 7am–dusk.

DIRECTORY

Banks There's a branch of the KBZ Bank with an ATM
opposite the *Shwe Thazin Hotel*.

Chin State

ချင်းပြည်နယ်
Squeezed in between Myanmar,
Bangladesh and the Indian states of
Mizoram and Manipur, remote and
impoverished **Chin State** is one of
Myanmar's least explored regions, with
thick jungles, mountainous terrain and
only rudimentary infrastructure. The
state's 500,000 or so Chin inhabitants
– including the famed women with
facial tattoos – are among Myanmar's
most persecuted minorities. Large
numbers converted to Christianity
during colonial times, and have
suffered widespread oppression from
the 1960s through to the present day,
with forced labour, torture, rape, acute
food shortages and extrajudicial
executions widely reported – as well as
attempts to forcibly reconvert Chin
Christians to Buddhism.

The region has been largely closed to
foreigners for decades, but over the past
couple of years things have changed
and Chin State has suddenly started to
open up, with permit-free independent
travel now permitted to many areas.
This is exciting news for adventure-
seekers, who now have a rare
opportunity to explore a part of Asia
seen by few other foreigners. The star
attraction of the region is **Mount
Victoria** (aka **Nat Ma Taung**), the highest
peak in Myanmar south of the
Himalayas. Elsewhere, the towns of
Hakha and **Falam** offer a glimpse of
small-town Chin life, and there's the
chance to meet some of the last
tattooed women in villages throughout

the area. If you're looking for a real Myanmar adventure, then you could try the gruelling (and rarely completed) trek of Chin State from Mount Victoria right through to Mrauk U (see box opposite).

ARRIVAL AND GETTING AROUND   CHIN STATE

Be aware that travelling in Chin State is not for the faint-hearted. Conditions are still **basic**, there are few roads, electricity and hot water are very hit and miss, and locals are utterly uncertain when it comes to interacting with foreign visitors. For these reasons, almost every traveller uses the services of a **tour company** with contacts in the region. Due to the lack of a road, you cannot cross directly between Mount Victoria and Hakha and Falam. Instead, you'll have to go all the way back down to the Ayeyarwady Valley, and then up into the hills on another road. You should allow at least a week to visit all of the places listed here, though ten days is better.

By bus The bus service is limited. If you're heading to Mount Victoria, there are a couple of buses and minibuses a day from Pakokku (near Bagan) to Kanpetlet. However, this isn't the best idea, as once you get to Kanpetlet you would need a car to get to the mountain trailhead, and there aren't any available here to rent. For Hakha and Falam, there are daily buses from Kalaymyo (west of Shwebo in northern Myanmar) that go to Hakha (9hr) via Falam (5hr).

By tour An increasing number of tour companies are adding Chin State to their itineraries. Perhaps the most experienced operator in Chin is the Yangon-based Pegu Travels (☎01 371937, ⓦpegutravels.com). Other good Yangon-based operators include Ayarwaddy Legend (☎01 252007, ⓦayarwaddylegend.com) and Khiri Travel (☎01 375577, ⓦkhiri.com). Numerous travel agencies in Bagan also offer two- to three-night trips to Mount Victoria.

Mount Victoria and around

နတ်မတောင် (ဝိတိုရိယတောင်) · $10 park fee

Practically the only place even slightly on the Chin tourist radar is **Mount Victoria** (Nat Ma Taung), most easily accessible from Bagan. Rising from dense forests, the upper reaches of the mountain form a so-called "sky island", with alpine plant and bird species characteristic of the Himalayas living alongside other endemic flora and fauna. The mountain and its surrounding are so biologically important that it has been made an ASEAN Heritage Park and been declared of Outstanding Universal Value by UNESCO.

Although the mountain is reasonably high at 3053m, it's a fairly easy five-hour return hike to the summit from the trailhead, which is a 45-minute drive from Kanpetlet village, around 20km to the east. The prime time of year to climb is from November to late February, when the views are at their best, the temperatures are pleasant and the rhododendron bushes are ablaze with colour. Most people visit the mountain as part of a pre-arranged tour booked in Yangon or Bagan, but if you come independently then guides can be arranged through one of the eco-lodges in Kanpetlet.

ACCOMMODATION

There is no accommodation on the mountain itself. Most people use Kanpetlet as a base, though the best available accommodation is all a short way out of town in the direction of the mountain trailhead.

Mountain Oasis Eco-Lodge 10 min out of Kanpetlet on the road to the trailhead. This friendly lodge offers ten basic wooden cottages with thatched roofs, small terraces and cold-water bathrooms (which really aren't fun at this altitude). Guides and picnic lunches can be organized here. $̄69

Hakha

ဟားခါး

HAKHA, the diminutive capital of Chin State, lies at an altitude of 1867m and has a cool – and at night even cold – climate. The town is notably less developed than most other regional capitals in Myanmar, and – as its population is mostly Christian – the town has a very different atmosphere to much of lowland Myanmar. You're far more

2

HIKING BETWEEN MOUNT VICTORIA AND MRAUK U

There aren't many parts of Southeast Asia where the line between tourist and fully fledged explorer can be crossed, but **Chin State** is one such place. If you really want to go where few – or, if the rumours are to be believed, no – Western visitors have been before, then this week-long trip on foot and by boat covering the breadth of the Chin State should do the trick. It has only been attempted a handful of times so far, and it's certainly not the easiest trip to make. The route generally begins from **Mount Victoria**, and finishes among the temples of Mrauk U. Along the way, the trail crawls up and down steep forested slopes and along the floors of remote valleys for around five days, and after this you'll need to hop onto a long-tailed boat for a two-day river ride to Mrauk U. Along the way, you can expect to stay overnight in villages that have never before hosted a Western tourist, and you'll probably get to meet quite a few tattooed ladies, too.

Needless to say, an experienced **local guide** is an absolute must. Two companies who can help to organize this groundbreaking but expensive trek are Yangon-based Pegu Travels (☎01 371937, ⓦpegutravels.com) and the highly regarded Kathmandu-based Kamzang Journeys (☎+977 9 8034 14745, ⓦkamzang.com).

likely to see churches than golden pagodas piercing the skies, and if you're in town on a Sunday it's well worth popping into one of them for a service. Otherwise, attractions here are limited to the interesting market (selling warm clothing and all sorts of delicious-looking fruits and vegetables) and the mountain peak that looms above the town, which offers a nice viewpoint – you can reach it with a long walk or short taxi ride (around K3000) from the centre.

ACCOMMODATION

Cherry Guest House 112 Bogyoke Rd ☎ 09 3350 2511. Based close to the clocktower in the centre of town, this very simple guesthouse is about as cheap a place as you'll find anywhere in Myanmar – and you'll shortly find out why. Rooms are plain, and the communal bathrooms have cold water only. Breakfast is not included. **K15,000**

Falam
ဖလမ်း

Spread along a soaring mountain ridge with memorable vistas over wave after wave of steep-sided valleys and peaks, there's something of a Himalayan hill-station atmosphere to **FALAM**. Dominated by the double spires of its Baptist church, it's a far more attractive and enticing destination than Hakha, its neighbour to the south, and you'll find it easy to spend a few days walking along the surrounding ridges and sitting in the teashops around the market, getting to know the local Chin people.

ACCOMMODATION

Holy Guest House B-215 Bogyoke Rd ☎ 09 400 305 703. A guesthouse in the centre of town with small, grungy rooms and shared cold-water bathrooms. Breakfast is not included in the room rate. **$10**

Southeastern Myanmar

KYAIKTIYO (GOLDEN ROCK)

Southeastern Myanmar

Stretching for a thousand kilometres from the turbid waters of the Gulf of Mottama to the sun-drenched islands of the Myeik Archipelago, Myanmar's panhandle is often overlooked by visitors in the rush to head north from Yangon. However, with Tanintharyi and the region's Thai border crossings now largely open to foreign visitors, this lush and beautiful region – peppered with intriguing sights and fringed with the least developed beaches in Southeast Asia – is crying out to be explored.

3

Generations of devout Buddhist monarchs have endowed **Mon State** with a gold-coated legacy. Not far from Yangon, the countryside around the historical Mon capital of **Bago** is full of golden *zedi* and dreamy reclining Buddhas. Further east, **Kyaiktiyo**, or the Golden Rock, is the most revered of the southeast's religious monuments, the precariously balanced pagoda-crowned boulder floating high above the Eastern Yoma Mountains.

With its drawn-out coastline and sheltered natural harbours, the southeast played an important role in Indian Ocean trade for centuries, exporting pottery, teak and other exotic products from the Burmese interior. While the port city of **Mawlamyine** came to prominence only under nineteenth-century British rule, it's the best place to get a sense of this mercantile heritage, with bustling markets and peeling godowns dotting the town centre. The countryside nearby is full of fascinating day-trips, from **Thanbyuzayat**'s sombre war cemetery to **Win Sein Taw Ya**, an over-the-top 180m-long reclining Buddha.

East of Mon State, **Kayin State** was the site of one of Myanmar's most violent **ethnic conflicts** (see p.382), with decades of fighting between Kayin nationalists and government troops leaving hundreds of people dead and tens of thousands more living as refugees in neighbouring Thailand before a ceasefire was signed in 2012. Today, the peaceful countryside around state capital **Hpa-An** belies the violence of the recent past, and the small town is now a great place to stay while exploring the dramatic mountains and Buddha-filled caves nearby.

In the far south, the **Tanintharyi Region** only opened up around 2013 and is today home to a string of dazzling deserted beaches around **Dawei**, while **Myeik** is a fascinating hub for all sorts of tropical industries, from cashew-nut factories to malodorous workshops fermenting fish for *ngapi* paste. Sail away from the coast, deep into the still quite difficult to access **Myeik Archipelago**, and it's likely you'll encounter yet more exotic sights: groups of nomadic sea gypsies riding the waves, and fishermen perched precariously atop rickety bamboo platforms, plucking fish straight from the bountiful waters of the Andaman Sea.

SHWEMAWDAW PAGODA, BAGO

Highlights

❶ Bago A backwater today, low-key Bago has a rich and fascinating history, the remnants of which lie scattered around town. **See p.143**

❷ Kyaiktiyo (Golden Rock) Buddhists flock to this gravity-defying golden boulder, purportedly held in place by a few extra-strong strands of the Buddha's hair. **See p.148**

❸ Hpa-An Clamber up jungle-shrouded mountains, explore holy caves and soak in clear pools near Kayin State's laidback capital. **See p.151**

❹ Mawlamyine Filled with colonial architecture and set amid pagoda-topped hills, Mawlamyine makes a perfect base for exploring the surrounding countryside. **See p.159**

❺ Bilu Kyun Buffalo carts and ancient buses rumble down palm-lined roads on Bilu Kyun, home to a plethora of interesting cottage industries and just a short boat ride from Mawlamyine. **See p.164**

❻ Dawei Beach-hop on the beautiful Dawei Peninsula – from endless stretches of sand to tiny beachside fishing villages, there's something for beach bums of all kinds. **See p.169**

❼ Myeik Archipelago Thread your way around the Myeik Archipelago, where the waters teem with flying fish and the hundreds of islands are blanketed with immaculate white sand. **See p.174**

HIGHLIGHTS ARE MARKED ON THE MAP ON P.142

HIGHLIGHTS

1. Bago
2. Kyaiktiyo (Golden Rock)
3. Hpa-An
4. Mawlamyine
5. Bilu Kyun
6. Dawei
7. Myeik Archipelago

Bago

ပဲခူးမြို့

While **BAGO** is a provincial town today, its outskirts retain hints of its magnificent and turbulent past. Formerly known as Pegu, the town was the capital of several Mon and Burmese kingdoms, and flourished as a bastion of Theravada Buddhism in the fifteenth century and as a regional trade entrepôt in the sixteenth. Each period of dominion brought with it a new layer of gilded **pagodas** and languorous **reclining Buddhas**, and today the admittedly noisy and chaotic centre makes a fine place to spend a day or two cycling between its gold-coated sights.

Some 80km from Yangon, Bago sits astride the Yangon–Mandalay railway and the old highway, making it a convenient stop-off between the two cities. If you really wanted to, you could also visit on a very rushed day-trip from Yangon.

Brief history

According to Buddhist legend, the newly enlightened **Siddhartha Gautama** made a flying trip to Lower Burma, which at that time was covered by seawater. Seeing a female *hamsa* sitting on the back of a male, perched on a tiny island of dry land, Buddha foretold that this spot would become the centre of a prosperous kingdom 1500 years later. Roughly on schedule, once the waters had receded, two Mon princes founded the town then known as Hanthawaddy in 825 AD. The **double hamsa** motif can be seen all over Bago today.

After centuries sandwiched uncomfortably between the armies of Bagan and Ayutthaya, the Mon kingdom moved its capital from Mottama, near Mawlamyine, to Bago in 1369. The town became a major religious centre under the fifteenth-century reign of devout Queen Shin Sawbu, who passed her throne to an alchemist monk named **Dhammazedi**, to whom the queen had married her daughter. During his 32-year reign, Dhammazedi entrenched Bago's position as a centre of Buddhist orthodoxy, expanding pagodas, funding pilgrimages and holding mass ordinations.

TRAVEL RESTRICTIONS

At the time of research, it was possible to travel overland to all of the towns featured in this chapter. **Permits** are still required for travel to the farthest reaches of the Myeik Archipelago, and the more enticing parts of this area are still only accessible to those on organized multi-day boat tours. Operators arrange permits, although it can take up to two weeks to receive them – you'll need to plan ahead. If you're just visiting the more accessible islands on a day-trip from Myeik or Kawthaung, then permits are no longer required.

After the Hanthawaddy kingdom collapsed in 1539 (see p.362), **King Bayinnaung** (also known as Bayintnaung) sacked the city in his struggle to annexe Lower Burma. The energetic monarch then set about rebuilding Bago as his capital, digging a moat filled with crocodiles (which are now long gone) and building the Kanbawzathadi Palace (see p.145). However, in 1599 Bago was razed again, continuing a pattern of destruction and reconstruction that has continued almost to the present – the town was last levelled by an earthquake in 1930. After the Bago River silted up in the sixteenth century, Bago lost access to the sea and ceded its position as a trade centre to Thanlyin (then called Syriam), and the town slowly slipped back into obscurity.

Shwemawdaw Pagoda

ေရွှေမော်ေတာ်ဘုရား• Pagoda Rd • Daily 5am–10pm • Entry covered by the Bago Archeological Zone ticket; camera fee K300

Visible for many kilometres around, **Shwemawdaw Pagoda**'s vast golden dome dominates Bago's skyline. Buddhist legend has it that a pair of merchant brothers built the monument to enshrine two of Buddha's hairs in 582 BC, with successive generations adding relics and extending the spire to its current height of 114m – making it taller than even Shwedagon in Yangon – and covering it with 1.5 tonnes of gold leaf.

The *zedi* has fallen victim to numerous **earthquakes** over the years. A large chunk of brickwork that collapsed in 1917 is dramatically embedded in its western side, sprouting incense sticks from cracks in its mortar. After the most recent earthquake in 1930, the pagoda lay in ruins for twenty years, until unpaid volunteers built the structure you see today in the early 1950s.

The four staircases leading to the pagoda are flanked by large chinthe with tiny golden Buddhas in their open mouths; the western staircase leads east to Hintha Gon Paya (see below) along a covered arcade. Shwemawdaw is the site of a major ten-day pagoda festival around the Tagu full moon, which falls in March/April each year.

Hintha Gon Paya

ဟင်္သာကုန်းဘုရား• Off Thanat Pin Rd, 500m east of Shwemawdaw Pagoda • Daily 5am–10pm • Free; camera fee K300

Its name meaning "Hamsa Hill", **Hintha Gon Paya** was once the only point of land above sea level around Bago, and the hill is believed to be the place where Buddha spotted the two *hamsa* that gave rise to his prophesy about Bago. King Bayinnaung constructed the complex in 1567, but the current tiered shrine is the creation of the hermit monk **U Khanti**, and dates from 1924.

In addition to decent views of the pagoda-stippled surroundings, the main reason to climb up here is for the chance to witness one of the **nat ceremonies** for which Hintha Gon is known. Transvestite *natdaws* (mediums) energetically channel the *nat* to the frenetic accompaniment of a traditional orchestra, purportedly bringing good luck to worshippers. Several *nats* are represented here, but foremost among them is **Bago Medaw**, a local Mon *nat* depicted as a woman wearing a buffalo skull. There are no set times for *nat* ceremonies, so whether one is taking place at the time of your visit is down to luck.

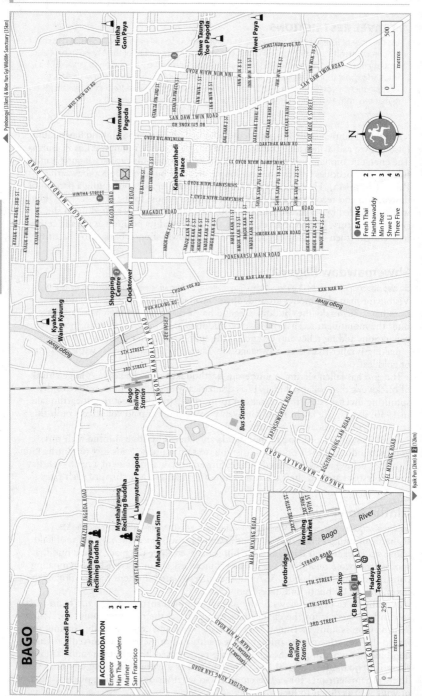

BAGO

Mahazedi Pagoda

■ ACCOMMODATION
Emperor	3
Han Thar Gardens	2
Mariner	1
San Francisco	4

● EATING
Fresh Thai	2
Hanthawaddy	1
Min Htet	3
Shwe Li	4
Three Five	5

3

Pyinbongyi (33km) & Moe Yun Gyi Wildlife Sanctuary (35km)

YANGON–MANDALAY ROAD

Kyakhat Waing Kyaung

Shwemawdaw Pagoda

Hintha Gon Paya

Shwe Taung Yoe Pagoda

Mwei Paya

SHWETAUNGYOE RD

INN WIN MAIN ROAD

SAN DAM TWIN ROAD

Kanbawzathadi Palace

SHINSAWPU MAIN ROAD 31

MAGADIT ROAD

HMORRAN MAIN ROAD

PONENARSU MAIN ROAD

KAM NAR LAM RD

HINTHA STREET

Shopping Centre

Clocktower

PAGODA ROAD

THANAT PIN ROAD

CHONE YOE RD

PUN RIAING RD

KAN NAR RD

Bago River

SEE INSET

YANGON–MANDALAY ROAD

5TH STREET

3RD STREET

Bago Railway Station

Bus Station

TAPINSHWEHTEE ROAD

Shwethalyaung Reclining Buddha

Myathalyaung Reclining Buddha

Laymyatnar Pagoda

Maha Kalyani Sima

MAHAZEDI PAGODA ROAD

SHWETHALYAUNG ROAD

YANGON–MANDALAY ROAD

MAHA MYAING ROAD

Kyaik Pun (2km) & (12km)

Morning Market

Footbridge

Bago River

STRAND ROAD

5TH STREET

Bus Stop

4TH STREET

3RD STREET

CB Bank

Hadaya Teahouse

Bago Railway Station

YANGON–MANDALAY ROAD

N

500
metres
0

250
metres
0

BAGO ARCHEOLOGICAL ZONE TICKET

Entrance to the Shwemawdaw Pagoda, Kanbawzathadi Palace, Shwethalyaung Reclining Buddha and Kyaik Pun is covered by the **Bago Archeological Zone ticket**, which costs K10,000 and is valid for a week from purchase. While you can see all these sights from the street, you won't be able to get up close without stumping up the cash – and it's particularly worthwhile at Shwemawdaw Pagoda. Tickets can be purchased at any of the sights covered here.

Kanbawzathadi Palace

ကမ္ဘောဇသာဒီရွှေနန်းတော် • Myintawtar Rd, 400m south of Shwemawdaw • Daily 9.30am–4pm • Entry covered by the Bago Archeological Zone ticket

Built in 1553 at the heart of King Bayinnaung's Bago, the original **Kanbawzathadi Palace** survived for less than fifty years before it was looted and razed by Rakhine troops in 1599. The palace lay in ruins for four centuries, until it was excavated and restored in the mid-1990s under General Khin Nyunt's sponsorship.

Today, the poorly maintained concrete throne halls are photogenic enough from a distance, but give little sense of the original scale of the palace buildings. More interesting are the jagged remains of the original teakwood columns, sent to Bayinnaung from around the country, and a few artefacts discovered during the excavation that are housed in a small **archeological museum** on the same site.

Mwei Paya

မြွေဘုရား • Off Shwetaungyoe Rd, 1.5km south of Hintha Gon Paya • Daily during daylight hours • Free

One of Bago's less orthodox religious sites, **Mwei Paya**, also known as the Snake Monastery, is home to a venerable Burmese python. Estimated to be an incredible 120 years old, the 5m-long, tree-trunk-thick female snake is believed to be the reincarnation of an abbot from a monastery in Hsipaw, who now divides her time between sleeping (or meditating, depending on your view) and eating chickens. The banknotes tucked by followers into her scaly folds have funded the rapid expansion of the monastery, which also hosts exciting **nat ceremonies** on full moon days.

Some 300m to the north of the monastery is the hilltop **Shwe Taung Yoe Pagoda**, or Sunset Pagoda, which is worth visiting for its great views over Bago.

Kyakhat Waing Kyaung

ကြိုခတ်ဝိုင်းကျောင်းတိုက် • 100m north of the market • Daily 7am–noon • Free

Sandwiched between the northwest corner of the moat and the Bago River, **Kyakhat Waing Kyaung** is Bago's biggest monastery. It formerly housed 1200 monks, though many were forced to return to their home communities after the crackdown that followed 2007's Saffron Revolution (see p.376), and today around five hundred remain. The monastery is best known for its 11am **lunchtimes**, where busloads of Thai tourists descend to give packets of instant noodles as alms to a long line of straight-faced monks. The whole spectacle of watching the monks filing past and then eating their lunch is rather surreal.

Shwethalyaung Reclining Buddha

ရွှေသာလျောင်းဘုရား • Mahazedi Pagoda Rd • Daily 5am–dusk • Entry fee covered by the Bago Archeological Zone ticket; camera fee K300

The tenth-century **Shwethalyaung Reclining Buddha** lies 2km west of the town centre. Built by King Migadepa in 994 AD to celebrate his conversion to Buddhism (a series of paintings on the back of the statue tells the full story), the 55m-long statue shows Buddha resting his head on an ornate pillow on the eve of his

MOE YUN GYI WILDLIFE SANCTUARY

A protected lake and wetland, the **Moe Yun Gyi Wildlife Sanctuary** ($1) is about a 45-minute drive north of central Bago. Its position on north–south migratory routes means that, between around October and March, it attracts masses of overwintering waders and waterbirds escaping the icy Siberian winter. As a result, it's regarded as one of the top birding sites in Myanmar. Around 125 species have been recorded here, including sarus cranes and swamp hens, masses of herons, egrets, darters and cormorants, as well as a variety of gulls.

Birdwatching boat trips ($20–30 per hour for one or two people) can be organized from the low-key *Moe Yun Gyi Resort* (☎052 70113, ⊕facebook.com/moeyungyiresort), which overlooks the lake and is just north of the village of Pyinbongyi. The resort also has quite overpriced accommodation ($90) in houseboats on the fringes of the lake, and there's a café, restaurant and karaoke bar.

3

enlightenment. The statue was abandoned after King Alaungpaya sacked Bago in 1757, and lay forgotten in the jungle until British railway contractors rediscovered it in 1880.

Like many of Bago's religious buildings, few traces of Shwethalyaung's antiquity remain, and the site is covered with a rather obtrusive canopy. Photographers may prefer to walk a few minutes south to the similarly proportioned **Myathalyaung Reclining Buddha**, built in 2002, which remains uncovered.

Maha Kalyani Sima

မဟာကလျာဏီသိမ် • Shwethalyaung Rd • Daily 5am–dusk • Free

It's easy to overlook this dilapidated monastery on your way to the other sights west of town, but **Maha Kalyani Sima** is the site of Myanmar's first **ordination hall**. Built in 1476 by King Dhammazedi, the hall commemorated the return of 22 monks he had sent to Sri Lanka, the orthodox home of Theravada Buddhism, in the hope of reinvigorating the country's *sangha* (monastic community). Find your way to the rear of the scruffy monastery buildings and you'll discover ten stone tablets with inscriptions in Pali and Mon, which describe the early history of Buddhism in the region. Like most of Bago's historic buildings, the hall has been rebuilt several times, with its latest incarnation reopened in 1953 by U Nu, then Prime Minister of Burma.

Mahazedi Pagoda

မဟာစေတီဘုရား • Mahazedi Pagoda Rd • Daily 5am–dusk • Free; camera fee K300

On the western edge of Bago, white and gold **Mahazedi Pagoda** is one of the most striking religious buildings in Bago, with steep whitewashed staircases leading to the base of the pagoda itself (although it's a men-only zone beyond the main terrace), and a few attractive shrines nearby. King Bayinnaung built the original structure in 1561 and he enshrined a fake tooth relic thought to be the sacred Tooth of Kandy in Sri Lanka here in the 1570s. When it was later discovered to have been an ox bone fake sent by the king of Kotte, Bayinnaung regally dismissed the tooth's sceptics and today it is a venerated relic in Sagaing's Kaunghmudaw Paya (see p.306).

Kyaik Pun

ကျိုက်ပွန်ဘုရား • Kyaik Pun Rd • Daily 8am–dusk • Entry fee covered by the Bago Archeological Zone ticket; camera fee K300

Around 4km south of the railway station, just west of the main Yangon road, **Kyaik Pun** consists of four 30m-high Buddhas representing Siddhartha Gautama and his three predecessors, all shown at the moment of their enlightenment, in *bhumisparsha* mudra with one hand touching the earth. The back-to-back arrangement of the statues, which can also be seen at the **Laymyatnar Pagoda** near Maha Kalyani Sima, seems to have originated with the Mon before spreading to Bagan and Thailand.

ARRIVAL AND DEPARTURE   BAGO

By bus The bus station is 1km southwest of the town on the Yangon–Mandalay Road. Tickets are available both from here and the bus company offices on the main road between the *Mya Nan Da* and *San Francisco* hotels (see below). Most buses will stop at both the bus station and in town by *Three Five* restaurant, but do check this when you buy your ticket. Many of the more foreigner-savvy hotels also sell bus tickets.
Destinations Hpa-An (hourly; 6hr); Kinpun (for Kyaiktiyo; hourly; 3hr); Mandalay (3 daily; 10–12hr); Mawlamyine (3 daily; 5hr 30min); Pyin Oo Lwin (2 daily; 10hr 30min);

Taunggyi (for Inle Lake; 2 daily; 12hr); Taungoo (3 daily; 4hr); Yangon (4 hourly; 1hr 30min–2hr).
By train Bago's railway station is just west of the town centre, on the north side of the main road. For Kyaiktiyo, take a Mawlamyine-bound train and get off at Kyaikhto. For Inle Lake, change at Thazi.
Destinations Dawei (daily; 22hr 30min); Kyaikhto (3 daily; 3hr); Mandalay (3 daily; 14hr); Mawlamyine (3 daily; 7–8hr); Naypyitaw (5 daily; 7–8hr); Taungoo (3 daily; 4hr 30min); Thaton (3 daily; 5hr); Thazi (3 daily; 10–11hr); Yangon (8 daily; 2hr); Ye (daily; 14hr).

GETTING AROUND

By motorbike taxi A short journey around town ought to cost no more than K500, and full-day tours can be arranged for a reasonable K3000 through the budget hotels –

although most drivers do not speak English.
By bicycle Bikes are available to rent from the *San Francisco* hotel for K3000/day.

ACCOMMODATION

Emperor 8 Main Rd ☎052 222 2108, ✉nyeinchanbgo @gmail.com. One of the nicer budget options in town. The small rooms are clean and colourful, though all suffer from a good amount of background noise from the nearby main road and mosque. One bonus is that you can check out at any time – handy if you're on the late bus to Mandalay. Breakfast is not included. $20
★**Han Thar Gardens** 34 Bullein Tar Zone Village, 12km south of Bago on the Yangon–Mandalay Rd ☎09 4281 77217, ✇hanthargardens.com. Several classes above anything else in Bago, this place has airy and beautiful deluxe rooms in the main building, with vast bathrooms. The cheaper superior rooms have less of a wow factor but are still attractive and spacious, and there is a small pool and sundeck. The only downside is the out-of-town location, next to a busy main road, though with a pretty on-site café serving excellent, largely organic

Burmese food (mains $7–8), you may not need to leave anyway. $140
Mariner 330 Pagoda Rd ☎052 201034, ✉hotel mariner.hm@gmail.com. Close to Shwemawdaw, this is one of the few foreigner-friendly hotels in the eastern part of town, with thirty bright rooms. It's housed on the top three floors of a building that also contains a shopping centre, hair salon and a café. You can expect to pay a little more for a pagoda view, but it's money well spent. $35
San Francisco 14 Main Rd ☎052 22265. *San Francisco* is understandably popular with backpackers, with twenty fan-cooled rooms and knowledgeable, helpful staff. The cheapest doubles with shared bathrooms are acceptable, while the more expensive rooms ($18) are really quite impressive considering the price. Breakfast not included. $14

EATING

Fresh Thai Icon Shopping Center on the Yangon–Mandalay Rd. This rooftop restaurant is based inside the new Icon Shopping Center, and serves tasty Thai dishes (mains K5000–6000) from a menu that's so exhaustive you'll forget what you wanted to order by the time you finish reading it. Daily 9am–10pm.
Hanthawaddy 192 Hintha St ☎09 4921 7309. Bago's most upmarket dining option, *Hanthawaddy* is housed in a villa with good views of Shwemawdaw from the upstairs balcony. The menu covers Burmese, Thai and Chinese dishes for K4000–6000. The

Burmese meals are the best. This place is popular with tour groups, and if it's busy you may be directed to their nearby sister restaurant, *Century*. Daily 10.30am–10.30pm.
★**Min Htet** Shwetaungyoe Rd, just north of Shwe Taung Yoe Pagoda. Locals flock to this simple restaurant at lunchtime for tasty Burmese-style curries (there's usually one vegetarian option on offer), accompanied by the usual trappings of salad, *ngapi* and vast quantities of rice. Expect to pay K1200 for a meal with tea. Mon–Sat 9am–6pm.

3

Shwe Li 194 Strand Rd ☎052 222 2213. In a quiet spot facing the river just off the main road, this Chinese restaurant serves authentic food (mains K2000–4000) to a primarily local clientele, who come for dishes such as fried pork with bamboo shoots. Just remember to bring your

mosquito repellent. No English spoken. Daily 10am–10pm.
Three Five 10 Main Rd ☎052 22223. Cavernous and popular Chinese restaurant with a long menu that includes interesting dishes such as chicken with crab (mains K3500–6000). Daily 8am–9pm.

DIRECTORY

Banks CB Bank, on the main road between *Three Five* restaurant and the *Emperor* hotel, has an ATM and currency exchange, as does the KBZ Bank inside the Icon Shopping Center near the clocktower.

Post office Bago's post office is tucked away in an unassuming bungalow south of Shwemawdaw – be prepared to ask for directions.

Kyaiktiyo (Golden Rock)

ကျိုက်ထီးရိုးဘုရား

One of the holiest places in the country, **Kyaiktiyo** is a major draw for Buddhist pilgrims, with thousands visiting every day during the November to March pilgrimage season. The site also pulls in substantial numbers of non-believers, who come to marvel at the huge gold-covered boulder – the **Golden Rock** – that is perched rakishly on a granite slab high up in the Eastern Yoma Mountains. On busy evenings, when the sinking sun tinges the sky a fiery orange, the rock glitters and glows and a thousand awed pilgrims whisper prayers to the breeze – it's truly one of the most magical places in Myanmar.

A Mon name, Kyaiktiyo means "pagoda on a hermit's head" – a reference to its legendary backstory. Burmese Buddhists believe that Buddha gave a strand of his hair to a hermit, who tucked it into his own topknot for safekeeping. The hermit later presented the hair to the king of Thaton on the condition that it be enshrined in a rock shaped like the hermit's own head. After a long search, the king managed to find a suitable rock at the bottom of the ocean and, with some supernatural help, transported it to its current location, where the hair has been holding it in place ever since. It's rumoured to be possible to pass a thread between the rock and its base by rocking the boulder gently back and forth, and yet the Golden Rock has managed to withstand several large earthquakes in its long history. Whether you believe the legend or not, it's easy to imagine that something more powerful than just geology is keeping the rock up there.

Ascending Kyaiktiyo

Trucks run from Kinpun to the mountaintop plaza (K2000 back of truck/K3000 front cabin) and Yathetaun truck stop (K1500 back of truck/K2000 front cabin) from 6am–6pm, departing when full and less frequently as the afternoon wears on; sedan chairs cost K20,000/person

The stony **trail** to the Golden Rock starts from the small town of **KINPUN**, from where a well-marked path leads 11km to the mountaintop. While the hike starts relatively gently, it turns into a long and sweaty climb – the rock sits at 1100m, 1000m above Kinpun itself – and takes at least four hours. The trail is well shaded by day but is poorly lit after dark, and it is not advisable to climb overnight. Villagers have set up bamboo stalls along the track, and water and snacks are widely available on the walk up – as are small children shouting *"mingalaba"* ("hello").

The huge majority of visitors to Kyaiktiyo settle for taking an open **truck** up the mountain from Kinpun, either to the mountaintop plaza or to Yathetaun truck stop – the fares explicitly include life insurance, which may give a sense of how exciting the drive can be. From Yathetaun truck stop, it's a 45-minute walk up a steeply switchbacked path to the Golden Rock. This is perhaps the best way of approaching the rock, as it gives a sense of how it would be to walk the entire pilgrim trail without quite as much physical exertion. Sedan chairs are also available from the mountaintop truck stop to the shrine itself, but it's a five-minute walk there so they're not really worth it. On descent, be aware that trucks from Yathetaun to Kinpun are far less frequent than those from the mountaintop – unless you are travelling with a group, you may end up waiting for hours for the truck to fill up. The first trucks usually leave around 6am, while the last trucks depend on demand but normally depart shortly before sunset. At the time of research there were proposals to build a cable car up the mountain, but fortunately this seems a long way off.

On the mountain

Ticket office daily 7am–9pm • Two-day pass K6000 • Dress appropriately (no shorts or revealing clothing)

Once at the top of the mountain, foreigners are required to pay a **government fee**, which buys a two-day pass. From the ticket office it's a short walk to the main complex, an expanse of tiles and minor shrines surrounding the Golden Rock itself. Men are allowed to cross the **footbridge** (without cameras or phones) to the Rock itself to add to its lustre (a tiny sheet of gold leaf; K1700), but women must stay a short distance away.

Pilgrims throng Kyaiktiyo both day and night, but activity is greatest early in the morning and at dusk, with people praying, lighting candles and making offerings. It is worth taking time to explore beyond the crowded main plaza, as several quiet trails lead across the mountains. For a short, sharp walk, follow the path down past *Yoe Yoe Lay* hotel to a T-junction. The left-hand path leads 2.5km downhill to **Moe Baw Waterfall**, while the right-hand path leads past a small **cave shrine** and dozens of macabre traditional medicine stalls, decorated with centipedes and goat skulls, up to **Kann Pa Sat**, a small pagoda with a large loudspeaker that broadcasts blessings. From Kann Pa Sat you can head straight back to the plaza (making a 1.5km loop), or continue along the ridge, past a row of helipads and through attractive wooded scenery to a series of smaller, improbably shaped, rock-and-stupa combinations. One of the more striking places to aim for is **Bodhi Taw Kaw**, 1.5km along the ridge from the plaza, where ranks of small Buddha statues seated on pedestals cover the hillside. The 3km trail ends in a winding set of steps that lead down to **Kyauk Ta Gyi**, a small shrine set deep in a wooded valley; from here, you'll need to retrace your steps to the plaza.

ARRIVAL AND INFORMATION
KYAIKTIYO (GOLDEN ROCK)

By bus Some buses run direct to Kinpun, stopping outside *Sea Sar* restaurant, while others stop 15km away in Kyaikhto and transfer passengers to Kinpun by truck (the price is included in the bus ticket). Outbound bus tickets can be purchased in Kinpun at the booths opposite *Sea Sar*, with most services finishing by mid-afternoon. If there aren't many buses heading in the direction you need from Kinpun, there are likely to be more passing Kyaikhto – although seats aren't always available on these.
Destinations Bago (hourly; 3hr); Hpa-An (3 daily; 4hr); Mawlamyine (daily; 4hr); Yangon (hourly; 5–6hr).

By train The nearest railway station to Kyaiktiyo is in Kyaikhto. All trains between Yangon and Mawlamyine stop here, most passing through inconveniently early in the morning, although there is one train in each direction around noon each day. From the station it's a 30min pick-up (K1000) or motorbike (K2500) ride to Kinpun.
Destinations Bago (3 daily; 3hr); Dawei (daily; 20hr); Mawlamyine (3 daily; 5hr); Thaton (3 daily; 2hr); Yangon (3 daily; 5hr).
Services The KBZ Bank on Kinpun's central junction has an ATM.

ACCOMMODATION

Those travelling on a budget are best off abandoning hope of a mountaintop stay – while **Kinpun** has some decent cheap accommodation, hotels **on the mountain** charge a robust premium. At the time of research, foreign travellers were not allowed to stay in the inexpensive pilgrims' hostels at the top.

KINPUN
Bwaga Theiddhi Hotel Kyaiktiyo Rd ☎ 09 778 076 097.

Based next to the truck stop, this modern multistorey hotel has smart rooms. It lacks character compared to the *Golden*

Sunrise, and the standard rooms ($40) only have shared bathrooms. $40

★**Golden Sunrise** Golden Rock Rd ☎ 09 598 723 301, ⊛ goldensunrisehotel.com. Located in a peaceful garden a 10min walk down the road from Kyaikhto, *Golden Sunrise*'s creative rooms and common areas incorporate lots of natural features, and the gardens are filled with twittering birds. There's a pleasant, rustic-looking restaurant on site. $47

Sea Sar Just off the main road ☎ 09 425 353 566. Tucked away behind *Sea Sar* restaurant and set around a lawn, the bungalows here are clean, decent and certainly better value than some of the budget competition. However, the cheapest rooms are in a separate block just down the road. These have fans and cold-water bathrooms only – and plenty of grime. No discount for single occupancy. $15

ON THE MOUNTAIN

Golden Rock Near Yathetaun truck stop ☎ 09 871 8391, ⊛ goldenrock-hotel.com. Set in lush grounds a 45min walk downhill from the mountaintop, this hotel offers the same level of comfort and service as its sister property, *Mountain Top,* but with a less convenient location and correspondingly lower prices. Make sure you get off the truck at Yathetaun truck stop, otherwise you face a long and very steep descent with your bags. Closed May–Oct. $90

Mountain Top Near the Foreigners' Registration Office ☎ 09 871 8392, ⊛ mountaintop-hotel.com. With comfortable, nicely designed rooms arranged on a steep slope, sunrise views over blue-green mountains and a pretty garden restaurant, this hotel is understandably popular with well-heeled foreign travellers. $135

Yoe Yoe Lay Mountaintop plaza ☎ 09 872 3082, ⊛ yoeyoelayhotel.com. On the opposite side of the plaza to the main approach, close to the Golden Rock itself, this is the cheapest foreigner-friendly accommodation in the area. The least expensive doubles are laughably small, with shared bathrooms and no windows, and at night the rush of pilgrims and the loud chanting can make it noisy – but then you did come to Golden Rock for the pilgrims. Closed May–Oct. $84

EATING

Kinpun has plenty of eating options, most of them touristy Burmese–Chinese places lining the road to the trail. Locals gravitate towards the small restaurants away from the main junction. As you might expect, food options **on the mountain** are more expensive and limited than in Kinpun. The cheapest are the canteens that cluster between the Golden Rock and Kann Pa Sat, but there are one or two more interesting options around.

KINPUN

Kaung San Kyaiktiyo Rd ☎ 057 23671. On the path leading to the mountain, *Kaung San* serves up tasty Burmese and Chinese dishes. Although the service can be a bit brusque, their *jin thouq* (ginger salad) is excellent. Prices for hot dishes start at K1500. Daily 6am–9pm.

Mya Yeik Nyo Overlooking the truck terminal. One of Kinpun's more atmospheric restaurants (thanks to their romantic lighting), with friendly staff and good food. A Burmese curry and rice set costs K3000, with other dishes starting from K2000. Daily 4am–9pm.

ON THE MOUNTAIN

A1 Opposite the Foreigners' Registration Office. With tables dotted around a pleasant tree-filled yard, *A1* serves up decently priced Burmese soups and salads, along with Chinese stir-fries. A meal will set you back around K3000. No alcohol. Daily 6am–9pm.

Mountain Top Restaurant Mountain Top hotel ☎ 09 871 8392. With white tablecloths, candles and a wine list, the patio here may feel a tad incongruous with the setting, but it's the most appealing place to eat on the mountain. The dishes on their Burmese–Western menu start at $6, and a full three-course meal will set you back around $20. Daily 6am–10pm.

Thaton

သထုံမြို့

Formerly an important Indian Ocean seaport and capital of a tenth-century Mon kingdom (see p.358), **THATON** is a sleepy little place today. With the port silted up for centuries and the city walls long gone, all that remains of Thaton's past is a collection of inscribed tablets discovered in the precincts of the main, and impressively large, pagoda, **Shwe Sar Yan Pagoda**. Nonetheless, Thaton is still a rewarding place to spend the day wandering through its neat streets and poking around the lively **market**, part of the attraction being that very few foreigners stop here. Energetic types may wish to climb up the covered staircase to **Mya Thapaint**

Pagoda, 1.5km due east of the market, for beautiful views over ranks of palm trees to the shimmering sea – now almost 16km to the west. The view is particularly rewarding at dawn and dusk.

ARRIVAL AND DEPARTURE   THATON

By train Thaton's railway station is a short walk west of the market, with tickets going on sale just before each departure.
Destinations Bago (3 daily; 5hr); Kyaikhto (3 daily; 2hr); Mawlamyine (3 daily; 2hr 30min–3hr); Yangon (3 daily; 7–8hr).

By pick-up Frequent pick-ups to Hpa-An (1hr) and Mawlamyine (2hr) leave regularly from the car park outside Shwe Sar Yan during daylight hours, with the last one leaving around 4pm. Both destinations cost K1500, or K4000 if you want to sit up front. There are also a few pick-ups to Kyaikhto (2hr 30min; K2000).

ACCOMMODATION

Thuwunnabumi Hotel 110 cnr Myathapaik Pagoda Rd & Hospital St ☎ 057 40932, ✺ thuwunnabumihotel .com. Only a month old at the time of research, this business-class hotel is excellent value for money (but

beware of creeping prices as it becomes more established). The rooms are cool and calm, and the gnome-like statues that fill the gardens are a welcome, if slightly bizarre, change from the Buddha statues everywhere else. ̄S̄35

EATING

Aung Shwe Sar Yan Rd. This typical Burmese restaurant, just north of Shwe Sar Yan's north gate, is the most popular in a small row of similar restaurants serving up excellent curries and mounds of rice. Vegetarian options are available. If you have trouble finding it, look out for the lime-green sign in Burmese. Mains K1000–1500. Daily 8am–7pm.

First Café Mountain Mya Thapaint Pagoda Rd ☎ 09 872 0904. On the road towards hilltop pagoda Mya Thapaint, this big thatched-roof café has something of a beach shack vibe, and is popular with local young people and Thaton's businessmen. It produces good Burmese curries, Chinese dishes plus real coffee and juices. A curry meal costs around K3000. Daily 9am–9pm.

Hpa-An and around

ဘားအံ မြို့

Just outside **HPA-AN**, the capital of Kayin State, a sheer limestone ridge pokes through the surrounding brilliant green rice paddies, imbuing the landscape with a kind of dramatic beauty. There's not much to see in the understated town itself, although the **markets** are bustling and **Shweyinhmyaw Paya** boasts wonderful views of the **Thanlyin River** sliding past. The main attraction here is the opportunity to get out into the countryside, where it's possible to poke around **caves**, climb up jungle-draped **Mount Zwegabin** and swim in spring-fed pools. **Kyauk Kalat Pagoda**, perched on a vertiginous finger of rock, will amaze even those suffering from pagoda overexposure, and there are numerous **Kayin villages** to explore as well. If you visit in December or January, you may catch the lively **Kayin New Year** celebrations, when Hpa-An hosts dancing and kickboxing competitions.

   Many people come here for a few days and end up staying longer, and the town is fast becoming a favourite among southern Myanmar's backpackers. When you do manage to tear yourself away, you'll have the fun option of catching a **riverboat** down the Thanlyin to Mawlamyine (see box, p.162).

Shweyinhmyaw Paya

ရွှေယင်မျှော်ဘုရား • Thida St • Daily 5am–10pm • Free

For the best views of the Thanlyin River and Mount Hpar-Pu's distinctive silhouette (see p.152), head down to the petite **Shweyinhmyaw Paya** at dusk to watch the sun set over the riverbank. The pagoda is also home to a statue of a giant green frog (frogs are an important symbol for the Kayin) and a *naga* – a reference to the story behind

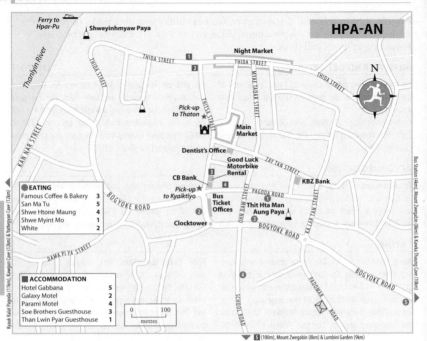

HPA-AN

Ferry to Hpar-Pu

Shweyinhmyaw Paya

Night Market

THIDA STREET
THIDA STREET
THIDA STREET

MYAE TADAR STREET

Thanlyin River

THIDA STREET

KAN MAR STREET

Pick-up to Thaton

Main Market

Dentist's Office

Good Luck Motorbike Rental

ZAY TAN STREET

CB Bank

KBZ Bank

Pick-up to Kyaiktiyo

BOGYOKE ROAD

Bus Ticket Offices

PAGODA ROAD

OHN DAW STREET

Thit Hta Man Aung Paya

KALAR TAN STREET

Clocktower

BOGYOKE ROAD

DAMA PLYA STREET

BOGYOKE ROAD

PADOMAR ROAD

SCHOOL ROAD

● EATING	
Famous Coffee & Bakery	3
San Ma Tu	5
Shwe Htone Maung	4
Shwe Myint Mo	1
White	2

■ ACCOMMODATION	
Hotel Gabbana	5
Galaxy Motel	2
Parami Motel	4
Soe Brothers Guesthouse	3
Than Lwin Pyar Guesthouse	1

Kyauk Kalat Pagoda (11km), Kawgun Cave (12km) & Yathaypyan Cave (12km)

Bus Station (4km), Mount Zwegabin (8km) & Kawka Thaung Cave (10km)

0   100
metres

5 (100m), Mount Zwegabin (8km) & Lumbini Garden (9km)

Hpa-An's name, which means "Frog Vomit". Kayin legend tells of a *naga* swallowing a frog that had a gem in its mouth. The gem magically stopped the *naga* from keeping his dinner down, and it vomited the frog onto the banks of the Thanlyin where Hpa-An stands today – immediately bestowing Myanmar's most memorable and least poetic place name upon the town.

Mount Hpar-Pu

ဟားပုတောင် · Ferry across the river K500/person (every 30min: daily 6am–6pm)

The nearest limestone peak to downtown Hpa-An, **Mount Hpar-Pu** is a quick boat trip across the Thalwin River from Shweyinhmyaw Paya. Once you're on the opposite bank, it's a short walk through vegetable fields to the nearest village, where there's an English sign pointing the way. The road leads to the foot of Hpar-Pu, before swinging right towards the river. Follow the road around to the bottom of the steps up the mountain – a sweaty twenty-minute climb from here ought to see you close to the summit. Note that as a landslide swept away a chunk of the mountain during the 2013 rainy season, it is no longer safe to climb to the very top, but it is still possible to get high enough for wonderful views of the river and out towards Mount Zwegabin.

Mount Zwegabin

ဇွဲကပင်တောင် · 10km south of Hpa-An · Tuk-tuk from Hpa-An K5000; motorbike taxi K2500

From certain angles, the limestone bulk of **Mount Zwegabin** erupts from the landscape like a giant molar tooth. While the 725m-high mountain may look impossibly steep from downtown Hpa-An, there are two beautiful paths to the summit that make it a rewarding half-day hike.

Most ascend the less direct and more scenic western side of the mountain, along a trail starting from **Lumbini Garden** (K1000), 3km east of Kyauk Kalat Pagoda, where 1100 Buddha statues have been arranged in picturesque rows. From here, it takes around two hours to climb the steep and winding path to the summit, with water and drinks available from a single stall en route and plenty of **macaques** for company. The trail down the eastern flank of the mountain is more direct, with relentless staircases leading to a small restaurant at the foot of the mountain, from where it's a straight, flat 1km walk to the Myawaddy Road. Whichever way you cross the mountain, it's advisable to arrange a pick-up at the other end to avoid a long wait.

For many people, **staying overnight** at the mountaintop monastery to watch sunrise is the highlight of a trip to Hpa-An. The monastery has two twin-bed rooms, which go to the first people to get to the summit, and a hall with sleeping mats. In either case, a payment of K5000 is expected. Simple meals are available at the monastery, but it's best to take snacks and water with you. Also, keep in mind that it can get surprisingly chilly at the top, so bring some extra bedding.

Note that Hpa-An's immigration department periodically clamps down on the practice of sleeping at the top – check at the *Soe Brothers Guesthouse* (see p.156) before you drag your backpack up here. There was also a proposal to build a cable car to the top of the mountain at the time of research, although whether it'll ever get off the drawing board is anyone's guess.

Kyauk Kalat Pagoda

ကျောက်ကလပ်ဘုရား· 10km south of Hpa-An, between Kaw Kyaik and Taw Bon villages · Daily during daylight hours · Free · Motorbike taxi from Hpa-An K2500; tuk-tuk K5000

Balanced on a bizarrely shaped limestone pinnacle with frangipani trees sprouting from cracks in the rock, **Kyauk Kalat Pagoda**, 7km south of Hpa-An, is the area's most arresting sight. On an island in the centre of an artificial lake, the site is part of a working monastery and is a shoe-free, vegetarian zone. Revered monk **U Winaya** (see box below) was a novice here in the 1920s, before he founded a monastery at Thamanya, 40km southeast of Hpa-An.

Saddan Cave

ဆဒ္ဒန်ဝှ· Daily Nov–April · K1000; boat trip K1500/person · Motorbike taxi from Hpa-An K3500, tuk-tuk K5000–7000

In a hard-to-find spot 28km south of Hpa-An, at the southern end of the jagged limestone ridge, lies **Saddan Cave**, the most dramatic of the region's caverns.

THE THAMANYA SAYADAW: U WINAYA

Years after his death, **U Winaya**, *sayadaw* of Thamanya Monastery, remains one of Myanmar's most respected religious figures – pictures of him decorate taxis across the country. A spiritual adviser and supporter of Aung San Suu Kyi, U Winaya was renowned for his humanitarian work. During decades of vicious fighting between the Karen National Liberation Army and government forces, the area surrounding Thamanya Monastery was a sanctuary of non-violence until the abbot passed away in 2003 at the age of 93.

Shockingly, in 2008 U Winaya's **tomb** was broken into and his body disappeared. Four days later, the monastery received an anonymous phone call notifying them that the abbot's body had been burned, and his remains left outside a small *zedi* near the edge of the monastery grounds. Many believe that this violation was part of a **yadaya**-inspired plot to help the government win a crucial referendum on constitutional reform that was held a few weeks later. *Yadaya* is a uniquely Burmese practice where steps taken now on the advice of an astrologer are believed to prevent future bad luck – a practice that senior generals in Myanmar's military government have been known to indulge in for years.

3

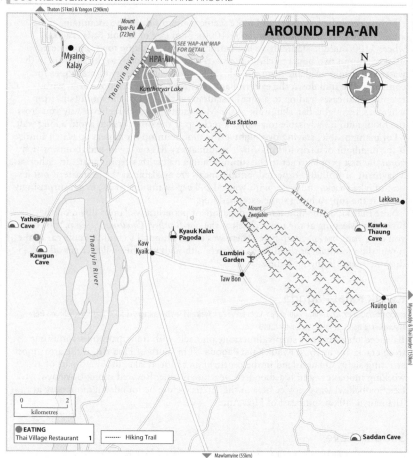

A complete golden *zedi* sits inside the cave entrance, but the Buddhist statuary quickly gives way to natural rock formations – stalactites drip from the ceiling like molten wax, and mushroom-like stalagmites emerge from the earthen cave floor. Bats roost in the erratically lit main cavern (take a good torch), which takes around fifteen minutes to walk through barefoot. On the far side, the path emerges beside a limpid forest pool, from where (between November and April only) you can take a short boat trip back towards the entrance. Note that the entire complex is off limits during the rainy season.

The cave's name comes from an elaborate Jataka story about one of Buddha's previous incarnations, in which he was the elephant king Saddan – keep an eye out for the elephant statues flanking the entrance.

Kawgun Cave

ကော့ဂွန်းဂူ • Daily 7am–dusk • K3000 • Motorbike taxi from Hpa-An K2500; tuk-tuk K5000

With walls covered in rippling mosaics of terracotta votive tablets, and fragments of aged stucco reliefs visible in the gaps, **Kawgun Cave**, 12km southwest of Hpa-An in Kawgun village, has been used by local Mon Buddhists since the seventh century, with each generation scraping away some of the old to make room for the new. While the shallow cave's walls are an impressive sight, many of the oldest statues have been destroyed by tremors resulting from work at the nearby cement factory, leaving only a few sandstone tablets of late Bagan-style carving and the rather average modern statuary intact. At weekends it gets very busy with local pilgrims and tourists, who help imbue a bit of life into the caves.

Yathepyan Cave

ရသေ့ပြိန်ဂူ • Daily 7am–dusk • Free • Motorbike taxi from Hpa-An K2500; tuk-tuk K5000

Near Kawgun village, 12km southwest of Hpa-An, the small **Yathepyan Cave** is filled with newish statues and a few timeworn reliefs, and has good views of Mount Zwegabin. Its most notable feature is the hole in the cavern roof, which has a pagoda covered in bird droppings directly below it. During King Anawrahta's eleventh-century campaign in Lower Burma, a hermit took refuge here with a golden Buddha statue. Newly converted to Theravada Buddhism, Anawrahta coveted the statue and tried to wrest it from the hermit, who burst up through the cave roof with the statue under his arm and flew to safety, supposedly creating the hole you see today.

Kawka Thaung Cave and around

ကော့ကသောင်ဂူ • Daily 8am–5.30pm • Free • Motorbike taxi from Hpa-An K2500; tuk-tuk K5000

Ten kilometres southeast of Hpa-An, a short distance east of the road to Mae Sot, is **Kawka Thaung Cave**. The cave itself is a shallow affair, its single chamber narrowing to a cramped meditation space for monks, and it has a shrine containing some tiny fragments of bone relic. The area beyond the cave is likely to hold your attention for longer – a photogenic row of monk statues leads to a second Buddhist cave (usually locked), a creepy-looking **nat shrine** and a swimming hole filled with cool, clear spring water, surrounded by teahouses.

ARRIVAL AND DEPARTURE

HPA-AN AND AROUND

By bus The bus station is 4km southeast of the central clocktower on Myawaddy Road. Many buses stop at both the bus station and near the clocktower, but check this when you buy your ticket. Bus tickets are available from the bus station, at the bus company offices near the clocktower and in most hotels. All Yangon-bound buses make stops at Bago and Kyaikhto (for Kyaiktiyo). Buses to Mawlamyine run until 4pm.

Destinations Bago (6 daily; 6hr); Dawei (daily; 8hr); Mandalay (daily; 15hr); Mawlamyine (1–2 hourly; 2hr); Naypyitaw (2 daily; 9hr); Yangon (6 daily; 9hr).

By pick-up Pick-ups to Thaton (frequent; 1hr) leave from a small lane just north of the mosque. A pick-up to Kyaiktiyo (stopping in Kinpun; K3500) leaves from Zay Tan St daily at 7am.

By shared taxi Cars to Myawaddy (5–6hr) leave when full from the clocktower.

By boat The boat journey between Hpa-An and Mawlamyine is one of southern Myanmar's most attractive journeys (see box, p.162).

GETTING AROUND

By tuk-tuk or motorbike taxi Taking a tuk-tuk to the sights that are farther afield is K5000 each way, although the drive to Saddan Cave is usually a little more expensive. A motorbike taxi will cost half that each way.

By motorbike Motorbikes can be rented from Good Luck Motorbike Rental Center (Thitsa St) for K6000–8000 per day, depending on the type you want.

By bicycle Bikes are available to rent from *Soe Brothers Guesthouse* for K2000/day (see p.156).

INFORMATION AND TOURS

Maps Both *Soe Brothers* and *Galaxy Motel* offer decent photocopied maps to guests. There's a fancier English map available from bookshops around town, but it's less useful than either of the free ones.

Tours Most guesthouses organize day-trips around the Hpa-An region, but perhaps the most popular one is the tuk-tuk tour led by *Soe Brothers*. The trip costs K30,000 per vehicle per day, so the more people you manage to squeeze into your tuk-tuk, the cheaper it will be – K5000 each is usual. Be aware that few of the drivers speak English. If you would like an English tour, the *Soe* *Brothers*' manager, La Shu, is an excellent guide, and a day scooting around on the back of his motorbike will cost around K15,000.

ACCOMMODATION

Hotel Gabbana B.E.H.S St ☎058 22425, ⊚hpa -anhotelgabbana.com; map p.152. The most upmarket hotel in the town centre, the *Gabbana* offers a smooth stay in its brightly painted rooms, which have purple sashes on the beds and decent bathrooms. It's a 5min walk from the town centre, which gives it the advantage of being quieter than most. $55

★**Galaxy Motel** 2/146 Cnr Thisar Rd & Thida St ☎058 21347; map p.152. At this wonderfully warm and welcoming town-centre hotel it's all about the staff, and in particular the manageress, Kim – where she gets the energy to keep smiling and answering the same old questions time and again about bus times is beyond us. The rooms themselves are carpeted, well maintained and have boiling hot water in the bathrooms. Do try and avoid the noisier rooms facing the road. $22

Parami Motel Pagoda Rd ☎058 21647; map p.152. Close to the centre of town, *Parami* has pleasant staff, and its best rooms ($30) are spacious and have high ceilings – those on upper floors have wonderful views over Hpa-An to Mount Zwegabin. The cheaper rooms are hardly the stuff of dreams – or not good dreams, anyway.

Taken altogether, it's still one of the better-value hotels in this price range. $12

★**Soe Brothers Guesthouse** 2/146 Thitsa St ☎058 21372, ⊚hsoebrothers05821372@gmail.com; map p.152. The rooms are decent in this long-time budget favourite – small, but cool and clean. The main draws are the staff, who are experts at dealing with travellers' needs, and the common areas that add to the fun and friendly atmosphere. Single rooms start at just $7, doubles with shared bathrooms are $18 and there are also some good doubles with attached bathrooms and plenty of space for $25. In high season there's also a small sleeping-mat dormitory upstairs, but this is only in use when all other rooms are full. No breakfast. Dorms $5, doubles $18

Than Lwin Pyar Guesthouse Thida St ☎058 21513; map p.152. You won't be able to miss this intense purple guesthouse, and that's no bad thing because it's an appealing backpacker hotel. Rooms are clean, although the cheapest are mere cells that share bathrooms (K13,000), and there's a great little roof terrace and plenty of traveller services on offer. K18,000

EATING

Hpa-An's **markets** are the most interesting and low-cost places to eat, although the offerings at both the morning and night markets are somewhat noodle-centric. Sweet-toothed travellers should seek out *bein moun* – crispy rice-flour pancakes smeared with jaggery syrup and sprinkled with coconut shreds.

Famous Coffee & Bakery Bogyoke Rd; map p.152. With freshly squeezed juices, proper coffee (that actually has a kick to it) and good pastries (around K500–1500), this a/c café is the place to come for a more familiar home-from-home breakfast experience. It's just a shame about the deafening road noise. Daily 7am–9.30pm.

★**San Ma Tu** Bogyoke Rd ☎058 21802; map p.152. This place has a well-deserved reputation for great Burmese food, which means it's often full of foreigners. Choose a vegetarian (K500) or meat (from K1500) curry from their wide selection, and it will be served with at least ten diverse and tasty side dishes, soup and tea. Rice is an additional K500. Daily 10am–9pm.

Shwe Htone Maung School Rd; map p.152. This bustling teahouse serves up delicious bowls of noodles, hot drinks, juices and sinful fried snacks throughout the day – prepare to become addicted to the banana fritters they serve at breakfast. English menu available. Daily 6am–10pm.

★**Shwe Myint Mo** 2 Pagoda Rd ☎058 21362; map p.152. Serving Burmese food with Indian undertones, as well as particularly tasty soups and salads, *Shwe Myint Mo* cooks up meals accompanied by numerous enticing side dishes. The tomato salad, slathered with peanut sauce, is simply superb. Plan on spending K2500 for a full meal. Daily 7am–9pm.

Thai Village Restaurant Near Yathepyan Cave ☎09 7936 28757; map p.154. It's a little touristy, but nevertheless the *Thai Village* is the best place to stop for a pleasant lunch in a garden setting (mains K3000–4000) while touring the caves and temples around Hpa-An. Staff will carefully explain exactly what each dish is. If you're having trouble finding it, look for the odd statue of a stereotypical Mexican man pointing off the main road, and then turn off and follow the wall. Daily 8am–10pm.

White Bogyoke St; map p.152. This scruffy but charming teahouse serves up great sugar parathas and crispy naan bread all day long. They also do a wonderful samosa *thouq*, but you'll need to get here early to sample it before they run out. Daily 6am–10pm.

DIRECTORY

Banks Both CB Bank on Thitsa Rd and KBZ on Zay Tan St offer currency exchange and have ATMs.

Post office Hpa-An's post office is on Padomar Rd, about 400m south of the roundabout. There's no English sign – look for the Myanmar flag outside.

Myawaddy

မြဝတီမြို့

One of the more convenient checkpoints on the Thai–Myanmar border, the border crossing between the busy town of **MYAWADDY** and Mae Sot in Thailand is relatively accessible from major cities on either side.

Migyaung Gon Pagoda

မိကျောင်းကုန်းဘုရား • Just off Nat Shin Naung St, 400m south of the main road • Daily 5am–10pm • Free

Just 1km southwest of the border, the central shrine at **Migyaung Gon Pagoda** rests on the back of a vast concrete crocodile, making it one of the more bizarre photo opportunities in Myawaddy, and the only one worth searching out if you're stranded here for a day. Women aren't allowed on the crocodile itself, where the chapels hold a collection of Burmese- and Thai-style Buddhas as well as murals relating the story of the pagoda's construction – a princess hid her jewels in a crocodile's nest for safekeeping, and later donated the jewels to the monastery.

ARRIVAL AND GETTING AROUND

By shared taxi Minivans to Mawlamyine (5hr) and Hpa-An (6hr) leave from the main road just beyond the border post when full. It costs K10,000 per person to either destination. A branch of Vega Travel (📞09 0440 9590), inside the immigration office, also arranges minivans to Yangon for K45,000/person.

By motorbike taxi A motorbike taxi costs K500/person for a ride anywhere in town.

ACCOMMODATION AND EATING

Myawaddy Hotel Bayintnaung St 📞058 50519. A great-value and well-run hotel a minute or two on foot from the border post. The rooms are plain and functional, but kept in good condition. As there's no lift, those on the fourth floor will bag you a $10 discount. The breakfast is very avoidable. $30

Ngwe Setkar Hotel Chit Kyi Yae St 📞058 50756. The only budget option in town that accepts foreigners, *Ngwe Setkar* is quite a hike from the border, but the rooms are decent enough for the night if you're a little tired. Breakfast not included. K12,000

DIRECTORY

Banks The KBZ Bank has an ATM as well as currency exchange upstairs – the rates are better than the branch of CB Bank opposite, but neither bank will exchange Thai baht. To change baht, you'll need to stop in at the Vega Travel desk inside the immigration office, or take your chances at one of the roadside booths.

MYAWADDY–MAE SOT BORDER CROSSING

Since the Myanmar government removed a rule requiring foreigners to leave their passports at the **Myawaddy–Mae Sot border crossing** in 2013, numbers of overland travellers using this border have increased dramatically. The Myanmar border post (daily 6am–5.30pm) is on the west side of the Moei River. Foreigners can use a small immigration office, rather than queuing with the locals. From here, it's a short walk over the Friendship Bridge to the Thai side of the border (6.30am–6.30pm Thai time) and a 50 baht pick-up ride to Mae Sot's bus station, from where there are direct buses to Bangkok (6 daily; 8hr) and Tak (hourly; 1hr 30min). From Tak there are direct buses to Chiang Mai, Chiang Rai, Lampang and Mae Sai.

Mawlamyine

မော်လမြိုင်မြို့

Sandwiched between a ridge of pagoda-topped hills and the island-filled estuary of the Thanlyin River, **MAWLAMYINE** is an absorbing base to spend a few days. The town is a diverting place to explore, with the centre dominated by a series of fascinating markets and the neighbourhoods beyond dotted with neat churches and extravagantly crumbling **colonial mansions** – even by 1904, Mawlamyine's atmosphere was already described as being "one of decay" by a British travel writer, V.C. Scott O'Connor. But it would be a shame not to venture into the surrounding region, whether to the picturesque island of Bilu Kyun or to one of the unusual religious sites nearby (see p.164). Finally, good travel connections make Mawlamyine an excellent starting point for forays south to Tanintharyi, or north along the Thanlyin River to Hpa-An in Kayin State (see box, p.162).

Brief history

3

For much of its history, Mawlamyine was overshadowed by nearby Mottama (formerly known as Martaban), which was a major Indian Ocean trade entrepôt until the mid-sixteenth century – even today, it remains one of the most multicultural towns in Myanmar. When the **British** annexed Tanintharyi (Tenasserim) after the First Anglo-Burmese War, Mawlamyine – then little more than a fishing village known to the British as Moulmein – was made capital of Lower Burma from 1827 to 1852. Located at the confluence of the Thanlyin, Gyaing and Ataran rivers, with a sheltered harbour on the Andaman Sea, the city became a wealthy teak port and home to a substantial British and Anglo-Burmese population.

Several generations of writer **George Orwell**'s (see p.337) family – including his mother – were born and grew up in the city, but by the time Orwell himself arrived here in 1926 to staff the police headquarters, its heyday was over and the timber mills and shipyards were closing down as trade shifted to Yangon. The town became a popular retirement spot for British civil servants until Ne Win's 1962 coup d'état led to an exodus of the British, Anglo-Burmese and Indian population.

Kyaikthanlan Pagoda

ကျိုက်သန်လန်ဘုရား • Viewpoint Rd • Daily 5am–10pm • Free

One of the few places visited by Rudyard Kipling during his three-day trip to Burma in 1889, **Kyaikthanlan Pagoda** is the self-same "old Moulmein Pagoda" immortalized in the opening lines of his poem, *Mandalay*. The oldest and tallest of the pagodas that line Mawlamyine's eastern ridge of hills, Kyaikthanlan has a tiled terrace that's a popular spot from which to watch the sun set over Bilu Kyun (see p.164) and the islands of the Thanlyin estuary. It also offers good views of the 1908 prison, which is a little less poetic.

The pagoda's name is thought to be a corruption of "Kyaikshanlan", meaning "Shan-defeating pagoda", and it's the earliest brick structure built here to celebrate the routing of the Siamese army in 875. The most pleasant way to reach it from town is along Kyaikthanlan Road, which becomes a covered staircase just east of its junction with Upper Main Road, passing several monasteries. Another attractive walkway joins Kyaikthanlan to Mahamuni Paya, a few hundred metres to the north.

Mahamuni Paya and around

မဟာမုနိဘုရား • Viewpoint Rd • Daily 5am–9pm • Free

The densely mirrored powder-blue interior of **Mahamuni Paya** is particularly beautiful at dusk. A replica of the Buddha at Mandalay's Mahamuni Paya (see p.289) sits in the

3

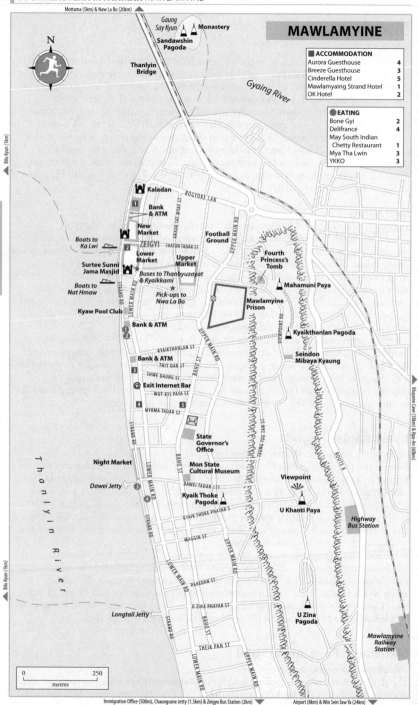

Mottama (5km) & Naw La Bo (20km)

Gaung
Say Kyun
Monastery
Sandawshin
Pagoda

Thanlyin
Bridge

Gyaing River

MAWLAMYINE

■ **ACCOMMODATION**
Aurora Guesthouse	4
Breeze Guesthouse	3
Cinderella Hotel	5
Mawlamyaing Strand Hotel	1
OK Hotel	2

● **EATING**
Bone Gyi	2
Delifrance	4
May South Indian	
Chetty Restaurant	1
Mya Tha Lwin	3
YKKO	3

Bilu Kyun (1km)

Kaladan

BOGYOKE LAN

Bank
& ATM

New
Market

Boats to
Ka Lwi

ZEIGYI

Lower
Market

Upper
Market

Football
Ground

Fourth
Princess's
Tomb

Mahamuni Paya

Surtee Sunni
Jama Masjid

Buses to Thanbyuzayat
& Kyaikkami

Boats to
Nat Hmaw

Pick-ups to
Nwa La Bo

Mawlamyine
Prison

Kyaw Pool Club

Bank & ATM

Kyaikthanlan Pagoda

KYAIKTHANLAN ST

Seindon
Mibaya Kyaung

Bank & ATM

THIT DAR ST

SHWE DAUNG ST

@ Exit Internet Bar

WUT KYI PAYA ST

MYOMA TADAR ST

State
Governor's
Office

Mon State
Cultural Museum

Night Market

DAWEI TADAR ST

Viewpoint

Dawei Jetty

Kyaik Thoke
Pagoda

U Khanti Paya

KYAIK THOKE PHAYAR S

Highway
Bus Station

MAGGIN ST

Longtail Jetty

PABEDAN ST

U ZINA PHAYAR ST

U Zina
Pagoda

Mawlamyine
Railway
Station

THEIK PAN ST

Khayone Cave (18km) & Hpa-An (60km)

Bilu Kyun (1km)

Thanlyin River

N

0   250
metres

central shrine, flanked by curved elephant tusks. Built in 1905 with donations from a wealthy local lady, its original tiles – hand-painted with peacocks – can still be seen on the walls of the corridor that circles the main chapel.

A few minutes' walk downhill from here, just west of Mahamuni Paya, is a forlorn, crumbling white stupa that marks the last resting place of **Fourth Princess**, the strong-willed and intelligent youngest daughter of King Thibaw and Queen Supalayat (see p.367), who was born in exile in India and came to her homeland for the first time as an adult.

Seindon Mibaya Kyaung

စိန်တုံးမိဖုရားကျောင်း • Viewpoint Rd • Daily during daylight hours • Free

The sky-blue and candyfloss-pink **Seindon Mibaya Kyaung** (also known as Yadanarbon Myint Kyaung) is centuries old and looks terribly dilapidated from the outside – even by Mawlamyine's standards. However, the main hall contains a wealth of lively red and gold teak reliefs, carved elephants' tusks and a cobweb-festooned period replica of a throne – the legacy of the monastery's royal connections. One of King Mindon's many widows, Queen Seindon, took refuge here after her husband's death in 1878 and paid for the building's construction. Today, the monastery is home to just nine monks, who have set up their living quarters among the faded finery – they'll turn on the lights for you in return for a small donation and a signature in their visitors' book.

U Zina Pagoda

ဦးဇိနဘုရား • Viewpoint Rd • Daily during daylight hours • Free

At the southern end of Mawlamyine's hills, a long, sweaty walk from Kyaikthanlan Pagoda, is the nineteenth-century **U Zina Pagoda**. The eponymous monk U Zina founded the monastery after discovering a cache of gemstones on this spot, having been shown the location in a dream.

The markets

Daily 6am–5pm

Local people somehow differentiate between the various markets that sprawl between Strand Road and Upper Main Road – for visitors, they seem to blur into one. The whole area is known as **Zeigyi** (not to be confused with Zeigyo, a separate part of the city, 6km to the south) and is divided into the Upper and Lower markets. The **Lower Market** is made up of a characterless modern complex on Lower Main Road (built after a two-day fire raged through its predecessor in 2008) and the dark, atmospheric and much more interesting covered **New Market**, just to the north. In the latter, porters stroll barefoot down the aisles and entire sections are devoted to betel leaves and *ngapi*; there's also the odd market bar, with stallholders nursing glasses of whisky and watching television. A small alleyway lined with gold and longyi shops links the Lower Market with the **Upper Market**, which is largely devoted to stalls selling gold, cosmetics and Chinese-made toys.

Mon State Cultural Museum

မွန်ယဉ်ကျေးမှုပြတိုက် • Corner of Baho St and Dawei Tadar St • Tues–Sun 10am–4.30pm, closed on public holidays • K5000

The modest collection on display at the two-floor **Mon State Cultural Museum** may be confusingly organized and poorly lit, but it's still well worth a visit. The highlights include a Mon crocodile-shaped harp, an eighteenth-century teak palanquin, and a beautiful palm-leaf fan set with gold and glass patterns, along with an informative series of displays about local industries.

Gaung Say Kyun

ခေါင်းဆေးကျွန်း • Daily during daylight hours • Free • Boat from Mawlamyine K1000 return

A short boat trip from the northern end of Mawlamyine, the pretty island of **Gaung Say Kyun** is forested with almost equal numbers of palm trees and pagodas. The island's name, meaning "Shampoo Island", dates from the Ava period, when the water for the king's annual hair-washing ceremonies was drawn from a **spring** here and transported to Inwa, 800km away. The spring is now covered by a pavilion that is usually kept locked, but a small tank at the side is accessible – local people sometimes still use the water for rinsing their hair, as it's thought to bring good luck. The nineteenth-century Mon-style **monastery** buildings are home to a small convent, a monastery and a meditation centre (although with the 2006 Thanlyin Bridge just 50m away, meditation is presumably far more challenging than it used to be), and the outlying *zedi* represent several different Buddhist traditions from Nepal to China, although the centrepiece is the Burmese-style **Sandawshin Pagoda**.

ARRIVAL AND DEPARTURE   MAWLAMYINE

By plane Some 8km southeast of town, Mawlamyine's small airport is supposedly served by a daily Myanmar Airways flight from Yangon (30min), but it actually operates on what is described as a "flexible" service – which means if there aren't enough customers, it doesn't take off.

By bus There are several bus stations in Mawlamyine. Buses to Yangon, Hpa-An and northern Myanmar leave from the Highway Bus Station on the eastern side of the hills, while southbound services depart from the Zeigyo bus station 6km south of the market. Buses to Thanbyuzayat and Kyaikkami depart from the southern end of the Zeigyi Market on Lower Main Rd until 4pm.

Destinations Bago (5 daily; 5hr 30min); Dawei (11 daily; 9hr); Hpa-An (1–2 hourly until 4pm; 2hr); Kinpun (for Kyaiktiyo; 2 daily; 4hr); Kyaikkami (hourly; 3hr);

Thanbyuzayat (hourly; 2hr); Yangon (3 daily; 8hr).

By shared taxi Minivans depart for Myawaddy (daily; 5hr) from the Zeigyo bus station between 8–10am. Book a seat in advance through your accommodation and you'll qualify for a free pick-up.

By train Mawlamyine's railway station is located 4km southeast of the market area on the eastern side of the ridge.

Destinations Bago (3 daily; 7–8hr); Dawei (daily; 15hr); Kyaikhto (for Kyaiktiyo; 3 daily; 5hr); Thaton (3 daily; 2hr 30min–3hr); Yangon (3 daily; 9hr); Ye (daily; 6hr).

By boat Chugging upstream along the Thanlyin River to Hpa-An (4hr) is a popular way to depart Mawlamyine (see box below). Boat services to Bilu Kyun are covered in the "Around Mawlamyine" section (see p.164).

GETTING AROUND

By motorbike taxi A short trip around town ought to cost K500. Longer trips start from K1000 (like from the market area to the Zeigyo bus station).

By bicycle Bikes are available to rent from *Breeze*

Guesthouse (K2000/day).

By motorbike Motorbikes can be rented from *Breeze Guesthouse* and Kyaw Pool Club, one block north of *Breeze*. Both charge around K10,000/day.

MAWLAMYINE TO HPA-AN BY BOAT

The three- to four-hour boat ride past bucolic villages of palm-thatch huts (K10,000) along the **Thanlyin River**, from the waterfront to the dramatic limestone scenery around Hpa-An, is one of the most memorable journeys in southern Myanmar.

Most choose to go from Mawlamyine to Hpa-An, leaving the best of the scenery to the end of the journey. Boats make the round trip from Mawlamyine to Hpa-An and back in a day – if there aren't enough people to run the first leg, then the boat will not do the second leg either. They generally leave Mawlamyine at 8.30am (with a hotel pick-up around 8am) and return around 1.30pm, with a 1pm pick-up from Hpa-An hotels; along the route, many stop briefly at a monastery.

There were once public ferries, but they stopped running a few years ago and now a couple of different private operators have stepped in to cover the trip. These services are aimed squarely at tourists, so don't expect to see any local colour on board. Make sure you bring snacks and water, and that you visit the toilets beforehand because there aren't any on board. The boat service stops between June and October.

INFORMATION AND TOURS

Maps Most of the hotels can provide city maps, although the *Cinderella Hotel*'s version is a cut above the rest, with photographs and information about local sights on the reverse – you can pick these up from the hotel reception.

Tours *Breeze Guesthouse* runs reasonably priced day-trips to Bilu Kyun (see p.164) and Nwa La Bo (see p.165).

ACCOMMODATION

Aurora Guesthouse 277 Lower Main Rd ☎057 22785. This lime-green guesthouse has a selection of cheap partitioned rooms with shared bathrooms (from $7), as well as a few much smarter en-suites. There's a pleasant shared balcony and the owner is gruff but helpful – it's a great budget option. Breakfast is not included. **$20**

Breeze Guesthouse 6 Strand Rd ☎057 21450, ✉breeze.guesthouse@gmail.com. This backpacker favourite has finally been given a bit of a renovation after many years. Its once grubby, cell-like rooms are now smart and white – though they're still so small it's like sleeping in a rabbit hutch. The bathrooms are also still communal. The most expensive rooms ($30) are large and old-fashioned, with shutters that swing open to let in the sea breeze, but they seem to be perennially booked up. The staff are knowledgeable, and its location in the centre of town is great. **$16**

★**Cinderella Hotel** 21 Baho St ☎057 24411, ⓦcinderellahotel.com. A few blocks east of Strand Rd, *Cinderella* is one of the best-value hotels in Myanmar. A small army of staff, some in white gloves, provides excellent service. The rooms are spacious and attractively decorated, the beds are comfortable and the hallways display a treasure-trove of Burmese handicrafts. The huge breakfasts are also particularly good, and there's unusually fast wi-fi. It also caters to backpackers, with spotless (though cramped) eight-bed dorms ($15). **$50**

Mawlamyaing Strand Hotel Between Lower Main Rd and Strand Rd ☎057 25624, ⓦmawlamyaing strandhotel.com. As you'd expect from Mawlamyine's fanciest hotel, the spacious rooms here are attractive and comfortable, though they're somewhat bland. There are two hotel restaurants (one inside and one open-air, the latter with nightly karaoke), and an excellent buffet breakfast is included. **$110**

OK Hotel 11–12 Thaton Tadar St, on the corner of Strand Rd ☎057 24677, ⓦokhotel-mlm.com. The tiled rooms here may not be particularly stylish, but they are clean and comfortable and each one comes with a/c and an en-suite bathroom – some with bathtubs. Since it's close to the market, rooms facing Thaton Tadar St can be very noisy – try to get one of the quieter rooms with great views over Strand Rd and the river. **$35**

EATING

Every day from 5pm onwards, a strip of **open-air food stalls** sets up along Strand Rd, just north of Dawei Jetty – it's a great spot to grab a bite to eat and watch the sunset. The food on offer, like barbecued skewers, fried rice, seafood and noodles, often doesn't taste as good as it looks (and some people report getting sick after eating here), but the atmosphere is great fun.

Bone Gyi Strand Rd ☎057 26528. Dishing up good Chinese food, this popular restaurant stays full of well-to-do Mawlamyiners until late in the evening, although as many come here to drink as to dine (there's even a wine list). It's a little more expensive than most Mawlamyine restaurants (mains K4000–7000), but the food quality is higher and worth the price. Daily 9am–9pm.

Delifrance Strand Rd, south of Dawei Jetty ☎09 566 0192. An imitation of the international chain, this small café serves decent coffee (espresso K1000), cake and sandwiches (K1000–1500), and has a small patio overlooking the hustle and bustle of Strand Rd and the river. Daily 9am–10pm.

★**May South Indian Chetty Restaurant** Strand Rd ☎09 4980 4047. This low-key restaurant is at its best (and busiest) around lunchtime, when it fills with market porters and office workers who come for the delicious Indian-inspired curries and biryani, served Burmese-style with fresh vegetables and side dishes. In the evenings foreign tourists can outnumber locals, but this place hasn't let its popularity get to its head – it retains a slightly chaotic and grubby feel. You can expect to pay around K1500 for a filling vegetarian meal and approximately K2500 for a meat-based one. Daily 10am–9pm.

Mya Tha Lwin Dawei Jetty, Strand Rd. A sizeable step up in quality from the bustling night market stalls next door, the busy and buzzy *Mya Tha Lwin* is a popular Chinese seafood restaurant where a main course will set you back around K3500. Daily 9am–11pm.

YKKO Dawei Jetty, Strand Rd ☎09 401 591 212. Clean and bright, with lovely views of the river, upmarket *YKKO* serves Thai food, barbecue and *kyay-oh* (noodle soup), along with an array of juices and coffee in its a/c dining room. Prices are higher than elsewhere in town – a plate of barbecued skewers will set you back approximately K3000. Daily 10am–10pm.

DIRECTORY

Banks Mawlamyine has plenty of banks and ATMs, with several on Strand Rd just south of the *Mawlamyaing Strand Hotel*, and more just north of *Breeze Guesthouse*. There is also an ATM at the *Cinderella Hotel*.

Post office Mawlamyine's large post office is housed in a building directly north of the State Governor's offices on Baho St.

Around Mawlamyine

The countryside around Mawlamyine is full of quirky side-trips – Buddhist **Khayone Cave** moonlights as a lively *nat* shrine; **Bilu Kyun** ("Ogre Island") contains nothing more fearsome than some really bad roads; and the vast, unfinished **Win Sein Taw Ya** reclining Buddha seems more like a monk's bid for immortality than a holy shrine. Further afield, there's the **Thanbyuzayat war cemetery** and the remains of the infamous World War II "Death Railway", as well as the seaside pagoda at **Kyaikkami**.

Bilu Kyun

ဘီလူးကျွန်း

Despite its disquieting name, Ogre Island – **Bilu Kyun** – is actually something of a rural idyll, rather than the haunt of man-eating giants. The largely Mon villages that dot this bucolic 32km-long island are linked by a web of rutted tracks, with more buffalo carts than cars. Islanders divide their time between fishing, growing rice and working in one of many **cottage industries**, and it's the chance to watch the latter that makes a visit here so absorbing.

There are several stories behind how the island got its name – the most likely one is that the head-hunting people who originally populated this area were pushed onto the island by the arrival of the more sophisticated Mon, who (fearing their neighbour's proclivities) called it Ogre Island.

Workshops on the island produce a wide range of home-grown products, from bamboo and banana-leaf hats to toddy (see box ooposite) and even rubber bands. The small factories generally welcome visitors and there's little pressure to buy, but as most places are hard to find, it's best to join a tour to get the most out of a day on the island (see below).

At the time of research, a huge new bridge connecting Bilu Kyun with the southern end of Mawlamyine was close to completion. Once finished, this island is likely to change quickly.

ARRIVAL AND DEPARTURE
BILU KYUN

Tours At the time of research it was not possible to stay on the island overnight. This, as well as the unreliable ferry timetable and slow island transport, means it's probably best to sign up for the *Breeze Guesthouse's* popular day-trip ($30pp, depending on group size), which takes in a good selection of the workshops and stops at a swimming hole – all transport and food are included. Most of the mid-range hotels will be able to organize more flexible private trips along the same lines, but you should agree a price in advance.

By ferry If you're determined to make the trip yourself, ensure you check the return ferry times in Mawlamyine before you hop on a boat. Government ferries depart from one of the two jetties on Strand Rd next to the

market. Ferries to Ka Lwi (Mon–Sat 2 daily; 1hr; K1500) at the northern tip of the island depart from the northernmost of the two, while boats from the southern jetty head to Nat Hmaw (Mon–Sat 3 daily; 2hr; K2000), halfway down the island's eastern shore. An additional private ferry service operates every day between the inconveniently located Chaungsone Jetty and Nat Hmaw.

By long-tail boat There's also a long-tail boat that sails straight across the channel to the island (daily 6am–6pm, departing when full; 20min; K3000) from a jetty on Strand Rd – the drawback here is that it drops you off at an isolated section of the shore, rather than in a village, so you'll need your own transport from there.

Nwa La Bo

နွားလပို့တောင်ဝ • Daily during daylight hours; closed during rainy season • Free

High up in the hills 20km north of Mawlamyine, **Nwa La Bo** – a stack of three slender gold-covered granite boulders, balanced end to end and crowned with a small pagoda – stands proudly overlooking the far-off Thanlyin River. From afar, the entire thing looks a little bit like a gigantic, golden gnome. Despite the fact that its creation purportedly pre-dates the Golden Rock at Kyaiktiyo, and regardless of its much more precarious placement, Nwa La Bo is far less revered than its more famous cousin, mainly because the rocks house less distinguished hair relics. Pilgrim numbers peak during the **pagoda festival** held in the second half of the Thingyan water celebration each year, and at weekends locals come here in greater numbers. There are a few more outcrops of rock nearby, but the hiking is limited – it's basically a pleasant, peaceful place to sit and watch swifts flitting above the shrine.

ARRIVAL AND DEPARTURE	NWA LA BO
By pick-up Pick-ups to Kyonka village (K1000), at the foot of the mountain, leave when full from outside the market on Mawlamyine's Lower Main Rd.	at 11am every day for the top of the mountain (K2000 return), leaving from just inside this entrance – unless there are enough visitors to fill subsequent trucks, you're
By motorbike taxi A motorbike taxi to Kyonka costs K5000 for the return trip, and a private taxi to Kyonka is around K25,000 with waiting time.	faced with a long (7km), unshaded walk to the top with no water available en route, although there is a small teahouse at the top. The 11am truck usually returns to Kyonka around
Kyonka to the summit Once in Kyonka, the entrance to Nwa La Bo is marked by a golden archway. A truck departs	noon or a little after, though it's best to confirm this with the driver.

Khayone Cave

ခရဲဉ့ • Daily 6am–dusk • Free • Hpa-An-bound buses pass the road to the cave, from where it's a 10min walk

Around 18km northeast of Mawlamyine on the road to Hpa-An, the otherwise flat landscape suddenly gives way to a single sheer-sided limestone karst hill. At its base is **Khayone Cave**. There are two small cave systems here, one reached by a road lined with a picturesque queue of life-sized monk statues, the other reached by a straight access road; the main cave is at the end of the latter.

While Khayone Cave is nominally Buddhist, arrive around 7–9am and you will coincide with the crowds of locals who come to pray to the local *nats* whose images stand alongside rows of golden Buddhas. Inside the entrance is the statue of a *zawgyi*, which visitors rub in the hope of driving away sickness; nearby is the effigy of an education-promoting *nat* riding on a *hamsa*, where students leave hopeful bunches of flowers before their exams. Like a sort of cave-bound clinic, Khayone is also the site of faith-healing sessions and regular morning seances, during which one of the three *nats* depicted sitting in a row by the cave's exit is said to possess a medium to counsel local women.

PALM WINE AND TODDY TAPPERS

Toddy, or palm wine, is responsible for hangovers everywhere from Nigeria to Papua New Guinea. All over Myanmar, where it's known as *tan-ye*, you'll see spindly bamboo ladders leading up spiky palmyra palms – a sure sign that a toddy collector is at work nearby. A collector, also known as a **tapper**, will fasten a bamboo tube around the cut stem of the tree's flowers, and gather the sweet, white sap that drips out. The sap is then left to ferment naturally for a few hours, producing a cloudy, lightly alcoholic beverage. Sweet and slightly sour, toddy must be drunk on the day it is produced, before it turns into vinegar. Happily for the toddy tappers, however, leftover toddy can be evaporated and turned into delicious and exceedingly addictive lumps of caramel-coloured **jaggery**, often served at the end of a meal and jokingly called "Burmese chocolate".

Kyaikmaraw Paya

ကျိုက်မရော့ဘုရား • Daily 6am–dusk • Free • Pick-ups for Kyaikmaraw leave from Maylamyine's Zeigyo bus station (hourly; 30min; K500)

The **Kyaikmaraw Paya**, in the small country town of Kyaikmaraw, around a twenty-minute drive east of Mawlamyine, was built in the mid-fifteenth century on the request of Queen Shinsawbu. The centrepiece of the complex is a large Buddha image, unusually sitting as if in a chair. Surrounding this are a number of more classically cross-legged Buddhas and, behind, there are two reclining ones. The temple complex is also notable for its beautiful stained-glass windows.

Kyauktalon Taung

ကျောက်တစ်လုံးတောင် • Daily during daylight hours • Free •

One of the more arresting features of the landscape around Mawlamyine, the **Kyauktalon Taung** is a thin, craggy needle of rock rising up out of the palm trees a thirty-minute drive south of Mawlamyine. It's topped with a couple of small *payas*, and the hot, sticky climb up to the summit takes around fifteen minutes, but is worth it for the stunning views over dense forests and a few scattered villages. On the opposite side of the main road is a lower Hindu version. A visit is easily combined with Win Sein Taw Ya, which is based just a few minutes to the southeast.

Win Sein Taw Ya

ဝင်းစိန်တော်ရ • Daily 7am–dusk • Free • Take a bus or pick-up (both K500) towards Thanbyuzayat from Mawlamyine's Zeigyo bus station and get off at Win Sein Taw Ya (hourly; 40min) – the junction is marked by a golden gateway topped with two large cranes, from where it's a 2km walk to the Buddha; alternatively, a motorbike taxi from Mawlamyine costs K8000 with wait time and a stop at Kyauktalon Taung, and a taxi is K20,000

Even if you've visited enough reclining Buddhas to last a lifetime, do make time to visit **Win Sein Taw Ya**, which lounges across a series of hillsides 22km south of Mawlamyine en route to Mudon. It's said to be the largest reclining Buddha in the world, and shows outlandish Myanmar at its very best. The eight floors inside are filled with dioramas depicting scenes from the Buddha's life, and images of the nasty kings of old having their way with groups of young women. A moment later, you'll come across depictions of sinners being impaled on spikes and boiled in lakes of lava, as payback for a lifetime of naughtiness.

The ninety-something-year-old monk who dreamed up this bizarre project recently passed away, but not before he'd begun constructing an even larger statue on the opposite side of the narrow valley – though there's currently no saying if or when it will ever be completed.

In late January every year a major festival takes place here to celebrate the birthday of the monk who created these artistic "masterpieces". It attracts throngs of itinerant salesmen, monks and the odd hermit, and is also the setting for a kickboxing tournament.

Thanbyuzayat and around

South of Mawlamyine, visitor numbers begin to thin out considerably. Even so, the small town of **Thanbyuzayat** is well worth visiting for its fascinating (though admittedly rather unsettling) history, and the nearby beach town of **Kyaikkami** is popular with local Burmese hoping to dip their toes in the ocean and seek blessings at the nearby Buddhist pilgrimage site. Further south lies laidback **Ye**, which is based firmly off the beaten track, where you'll find four very large Buddha statues and a lovely lake setting – it's an excellent place to relax.

THE DEATH RAILWAY

When Japan seized control of Burma in 1942, the supplies and troops needed to maintain their forces had to be shipped in by sea. The battles of the Coral Sea and Midway that spring reduced Japanese naval strength, and the long voyage to Burma was thought to leave the precious fleet vulnerable. An alternative was required, and the **Burma–Siam railway** – a route previously surveyed by the British government of Burma in the 1880s – was revived. In July 1942, construction started simultaneously from Ban Pong in Thailand and Thanbyuzayat in Burma.

The Japanese aimed to complete the 420km-long railway in just fourteen months, despite the difficulties posed by the mountainous, jungle-covered terrain. It is estimated that 60,000 Allied POWs and 180,000 *rōmusha* (Asian civilian labourers, primarily from Indonesia) worked on the project, hacking through the Tenasserim Hills with primitive tools. By the time the railway was completed in October 1943, over 12,000 POWs and around 90,000 *rōmusha* had died from maltreatment, sickness and starvation.

In the end, the railway was in operation for just over twenty months before an **Allied bombing raid** put it out of action. A 130km-long stretch is still in use in Thailand, but inside Myanmar the tracks have been slowly reclaimed by the rainforest. The Myanmar government periodically announces plans to rebuild the railway, but as yet this hasn't moved beyond the drawing table.

3

Thanbyuzayat

သံဖြူဇရပ်မြို့ • Buses to Thanbyuzayat (hourly 6am–4pm; 2hr) run from Lower Main Rd beside Mawlamyine's market

THANBYUZAYAT, 64km south of Mawlamyine, was the end point of World War II's infamous "Death Railway" (see box above), constructed by the Japanese using forced labour at appalling human cost.

Thanbyuzayat War Cemetery

သံဖြူဇရပ်စစ်သင်္ချိုင်း • Daily during daylight hours • Free

The beautiful **Thanbyuzayat War Cemetery** is a moving memorial to the Death Railway. A kilometre west of the clocktower, the cemetery contains the graves of 3771 Commonwealth and Dutch soldiers, who died during the construction of the railway and in air raids following its completion. Bronze plaques, often with heart-breaking inscriptions from bereaved mothers and wives, mark each grave.

Kyaikkami

ကျိုက္ခမီမြို့

Some 85km south of Mawlamyine, the tidy little coastal town of **KYAIKKAMI** juts into the murky waters of the Gulf of Mottama. The British annexed this town after the First Anglo-Burmese War, naming it **Amherst**, and it became a popular seaside resort for Mawlamyine's expatriate and Anglo-Burmese community – even today, there are still one or two bright colonial buildings around town. Though the muddy waters surrounding the little beach won't appeal to travellers, and there is no accommodation licensed to accept foreigners, the town fills up at weekends with fun-seeking Burmese people from nearby areas.

Yele Paya

ရေလယ်ဘုရား • Daily dawn–dusk • Free

Today, most visitors come to Kyaikkami to visit **Yele Paya**, a picturesque seaside pagoda situated 1km from town at the tip of a small peninsula. Local Buddhists believe that the pagoda, reached along a covered causeway, contains a Buddha image that floated here from Sri Lanka, as well as several hair relics. These treasures are covered with an unusual tiered shrine, which is encircled by rows of Mandalay-style Buddhas. Note that women are not allowed to enter the main chapel, and must instead use a designated "Lady Worship Area" to the side of the main one.

ARRIVAL AND DEPARTURE   KYAIKKAMI

By bus and pick-up Buses to Kyaikkami depart from outside Mawlamyine's main market, on Lower Main Rd (K1000; hourly; 3hr). From Thanbyuzayat, pick-ups leave from the clocktower (K300; hourly; 1hr).

Ye

ရေး

The quiet, rural town of **YE** is a surprising little place. It's well off the usual tourist trail, and while you can tick off its major sights in a day, it's worth staying a little longer to devote time to more relaxed pastimes, like cycling out into the countryside.

The town centres on an attractive lake, which you can circumnavigate in half an hour or so. At one end, a small footbridge leads to a temple that's been suspended on stilts over the water. Locals visit the lake each evening to feed handfuls of multicoloured popcorn to hundreds of large carp, which gather in swarming masses with their mouths agape, like shoals of toothless piranhas.

Ye is only a short way inland from the coast, but its beaches tend to be shallow and slightly muddy – if you're desperate to lay out your beach towel, keep heading south towards Dawei and Myeik.

Ko Yin Lay

ကိုရင်လေး • Daily 6am–7pm • Free • Motorbike taxi from Ye K35,000

A twenty-minute drive north of Ye is **Ko Yin Lay**, a low hill otherwise known as "Banana Mountain". While it doesn't have as many banana plants as the name suggests, it does have four very large sitting Buddha statues arranged around a tower – and an equally large reclining version was under construction at the time of research. The sitting Buddha statues are hollow, and you can climb the nine flights of stairs inside for lovely views out over the surrounding countryside. There are several other smaller temples on the same site.

ARRIVAL AND DEPARTURE   YE

By bus Buses to Ye will drop you off at the bus station, a K500 motorbike taxi ride from the town centre.
Destinations Dawei (4 daily; 4hr); Mawlamyine (8 daily; 4hr).

By train There's one very slow train to Dawei per day at 10.30am, and just two trains per day to Mawlamyine.
Destinations Dawei (daily; 8–10hr); Mawlamyine (2 daily; 6hr).

ACCOMMODATION

May Shan II Guest House Strand Rd ☏ 09 870 1427. You should only come here as a last resort, as this lakeside guesthouse is a bit overpriced. Rooms with shared bathrooms cost less at K15,000, but all of them look older than they are. The sign outside is in Burmese script only, and breakfast isn't included. **K35,000**

Starlight Guest House Strand Rd ☏ 09 2557 13253, ⓦ starlight-guesthouse.com. Run by Dave, an American, and his charming local wife, the welcoming

Starlight is a league above everything else in Ye. The small rooms are painted in calming buttercup colours and have pretty bunches of flowers. Breakfast each morning on the terrace overlooking the lake is a delight. A huge amount of travel-related information is available here, and staff can organize day-trips to nearby beaches, villages, mangrove swamps and other attractions. Book ahead. **K30,000**

EATING

Rot Sar Restaurant Strand Rd. Tasty and spicy Thai–Burmese dishes are served up in this very simple, fairy light-illuminated setting beside the tranquil lake. The stir-fried vegetable dish (mains K15,000) will provide almost an entire garden's worth of greens – and certainly your five a day. Daily 9am–9pm.

Dawei and around

Off-limits to foreign visitors for almost fifty years, the **Tanintharyi Region**, Myanmar's southernmost territory, finally opened to travellers in 2013. Having spent decades in isolation, Tanintharyi's coastline is tantalizingly undeveloped – something it has in common with the region's infrastructure. From the beaches outside laidback **Dawei** to the bustle of **Myeik** and the idyllic **Myeik Archipelago** beyond, Myanmar's Andaman coastline will one day be a huge draw for beach bums and hotel developers alike. For now, the region is still waiting for its day in the sun – go now before everyone else catches on.

Dawei

ထား:ဝယ်မြို့
Although **DAWEI** is eclipsed by its better-known neighbour, the Myeik Archipelago, its isolated stretch of coastline is home to some of the region's best and most accessible **beaches**. Fishing villages spill right down to the gloriously clear water around **San Hlan**, a lone gold pagoda looks out over the Andaman Sea at **Shin Maw**, and unlikely-looking sandy tracks lead to gorgeous stretches of sand almost everywhere. And, save for the fishermen, there's seldom another person in sight. There's very little to distract you from heading to the seaside here, though it makes a convenient base for trips around the south with plenty of good hotels and decent transport connections.

The only shadow on the horizon for Dawei is the question of how long its temptingly undeveloped shoreline will remain intact. The Myanmar government, Thailand and Japan have started work on a joint project to create the largest industrial zone in the country – one of the largest in Southeast Asia (see box, p.170) – and the opening of the **Htee Kee–Phu Nam Ron border crossing** with Thailand (see box, p.172) has also led to a surge in tourism. At least for the moment, these developments have had relatively little impact on the beaches.

Shwe Taung Zar Pagoda

ရွှေတောင်စားဘုရား • Daily 5am–10pm • Free
The only real sight within Dawei itself is **Shwe Taung Zar Pagoda**, the town's most important, and slightly zany, Buddhist temple. At the centre of the complex stands the tapering pagoda, surrounded on all sides by further shrines. In one corner is a small museum containing an odd collection of old cannons, golf tournament trophies and various swords and statues.

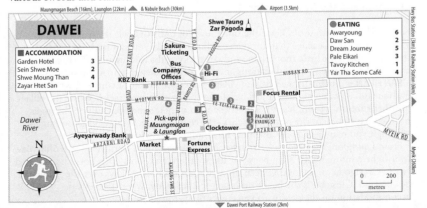

DAWEI

Maungmagan Beach (16km), Launglon (22km) ▲ & Nabule Beach (30km)   ▲ Airport (3.5km)

ACCOMMODATION
Garden Hotel	3
Sein Shwe Moe	2
Shwe Moung Than	4
Zayar Htet San	1

●**EATING**
Awaryoung	6
Daw San	2
Dream Journey	5
Pale Eikari	3
Tavoy Kitchen	1
Yar Tha Some Café	4

Shwe Taung Zar Pagoda

Sakura Ticketing

Bus Company Offices

KBZ Bank

Hi-Fi

NIBBAN RD

Focus Rental

MYOTWIN RD

YE-YEIKTHA RD

Dawei River

Pick-ups to Maungmagan & Launglon

PALAUKKU KYAUNG ST

Ayeyarwady Bank

ARZARNI ROAD

Clocktower

ARZARNI ROAD

Market

Fortune Express

N

MYEIK RD

0   200
metres

Dawei Port Railway Station (2km)

Hwy Bus Station (3km) & Railway Station (4km)   Myeik (260km)

3

DAWEI SPECIAL ECONOMIC ZONE

Along the northern edge of Nabule Beach, 30km northwest of Dawei, a wide, sandy road leads to the isolated shoreline. On either side of it, a series of signs stands in front of various scrubby, deserted plots, ambitiously announcing the "LNG Terminal – 35 Acres" and "Main Port 2km". This is the **Dawei Special Economic Zone (SEZ)**.

In 2008, the Myanmar and Thai governments signed a deal to develop this stretch of coast into a huge industrial estate and **deep-sea port**. With a highway, railway and pipeline leading directly to Bangkok, 350km to the east, the development would allow firms from across Southeast Asia to bypass the busy waters of the Straits of Malacca.

Local people, fearing that they stand to lose their land and livelihoods, and that the benefits will mostly go to overseas businesses rather than local ones, have established the Dawei Development Association to monitor the SEZ. So far there have been accusations that farmers have been forced to give up their cashew and betel-nut plantations without fair compensation, and an increase in complaints of land grabs as developers rush to find a foothold in the area.

In 2013, the project was put on hold after failing to gather sufficient financial backing, but in early 2015 the Thai and Myanmar governments announced that they were resurrecting the project with the assistance of Japan. The first stage of development involves the construction of a new road to Thailand, the creation of a small port and various infrastructure and telecommunications projects, due by 2020. For now, it's possible to visit the project **showroom** near Nabule to get a flavour of what the future here will look like.

Maungmagan Beach and around

မောင်းမကန်

Maungmagan, the best known of Dawei's beaches just 16km north of town, is the only one that's set up for visitors, with a string of restaurants lining the sand and an excellent guesthouse or two nearby (see p.171). It's strange, then, that it's also one of the less attractive beaches in the region, with darker sand, more rubbish than elsewhere, and – at low tide at least – a wide expanse of muddy sand that gives the distinct feeling of bathing in an estuary.

Still, Maungmagan is a good base for exploring the surrounding area, which includes the site of the proposed **megaport** (see box above), lots of pretty villages set amid groves of cashew trees, and a 12km-long beach at **Nabule** (pronounced "Nabu-lay"), which is one of the more attractive beaches in southern Myanmar. If you head south along the coastal road from Maungmagan, you'll reach **Myaw Yit Pagoda** after 11km, a collection of *zedi* at the end of a causeway on a rocky section of shore.

Launglon and the Dawei Peninsula

လောင်းလုံ

Some 22km southwest of Dawei the small town of **LAUNGLON** is the gateway to a string of fantastic beaches that dot the coastline – if only you can find them. Most of the access roads are little more than sandy or rocky paths leading over the hills to the coast, so be prepared to ask directions and for fairly challenging road conditions.

SAN HLAN is a palm-fringed fishing village 5km southwest of Launglon, with a harbour full of wooden boats and a beach covered with drying racks. While the village is rather rubbish-strewn, it's still a pretty spot, and there's the possibility of hiring a fishing boat to one of the nearby beaches – **Pa Nyiq** or **Shan Maw** make good targets, although you may need some Burmese to communicate what you're after.

From Launglon, the peninsula stretches for a further 50km until you reach **Shin Maw** (not to be confused with Shan Maw) at the southern end. This open horseshoe-shaped bay has a pagoda on its southeastern tip, with beautiful open views over the Andaman Sea beyond. Close by is the beautiful beach at **Zat Sar Aw**, where the only accommodation on the peninsula can currently be found.

Perhaps the most drop-dead gorgeous of all the beaches is **Po Po Kyak** or "Grandfather Beach", which is around a two-hour motorbike ride from Dawei. It's a vast curl of tinsel-white sand backed by lush jungle, with a small river at one end. For the moment it's completely undeveloped, so take food and water with you.

ARRIVAL AND DEPARTURE

DAWEI AND AROUND

By plane Dawei's small airport has daily flights to Yangon. At the time of research there were no flights south to Myeik, but this is likely to change. The terminal is 3.5km north of the town centre (K1500 by motorbike taxi, K4000 by tuk-tuk). Tickets are available from Sakura Ticketing Centre, at the junction between Pagoda Rd and Ye Rd (☎ 059 22444).

Destinations Yangon (daily; 1hr).

By bus Buses stop at Dawei's Highway bus station, a 15min drive east of town (K4000 by tuk-tuk or K1500 on a motorbike taxi). Tickets are available from the bus company offices that are concentrated on Ye Rd, just north of the junction with Nibban Rd. Minibuses to the Htee Kee–Phu Nam Ron border crossing (see box, p.172) depart from Dawei daily. Book a seat in advance through your accommodation.

Destinations Htee Kee–Phu Nam Ron (daily; 3hr);

Mawlamyine (11 daily; 6–7hr); Myeik (7 daily; 6–7hr); Yangon (11 daily; 12hr); Ye (11 daily; 4hr).

By train Dawei has two railway stations: the main one, 6km east of the main market (K2000 by motorbike or K4000 by tuk-tuk), and Dawei Port, 2.5km south of town – it's best to get off at the main station (the first one you arrive at southbound), as the shunt between stations takes eons. A single train departs each day at 6am for Ye (rumoured to be the slowest train in the country), where everyone switches trains before heading on to Mawlamyine and Yangon.

Destinations Ye (daily; 9hr).

By boat It used to be possible to travel between Dawei, Myeik and Kawthaung by boat. These services stopped a couple of years ago, but it's worth asking around to see if they've restarted.

GETTING AROUND AND INFORMATION

By motorbike taxi A trip to the airport or bus station will set you back K1500, while the long ride out to Maungmagan costs around K15,000.

By pick-up Pick-ups to Maungmagan and Launglon (both K1500) leave from around the market on Arzarni Rd.

By tuk-tuk A short trip around town will cost K1000–1500. A tuk-tuk to Maungmagan will cost a fairly steep K15,000.

By motorbike Given the excellent potential for day-trips

around Dawei, renting a motorbike is a useful option. Focus Rental Service (688 Pakoku Kyaung Rd; ☎ 09 422 190 130) rent out motorcycles for K8000/day. They supply maps of the Dawei Peninsula, with all the beaches and drive times between them marked.

Information Run by a locally based expat, the Southern Myanmar website (ⓦ southernmyanmar.com) is regularly updated with information about the region.

ACCOMMODATION

DAWEI

Garden Hotel 88 Ye Rd ☎ 059 22116, ⓦ gardenhotel dawei.blogspot.com. Housed in an 1842 villa, this hotel is much larger than it looks from the street. The lofty rooms range from cramped $15 singles with fans and shared bathrooms to attractive (though still a/c-free) $35 rooms. Breakfast not included. $20

Sein Shwe Moe 577 Ye Yeiktha Rd ☎ 059 24073. While its owners may be a little slow to smile, this small, lemon-yellow hotel is extremely clean, and though the rooms are small, they're very cheap – the four single rooms with fans are just K10,000. Breakfast not included. K16,000

★**Shwe Moung Than** 665 Pakaukku Kyaung St ☎ 059 23764, ⓔ shwemaungthan22@gmail.com. This smart hotel ticks all the boxes. The comfortable rooms are bright and decently sized, and the staff are incredibly helpful. Rooms vary in size, but all are clean and good value for money. $20

Zayar Htet San 566 Ye Yeiktha Rd ☎ 059 23902, ⓔ hotelzayarhtetsan@gmail.com. Reminiscent of a Cubist painting from the outside, *Zayar Htet San* certainly stands out on this quiet street. Once inside, the rooms are comfortable and nicely designed, with wooden floors and tasteful decoration, and are very good value overall. The in-house restaurant, however, is worth missing. $40

MAUNGMAGAN

Coconut Guesthouse Maungmagan ☎ 09 423 713 681, ⓔ cocoguesthouse95@gmail.com. While there are a few places to stay in Maungmagan, this is the pick of the bunch, with ten simple, fan-cooled rooms in bungalows a short walk from the beach. With charming staff and a chilled-out restaurant on-site (breakfast not included), it's a good enough reason to stay in Maungmagan. The beach is a 5min walk away. $25

HTEE KEE–PHU NAM RON BORDER CROSSING

Opened in August 2013, the border crossing between **Htee Kee** in Myanmar and **Phu Nam Ron** in Thailand is the closest crossing point to Bangkok, and is being increasingly used by tourists as an entry/exit point between the two countries. Minibuses have a monopoly on the route between Dawei and Htee Kee (3hr; K20,000), and you can book them from the bus offices on Ye Road. Once you're stamped out of Myanmar at Htee Kee, it's 5km through no-man's-land to the Thai border post at Phu Nam Ron, which you can cover either on foot or by hitchhiking. From Phu Nam Ron, there are buses to Kanchanaburi (2hr), and thence to Bangkok.

ZAT SAR AW

Myanmar Paradise Beach Zat Sar Aw beach, Maungmagan ☎ 09 4985 1256, ⓦmyanmarparadise beach.com. Way out towards the very end of the Dawei Peninsula and currently the only place out here to stay, the *Myanmar Paradise Beach* has individual wooden bungalows with terraces and hammocks set on a sublime sweep of palm-backed white sand. Basically, it has the whole beach bliss thing down. You'll need to call to organize transport out to them. K30,000

EATING

DAWEI

Awaryoung Corner of Arzarni Rd and Pakaukku Kyaung St ☎ 059 21887. A popular teahouse with outdoor seating, *Awaryoung* produces a good range of snacks and excellent noodle salads. English menu available, mains K1000–1500. Daily 7am–10pm.

★ **Daw San** 506 Hospital Rd ☎ 09 4987 2584. A low-key Burmese restaurant, which dishes up delicious curries all afternoon. The beef curry is particularly good, but there are plenty of vegetarian options available too. A meal with side dishes will cost around K2500. Daily 11am–8.30pm.

Dream Journey 661 Pakaukku Kyaung St ☎ 09 500 7091. This café serves up reasonably priced cheesecake, fruity yoghurt and coffee (espresso K500) – the latter is particularly popular with fatigued teachers from the school opposite. The helpful owner, Zin Wai, speaks excellent English. Daily 7am–10pm.

Pale Eikari 572 Ye Yeiktha Rd ☎ 059 21282. A kind of upmarket beer station, this garden restaurant is a popular nightspot with well-to-do locals dining on fairly average, but quite expensive, Chinese and Thai food (mains K6000–7000) and enthusiastically drinking draught beer. Daily 6am–10pm.

Tavoy Kitchen 234 Phyar Rd ☎ 09 455 192 525. With candle-lit tables, plenty of delicious tamarind and plum juices and a short list of neatly presented, if slightly toned down, Thai dishes (mains K5000–6000), this is easily the most popular place with foreign tourists. The free local sweets to finish off your meal are a nice touch. Mon–Sat 10am–3pm & 5–11pm, Sun 5–11pm.

Yar Tha Some Café Myotwin Rd ☎ 09 968 291 318. This small café is aimed squarely at passing travellers and has a very unexpected, and rather welcome, selection of cakes, coffees and juices (all around K600–800). Daily 9am–9.30pm.

MAUNGMAGAN

★ **Esso Restaurant** Southern end of the beach. *Esso* might just be a simple beachshack restaurant overlooking the sands of Maungmagan, but their curry crab (K7000) and prawns with cashew nuts (K6000) could easily turn out to be among the best meals you'll have in southern Myanmar. Wash them down with fresh coconut juice and you have the making of a meal fit for a beach-bum king. Daily 8am–9pm.

DIRECTORY

Banks KBZ Bank (Nibban Rd) and Ayeyarwady Bank (Arzarni Rd) both have ATMs; the former also offers currency exchange. Neither ATM currently accepts MasterCard.

Myeik and around

မြိတ်မြို့

Thanks to its location far from the reins of power, **MYEIK** – Tanintharyi's largest city – enjoys a rather exotic reputation, as it's surrounded by tropical waters and floating villages of Salone sea gypsies. And in many ways, the town lives up to expectations. With its crumbling colonial architecture, bustling fish markets, hilltop pagoda and busy waterfront, Myeik is at the very least an interesting place to explore. Entire neighbourhoods are given over to drying fish and the making of *ngapi* (fermented fish paste), and you'll have the chance to poke around nearby shipyards and cashew-nut factories – although you'll need a guide to find most places.

It sprawls around the estuary of the Tanintharyi River, with Strand Road looking out over the busy waterways to the **Twin Islands** (Padaw Taung and Pathet Taung), now linked by reclaimed land and home to a large fish factory. As interesting as the town of Myeik is, the real reason people come here is for the **Myeik Archipelago** to the south (see p.174). These islands have been tempting explorers and adventurers for decades, but until very recently they've remained largely out of bounds to foreigners. Now, permit restrictions have been lifted and the first stirrings of a tourist industry are emerging – although much of the archipelago remains very difficult and expensive to get to.

Brief history
Like most of Tanintharyi, Myeik (formerly known as Mergui) was part of the Bagan Empire until its collapse in 1287. From then until the mid-eighteenth century, the town belonged to Siam, with a few short interludes of Burmese rule. The port flourished as result of its location, poised between the Indian Ocean and the South China Sea. Traders would travel from Myeik up the Tanintharyi River to Tanintharyi town (the town, river and region all share the same name), 80km to the southeast, and across the hills to Siam proper. After the Konbaung dynasty sacked Ayutthaya in 1767, Myeik returned to Burmese rule, until the British annexation of Tanintharyi in 1826.

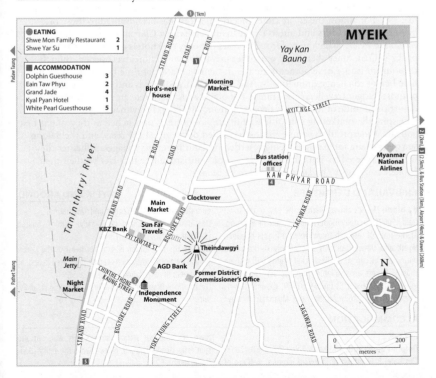

Theindawgyi and around

သိမ်တော်ကြီး • Between Bogyoke Rd and Yoke Taung St • Daily 5am–10pm • Free

At the top of a modest hill, **Theindawgyi** is Myeik's oldest and most important pagoda. It's particularly lively in the evening, when locals visit in the hope of catching a rare breeze. Of particular architectural interest is the **ordination hall**, its teak ceiling carved with hermits and parrots. Just south of the compound, on the road that runs along the hilltop, is the British-era **District Commissioner's office**, still in government service, and opposite a small building that was formerly the town's arsenal.

Twin Islands

Daily during daylight hours • Free • Long-tail boats (K5000–6000 return) head out to both islands from just south of the main jetty

They're hardly the stuff of tropical beach fantasies, but the **Twin Islands** are still worth a visit. The northernmost island, **Padaw Taung**, is home to a standing Buddha statue and several small stupas, while **Pathet Taung**'s resident Buddha is a large reclining version. It's not possible to walk from one to the other. In theory the Twin Islands are off-limits to foreigners, but in reality this is rarely enforced.

Myeik Archipelago

မြိတ်ကျွန်းစု

The islands of the **Myeik Archipelago** are the stuff of legend. Part of one of the least-known archipelagos in Southeast Asia, the gorgeous, largely uninhabited islands are fringed with white-sand beaches and cloaked in jungles and mangrove forests, which are home to gibbons, tiny mouse deer and monitor lizards, as well as (quite possibly) any number of smaller creatures that are as yet unknown to science.

The islands have retained their near-pristine condition as they were almost totally closed to outsiders for decades. They finally opened to dive boats for the very first time in 1996. For almost the entire time since then, access has been limited to those on **live-aboard boat tours** and guests of the luxury *Andaman Club* and low-key *Myanmar Andaman Resort*, which were for many years the only two **hotels** on the islands (see pp.175–176). Since then, only one other privately owned hotel has opened, though rumours of future developments are rife. It's only a matter of time before the situation here begins to change dramatically. And while the live-aboards and resorts are easily out of most budget travellers' price range, the big news is that there are now affordable day-trips to some of the islands departing from Myeik and Kawthaung (see box, p.175).

Despite the marketing spiel, the islands are not quite as untouched as they might first appear. Widespread dynamite fishing has killed off many of the reefs, and the **Salone sea gypsies** are increasingly being resettled on land in scruffy villages. Whether they will be subjected to "human zoo-style" ethnic tourism, a fate that has befallen their Moken cousins in Thailand, remains to be seen.

ARRIVAL AND DEPARTURE

By plane Myeik's airport, 4km to the east of the town (taxi K5000), has daily flights to Yangon and Kawthaung. At the time of research there were no flights between Myeik and Dawei, but this is generally considered a temporary hiccup so it's likely that flights will resume shortly. Tickets are available from the Sun Far Travels office on Pyi Tawtar St (☎ 059 41160, ⬤ sunfartravels .com). Air KBZ, Apex Airlines and Myanmar Airways operate daily flights to Yangon and Kawthaung. Destinations Kawthaung (2–3 daily; 45min); Yangon (2–3 daily; 2hr).

By bus The bus station is 4km northeast of the centre (K1000 by motorbike); tickets can be purchased here or at offices near the fire station on Kan Phyar St. Destinations Dawei (7 daily; 6–7hr); Kawthaung (11 daily; 9hr).

ACCOMMODATION

MYEIK

Dolphin Guesthouse 139 Kan Phyar Rd ☎ 059 42868. This hotel is in rather an awkward location, well out of town near the bus station, but it's very well run and spotlessly clean, if rather bland. Avoid the noisy road-facing rooms. $25

TOURING THE MYEIK ARCHIPELAGO

DAY-TRIPS

Most people visit the islands on a day-trip out of Myeik. Permits are no longer required to do this, and the trips are easy to organize – though they don't run between around May to September.

From **Myeik**, two standard trips ($80 per person) are offered, combining snorkelling, village visits and a bit of beach time into one busy day. Tours are sold through most travel agencies and hotels in Myeik, and everyone piles onto boats together. The big problem with these trips is that you spend as much time on the boat as you do on the beach or in the water, and – as you only have time to reach the islands closer to the mainland – the beaches are not the best. At low tide, many of these beaches become very shallow and muddy, and the snorkelling around them is mediocre with very low visibility and little coral. Treat these trips more as a fun day out rather than a genuine chance to explore the islands. Agents in Myeik also sell a kayaking day-trip: you go by speedboat out to one of the islands, where you can paddle around the mangroves ($60).

From **Kawthaung**, it used to be possible to do overnight camping trips on the beach ($170), but these were suspended at the time of research due to permission issues. It's best to check whether these have started up again, as they're certainly worthwhile.

LIVE-ABOARD BOATS

The most rewarding way of experiencing the islands is on a **live-aboard boat**. These are luxury motor yachts, so conditions are decidedly idyllic with comfortable bedrooms and great food – the general idea is that you sit back and do nothing while sailing from one blissful beach or colourful coral reef to another.

A One Diving ☎+66 (0)818 915510, ⍉a-one -diving.com. This is a Ranong-based operator offering live-aboard dive tours. Trips to the archipelago start from $850/person for a five-day tour, including all expenses except park and visa fees.

Burma Boating ☎+66 (0)210 70445, ⍉burma boating.com. Thailand-based operator offering luxurious live-aboard tours from $2600/person for a six-day trip, including everything except park and visa fees.

Moby Dick Adventures ☎013 800382, ⍉islandsafarimergui.com. With offices in Yangon and Kawthaung, Moby Dick specializes in "island safaris" where the focus is on kayaking and snorkelling rather than diving. A five-day trip will set you back $1110/person.

The Smiling Seahorse ☎+66 (0)860 110614, ⍉thesmilingseahorse.com. Based in Thailand, the French-run *Smiling Seahorse* sails to some of the remoter parts of the archipelago. Six-day, fifteen-dive trips around the archipelago start at $1050, not including equipment rental or park and visa fees.

Eain Taw Phyu 42 Kan Phyar Rd ☎059 42055, @eaintawphyu.hotel@gmail.com. This is the closest Myeik gets to a boutique hotel. The icy white rooms are accented with rich, dark woods, and have been given a splash of colour with fresh tropical orchids. The cheapest rooms get a lot of road noise, so opt for the slightly more expensive ones that overlook the decent swimming pool, at the back of the palm-filled garden. $65

Grand Jade 28–30 Baho Rd ☎059 41906. You can hardly miss this modern, nine-storey hotel right in the heart of town. The large rooms are impressively well equipped, but it's the floor-to-ceiling windows with sea views that really steal the show. $60

Kyal Pyan Hotel 58 C Rd ☎059 42135. A rather unprepossessing exterior gives way to what are actually surprisingly pleasant, large and well-maintained rooms. The cheapest single rooms (K15,000) are pretty grubby, though. K35,000

White Pearl Guesthouse 97–98 Middle Strand Rd ☎092 5288 8812, @whitepearlmyeik@gmail.com. The go-to hotel of choice for all budget travellers passing through Myeik, the *White Pearl* has two types of rooms. Economy rooms are cement-walled cells with shared bathrooms ($14), while the standard rooms are much smarter and have attached bathrooms and partial seaviews. $30

MYEIK ARCHIPELAGO

Andaman Club Thahtay Kyun Island ☎01 377891, ⍉andamanclub.com. A 15min motorboat ride from Kawthaung, this private island resort has everything from an 18-hole golf course to a casino. The staff are keen and the rooms are perfectly comfortable, with great views available from the seafront ones – although the hotel is frequently empty, and doesn't quite realize its potential

3

> ## THE BIRDS
>
> At dusk each day, clouds of swiftlets stream into an anonymous house on Strand Road. The suburban-looking home, its windows boarded over, is home to a **bird's-nest farm** – one of Myeik's weirdest industries. The story goes that a flock of swifts moved into the roof of the house. The entrepreneurial owner, realizing the value of his new tenants, moved out and turned his house into a man-made "cave", where the swifts could build their valuable nests, and he could sell them to Chinese gourmands keen to enjoy a bowl of bird's-nest soup.
>
> Landlords hoping to repeat his success have built structures without windows to replicate the darkness of the birds' natural homes, and play recordings of swifts' calls each day around dusk, which you'll hear throughout Myeik and Kawthaung, in the hope of attracting the birds.

for Bond-style glamour. No Myanmar visa necessary. **$100**

Boulder Bay Eco Resort Boulder Island ☎ 01 380382, ⓦ boulderasia.com. Newly opened eco-resort in the southern part of the archipelago. The cottages here are understated and comfortable, while the beach out front is worthy of a hundred stars. Activities on offer include diving, snorkelling, village visits and island hopping. Closed May–Oct. **$480**

Myanmar Andaman Resort Macleod Island ☎ 09 797 627 627, ⓦ www.myanmarandamanresort .com. Designed along eco-lodge lines, this attractive small hotel and its established dive centre offer beach bliss. Accommodation is either in luxurious cottages or in even more impressive rooms ($360), and rates include transfers, meals and most activities. Closed May–Oct. **$300**

EATING

Each evening a **night market** sets up on Strand Road south of the boat jetty from 5–10pm. It's an attractive place to eat, with views out to the Twin Islands, and the food is mostly focused on skewers, fried rice and salads – a meal will cost around K2000. There's also a small **morning market** (daily 6–11am) off C Rd, just south of the *Kyal Pyan* hotel. Dodge your way past the fish-sellers at the entrance and you'll find a range of delicious snacks on sale – try the *kawb moun*, a coconut-heavy batter cooked in an iron bowl until the edges are crispy and the centre is still moist.

Shwe Mon Family Restaurant Chinthe Thone Kaung St. A traditional Burmese curry buffet is on offer all day, every day here, but you'll need to arrive early to have much of a choice. Their pennywort salad is excellent, and a curry and rice combo will cost around K2000. Daily 10am–8pm.

Shwe Yar Su Strand Rd, 1km north of the town centre ☎ 05 941986. This is a well-regarded seafood restaurant and beer station, with a menu that basically comprises every creature that's ever paddled in the ocean. Among the more unusual offerings are giant mantis prawns and horseshoe crab eggs. Mains K2000–6000. Daily 3–11pm.

DIRECTORY

Banks There's a branch of AGD Bank on Bogyoke Rd, near the Independence Monument, with ATM and foreign exchange. KBZ Bank on Pyi Tawtar St also has an ATM.

Kawthaung

ကော့သောင်းမြို့

If you're in **KAWTHAUNG**, in the extreme south, you are likely to be focused either on getting to Thailand or starting the long journey north to Yangon. The small town isn't especially exciting, but there are a few things to see if you find yourself stuck here between connections.

While Kawthaung's outskirts sprawl along the coastline, the centre of town is compact and easy to navigate on foot. As you arrive at the jetty you'll see the **clocktower**, 100m inland – Airport Road curves uphill southwest of here, and the main market sits a block to the north. It's possible to stroll around the southernmost point of mainland Myanmar at **Bayinnaung Point** (originally named Victoria Point by the British, and renamed after the Burmese king who sacked Ayutthaya in 1564) and to the north of town is the **555 Viewpoint**, which offers great views of the islands and away across the border to Ranong.

Further afield, **Maliwan Waterfall** lies 40km overland to the northeast, and you can sunbathe at **Palutonetone Beach** on Thane Island 7km northwest, which is reached across a bridge from the mainland.

ARRIVAL AND DEPARTURE KAWTHAUNG

By plane Kawthaung's airport is 11km north of town (K3000 by motorbike taxi, K7000 in a tuk-tuk). Air KBZ, Apex Airlines and Myanmar Airways all operate daily flights to Yangon that stop briefly in Myeik.
Destinations Myeik (2–3 daily; 45min); Yangon (2–3 daily; 3hr).

By boat Boats to Ranong in Thailand (30min; 100 baht) depart from a temporary-looking jetty just north of where the fast boats arrive.
By bus There's a daily big bus to Myeik as well as twice-daily minibuses (9hr).

GETTING AROUND

By motorbike taxi and tuk-tuk A motorbike taxi around town will cost K1000, while the return trips out to Palutonetone Beach or 555 Viewpoint will cost K3000–3500 with waiting time. The longer journey out to Maliwan

Waterfall costs K8000–10,000, depending on your haggling skills. Tuk-tuks will cost at least double the motorbike taxi fare.

ACCOMMODATION

Honey Bear Hotel Strand Rd ☎ 059 51352. Right on Strand Rd, the front rooms here are noisy and have partially obscured sea views (there's an island in the way). It's pleasant enough inside, and this place is still the most conveniently located of Kawthaung's hotels, but keep in mind that the pricey en-suite rooms don't have hot water. $45

★ **Penguin** 339 Sabel St ☎ 059 51145, ⓦ penguinhotel kawthaung.wordpress.com. This extravagantly tiled guesthouse is tucked away in a backstreet, a sweaty 10min walk uphill from the jetty. Rooms are clean and neat, and there's a small restaurant downstairs. The hotel accepts US dollars, baht and kyat, with baht prices offering the best value for money. $30

EATING

J-Bon Coffee and Cold Airport Rd, 200m uphill southwest of the clocktower. This excellent teahouse, near the northern entrance to Bayinnaung Point and set in a leafy yard, offers a better-than-usual selection of cold drinks and teahouse snacks – their noodle salad is delicious – as well as a fine cup of Burmese coffee and lime. Mains around K2500. Daily 6am–6pm.
Love Coffee Shop Opposite the jetty. The first place you'll see as you get off the boat at the jetty, this little coffee shop has been serving good iced coffee and fried rice

to visa-runners for years. Mains K1500–2500, English menu. Daily 9am–9pm.
★ **Penguin** Near the clocktower. Down an anonymous side street (one block away from the clocktower towards the jetty, on the south side of the road), *Penguin* is the busiest restaurant on Kawthaung's dining scene – it's best to get here early before they run out of their delicious curries, seafood and side dishes (mains K2500). Vegetarian options available. Daily 9am–9pm.

DIRECTORY

Banks There's a KBZ Bank and ATM on Airport Rd near the *Kawthaung* hotel. To change baht you'll need to chance it at

one of the counters along Strand Rd.

KAWTHAUNG–RANONG BORDER CROSSING

The **Kawthaung–Ranong border crossing** straddles the Kra Buri or Pakchan River. Boats (100 baht one-way) cruise from one side to the other while the crossing is open (daily 6am–5.30pm, Myanmar time). There's one short stop on the edge of town, close to Kawthaung for Myanmar passport control, and another closer to Ranong for citizens of ASEAN member states, before you reach Thai passport control. Once you're outside the Thai border post, there are ATMs and it's about a 20 baht pick-up ride to Ranong bus station.

Central Myanmar

WATER FOUNTAIN PARK, NAYPYITAW

Central Myanmar

Stretching between the Shan Hills to the east and the Ayeyarwady River to the west, the lightly populated plains of central Myanmar (which includes parts of Bago, Mandalay and Magwe regions) comprise a flat and relatively featureless expanse of countryside whose modern-day somnolence belies its pivotal role in the history of the nation. The heartland of Bamar identity, the region is home to three of the country's former capitals – Pyay, Bagan and Taungoo – each of which successively controlled empires stretching across large parts of Myanmar, and sometimes beyond.

Today, many visitors to Myanmar fly straight from Yangon to the temples of Bagan (covered in chapter 5), and completely miss out on everything the rest of central Myanmar has to offer. If you have time on your hands, a road trip through this often parched region is incredibly rewarding, revealing the ruins of ancient capitals, gold-soaked pagodas, rock-hewn Buddhas, charming small towns and, perhaps most intriguing of all, Myanmar's new capital, Naypyitaw – a surreal city that speaks volumes about the vanity and insecurity of Myanmar's ex-military government.

There are two possible roads leading north from Yangon across this region. The Yangon–Mandalay Expressway, the fastest route north, allows you to stop in the moated town and former capital of **Taungoo** with its clutch of temples, fine lake views and hints of former glory, while further north personable **Meiktila** has plenty of small-town charm, a beautiful lakeside setting and a further sprinkling of colourful shrines. Midway between the two, the nation's bizarre new capital, **Naypyitaw**, is essential viewing for Myanmar at its most brazenly outlandish.

Alternatively, you can opt for the much slower road north from Yangon along National Highway 2. **Pyay**, one of the more enchanting towns in the country, is home to another major temple complex and the enigmatic remains of the ancient Pyu capital of **Thayekhittaya** (Sri Ksetra). The little-known ruins of **Beikthano**, the oldest of the historic Pyay city-states, lie half-buried in the undergrowth to the north of here, close to the lively town of Magwe.

Yangon to Mandalay

The modern **Expressway** between Yangon and Mandalay offers a swift and relatively painless route to both Mandalay and Bagan, although the personable towns of **Taungoo** and **Meiktila** offer an enjoyable slice of traditional Burmese small-town life if you fancy breaking the journey. Halfway between Yangon and Mandalay, the nation's new capital of **Naypyitaw** is required viewing if you're interested in the consummate madness of Myanmar's ruling military junta and the surreal excesses of modern urban planning gone wrong – although it doesn't have a lot to recommend it otherwise.

Ministries in motion p.187
Thayekhittaya (Sri Ksetra) orientation p.194

Ancient city of Beikthano p.196
Village life in Yenangyaung p.197

AKAUK TAUNG

Highlights

① Cycling the backroads Hire a bicycle and pedal down Taungoo's quiet backroads, past rustic farming villages, rice fields and tiny hidden pagodas. **See p.184**

② Fountain Garden The Day-Glo pink and green "dancing" fountains of Naypyitaw's Fountain Garden might be the most surreal sight in a city that specializes in surreal. **See p.187**

③ Shwesandaw Pagoda, Pyay Be wowed by one of the most beautiful pagodas in the country, with its views over a giant Buddha statue and collection of ancient relics. **See p.193**

④ Thayekhittaya (Sri Ksetra) Explore the sprawling remains of a once great city, and at the same time enjoy a glimpse into rural life in Myanmar. **See p.193**

⑤ Akauk Taung Take a slow boat down the Ayeyarwady River to admire the Buddhas hewn into the rock face by bored tax collectors. **See p.195**

⑥ Beikthano Veer off the beaten track and delve into days long past at the little-known archeological site of Beikthano. **See p.196**

⑦ Yenangyaung Get under the skin of rural life in Myanmar in Yenangyaung, where you can spend time visiting farming villages and supporting local communities. **See p.197**

HIGHLIGHTS ARE MARKED ON THE MAP ON P.182

Taungoo

တောင်ငူမြို့

Just off the old Yangon–Mandalay road (National Highway 1), and only 10km east of the newer (and faster) Yangon–Mandalay Expressway, the bustling little provincial city of **TAUNGOO** (aka Toungoo) has a cluster of low-key sights and heaps of friendly, off-the-beaten track character – as well as one of the region's most appealing guesthouses. Taungoo's engagingly small-town atmosphere belies its considerable significance in the history of Myanmar as the centre of the **Taungoo dynasty** (see p.362), for a time one of the largest empires in the history of Southeast Asia. Little remains of the city's glory days, however, the royal palace having been obliterated by Japanese bombers during World War II.

The heart of Taungoo is the original **moated city** – parts of the original moat survive, along with a few fragments of the original city walls. Imposing new eastern and western **gates** were built in 2010 to celebrate the city's five-hundredth birthday, with a large statue of Taungoo's founder, King Mingyinyo, erected just outside the east gate for good measure. In the southwestern corner of the walled city, the fine **Kandawgyi Lake** is a pleasant spot for a bike ride or stroll, with an attractive string of cafés along its eastern

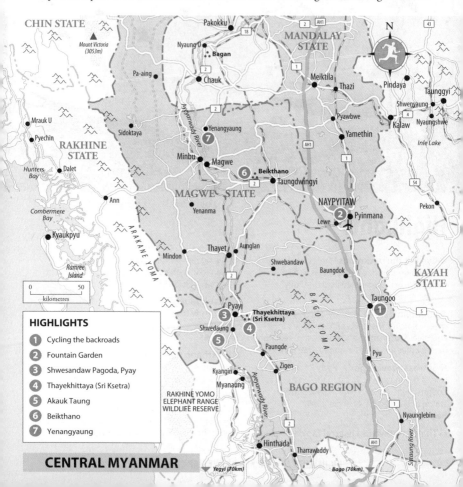

HIGHLIGHTS

1. Cycling the backroads
2. Fountain Garden
3. Shwesandaw Pagoda, Pyay
4. Thayekhittaya (Sri Ksetra)
5. Akauk Taung
6. Beikthano
7. Yenangyaung

CENTRAL MYANMAR

side and the fanciful temple-style roofs of the *Royal Kaytumadi* hotel (see p.185) rising across the water.

Shwesandaw Pagoda

ရွှေဆံတော်ဘုရား • Daily 6am–9pm • Free

The most impressive of Taungoo's various temples, the **Shwesandaw Pagoda** sits more or less in the centre of the old walled city, its large gilded stupa rising high above the surrounding streets. The stupa was built in 1597 on the site of a much older structure, which is said to have contained hair relics of the Buddha (the temple's name means "Golden Sacred Hair Relic").

   The most interesting approach is from the east via a long covered walkway, which is initially lined with shops selling assorted religious items, before passing through a pretty jumble of stupas and monastic quarters. From here, a short flight of steps leads up to a stupa, which is very similar in outline to the Shwedagon in Yangon, with eighty-odd miniature stupas stacked up around its lower two terraces. Various statues in glass cabinets stand around the terrace, showing scenes from the life of the Buddha and processions of kings and monks, and murals depict the gory punishments awaiting sinners in hell. A striking Mandalay-style Buddha sits in the shrine on the west side of the stupa, gifted to the temple in 1912 by a retired civil servant who donated his own body weight in silver and bronze. On the opposite (eastern) side of the stupa, there's a large, recently constructed reclining Buddha.

Myasigon Pagoda

မြစည်းခုံဘုရား • Daily 7am–8pm • Free • The museum is usually locked, but you can ask someone to unlock it for a donation of around K1000

4

Close to the southern edge of the walled city centre, the glitzy **Myasigon** (or Mizagon) **Pagoda** offers a complete contrast to the traditional Shwesandaw. The temple's small stupa seems almost an afterthought to the adjacent shrine, with its huge gilded Buddha ensconced in a shiny-bright pavilion covered in dazzling glass mosaics. Outside, the terrace surrounding the stupa is home to an unusually kitsch model of Kyaiktiyo (the Golden Rock; see p.148), complete with miniature steps and shrines rising out of a sculpted forest, plus a couple of tiny, doe-eyed elephants.

   In the northwest corner of the terrace, a cream-coloured building houses a small **museum** containing various Buddhas and other religious artefacts, a statue of the three-headed elephant Erawan (the mount of Indra), plus a few old colonial-era notes and coins and a very dusty old soda bottle. Though the museum's usually kept locked, you can get a decent look through the window slats if you don't manage to find someone with a key.

Kandawgyi Lake

ကန်တော်ကြီး

The western side of the old town is dominated by the large and pretty **Kandawgyi Lake**, which dates from the sixteenth century. It's flanked on all sides by grand, old trees, and there's a landscaped garden and children's amusement park towards the northern end – this is one of the best places in town for an evening promenade. Also look out for the cafés dotted around the eastern edge.

Kaunghmudaw Pagoda

ကောင်းမှုတော်ဘုရား • 1.5km west of town (follow the road out of the west gate)

Set in beautiful countryside west of Taungoo centre, the pretty **Kaunghmudaw Pagoda** makes a good target for a leisurely out-of-town bike ride. Flamboyantly roofed stairways lead from the north and east to the terrace and the small but elaborately sculpted gold stupa, with leering chinthe standing guard at each corner, surrounded by the usual impressive bo tree, bell, prayer pole and inevitable model of the Kyaiktiyo (see p.148).

TAUNGOO

■ ACCOMMODATION
Amazing Kaytu	1
Mother's House Hotel	3
Myanmar Beauty Guesthouse II, III & IV	4
Royal Kaytumadi Hotel	2

● EATING
Aung Moe Hein	1

ARRIVAL AND DEPARTURE

TAUNGOO

By bus Buses stop at various bus company offices along National Highway 1. A motorbike taxi to *Myanmar Beauty Guesthouse* or *Mother's House Hotel* (see below) costs around K1500 with luggage.

Destinations Bago (hourly; 5hr); Hpa-An (2 daily; 7hr); Kalaw (daily; 10hr); Mandalay (2 daily; 7hr); Meiktila (hourly; 5hr); Naypyitaw (hourly; 2hr 30min); Thazi

(hourly; 5hr); Yangon (hourly; 5hr).

By train The railway station is on the south side of the centre, just inside the city walls.

Destinations Bago (3 daily; 4hr 30min); Mandalay (3 daily; 8–9hr); Naypyitaw (3 daily; 2hr 30min); Thazi (3 daily; 6hr); Yangon (3 daily; 7hr).

GETTING AROUND

By bicycle Central Taungoo is compact enough to be covered on foot, but renting a bicycle (for around K3000/day) from *Myanmar Beauty* is a nice way to explore,

especially if you want to go out to Kaunghmudaw Pagoda.
By motorbike taxi A motorbike taxi from one of the out-of-town guesthouses to the centre costs around K1500.

ACCOMMODATION

Amazing Kaytu Off Yangon–Mandalay Rd ☎054 23977, ⊛amazing-hotel.com. Neat, modern little hotel set slightly off the main road and just a short walk from the town centre. Standard rooms upstairs (with TVs, a/c, hot water and fridges) are pokey and old-fashioned; superior rooms downstairs cost just $6 extra and are much more attractively decorated, with prints of flowers and plants on the walls – though they're still on the small side. $40
Mother's House Hotel 501 Yangon–Mandalay Rd, 3km south of town ☎054 24240, ⊜motherhousehotel @gmail.com. A reasonable place, although slightly too close to the main road for complete comfort. Cheaper rooms (with hot water, a/c, TVs and fridges) are pleasant

enough, although it's worth paying an extra $5 for one of the larger and more attractive wood-panelled bungalows around the back. There's also a small restaurant attached, though it's right on the road. $30
★Myanmar Beauty Guesthouse II, III & IV 3km south of town, just off the east side of the Yangon–Mandalay Rd ☎054 25073 or ☎09 784 040 402. Overlooking the fields south of town, this lovely guesthouse justifies a stopover in Taungoo all by itself. Rooms are spread over three separate wooden buildings. Those in building *II* (en-suite, cold water only) are simplest and cheapest, but perfectly adequate – though they're not always keen to rent them to foreign visitors; those in *III*

($30) are more attractively furnished and have hot water, a/c and little balconies; while those in *IV* ($49) are full of interesting knick-knacks and have beautiful views over rice paddies, far-off mountains and a large pond (and there are no TVs to spoil the peace). All rates include a spectacular breakfast featuring a huge spread of local fruits, samosas and all sorts of wonderful sticky-rice concoctions. They also have creaky old bikes for rent (K3000/day). **$25**

Royal Kaytumadi Hotel Taw Win Kaytumadi Rd

☎ 054 24761, ⓦ kmahotels.com. Taungoo's fanciest hotel (owned by a company with strong ex-military government links) occupies a string of quaint pagoda-style bungalows dotted around extensive gardens in a beautiful location right next to the lake. Rooms (try to get one facing the water) are nicely decorated with wooden floors and chintzy furniture, and facilities include a big pool, plus a gym and spa. Cheaper rooms face the road and can be noisy. **$85**

EATING

Aung Moe Hein Off Bo Hmu Po Kun Rd. This cheap, open-fronted beer station-style place is a solidly Burmese affair rather than a tourist-orientated restaurant. The menu is in Burmese only and staff speak little English, which means that for most people it's going to be a point-and-guess ordering experience. Expect plenty of chicken and pork curries, as well as the usual Chinese basics. The sign is in Burmese only, so you'll likely need to ask someone to point it out. Mains mostly K2000–2500. Daily 8.30am–10pm.

DIRECTORY

Banks There are ATMs at the AGD Bank and Ayeyarwady Bank on the main Yangon–Mandalay road just east of town, and at the AGD Bank and CB Bank close to one another on the same road just south of the market. There's also a KBZ ATM in the middle of the old town.

Naypyitaw

4

နေပြည်တော်

Quite possibly the world's weirdest capital, the newly created city of **NAYPYITAW** (aka Nay Pyi Taw, Nay Pyi Daw or Naypyidaw – meaning "Abode of the Kings") occupies a strategic location between Yangon and Mandalay, and was built largely in secret and unveiled in 2005 as the brainchild of Myanmar's military government (see box, p.187). The official reason given for the sudden relocation was a lack of space in Yangon, although rumours suggest the decision to move the capital was taken by Senior General Than Shwe, after his personal astrologer warned him of the possibility of an invasion from the sea. The location of the new capital – complete with a substantial military presence – close to the historically turbulent Shan, Kayah and Kayin states may also have been a factor in the decision.

For the average visitor, Naypyitaw is interesting mainly as a study in contemporary **urban planning** at its most OTT – and for the gaping disconnect between the city and the rest of Myanmar. Spread over an area that's estimated to be over six times the size of New York, the new capital is simultaneously outlandish, brazen and faintly lunatic – a vast wilderness of eight-lane highways (largely deserted, except when the motorcade of a passing general or visiting dignitary shatters the silence), supersized roundabouts, grandiloquent government buildings and overblown hotels more reminiscent of the modern cities of the Arabian Gulf than anything remotely Burmese.

The city is divided into specific, dedicated **zones**. The ministerial zone contains all the government ministry buildings and is generally out of bounds to foreigners without a specific invite. The diplomatic zone is, as the name suggests, where the foreign diplomatic community is supposed to be based, except that, aside from the embassy of Bangladesh, all the embassies and diplomats have chosen to remain in Yangon. The hotel zone contains a ridiculous number of massive hotel complexes, few of which are ever full. This is the area where you will stay. The shopping zone contains not much at all, but is basically the centre of the city. Finally, there's the heavily fortified military zone, which is where the generals luxuriate in their palatial houses. This area is absolutely out of bounds to civilians. City life, such as it is, is confined to a few stringently demarcated market zones plus a couple of modern malls, while specific sights, barring the vast Uppatasanti Pagoda, are few.

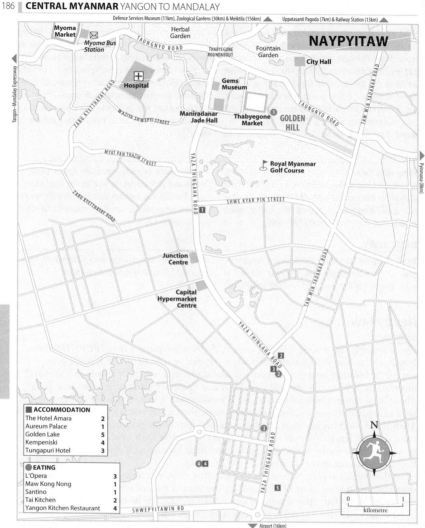

NAYPYITAW

Myoma Market

Herbal Garden

Myoma Bus Station

TAUNGNYO ROAD

THABYEGONE ROUNDABOUT

Fountain Garden

City Hall

Yangon–Mandalay Expressway

Hospital

ZABU KYETHAVIN ROAD

WAZIYA SHWEPYI STREET

Gems Museum

Maniradanar Jade Hall

Thabyegone Market

GOLDEN HILL

TAUNGNYO ROAD

LAW WIN YADANAR ROAD

MYAT PAN THAZIN STREET

YAZA THINGAHA ROAD

Royal Myanmar Golf Course

ZABU KYETTHAYAY ROAD

SHWE KYAR PIN STREET

1

Junction Centre

Capital Hypermarket Centre

YAZA THINGAHA ROAD

LAW WIN YADANAR ROAD

2

3
2

4

ACCOMMODATION

The Hotel Amara	2
Aureum Palace	1
Golden Lake	5
Kempeniski	4
Tungapuri Hotel	3

EATING

L'Opera	3
Maw Kong Nong	1
Santino	1
Tai Kitchen	2
Yangon Kitchen Restaurant	4

4 4

YAZA THINGAHA ROAD

5

SHWEPYITAWIN RD

N

0   1
kilometre

Airport (16km)

Pyinmana (8km)

Uppatasanti Pagoda

ဥပ္ပါတသန္တိစေတီတော် • Yaza Htarni Rd, around 9km from Thabyegone Roundabout • Daily 6am–9pm • Free; the $5 foreigners' entrance fee was not being asked for at the time of writing • A taxi/motorbike taxi from the Yaza Thingaha Rd hotels will cost around K15,000/K8000 return, and there's usually an hour wait

Naypyitaw's most prominent monument, the **Uppatasanti Pagoda** (although local pronunciation makes it sound more like "Uppatadaani") looms above the city's largely flat and featureless hinterlands, and is visible for many kilometres in every direction. Completed in 2009, the pagoda was offered as a merit-making act by the man responsible for the city, Senior General Than Shwe, and his wife (displaying a distinct parallel with Burmese kings). The name, roughly translating as "protection against calamity", derives from a sixteenth-century Buddhist sutra designed to be recited at times of crisis, and particularly when confronted with the threat of foreign invasion – a telling allusion to Naypyitaw's founding *raison d'être* and the prevailing paranoid fear of invasion.

A near-copy of the Shwedagon in Yangon (although it comes in at a symbolic 30cm shorter), the Uppatasanti is impressively huge from a distance, although less remarkable close up when the shoddiness of the workmanship, including lots of cheap gold paint with red and white smears, becomes apparent – only the topmost section of the spire is properly gilded. Three grand staircases lead up to the **terrace** (although only the eastern stairs are usually open, and most visitors take the lift). The terrace itself is huge, windswept and depressingly bare, with only a couple of token Buddha statues and a single huge prayer pole to relieve the emptiness, although the sweeping views partly compensate.

The pagoda's chief peculiarity is that it's hollow. A huge square pillar stands in the centre of the green-and-gold **interior**, as if carrying the weight of the stupa on its shoulders. Fine carvings showing scenes from Buddhist mythology, history and the life of the Buddha are arrayed around the sides. Visit around sunset, when most pagodas across Myanmar are humming with activity, and what will likely strike you about the Uppatasanti is the dearth of people – a far cry from the Shwedagon.

In a small pen near the bottom of the eastern stairs you'll find the pagoda's celebrated menagerie of five **white elephants** (see p.82), which can often be seen here munching on bamboo (although they're sometimes taken off for exercise elsewhere), plus a couple of smaller ordinary elephants. Locals regard these rare creatures as being extremely auspicious, though sceptical foreigners may feel the animals provide an apt symbol of Naypyitaw itself – given that it's essentially nothing but an enormous white elephant of a slightly different kind.

Fountain Garden

4

ရေပန်းဉယျာဉ် • Taungnyo Rd • Daily 8am–9pm • K700

Just east of Thabyegone Roundabout, and providing a pleasant change of scene from the concrete wasteland outside, is the pretty ornamental **Fountain Garden**, set either side of the small Ngalait River; a pair of small bridges traverse the water, employing an enjoyably wobbly, jungle-style design. Lush clumps of bougainvillea, palms and topiary trees abound, along with assorted pavilions, a playground with water slide, and a musical clock, none of whose four faces can agree on the correct time.

Although it's worth a visit at any time of the day, this garden really comes into its own around dusk and shortly after dark, when the fountains light up in fluorescent

---

MINISTRIES IN MOTION

Myanmar's new **capital** was constructed amid cloak-and-dagger secrecy between 2002 and 2005, at an estimated cost of around $4 billion on a greenfield site between the old Yangon–Mandalay highway and the small towns of Pyinmana and Lewe. Following its unveiling, government ministries were moved en masse from Yangon, with staff being given 48 hours to relocate (though their families were temporarily banned from following). Meanwhile, the foreign diplomatic community remains stubbornly entrenched in Yangon – so far the only embassy to have moved into the city's designated diplomatic zone is that of Bangladesh.

The city's long-suffering bureaucrats, summarily transferred from Yangon, now occupy Lego-like swathes of dormitory suburbs, their roofs colour-coded to signify the status of the officials within, while the ruling elite have ensconced themselves in the city's fiercely guarded **military zone** (strictly off limits to casual visitors), allegedly complete with many kilometres of tunnels and bunkers, and eight-lane highways designed so jets can land on them. There is also a vast military parade ground in this zone, overseen by statues of kings Anawrahta, Bayinnaung and Alaungpaya – Myanmar's three greatest empire-builders, and greatly beloved of the army bigwigs – often featuring in militaristic propaganda, though inaccessible to the average citizen.

Surprisingly, Naypyitaw's population is already nudging the million mark, making it Myanmar's third-largest city and one of the world's fastest-growing urban centres – although you'd hardly guess this, given the largely deserted and decidedly moribund atmosphere. The entire place still feels very much like a work in – perhaps permanent – progress.

shades, Euro pop blasts out of loud speakers and the fountains "dance" to the thudding beats while an appreciative audience of locals ooh and aah.

Gems Museum

ကျောက်မျက်ရတနာပြတိုက် • Yaza Thingaha Rd, 400m south of Thabyegone Roundabout • Tues–Sun 9am–4pm • $5

Next to the distinctive, flying-saucer-shaped Maniradanar Jade Hall exhibition centre, the modest, one-room **Gems Museum** serves up a decent overview of Myanmar's gem production. On show are assorted rubies, sapphire, lots of jade and the country's largest pearl, although few visitors find it worth the inflated admission price.

Defence Services Museum

စစ်သမိုင်းပြတိုက် • Zeyathiri Township • Mon–Thurs, Sat & Sun 10am–4pm • $20

Even compared to the size of Naypyitaw, the **Defence Services Museum** is incredibly grand in scale, based some 10km northeast of the city centre. Spread across its simply enormous six hundred acres are several aircraft hangars stuffed with military hardware and history, as well as a lake showcasing multiple examples of Myanmar's navy ships. Almost all of the displays push the military's propaganda, so it's an interesting place to visit – if only to get an idea of how the country's generals view the world.

Zoological Gardens and Safari Park

တိရစ္ဆာန်ဥယျာဉ်နှင့် ဆာဖာရီဥယျာဉ် • Zeyar Thiri, a 45min drive northeast of the centre • **Zoological Gardens** Tues–Sun 8.30am–8pm • $10 • **Safari Park** Tues–Sun 8.30am–4.30pm • $20 • A taxi to the zoo will cost around $25–30 return

Naypyitaw's **Zoological Gardens and Safari Park** claim to be the largest in Southeast Asia, and are home to over six hundred animals, including white tigers, leopards, elephants, kangaroos and, most famously, a group of penguins living in a specially built air-conditioned cage. Unfortunately, the zoo has deteriorated since it opened and the animals are no longer well cared for, so it is worth avoiding.

ARRIVAL AND DEPARTURE NAYPYITAW

By plane Naypyitaw's shiny new airport is 16km southeast of the centre. A taxi from here into town (there are no buses) will cost around K10,000.

Destinations Bangkok (6 weekly; 2hr); Heho (daily; 40min); Mandalay (3 daily; 50min); Yangon (5 daily; 1hr).

By bus The main Myoma Bus Station is on Yan Myo Thant Sin Rd, around 6km northwest of the hotel zone. Approaching from the south, you may be able to hop off on Yaza Thingaha Rd, where most of the city's hotels are located.

Destinations Kalaw (daily; 5hr); Lashio (daily; 13hr); Mandalay (7 daily; 4hr); Mawlamyine (2 daily; 11–12hr); Meiktila (7 daily; 3hr); Pyin Oo Lwin (2 daily; 8hr); Taungoo (hourly; 2hr 30min); Yangon (10 daily; 6hr).

By train The huge railway station is in a hugely inconvenient location 14km north of Uppatasanti Pagoda, a K17,000 taxi journey from town.

Destinations Bago (5 daily; 7–8hr); Mandalay (2 daily; 6–7hr); Taungoo (3 daily; 2hr 30min); Thazi (3 daily; 3hr); Yangon (3 daily; 9–10hr).

GETTING AROUND

By motorbike taxi Naypyitaw is way too big to even think about walking around. Motorbike taxis hang out around many of the hotels, Capital Hypermarket Centre, Junction Centre and Myoma Market – count on around K4000 for the trip from Myoma Market to the Yaza Thingaha hotels, or around K10,000 for a half-day tour of the city.

By taxi There are usually taxis for hire outside the Capital Hypermarket Centre, or you can book one through your hotel.

ACCOMMODATION

All accommodation is located in what is known as the Hotel Zone, which lines **Yaza Thingaha Road**, and none of it is small or subtle. Most of the hotels still seem as if they're fresh out of their wrappings, although the lack of visitors can make them feel decidedly moribund. There are no budget places to stay, although the massive glut of accommodation at least means that most places are excellent value.

The Hotel Amara 11 Yaza Thingaha Rd ☏ 067 422201, ⓦ thehotelamara.com. A very good-value option, where even the cheapest rooms have polished wooden floors and elegant bedspreads. Pricier rooms are stretched out along a man-made lake and, as with all the hotels in Naypyitaw, there is an abundance of space. $55

Aureum Palace Yaza Thingaha Rd ☎067 420746, Ⓦaureumpalacehotel.com. This is an impressive resort, with appealing contemporary Asian styling and attentive service. Accommodation is scattered around extensive grounds overlooking a small lake; rooms are bright and spacious, and come with desks, wardrobes, tables and comfy chairs. Facilities include a big (although shallow) pool, gym and spa. Also goes by the name *Shwe Nan Taw Hotel*. $59

Golden Lake Yaza Thingaha Rd ☎067 434022, Ⓔthegoldenlakehotelnpt@gmail.com. The cheapest option in the city has English-speaking staff and simple, but surprisingly smart, rooms set in a concrete block overlooking nothing in particular. Even so, it's a good deal.

Rooms without bathrooms cost just K21,000, and it also has smarter suites and villas. K31,000

Kempinski Shwe Pyi Taw Win Rd ☎067 8106061, Ⓦwww.kempinski.com. This is the top choice of diplomats and movers and shakers. The enormous *Kempinski* has contemporary chic business rooms and a pool, as well as the appropriately named *Diplomat Bar* and the superb *Yangon Kitchen Restaurant* (see below). Frequently offers big discounts if you book online. $174

Tungapuri Hotel 9/10 Yaza Thingaha Rd ☎067 422020, Ⓦtungapurihotel.com. Feeling more lived-in than most along Yaza Thingaha, this hotel has some of the city's cheapest rooms, plus good attached Thai (see below) and Chinese restaurants. Usually, a discount of around thirty percent is given almost before you can open your mouth to ask for a room. K35,000

EATING

★**L'Opera** Nirvana Hotel, Yaza Thingaha Rd ☎067 422253, Ⓦoperayangon.com. This is the best Italian restaurant In Naypyitaw, and may even be one of the best restaurants in the entire country. The chefs at *l'Opera* serve up beautifully presented dishes such as linguini with cuttlefish ink and beef tenderloin with black truffle sauce. There's also a huge open-plan wine cellar. Needless to say, there aren't many backpackers eating here. Mains K15,000–43,000. Daily 10am–10.30pm.

Maw Kong Nong Golden Hill, near Thabyegone Market. This big hilltop beer station is one of the few places in central Naypyitaw resembling a local Burmese restaurant, and it has decent traditional food (with an English menu) such as the usual Shan noodles, plus dishes like fried chicken with green mustard, fried pork with bamboo shoots, and Shan meat and vegetable salads. Choose from what's shown in the cabinet (two meat plus one veg dish for K2500) or go à la carte (mains around K5000). There's another branch, *May Kong Nong II*, with over thirty different curries ready in the glass cabinet, at the bottom of the hill. Daily 10am–midnight.

Santino Golden Hill, near Thabyegone Market.

Bright, modern restaurant serving up a huge selection of Western, Thai, Japanese and Burmese dishes (mains K4000–6000), plus good Western and Burmese breakfasts. There's also a small in-house bakery and good coffee. Daily 7am–10pm.

Tai Kitchen Next to the Tungapuri Hotel, Yaza Thingaha Rd ☎067 422282. Large and pleasantly lively restaurant serving up a big menu of authentic Thai cuisine, plus a few traditional Shan dishes – the *pad thai* (K5500) is as good as you'll get in Myanmar, and there's a good drinks list and coffee selection too. Mains K5000–8000. Daily 8am–10pm.

★**Yangon Kitchen Restaurant** Kempinski Hotel, Shwe Pyi Taw Win Rd ☎067 8106061. Fancy dining on Norwegian salmon or duck confit? The *Yangon Kitchen*, inside the upmarket *Kempinski Hotel*, is one of the most exclusive restaurants in Myanmar, and the food and presentation couldn't be further away from the curries and salads that most Burmese eat on a day-to-day basis. Inside, you're likely to encounter large parties of military top brass with jackets covered in medals, and the perfumed wives of various diplomats. Mains K18,000–25,000. Daily noon–3pm & 6–10.30pm.

DIRECTORY

Bank There are several ATMs at both the Capital Hypermarket Centre and Junction Centre, as well as at

several of the hotels. There's also a moneychanger in the Capital Hypermarket.

Meiktila

မိတ္ထီလာမြို့

The attractive lakeside town of **MEIKTILA** is an agreeable place to break the journey north from Yangon to Mandalay. The town stands at something of a crossroads, with connections west to Bagan, east to Inle Lake and north to Lashio, as well as to Mandalay and Yangon. It's also one of central Myanmar's prettiest and most enjoyably low-key destinations, with its shrine-studded lake, bustling market and tree-lined

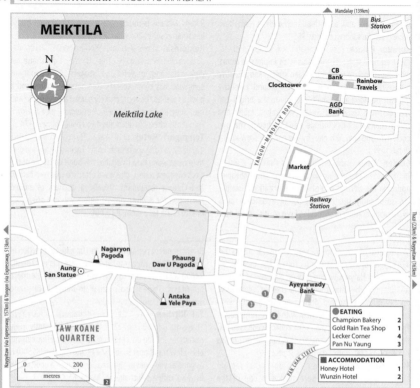

MEIKTILA

N

Bus Station

Meiktila Lake

Clocktower

CB Bank

Rainbow Travels

AGD Bank

YANGON–MANDALAY ROAD

Market

Railway Station

Thazi (22km) & Naypyitaw (163km)

Naypyitaw via Expressway, 157km) & Yangon (via Expressway, 513km)

Nagaryon Pagoda

Aung San Statue

Phaung Daw U Pagoda

Antaka Yele Paya

Ayeyarwady Bank

TAW KOANE QUARTER

PAN CHAN STREET

0   200
metres

● EATING
Champion Bakery	2
Gold Rain Tea Shop	1
Lecker Corner	4
Pan Nu Yaung	3

■ ACCOMMODATION
Honey Hotel	1
Wunzin Hotel	2

4

streets – although present appearances belie the town's turbulent past. The town is famously the site of one of Southeast Asia's bloodiest conflicts when, between February and March 1945, British forces killed 20,000 Japanese soldiers in a final battle for the control of Burma, devastating the town. Later, catastrophic fires enveloped Meiktila in 1974 and 1991, while in March 2013 the town hit the international headlines when **Buddhist mobs** went on the rampage against their Muslim neighbours (formerly comprising around thirty percent of the population), killing over forty people and forcing an estimated 12,000 others from their homes while government security forces, it's alleged, stood by and watched.

Meiktila Lake

မိတ္ထီလာကန်

In the middle of town is **Meiktila Lake**, fringed with shrines and stupas and crossed by two bridges. Next to the southern bridge you'll immediately notice Meiktila's most memorable landmark, the striking (in a Disney way rather than a beautiful way) **Phaung Daw U Pagoda**, constructed in the form of a large boat, with soaring stern and the head of a mythical karaweik (aka *karavika*) bird. Inside, the temple's single wood-panelled hall is largely bare, save for a single gold stupa and a few entertaining paintings illustrating moral fables from ancient and modern Burma.

Crossing the bridge, you'll see (on your left) the diminutive **Antaka Yele Paya**, comprising a small stupa and shrine perched amid the waters of the lake, connected to the shore by a long wooden footbridge. At the time of research it was undergoing restoration, but you could still walk to it. Continuing along the main road just past here you'll reach the **Nagaryon Pagoda**, built in honour of the Japanese soldiers killed in Meiktila during World War II. A gilded statue of Aung San stands outside.

The market

East of the Yangon–Mandalay road, north of the railway station • Most stalls open daily 8am–6pm

It's worth having a wander through Meiktila's sprawling and enjoyably ramshackle **market**, where hundreds of hawkers sit beneath lopsided parasols and sell vegetables and other produce, and shopkeepers measure rice, pulses, tea and spices from cut-down oil drums.

ARRIVAL AND INFORMATION   MEIKTILA

By bus and motorbike taxi The bus station is just northeast of the clocktower at the northern end of town, although services usually also drop off passengers along the main road. On arrival, there are plenty of motorbike taxis available to ferry you across town, although the place is small enough that you could just walk. Agents selling bus tickets can be found all along the road running east from the clocktower.

Destinations Bagan (daily; 3hr 30min); Lashio (5 daily; 10–11hr, with some services continuing to the Chinese border at Muse); Magwe (2 daily; 4hr 30min); Mandalay (7 daily; 3hr); Naypyitaw (7 daily; 3hr); Sittwe (daily; 26hr); Taunggyi (3–4 daily; 4hr); Yangon (6 daily; 9–10hr).

By train The railway station is more centrally located than the bus station, just southeast of the market, although it's situated on a small branch line with limited services. To reach Yangon, Mandalay or Lake Inle it's much easier to go to nearby Thazi – where regular pick-ups run from the bus station (45min), leaving when full – and pick up a train there.

Services There are ATMs at the CB Bank, next to Rainbow Travels, at the AGD Bank opposite, and the Ayeyarwady Bank.

GETTING AROUND

By motorbike taxi Meiktila is easily walkable, although there are plenty of motorbike taxis (identifiable by their drivers' official jackets) around town. Count on K500–1000 per journey.

ACCOMMODATION

Honey Hotel Pan Chan St, near the lake ☎ 064 23588. Medium-sized hotel in a peaceful spot overlooking the lake. Rooms (all large with a/c and – in theory if not always in practice – hot water) are a bit grubby but perfectly ok for a night, if you don't mind the rock-hard mattresses and feral dogs in the street outside. $5 extra gets you a TV and minibar. **$35**

Wunzin Hotel Taw Koane Quarter ☎ 064 23848. In a quiet location just across the lake (and next to the one and only court of Meiktila Tennis Club – rackets available), this good-value hotel has large, and starkly furnished, rooms in the main building with lake views, lots of sunlight and decent bathrooms ($50). The cheaper rooms are smaller, smellier and lack lake views, but are otherwise clean and quiet. It also goes by the name of *Floral Breeze Hotel* or a combination of both names. **$30**

EATING

There's a convivial little cluster of teahouses and cafés along the street around the *Gold Rain Tea Shop*, while towards dusk dozens of food stalls set up here, creating one of the region's most appealing **night markets**. For breakfast *mohinga*, there's a good stall about five buildings west of the *Pan Nu Yaung* restaurant.

Champion Bakery Yangon–Mandalay Rd. Stock up here for a long road journey with fresh breads, cakes, sandwiches and biscuits. Sandwiches are around K500–1000. Daily 7am–9pm.

Gold Rain Tea Shop Off Yangon–Mandalay Rd. One of a cluster of lively teahouses along this side street, with tables set out on the broad pavements and serving up tea, coffee and enormous Chinese-style buns stuffed with minced chicken or pork. Nothing you eat here is likely to cost more than K1500. Daily 6am–8pm.

Lecker Corner Off Yangon–Mandalay Rd. This smart restaurant has taken Meiktila's limited eating scene several notches upmarket. A small army of staff will greet you here, and the menu includes a big list of authentic Thai dishes plus a slightly shorter and less interesting Chinese selection, backed up by a long drinks list. Mains K2500–5000. Daily 10am–9pm.

Pan Nu Yaung Yangon–Mandalay Rd. Popular local restaurant dishing up cheap rice and noodle snacks, including *mohinga* (K500–1000), alongside Thai, Burmese and Chinese mains, with most dishes going for K1500–3500. The sign is written In Burmese only, but confusingly there's a bright red sign out front saying "Dot" in English. Daily 8am–9pm.

Yangon to Bagan

Journeying between Yangon and Bagan, most travellers nowadays either fly or take an express bus via the Yangon–Mandalay Expressway. With more time on your hands, you could follow the slower route along the old Yangon–Bagan highway via the riverside city of **Pyay**, one of the country's oldest settlements and also the starting point for the long bus journey to Ngapali. Further north, and a short way off the main route, the near-forgotten remains of the ancient city of **Beikthano** will please history buffs, while **Magwe** sees few visitors but has bus connections west to Sittwe and Mrauk U – although these are still the preserve of the adventurous few.

Pyay and around

ပြည်မြို့

With one of central Myanmar's finest temples, the **Shwesandaw Pagoda**, and the ruins of ancient **Thayekhittaya** (Sri Ksetra) nearby, **PYAY**, the largest city on the old Yangon–Bagan highway, is easily the most enjoyable town to visit in central Myanmar. Pyay, which is pronounced variously as either "Pay" or "Pea", lies around 275km north of Yangon (350km south of Bagan) and has a gorgeous setting on the banks of the Ayeyarwady River.

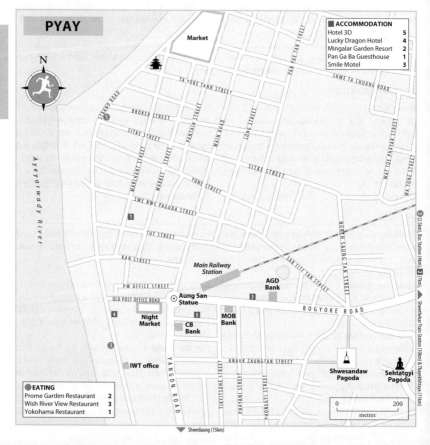

PYAY

Market

N

ACCOMMODATION
Hotel 3D	5
Lucky Dragon Hotel	4
Mingalar Garden Resort	2
Pan Ga Ba Guesthouse	1
Smile Motel	3

SPENKO ROAD

TA YOKE TANN STREET

SHWE TA CHUANG ROAD

PAN PAE TAN STREET

BROKER STREET

SITKE STREET

PANTAIN STREET

MAIN ROAD

LON STREET

SITKE STREET

WATT GE PHAYAR STREET

MA YONE STREET

MERCHANT STREET

MARKET STREET

YONE STREET

SWE NWE PAGODA STREET

TUT STREET

NORTH SAUNG TAN STREET

KAN STREET

A y e y a r w a d y   R i v e r

Main Railway Station

SAR TITE TAN STREET

AGD Bank

PW OFFICE STREET

OLD POST OFFICE ROAD

Aung San Statue

Night Market

CB Bank

MOB Bank

BOGYOKE ROAD

IWT office

YANGON ROAD

TIKYI SONE STREET

PHAYANI STREET

PHONEGYI STREET

ANAUK ZAUNGTAN STREET

Shwesandaw Pagoda

Sehtatgyi Pagoda

EATING
Prome Garden Restaurant	2
Wish River View Restaurant	3
Yokohama Restaurant	1

0   200
metres

(2.5km); Bus Station (4km); (7km); Shwebonbar Train Station (10km) & Thayekhittaya (11km)

Shwedaung (15km)

One of the oldest settlements in Myanmar, Pyay's history stretches back to the days of ancient Sri Ksetra (see p.358). The town subsequently developed into a major centre during the colonial era after being captured by the British in 1825 (who named it "Prome") and then retaken in 1852 during the Second Anglo-Burmese War. Burma's first railway line was completed here in 1877, connecting colonial Prome with Rangoon, while at the end of the colonial period the city was the scene of major fighting between British and Japanese forces during World War II.

The market

Strand Rd, 10min walk north of the centre • Most stalls open daily 8am–6pm

North of the centre is Pyay's large, interesting and slightly chaotic **market**. A long row of *thanaka*-wood vendors sit lined up along the waterfront at the front of the market – the Shinmadaung *thanaka* tree (one of several used to produce *thanaka* paste; see box, p.7) grows abundantly in the Pyay district, and although mass-produced *thanaka* creams are widely available, many Burmese still prefer to grind their own. There's a large **Chinese temple** on the corner of Ta Yoke Tann Street on the south side of the market.

Shwesandaw Pagoda and around

ရွှေဆံတော်စေတီ • Bogyoke Rd • Daily 6am–9pm • K3000

The main sight in town is the **Shwesandaw Pagoda** ("Golden Hair Relic Temple"), which rises high above the southern side of Bogyoke Road, to which it's connected by 160 steep stairs lined with shops (there's also a lift, although – as ever – it's much more fun to walk). The majestic central stupa, said to contain a couple of the Buddha's hairs, is one of the largest and most dazzling in the country – a metre taller than the Shwedagon in Yangon itself, with every surface gilded and polished to a glittering, golden sheen. The spire, topped (unusually) with not one but two *hti*, is uncharacteristically large in relation to the bell below, giving the whole thing a distinctively slender outline – particularly spectacular when floodlit at night.

In the northeast corner of the courtyard the small and dusty **Pyay Shwe San Daw Museum** (donation) houses assorted monastic artefacts, including a beautiful miniature *karaweik* and a couple of intricately carved ivory tusks. Also on display are a few interesting old photos, including shots of the Gurkha Rifles entering Prome in 1945.

Slightly further around (heading clockwise), a tiny model of the stupa sits in what looks like a giant birdcage, with good views of the Sehtatgyi Pagoda (see below) to the rear. On the south side of the terrace, a shrine holds a replica of the Buddha's Tooth Relic from Sri Lanka – which is said to have been stored alongside the original tooth in Kandy (the second city of Sri Lanka and home of its most important Buddhist shrine), and thus to have been similarly charged with spiritual power.

Just east of the temple, you can't fail to see the enormous **Sehtatgyi Pagoda** ("Big Ten-Storey") Buddha, seated in the earth-witness mudra facing the Shwesandaw, his eyes more or less level with the temple terrace, and clearly visible from it.

Thayekhittaya (Sri Ksetra)

သရေခေတ္တရာ • Pyay Rd • Daily 9am–4pm • $5 • Ox-cart tours around K8000 per cart, depending on the number of people • A motorbike taxi to the site costs around K3000 each way

Some 8km east of Pyay lie the scant remains of ancient **Thayekhittaya** – or **Sri Ksetra**, as it was known in its heyday – the great Pyu city that held dominion over large swathes of central Myanmar between the fifth and ninth centuries (see p.358). The slight aura of desolation that hangs over the impressively large site is haunting, offering faint hints of the once great city now virtually erased from the map. Thayekhittaya's glory days may be long gone, but in 2014 UNESCO recognized its historical importance by making it (along with Beikthano and Halin) a World Heritage Site – the first in Myanmar.

Thayekhittaya's most impressive monuments are a trio of enormous **stupas**, said to be three of the nine commissioned by the city's founder, King Duttabaung. These are

THAYEKHITTAYA (SRI KSETRA) ORIENTATION

Most of Thayekhittaya's remains are contained within a designated **archeological park**, although two of the three big stupas – **Payagyi** and **Payamar** – lie outside it, and can be visited for free. The fragmentary ruins cover a sizeable area. Bikes and cars carrying tourists aren't allowed into the site, so you can either **walk** (although really it's too big to cover the entire site comfortably on foot) or charter an **ox-cart**, which are hired out for a set period of three hours. These are fun for about the first ten minutes, but tediously slow and pretty uncomfortable for the next two hours and fifty. You might prefer to go for a shorter circuit instead, even if you can't negotiate a discount on the full fare. Ox-carts can be organized through the site ticket office. If you do walk, there are plenty of signs and strategically placed maps to point you in the right direction. A very doable 1hr 30min walk begins at the museum and ticket office, and continues to the old palace, some of the former walls and the Rahanda Gate before heading back to where you started via the Payahtaung Pagoda.

among the oldest stupas in the country, characterized by their huge size and rather primitive shapes – the complete antithesis of later Burmese designs. Apart from the stupas, most of the ruins are, architecturally speaking, fairly underwhelming, although some of the later structures offer tantalizing glimpses of the glorious Burmese style that would subsequently flower in Sri Ksetra's successor kingdom of Bagan. Among the best reasons to visit is the chance to wander at will amid the beautiful landscape, which has lakes laden with water lilies, tiny farming villages and fields full of crops. It's all especially beautiful first thing in the morning or after 3pm, when the light softens and turns gold.

Payagyi Stupa

The first of the three stupas you reach is the **Payagyi**, right next to the main road about 1km before the entrance to the site proper. Dating from the sixth or seventh century, the stupa is said to contain the big toenail of the Buddha's right foot; it's also known as the Maha Zedi ("Great Stupa") or Sai Sai ("Slowly Slowly") Pagoda, on account of the length of time it took to construct. Seated on three circular terraces with a diminutive gilded *hti* on top (a later addition), the sheer size of the thing is impressive, although its rudimentary conical shape (made slightly lopsided by the ravages of time) is a world away from the elegant designs of Bagan. The faint remains of some discoloured original plaster can still be seen clinging to its sides.

Payamar Stupa

A second huge stupa, the **Payamar**, lies about 100m past the entrance to the archeological site, off on the left-hand side of the road and attractively situated among paddy fields. Also attributed to King Duttabaung, it's very similar in size, shape and date of construction to the Payagyi stupa, although in slightly worse condition, its brickwork now sprouting small tufts of vegetation.

The museum

Tues–Sun 9.30am–4.30pm • $5

The small **museum** at the entrance to the site contains old Pyu inscriptions and burial urns, silver coins and assorted beads, plus statues of a couple of Hindu deities and other Indian-influenced figures – proof of the strong cultural contact between Sri Ksetra and the subcontinent. Unfortunately, many of the more impressive finds have been carted off to the National Museum in Yangon, which now has extensive displays on the ancient city.

The archeological park

Immediately beyond the museum lie the extensive, carefully reconstructed walls of the former **palace** area, more or less in the middle of the old city. A ten-minute cart ride southwest brings you to the **Rahanda** (or "Yahanda") **Gate**. The actual gate has pretty much disappeared, although you can still see the collapsed, earth-covered remains of the original brick **city walls** on either side. Just past the gate, outside the walls, is the narrow **Rahanda Cave Pagoda**, with a triangular, brick-vaulted roof and eight small, seated Buddhas looking back towards the city inside the walls.

Continuing southeast around the outside of the walls brings you to the (probably) fifth-century **Bawbawgyi Stupa**, the most impressive of Thayekhittaya's three giant stupas and one of the oldest Buddhist monuments in the country – and indeed anywhere else in Southeast Asia. Standing 46m tall with almost sheer sides and a flattish top, it looks quite unlike any other such structure in Myanmar, although it bears a passing resemblance to the famous Dhamek Stupa at Sarnath in India, from where inspiration for this prototypical Burmese stupa may have come.

A couple of minutes further east is the tenth-century **Bei Bei Pagoda**. Dating from the twilight years of Sri Ksetra, this diminutive square brick shrine shows clear evidence of the emerging Bagan style, with characteristic flamed-shaped door pediments and the remains of a tall stupa. Just south of here is another small brick shrine, the **Lay Myet Hna**, its walls held together in a cage of big red girders.

Re-entering the walls and heading north, you'll reach the small eighth-century **East Zegu Pagoda**, with its four entrances (all now bricked up) and heavily moulded brick doorways and pilasters, although the original roof has now been replaced by a large concrete daub. One final hop north brings you to the **Payahtaung Pagoda**, just east of the museum. Dating from the tenth or eleventh century, this is the largest and finest of Thayekhittaya's shrines: a big square brick box, each of its four sides penetrated by a solitary undersized door. A mini-stupa sits on one corner of the roof next to three superimposed terraces, which look as if they once supported a rooftop stupa-spire.

Shwemyethman Pagoda

ရွှေမျက်မှန်ဘုရား • Regular pick-ups run from Pyay to Shwedaung

A popular half-day trip from Pyay (or an easy stop on the journey to or from Yangon) is to the **Shwemyethman Pagoda** in the town of Shwedaung, 15km south of Pyay on the Yangon highway. The temple is famous for its bespectacled Buddha: a huge seated image wearing a natty pair of round spectacles and bearing a faint but unmistakable resemblance to John Lennon. One theory holds that the statue was first equipped with eyewear by King Duttabaung in the fourth century after he went blind – whereupon the monarch promptly regained his sight. However, as glasses weren't invented until eight hundred years later, this seems a rather unlikely story. Another theory is that the glasses were added to the statue to provoke local interest in the Buddhist faith (although the statue's original spectacles were stolen long ago and the image now wears modern replacements). Whatever its origins, the statue is believed to have the power to cure poor eyesight and other ocular diseases – a case near the statue is full of glasses discarded by visitors who claim to have had perfect vision restored during a visit to the temple.

Akauk Taung

အကောက်တောင်

A fun and off-beat half-day adventure from Pyay takes you to **Akauk Taung** ("Tax Hill"), where generations of tax collectors, when not taxing boats carrying cargo down the Ayeyarwady River, filled their time carving dozens of Buddha images into the cliff faces above the sluggish river waters. Most of the carvings were made around the mid-nineteenth century, but there are a few much newer ones as well – and you have to wonder at the dexterity needed to create such delicate art on the fragile-looking cliffs.

As interesting as the carvings are, many find the journey there just as much of a highlight. You have to hire one of the traditional riverboats in Htonbo (for K15,000 per person) and float downstream to the cliffs where the carvings are. The trip takes about an hour on average, and you can scramble out at one point to make a short, sharp climb up the slope to a small pagoda, which offers good river views.

4

ANCIENT CITY OF BEIKTHANO

Thayekhittaya (Sri Ksetra; see p.193) might have been the largest and most important of the string of so-called Pyu city-states that dominated the plains of Myanmar for a thousand years, but the original was **Beikthano**, founded around 200 BC. Despite being part of Myanmar's first UNESCO World Heritage Site, Beikthano remains very little known even within the country. The site is around 20km west of Taungdwingyi, which is around the halfway point between Pyay and Bagan.

At its height, the city was likely to have been the capital of the first politically unified state in Myanmar, covering some 740 acres and walled in its entirety. Today, much of the site is buried under a thick brush of trees, and is still awaiting excavation. However, some sections of the old city walls and a series of walled compounds are visible, and there's also a small museum. A member of staff from here will usually be happy to show you around the archeological site.

The site is best visited while travelling between Pyay and Bagan in either a rented car or a taxi, and you can use Magwe as an overnight stop (see opposite).

There's no direct public transport from Htonbo to Pyay – you'll have to take a bus and then truck hop. You should be able to find transport in Pyay heading to either Padaung or, better, Oke Shit Pin, and from there it's likely you'll encounter something continuing on to Htonbo. Not surprisingly, most people end up hiring a taxi for a half-day trip from Pyay (3hr return drive; K55,000).

ARRIVAL AND DEPARTURE
PYAY AND AROUND

By bus The bus station is 4km east of the centre along Bogyoke Rd – to get there from the centre, either hop on one of the pick-ups that shuttle up and down Bogyoke Rd or catch a motorbike taxi (K1500). The only bus to Bagan currently leaves in the late afternoon; alternatively, catch a bus to Magwe and pick up a connection there. The buses to Ngapali and Sittwe are minibuses.

Destinations Bagan (daily; 10–12hr); Magwe (4 daily; 5hr); Mandalay (2 daily; 13hr); Ngapali (2 daily; 12hr); Nyaung U (daily; 8hr); Sittwe (daily; 28hr); Yangon (6 daily; 6–7hr).

By train Nightly services to Yangon leave from the main station in the middle of town. There's also an overnight service to Bagan departing from Shwethekar Station, around 10km east of the centre.

Destinations Bagan (daily; 10hr); Yangon (daily; 8hr 30min).

By boat There used to be twice-weekly IWT government ferries to Yangon, Bagan and Mandalay, but they weren't running at the time of research – it's worth checking whether they're operating again. The office is the small, green shack on Strand Road.

ACCOMMODATION

Hotel 3D 1448 Shwe The Tann St ☎09 973 939 395. Modern but bland town-centre hotel that's comfortable and filled with staff who politely bow whenever a guest walks past. Although it's based almost overlooking the night market, it's on a quieter side street. **$30**

★**Lucky Dragon Hotel** 772 Strand Rd ☎053 24222. Unexpectedly upmarket mini-resort in the heart of Pyay, with accommodation in attractive white chalets spread out down a long, thin garden, plus a smallish pool. Rooms are surprisingly stylish, with parquet floors, cool white decor and smart, modern bathrooms. Excellent value. **$55**

Mingalar Garden Resort 10–11 Bogyoke Rd ☎053 28661, ⊛mingalargardenresort.com. This resort-style hotel is based well out of town, but just a short walk from the Payagyi Stupa. The highlight is the landscaped gardens, which

have interconnecting ponds and a large carp-filled lake. The rooms, which are in individual wooden bungalows with little terraces, are comfortable in a minimalist kind of way, but lack the wow factor that the room rates might indicate. **$80**

Pan Ga Ba Guesthouse Merchant St ☎053 26543. In a wonderful old timber building, this is as much a homestay as a guesthouse and the family running it will fuss endlessly over you – and quite possibly invite you to eat with them. Rooms are very simple and hot water comes by the bucket. **K22,000**

Smile Motel 10–11 Bogyoke Rd ☎053 25142, ⊛smilemotel333@gmail.com. This place, on the noisy main road, would put a smile on your face if it was about half the price, and the rooms are quite musty and uninspiring. The cheapest rooms, though small, are actually quieter and better value. No breakfast. **$24**

EATING

Pyay has an above-average range of eating options compared to most places of a similar size, and the centre tends to stay lively until relatively late – particularly the busy string of restaurants along Yangon Road south of the Aung San statue. There's also a small but excellent **night market** spread along Old Post Office Rd west of the statue.

Prome Garden Restaurant Yangon Rd ☎053 25629. On the main road to Yangon, but well out of the town centre, this large garden restaurant has tables set out under the trees and is one of the classiest places to eat in Pyay. The high-quality Chinese food is as delightful as the setting, and the menu includes items such as steamed duck with asparagus sauce or pork slow-cooked with bean curd in an earthen pot. Mains K5500–6500. Daily 9am–11pm.

★**Wish River View Restaurant** Strand Rd ☎09 252 422 828. Lively restaurant with lovely views of the spotlit river. The sophisticated menu is filled with excellent Thai curries and fresh fish served in imaginative ways – try the prawn kebabs or catfish stew. Mains around K4000–6000. Daily 5–11pm.

Yokohama Restaurant Strand Rd, near the market ☎09 423 670 456. This is a bright, modern restaurant with English-speaking staff, offering authentic Japanese fare like *tonkatsu*, *tori teriyaki*, *ebi* tempura and so on. Small dishes are K1500–2000, larger set meals range from K3000–5000. It's well worth the short (but dark – take a torch) walk from the town centre. Daily 11.30am–2pm & 5–10pm.

DIRECTORY

Banks There are plenty of ATMs around town including at the CB Bank, AGD Bank and MOB (though the latter doesn't take MasterCard); there's also a second CB Bank ATM at the *Lucky Dragon Hotel* (see p.196).

Magwe

မကွေး

Sprawling along the east bank of the Ayeyarwady River some 240km north of Pyay and 175km south of Bagan, **MAGWE** (or "Magway") is a busy provincial centre and the capital of Magwe Region, home to a large university and an impressive 2.5km bridge over the river. There's not much to interest the casual visitor, although if you're travelling between Bagan and Pyay you might want to stop for an hour to have a look around the dusty market and the **Mya Tha Lun** pagoda, perched on a hilltop north of the centre. **Nga Ka Pwe Taung**, half an hour's drive over the river, is also worth visiting for its series of bubbling mud pools, formed by butane gas seeping from the ground.

ARRIVAL AND DEPARTURE	MAGWE

By bus The bus station is around 2km east of the centre down Pyi Taw Thar Rd (around K1000 by motorbike taxi, or a little less in a shared pick-up).

Destinations Bagan (3 daily; 4hr); Mandalay (daily; 8hr); Meiktila (2 daily; 4hr 30min); Mrauk U (daily; 10hr); Pyay (4 daily; 5hr); Sittwe (daily; 15hr); Yangon (daily; 12hr).

ACCOMMODATION

Htein Htein Tar 17th St ☎063 23499. The rooms here are comfortable, quiet and come with a/c, TVs and fridges, but if you're travelling as a couple they're a bit overpriced – singles are much better value at $30. $60

Nan Htike Thu Hotel Strand Rd, south of the bridge ☎09 5632 8204, ⓦfacebook.com/nanhtikethumagway. This is a smart, modern and competitively priced 68-room hotel with well-equipped rooms and a nice pool. $45

VILLAGE LIFE IN YENANGYAUNG

Yenangyaung is a small town basically in the middle of nowhere – a two-hour, 50km drive northeast of Magwe, or about 100km southeast of Nyaung-U. But if you really want to get under the skin of rural life in Myanmar, this is a great place to do it. Not only will you have the opportunity to explore the surrounding farming villages and go boating down the river, but you can do it all while based in a truly standout new guesthouse that supports local education and community projects – which you can also visit. Buses run to Yenangyaung from Magwe and Nyaung-U, and guesthouse staff can provide transport advice.

★**Lei Thar Gone Guesthouse** On the edge of town ☎060 21620, ⓦleithargone-guesthouse.com. Mounted atop a rocky crag with views over the hot plains and the shimmering Ayeyarwady River, *Lei Thar Gone* is a wonderfully relaxed place. There are contemporary stone-lined rooms, filled with thoughtful touches such as welcome messages scribbled onto glossy green leaves, and the meals they prepare here are a real highlight. $40

Bagan and around

BAGAN

Bagan and around

As the white heat of the day fades into dusk, around two thousand ancient Buddhist temples begin to glow a fiery red – just as they have every evening for hundreds of years. Bagan, the heartland of the first great pan-Burmese empire, is for many the real showpiece of Myanmar, and its legendary temples blanket the scorched and scrubby plains in an astonishing profusion of Buddhist architecture. They lie scattered over an area of almost seventy square kilometres, constructed during one of history's most extravagant building booms.

The sheer scale and density of **Bagan**'s monuments are almost guaranteed to overwhelm – its riches are such that many superb temples (which would be star attractions almost anywhere else) often fail to merit even a mention in most tourist literature. Its architecture comprises an extended variation on a few basic themes, with a handful of recurrent styles and structures that have gradually evolved over time – much of the pleasure of exploring its myriad temples is in unravelling the underlying motifs and meanings that underpin them.

Bagan is also the jumping-off point for visits to the quirky *nat* shrines at **Mount Popa**. There's none of the architectural wonder here, but this place offers a fascinating glimpse into Burmese spirituality with its throngs of excited pilgrims. Nearby, you can visit **Salay** to see more of historic Myanmar, where you'll find carved wooden monasteries, tumbledown temples and a museum-worthy collection of colonial architecture – needless to say, it's an excellent place for an off-the-beaten-track adventure. To the north is **Pakokku**, a bustling town that owes little to tourism yet has a number of extravagant temples.

Bagan

ပုဂံ

BAGAN is unquestionably one of Asia's – indeed the world's – great sights: a vast swathe of temples and pagodas rising from the hot, flat plains bordering the Ayeyarwady River, the landscape bristling with uncountable shrines and stupas which carpet the countryside in an almost surreal profusion and stretch as far as the eye can see. As an architectural showpiece, Bagan (or "Pagan", as it's also sometimes Romanized) is rivalled only by the roughly contemporaneous temples of Angkor in Cambodia, but while the major monuments of Angkor have now disappeared under a flood of coach parties, the temples of Bagan remain, in comparison, fairly uncrowded and retain much of their prevailing magic and mystery – for the time being, at least.

Greater Bagan comprises three main areas. You'll find most of Bagan's cheap accommodation in lively **Nyaung U**, which is a typical dusty, noisy Burmese town

TAUNG KALAT (MOUNT POPA)

Highlights

❶ Shwezigon Pagoda One of the oldest, grandest and most revered of all Bagan's temples, still busy with worshippers after almost a thousand years. **See p.203**

❷ Ananda Paya An enormous mountain of stone, embellished with terraces, stairways and stupas, and topped with a spire. **See p.209**

❸ Sunset over Bagan Climb to the top of one of Bagan's ancient monuments, and watch the sunset over the innumerable temples dotting the plains below. **See p.216**

❹ Sulamani Paya A red-brick jewel of a temple – perhaps the most perfect of all Bagan's myriad monuments. **See p.217**

❺ Hot-air balloon ride Take a ride in a hot-air balloon, and enjoy a champagne breakfast as the morning sun catches Bagan's golden temples. **See p.228**

❻ Taung Kalat and Mount Popa A colourful cluster of shrines and temples, perched dramatically atop an ancient volcanic outcrop and celebrating the wonderful world of the *nat* spirits. **See p.228**

❼ Salay Expect to see tumbledown temples and fading colonial architecture in off-the-beaten-track Salay. **See p.231**

HIGHLIGHTS ARE MARKED ON THE MAPS ON P.202 & PP.204–205

5

that today relies heavily on tourism, while around 5.5km down the road is the historic walled city of **Old Bagan**, which is home to a cluster of upmarket resort hotels and the greatest concentration of historic monuments. Around 4.5km further south, somnolent **New Bagan** (Bagan Myothit) was originally constructed by the former military government to rehouse families living around the ruins of Old Bagan, and today the town's economy is almost entirely built around tourism. There are dozens of hotels and restaurants scattered throughout the area, though they're mainly mid-range and upmarket. There are also a few further places to sleep, eat and shop in the roadside villages of **Wet Kyi Inn** (midway between Nyaung U and Old Bagan) and **Myinkaba** (between Old and New Bagan).

Stretching inland from here away from the river, the **Central Plain** is where you'll find many of Bagan's finest temples. The entire area (covering around forty square kilometres) is protected as the **Bagan Archeological Zone**, although there's no physical evidence of a demarcated area on the ground.

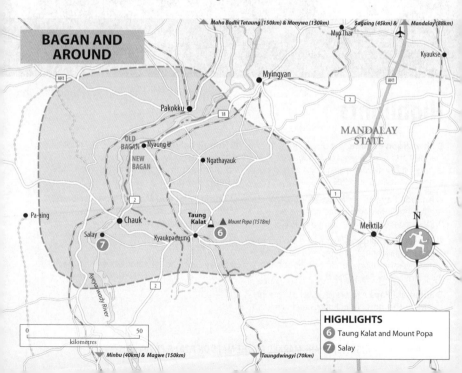

HIGHLIGHTS
6 Taung Kalat and Mount Popa
7 Salay

Nyaung U

5

ညောင်ဦးမြို့

The heart of the busy (if unremarkable) small town of **NYAUNG U** looks surprisingly untouched by the thousands of tourists who descend on it every year. The centre of town is marked by the roundabout at the junction of Anawrahta and Main roads (both of which lead down to Old Bagan), and next to it you'll find the town's attractive **market**. There are also a few temples in the town itself, most notably the superb **Shwezigon**, one of Bagan's finest monuments, and the mural-covered **Kyansittha Umin** nearby.

Sapada Pagoda

ဆပဒဘုရား • At the junction of Anawrahta and Kyaukpadaung roads

Marooned in the middle of a roundabout, the small **Sapada Pagoda** is a good example of the Sri Lankan-style stupa that was popular in the early days of Bagan, with its distinctive box-like *harmika* (relic chamber) separating the slightly bulbous dome and the top-heavy spire above – later Burmese stupas (see p.390) would replace the *harmika* with a lotus-shaped *amalaka*, achieving a far more satisfyingly seamless and organic form.

Shwezigon Pagoda

ရွှေစည်းခုံဘုရား • Shwezigon Pagoda St • Daily 6am–9pm

The most important pilgrimage site in Bagan, the **Shwezigon Pagoda** feels quite different from the other temples in the area. It's closer in appearance and atmosphere to the great working temples of Yangon than the historic monuments elsewhere in the city, with its enormous gilded stupa surrounded by a colourful complex of subsidiary shrines. Despite its relatively modern appearance, the Shwezigon is one of Bagan's oldest monuments, begun by King Anawrahta (1044–77) to enshrine (it's said) a collarbone and a tooth of the Buddha brought from Sri Lanka – although it wasn't finished until the reign of his son Kyansittha (1084–1112) in around 1089.

Long covered passages, each flanked by a huge pair of white chinthe, lead into the temple from the south and east – although you should beware the shopkeepers on the southern side, where most tourists enter, as they're probably the most cut-throat in Bagan. Inside, the complex is dominated by its vast **stupa**, set atop three battlemented terraces, with elaborate red-carpeted staircases flanked with lions rising to the summit. The stupa is actually built mainly of sandstone rather than the usual brick, although you can't see this since the whole thing (including the terraces) is dazzlingly gilded right

2016 BAGAN EARTHQUAKE

August 24, 2016 began just like any other day in Bagan, with tourists drifting between ancient temples and horse carts trotting down bumpy tracks – but then an **earthquake** hit at a depth of 84km just to the southwest of Bagan, measuring 6.8 on the Richter scale.

Only one person was killed (in nearby Pakokku), but Bagan's famous temples didn't escape so lightly – or at least that's how it first appeared. Around four hundred temples were visibly damaged in the quake, but experts quickly revealed that much of the damage was not to the ancient bricks and art, but to the shoddy **restoration attempts** implemented by the former military government in the mid-1990s. Back then, the work had been so badly done that when the earthquake hit, much of it simply crumbled and fell to the floor, while the original structures (which had already survived countless tremors) remained undamaged underneath.

The potential silver lining to all this is that Bagan, which has for so long been denied UNESCO World Heritage status thanks to this poor-quality renovation work, is now being renovated by experts and could potentially obtain its World Heritage listing as early as 2018. While this work takes place, you can expect many of the temples to be covered in scaffolding or temporary structures.

5

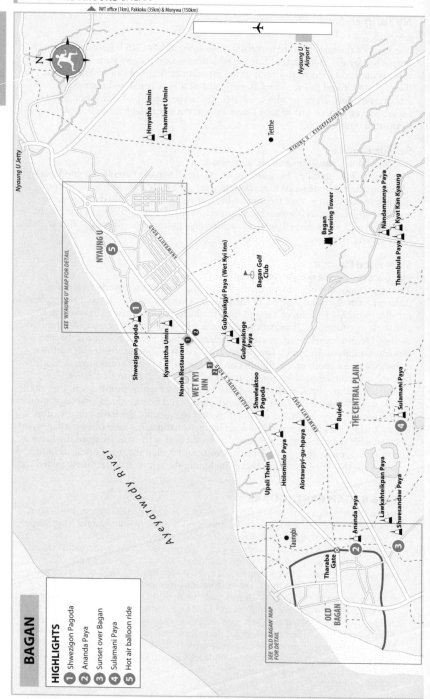

IWT office (1km), Pakkoku (35km) & Monywa (150km)

N

Nyaung U Jetty

Hmyatha Umin

Thamiwet Umin

Tetthe

NYAUNG U–KYAUKPADAUNG ROAD

Nyaung U Airport

Bagan Viewing Tower

Nandamannya Paya

Kyat Kan Kyaung

Thambula Paya

SEE 'NYAUNG U' MAP FOR DETAIL

ANAWRAHTA ROAD

NYAUNG U

5

Gubyaukgyi Paya (Wet Kyi Inn)

Bagan Golf Club

Shwezigon Pagoda

1

Kyansittha Umin

Nanda Restaurant

1 2

WET KYI INN

2 1

Gubyauknge Paya

BAGAN–NYAUNG U ROAD

Shweleiktoo Pagoda

Sulamani Paya

THE CENTRAL PLAIN

ANAWRAHTA ROAD

Buledi

4

Sulamani Paya

Ayeyarwady River

Upali Thein

Htilominlo Paya

Alotawpyi-gu-hpaya

Lawkahteikpan Paya

Shwesandaw Paya

Ananda Paya

Taungbi

Tharaba Gate

2

3

OLD BAGAN

SEE 'OLD BAGAN' MAP FOR DETAIL

BAGAN

HIGHLIGHTS

1 Shwezigon Pagoda
2 Ananda Paya
3 Sunset over Bagan
4 Sulamani Paya
5 Hot air balloon ride

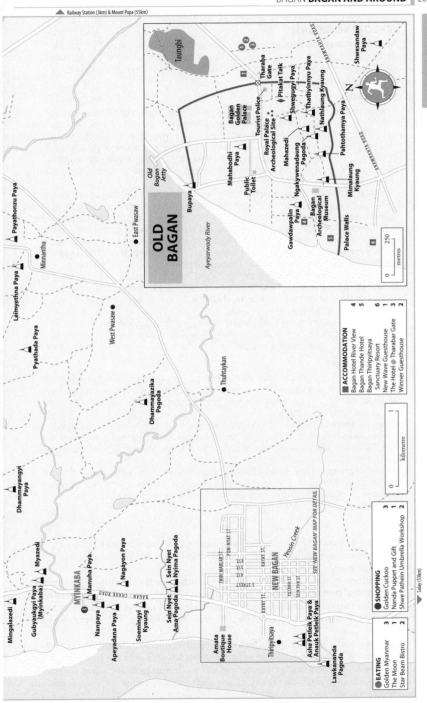

Railway Station (3km) & Mount Popa (55km)

OLD BAGAN

Ayeyarwady River

Old Bagan Jetty

East Pwasaw

West Pwasaw

Minnanthu

Thuhtaykan

Taungbi

Tharaba Gate

Bupaya

Mahabodhi Paya

Public Toilet

Tourist Police

Bagan Golden Palace

Royal Palace Archeological Site

Pitakat Taik

Shwegugyi Paya

Thatbyinnyu Paya

Nathlaung Kyaung

Pahtothamya Paya

Mahazedi

Ngakywenadaung Pagoda

Mimalaung Kyaung

Gawdawpalin Paya

Bagan Archeological Museum

Palace Walls

Shwesandaw Paya

Payathonzu Paya

Leimyethna Paya

Pyathada Paya

Dhammayazika Pagoda

Dhammayangyi Paya

Mingalazedi

Myazedi

Gubyaukgyi Paya (Myinkaba)

MYINKABA

Manuha Paya

Nanpaya

Apeyadana Paya

Soemingyi Kyaung

BAGAN - CHAUK ROAD

Nagayon Paya

Sein Nyet Ama Pagoda

Sein Nyet Nyima Pagoda

Amata Boutique House

Thiripyitsaya

Lawkananda Pagoda

Ashe Petleik Paya & Anauk Petleik Paya

NEW BAGAN

Yeotin Creek

THIRD MARKET ST

KAYAY ST

KAYAY ST

3 STREET

3 ST

4 ST

5 ST

POE NYA ST

YUZANA ST

SEIN PAN ST

SEE NEW BAGAN MAP FOR DETAIL

Salay (53km)

● EATING
Golden Myanmar   3
The Moon   1
Star Beam Bistro   2

● SHOPPING
Golden Cuckoo   3
Nanda Puppet and Gift   1
Shwe Pathein Umbrella Workshop   2

■ ACCOMMODATION
Bagan Hotel River View   4
Bagan Thande Hotel   5
Bagan Thiripyitsaya
Sanctuary Resort   6
New Wave Guesthouse   1
The Hotel @ Tharabar Gate   3
Winner Guesthouse   2

0   250
metres

0   kilometre   1

5

EXPLORING BAGAN

The **architectural background** to the temples of Bagan is covered in detail in Contexts (see box, p.390), which provides a fuller overview of the various styles and features of the myriad monuments and their historical context. The **history** of Bagan is also covered in Contexts (see p.359).

ITINERARIES

There are endless different ways of tackling the temples of Bagan, with monuments clustered so thickly on the ground that fixing on a particular itinerary is a matter of personal taste rather than practical necessity. It's best to take your time – rush in Bagan, and you're likely to become rapidly templed out and terminally stupa-fied. You'll need at least **three days** to get to grips with the major monuments, and getting on for **a week** to properly explore all the places covered here. Keep in mind that a thorough investigation of the whole site could take the best part of a year.

That said, a few pointers might prove useful. The monuments of **Old Bagan** make a logical starting point, the site's densest and most diverse collection of temples including the landmark Thatbyinnyu and Gawdawpalin, along with a host of other fascinating buildings. The temples of the **Central Plain** – including the stunning Shwesandaw, Dhammayangyi and Sulamani – will fill a second day, perhaps with the Mingalazedi and Dhammayazika Pagoda included, while a third day can be spent exploring the area between **Nyaung U** and **Old Bagan**, particularly the magnificent Shwezigon Pagoda and Htilominlo Paya, and the mural-covered Upali Thein and Gubyaukgyi Paya. A further string of temples stretches south of Old Bagan through **Myinkaba** village to **New Bagan**, and there's another cluster of absorbing little monuments around the village of **Minnanthu**, which is somewhat off the beaten track, and a perfect place to escape the modest crowds.

It's also worth remembering that there are around two thousand further temples not covered in the accounts here, and it's also fun to leave your guidebook in your hotel room and go off exploring – you're more or less guaranteed to have most places entirely to yourself.

PRACTICALITIES

Many of Bagan's less-visited temples are kept **locked**, particularly those containing delicate murals or valuable artefacts. In most places, someone will magically appear to unlock the temple for you; occasionally you might have to ask around to find the keyholder. A tip of around K500 generally suffices.

A decent **torch** is pretty much essential if you want to properly appreciate Bagan's many remarkable temple murals. If you don't have one, you can sometimes borrow one from the temple keyholder or resident hawker. A tip is obviously expected – again around K500 is fine.

Note that **photography** of Bagan's fragile murals is expressly forbidden inside the more popular temples. In less busy temples you might be allowed to take photographs, although given the damaging effects of flash on the temple's delicate, centuries-old paintings, the responsible thing to do is to keep your camera in your bag.

down to the pavement. Fine glazed tiles depicting various Jataka scenes are set around the base (although many are now missing), while double-bodied lions guard each corner.

Large shrines sit at the bottom of the four staircases, each containing an impressive standing **gilded bronze Buddha** (the four largest in Bagan), modelled after the Indian Gupta style – although they're rather difficult to see behind their protective grilles. Exiting the northern side of the temple, the path leads down to the water, with fine river views.

The temple is the site of a major **festival** during the Burmese month of Tazaungmone (in October or November), during which pilgrims from all over the country converge on Nyaung U, and Shwezigon transforms into an enormous country fair, complete with puppet shows, open-air theatre, dance performances and so on, plus handicraft and food stalls aplenty.

THE NATS OF SHWEZIGON

The Shwezigon is interesting historically for its role in the development of Burmese Buddhism. Aware of his people's love of the old **nat spirits** (see p.386), the savvy King Anawrahta decided to encourage interest in the new Theravada Buddhist faith by placing images of the 37 most revered *nats* on the lower terraces of the stupa, believing that people would be won over to the new Buddhist faith more easily if it incorporated aspects of their traditional beliefs – and thus setting a precedent for the combined *nat* and Buddhist shrines that can still be found throughout Myanmar to this day (nowhere more so than at nearby Taung Kalat and Mount Popa).

The *nats* of Shwezigon, meanwhile, having fulfilled their original function, are now relegated to a subsidiary shrine – signed **"Shrine of Bodaw Indra and 37 Nats"** – tucked away in the far southeast corner of the temple compound. You may be able to find someone to open it for you for a tip, offering you a surreal glimpse of the 37 small gilded images of assembled *nat* notables lined up solemnly in glass cases – and looking decidedly neglected compared to their glory days sitting enthroned upon King Anawrahta's magnificent stupa.

Kyansittha Umin

ကျန်စစ်သားဥမင် • Signed off Main Rd a few metres past the entrance to the Shwezigon Pagoda's southern covered terrace • Daily 8am–6pm

Almost in the shadow of the Shwezigon Pagoda, the modest **Kyansittha Umin** is easily missed but worth a look for its unusual murals. The name means "Cave of Kyansittha" in honour of King Kyansittha, although the building most likely dates back to the rule of his father, Anawrahta. The small rectangular brick building (not actually a cave) was apparently used as a monastic residence, although it's difficult to see how anyone would have managed to live in the cramped interior, bisected by a grid of narrow passages which are now propped up with steel frames following earthquake damage in 1975.

Virtually every interior surface is covered with fine **murals** in subdued whites, browns and yellows, depicting various scenes from daily life and Buddhist mythology. Particularly interesting are the paintings of Mongol soldiers (on the rear wall roughly opposite the entrance) – a memento of the repeated Mongol incursions into Myanmar in the late thirteenth century. The invaders are instantly recognizable thanks to their distinctive hats, like upturned fruit bowls decorated with fancy plumes.

Nyaung U to Old Bagan

Myriad monuments dot the area between Nyaung U and Old Bagan, although relatively few are of sufficient interest to feature on most tourist itineraries. They do, however, include two of Bagan's finest temples – the flamboyant **Htilominlo Paya**, midway between Nyaung U and Old Bagan, and the magnificent **Ananda Paya**, just outside the latter.

Gubyaukgyi Paya (Wet Kyi Inn) and around

ဂူပြောက်ကြီးဘုရား • Off Anawrahta Rd • Daily 8am–6pm

Not far from Nyaung U is the thirteenth-century **Gubyaukgyi Paya** ("Great Painted Cave Temple" – not to be confused with the identically named temple in Myinkaba), signed off Anawrahta Road as "Nge Gu Pyauk Gyi". Traces of fine plasterwork can still be seen on the exterior, which has an unusual pyramidal spire above – perhaps inspired by the one at the Mahabodhi temple in Old Bagan. Inside are many fine murals showing assorted Jataka scenes, arranged mosaic-like within dozens of small square panels.

A certain Dr Thomann from Germany, who visited in 1899, authored one of the first books ever written on Bagan. Sadly, as well as writing about the area, he also felt it acceptable to remove many of the paintings that were originally here, and sell them in

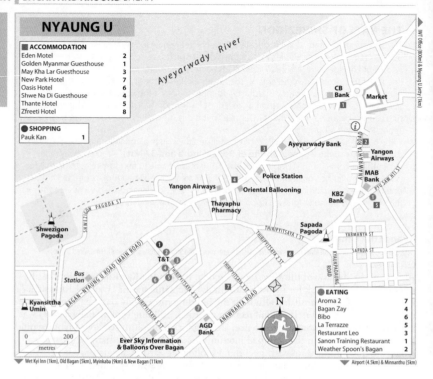

NYAUNG U

■ **ACCOMMODATION**

Eden Motel	2
Golden Myanmar Guesthouse	1
May Kha Lar Guesthouse	3
New Park Hotel	7
Oasis Hotel	6
Shwe Na Di Guesthouse	4
Thante Hotel	5
Zfreeti Hotel	8

● **SHOPPING**

Pauk Kan	1

● **EATING**

Aroma 2	7
Bagan Zay	4
Bibo	6
La Terrazze	5
Restaurant Leo	3
Sanon Training Restaurant	1
Weather Spoon's Bagan	2

Ayeyarwady River

CB Bank
Market
Ayeyarwady Bank
Yangon Airways
Police Station
Yangon Airways
Oriental Ballooning
MAB Bank
KBZ Bank
Thayaphu Pharmacy
Sapada Pagoda
Shwezigon Pagoda
T&T
Bus Station
Kyansittha Umin
AGD Bank
Ever Sky Information & Balloons Over Bagan

ANAWRAHTA ROAD
SHWEZIGON PAGODA ST
THIRIPYITSAYA 1 ST
THIRIPYITSAYA 2 ST
THIRIPYITSAYA 3 ST
THIRIPYITSAYA 4 ST
THIRIPYITSAYA 5 ST
BAGAN–NYAUNG U ROAD (MAIN ROAD)
YARMANYA ST
SAPADA ST
KYAUKPADAUNG ROAD
PYU SAW HTI ST

N

0   200
metres

INT Office (800m) & Nyaung U Jetty (1km)

▼ Wet Kyi Inn (1km), Old Bagan (5km), Myinkaba (9km) & New Bagan (11km)   ▼ Airport (4.5km) & Minnanthu (5km)

auctions abroad. The holes where the naughty German removed large sections of plaster are still gapingly obvious.

Around 250m past the Gubyaukgyi, the **Gubyaukge Paya** (signed off Anawrahta Rd as "Gu Byauk Nge – Wet Kyi Inn") is very similar both in style and name, with further fine exterior plasterwork and some well-preserved murals within.

Htilominlo Paya

ထီးလုံမင်းလိုဘုရား • Main entrance off the Bagan–Nyaung U Rd • Daily 8am–6pm

Roughly halfway between Nyaung U and Old Bagan, the **Htilominlo Paya** is one of the last and finest of Bagan's temples, and a perfect example of the city's late-period architecture. The temple was constructed by King Htilominlo (aka Nantaungmya, who ruled from 1211–35), the youngest of the five sons of King Narapatisithu. According to legend, the five princes were placed around a white umbrella and Htilominlo was elected ruler when the umbrella fortuitously tilted in his direction. The grateful young king subsequently commemorated the event by building a temple on the site of his decisive ceremony. History suggests that the umbrella's judgement may have been flawed, however, since Htilominlo turned out to be one of Bagan's less effectual rulers, more interested in temple-building than in overseeing affairs of the realm.

His temple is undeniably impressive, even so, built in the characteristic double-cube structure reminiscent of the Sulamani and Thatbyinnyu temples (even if the entire inner courtyard has been transformed into a miniature tourist bazaar packed with assorted shops and stalls). The exterior is notable for its exceptionally fine stucco carvings, featuring dozens of ferocious *kirtimukha* arranged around the cornice, spewing upside-down lotuses out of their gaping, fang-filled mouths. Four large gilded Buddhas sit inside, with extensive geometrical murals covering the walls.

Upali Thein

ဥပါလိသိမ် • Next to Bagan–Nyaung U Rd, 250m west of the Htilominlo Paya • Daily 8am–6pm

Erected during the reign of King Kyazwa (1235–50), the small but striking **Upali Thein** is one of Bagan's few surviving ordination halls (*thein*). The building looks unlike any other in Bagan – its steeply ridged roof and lean-to aisles were possibly modelled after now-vanished wooden buildings of the period, with two tiers of quaint, lozenge-shaped battlements (an eighteenth-century addition) and a tiny spire on the top.

A steel frame supports the lopsided **interior**, which was damaged during the 1975 earthquake, and there's a single Buddha statue at the end. The walls are decorated with intricately detailed murals depicting various Jataka scenes in pale greens, dark reds and whites. These are not original, however, as they were added in the eighteenth century, and the figures are much larger than those in traditional Bagan paintings.

Alotawpyi-gu-hpaya

အလို့တော်ပြည့်ဝူ့ဘုရား• Halfway between Nyaung U and Old Bagan, right next to Anawrahta Rd • Daily 7am–9pm

The eye-catching **Alotawpyi-gu-hpaya** is one of the few temples between Nyaung U and Old Bagan still in daily use, normally busy with locals and offering a lively contrast to the time-warped monuments surrounding it on all sides. Usually, relatively few tourists stop by. Built in the twelfth century by King Kyansittha, the ancient shrine has latticed brick windows and a pure early-period style, while the incongruously glitzy gilded stupa above has a distinct touch of Hollywood about it – altogether, the building seems a bit like a very elderly lady in an outrageously loud hat. The modern tiled **interior** is very much that of a working temple rather than an archeological monument, its walls decorated with crude but colourful orange and brown murals of identikit Buddhas lined up in rows. A large stupa stands directly behind the temple, with traces of green glazed tiles still visible on its bell.

Ananda Paya

အာနန္ဒာဘုရား• Just east of Old Bagan • Daily 8am–6pm

Built between 1090 and 1105 during the reign of King Kyansittha, the **Ananda Paya** is one of the largest and most stunning of all the Bagan temples, its landmark spire rising 52m high above the surrounding plains. The Ananda is generally considered the culminating masterpiece of early-period Bagan architecture, although it also hints at the city's later architectural style with its six rooftop terraces and soaring spire, which give it a lofty profile quite unlike earlier, horizontally challenged, designs. The ground plan (a Greek cross embedded in a square) is also innovative, with four entrances rather than the customary one, and the absence of the usual brick-latticework fill inside the window frames allows far more light inside compared to the atmospheric gloom which had previously been the norm in Bagan's shrines.

The exterior

Before plunging inside, it's worth strolling around the temple to have a look at the building's superb **exterior**. The four imposing entrances are richly decorated with miniature stupas and extravagant flame-shaped door and window pediments – and just above, the corners of the six terraces are crowded with assorted miniature stupas and statues of lions and Buddhas. Fine glazed tiles depicting various Jataka scenes (the largest such collection in Bagan) run around all six terraces; those adorning the base of the temple depict (on the western side of the building) the Buddha's victory over Mara and his monstrous army and (on the eastern side) *devas* holding auspicious symbols. Look out, too, for the unusual double-bodied chinthe that sit at ground level guarding the corners of the structure.

The interior

The Ananda boasts one of Bagan's finest **interiors**. The four entrances are each protected by a pair of door guardians seated in niches. Beyond, there's an unusual double ambulatory (one ambulatory enclosed within the other), with huge teak doors hung at each of the four entrances to the outer ambulatory and numerous ornate niches lining the ambulatory walls, with small carvings within including Buddha figures and scenes from his life.

Four enormous **Buddhas** stand on each side of the temple's central core, with further pairs of guardian figures in front. The Buddha statues on the north and south sides are original (in the *dharmachakra*, or teaching, mudra). The other two are replacements in the later Konbaung style for original statues destroyed by fire in the 1600s. Sitting at the feet of the western Buddha (in the *abhaya* – "have no fear" – mudra) are two lacquer figures said to depict King Kyansittha and Shin Arahan (see p.385). The eastern Buddha – with arms by its sides and hands outstretched – is unusual in that it doesn't conform to any recognized mudra. The small object between the image's fingertips is said to be a herbal pill, perhaps symbolizing the cure from suffering offered by the Buddha's teachings. Quirkiest of all is the face of the southern Buddha, which changes from a pensive pout to a cheesy grin as you walk away from it.

Old Bagan

ပုဂံမြို့ဟောင်း

The monuments clustered within the ancient walled city of **OLD BAGAN** are without doubt the finest in Bagan, and this is an excellent place to start exploring the Archeological Zone. The sights here are also remarkably diverse, covering all the various periods and styles of Bagan, from the historic **Bupaya** and bunker-like **Pahtothamya Paya** through to the flamboyant late-style **Gawdawpalin Paya**, as well as several curiosities including the *nat*-inspired **Tharaba Gate**, the ersatz-Indian **Mahabodhi Paya**, the **Pitakat Taik** library and the Hindu **Nathlaung Kyaung** shrine – not to mention the magnificent **Thatbyinnyu Paya**, one of Bagan's greatest temples.

Tharaba Gate

သရပါ တံခါး

Approaching from Nyaung U, the entrance to the formerly walled city of Old Bagan is via the quaint **Tharaba Gate**, the only one of Old Bagan's twelve former gateways to survive. Sections of the original city walls, constructed by King Pyinbya (846–76) in 849, can still be seen on either side. Casting aside Buddhist orthodoxy, the gate is dedicated to the two Mahagiri (see box, p.230) **nat spirits**, popularly known as Maung Tinde ("Mr Handsome"), whose image stands in a niche on the left-hand side of the gate, and his sister Shwemyethna ("Golden Face") opposite.

Bagan Golden Palace

ရွှေနန်းတော် • Daily 6am–8pm • $5

A shameless eyesore in the heart of historic Bagan, the **Bagan Golden Palace** complex claims to re-create the royal splendour of Bagan's former kings, complete with overblown pseudo-traditional architecture, extraneous quantities of gilded paint and other stylistic nonsense – although it's really just an OTT shopping and entertainment venue designed to squeeze easy dollars out of the passing coach-party trade. The inflated entrance price gives you full access to the complex's overpriced souvenir shops and so-called "bazaars", but not much else.

Royal Palace Archeological Site

ဆဝဒဘုရား

Opposite the ersatz Bagan Golden Palace, the **Royal Palace Archeological Site** protects the uninteresting remains of Bagan's original palace complex. It's not currently open to visitors, which is no great shame, and you can in any case get a decent view of the modest excavations by peering through the roadside fence.

Mahabodhi Paya

မဟာဗောဓိဘုရား • Daily 8am–6pm

Looking like an exotic foreign stranger amid the surrounding Bamar- and Mon-style temples, the **Mahabodhi Paya** is built in imitation of (and named after) the great Buddhist temple at Bodhgaya in North India, erected on the site of the bodhi tree under which the Buddha gained enlightenment. Built during the reign of Htilominlo, the temple is dominated by its mighty pyramidal tower, subdivided into horizontal niches filled with hundreds of small seated Buddhas gazing placidly down at the passing tourists below. It all looks very Indian, although the temple is far from an exact copy of the Bodhgaya original – whether this was the result of an intentional redesign or the consequence of dodgy building contractors remains unclear.

On the north side of the Mahabodhi, the fragmentary brick ruins of the **Ratana-Gara** ("Gem House") house Bagan's only extant examples of glazed painted tiles, although they're so badly worn that they're virtually indecipherable.

Bupaya

ဘူးဘုရား • Daily 7am–9pm

Commanding the Ayeyarwady from atop a high bluff overlooking the water, the **Bupaya** ("Gourd Stupa") is Old Bagan's most popular place of local worship, with an atmosphere of cheerful Burmese hustle and bustle that's quite different from other temples hereabouts. The small complex's major feature is its unusual **gilded stupa**, raised above the water on a crenellated white terrace, with steps leading down to the river below. Said to date back to the reign of the semi-legendary third king of Bagan, Pyuswati (162–243), the stupa's distinctively bulbous, gourd-shaped outline is typical of early Pyu architecture – although what you see now is actually a reconstruction, as the original was toppled during the 1975 earthquake.

Gawdawpalin Paya

ကန်တော့ပလ္လင်ဘုရား • Daily 8am–6pm

A skinny supermodel amid the venerable monuments of Old Bagan, the **Gawdawpalin Paya** was begun during the reign of Narapatisithu (1174–1211) and completed by his son, Htilominlo – and then seriously damaged in the 1975 earthquake, although it's since been patched up. With a superb late-period double-cube structure, it looks like a taller, slimmed-down version of the Thatbyinnyu, with a slender spire reaching a height of 55m – it's one of the loftiest in Bagan. Fine stuccowork showing the usual *kirtimukha* with pearls and garlands decorates the exterior, although the interior is disappointingly plain, save for some traces of floral murals around the four main entrances.

Bagan Archeological Museum

ရှေးဟောင်းသုတေသနပြတိုက် • Tues–Sun 9.30am–4.30pm • K5000 • No photography

Given the wealth of attractions on offer in Bagan, the **Bagan Archeological Museum** may seem rather a let-down (and it's also a very unsightly building).

Entering the museum, the main hall on the **ground floor** has some fine sandstone Buddhist carvings from the Gubyaukgye and Nagayon temples in Myinkaba, as well as a pair of fine pillar inscriptions erected by Kyansittha. The attached "Showroom of Bagan Period Literature" is full of pillar inscriptions recording the various buildings donated by local notables to Bagan's monastic community, along with accompanying lands, slaves and the occasional cow. Here, you'll also find the museum's most important exhibit, the **Myazedi inscription**, which is one of a pair of identical carvings – the other being at the Myazedi temple in Myinkaba (see p.220). Also on the ground floor, the "Bagan Period Arts and Crafts" showroom is worth a quick look for its rare cloth painting and models of outlandish Bagan-era hairstyles, plus a mishmash of other artefacts including some interesting stone carvings and the inevitable pots.

5

Pickings are thinner up on the **first floor**, although the "Buddha Images" room is worth a quick peek as it includes further images from the Nagayon Paya, an eleventh-century Buddha fashioned from an alloy of five metals (now protected by stout golden bars), and some fine wooden, stone and lacquer Buddha images.

Mimalaung Kyaung

မီးမလောင်ကျောင်း • Directly behind the drink stalls opposite the Bagan Archeological Museum • Daily 8am–6pm

The engaging **Mimalaung Kyaung** ("The Temple Which Fire Cannot Burn") is one of Old Bagan's prettiest monuments. Built in the reign of Narapatisithu, the small temple acquired its soubriquet after surviving a devastating conflagration in 1225. Its fire-resistant qualities are enhanced by the unusually high platform on which it's built, reinforced with huge buttresses and ascended via a small staircase lined with a large pair of cheerfully grinning chinthe. The small **shrine** on the platform at the top is similarly unusual, topped with a fancifully sculpted roof and slender spire. Its elevated position also provides one of the finest **views** in Old Bagan, with the monumental Thatbyinnyu close by, the Ananda temple rising behind and various other monuments dotted below.

Pahtothamya Paya

ပုထိုးသားများဘုရား • Follow the dirt road in front of the Mimalaung Kyaung for around 250m • Daily 8am–6pm

Built sometime in the tenth or eleventh century, the brooding **Pahtothamya Paya** is a low-set, heavy structure in classic early-period style, with tiny latticed-brick windows and an incongruously slight and inconsequential Sri Lankan-style stupa plonked on top – typical of the city's oldest temples before the curved shikhara-style tower became the superstructure of choice. Entrance to the **interior** is through an arched antechamber that looks rather like the inside of a capsized ship. Blackened mosaic-style murals line the walls, while a brooding Buddha sits in near-darkness in the central shrine. Past here, a gloomy and intensely atmospheric **ambulatory** leads around the shrine. Shine a torch, and the walls come alive with marvellously detailed murals – some of the oldest in Bagan – captioned in Mon and including scenes showing Prince Siddhartha on a boating trip and a fine panel depicting the legendary visit of Kaladevila to the infant Buddha-to-be, the sage splendidly bearded and clad in an extravagant red cloak, holding the tiny Prince Siddhartha aloft in one hand.

Nathlaung Kyaung and around

နတ်လျှောင်ကျောင်း • Daily 8am–6pm

The modest **Nathlaung Kyaung** is one of the oldest temples in the city, possibly dating from the reign of Anawrahta, or perhaps as much as a century earlier. It's also notable for being Bagan's only Hindu temple, built for Indian merchants visiting the city and dedicated to Vishnu (the name means "Temple Where The Nats Are Confined" – perhaps a reference to the foreign Hindu deities contained within). The compact square structure, topped with an elaborately moulded spire, is now somewhat reduced from its former dimensions, the original entrance hall having disappeared long ago. Niches lining the exterior formerly housed images of the ten incarnations of Vishnu, although only seven survive, all pretty battered. Also note the dramatic flame-shaped pediment over the entrance, which is perhaps the oldest of its kind in Bagan and marks the first appearance of what would become one of the city's most distinctive architectural motifs.

Inside, a small ambulatory surrounds a single shrine. Facing the entrance is a modern sculpture of Vishnu reclining on the cosmic serpent Anata-Sesha, whose successive coilings and uncoilings are said to alternately move time forward and instigate creation, and then reverse it, causing the universe to end. Smaller images of the three major gods of the Hindu pantheon – Brahma, Vishnu and Shiva – hover above. Further images of Vishnu adorn the three other sides of the shrine, each holding a disc, mace, trident and lotus.

Standing directly opposite the Nathlaung Kyaung is the **Ngakywenadaung Pagoda**, a small, unusually bulbous stupa looking like a miniature version of the nearby Bupaya. Traces of the green glazed tiles that originally covered it can still be seen.

Thatbyinnyu Paya and around

သဗ္ဗညုဘုရား• Daily 8am–6pm

Dominating the skyline of Old Bagan is the monumental **Thatbyinnyu Paya**, one of the largest temples anywhere in Bagan. It's also the tallest, rising to a height of around 66m, although it's the sheer mass of the building that really impresses. Built by King Alaungsithu (ruled 1112–67), the temple marks an important transitional point between Bagan's early and late styles. This was Bagan's first fully fledged "double-cube" two-storey temple, with the main shrine placed on the upper storey and the traditional ground-floor shrine replaced with a "solid-core" structure in order to support the extra weight of the additional storey above. Each of the two storeys is topped with three terraces (now with flat roofs rather than the pitched lean-to roofs of earlier temples) and adorned with crenellations and corner stupas. Entrances are placed at each of the cardinal points – the so-called "four-faced layout" (with a slightly larger eastern portico) typical of late-period Bagan style and which, unlike earlier temples, often only had a single entrance. The **interior** has nice traces of geometrical floral murals inside the west entrance, but is otherwise disappointingly plain.

On the northeast side of the temple, look out for the small "**tally temple**" (*gayocho*). One brick out of every ten thousand used in the construction of Thatbyinnyu was set aside for counting purposes and a whitewashed temple was built with the resultant bricks – the surprising scale of the resultant structure gives a good idea of quite how many bricks were consumed by the mother temple. Around 100m south of the temple, you should also look out for the small surviving stretch of Old Bagan's crumbling **city walls**, which offers fine views over the surrounding monuments.

Shwegugyi Paya

ရွှေကူကြီး• Daily 8am–6pm

Built in 1140 during the reign of Alaungsithu, the **Shwegugyi Paya** is one of Old Bagan's most elegant temples, relatively small but perfectly formed. Like the nearby Thatbyinnyu, the Shwegugyi exemplifies the transition between Bagan's weighty Mon- and Pyu-influenced early style and the lighter, airier and more upwardly mobile late style, with its graceful curvilinear tower and stupa finials rising needle-like from the temple's roof.

Unusually, the main entrance is on the north side (rather than the customary east), presumably in order to face the nearby royal palace. A large Buddha sits facing the main entrance, opposite which (on your right as you enter) stands a pair of ancient Pali **inscriptions** recording, among other details, the temple's construction, which it is claimed took just seven months. Elsewhere traces of fine plasterwork decoration are still visible, along with three smaller Buddha figures in the ambulatory, roughly caked in gold leaf applied by dutiful worshippers.

ALAUNGSITHU AND NARATHU

The Shwegugyi Paya stands on an unusually high brick platform. According to one (particularly implausible) legend, this rose spontaneously from the ground in tribute to **King Alaungsithu**'s accumulated spiritual merit prior to the temple's construction in 1140. Twenty-three years later, it is said, the elderly and ailing king was brought back to Shwegugyi and left to die. When the king began showing unwelcome signs of recovering from his illness, his son and heir-apparent **Narathu** decided to hasten him on his way by smothering him to death in his own bedclothes, thereby murdering Alaungsithu in the temple that his own merit had helped to create. The moral of the story remains unclear.

5

The temple is also one of Bagan's most popular **sunset-viewing spots** (see box, p.216), offering splendid views from its narrow upper terraces – although space is at a premium, and the crowds are unrelenting.

Pitakat Taik
ပိဋကတ်တိုက် • Daily 8am–6pm

The unusual **Pitakat Taik** is thought to be the library built by King Anawrahta (ruled 1044–77) to house the thirty sets of the Tripitaka (the major sacred texts of the Buddhist canon) seized during the looting of the city of Thaton in 1057, and which Anawrahta is said to have borne home in triumph on the 32 white elephants of the vanquished King Manuha. The basic plan of the building is similar to that of the traditional Bagan temple, with the addition of three small staircases leading up to the low platform on which the building is set. The crowning spire and extravagant peacock-style finials adorning the five-tiered roof were added by King Bodawpaya in 1783.

The Central Plain

The **CENTRAL PLAIN** is Bagan at its most iconic: untrammelled by human habitation, its hundreds of temples rise out of the sandy, scrub-covered plains like the archetypal remnants of some remarkable lost civilization. The scale of the temples and stupas here is nothing short of astounding; they feature several of Bagan's most majestic monuments, including the landmark **Shwesandaw Paya**, the super-sized **Dhammayangyi Paya** and the exquisite **Sulamani Paya** – perhaps the most perfect of all Bagan's temples.

Shwesandaw Paya
ရွှေဆံတော်ဘုရား • Off Anawrahta Rd, roughly opposite the Ananda Paya • Daily 8am–6pm

Built around 1057 during the reign of Anawrahta, the **Shwesandaw Paya** ("Golden Sacred Hair Relic") was the very first of Bagan's great monumental stupas. It was constructed to enshrine a hair relic of the Buddha presented to Anawrahta by the king of Bago in gratitude for his military assistance in fending off a Khmer invasion. The design of the stupa established a model subsequently followed throughout Bagan, with a series of square terraces (decorated with rounded battlements) supporting a huge bell-shaped stupa (*anda*). The stupa itself sits on an octagonal base, providing a structural transition between the square terraces and round superstructure. Steep staircases lead up all four sides of the structure, providing access to the various terraces; these were formerly lined with glazed tiles illustrating the Jatakas, although most have now vanished. The stupa is one of Bagan's most popular **sunset-viewing spots** (see box, p.216), although the marvellous views over Old Bagan are slightly compromised by the eyesore Archeological Museum, and the relatively narrow terraces get horribly packed come sundown.

Right next to the stupa, inside the temple compound, look out for the **Shinbinthalyaung Temple**, a long, low, brick building housing Bagan's largest reclining Buddha (18m long) in *parinibbana* pose.

Lawkahteikpan Paya
လောကထိပ်ပန် • Around 150m north of the Shwesandaw Paya • Daily 8am–6pm

The diminutive **Lawkahteikpan Paya** is easily missed but worth a look for its fine murals. Black-and-white Jataka strip paintings decorate the sides of the entrance hall, with two Buddha footprints on the ceiling above, while the shrine's gilded Buddha image is framed by a series of larger and more colourful painted scenes showing the usual events from the life of the Buddha, including the ever-popular Temptation of

FROM TOP SHWEZIGON PAGODA (P.203); BULLOCKS AND CART, BAGAN >

SUNSET-VIEWING TEMPLES

Sitting high on the terrace of an ancient temple watching the sun set over the plains below is one of Bagan's **essential experiences**, although the decision in 2013 to close many of the temples' upper terraces for conservation purposes means that the choice of sunset-viewing perches is now somewhat limited – and the most popular places can get unbearably crowded.

You'll find that horse-drawn carriage drivers can often point you in the direction of lesser-known viewing spots, but it's often best not to follow their instructions as some temples have delicate embellishments that could easily be damaged if you climb on top of them. In reality, you'll find the sunsets are often just as enjoyable when you're seated beneath one of the nearby acacia trees.

The classic place to watch the sun go down is the **Shwesandaw Paya** (see p.214), which is strategically located close to many of Bagan's landmark monuments, though it can get appallingly busy – make sure you arrive early. The same can be said for the almost equally popular **Shwegugyi Paya** (see p.213) in Old Bagan; nearby, largely crowd-free alternatives include the **Mahazedi** stupa and the **Mimalaung Kyaung** (see p.212). The **Shweleiktoo Pagoda** offers just as good views, and is usually a bit less crowded. In the Central Plain, the spacious terrace atop the **Pyathada Paya** (see p.217) offers plenty of room and fewer crowds, although it's now being steadily discovered by the coach-party brigade. Another popular spot is the well-positioned **Buledi**, a large stupa off Anawrahta Road between Nyaung U and Old Bagan, although again space is at a premium (to reach it, take the dirt road just east of the Alotawpyi-gu-hpaya, following the sign to "Bulethi/Sulamani").

One final option is the government's eyesore **Bagan Viewing Tower** (daily 6am–10.30pm; K5000). It's overpriced, rather too far from the major landmarks and not nearly as atmospheric as the temples, although it does have the advantage that, being on it, you won't have to look at it.

Mara (at the top of the arch behind the image on the right-hand side); Mara himself is seated grandly on top of a white elephant.

Dhammayangyi Paya

ဓမ္မရံကြီးဘုရား • Follow the dirt track off Anawrahta Rd opposite the track leading to the Ananda Paya • Daily 8am–6pm

A brooding presence amid the monuments of Bagan's Central Plain, the huge **Dhammayangyi Paya** is cloaked in sombre legend. Built by the homicidal **King Narathu** (ruled 1167–71), the Dhammayangyi's construction was planned as a grandiose act of royal merit-making, which, Narathu apparently hoped, would be sufficient to wipe out the bad karma accumulated following the murder of his father (see box, p.213), brother and wife. In the event, Narathu himself was assassinated just two years after taking the throne by an eight-man hit squad despatched from India by the unhappy father of his murdered bride.

Modelled after the Ananda Paya, the Dhammayangyi is instantly recognizable not only for its sheer size but also for its distinctive outline. The temple is unique among later Bagan monuments in that it lacks an upper storey, compensating instead with a series of no fewer than six steep terraces (rather than the usual three) placed on top of the shrine, giving it a uniquely ziggurat-like appearance. The collapse of the original shikhara-style spire that formerly crowned the edifice further accentuates the building's pyramidal profile.

The **exterior** is notable for its superb masonry – it's said that Narathu ordered the bricks to be fitted together so tightly that not even a needle could be inserted between them (and lopped off the hands of any workmen who failed to achieve the necessary close-fitting finish). The stark **interior** boasts a few traces of murals around the four entrance porches, but is otherwise bare and faintly melancholy, with high corridors and the squeaking of bats and cooing of doves in the darkness overhead. There was originally a double ambulatory, although the entrances to the inner ambulatory have been mysteriously sealed up. One tradition says that this was an act of revenge against

5

the godless Narathu, although a more prosaic explanation is that the inner corridor was bricked up in order to prevent the huge structure from collapsing. A pair of Buddhas sit opposite the western entrance, with the historical Gautama and the future Maitreya placed next to each other – Bagan's only example of two major Buddha images placed side by side. Two stone inscriptions in Pali recording the temple's construction can be seen directly behind the paired images.

Sulamani Paya

စူဠာမဏိဘုရား• Turn left along the dirt track at the fork just before you reach the Dhammayangyi Paya, or take the earlier dirt track off Anawrahta Rd signed to "Bulethi/Sulamani" • Daily 8am–6pm

Sitting in splendid isolation more or less at the dead centre of the Archeological Zone is the magnificent **Sulamani Paya**, built by King Narapatisithu in around 1183. The Sulamani isn't the biggest or tallest of the Archeological Zone's myriad temples, but for many people it's the most beautiful of all Bagan's monuments and the iconic example of the city's late-style architecture in all its flamboyant finery. The double-cube structure was perhaps modelled on that of the Thatbyinnyu Paya (and subsequently copied by other temples such as the Gawdawpalin and Htilominlo), although none quite matches the Sulamani's perfect proportions, with two storeys of equal height each topped by three terraces, striking a delicate balance between the vertical and horizontal. The graceful shikhara above is actually a reconstruction following the 1975 earthquake – close up you can see how much newer the bricks are, compared to the rest of the building, although from a distance it looks fine.

The **exterior** boasts fine plasterwork along with unusual green and yellow glazed decorative tiles (also visible above some of the doors). **Inside**, the temple's entertaining murals are an eighteenth-century Konbaung-era addition, with large figures (including a couple of huge reclining Buddhas) painted in an engagingly naïve style.

Pyathada Paya

ပြိဿဒါးဘုရား• Follow the dirt road past the Sulamani Paya for around 750m • Daily 8am–6pm

Buried away amid a labyrinth of dirt tracks in the depths of the Central Plain, the **Pyathada Paya** is a singularly odd-looking late-period temple, with a large lower level and a small and decidedly cursory rooftop shrine – it actually looks as if only the lower half was finished, and that the builders originally intended to build a much larger upper storey. Whatever the reason, by serendipitous chance this has resulted in an unusually large and spacious rooftop terrace, almost as if expressly designed for sunset viewing (see box, p.216), which is what the temple is now best known for.

Dhammayazika Pagoda

ဓမ္မရာဇိကဘုရား• 3km northeast of New Bagan, off the Minnanthu Rd • Daily 8am–6pm

Stranded way out at the very edge of the Archeological Zone, a considerable distance from any other major monument, the **Dhammayazika Pagoda** is a bit of a hike to reach but well worth the effort. Sitting in an attractive garden-style compound, the impressively large gilded pagoda was built during the reign of Narapatisithu in 1198 to enshrine holy relics presented by the ruler of Sri Lanka. The complex is notable mainly for its unusual **pentagonal layout**, a design that can also be found at a few other Bagan temples, but nowhere else in the Buddhist world. It's thought that the five-sided structure resulted from the desire to provide a shrine to the future Buddha Maitreya alongside the four Buddhas of the present world cycle – Kakusandha, Konagamana, Kassapa and Gautama (see box, p.74) – who are commonly found in most Bagan temples, one at each cardinal point. Five gateways lead into the five-sided enclosure, with the central stupa sitting on a pentagonal terrace. Standing around the base of the stupa are five large and beautifully decorated shrines, each with a gilded Buddha and traces of Konbaung-era murals inside, while four lions and a pair of seated guardian figures keep watch on the roofs above, topped with intricately carved little

5

shikhara-style towers. Fine stucco decoration and glazed Jataka panels can be seen around the stupa terraces, which are also studded with an unusual number of dragon-mouthed waterspouts.

Around Minnanthu

The cluster of low-key monuments between the Bagan Viewing Tower and the small village of **MINNANTHU** isn't the most exciting in Bagan, although it's the quietest area within the Archeological Zone and you'll most likely have many of the temples here largely to yourself. Small examples of late-period architecture predominate, with some superb murals.

Nandamannya Paya and around

နန္ဒမညာဘုရား • 1km north of Minnanthu • Daily 8am–6pm (if the temple's locked, ask at the Payathonzu Paya for someone to let you in)

The modest **Nandamannya Paya**, built in 1248 during the reign of Kyazwa, is of interest mainly for its murals – they're some of Bagan's most famous. These include a fine painting of the **birth of the Buddha** showing Prince Siddhartha emerging from the hip of his mother, Queen Maya, and a well-known depiction of the **Temptation of Mara**, in which scantily clad nymphs attempt vainly to rouse the Buddha from his meditation (face the shrine's Buddha statue and the Mara mural is behind you in the left corner at around waist height, while the birth of the Buddha is on your right, to the left side of the window).

Behind the Nandamannya look out for the odd little **Kyat Kan Kyaung**, a modern monastic building placed in a large hole in the ground in order to minimize outside distraction.

Thambula Paya

သမ္ဗူလဘုရား • 200m south of the Nandamannya Paya • Daily 8am–6pm (If the temple's locked, ask at the Payathonzu Paya for someone to let you in)

Similar in appearance to the nearby Nandamannya, the pretty little late-style **Thambula Paya** (1255) is home to another superb tranche of murals – and for once the airy interior, with its high ceilings and tall pointed arches, is sufficiently light that you probably won't need a torch to see them. A profusion of densely detailed paintings covers virtually every surface, and includes floral decorations, miniature mosaic-pattern Buddhas and, in the west portico and elsewhere, several intricately painted inscriptions. The murals in the north porch are especially fine, and look out too for the unusual painting of a boat race inside the south porch.

Payathonzu Paya

ဘုရားသုံးဆူ • 300m south of the Thambula Paya • Daily 8am–6pm

A true curiosity, the unique **Payathonzu Paya** ("Temple of Three Buddhas") comprises three identical small, tower-topped shrines joined together in a line and connected by a single corridor. The shrines house some of Bagan's most unusual **murals**, which are light enough to see without a torch. Entrance is via the middle shrine; this and the shrine to your left (the eastern shrine) are richly decorated with unusual paintings showing a pronounced Mahayana or possibly even Tantric Buddhist influence, with many-armed figures, embracing couples, strange mythological animals and (in the eastern shrine) a small picture of a three-headed Brahma. At the opposite end of the temple, the walls of the western shrine are entirely bare, suggesting that the temple wasn't finished.

Leimyethna Paya

လေးမျက်နှာဘုရား • 200m south of the Payathonzu Paya • Daily 8am–6pm

Sitting on a platform reached by a rustic stairway roofed in corrugated iron, the **Leimyethna Paya** ("Temple of the Four Faces") is a fine late-period temple, built in 1223 by a minister of King Htilominlo. The intricately designed shrine features a mass of decorative pediments, miniature corner-stupas and moulded terraces, with a fine shikhara above. Inside, the light, airy interior is brightly decorated, with many mosaic-pattern black and gold Buddhas in the four porches and colourful, engagingly naïve-style murals on the interior walls and central cube, quite different from those at other temples nearby.

Myinkaba to New Bagan

The monuments stretching south of Old Bagan through the village of **MYINKABA** and on into **NEW BAGAN** are a bit of a mishmash, lacking the stellar attractions of other parts of Bagan but offering an interesting cross section of Bagan architecture through the ages. They include the small but architecturally significant shrines of **Nanpaya** and **Apeyadana Paya**, as well as the majestic **Mingalazedi**.

Mingalazedi

မင်္ဂလာစေတီ • Bagan–Chauk Rd, just south of Old Bagan • Daily 8am–6pm

Just south of the Old Bagan city walls, the **Mingalazedi** ("Blessing Stupa") was built during the reign of King Narathihapate (ruled 1256–87) – the last major monument to be constructed in Bagan before the Mongol incursions of 1287 sent the kingdom plummeting into decline. One of the finest of all Bagan's late-style stupas, the Mingalazedi is reminiscent in outline of the famous Shwedagon in Yangon, whose proportions it is said to have copied. Fine glazed tiles depicting Jataka scenes are displayed around the base of the stupa (there were originally 1061, of which 561 remain), while staircases (now closed) lead up through three terraces, their corners decorated with Indian-style *kalasa* (nectar pots).

The stupa's creator, **Narathihapate**, is remembered chiefly for his notorious gluttony (three hundred dishes per meal were considered obligatory) and for his subsequent headlong flight from the invading Mongols, which earned him the sobriquet of *Tayok-pyay-min*, roughly translated as "The King who ran away from the Chinese".

Gubyaukgyi Paya (Myinkaba)

ဂူပြောက်ကြီးဘုရား • Bagan–Chauk Rd • Daily 8am–6pm • To reach it, turn left on the road downhill just at the beginning of Myinkaba village (if you reach the *Sar Pi Thar* restaurant you've gone too far) – it's directly in front of the Myazedi, easily spotted thanks to its distinctive gilded stupa

Colourful murals – some of the oldest in Bagan – can be found at the small but florid **Gubyaukgyi Paya** (not to be confused with the identically named temple in Wet Kyi Inn), built around 1113 by Prince Rajakumar (aka Yazakumar), a son of King Kyansittha, in honour of his recently deceased father. The temple also offers an intriguing snapshot of Bagan architecture in evolution. Early-period hallmarks – the low-set, single-storey structure with an interior kept deliberately dark thanks to the almost completely bricked-up windows (carved here into unusual geometrical designs) – dominate, although there are hints of the emerging late-period style in the large shikhara and small rooftop shrine; the latter would subsequently develop into the fully fledged second storey characteristic of Bagan's later "double-cube" temples.

The **exterior** features some exceptionally fine stuccowork and carving, particularly around the elaborate window frames and pediments. Not much light gets into the gloomy **interior**. The best paintings – showing various Jataka scenes captioned in Mon – are in the ambulatory around the shrine, although it's very dark and you won't see anything without a torch.

Myazedi

မြစေတီဘုရား • Bagan–Chauk Rd • Daily 8am–6pm

Immediately behind the Gubyaukgyi stands the contrasting **Myazedi** ("Jade Stupa"), centred on a large, brilliantly gilded stupa. A busy, modern, working temple, it's of

5

minimal architectural distinction but is notable as the home of one of the two so-called **Myazedi inscriptions** (the other one being in the Bagan Archeological Museum). Carved onto a large pillar on the south side of the stupa (now protected behind bars in an ugly little concrete shelter), the inscription records the creation of the adjacent Gubyaukgyi temple by Prince Rajakumar, with the text repeated in four different languages – Pyu, Mon, Pali and Burmese – on each side of the square pillar. It's the longest extant inscription in Pyu ever discovered, while the parallel translations on the pillar's four faces served (like a kind of Burmese Rosetta Stone) as the basis for the deciphering of the previously untranslatable Pyu script in the early twentieth century.

Manuha Paya

မနူဟာဘုရား• Bagan–Chauk Rd • Daily 7am–9pm

Bang in the centre of Myinkaba village, the large and always lively **Manuha Paya** actually dates all the way back to 1059, despite its relatively modern appearance. According to legend, the temple was endowed by the captive Manuha, the former king of the Mon city of Thaton (see p.358), who had been brought back to Bagan by the all-conquering King Anawrahta and held prisoner in Myinkaba.

The temple itself is one of the earliest two-storey structures in Bagan, looking a bit like the Thatbyinnyu but smaller and dumpily proportioned. A huge golden alms bowl stands in the entrance hall, with three huge Buddhas squeezed into a trio of tiny shrines behind – their cramped living quarters are said to symbolize the captivity and reduced circumstances of Manuha himself. A large reclining Buddha occupies a fourth, slightly larger, shrine at the back of the temple.

Nanpaya

နန်းဘုရားကျောင်း• Directly behind Manuha Paya • Daily 8am–6pm • To reach it, exit the courtyard of Manuha Paya via the steps in the southwest corner and turn left; alternatively, follow the small track around the Manuha Paya wall on the left side of the temple through the red and gold arch and you'll see it almost immediately on your left

Like the adjacent Manuha Paya, the **Nanpaya** ("Palace Temple") is closely associated with Manuha, the deposed king of Thaton. One legend states that Manuha lived here during his years of exile; another, that it was built on the site of Manuha's former residence by his grandson during the reign of Narapatisithu, although the temple's distinctively low and heavy-set early-period design style suggests that it's at least a century too old for this particular theory to be true.

Whatever its provenance, the Nanpaya is one of Bagan's more offbeat structures. It's unusual chiefly for being constructed largely of sandstone rather than the customary brick, while the stumpy shikhara-style curvilinear tower on top may have been the first of its kind in Bagan, setting a trend for rooftop towers rather than stupas which would henceforth be the city's defining style. Note too the finely carved floral frieze running around the base of the windows, with tiny *hamsa* inserted within each swirl of leaves.

The **interior** is similarly interesting, with a unique open-plan arrangement featuring four massive sandstone pillars. Etched onto the pillars are some of Bagan's finest carvings. Gape-mouthed *kirtimukha* are shown on two sides of each pillar, while the other sides sport three-headed images of the Brahma (often co-opted into Buddhist mythology) holding a pair of lotus flowers. A now-vanished Buddha statue originally stood in the centre.

Apeyadana Paya

အပါယ်ရတနာဘုရား• Bagan–Chauk Rd, just south of Myinkaba village • Daily 8am–6pm

Named after (and possibly commissioned by) King Kyansittha's first wife, the diminutive **Apeyadana Paya** (or Abeyadana) is a superb example of Bagan's early-period architecture, its exterior decorated with fine brick-lattice windows and with a Sri Lankan-style rooftop stupa above (very similar to the one at the Pahtothamya in Old Bagan, which was built at roughly the same time). Inside sits an image of the Buddha flanked by his two chief disciples, Sariputra and Mogallana, while many beautiful **murals** adorn the entrance hall and very dark ambulatory (bring a torch). Queen Apeyadana, originally from Bengal in India, was possibly a Mahayana Buddhist, which perhaps explains the presence of murals depicting assorted Mahayana Bodhisattvas and Hindu gods including Vishnu, Shiva, Brahma and Indra.

Nagayon Paya

နဂါးရဲ့ဘုရား• Bagan–Chauk Rd, 200m south of the Apeyadana Paya • Daily 8am–6pm

Built during the reign of Kyansittha, the **Nagayon Paya** is a superb example of Bagan's early style at its most flamboyant. The entire temple has a slightly theatrical look, raised on an eye-catchingly high terrace and done up with a showbiz super-abundance of mini-stupas, pretty geometrical lattice windows and lots of the characteristic flame-shaped pediments so beloved of Bagan's architects – the steeply pitched double pediment over the main entrance is particularly *de trop*. Best of all is the fine curved central tower, raised up on three high terraces and looking like a trial run for the great tower of the Ananda Paya, the crowning masterpiece of Kyansittha's reign.

Inside, there's the usual shrine-plus-ambulatory layout, with a large gilded standing Buddha, his head protected by the hood of the *naga* snake-king Mucalinda (the temple's name means "Protected by the Naga Serpent"), with two smaller images standing to either side. Badly eroded paintings line the dark ambulatory (torch needed) along with finely carved Buddha statues in niches, although many of the images formerly located here have now been carted off to the Bagan Archeological Museum.

Soemingyi Kyaung

စိုးမင်းကြီးေကျာင်း• Bagan–Chauk Rd, roughly midway between Myinkaba and New Bagan • Daily 8am–6pm

Built in the early thirteenth century, the **Soemingyi Kyaung** is one of the few surviving monastic buildings in Bagan, most such foundations having been constructed in wood and long since vanished. Not much remains of the original monastery, bar a small courtyard with cells on its north and south sides and a small shrine. The bases of two staircases (at the courtyard's southeast and southwest corners) can also be seen. These would originally have led up to a now-vanished wooden roof, and offer impressive views over nearby temples, including a huge stupa immediately to the north.

Sein Nyet Ama and Sein Nyet Nyima pagodas

စိန်ညက်အစ်မ/ စိန်ညက်ညီမ• Bagan–Chauk Rd, two-thirds of the way towards New Bagan • Daily 8am–6pm

The so-called "Seinnyet Sisters" – Sein Nyet Ama and Sein Nyet Nyima – are an impressive pair of contrasting late-period structures standing next to one another close to the main road. The towering **Sein Nyet Ama Pagoda** (the *ama*, or elder, sister) is said to have been built in the eleventh century by Queen Seinnyet, although stylistically it looks much later, with its fine curvilinear spire set at the top of four steep terraces.

The adjacent **Sein Nyet Nyima Pagoda** (*nyima* meaning "younger sister") is slightly smaller, with a massive conical spire decorated with deeply incised rings and traces of fine carvings and stucco *kirtimukhas* around the bell below, with Buddha statues sitting in niches on each side.

Ashe Petleik Paya and Anauk Petleik Paya

အရှေ့ဖက်လိပ်ဘုရား၊ / အနောက်ဖက်လိပ်ဘုရား• Next to the road running down to the Lawkananda Pagoda • Daily 8am–6pm • To reach it, follow the road through the big red arch on the right a few metres past the *Floral Breeze Hotel* (with an easily missed sign to the Lawkananda)

The twin Anauk ("Western") Petleik and Ashe ("Eastern") Petleik temples are thought to date from the reign of Anawrahta, making them two of the oldest buildings in Bagan. Both have suffered massively from the ravages of time, however, and were largely rebuilt in 1905.

5

The first temple you'll see, the **Anauk Petleik Paya**, is the slightly better preserved of the two, with a Sri Lankan-style bell-shaped stupa that's missing the top of its spire. The adjacent **Ashe Petleik Paya** is even more fragmentary, topped by a large stupa that's now little more than a hunk of shapeless brick. The shrines are of interest principally for their remarkable collection of **unglazed tiles** stored within and depicting the usual Jataka scenes (these formerly comprised a complete cycle of all 547 Jataka stories, although many of the tiles are now missing).

Lawkananda Pagoda

လောကနန္ဒစေတီတော် • Just southwest of New Bagan • Daily 7am–9pm • Accessed by continuing past the Ashe Petleik Paya and Anauk Petleik Paya to the end of the road

Set majestically above the river, the large and dazzlingly gilded stupa of the **Lawkananda Pagoda** ("Joy of the World") dates back to the reign of Anawrahta, making it one of Bagan's oldest such structures – although it's been rebuilt since. Enshrining a replica of the Buddha's tooth presented to Anawrahta in 1059, the pagoda remains a popular place of local worship. The temple stands close to what was once Bagan's main harbour and still commands beautiful Ayeyarwady views, although the river's somewhat quieter now than it was in Anawrahta's heyday, when the docks below would have been busy with shipping from the Mon provinces, Rakhine, Sri Lanka and elsewhere.

ARRIVAL AND DEPARTURE

BAGAN

By plane The airport is around 4km southeast of Nyaung U. A taxi into Nyaung U costs K7000, and a ride to New Bagan or Old Bagan will set you back around K10,000. On the way back to the airport, you should be able to wangle a cheaper fare that's been cut by up to a quarter. Mann Yadanarpon Airlines (☎061 61063), Yangon Airways (☎061 60475) and Golden Myanmar Airlines (☎061 61219) are among the companies offering flights into Bagan from Mandalay (around $60) and Yangon (around $120). There's a K1000 departure tax on all flights. Tickets can be bought either from the airline offices in town or from many local travel agents.

Destinations Heho for Inle Lake (7 daily; 40min); Mandalay (4–7 daily; 30min); Ngapali (5 daily; 1hr 20min); Yangon (many daily; 1hr 20min).

By bus The bus station is on Main Rd in Nyaung U, close to the Shwezigon Pagoda and not far from Thiripyitsaya 4 St and some of the Main Rd guesthouses. If you're heading on to Wet Kyi Inn, Old Bagan or New Bagan, you'll need to hire a taxi or pick-up (around K5000 to Old Bagan or K7000 to New Bagan) or hop on a (slightly cheaper) motorbike taxi. Tickets for express buses can be bought from any of the myriad tour operators in Nyaung U, plus a couple in New Bagan (see p.223). For Pakokku (1hr) there are only very crowded local minibuses that leave about every hour throughout the day from the market area rather than the bus station. If you're heading to Monywa, you'll have to change in Pakokku.

BAGAN TO MANDALAY BY BOAT

A popular way of travelling between Bagan and Mandalay (or vice versa) is by taking a **cruise boat** along the Ayeyarwady – some people find this a rewarding experience, although the size of the river means that for significant parts of the route the riverbanks are far distant and you don't actually see much save water on either side. Boats depart either from the jetty in Nyaung U (northeast of the market) or in Old Bagan (outside the old walls, to the north), depending on water levels. Services leave at around 5.30am, taking roughly 10–12hr to reach Mandalay.

The two main operators are **Malikha River Cruises** (☎09 7314 5748, ⊛malikha-rivercruises .com), **RV Shwe Keinnery** (☎09 402 745 566) and **Myanmar Golden River Group** (⊛mgrgexpress.com); all operators charge $32 from Bagan to Mandalay and $42 going the other way, and prices include breakfast and lunch. The MGRG boats are slightly more spacious and comfortable than the other two, although there's not much in it. The three operators offer at least one departure daily between them, although the vagaries of the various schedules mean that it's impossible to generalize about exactly which leave when. Tickets are most easily booked either through your accommodation or through a local tour operator.

Destinations Kalaw (3 daily; 8hr); Magwe (5 daily; 4hr); Mandalay (5–6 daily; 7hr); Meiktila (2 daily; 3hr 30min); Nyaungshwe (2 daily; 8hr 30min); Pakokku (hourly; 1hr); Pyay (daily; 8hr); Taunggyi (2 daily; 9hr); Yangon (5 daily; 10hr).

By taxi If you can get a group together, taxis (seating three, or four at a squeeze) are a convenient and reasonably affordable option for travel further afield. Count on spending around $200 to Mandalay, or $250 to Inle Lake.

By train The railway station is 5.5km southeast of Nyaung U, past the airport (around K7000 by taxi). The only licensed ticket seller anywhere in Bagan is located, rather improbably, at Blue Sea (☎061 60949 or ☎09 204 0135), a frozen-food and fish wholesaler on Main Rd in Nyaung U.

Destinations Mandalay (daily; 8hr); Pyay (daily; 10hr); Yangon (daily; 19hr).

GETTING AROUND

Bagan's sights are spread out over a considerable distance, so it's more than likely you'll need some form of transport to explore it all.

By bike Cycling is an enjoyable way to explore Bagan, although most of the bikes available for rent lack gears and are often not in the best shape, which can make pedalling even fairly modest distances hard work – the sandy backroads between outlying temples can also snag wheels and sap your strength with surprising rapidity. If you're cycling between Nyaung U and Old Bagan, note that the wide and relatively traffic-free Anawrahta Rd offers a more peaceful ride than the narrower and busier Nyaung U–Bagan Rd via Wet Kyi Inn. There are bikes for rent all over Bagan for K4000/day.

By e-bike Tourists aren't allowed to ride motorbikes in Bagan, although renting an e-bike (which is like a cross between an electric bicycle and a moped) offers a reasonable (if slightly slower) alternative, and saves you the effort of cycling. Chinese-made e-bikes are available to rent from many places in Nyaung U and New Bagan – small electric motors (operated via a moped-style handlebar throttle) give you a cruising speed of around 20–30km/hr, depending on the size of the bike. That said, you might want to take your bike for a test drive before committing to it. E-bikes generally cost around K8000/day, or K9000/day for slightly larger and more powerful models.

By horse-drawn carriage The classic way to tour Bagan is by horse-drawn carriage – a romantic, if not terribly comfortable, way of exploring the sights, saving you the bother of navigating your own way and allowing you to cut along the sandy backroads which are hard work on two wheels. Rates start from as little as K25,000/day or K15,000/half day, and you can book through your hotel or a local tour operator, or even approach a driver directly – in Nyaung U they can often be found hanging around at the top end of Thiripyitsaya 4 St and around the bus station.

By taxi For maximum speed and comfort, you can hire a taxi to explore the temples, although you'll miss out on a lot of the atmosphere of the archeological site while stuck inside a vehicle. Rates are around K35,000/day, or K20,000/half day.

By tourist bus At the time of research, the authorities were experimenting with a hop-on-hop-off tourist bus. The buses run around a dozen times a day, and take a circular route around the main temples and hotel areas of Bagan. Buses run to a strict timetable and tend to depart each bus stop on time. For more on the service – and to check if it has become a permanent fixture – see ⓦwonderbagan.com.

INFORMATION AND TOURS

Tourist offices There are tourist offices in both Nyaung U, on Anawrahta Rd, and New Bagan on Bagan–Chauk Rd (daily 9.30am–4.30pm, although this can change; ☎061 65040). There's not much actual information available, although staff can arrange taxis to tour Bagan and to the airport (K5000/6000/7000 from Nyaung U/Old Bagan/New Bagan respectively). They can also provide guides (see below). The office in New Bagan is by far the most helpful.

Guides Guides can be hired through Bagan's two tourist offices or through most tour operators around town. Professional licensed guides cost $35/day. Local guides can be hired for $20/day, although their services are likely to be considerably more hit and miss.

Tours Ever Sky (Thiripyitsaya 5 St, Nyaung U; ☎061 60895, ⓔeverskynanda@gmail.com) is a helpful and reliable general tour operator, offering trips around Myanmar, car rental, ticket purchasing services and more. Tourist Information & Travelling Services (T&T; Thiripyitsaya 4 St, Nyaung U; ☎09 4037 19542, ⓔsm.somkiat@gmail .com) is also a good, long-established travel agent offering car rental, bus tickets and local tours. They also offer fortune telling, which might be worth considering before a long bus journey.

ACCOMMODATION

Bagan is no bargain, thanks to the number of visitors. The cheapest accommodation is clustered in **Nyaung U**, although inexpensive accommodation is rare. Similar places stretch down the main road into the village of **Wet Kyi Inn**, about 1km

5

south. **New Bagan** has a decent range of mid-range options, while **Old Bagan** is home to a cluster of upmarket resorts – attractive, if rather pricey for what you get, and also mostly generic – though there are a couple of more appealing exceptions. Rooms at the places listed here all come with a/c.

NYAUNG U AND AROUND

Eden Motel Anawrahta Rd, near the market ☎061 60639; map p.208. Lacklustre budget option offering cheap en-suite rooms with hot water – it's not much more than a useful stopgap for a night. There are similar rooms at a similar price in the *Eden Motel II* block over the road. **$25**

Golden Myanmar Guesthouse Main Rd ☎061 60901; map p.208. This is a long-running guesthouse with bright, clean rooms – though many are showing their age. Staff are very friendly, and there's an in-house travel agency that can organize onward transport and local guides. **$20**

May Kha Lar Guesthouse Main Rd ☎061 60304; map p.208. Sky-blue guesthouse with potted plants in the courtyard and wood-panelled, slightly gloomy rooms split between two blocks. It's worth paying $5 extra for a larger, quieter room in the block furthest from the road. This is the best of the budget hotels on Main Rd. **$20**

New Park Hotel Off Thiripyitsaya 4 St ☎061 60322, ⓦnewparkmyanmar.com; map p.208. Popular, and very good, budget option in an excellent location on a quiet backstreet. Rooms come in three different classes, but all are spotless, bright and have an attached bathroom – the best are the $30 garden-facing rooms, which have terraces and "sleep-easy" chairs. The owner has lots of useful travel advice and sells bus tickets and tours. **$25**

Oasis Hotel Anawrahta Rd ☎061 60923, ⓦoasishotelbagan.com; map p.208. Appealing hideaway hotel, with a string of thatched concrete bungalows arranged beside a narrow, jungle-like garden and a delightful little swimming pool. The simple rooms are cool, comfortable and have

rustic brown-brick bathrooms. It's worth paying a bit more for one of the quieter rooms at the far end of the garden ($100–120). **$80**

Shwe Na Di Guesthouse Main Rd ☎061 60409; map p.208. This is not the most inspiring place, although its rates are a reasonable deal by Bagan standards and it's very popular with Burmese visitors. Cheaper rooms with basic shared bathrooms (cold water only) are little more than boxes, although they're cleaner than those in most other establishments nearby. There are also smarter and pricier en-suite rooms around the back ($30). **$20**

Thante Hotel Pyu Saw Hti St ☎061 61116; map p.208. Long-running option close to the centre of Nyaung U, with accommodation in spacious, old-fashioned bungalows spread around pleasant gardens complete with a good-sized (albeit very shallow) pool. The comfortable rooms are dated in a charming, "floral bedspread" kind of way, and are a reasonable choice – although rates are on the high side. **$65**

Zfreeti Hotel 407 Thiripyitsaya 5th St ☎061 61003, ⓦzfreetihotel.com; map p.208. Set in a pair of good-looking brick buildings, this is one of Nyaung U's more stylish hotels – and yet it's very reasonably priced. Standard rooms are white, bright, neat and clean; deluxe rooms ($10–20 extra) are a little more stylish. A small pool and garden complete the package. **$70**

WET KYI INN

New Wave Guesthouse Main Rd ☎061 60731; map pp.204–205. This is one of Wet Kyi Inn's best options, with bright, comfortable and well-decorated rooms at a reasonable price. **$40**

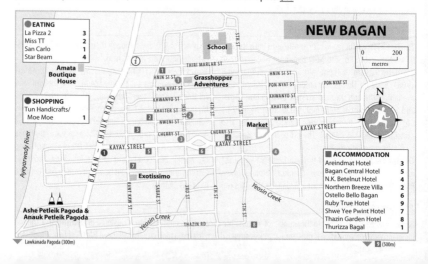

● EATING	
La Pizza 2	3
Miss TT	2
San Carlo	1
Star Beam	4

● SHOPPING	
Tun Handicrafts/ Moe Moe	1

NEW BAGAN

■ ACCOMMODATION	
Areindmat Hotel	3
Bagan Central Hotel	5
N.K. Betelnut Hotel	4
Northern Breeze Villa	2
Ostello Bello Bagan	6
Ruby True Hotel	9
Shwe Yee Pwint Hotel	7
Thazin Garden Hotel	8
Thurizza Bagal	1

Winner Guesthouse Main Rd ☎ 09 402 501 091; map pp.204–205. This is one of the better choices among Wet Kyi Inn's modest array of budget options. Cheaper rooms are bare but clean, and share tolerable communal bathrooms with hot water. Smarter en-suite rooms ($20) are significantly brighter and more appealing, so long as you don't mind the strange metal beds that look like they've been pilfered from a local intensive care unit. $15

OLD BAGAN

★ **Bagan Hotel River View** Behind the Gawdawpalin Paya ☎ 061 60316, ⊛ kmahotels.com; map pp.204–205. In a superb location right behind the Gawdawpalin Paya, this rustic resort-style complex rivals *The Hotel @ Tharabar Gate* as Old Bagan's top address. Accommodation is in a cluster of low-slung red-brick buildings, and the friendly staff serve breakfast underneath the trees overlooking the river. There's also a banana-shaped pool and a spa. $135

Bagan Thande Hotel Behind the Bagan Archeological Museum ☎ 061 60025, ⊛ thandehotel.com; map pp.204–205. This is the cheapest option in Old Bagan, with accommodation in uninspiring bungalows and rooms with old-fashioned furnishings and dated bathrooms. Go for the $120 rooms if you can, which have at least a touch of character, and make sure you check out the pool and spa. $80

Bagan Thiripyitsaya Sanctuary Resort Just south of Old Bagan, off Anawrahta Rd ☎ 061 60048, ⊛ thiripyitsaya-resort.com; map pp.204–205. This is a top-dollar resort hotel occupying a prime position in a very peaceful location just outside the old city walls – with magnificent river views to boot. Unfortunately it doesn't quite live up to its magnificent setting, as the rooms are more functional than inspiring – and those with river views come with a hefty $80 surcharge. A pleasant spa, splendid riving-facing pool and cooking and meditation classes all help compensate, though. $135

★ **The Hotel @ Tharabar Gate** Tharaba Gate ☎ 061 60037, ⊛ tharabargate.com; map pp.204–205. If you're looking for a real "wow" factor, then you can't go wrong with this hotel in Old Bagan. The modern rooms are decorated with traditional paintings and artefacts, and the pretty flower gardens and pool come complete with a collection of stone elephants and wooden crocodiles. After a day exploring Bagan's temples, you'll no doubt appreciate the spa. $245

NEW BAGAN

★ **Areindmat Hotel** 2nd St ☎ 061 65049; map p.224. This is the most impressive of New Bagan's hotels, with rooms set around a grassy courtyard centred on a lily-covered pond and a tree covered in hanging decorations. Hindu art and sculptures fill the space, and the rooms have wooden furnishings and large rain showers. There's also a

lush swimming pool and a semi-alfresco dining area. One of the best around. $140

Bagan Central Hotel 15/16 Kayay St ☎ 092 5713 6019; map p.224. Dated hotel with a design so seriously odd it verges on retro-chic, although somehow it all works. Accommodation is in a cluster of bungalows (faced with knobbly bits of petrified wood) set around a "garden" cobbled with black bricks, while rooms come with heaps of gloomy wood panelling and quasi-Victorian furnishings like some kind of Gothic film set. The rooms are all identical, but the less you pay the closer you'll find yourself to the noisy main road. It's comfortable, even so, and very reasonably priced. $35

N.K. Betelnut Hotel Kayay St ☎ 061 65054; map p.224. Attractive guesthouse-style hotel with simple but well-equipped wood-panelled rooms and pretty cabanas out front faced with split betel tree trunks (hence the name). The position, right by the busy road, can make it a bit noisy, but the genuinely warm welcome partly compensates for a disturbed night's sleep. $35

Northern Breeze Villa 162 Cherry St ☎ 061 65472, ⊛ northernbreezehotel.bagan@gmail.com; map p.224. At current rates this place, which has small, clean and modern rooms, is a bargain. It's thoughtful touches like stone showers, art on the walls and a breakfast area amid weaver-bird nests that really set it apart from similarly priced competition. $40

★ **Ostello Bello Bagan** Main Rd ☎ 061 65069, ⊛ ostellobello.com; map p.224. This is a fabulous new Italian-owned hostel that's in a class above the rest. Dorms ($26) have between four and eight beds made of nicely faded wood and topped with good mattresses. Each room has its own bathroom. There's a travel desk, a bar with happy hour and a busy restaurant serving pizzas and other traveller favourites, and they also host party nights and events. With all this on offer, it's hardly a surprise to hear that *Ostello Bello* has completely cornered the Bagan backpacker market. $69

★ **Ruby True Hotel** Myat Lay Rd ☎ 061 65065, ⊛ rubytruebagan.com; map p.224. Delightful garden hotel with woven bamboo rooms set under the pink and purple blossoms of bougainvillea trees. Rooms are kitted out with desks, fridges, bedside tables and wardrobes, but the real highpoint of a stay here is the staff, who take the typical Burmese kind, helpful attitude to new levels of warmth. It's in a quiet area a 10min walk from central New Bagan. A great find. $80

Shwe Yee Pwint Hotel Kant Kaw St ☎ 09 519 3420, ⊛ shweyeepwinthotel.com; map p.224. Attractive hotel arranged around a pair of walled garden courtyards, with a further selection of rooms in a less attractive block on the other side of the road. Rooms are well equipped, if uninspiring, and there's also a good-sized pool plus spa. Reasonable value, though unlikely to set the pulse racing. $130

5

Thazin Garden Hotel 22 Thazin Rd ☎01 245 413, ⓦ thazingarden.com; map p.224. If you don't mind the overdose of tack, with gold-painted "royal" bed heads and bathrooms coated in marble, then this is one of New Bagan's better options. It's in a very peaceful location on the edge of town, set around a square of lush garden. Rooms come with either garden or temple views. Decent value. **$125**

Thurizza Bagal Thiri Marlar St ☎061 65229, ⓔ thirimarlarhotelbagan@gmail.com; map p.224. One of the best deals in New Bagan, set around a pretty little garden-patio and offering a genuine touch of class at sensible rates. Standard rooms are quiet, clean and nicely furnished, while superior rooms ($60) are well decorated and have wooden floors and attractive bathrooms. Used to be known as the *Thiri Marlar Hotel*. **$38**

EATING

There's a decent spread of places to eat throughout Bagan, although most are fairly humdrum, offering generic menus of pseudo-Western, sort-of Thai, insipid Burmese and so-so Chinese, often at above-average prices. Look out, though, for the delicious tamarind flakes wrapped in paper, a local speciality, which are served free at many places after meals as a digestive aid. The main cluster of restaurants is in **Nyaung U** along Thiripyitsaya 4 St (aka "Restaurant Row"), with further places spread along Main Rd and down into the nearby village of **Wet Kyi Inn**. In **New Bagan**, a bunch of similar-style places flanks the roundabout right in the middle of town about halfway up Kayay St, while in **Old Bagan** there's a fun little group of vegetarian-leaning restaurants near Tharaba Gate. There are no real Western-style bars, although many of the restaurants are also nice places to drink.

NYAUNG U

Aroma 2 Thiripyitsaya 4 St ☎09 204 2630; map p.208. This place specializes in Indian food, with seating on a large terrace that the many lanterns fail to fully illuminate. Food is reasonable enough and meals come with a nice spread of home-made chutneys (including an excellent tamarind pickle). They proudly advertise their lack of wi-fi and suggest that you pretend it's 1995 and talk instead – wise words, indeed. Meat mains K5000–6000, vegetarian mains K2500–3500. Daily 11am–3pm & 6–10pm.

Bagan Zay Thiripyitsaya 4 St ☎06 1246 2057; map p.208. With claret-coloured curtains and a blushing red bar, this restaurant doesn't just have the looks to make it stand out from the pack but the food as well, which is described as modern Myanmar cuisine and includes dishes such as grilled bullfish filets with lentil galettes (mains K4000–6000). Daily 9.30am–11pm.

Bibo Off Thiripyitsaya 4 St ☎09 402 555 241; map p.208. The super-friendly service from owner Thant Zaw Aung and his wife makes eating here a real pleasure. The menu covers Myanmar salads, soups and curries, plus a few Western dishes and a good selection of Thai curries and soups (mains K3000–5000) – not terribly authentic, but tasty enough, and competitively priced. Drinks include a good cocktail selection (K2000–3000 each), which are incredibly cheap during the two-for-one happy hour (5.30–7.30pm). Sometimes closes early, when the last customers leave. Daily 8am–9pm.

★**La Terrazze** Thiripyitsaya 4 St ☎09 259 010 913; map p.208. If you're hankering after olive oil, balsamic vinegar, parmesan, pancetta and home-baked foccacia, head for this impressive Mediterranean-flavoured restaurant, which is one of the more upmarket places to eat in Bagan. The well-chosen menu (mains K7000–9000) includes risotto, lasagne and a couple of fish and meat

secondi, plus excellent salads – the *insalata Siciliana* is a joy. Daily 11.30am–9.30pm.

Restaurant Leo Thiripyitsaya 4 St ☎09 402 559 018; map p.208. *Leo's* is a small, open-fronted, lime-green place that's the current flavour of the day with travellers. Diners eat surrounded by potted plants and art, which helps give a relaxed vibe. The menu is limited but very well chosen and presented, and includes a selection of Thai and Myanmar curries, sandwiches and pasta dishes. Mains K4000–5000. Daily 10am–10pm.

★**Sanon Training Restaurant** Pyu Saw Hti St ☎09 451 951 950, ⓦ sanon-restaurant.org; map p.208. A garden restaurant decorated with tear-shaped lamps, the *Sanon Training Restaurant* is part of a project in which disadvantaged local youths are trained in the business of high-end catering – and the results are outstanding. A blend of modern Myanmar and Western cuisine results in dishes such as roast duck with pumpkin and bean salad, fiercely fiery river prawns, beer-battered fish and Irrawaddy fish cakes with glass noodles. Once you're done with that lot, then take our advice and finish with a lime mousse. Daily specials are K5500. Mains K4000–6000. Daily 11am–10pm.

★**Weather Spoon's Bagan** Thiripyitsaya 4 St ☎09 4309 2640; map p.208. This unpretentious and ever busy little café is one of the better places to eat in Bagan (and much better than the British chain whose name the owner has adopted). The superb and entirely authentic Thai cuisine (mains K3000–4000) would put many a Bangkok restaurant to shame, while the Western food, including excellent burgers (K4500), is equally good. There's also an above-average selection of international vegetarian dishes plus assorted Chinese fare, all at super-competitive prices. Also has what's likely to be the best wi-fi connection in Bagan. Daily 9am–10pm.

OLD BAGAN

Golden Myanmar Near Tharaba Gate, opposite Pyi Yar; map pp.204–205. A haven of local-style dining amid touristy restaurants that surround it on all sides. There's no menu, but set meals (K4000) offer a huge spread of fifteen or so dishes including pork, chicken, beef and fish and come with assorted vegetable sides (and condiments) such as tasty tofu, crunchy tea-leaf salad and other Burmese delicacies. Daily 10am–8.30pm.

The Moon Near Tharaba Gate ☎09 4301 2411; map pp.204–205. The original of the cluster of homespun little vegetarian cafés just outside Tharaba Gate. The veg-only menu (mains K2500–3500) features all sorts of Asian and Western options, including soups, salads, burgers, curries and stir-fries – anything from mung bean soup and gazpacho through to deep-fried gourd, tamarind-leaf curry and papaya soup with yoghurt. The daily specials are chalked up on the blackboard. Daily 9am–9.30pm.

Star Beam Bistro Near Tharaba Gate, close to The Moon café; map pp.204–205. The original branch of this well-regarded local restaurant chain, although most people now go to their newly opened premises in New Bagan (see opposite); this one has become more of a café than a restaurant. Serves sandwiches, snacks and good coffee. Daily 11am–9pm.

NEW BAGAN

La Pizza 2 Kayay St; map p.224. Colourful Pathein umbrellas welcome you to this very popular pizza restaurant (mains K7000–11,000) right in the centre of town. Among the standard pizza toppings that can be found in any pizzeria anywhere on the planet, they have a few local specials like tea-leaf pizza. Daily 11.30am–9.30pm.

Miss TT 3rd St; map p.224. A cute little timber-lined, flower-filled café serving caffeine boosts such as espressos and cappuccinos as well as ice creams to soothe on a hot day. Coffees from K1000. Daily 8am–8pm.

San Carlo 3rd St ☎061 65253; map p.224. Above-average Western food from an Italian-trained Burmese chef, including a big selection of pizza and home-made pasta (K3500–5000) with proper mozzarella, parmesan, salami and so on. The dining room is covered floor to ceiling in paintings depicting local scenes. Daily 8am–10pm.

★**Star Beam** Near New Bagan Market, behind NLD Party Office ☎09 401 523 810; map p.224. Internationally trained chef Myo Myint turns out a short but delicious menu (mains K3500–6000) of superior local and international dishes, including Rakhine fish and Myanmar prawn curries alongside a few Western dishes – the freshly baked bread given out with the meals is a tasty touch. Daily 11am–9pm.

SHOPPING

There are plenty of shops in Bagan, though there are few places that really get the pulse racing. **Lacquerware** is the main local craft, particularly in Myinkaba village, which is stuffed to the gills with lacquer workshops and showrooms. There are a few **woodcarving** shops in Nyaung U along Thiripyitsaya 4 St. Bookshops are sadly rare, but some of the restaurants and guesthouses offer book swaps.

Golden Cuckoo Myinkaba village (follow the dirt road down the right-hand side of the Manuha Paya) ☎061 65156; map pp.204–205. The most enjoyable of Myinkaba's many lacquerware workshops, run by the same family for four generations and offering absorbing workshop tours without any sales patter or pressure to buy. Cheaper items (with seven layers of lacquer; from around

K10,000) are displayed in the showroom at the front, while the top-quality fourteen-layer pieces are kept in two rooms at the back (look out for the lacquer iPhone cover, motorbike helmet and guitar). Daily 7.30am–7.30pm.

Nanda Puppet and Gift Nanda Restaurant, Main Rd, Wet Kyi Inn ☎061 60790; map pp.204–205. Small selection of attractive traditional wooden puppets, plus

CULTURAL SHOWS

Several places around Bagan run nightly cultural shows featuring traditional puppets and/or dancing.

Amata Boutique House Thiripyitsaya Quarter, New Bagan ☎061 65099, ⓦamatabtqhouse.com. Performances nightly from Oct to March starting with a 30min puppet show followed by an hour of traditional Shan and Karen dancing. Free with a meal in the restaurant (with Asian mains for around K6000–7000). Daily 7–8.30pm.

Bagan Golden Palace Main Rd, Old Bagan. In the past this place staged nightly dance shows with dinner

in season ($24 with buffet or $10 entrance plus à la carte meal), but these had stopped at the time of research. They're likely to start again, so it's worth checking.

Nanda Restaurant Bagan–Chauk Rd, Wet Kyi Inn ☎061 60790. Enjoyable 40min puppet shows, free with a drink or meal at the restaurant (although the pedestrian Chinese food is expensive, with mains at around K5500–7000). Shows are put on whenever a tour group turns up to eat (and that's most lunch times).

5

BALLOONING IN BAGAN

There's perhaps no better way to see the temples of Bagan than by floating in the dawn light high above the temples in a **hot-air balloon** – although trips don't come cheap. Three operators run trips (all cost the same and leave from the same area at the same time), though they get booked up quickly, and in high season particularly it's a good idea to reserve as far in advance as possible. Flights cost from $330 per person, last around an hour and finish with a champagne breakfast.

Balloons over Bagan Near Hotel Zfreeti, Nyaung U ☎061 60713, ⓦ balloonsoverbagan.com.
Golden Eagle Balloon ⓦ bagan-balloon.com.

Oriental Ballooning 76A Lanmadaw Rd, Nyaung U ☎09 250 505 383, ⓦ orientalballooning.com.

a few other fine woodcarvings. Daily 9am–9.30pm.
Pauk Kan Thiripyitsaya 4 St ☎065 01143; map p.208. One of several woodcarving workshops along Restaurant Row. Most of the modern carvings on display are fairly stereotypical (the inevitable elephants and Buddhas, although they also have a small selection of far more attractive antique pieces on display – mostly on the larger side. Daily 7am–10pm.
Shwe Pathein Umbrella Workshop Wet Kyi Inn ☎09 4934 0854, ⓦ myanmarhandmade.com; map pp.204–205. It's difficult to miss this shop, thanks to the spectacularly

large and colourful Pathein-style parasols (see box, p.106) laid out in front of it next to the road – the resident artisans can also usually be seen at work inside. Cotton parasols range from K8000 up to K150,000, and they also do colourful silk parasols for around K5000–8000. Daily 7am–9pm.
Tun Handicrafts/Moe Moe Bagan–Chauk Rd, New Bagan ☎061 65063; map p.224. Upmarket showroom devoted to high-quality but expensive lacquerware. Smaller pieces start at around K15,000, while larger pots run into the hundreds of dollars – although they might be susceptible to bargaining. Daily 8am–9pm.

DIRECTORY

Banks All the banks marked on our Nyaung U map (see p.208) have ATMs. There's a foreign exchange counter at the AGD Bank on Thiripyitsaya 4 St, at the CB Bank on Main Rd and at the MAB Bank on Anawrahta Rd.
Internet Connections can be erratic and brain-crushingly slow here – the enhanced wi-fi connection at *Weather Spoon's Bagan* (see p.208) is generally reckoned the fastest and most reliable in town. Dedicated internet

cafés are increasingly rare.
Post office Anawrahta Rd, Nyaung U (signed "Telecommunications Centre"; Mon–Fri 9am–5pm, Sat 9am–noon).
Spas Spa treatments are available at many of the more upmarket hotels and also at the Blossom Spa at the *Amata Boutique House* in New Bagan (see map p.224), which operates 10am–9pm daily.

Around Bagan

There's an interesting crop of attractions in the area surrounding Bagan. Pick of the bunch is the dramatic **Taung Kalat** rock, the epicentre of Burmese *nat* worship, dotted with shrines to the unruly lords of the spirit realm. Visits to Taung Kalat can be combined with hikes up the adjacent **Mount Popa** or, alternatively, with a visit to **Salay**, south of Bagan, with its superb wooden monastery and cluster of Bagan-era monuments. Heading in the opposite direction, the riverside town of **Pakokku**, just to the north of Bagan, is home to a colourful trio of modern temples that are worth a half-day visit. All of these towns offer the sort of tantalizing glimpse of local life that can often be sadly missing in Bagan.

Taung Kalat

တောင်ကလပ်

Easily the most interesting excursion from Bagan is the half-day trip to **Taung Kalat** ("Pedestal Hill"), a dramatic little sheer-sided, temple-topped plug of volcanic rock around an hour's drive from Nyaung U (it's usually, if erroneously, referred to as **Mount**

Popa, although strictly speaking the mountain itself is the adjacent 1518m-high massif with its summit 4km to the east).

Taung Kalat (and Mount Popa) are famous throughout Myanmar as the home of the **nat spirits** (see p.386), attracting thousands of pilgrims who come and pay their respects to (and perhaps request a cheeky favour of) the resident *nats*. Things are particularly busy during the full-moon festival seasons of Nayon (May/June) and Nadaw (Nov/Dec).

According to **tradition**, you shouldn't wear red, black or green when visiting the mountain, nor should you bring meat, especially pork – a rule that's possibly in deference to the Muslim sensibilities of Byatta (see box, p.230), one of the *nats* said to reside on the mountain.

Entrance to the shrines is free. It takes around twenty minutes to climb to the summit of the rock, and for most people an hour or two is sufficient to explore the site.

Nat Temple

Before heading up the steps, be sure to visit the quirky **Nat Temple**, directly opposite the main stairway. Slightly kooky near life-size mannequins of assorted *nats* can be found here, standing along the back wall of the shrine inside a glassed-in corridor, many with banknotes stuffed into their hands. More or less at the centre of the gallery stands **Mai Wunna** (see box, p.230), the "Queen Mother of Popa", flanked by her sons **Min Gyi** and **Min Lay**. A few figures down to the right is the eye-catching **Min Kyawzwa**, the "Drunken Nat", mounted on a horse and festooned with rum bottles and packets of cheroots in honour of his misspent life drinking, cockfighting and hunting. Further along is an image of the elephant-headed **Ganesh**, one of several Hindu gods inducted into the Burmese *nat* pantheon (where he is known as Maha Peinne).

To the summit

From the temple, head between the pair of large white elephants opposite and up the main steps. There are **777 steps** up to the top, covered all the way. The lower third of the stairway is lined with numerous shops, beyond which is a footwear stall where you'll have to leave your shoes. The climb is punctuated by the incessant requests for "donations" for cleaning by locals who keep the stairs clear of monkey poo and other rubbish, while the monkeys themselves are very much in evidence, and fond of snatching food from the unwary.

Further *nat* shrines dot the steps on the way up. The most interesting is the one just above the footwear stall, signed "**Nat Nan**", featuring a parade of *nats* with helpful English signs. Figures here include (from left to right) Myin Phyu Shin (aka Aung Zawmagyi, "Lord of the White Horse"), a messenger said to have been executed for delivering an important royal communiqué too slowly, along with a family group showing Byatta (see box, p.230) and two images of his wife and sons.

The **summit** of the rock (737m) is covered in a dense cluster of Buddha and *nat* shrines, often crammed together shoulder to shoulder in the same shrine.

Mount Popa

ပုဂ္ဂ:တောင် · The quickest way to access Mount Popa is along the road past the *Popa Mountain Resort*. Any of the Bagan tour operators (see p.223) should be able to arrange trips up the mountain, and guides are also usually available for hire through the *Popa Mountain Resort*

Rising immediately to the east of Taung Kalat, the thickly forested slopes of the **Mount Popa** massif (1518m) comprise the eroded remains of a massive, extinct stratovolcano, topped with an enormous caldera some 1.6km wide and 850m deep. Often described as Myanmar's Mount Olympus, the massif is still considered the spiritual home of the country's four Mahagiri *nats*, and the *nat* shrine about halfway up the mountain remains a popular place of pilgrimage.

5

THE MAHAGIRI NATS

Mount Popa is associated with many spirits, but particularly with the four **Mahagiri** ("Great Mountain") *nats* – Mai Wunna and her husband Byatta, and Maung Tinde and his sister Shwemyethna – all of whom are popularly believed to live on the mountain.

MAUNG TINDE AND SHWEMYETHNA

The first of the Mount Popa legends concerns **Maung Tinde** – aka Nga Tin De, Min Mamagiri ("Lord of the Great Mountain"), Eindwin Nat or simply "Mr Handsome" – and his sister **Shwemyethna** (aka Hnamadawgyi, Saw Me Ya, Myat Hla and "Golden Face" – although another version of the tale says that the sister was actually Thonbanhla, a different *nat* entirely). Legend recounts that the king of Tagaung, fearful off Maung Tinde's supernatural powers (which included the ability to snap the tusks of an elephant with his bare hands), wed Shwemyethna in order to lure her brother to the palace, whereupon he was promptly tied to a tree and burnt to death – only for his sister to leap into the flames with him. The expired siblings subsequently reappeared as malevolent spirits, haunting the tree where they had died, until the king ordered it cut down and flung into the Ayeyarwady, along which it floated to Bagan. The two spirits then appeared in a dream to the king of Bagan asking him for a place to dwell, offering in return to guard the city. The king had the remains of the tree carried to Mount Popa, where the spirits of Maung Tinde and Shwemyethna are still said to reside, while shrines to the *nats* were erected at Tharaba Gate in Bagan (see p.210), where they remain to this day.

MAI WUNNA AND BYATTA

The second legend relates to **Mai Wunna** ("Miss Gold" – aka Popa Mai Daw, the "Queen Mother of Popa") who is said to rule over Mount Popa, on which her spirit dwells. Mai Wunna was a flower-eating ogress who became enamoured with **Byatta**, an Indian Muslim with supernatural powers, who had been ordered by King Anawrahta to collect flowers ten times daily from the mountain. Mai Wunna's advances resulted in Byatta neglecting his duty and being executed by the king, but not before she had produced two sons, **Min Gyi** and **Min Lay** (aka Shwe Hpyin Naungdaw and Shwe Hpyin Nyidaw).

Mai Wunna, it is said, subsequently died of a broken heart, while her sons were taken away by the king, and were later themselves executed for dereliction of duty while in his service, becoming *nats* in their turn – their shrine at Taungbyone, near Mandalay, is now the site of one of Myanmar's biggest *nat pwè* (spirit festivals; see box, p.298).

Assorted trails snake through the forest swathing the mountainside, which is home to profuse vegetation and numerous orchids – the name Popa is believed to come from the Pali/Sanskrit *puppa*, meaning flower, and flowers also loom large in the local legend of Mai Wunna and Byatta (see box above). It takes around four hours to reach the summit – guides can be arranged through the *Popa Mountain Resort*, halfway up the mountain, for $24.

ARRIVAL AND DEPARTURE TAUNG KALAT

By pick-up If you're heading to Taung Kalat from Bagan by public transport, a pick-up leaves the bus station in Nyaung U daily at 8am (2hr 30min), returning at 1.30–2pm – although you might have to change to another pick-up at Kyaukpadaung, just over halfway to the mountain, if there aren't enough passengers. It drops you in the village at the foot of the rock.

By car It's far preferable to either rent your own car (1.5hr; around K35,000) or take a seat in a shared taxi. Memory Share Taxi Service (Main Rd, Nyaung U ☎09 204 3579, ✉kohtaybgn@gmail.com) runs daily shared taxis to Mount Popa at 9am for K10,000/person. Any hotel can book you a seat.

ACCOMMODATION AND EATING

Popa Mountain Resort 1km east of Taung Kalat (4km by road) ☎01 399 334, ✉myanmartreasure resorts.com. A neat little mountain retreat, affordably priced and offering the perfect base for treks up Mount Popa. Accommodation is in a string of individual bungalows, nicely furnished with wooden floors, wicker furniture and a slight colonial ambience; pricier rooms have stunning views of Taung Kalat below.

Non-guests can pay $2 to use the pool and admire the view. **$100**

Yangon Restaurant A 5min drive from Taung Kalat on the road to Bagan. There are loads of cheap and quick places to eat at the base of Taung Kalat, but if you're arriving with a private driver from Bagan then you will invariably stop and eat at *Yangon Restaurant* a short drive away. Despite catching most of the tourist trade, this restaurant's Burmese and Thai dishes are very tasty. Mains around K4000. Daily 8am–6pm.

Salay
၀ဇလ

Around 50km south of New Bagan, just south of the town of Chauk on the banks of the Ayeyarwady, **SALAY** (aka "Sale") had a brief flowering of importance as a satellite of Bagan in the twelfth and thirteenth centuries, before falling back into relative obscurity. Just before the close of the nineteenth century, the British discovered **oil** buried under the ground around here and the town became rich on black gold and the passing river trade. This sudden influx of wealth allowed the inhabitants to build majestic Burmese-Victorian townhouses – a number of which still stand, in various states of decrepitude. Salay is today home to around fifty active monasteries, as well as over a hundred Bagan-era monuments. Note that there is nowhere to stay in Salay.

Yoke Sone Kyaung
ရုပ်ပုံကျောင်း • Tues–Sun 9.30am–4.30pm • K5000

Salay's main attraction is the impressive **Yoke Sone Kyaung** (aka "Youqson Kyaung"). Built in 1882, the unusual wooden structure consists of a large platform, raised on pillars, with a cluster of intricately carved wooden shrines on top. Flamboyant woodcarvings along its outer walls show scenes from the Jataka and Ramayana. The monastery is also home to the small **U Pone Nya Museum**, named after the celebrated nineteenth-century Burmese writer and containing assorted exhibits from other sites in Salay, including further fine woodcarvings.

Opposite the Yoke Sone Kyaung is a colonial-era library complex consisting of two separate buildings (one building dates from 1922 and the other from 1926) attached to one another via a very short enclosed iron bridge. Today, it serves as a library for the nearby monasteries. Due to the dearth of tourists in Salay the museum is often kept locked up, but even if there's nobody around to open it up, you can still walk around the outside.

Other monuments

On the opposite side of the road from the Yoke Sone Kyaung is the **Sar Sanatan Khon** monk training school, and the tumbledown white monastery, covered in plants and vines, dates from the 1860s. Right next to this is another wooden monastery, adorned with a few carvings and stone lions standing guard outside.

Beyond is a cluster of other temples: some gaudy and new, some majestic and ancient. These include the **Payathonzu**, an unusual tripartite temple similar to its namesake in Bagan (see p.218). Close by, the **Man Paya Pagoda** is home to the 7m-tall **Shinbin Maha Laba**, the largest lacquer Buddha image in Myanmar, said to date back to the thirteenth century.

Around 6km south of town, the **Shinpinsarkyo Pagoda** boasts some fine murals and a thirteenth-century wooden Buddha, while a further 1.5km beyond, so-called **Temple 99** has further excellent Jataka murals in its small thirteenth-century shrine. It's also worth devoting some time to exploring the small town centre, with its collection of mildewed colonial buildings.

| **ARRIVAL AND DEPARTURE** | **SALAY** |

By bus and pick-up From Bagan, take one of the frequent buses to Chauk and change there for a hugely overcrowded and slow pick-up truck to Salay. It will stop in every village between Chauk and Salay, but you'll get there eventually.

5

By car A trip by car to Salay from Bagan costs around $35–40 for a half-day, or around $60–70 for a day-long tour also including Mount Popa. To book, ask in travel agencies and hotels around Bagan.

EATING

★**Salay House** 481 Strand Rd ☎09 797 222 122, ⓦ salayhouseburma.com. In the centre of town, and overlooking the river, this colonial building has been impeccably restored by the wonderful Win Thidakhine and her husband, and turned into a café and craft shop. They serve fruit juices and daily specials such as vegetarian curries and pickled tea-leaf salads, and Win, who speaks English and German, also conducts historical walking tours of the town and is in the process of setting up day-trips from Bagan. Upstairs, the couple have assembled a little museum-like re-creation of a colonial Englishman's house, complete with pith hats, gramophones and King George VI commemorative plates.

Pakokku and around

ပခုက္ကူ

A large, leafy town on the north bank of the Ayeyarwady around 30km northeast of Bagan, **PAKOKKU** hit the international headlines in 2007 when local monks took to the streets to protest against skyrocketing fuel prices, kick-starting the nation's ill-fated "Saffron Revolution" (see p.376). Things are a lot quieter now, while the opening of a huge new **bridge** (the longest in Burma) over the river in 2011 resulted in the demise of the old ferry service to Bagan, meaning that most travellers now pass straight through. The town is still a worthwhile destination for a half-day trip, however, offering a trio of temples and an interesting slice of traditional life compared to touristy Nyaung U down the river.

Thihoshin Pagoda

သီဟိုဠ်ရှင်ဘုရား

The eye-poppingly glittery **Thihoshin Pagoda**, in the centre of town, is instantly recognizable thanks to the large clocktower next to the main entrance, and its interior is dazzling, with virtually every surface covered in multicoloured glass mosaics. The large courtyard at the back is home to a modest **museum** (free), piled high with assorted exhibits in glass cases including the usual old Buddhas, banknotes, bells, palanquins, lacquerware and a considerable quantity of dust.

Shwegugyi Pagoda

ရွှေဂူကြီးဘုရား • Just under 1km down the road from Thihoshin Pagoda

Like the Thihoshin Pagoda, the **Shwegugyi Pagoda** is a study in Burmese kitsch, its main shrine decorated with abundant white-and-orange frills and flourishes, with a slender golden stupa on top. The interior is contrastingly plain, save for the temple's prized **Tangetawgyi Buddha**, framed against a hundred-year-old woodcarved backdrop, its mass of intricate filigree populated by 136 little people along with various birds and animals. The top of the carving depicts the Buddha's descent from the Trayastrimsha heaven to earth after preaching to the gods above, accompanied by Indra and Brahma – a favourite subject of Burmese artists.

Also inside the shrine is a cabinet of curiosities, which includes eight swordfish bills of various sizes. Nobody can explain how or why they are here, but it's likely they were traded or a gift.

Shwe Mo Htwa

ရွှေမိုးထွာ • Around 3km east of the town centre beside the river

The town's third major temple is the **Shwe Mo Htwa**, a pretty little complex with a dense cluster of spiky-roofed shrines painted in various shades of gold and green, all arranged around a large courtyard dotted with prayer poles and planetary posts. The temple stands on the edge of town overlooking the Ayeyarwady, with sweeping views up- and downriver.

Pakhangyi

ပခန်းကြီး

A twenty-minute drive from Pakokku on the road to Monywa is **Pakhangyi**. In and around this town you'll find a nineteenth-century dark-wood monastery, scattered old stupas and remnants of ancient walls that are slowly being gobbled up by vines and creepers. A happy hour or so can be spent exploring the area and making exciting discoveries.

ARRIVAL AND DEPARTURE   PAKOKKU

By minibus/pick-up Three minibuses (daily; 1hr) depart at 9am, noon and 3pm for Pakokku from Nyaung U, dropping off near the market; alternatively, you can catch a pick-up (1hr 30min), also from near the market. Heading to Monywa (daily; 3hr), there are a couple of minibuses plus regular but slower and more uncomfortable pick-ups. Both depart from close to Pakokku's market area. There are also buses here to Shwebo (daily; 6hr).

By car A half-day trip to Pakokku from Bagan costs around $35/40 by car.

ACCOMMODATION

Mya Yatanar Inn 75 Lanmataw Rd ☏ 09 785 321 457. This friendly homestay is in the town's old quarter, close to the river on a shaded, tree-lined street, and is a throwback to a different era of backpacking: cheap, very basic, but with heaps of character. The highlight of a stay here is sitting on the terrace in the evening with Myi Myi, the gentle lady who has been hosting travellers here for 35 years, and listening to her and her family telling stories. Ask them to show you the old guestbook, which contains an entry by a now well-known Hollywood star. **K20,000**

Thu Kha Hotel Myoma Rd ☏ 062 23077, ✉ thukha717 @gmail.com. This hotel might be only a couple of years old, but it's already looking pretty tatty and the rooms can be noisy. Even so, it's undeniably more comfortable than *Mya Yatanar*, but lacks any of the character. **$35**

Inle Lake and the east

KAKKU

Inle Lake and the east

The southern half of Shan State and neighbouring Kayah State – stretching roughly from Kalaw and Inle Lake east to Kengtung and the Thai border, and south to Loikaw – is certainly Myanmar's most diverse and arguably its most rewarding area to travel in, despite the occasional difficulties of getting from A to B. Scenically, this is one of the country's most spectacular destinations, from the sublime pine-clad hills of Kalaw and the rolling uplands around Kengtung through to Inle Lake itself, a serene oval of water nestled between cloud-capped mountains. The region also offers an extraordinary ethnic tapestry of tribes, including the majority Shan, the Intha lake-people of Inle, the brightly red-turbanned Pa-O, the longhouse-dwelling Loi and the long-necked Kayan (Padaung). You could easily spend a week or longer just exploring the tourist hotspots around Inle and Kalaw, although further-flung Kengtung and Loikaw offer the chance to get right off the beaten track, while there are also plenty of opportunities to trek or cycle deep into the heart of the beautiful countryside almost everywhere.

The region's main attractions are all located in a relatively small area (though some awful public transport can make it feel much bigger than it actually is) in the southwest corner of Shan State. Gateway to the region is the old colonial hill station of **Kalaw**, with its refreshingly crisp climate and gorgeous backdrop of forested hills. It's also the starting point for numerous **treks** into the beautiful surrounding countryside, including the memorable two- or three-day hike down to Inle Lake, which offers marvellous landscapes and the chance to delve into local ethnic-minority culture en route. North of Kalaw, the pretty little lakeside town of **Pindaya** is home to the memorable Shwe Oo Min Cave, filled with thousands upon thousands of golden Buddhas.

Further east, the laidback tourist town of **Nyaungshwe** functions as the main base for excursions by boat or bike on or around beautiful **Inle Lake**, just a few kilometres to the south, and has a good selection of places to stay and a brilliant array of eating and drinking venues (although there are plenty of mainly upmarket places if you fancy

KENGTUNG MARKET

Highlights

❶ Inle markets Increasingly touristy but somehow still very traditional, Inle's itinerant markets move around the area on a regular five-day cycle, selling everything from fruit and flowers through to ethnic-minority headgear and cheesy souvenirs. **See box, p.241**

❷ Hiking around Kalaw There are plenty of trekking opportunities in the verdant hills around Kalaw, including the hike to Inle Lake – one of Myanmar's most memorable journeys. **See box, p.243**

❸ Shwe Oo Min Cave Remarkable cave complex, high above the peaceful lakeside town of Pindaya, stuffed to the gills with an extraordinary array of golden Buddha statues. **See p.246**

❹ Boat trips on Inle Lake Spend a day exploring the lake's stilted villages, floating gardens and water-fringed pagodas. **See p.260**

❺ Kakku This magical religious site features a remarkable array of over two thousand slender stupas rising from a remote hillside in the countryside south of Taunggyi. **See p.264**

❻ Pan Pet Rewarding interactions with Myanmar's famous long-necked Kayan (Padaung) ladies in the unspoilt village of Pan Pet, deep in the heartlands of remote Kayah State. **See p.269**

❼ Kengtung Way off the beaten track in Myanmar's far east, Kengtung boasts a pretty lake, plentiful pagodas and rewarding treks through colourful ethnic-minority villages. **See p.270**

HIGHLIGHTS ARE MARKED ON THE MAP ON P.238

staying on the lake itself). Northeast of Nyaungshwe is **Taunggyi**, the bustling capital of Shan State, little visited by foreigners but offering a complete change of pace and scenery; as well as hosting one of Myanmar's most spectacular festivals, it's also a convenient jumping-off point for visits to the stupa-swathed hillside at **Kakku**. Striking east of Taunggyi, you'll need to get on a plane to reach remote **Kengtung**, well off the tourist trail but offering a rewarding clutch of Buddhist pagodas and hill-tribe treks; it's also a handy staging post if you're heading to (or coming from) northern Thailand via the border town of **Tachileik**.

South of Taunggyi, **Kayah State** is now beginning to establish itself on the tourist radar, with plenty of foreigner-licensed accommodation now available in the enjoyably laidback state capital of **Loikaw**, from where it's possible to take a day-trip out to local Padaung and Karen villages.

Note that Pyin Oo Lwin, Hsipaw, Lashio and other parts of **northern Shan State** are featured in the Northern Myanmar chapter (see p.310).

Kalaw and around

ကလော

Gateway to the Inle region, lofty **KALAW** (pronounced Kah-*lore*) was established back in colonial times by British officers and administrators seeking an escape from the heat of the plains and has changed little in essence since. Less touristy and considerably more sedate than nearby Nyaungshwe, the town continues to serve as a breezy hill resort catering to a relatively well-heeled crowd of domestic and foreign tourists attracted by the refreshingly temperate climate and verdant upcountry scenery.

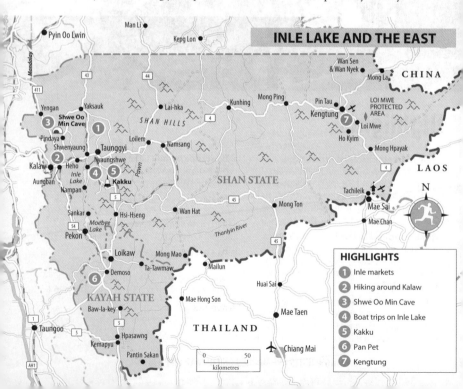

INLE LAKE AND THE EAST

HIGHLIGHTS

1. Inle markets
2. Hiking around Kalaw
3. Shwe Oo Min Cave
4. Boat trips on Inle Lake
5. Kakku
6. Pan Pet
7. Kengtung

TRAVEL RESTRICTIONS

The main closed-off area in this chapter is the wide swathe of land **between Taunggyi and Kengtung**. Foreigners are not permitted to visit this area, but can take flights between the two towns. In addition, to get anywhere at all from Kengtung, you'll need government permission, though this is free and fairly simple to arrange. Much of **Kayah State** remains off limits, although the state capital Loikaw and nearby villages are now freely open to independent travellers (see p.266).

6

There's still a distinct hint of an old-school subcontinental hill station about the place, both in the numerous (albeit dilapidated) colonial buildings which dot the centre, and in the sizeable local population of Nepalis and Indians, who first arrived as road- and rail-builders during British times and whose descendants remain in Kalaw to this day. The gorgeously green and craggy pine-studded hills which ring the town in every direction have a certain foothills-of-the-Himalayas feel too, as does the invigorating **climate**, pleasantly mild and sunny by day but often surprisingly chilly by night, especially during the winter months – this is one of the few places in Myanmar you'll appreciate a decent coat and woolly hat.

Most visitors to Kalaw come **to trek** (see p.243) – either following the well-beaten trails down to Inle Lake or, increasingly, to hike amid the stunning countryside around town or down to Pindaya. In town itself, a clutch of low-key sights – most notably the fine **Shwe Oo Min Paya** Buddha caves – can easily fill a day, or possibly two, perhaps combined with shorter rambles into the hills around town.

Aung Chan Tha Zedi

အောင်ချမ်းသာစေတီ • Khone Thae St • Daily 4am–9pm • Free

Poking up from the very centre of town is the impossible-to-miss stupa of the **Aung Chan Tha Zedi**, covered from tip to toe in tessellated mirrors which glint magically during sunrise and sunset. All this said, there's no real need to step inside the rusty gates guarding the complex – the views from around the market or the *Morning Star* teahouse (see p.244) are good enough.

Kalaw market

ကလောဈေး • Entrances on Union Highway and Khone Thae St • Daily 6am–5pm

Right next to the Aung Chan Tha Zedi, Kalaw's **market** is particularly lively when Inle Lake's peripatetic market (see box, p.241) lands here every fifth day, with stalls spilling out onto neighbouring streets. Even when the travelling market's not in town it's still worth a browse, with ramshackle tarpaulin-covered stalls stacked up with piles of tea, spices and bits of dried fish pounded into little circular wafers. There are also a few stalls selling traditional Burmese antiques and collectibles including opium pipes, metal *tattoo* sticks, Shan-style jewellery, puppets, lacquerware and palm-leaf books.

Thein Taung Kyaung

သိမ်တောင်ကျောင်း • Accessed from Union Highway • Daily 24hr; museum open on request • Free

North of the market, it's worth dragging yourself up the 270-odd steps of the covered staircase leading to the small **Thein Taung Kyaung** monastery, perched on a ridgetop high above town. There's not much to see once you've made the ascent bar a huge bo tree wrapped in flowering epiphytes and a small but eye-catching golden stupa designed in emulation of the Mahabodhi Paya in Bagan (see p.211). The views, however, are predictably good, with sweeping vistas over town and into

6

KALAW

0   200
metres

Thein
Taung
Kyaung

THEIN TAUNG PAGODA STREET

Bus
Tickets

Bus
Tickets

Fire Station

UNION HIGHWAY (NH4)

Soe Thein
Massage

NATSIN ROAD

THIRI MANGALAR STREET

UNION HIGHWAY (NH4)

KBZ
Bank

Market

Sikh Temple

Heho Airport, Inle Lake & Pindaya

Aung Chan
Tha Zedi

ZATILA STREET

TATANA

AUNG

Eagle Trekking

A1 Trekking

KHONE THAE STREET

Green Discovery

Pick-ups to
Taunggyi

DRINKING
Hi Bar   1

AUNG THA CHAN STREET

Sam's Family

MIN STREET

ZAW TIKA ST

AUNG THA PYAY STREET

N

Shwe Lin
Lun Paya

Naing Naing

STATION STREET

Hsu Taung
Pye Paya

THIDAR STREET

CHERRY STREET

Police Station

Hnee Pagoda (2.3km)   8 (1km) &   Shwe Oo Min Paya (1.8km)   Train Station (400m), 9 (1km), 10 (1km) & 11 (1.4km)

ACCOMMODATION	
Dream Villa	7
Eastern Paradise	3
Golden Kalaw Inn	5
Golden Lily	4
Honey Pine	1
Morning Glory Inn	10
Pine Breeze	6
Pine Hill Resort	8
Royal Kalaw Hills Resort	9
Thitaw Lay House	11
Winner	2

EATING	
Aung Nyein Chan Aung	7
Everest	5
Ma Hnin Si	3
Morning Star	4
Pyae Pyae	1
Red House	6
Sprouting Seeds	8
Thirigayhar	2

SHOPPING	
Rural Development Society	1

the hills beyond, and you can also take off into the countryside on tracks leading away behind the complex.

Around Kalaw

There are a couple of diverting sights hidden away amid the gentle hills south of Kalaw, easily combined into a pleasant two- to three-hour ramble. The highlight is the Buddha-filled cave of the **Shwe Oo Min Paya**, while the quaint **Hnee Pagoda** is also worth a detour. Much of the area is occupied by a large military zone, with an incongruous golf course inserted in the middle, although the main roads through it are open to all, despite the occasional checkpoint.

Shwe Oo Min Paya

ရွှေဥမင်ဘုရား • Shwe Oo Min Rd • Cave daily 6.30am–5.30pm • Free • From town, take Min St south and follow the road as it veers right (becoming University Rd) after about 500m, then turn right again after 500m onto Shwe Oo Min Rd

Just over 1km south of town, the extraordinary Buddha-filled cave of **Shwe Oo Min Paya** is well worth a look, especially if a visit to the eponymous Buddha cave in Pindaya (see p.246) isn't on your schedule. Dozens of golden pagodas stand clustered in front of the entrance to the **main cave**, inserted into a jungle-covered rock face. Inside, the cave is stuffed with hundreds of Buddhas inserted into every available space, like some surreal, subterranean Buddha warehouse, with images in every conceivable size and style – although virtually all are seated, with just a couple of standing and reclining figures. The adjacent **upper cave** is significantly smaller and claustrophobic, with narrow (and sometimes treacherously slippery) stairs leading up and down between further statues, and a large empty space at the far end, still waiting to be filled with images.

6

INLE MARKETS

A number of **markets** in the Inle Lake area operate on a rotating five-day cycle, moving around different towns and villages. With the possible exception of the very touristy Ywama "floating market", they're fascinating places (particularly early in the morning), where people from remote villages come to sell their produce or livestock and buy essential goods. The products on sale at most markets are generally geared to locals – fruit, veg, clothing, fishing equipment and the like. You'll also find fabrics including longyi and the headscarves used by local ethnic-minority women, while the more tourist-oriented markets sell a range of local antiques and cheesy souvenirs too.

Three or four markets take place simultaneously on each of the five days; in the schedule below, the last place listed for each day is either on or around Inle Lake.

Day 1 Kalaw/Shwenyaung/Inthein
Day 2 Nyaungshwe/Pindaya/Nampan
Day 3 Than Taung/Heho/Kyone/Taung Tho
Day 4 Aungban/Taunggyi/Ywama
Day 5 Pwe Hla/Maing Thauk/Phaung Daw Oo Paya.

Hnee Pagoda

ဦးဘုရား • Hnee Pagoda Rd • Daily 24hr • Free • From town, take Min St south and turn right onto Cherry St; continue straight uphill for 1km and then straight on at the junction with Damasatkyar Rd for another 400m to reach the complicated road junction in front of the Junction Rose hotel; from here, take the small road on your right, which brings you to the back of the pagoda after another 800m. If you're approaching from Shwe Oo Min Paya, follow the road as it loops west past the cave, through the golf course, then swings north through a checkpoint to reach the Junction Rose hotel

Around 2.5km southwest of central Kalaw, the hilltop **Hnee Pagoda** ("Bamboo Pagoda") sits amid rolling countryside that simply begs to be delved into. The main hall is home to the pagoda's revered Buddha statue, made of bamboo (hence the temple's name – although the original material is now invisible beneath the inevitable layers of gold leaf) and said to be more than five hundred years old. The hall doubles as a local dispensary, bookstore and teashop – the little old ladies who work here will probably offer you a cup of green tea and a plate of edible pickled tea leaves and nuts to round off your visit.

ARRIVAL AND DEPARTURE

KALAW AND AROUND

BY PLANE

Heho airport is around 35km east of Kalaw. Most people landing there are heading towards Inle Lake, which makes it hard to find people to share a cab to Kalaw (1hr); cabbies may start the bidding at around K40,000, though K30,000 –35,000 is a fairer amount for the distance. The only alternative is to walk the 2km or so to the main road and wait for a passing bus – this can take a while to arrive, and even if you're lucky enough to get a seat you'll probably have to change in Aungban. From Kalaw back to the airport, taxi prices are often a little cheaper; plane tickets can be purchased from agencies on Kalaw's Union Highway. **Destinations** Kengtung (2 weekly; 40min); Lashio (1 daily; 50min); Mandalay (5 daily; 35min); Nyaung U, for Bagan (1–2 daily; 40min); Tachileik (1–3 daily; 50min); Thandwe, for Ngapali (3 daily; 1hr); Yangon (6–7 daily, plus additional services via Mandalay and/or Nyaung U; 45min).

BY BUS, MINIBUS AND PICK-UP

Hardly any buses originate in Kalaw itself, with most passing through in transit en route to or from Taunggyi. Services stop at the various bus company offices along the main road, where you can also buy tickets, although you might find it easier to book either via your hotel or through any of the tour and trekking operators around town (see p.242). Pick-ups to Taunggyi (2hr 30min) leave from just southwest of the Aung Chan Tha Zedi, travelling via the turn-off to Heho airport (1hr 15min) and Shwenyaung (2hr), at the junction of the road to Nyaungshwe; vehicles tend to leave when full and are most frequent in the morning from around 7am to 8.30am.

To Nyaungshwe A few minibuses and buses (originating in Mandalay) pass through Kalaw en route to Nyaungshwe, although reserving a seat can be tricky. Alternatively, catch a local pick-up or minibus from the transport stop just southwest of the Aung Chan Tha Zedi to Shwenyaung (2hr), from where you can catch another pick-up or a taxi to Nyaungshwe (30min).

To Pindaya To reach Pindaya you'll have to take a pick-up or minibus (or motorbike taxi) to Aungban (30min; K1000),

6

and then a second pick-up (1hr; K3000) onto Pindaya, although if you're trying to do this as a day-trip from Kalaw note that transport back to Aungban from Pindaya tends to dry up in the afternoon, in which case your only way out will be by taxi.

Destinations Bagan (2 daily; 6–7hr); Loikaw (1 daily; 7hr); Mandalay (6 daily; 6hr); Naypyitaw (2–3 daily; 7hr); Taunggoo (3–4 daily; 9hr); Thazi (6 daily; 4hr); Yangon (8 daily; 10hr).

BY TAXI

The frustrating public transport connections to Inle and Pindaya tempt some to bite the bullet and splash out on a cab: count on K35,000 to either Pindaya (same fare

one-way or return) or Nyaungshwe, or at least K50,000 to visit the cave at Pindaya and then continue on to Nyaungshwe.

BY TRAIN

Kalaw's station, just over 1km south of the centre, sits on an extremely slow train line running from Thazi on the main Yangon–Mandalay line to Shwenyaung (a 30min ride by pick-up or taxi from Nyaungshwe). The views on this route are quite superb – some of the best in the land, indeed – though the wooden seating and bumpy journey (how can train lines have potholes?) will leave you with buns of steel. Destinations Shwenyaung (1 daily; 3hr 30min); Thazi (1 daily; 7hr 15min).

GETTING AROUND

Bicycle rental Naing Naing (see below) has an excellent selection of bikes, including gearless runarounds

(K3000/day), basic mountain bikes (K5000/day) and "deluxe" bikes ($12/day).

TREKKING AND TOUR AGENCIES

For more details about the trek to Inle Lake (see box opposite); when booking a trek, always check exactly what is and isn't included (boat and taxi fares, luggage transfer and so on). Day-treks and bike rides normally go for around $20 per person per day, while for overnight tours you'll have to add in the price of meals and accommodation (around another $10 per person).

A1 Trekking Khone Thae St ☎09 4958 5199, ✆A1 trekking.blogspot.com. Friendly, clued-up operator running two- and three-day Inle treks, as well as one- to three-day hikes around Kalaw, with a maximum of six people per group.

Eagle Trekking Aung Chan Tha St ☎09 428 312 678, ✉eagletrekking@gmail.com. Wide range of treks (maximum six people per group) including two- to five-day Inle itineraries, half- and full-day walks around Kalaw and two- and three-day treks to Pindaya. Also organizes birdwatching day-trips, one-day bike rides to Inle and combination bike-plus-hike tours.

Green Discovery Khone Thae St ☎09 428 318 216, ✆greendiscoverymyanmar.com. Well set-up tour operator offering a mix of trekking and cycling tours,

including the usual Inle treks plus three-day hikes to Pindaya. They also run one-day bike rides on quality mountain bikes to Inle and/or Pindaya, as well as various trekking-plus-cycling combinations.

Naing Naing Min St ☎09 428 312 267, ✉naing .cc@gmail.com. Kalaw's leading specialist biking operator, running one- and two-day tours to Inle (plus a cycling-plus-hiking two-day itinerary), as well as three-day rides from Kalaw or Inle to Mandalay or Bagan. They also arrange standard two- and three-day treks to the lake.

Sam's Family Aung Chan Tha St ☎081 50377, ✉samtrekking@gmail.com. Operated from the dining tables of a small restaurant, this reliable and long-running family business offers standard Inle treks, often at cheaper prices than the competition.

ACCOMMODATION

Accommodation in Kalaw caters to a relatively well-heeled crowd and there's a chronic lack of real budget options, although plenty of mid-range places. Given the often chilly climate, a/c isn't really necessary, although it comes as standard in most places, while the heaters provided in some more upmarket establishments are a definite bonus on cold nights.

Dream Villa Zatila St ☎081 50144, ✉dreamvilla hotel@gmail.com. One of the nicer places in the town centre, in a big fancy white building on a quiet backstreet. Inside it feels a bit like a Burmese Swiss chalet, with cosy wood-panelled rooms, which come with fridge, kettle and flatscreen TV (but no heater). Nice enough, but pricey for what you get. $50

Eastern Paradise Thiri Mangalar St ☎081 50315, ✉easternmotel@gmail.com. Dated but acceptable option, although the decor might remind you of childhood visits to an elderly relative and the rooms are a bit gloomy – $5 extra gets you one of the brighter ones upstairs. $25

Golden Kalaw Inn Natsin Rd ☎081 50311, ✉golden kalawinn@gmail.com. Reliable if uninspiring option with

TREKKING TO INLE LAKE AND AROUND KALAW

If there's one must-do activity in eastern Myanmar, it's the **multi-day trek** from Kalaw to Inle Lake, offering a memorable combination of striking scenery and a glimpse into some of Myanmar's minority cultures, all in one. While it's quite possible to walk from the lake to Kalaw, few people do it this way – heading from west to east, it's downhill most of the way, and you get the lake as a reward at the end.

ARRANGING A TRIP

Numerous tour operators in Kalaw (see opposite) arrange Inle treks, providing a guide, super-simple village accommodation, and three meals per full day. Your main choice will be whether to plump for a **two-** or **three-day** trip; the two-day trek is essentially the three-day trek minus the first day, which you'll cover by taxi instead. Some operators have four-day options, though three is enough for most travellers. The walk is long and pretty easy, so all you need is decent footwear – in the dry season, it's just about possible to make the trek in flip-flops. Also useful are a hat, sunblock and mosquito repellent (the area was malaria-free at the time of writing, but better safe than sorry). A torch and a towel also come in handy.

Prices vary depending upon how many there are in your group; agencies will usually be able to lump you in with others. Rates vary quite widely – anything from $20 to $30 per person per day. Always check if quoted prices include the boat ride across the lake (around $15 for the whole boat), transfer of baggage from Kalaw to Inle (around $4) and the Inle entrance fee ($10). You'll also need to factor in the cost of a taxi (around $15 per vehicle) if you're doing the two-day option.

THE WALK

Those on three-day treks will spend their **first day** on a semicircular route around town. This contains the only real forest on the trail, a small section that's only ever tricky after rain. Once through this, you'll emerge into a swathe of tea plantations, and weave from village to village along country trails – **Pa-O** and **Danu** people are most numerous in this area. The **second day** (or the first, if you're on a two-day trip) is mostly flat, with more villages and plenty of agricultural activity: rice, chilli, sesame and potato are among the crops grown in these parts. The **final day** sees the big drop down into Inle, with water buffalo tramping along the dusty trails and the lake itself visible for some of the walk.

OTHER OPTIONS AROUND KALAW

The increasing numbers of people tramping from Kalaw to Inle has prompted some operators to investigate alternative routes around Kalaw in an effort to escape the crowds. The two- or three-day trek **to Pindaya** is becoming increasingly popular, while there are also some rewarding day-treks **around Kalaw** (usually going for around $20 per person). In addition, a growing number of operators are now offering **cycling** trips around Kalaw, down to Inle Lake or Pindaya, or even further afield, while some also offer combined **cycling-plus-trekking** tours.

If you fancy a little taster of the countryside around Kalaw before signing up for a trek, try walking uphill to the west of town, past the *Pine Breeze* hotel; turn right at the junction, then left to wrap around the pagoda on a dirt path. A mere fifteen minutes from Kalaw, you're already in the countryside, with easy paths leading to small villages and across the hills beyond.

---

smallish but clean and comfortable rooms (those upstairs are brighter, and at the same price), plus good Western and Myanmar-style breakfasts. $25

Golden Lily Natsin Rd ☎ 081 50108, ✉ aungharri @gmail.com. Long-running backpacker favourite with a mixed bag of rooms. Budget doubles with shared bath – essentially a couple of beds jammed into a small and shabby wooden box – are unquestionably cheap but not at all cheerful. The wood-panelled en-suite rooms ($18) are gloomy but otherwise much nicer, opening out onto a grand balcony with sweeping hill views. $11

Honey Pine Zatila St ☎ 081 50728, ✆ honeypinehotel .blogspot.com. One of the better lower mid-range options in town, with neat, clean, pine-panelled fan rooms equipped with fridge, kettle and flatscreen TV (although rooms downstairs can be a bit dark). Superior rooms ($10 extra) come with a/c and bathtub. $35

Morning Glory Inn 16 East Circular Rd ☎ 081 50847, ✆ morninggloryinnkalaw.com. Set around a dinky half-timbered colonial house (in whose neat little dining room you'll eat your breakfast), with accommodation in red-and-white chalets dotted around the extensive gardens shelving

6

down into the valley below. Rooms themselves are comfy but rather plain, although the price is fair, and each comes with a little veranda from which to enjoy the fine views. $35
Pine Breeze Thittaw Rd ☎081 50459, ✉pinebreeze hotel@gmail.com. Among the town's newer options, occupying a slightly elevated position up a side street just west of the centre. Downstairs rooms are the cheapest; $10 extra gets you one of the brighter upstairs rooms, most of which have great views (plus balconies in some), as does the top-floor breakfast room. $35
★**Pine Hill Resort** Oo Min Rd ☎081 50079, ⌨myanmarpinehill.com. One of Kalaw's most beguiling places to stay, set in and around a lovely old colonial bungalow with bags of period character and atmosphere, with bright, pine-laden rooms arranged around immaculately manicured lawns and gardens. It's located in a quiet area 2km south of the town centre – a plus for some, a minus for others. $95
Royal Kalaw Hills Resort East Circular Rd ☎081 50851, ⌨royalkalawhillsresort.com. A real taste of colonial-era Kalaw, occupying a hundred-year-old country

house straight out of darkest Surrey plus a couple of new buildings sympathetically designed in keeping with the original, all wrapped up in picture-perfect terraced gardens. Rooms in the new buildings are smartly furnished in quasi-period style, although it's the (significantly more expensive) rooms in the original villa which are the real stunners – each an exquisite little Edwardian period piece full of time-warped atmosphere and character. $150
Thitaw Lay House Forest Rd ☎081 50846, ⌨thitaw layhouse.com. Attractive mid-range guesthouse in a soothingly rustic setting surrounded by woodland a 15min walk from town. Accommodation is in a pair of large and attractively appointed wooden bungalows and a slightly larger studio, and rates include a good buffet breakfast featuring quality home-baked items. $50
Winner Union Highway ☎081 50025, ✉winnerhotel .kalaw@gmail.com. Reliable and competitively priced budget option, with attentive service and a range of rooms including smallish but OK fan-only doubles, plus bigger and quieter a/c doubles (from $30) set away from the main road. $20

EATING

Aung Nyein Chan Aung Station St ☎081 50662. If you fancy eating in a place where locals are guaranteed to outnumber tourists, this is your spot. There are no prices on the menu for their mix of Burmese, Shan and Chinese dishes, but it'll generally come to K2500–3000 or so for a set of rice, main and sides. The Burmese food is served from 10.30am; as ever, the earlier in the day you eat it, the less time it has had to sit around acquiring germs. Daily 8.30am–10pm.
Everest Aung Chan Tha St ☎081 50348. Popular North Indian restaurant serving a wide range of meat and veg curries and thalis (mains around K4000) alongside the classic Nepalese-style dhal bhat – not the best Indian food you'll ever have, although the attentive service and lively atmosphere make it a nice place for an evening meal. Daily 9am–9pm.
Ma Hnin Si Station St ☎081 50727. Understated but gorgeous little teahouse – with its mocha-coloured tables and kindergarten-size chairs, mint-coloured interior and

hand-painted signs, it's like a little work of art that simply begs to be photographed. Try some of the speciality deep-fried Indian savouries with your tea. Daily 6am–8pm.
Morning Star Khone Thae St ☎081 50443. Mauve tables, lime-green chairs and sky-blue doors give this place the colour of a Caribbean beach shack. The fare, however, is pure Indian, including sugary Indian sweets and (in the mornings) delectable *chapati puri* (K400) – sitting outside with a view of the glittering glass stupa of the Aung Chan Tha Zedi opposite is a fine way to start the day. Daily 6am–7pm.
Pyae Pyae Union Highway ☎081 50798. Pint-sized little venue on the main road a short walk west of the centre, popular with tourists and locals alike on account of its excellent Shan noodles (K1000) served in a variety of soups, and salad. Daily 6am–9pm.
★**Red House** Min St ☎09 771 357 407. Set in a fine old colonial building (the red house of the name), this stylish new venue has brought a welcome dash of culinary chic to town, with a mainly Italian menu (mains K6600–8800) of

---

CHEWING BETEL, KALAW-STYLE

Kalaw is one of the better places in the land to give the chewing of **betel nut** parcels (see box, p.10) a go. While most travellers find the taste diabolical (and it's also carcinogenic), the fare on offer in Kalaw can be surprisingly pleasant to munch on. Sweeter, tastier ingredients such as **green papaya** and **coconut** are often added to the regular mix, while locals like the betel nuts themselves lightly roasted, adding yet another nuance to the taste. Dozens of shacks and tiny shops will sell you this local oddity, with the stretch south of the market a particularly happy hunting ground; figure on around K200 per parcel and, as ever, remember to spit out the first few times your mouth starts to fill with saliva, as the slaked lime can destroy your liver, as well as your teeth.

pizza and pasta plus real mozzarella, *frittata* and warming bowls of minestrone perfectly suited to chilly Kalaw, plus good coffee. Daily 11am–10pm.

Sprouting Seeds Thidar St ☎09 767 472 669. Cute little good-lifer vegetarian café, with soothing hill views from the attached garden. Food features a small but well-chosen selection of international flavours featuring "small bites" (K3000–4000) such as tea-leaf salad, guacamole and bruschetta alongside a few Asian-style mains (K5000–6000). They also do a good range of hot and cold drinks,

plus bakery items, home-made yoghurt and ice cream. Tues–Sun 9am–7pm.

Thirigayhar Union Highway ☎081 50216. Fun restaurant in a creaky and enjoyably time-warped old wooden house next to *Pyae Pyae*. The menu features an eclectic mix of Burmese, Shan, Chinese and European food (mains K6000–7500), including local dishes such as *zat byat byat* (spicy minced meat mixed with tomato and basil; K4000) and the curious-tasting peanut soup with mustard leaves. Daily 10am–10pm.

DRINKING

Hi Bar Khone Thae St. A genuine (if tiny) Western-style bar. It might be rough around the edges, but it has cheap

whisky sours (K1000) and on most nights a battered guitar is passed around for entertainment. Daily 5–11pm.

SHOPPING

Rural Development Society Min St ☎081 50747. Fair-trade shop selling inexpensive locally made souvenirs including jewellery, longyi and funky pompon hats. All

profits go towards development projects in surrounding minority villages. Daily 9am–5pm.

DIRECTORY

Bank There's a branch of KBZ Bank plus ATM on Min Rd. **Massage** Soe Thein offers traditional Pa-O massage for K8000/hr, from a first-floor room on the Union Highway

(daily 9.30am–6pm).
Post office Union Highway, Mon–Fri 9.30am–4.30pm.

Pindaya

ပင်းတယ

Few places in Myanmar make as dramatic a first impression as **PINDAYA**, as the road from Aungban begins its swooping descent into town, suddenly revealing the serene blue square of Pone Taloke Lake at the foot of the hills below, backdropped by a craggy limestone ridge studded with stupas and stairways. It's here, high up on the ridge above town, that you'll find one of the region's most memorable sights, the spectacular **Shwe Oo Min Cave**, a huge natural cavern filled with thousands upon thousands of gleaming Buddha statues – like some kind of surreal Aladdin's cave, Burmese-style. Most travellers visit the cave on a day-trip from Inle or Kalaw, although staying the night at Pindaya allows you to see the cave at the crack of dawn, before the tour buses arrive, and also gives you the chance to spend some time getting under the skin of one of eastern Myanmar's most serene and scenic towns.

Pindaya itself isn't much more than an overgrown lakeside village, and none the worse for it, although the lively little market offers a modicum of mercantile excitement. Centrepiece of the town is pretty **Pone Taloke Lake**, with the gilded stupas and old wooden buildings of the **Kantha Kyaung** monastery at its northern end. Paths around the lake offer beautiful strolls at any time of day, while after dark the waters are attractively framed by the lights of the town.

Beyond here stretches a bucolic landscape of rich red earth and rolling hills, less dramatically craggy than the landscapes around Kalaw but with its own more

---

PINDAYA ENTRY FEE

A K2000 **entry fee** was formerly levied on all foreign visitors to Pindaya (except those hiking in from Kalaw). This was not being charged at the time of writing, although it's possible that it may be reinstated (and, if so, most likely increased) in the future.

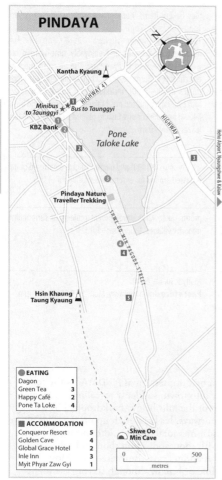

PINDAYA

Kantha Kyaung

Minibus to Taunggyi — Bus to Taunggyi

KBZ Bank

Pone Taloke Lake

HIGHWAY 41

Pindaya Nature Traveller Trekking

SHWE OO MIN PAGODA STREET

Hsin Khaung Taung Kyaung

● EATING
Dagon	1
Green Tea	3
Happy Café	2
Pone Ta Loke	4

■ ACCOMMODATION
Conqueror Resort	5
Golden Cave	4
Global Grace Hotel	2
Inle Inn	3
Myit Phyar Zaw Gyi	1

Shwe Oo Min Cave

0 — 500 metres

Hebo Airport, Nyaungshwe & Kalaw

understated charm. Arid for most of the year, the region explodes into a patchwork of green after the rains, making this one of Shan State's most important agricultural zones. In and around town, you'll probably see some of the many **Danu** and **Pa-O** who live in the area, resplendent underneath colourful headdresses.

Shwe Oo Min Cave

ရွှေဥမင်ဂူ • Daily 6am–6pm • K3000

Hidden away in the towering limestone escarpment high above town, the spectacular **Shwe Oo Min Cave** is one of eastern Myanmar's great sights: a cavernous, sepulchral cave, crammed floor to ceiling with over nine thousand Buddha statues, gleaming magically in the dim light. There has apparently been a pagoda at the cave's entrance since the third century BC, and townsfolk like to regale visitors with the legend that the grotto was inhabited by a giant spider which took a fancy to local princesses and imprisoned them here – perhaps one reason why the statues inside the cave only date back to the late eighteenth century. More are being added all the time by Buddhist pilgrims and an assortment of international organizations. Statues are made of various different materials – wood, marble, cement and more – almost all carved in the seated position. Devotees touch the knees of images for blessing, which accounts for the rubbed-off gold leaf on the legs of many of the statues.

The **cave** itself divides into several distinct areas. The first section, in the highest and most cavernous part of the cave, is far and away the most spectacular, with Buddha statues crammed into every available space and stacked up virtually to the roof. Towards the back, the aptly named "The Maze" has winding walkways threading their way disorientatingly between further masses of statuary, with superb views across the entire main cave from the raised section at the very back. From here, further steps lead down into the depths of the cave, which becomes warmer and muggier as you descend, although the further reaches of the cave are less atmospheric – and less crowded with statues – than those near the entrance.

There are a couple of other things to see while you're up by the cave. One is the serene **monastery** just alongside – the whitewashed walls and rarefied air make it feel almost Tibetan. Then there's **Alegu**, the biggest Buddha on the mountainside at over 12m in height, sitting in a side-hall a little further along.

GETTING TO SHWE OO MIN CAVE

The easiest way to reach the cave is by **taxi** or **motorbike**. These can drop you at the bottom of the lift up to the cave, taking virtually all the effort out of a visit. If you want to **walk**, there's an extensive – and surprisingly confusing – network of covered staircases leading up to the cave from various directions (you might find it helpful to take a picture of the mountainside before you head on up, which you can then use as a reference to aid navigation once you're there and when coming back down). The shortest but steepest ascent is via the staircases directly below the cave – a breathless ascent up around five hundred steps. It's much nicer to walk up via the **Hsin Khaung Taung Kyaung** monastery (see below). The climb to Shwe Oo Min is much gentler following this route, and the path itself is peaceful and with lovely views – far nicer than yomping along the busy main road to the cave. However you get there, it's best to visit the cave **either early or late in the day**, when the worst of the tour groups have gone – and ideally when they open at 6am, when you're pretty much guaranteed to have them almost entirely to yourself.

6

Hsin Khaung Taung Kyaung

ဆင်ခေါင်တောင်ကျောင်း • Daily 24hr • Free • Accessible on a variety of paths from Shwe Oo Min Pagoda St, about a 15min walk south of town

The large teak-wood **Hsin Khaung Taung Kyaung** is well worth a visit if you're in Pindaya for more than just a few hours. It's quite easy to visit this monastery on your way to or from Shwe Oo Min (see box above) – it's downhill to the north of the cave, along a dirt track from one of the covered arcade exits.

ARRIVAL AND DEPARTURE
PINDAYA

BY PLANE

Heho airport (see p.241) is 65km from Pindaya; a taxi will set you back at least K45,000–50,000. If that's too steep, you could walk the 2km south to the main road and find a bus or pick-up heading west to Aungban (1hr 30min); from there, it's easy to find a pick-up for the remaining 1hr journey to Pindaya. Heading from Pindaya to the airport, you could make use of the few daily buses to Taunggyi (see below), though obviously these may not depart at times appropriate for you, and you'll have to make your own way from the main road to the airport.

BY BUS, MINIBUS AND PICK-UP

Pindaya doesn't crop up on many bus schedules. There are two daily buses (6am & 7am) plus minibuses (6am & 2pm) to Taunggyi (3hr 30min), departing from the junction outside the *Dagon* restaurant/beer station (see p.248).

To Kalaw To reach Kalaw you'll have to take a pick-up to Aungban (1hr; K3000), and then a second pick-up or

minibus (or motorbike taxi) on to Pindaya (30min; K1000 by minibus/pick-up); note that transport to Aungban tends to dry up in the afternoon, in which case your only way out will be by taxi.

To Nyaungshwe Heading to Nyaungshwe, first catch a bus/minibus heading towards Taunggyi and get off at Shwenyaung (3hr), from where it's a 30min ride by taxi (K10,000) or pick-up (K1000) to Nyaungshwe. Travelling in the opposite direction is tricky: first get to Shwenyaung, then hope you can get a seat on a passing bus, minibus or pick-up to Aungban (1hr 30min), where you'll need to change onto another pick-up for the final 1hr leg of the journey to Pindaya.

BY TAXI

Given the difficulty in reaching Pindaya by public transport, taking a taxi is a tempting option. Count on around K30,000–35,000 to Kalaw, a bit more to Nyaungshwe.

ACCOMMODATION

Conqueror Resort Shwe Oo Min Rd ☏ 081 66355, ⓦ conquerorresorthotel.com. Sprawling resort complex, with accommodation dotted around the attractive gardens in a mix of bamboo, wood and brick bungalows vaguely inspired by local architectural styles. Rooms are large and stuffed full of chintzy furniture, with verandas front and back, while facilities include a spa, restaurant and a good-sized pool. **$85**

Global Grace Hotel Shwe Oo Min Rd ☏ 086 22447, ⓦ globalgracehotelpindaya.com. A reliable mid-range option. Standard rooms in the main building are bright and light, with great lake views and balconies – although the fittings are looking a bit battered. Deluxe rooms ($10 extra) in the annexe are more modern and smartly furnished but contrastingly dark and viewless. **$40**

6

TREKKING AROUND PINDAYA

The two- to three-day trek from **Kalaw to Pindaya** is becoming an increasingly popular alternative to the Kalaw to Inle Lake route; it's normally done starting in Kalaw, which means you're walking downhill for most of the way. There are also a number of rewarding treks **around Pindaya** itself, such as the five-hour hike up to Yazagyi, a Kayan (Padaung) village up in the mountains. One- to three-day treks can be arranged through U Zaw Min Htike at **Pindaya Nature Traveller Trekking** on Shwe Oo Min Pagoda St (☎09 431 5490, ✉nature travellerpindaya@gmail.com; around $25 per person per day), and through the *Golden Cave* hotel on the same road (☎081 66166, ✇goldencavehotel.com; K10,000 for a half-day trek, K18,000 for a full day, K40,000 for two days).

Golden Cave Shwe Oo Min Rd ☎081 66166, ✇golden cavehotel.com. Dated but personable mid-range choice, with accommodation in the main building and in chalets dotted around the shady gardens. Rooms are spacious and enjoyably old-fashioned, with little balconies, wood-panelled walls and the sort of bedspreads your granny used to have. Staff can also arrange treks (see box above). $47

★**Inle Inn** Mahabandoola Rd ☎081 66029, ✇pindaya inleinnmyanmar.com. Pindaya's top accommodation choice, by a country mile, occupying an intimate little complex designed to resemble a traditional Burmese village (albeit far cleaner and more luxurious than any local village you're ever likely to see) set in gorgeous gardens. Accommodation is in a mix of rustic "huts" and larger suite-sized chalets with fireplace (lit nightly on request) and lovely wood-panelled bathtubs, and there's also a wonderfully airy bamboo and wood restaurant, plus a small pool, gym and spa. Huts $95, chalets $120

Myit Phyar Zaw Gyi 106 Zaytan Quarter ☎081 66325. Pindaya's only real budget option, centrally located close to the market, lake and several restaurants. Rooms are well past their best but are clean and reasonably well maintained. Rooms facing the lake have nice views, although can get quite noisy. Good single rates ($15). $25

EATING

Dagon Shwe Oo Min Rd. Either a restaurant or a beer station, depending upon whether you're looking at the signboard or the menu, but it functions pretty well in both regards. As well as selling draught beer, it's one of the town's more reliable places for food, with simple dishes such as fried rice or noodle soup (mains around K1500). Daily 7am–10pm.

★**Green Tea** Shwe Oo Min Rd ☎081 66344. A bit of a surprise in low-key Pindaya, this unexpectedly grand two-story wooden lakeside restaurant pulls in the coach parties at lunch but is a lot quieter and more pleasant after dark. Food features a fairly stereotypical range of European and Asian (Chinese, Thai and Vietnamese) dishes, plus a few local options including Myanmar chicken and pork curries (K5500) and Danu-style mashed rice with potato and fish (K2000). Daily 9am–4pm & 6–9pm.

Happy Cafe Shwe Oo Min Rd ☎093 623 3738. Not the best-looking teahouse in town, but the only one with an English sign and a lake view, making it a nice place to linger over a drink. Daily 6am–5.30pm.

Pone Ta Loke Shwe Oo Min Rd. Cute little café-cum-crafts shop serving up a short but authentic selection of Burmese dishes, including generous and inexpensive Myanmar curry spreads (K3000), plus local specialities like Inthar-style rice with fish and Danu-style rice with mashed potato. Daily 10am–8pm.

DIRECTORY

Banks There's a KBZ Bank at the northeast corner of the lake, although it's best to bring all the money you need in case their ATM's out of service.

Nyaungshwe

ညောင်ရွှေ

The small town of **NYAUNGSHWE** is the main base for visitors to **Inle Lake**, whose waters begin just a few kilometres to the south. The town has been one of the most visible beneficiaries of Myanmar's recent tourism boom, and the sudden inflow of cash has brought jolting changes to the formerly sleepy streets, as made evident by the mushrooming number of hotels and restaurants, as well as the multistorey buildings which poke incongruously from the rustic surroundings. However, Nyaungshwe has so

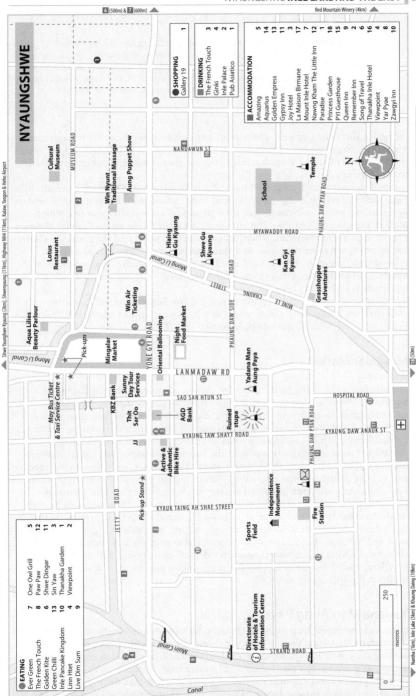

6 (500m) & 7 (600m) ▲

Red Mountain Winery (4km) ▲

NYAUNGSHWE

Shwe Yaunghwe Kyaung (2km), Shwenyaung (11km), Highway NH4 (11km), Kalaw, Yangon & Heho Airport

● SHOPPING
Gallery 19	1

● DRINKING
The French Touch	3
Ginki	4
Inle Palace	2
Pub Asiatico	1

▲ ACCOMMODATION
Amazing	5
Aquarius	14
Golden Empress	13
Gypsy Inn	11
Joy Hotel	3
La Maison Birmane	17
Mount Inle Hotel	7
Nawng Kham The Little Inn	12
Paradise	1
Princess Garden	18
PYI Guesthouse	15
Queen Inn	9
Remember Inn	2
Song of Travel	6
Thanakha Inle Hotel	16
Viewpoint	4
Yar Pyae	8
Zawgyi Inn	10

● EATING
Ever Green	7	One Owl Grill	5
The French Touch	8	Paw Paw	12
Golden Kite	6	Shwe Dingar	11
Green Chilli	13	Sin Yaw	3
Inle Pancake Kingdom	10	Thanakha Garden	1
Linn Htet	4	Viewpoint	9
Live Dim Sum	2		

Nantha (1km), Inle Lake (5km) & Khaung Daing (10km) ▼

0 — 250 metres

6

INLE LAKE ENTRY FEE

There's a $10 **entry fee** to the Inle Lake area, payable in either dollars or kyat; this is most commonly levied at a booth as you approach Nyaungshwe from the north. Your bus, taxi or pick-up driver will pull over (he'll get into trouble if he doesn't), and you may not even have to leave your seat during the purchase process. Those hiking in from Kalaw probably won't have to pay, and in any case you almost certainly won't be required to show your entry ticket at any time after purchase.

---

far ridden these changes well, and with its lazy charm barely diluted it remains one of Myanmar's most enjoyable places to kick back for a few days, or longer, helped by a good selection of accommodation in all price ranges and an excellent range of places to eat and drink.

Top of most visitors' bucket lists, naturally, is the memorable **boat trip** out onto Inle Lake itself (see box, p.260), easily arranged at just about any guesthouse, hotel or travel agent around town. In Nyaungshwe itself attractions include the enjoyable **Mingalar Market**, the splendid old royal teak mansion now housing the town's **Cultural Museum**, and some pretty **monasteries**, while just outside town you'll find the personable **Shwe Yaunghwe Kyaung** and the idyllic **Red Mountain Winery**. It's also easy and very enjoyable to take off by **bike** around Inle Lake for an alternative, land-side view of the waters, with possible destinations including the pretty village of Maing Thauk and the hot springs of Khaung Daing.

Nyaungshwe gets particularly busy during the **Fire-Balloon Festival** in nearby Taunggyi (see box, p.264), which takes place in November, and during the Phaung Daw Oo Paya Festival (September/October).

Mingalar Market

Daily 6am–5pm

Despite being slap-bang in the centre of eastern Myanmar's biggest tourist honeypot, **Mingalar Market** offers an enjoyable and surprisingly authentic slice of local life – rather more authentic and less touristed, in fact, than some of the Inle Lake markets, although things do get busy when the rotating five-day market (see box, p.241) arrives in town, taking up every available space in the market itself and spilling out onto the surrounding streets. At other times the market remains a low-key affair, with ramshackle stalls set below low-flying ropes and sagging sheets of tarpaulin, along with dozens of local seamstresses hunched over old-fashioned, pedal-operated sewing machines. There are also plenty of colourful food and flower stalls, manned (or, more accurately, womaned) by the local Shan and Intha who descend daily on the market to sell their wares, seated behind piles of tea leaves, watermelons, pumpkins, avocados and dangling hands of huge red bananas. The market's one concession to tourism is an interesting little cluster of handicraft stalls on its eastern side, selling a good selection of Shan-style jewellery, traditional palm-leaf books, *tattoo* sticks, opium scales and pipes, traditional puppets and so on.

Yadana Man Aung Paya

ရတနာမာန်အောင်ဘုရား• Entrances on Main Rd & Phaung Daw Side Rd • Daily 6am–9pm • Free, though small donation expected

The **Yadana Man Aung Paya** is the most interesting of the Buddhist monuments dotting the centre of Nyaungshwe, centred on a brilliantly gilded eight-tier octagonal golden stupa planted on a tall square base. Inside, four Buddhas sit at the cardinal points amid a quaint medley of assorted bric-a-brac displayed in glass cases, including opulent antique lacquerware, metalwork, figurines and opium pipes.

It's also possible to scramble up to the top of the earth- and scrub-covered remains of a **ruined stupa** immediately to the west for fine views out over Nyaungshwe and the surrounding hills.

The Monastery Quarter

ဘုန်းတော်ကြီးကျောင်းရပ်ကွက် • East bank of Mong Li canal • Daily 24hr • Free

Hugging the east bank of the small Mong Li canal is a trio of **monasteries**, each of them housing more than a hundred monks. While none of them is particularly interesting in an architectural sense, it's quite an experience to pass by at prayer time (early morning being your best bet) in order to take in the ethereal sound of monotonous, synchronized chanting.

Cultural Museum

ယဉ်ကျေးမှုပြတိုက် • Museum Rd • Tues–Sun 10am–4pm • K2000

The most intriguing sight in town is the **Cultural Museum** out to the northeast of the centre. An odd mishmash of teak ruins, brick add-ons and Buddhist flourishes, supposedly modelled on the palaces of Amarapura and Mandalay, it has passed through several different incarnations since its completion in 1923. The main hall was originally built as the palace of **Sao Shwe Thaik**, the last *saopha* (sky lord) of Nyaungshwe. An ethnic Shan himself, Sao Shwe Thaik became the first president of independent Burma in 1948, holding that post until 1952 and continuing as a prominent political figure in the new Union before being arrested following the military coup in 1962, dying in prison later the same year.

The Shan became increasingly marginalized under the subsequent military junta, and the palace building, after a time as the Museum of Shan Chiefs, was transformed into a Buddha Museum, its Shan identity erased. The times are a-changing, however, and a Shan flag now flutters happily outside, while old Shan ceremonial accoutrements including the royal throne and furniture have been put back on display, together with a few elaborate, sequinned royal costumes and some evocative photographs of Shan rulers and visiting dignitaries, including a very grumpy-looking future King Edward VII, labelled "Wale Prince (Crown Price of British)". It's the superb **interior**, however, which really catches the attention, particularly the cavernous audience hall and interconnected throne room, with mighty teak columns and carved wooden walls, screens and creaky floors – one of the most memorable of Myanmar's many fine timber constructions.

NYAUNGSHWE BY BICYCLE

Nyaungshwe is surrounded by stunning countryside, best explored either on foot on a trek (see p.253) or by **bicycle**. There are a number of rewarding destinations to aim for, including the Red Mountain winery (see box, p.256) and the Khaung Daing hot springs (see p.261) – you can actually work both into a circular route by taking a boat (around K8000 after haggling) between the village of Maing Thauk and Khaung Daing.

For an introduction to the area on two wheels, try the enjoyable 22km round-trip from Nyaungshwe to **Maing Thauk**, starting south of Nyaungshwe at Nantha village (see p.252). You'll enter the village immediately after passing the Buddha statue; take a left turn at the tiny T-junction. After passing through a tunnel-like thicket of bamboo, the road veers left; turn right instead, onto a dirt track just before the small bridge. This path heads through bucolic scenery to a small village, after which you'll be spat back out onto the main road to Maing Thauk. If you're heading in the opposite direction, the path back to Nyaungshwe starts almost opposite *Aung Thit Sar*, a tiny juice bar just north of a distinctive pink-painted building.

Nantha

 နန်းသာ • 1km south of town

It's well worth the short walk south to the small village of **Nantha**, a charming place that provides an Inle Lake vibe without the need to leave dry land – stilt-housing, friendly locals and a rural atmosphere whose tranquil air is broken only by the regular put-putting of boat engines. Look hard enough and you'll find a tiny teahouse and small shop; far easier to spot is the huge **Buddha statue** sitting at the village's north end.

6

Shwe Yaunghwe Kyaung

Around 2km north of Nyaungshwe on the road to Shwenyaung • Daily 6am–6pm • Free

It's well worth making the short excursion from Nyaungshwe to visit the pretty **Shwe Yaunghwe Kyaung** monastery, centred on a gorgeous old teak hall whose distinctive oval windows seem to have been designed specifically to frame shots of the monks meditating within. Look out too for the small **shrine** behind, with antique tiled floors and richly red-painted walls dotted with hundreds of tiny Buddhas set in niches. Unfortunately, the whole place can get overrun with coach parties – best to visit early or late in the day.

ARRIVAL AND DEPARTURE
NYAUNGSHWE

BY PLANE

Transport to/from town A taxi to or from Heho airport, around 35km northeast of Kalaw, costs around K20,000 and takes an hour (given the number of tourists heading to Nyaungshwe, it should be possible to find other people with whom to share the fare, at least when arriving). By public transport you'll have to walk (or take a taxi) 2km south to the main road, find something heading east towards Taunggyi, get off at Shwenyaung, then catch a pick-up (K1000) the rest of the way.

Tickets Plane tickets can be arranged through most of the tour and trekking operators around town, including specialist flight agent Win Air Ticketing and Travel Services on Yone Gyi Rd (☎081 209 920, ✉wintravel9@gmail.com).

Destinations Kengtung (3 weekly, plus additional services via Yangon; 35min); Lashio (6 weekly; 50min); Mandalay (5 daily; 35min); Nyaung U, for Bagan (1–2 daily; 40min); Tachileik (1 daily; 1hr).

BY BUS, MINIBUS AND PICK-UP

Many buses bypass Nyaungshwe, dropping passengers off at Shwenyaung, 12km to the north, where the Nyaungshwe road turns off from the main Taunggyi highway. From Shwenyaung it's 30min to Nyaungshwe by pick-up (K1000) or taxi (K10,000). Even if you've been booked on a service direct from Nyaungshwe it's possible that you'll have to change vehicles at Shwenyaung. Leaving Nyaungshwe, it's generally easiest to buy a ticket through your hotel, although there are also numerous tour agents around town selling tickets (May Bus Ticket Centre, opposite the northwest corner of the market, is one reliable place).

To Bagan and Yangon There's a choice of daytime and overnight buses to Bagan and Yangon; express services to the latter are run by JJ (c/o Sun Goddess Travel & Tour, near the *French Touch* restaurant; 6am; K27,000) and nearby Thit Sar Oo (6.30pm; K20,000).

To Kalaw The short hop to Kalaw can be surprisingly tricky unless you can find a free seat on a long-distance bus (or are prepared to pay the full fare to its final destination). The only other option is to catch a pick-up to Shwenyaung and then try to flag down a passing bus or pick-up on the main road (and you may need to change again at Aungban). Given all this, you might decide just to hire a taxi for the entire journey (see below).

To Loikaw There's a once-daily bus at 9am to Loikaw via Aungban.

To Pindaya Heading to Pindaya, you'll first need to take a taxi (K10,000) or pick-up (K1000) to Shwenyaung (30min), then hope you can get a seat on a passing bus, minibus or pick-up to Aungban (1hr 30min), where you'll need to change onto another pick-up for the final 1hr leg of the journey to Pindaya (1hr; K3000).

To Taunggyi Pick-ups to Taunggyi depart when full from the stand on Yone Gyi Rd west of the market.

Destinations: Bagan (5 daily; 8hr); Loikaw (1 daily; 7hr); Mandalay (5 daily; 7–8hr); Yangon (8 daily; 12hr).

BY TAXI

Count on around K35,000 one-way to Kalaw, K40,000 to Pindaya, and at least K50,000 to combine the two.

BY TRAIN

There's a once-daily train between Shwenyaung and Thazi (11hr 30min), which passes Kalaw (3hr 30min) on the way – it's exceptionally scenic, and exceptionally hard on your bottom.

GETTING AROUND

By bicycle Nyaungshwe is small and easily navigable on foot, though it's best to strike out into its rural environs by bicycle (see box, p.251), rentable from places all over town (K2000–3000/day). Bar the kick-ass bikes at Active & Authentic (see below), these are pretty much all the same; just be sure to check the state of the tyres and brakes before setting off.

By boat For information on boat trips from Nyaungshwe, see the Inle Lake section (see box, p.260).

TOURS AND ACTIVITIES

BALLOONING

Oriental Ballooning Lanmadaw Rd ☎09 250 089 443, ⓦorientalballooning.com. Enjoy the ultimate view of Inle Lake and the surrounding hills during an early morning flight (usually 1–2hr, depending on wind speeds) flown by experienced, UK-licensed pilots in state-of-the-art balloons. Flights cross the lake, offering bird's-eye views of the villages, boats and floating gardens below, before landing somewhere in or around Nyaungshwe. Mid-Oct to mid-March only; $390 per person.

CYCLING

★**Active & Authentic** Kyaung Taw Shayt Rd ☎094 2102 8796, ⓔaat.toursmyanmar@gmail.com. There are umpteen places in which to rent a bike in town, but this one is a cut above the rest. For a start, they have bikes which would make a Dutchman go weak at the knees: a little pricey at K12,000 for the day (or K7000 for half a day), but worth it if you're planning a long trip. They also rent out glasses and helmets, and can arrange excellent half-day (from $30pp) and full-day (from $50) tours. Daily 8am–9pm.

Grasshopper Adventures Phaung Daw Pyan Rd ☎09 775 773 435, ⓦgrasshopperadventures.com. Local branch of the leading worldwide cycle-tour operator, offering rewarding one-day tours ($80) around Inle Lake, featuring a mix of biking, boating and kayaking.

COOKING CLASSES

Myo Myo/Linn Htet Cooking Class Sike Pyo Village ☎042 832 6575. Rewarding cookery classes managed by the same family that runs Linn Htet restaurant (see p.255), offering the chance to rustle up a couple of Burmese curries, plus soup and rice. Classes (K20,000) are held morning and afternoon at Sike Pyo Village just outside town; enquiries and booking via the Linn Htet restaurant. Morning classes also feature a visit to the local market.

SPAS AND MASSAGE

Aqua Lilies Off Museum Rd ☎09 428 363 584. The town's best spa option, offering a wide range of treatments (K13,000–17,000/hr) including traditional Burmese anainte, Swedish, aromatherapy and four-hand massages. Daily 9am–9pm.

Khaung Daing Natural Hot Spring Nyaung Wun Village ☎094 936 4876. Excellent hot-spring resort within cycling distance to the west of town (see p.261).

Win Nyunt Off Myawady Rd. Far cheaper than Aqua Lilies (see above), this place offers traditional massage from K7000/hr in a ramshackle building just south of the museum. Daily 8am–8pm.

TREKKING

Pyone Cho c/o Lotus Restaurant, Museum Rd ☎09 428 313 717, ⓔpyonecholotus@gmail.com. One of the town's most experienced trekking operators, Mr Pyone Cho runs day treks in the hills overlooking Lake Inle to the east of Nyaungshwe (K12,000 per person in a group of two) plus two- and three-day treks to Kalaw ($50 per person for two days, or $65 for three days in a group of two, including all transport, luggage transfers, food and accommodation). He can usually be found most evenings in the Lotus restaurant just west of the market.

Sunny Day Tour Services West of the market ☎09 428 372 118, ⓔhtwe.sunny@gmail.com. Efficient and knowledgeable tour and trekking operator, offering day-treks in the hills east of town ($12 per person) plus two-day treks (around $45) around Nyaungshwe, and two- and three-day treks to Kalaw ($50 for two days, $60 for three days, all-inclusive). Daily 7am–8pm.

6

ACCOMMODATION

Nyaungshwe has an increasingly wide selection of accommodation, including plenty of budget places. All places listed have a/c unless stated otherwise; you may have to forego it in cheaper places, although given the town's fairly cool climate it's not essential, especially in the cool winter months.

Amazing Yone Gyi Rd ☎081 209477, ⓦamazing-hotel.com. Attractive upmarket hotel in a good central location next to a slightly grubby little canal. Ersatz Burmese decorative touches lend the place a modicum of style, while the bright, spacious rooms come with sunny window seats and balconies – although service could be sharper, given the price. There's also a small spa, good restaurant and free bikes for guests. **$100**

Aquarius 2 Phaung Daw Pyan Rd ☎081 209352, ⓔaquarius352@gmail.com. An understandably popular

6

option, set around a lush greenery-stuffed courtyard and a quaint wooden restaurant. The cheaper fan-only rooms are simple but good value, and there are also more modern a/c rooms (for $15 more) in the bright new, vaguely pueblo-style block around the back. $20

Golden Empress Phaung Daw Pyan Rd ☎081 209037, **@**goldenempresshotel@gmail.com. Reliable and characterful mid-range option, with plenty of traditional Burmese style, from the antique-strewn lobby to the cosy wood-panelled rooms – although it's well worth paying an extra $5 for one of the significantly bigger, brighter and quieter rooms upstairs. $40

Gypsy Inn Kann Nar Rd ☎081 209084, **@**gypsyinn hotel@gmail.com. One of the cheapest options in town, and a decent choice if you don't mind the constant roar of boats motoring up and down the adjacent canal. The cheapest (fan-only) rooms are basic and share bathrooms, but are reasonably comfortable and well-maintained given the price; pricier en-suite rooms ($25) come with a/c. Dorms $8, doubles $14

Joy Hotel Jetty Rd ☎081 209083, **@**joyhotel inle@gmail.com. A good canal-side cheapie, with great people-watching from the upstairs breakfast terrace. Rooms are past their best, but comfortable enough; en-suite doubles are a couple of dollars more than those with shared-bath, while shared-bath singles go for just $8. $16

La Maison Birmane Kyaung Daw Anauk St ☎081 209901, **@**lamaisonbirmane.com. Intimate little boutique hotel, designed in faux-Burmese village style, with ten stylishly minimalist rooms of varying sizes, styles and prices set around a lush garden. It fills up quickly, so book as far in advance as you can. $85

Mount Inle Hotel Yong Gyi St, 1.5km east of the centre ☎09 449 722 577, **@**mountinle.com. Suave new boutique hotel mingling Shan, Thai and Balinese influences in its cool contemporary design, with bright green-and-white wood-floored rooms arranged around a neat garden, and good views from the attached balconies. Free bikes for guests, and they also run good cooking classes. Given the style, prices are a bargain. $50

Nawng Kham The Little Inn Phaung Daw Pyan Rd ☎081 209195, **@**noanhom@gmail.com. Cheery and competitively priced little family-run guesthouse with a few simple but inexpensive fan rooms (plus more expensive a/c doubles for $10 more) set alongside a little strip of garden. $20

Paradise Museum Rd ☎081 209321, **@**inleparadise .com. Long-running upper-mid-range option in a rustic resort-style complex – dated, but pleasant enough, in a slightly humdrum sort of way. Choose between one of the old-fashioned wooden garden chalets, or the more state-of-the-art cream-coloured rooms in the main building. $75

★**Princess Garden** Mine Li Quarter ☎081 209214 or ☎09 514 8418, **@**princessgardenhotel@gmail.com. Set in delightful gardens with a surprisingly large swimming pool, this is a restful and friendly little retreat that books up well in advance during peak season – hardly surprising, given the bargain prices. Wood-floored rooms and slightly fancier bungalows are attractively decorated, while breakfast is served on a terrace with fine views of the surrounding fields and hills. Rooms $30, bungalows $40

PYI Guesthouse Phaung Daw Pyan Rd ☎081 209076, **@**pyi.nsmm@gmail.com. Super-friendly mid-range guest-house. Rooms in the main red-brick building are big, modern and rather bare but sparklingly clean, albeit the very flimsy duvets could do with an upgrade. There are also some smarter and more generously furnished wood-floored chalets ($10 extra), with proper blankets, around the back. $50

Queen Inn Win Quarter ☎081 209544, **@**queen.inle @gmail.com. Neat little hotel in a nice location by the canal. The big if rather bare rooms are decent value at the price (while singles cost just $15), while a handful overlook the canal itself – great for boat-watching, albeit noisy. $25

Remember Inn Museum Rd ☎081 209257, **@**rememberinn.jimdo.com. Enduringly popular budget choice with unusually bright and spacious rooms, slightly past their best, but still very comfortable and competitively priced (although the boxy bungalows in the garden outside are significantly less appealing). Breakfast is served on a sunny upstairs terrace, with a choice of Western or various Burmese options including good *mohinga*. Rooms $20, bungalows $35

Song of Travel Aung Chan Tha St ☎081 209731, **@**songoftravel.com. Funky new hostel occupying an utterly bizarre-looking building resembling a gigantic ghetto blaster. Accommodation is in well-equipped 14-bed a/c dorms, and facilities include a neat little café and what staff claim is the "best wi-fi in Nyaungshwe". Guests get free use of a bike. Dorms $14

★**Thanakha Inle Hotel** 80 Nan Thae St ☎081 209928, **@**thanakha-inle-hotel.com. Nyaungshwe's stand-out accommodation option, in a cheery banana-coloured building set around a lush palm-filled courtyard right next to the main canal to Lake Inle. The spacious and attractively designed rooms come with a distinct dash of Japanese-style minimalist chic and a choice of mountain, canal or garden views, while facilities include a cool rooftop lounge and a breezy waterfront restaurant. $130

Viewpoint Taik Nan Bridge ☎081 209062, **@**inleview point.com. Nyaungshwe's fanciest accommodation option, with 24 stilted cottages set on platforms dotted across the hotel's private lake – like a miniature version of the big Lake Inle resorts. The traditional Shan-style, concrete-free constructions feature wooden beams, local limestone, mud and rice straw, and paints made from laterite mud and natural wax, although the rustic materials don't compromise comfort levels or the generally luxurious ambience. Noise from passing boats may intrude, although for many people it's all part of the experience. There's also a spa, bar and a good restaurant (see p.256) attached. $130

Yar Pyae Nandawun St ☎081 209941, ✉yarpyae hotel@gmail.com. One of Nyaungshwe's better mid-range options. Outside it's an ugly three-storey

pink-painted box; inside, the spacious wood-floored rooms offer plenty of unassuming creature comforts and are well equipped with flatscreen TV, kettle and fridge. Does the job and does it at a very reasonable price. $30

Zawgyi Inn 122 Nandawun St ☎081 209929, ✉zawgyi inn@gmail.com. Peaceful and friendly little family-run guesthouse with spacious, neat and immaculately clean – albeit slightly bare – fan rooms with little verandas overlooking a pretty, plant-filled courtyard. $25

EATING

Nyaungshwe is up there with the best places to eat in Myanmar, with plenty of international options alongside the usual curries, rice and noodles. As well as the places listed below, the town's **night market**, just south of MIngalar Market, is also an enjoyable place to eat, with stalls selling good chapati and curry, barbecued chicken sticks and Shan noodles. The fun starts just after sundown.

Ever Green Yone Gyi Rd ☎094 4801 6338. Staffed by Nyaungshwe's most manic bunch of waitresses, this cute little place serves decent Shan coffee and assorted juices, along with a modest selection of mains (K2500–4500) including stir-fries, curries and pasta, plus good fish and chips made with fish from the lake. Daily 8am–10pm.

The French Touch Kyaung Taw Shayt Rd ☎09 525 1365. An artsy, loungey place that doubles as a gallery of sorts, and serves up good "Shan fusion" cuisine (K3500–5500) alongside more expensive European-style dishes (K6000–8000) including pizza and pasta, plus French-style soups, salads, waffles and puddings. Also a good place for breakfast, a quick coffee, or something stronger (see p.256). An interesting documentary on the Inle region is screened nightly at 7pm. Daily 7am–10pm.

Golden Kite Yone Gyi Rd ☎081 209327. Perhaps the best of the town's assorted faux-Italian eateries, with a reliable selection of pizzas (K7400) cooked in a real wood-fired oven, and pasta (K5000–6000) freshly made every day. Daily 9am–10pm, sometimes later.

Green Chilli Hospital Rd ☎095 214101. Elegant little place with a faintly colonial feel and a mainly Burmese menu majoring in local Intha specialities such as *kin-baung-kyaw* (deep-fried spring onion with tamarind), Intha-style whole stuffed fish, and crispy yellow tofu (mains K5000–6000). Daily 10am–10pm.

Inle Pancake Kingdom Win Quarter ☎081 209288. This place has been around since the 1990s. It was originally a milkshake café, and these are still the best things on the menu (K1500–2000). The pancakes (K2000–4000) are reasonable too, with plenty of fruity, savoury and sweet options. Daily 9am–9pm.

Linn Htet Yone Gyi Rd ☎081 209360. Looking like a proper Burmese restaurant compared to most of the foreigner-focused eateries in town, this place is as popular with locals as with tourists on account of its incredibly

filling meat, fish and veg curry sets (K3000), ranging from pork, beef, fish and chicken through to mutton tripe, sardines and tofu – if you can finish the lot you must have been pretty hungry. Daily 11am–9pm.

Live Dim Sum Yone Gyi Rd ☎09 428 136 964. Small dim sum restaurant offering relief to tired tastebuds which have had one too many bowls of Shan noodles. Individual dim sum dishes cost K1700–3000, or try one of their platters (K3500), with a choice between fried (K3700) or steamed (K4000) dim sum; there are also some good Chinese dishes on the menu (around K4000). Daily 10am–9pm.

One Owl Grill Yone Gyi St ☎09 262 972 841. Cool urban-style bistro serving up excellent (if relatively pricey) meaty Western fare (mains K5000–8000), including great burgers and other carnivorous mains. Also does a good range of breakfasts (from K3000), including the naughtily named English-style "Breakzit", plus cheap happy-hour cocktails (from K1500; 2–6pm). Daily 9am–11pm.

Paw Paw Phaung Daw Pyan Rd ☎959 778 779 627. Rustic little bamboo-shack restaurant, run by a lovely family and offering a great escape from the hustle and bustle of central Nyaungshwe. The short but sweet menu features traditional Shan home-cooked dishes including curries, stir-fries and deliciously flavoursome salads (mains K3000–5000). Daily 10am–11pm.

Shwe Dingar Lanmadaw Rd ☎099 102 4411. This large and lively teahouse, constructed almost entirely out of corrugated iron, bits of tarpaulin and Coca-Cola signs, is a fun and usually tourist-free venue, serving up the usual drinks alongside assorted snacks and simple noodle dishes. No English sign, although it's hard to miss. Daily 6am–7.30pm.

★**Sin Yaw** East side of the market ☎09 428 338 084. Lively local restaurant with almost manically friendly staff and a great selection of traditional Shan dishes (mains K4000–4500, including Inle Lake fish curry, Shan-style

6

RED MOUNTAIN WINERY

One of the most enjoyable side-trips from Nyaungshwe is to the **Red Mountain Winery** (daily 9am–6pm; free; ⓦredmountain-estate.com), 5km by road southeast of town, off the road to Maing Thauk. Following harvest time in February and March, a range of wines is produced, including Pinot Noir, Tempranillo, Sauvignon Blanc, Chardonnay, two varieties of Shiraz, a rosé, a white muscat and tawny port. Bottles cost from around K9000, or you can opt for a bargain four-glass sampler set for $3 in the winery's outdoor pavilion, enjoying wonderful views.

The best way of getting to the winery is by bicycle; it's less than an hour's ride from Nyaungshwe. It's not far by motorbike taxi, though since it's hard to find another one for the return journey, you may be looking at a fare of up to K10,000, including waiting time.

chicken with green pepper, long beans and basil, and a lip-smackingly good yellow tofu with lemon coriander sauce. Daily 10am–10.30pm.

★**Thanakha Garden** Thazi St ⓣ09 428 371 552. Attractive garden restaurant (particularly when candlelit after dark) serving up quality food from a menu that's mainly Asian, with a healthy sprinkling of Western dishes – burgers, fish and chips, sandwiches and waffles. Burmese and local Shan-style dishes are well represented, with dishes including Inle-style steamed fish and Inle Lake tomato salad with pounded peanuts and lime juice, and there are also curries, stir-fries, tasty

salads and a good drinks list to boot. Mains K3000–6000. Daily 11am–9.30pm.

Viewpoint Taik Nan Bridge ⓣ081 209062. Swanky (for Nyaungshwe) restaurant at the town's top hotel (see p.254), reached via a sweeping Hollywood staircase and with breezy views of the town, hills and chattering boats below. Shan cuisine is the speciality, with a range of set menus (K20,000–25,000) including vegetarian and barbecue options alongside "Shan tapas" and various other Burmese and Asian mains (around K7500). Daily 9am–1pm & 6–10pm.

DRINKING

The French Touch Kyaung Taw Shayt Rd ⓣ09 525 1365. This loungey café (see p.255) is a decent place for cocktails (K4500) and other tipples, with people-watching out front, or more secluded seating in the garden behind. Daily 7am–10pm.

Ginki Sao San Htun St ⓣ09 306 66456. Sexy new bar-restaurant in a pretty two-storey wooden house mixing colonial style with a contemporary chillout chic. Drinks include cheap Mandalay beer, wines by the glass (from K2500) and a cornucopia of cocktails, plus there's also a good selection of grilled and barbecued mains (K5000–7000) if you want to eat. Daily 10am–11pm.

Inle Palace Yone Gyi Rd ⓣ094 2834 4972. Cute and colourful two-storey bar with green-painted bamboo-log walls, colourful paper lanterns and a nice street-side

balcony. Drinks include cheap Mandalay beer, local Red Mountain and Aythaya wines (from K2500), and cocktails (K3000–4000; three-for-two during 4–8pm happy hour), plus plenty of other options. Daily 8am–10pm.

Pub Asiatico Museum Rd ⓣ09 452 096 741, ⓦpub-asiatico.asia. Looking like it's been airlifted straight out of uptown Yangon, this big modern bar-pizzeria offers an unexpected haven of urban cool amid the dusty streets of Nyaungshwe, plus sunset views from the rooftop terrace. The big drinks selection features exotic (for Myanmar) beers including Corona and Hoegaarden, a decent wine selection (glasses from K2400) and cheap cocktails (K2000–3000) during the daily happy hour (3–7pm). Also serves up passable if rather pricey pizzas (K7600–10,000). Daily 11.30am–11.30pm.

ENTERTAINMENT

Aung Puppet Show Ahletaung Kyaung Rd. Pulling strings in Nyaungshwe since 1995, the Aung Puppet Show puts on nightly performances (lasting 30min) of traditional Burmese puppetry in its tiny backstreet theatre, offering an

enjoyably intimate taste of this ever-popular artform. Entrance K5000. They also sell the puppets (K10,000–40,000); the shop is open around 8.30–9pm. Nightly 7pm & 8.30pm.

SHOPPING

Gallery 19 Shwe Chan Thar St. Sells the striking work of Taunggyi-based photographer Kyaw Kyaw Win (prints from around $20), with images of local people and landscapes,

along with assorted paintings by other regional artists. Tues–Sun 9am–8pm.

FROM TOP HILL-TRIBE WOMEN, NEAR INTHEIN (P.260); NAUNG TUNG LAKE, KENGTUNG (P.271) >

Inle Lake

အင်းလေးကန်

Majestic **INLE LAKE** is one of Myanmar's undoubted highlights. The lake itself is beautiful, a placid expanse with forested mountains on its eastern and western sides, while dotting the periphery of the waters is a marvellously photogenic chain of stilted villages and small towns inhabited by the local **Intha** people (see box opposite), with innumerable buildings rising out of the lake, complete with "streets" of water and boats for traffic – among Myanmar's most memorable, and surreal, sights.

While the lake is very firmly on the beaten path, its size is such that you only really notice just how many other foreigners are around when your boat pulls up at one of the stops. Even now, its **markets** are aimed more at villagers of the various ethnic groups that live in the area – among them Shan, Pa-O, Kayah and Danu – than they are at tourists. Most visit these markets as part of a **boat trip** (see box, p,000), while other sights hereabouts include the beautiful **Phaung Daw Oo Paya**, **Ngaphe Kyaung** (the former "jumping cat" monastery) and the lovely **hot springs** near Khaung Daing. Note that the sights have been listed here in an order heading vaguely clockwise around the lake, which is the route that most boatmen take. A good time to be around is during the **Thadingyut Festival of Lights** in October, when locals decorate their houses with lanterns and candles – a magical sight during a night-time boat ride through the stilt villages.

INLE LAKE

Shwenyaung (10km), Highway NH4, Kalaw & Yangon

Shwe Yaunghwe Kyaung

Nyaungshwe

Nantha

ACCOMMODATION

Golden Island Cottages	5/7
Inle Princess Resort	2
Inle Resort	3
Ngwe Zin Yaw	6
Paramount Inle Resort	1
Sanctum Inle Resort	4

EATING

Golden Kite	3
Green Chilli	4
Inle Heart View	1
Ngwe Zin Yaw	2

Red Mountain Winery

Khaung Daing Hot Springs

Myatheintan

Khaung Daing

Maing Thauk

Thit Tha Kyaung

Inle Lake

Than Taung

Ngaphe Kyaung

Thale U

Floating Gardens

Ywama

Phaung Daw Oo Paya

Tha Lay

Inthein

Nyaung Oak

Shwe Inn Thein Paya

Nampan

In Paw Khone

0   2
kilometres

Taung Tho (14km) & Sankar (35km)

The lake is, sadly, suffering from ever-increasing **pollution** – it's hard to imagine that, just one generation ago, its waters were clean enough to drink. These days, a greater proportion of the vessels that work the lake are motorized, locals are producing more litter, and chemicals from the floating gardens (and locals washing their clothes) are seriously impairing the quality of the water, and the size of the fish stock.

Maing Thauk and around

မိုင်းသောက်

The charming village of **MAING THAUK** is usually omitted from boat tours of the lake except on every fifth day, when the peripatetic Inle market arrives (see box, p.241), filling the village with a photogenic throng of commerce. Now a rustic backwater, Maing Thauk was formerly the headquarters of the colonial British administration in southern Shan State before it was moved to Taunggyi in 1894, although nothing remains of the original Fort Stedman (as it was known).

The village is split into two halves: one for landlubbers, and a "floating" section reachable via a long wooden bridge, looking a bit like a scaled-down version of the famous U Bein Bridge (see p.301)

"SONS OF THE LAKE" – THE INTHA PEOPLE

The **Intha** people – "sons of the lake" – are descendants of Mon from the far southeast (though they're now categorized as a subgroup of the Shan). Lacking land of their own, the Intha have taken to life on the water with a will, not only setting up house upon it but also constructing the remarkable patchwork of **floating gardens** which now cover large parts of the southern lake, producing abundant crops of fruit, flowers and vegetables. **Fishing** is the other local economic mainstay, and you'll doubtless see some of the lake's endlessly photographed Intha fishermen in their long, narrow boats, a large conical hooped net (sometime taller than the fisherman himself) to hand. The Intha are also famous for their unique style of **leg-rowing**, standing on one leg and using the other to push the oar (leaving an arm free to manipulate the net) in a precariously balanced feat of floating contortionism. Not surprisingly, the strange and seemingly timeless image of these traditional figures perched stork-like upon the sterns of their boats, net in hand, oar dangling from a leg, has become one of the signature images not only of Inle, but of Myanmar itself.

6

in Mandalay. The village can also be reached as part of an enjoyable **bike ride** from Nyaungshwe (see box, p.251).

Thit Tha Kyaung
တောရဘုန်တော်ကြီးကျောင်း

Sitting pretty up a steep hill to the east of Maing Thauk is the gorgeous **Thit Tha Kyaung** "forest monastery". From lake level you'll be able to make out the stupa at its front; the lake views from here are excellent, if somewhat sullied by electricity wires, while the monastery itself provides some great photo opportunities. It's a long, sweaty walk here from Maing Thauk, one that will take almost an hour; coming by bike, you'll have to drag the thing up the last few hundred metres, though coming back down is joyfully fast.

Nampan
နန်းပဝမ်

One of the lake's larger villages, **NAMPAN** is the first stop on most boat tours. Here you'll probably be directed towards weaving workshops, goldsmiths or cheroot factories, though if you get the chance it's well worth going for a walk between the beautiful stilt houses. There are a couple of good lunch spots hereabouts (see p.262), and those not yet temple-tired could ask to be dropped off at **Alodaw Pauk** shrine, one of the oldest religious structures in the area.

Phaung Daw Oo Paya
ဖောင်တော်ဦးဘုရား • Daily 24hr • Free; camera K500, video K500

Boats converge on the tiered lakeside **Phaung Daw Oo Paya**, west of Nampan and south of Ywama, to the extent that you might need to climb over a logjam of them in order to reach the shore. The pagoda building is nothing special, but men crowd around to add gold leaf to the revered group of five small Buddha figures at the centre of the main hall – already so coated that they've been transformed into what look like a little heap of golden boulders. Women aren't allowed to apply gold leaf, and will have to hand it over to a male assistant.

Ywama

North of Phaung Daw Oo Paya en route to Inthein you'll probably pass through **YWAMA**. It's an undoubtedly pretty little village, but also one of the most touristy on

6

INLE LAKE BY BOAT

A **boat trip** on the placid waters of Inle Lake is not only a beautiful and thoroughly enjoyable experience, but by far the best and easiest way in which to see the various sights around the lake, and take in its unique way of life. Most trips from Nyaungshwe follow a fairly standard route. Your boat will first spend some time chugging along the canal joining Nyaungshwe to the lake. As soon as you hit the lake proper, you'll see a bunch of "fishermen" (their boats surprisingly devoid of fish) posing for pictures in return for cash – easily ignored, since you'll get plenty of chances to snap real fishermen later on.

Heading around the lake, trips normally head to **Nampan** at the southern end of the lake – with most likely a stop at **Maing Thauk** if it's market day there – and then continue on to **Phaung Daw Oo Paya**, with possibly a side-trip to **Inthein** and a stroll on the **floating gardens** (see box, p.262), before ending at **Ngaphe Kyaung**. If you're leaving Ngaphe Kyaung before 4.30pm you could ask your boatman to also include the **Khaung Daing hot springs**. There are several options for **lunch** at Nampan and around Phaung Daw Oo Paya.

On the way around, your boatman will inevitably call at various floating **cottage industries**: lotus-fibre weavers, goldsmiths, cheroot-makers, boat-builders and the like. These are all free to visit, and there's little pressure to buy souvenirs, but feel free to tell your boatman if you've tired of these soft-sell activities.

PRACTICALITIES

Pretty much all hotels, guesthouses and travel agencies in Nyaungshwe can arrange boat trips, though you might be able to get a slightly cheaper price by haggling with the numerous boatmen who hang out around the main canal in Nyaungshwe. The standard price is around K18,000–20,000 per boat for a full-day trip (plus an extra K5000 if you want to visit Inthein). Boats fit a maximum of five people, though three or four is far more comfortable. Ask if your vessel has life jackets and cushioning on the seats. You'll all be seated in a line and essentially unable to talk to each other over the jagged rattle of the engine – bring a hat (the boats have no cover), sunblock and water. Clothing with long sleeves can also come in handy during the often chilly early mornings. Tours can take most of the day, meaning that an early start is advisable: pre-sunrise departures are popular, though some prefer to start later on and return at dusk.

---

the lake and very much on the coach-party (or, in this case, boat-party) circuit. This is particularly the case on days when the village hosts the rotating Inle market (see p.241), which here features a photogenic **floating market** section, although tourists now generally outnumber locals. Even on non-market days the place gets rather more foreign visitors than it really knows what to do with.

Inthein

အင်းတိန်

The canal ride west from Ywama to the over-touristy village of **INTHEIN** (also romanized as Indein) starts among reed beds before continuing between more solid banks with jungle on both sides: a striking contrast to the wide-open space of the lake. Just behind the village, at the base of a hill, is **Nyaung Oak**, a set of picturesquely overgrown stupas with carvings of Buddhas, chinthe, devas, elephants and peacocks. Head uphill along a covered walkway to reach **Shwe Inthein Paya**, a collection of seventeenth- and eighteenth-century stupas which are being slowly and heavy-handedly restored. On the way down, look out for a path on the left which runs through a bamboo forest back to the riverside.

Ngaphe Kyaung

ငါးဖယ်ကျောင်း • Daily 24hr • Free

Previously referred to as the "jumping cat" monastery, **Ngaphe Kyaung** was formerly famed for its felines, which resident monks had trained to jump through hoops in

> ## INLE'S "LONG-NECKED LADIES"
>
> If you're taking a boat trip on Inle Lake you'll probably be offered the chance to visit some of the long-necked **Kayan (Padaung) ladies** who have set up home among the Intha around the lake. Some tourists find the experience uncomfortably fake and voyeuristic – and it's certainly not a patch on the tours to Kayan villages around Loikaw (see p.269) – although bear in mind that the Inle tourist trade offers the Kayan the chance to make good money by selling their handicrafts, and there's no sign of the exploitation suffered by the Kayan served up to tourists at refugee camps in northern Thailand. There's no fee to enter their homes or to take photographs, although of course it's only fair to buy something in return.

exchange for edible rewards. This is what most people still come for, though the current crop of cats hasn't been trained to do anything at all – except possibly slink around and hide in corners. Relieved of its cat-fancying crowds, the monastery is now an enjoyably peaceful place to stop during a tour of the lake, centred on a gorgeously atmospheric teak hall filled with a stately array of beautifully carved Buddhas. The small **market** at the back of the monastery is also a good place to hunt for souvenirs.

Khaung Daing hot springs

ခေါင်တိုင်ရေပူစမ်း • Daily 8am–6pm • $7 • Around 9km south of Nyaungshwe, K15,000 return by taxi

Located off the west side of the lake, and easily reachable under your own steam from Nyaungshwe, the soothing **Khaung Daing hot springs** are a real indulgence, looking like a rather fancy upmarket resort complete with cocktail bar, restaurant and spa. The best time to be here is around sundown, when the shadow from the mountains to the east starts to inch, then race, across the surrounding fields.

South to Sankar and Moebye Lake

From the southern end of the lake, a canal leads down to the village of **Taung Tho**, (around 15km south of Nampan) whose market (see box, p.241) is a far more authentic affair than others around the lake. Past here the canal continues for a further 30km or so, through a sylvan landscape dotted with Shan and Pa-O villages before reaching remote **Moebye Lake**. The hills here would make for excellent hiking territory, but conceal a substantial opium trade: an estimated five tonnes of the stuff per year, with the crops protected by local militia.

The main attraction hereabouts is the pretty village of **SANKAR** (also spelt Samkar), close to the northern end of Moebye Lake, comprising a mix of stilted and shoreline houses. Directly across the lake from here is the nearby **Tharkong Pagoda**, with a modern temple complex surrounded by a photogenic array of crumbling red-brick stupas, some of them seeming to emerge directly from the lake (if water levels are sufficiently high), like some kind of half-drowned Burmese Atlantis. It's around six hours return from Nyaungshwe to Sankar (count on about K50,000 per boat), a long time to spend on the water.

Beyond Sankar, one adventurous possibility is to continue south by boat down Moebye Lake to the town of Pekon (another 2hr 30min), then by road (1hr) to Loikaw – although the journey will set you back a minimum of $75.

GETTING AROUND   **INLE LAKE**

By boat For details of boat trips on Inle Lake, see the "Inle Lake by boat" box (see p.260).

By bicycle It's possible to hit a few of the sights around the lake by bike (see box, p.251). For longer trips, ask at Active & Authentic (see p.253), who also run good bike tours.

6

INLE'S FLOATING GARDENS

Large areas around the shores of southern Inle Lake are covered in a huge tapestry of **floating gardens**, tended by the area's Intha farmers. Each "garden" comprises a long, thin strip of cultivable land, created using mud dredged up out of the lake layered on a bed of weeds and anchored in place using bamboo poles. The lake's nutrient-rich waters allow a wide range of vegetables, fruit and flowers to be grown, with much of the surplus turning up in markets around the lake. So successful have the floating gardens proved that large areas of lake have now vanished beneath them and local farmers have been forbidden from constructing any more – although it's said that new ones are still occasionally knocked up under cover of darkness, or when the eye of authority is turned elsewhere.

ACCOMMODATION

More than a dozen upmarket resorts dot the shores of the lake, some of them accessible only by boat, meaning that once you're in them, you're essentially stranded after dark. Rates usually include pick-up/boat transfer from Nyaungshwe, or sometimes Heho airport.

★**Golden Island Cottages** Nampan and Thale U ⓣ081 209550, ⓦgichotelgroup.com. One of the most affordable options around the lake – two, in fact, since they have locations in both Nampan and Thale U. Both are staffed by Pa-O people, and feature decent stilt-house rooms boasting gorgeous lake views; the Nampan location is set above the lake, while the one in Thale U is closer to shore. $92

Inle Princess Resort North of Maing Thauk ⓣ081 209055, ⓦinle-princess.com. A dreamily beautiful, undeniably romantic place designed with rare attention to detail – with prices to match. The furnishings and fabrics are all top-notch, the lily-filled ponds could tempt out the artist in you, and the on-site restaurant is fantastic. $265

Inle Resort Near Maing Thauk ⓣ09 515 4444, ⓦinleresort.com. Terrific option near to Maing Thauk, occupying a gigantic complex set around a restaurant that feels more like that of an ocean liner. Their cottages are affordable, but you'll have to splash out far more for a deluxe room or villa with lake view. The place is actually accessible by land as well as boat, meaning that you're not entirely trapped. $115

Ngwe Zin Yaw Near Phaung Daw Oo Paya ⓣ095 211996. The only lower-end option on the lake, this place functions primarily as a restaurant (see p.263) but also has a few simple rooms. $40

Paramount Inle Resort Khaung Daing ⓣ094 936 0855, ⓦparamountinleresort.com. Near the village of Khaung Daing and its hot springs, this is the best option at this price level. While its rooms aren't exactly huge, they're pleasantly decorated, and all have appealing balconies with lake views. $140

★**Sanctum Inle Resort** Maing Thauk Village ⓣ09 252 818 800, ⓦsanctum-inle-resort.com. Something a bit different from the other Inle resorts, centred on a huge white, faintly Tuscan-looking building set in spacious lakeside gardens. Inspired by the monastic ideals of quiet contemplation and spiritual calm, the resort's deep verandas, cloisters and tree-shaded paths exude a sense of rustic peace, while the spacious, understated but quietly luxurious rooms offer further balm to the soul. Facilities include the classy *The Refectory* restaurant and *Cloister Bar*, and there's also a gorgeous pool, plus an idyllic spa in which to tickle your inner nun. It's pricey at published rates, although discounts are often available online. $284

EATING

Boat trips can take up the whole day, so it's fortunate that there are plenty of places to eat on the lake, especially in and around **Nampan** village (see p.259), and in stilt houses abutting the **Phaung Daw Oo Paya**. If you want to dine anywhere specific, however, let your boatman know – otherwise, you may well be taken to a commission-friendly place of his choosing.

Golden Kite Nampan village ⓣ081 209327. Like *Green Chilli*, this is a Nampan-based twin to a more established Nyaungshwe restaurant (see p.255). This time the food isn't quite as good, but the charming above-the-lake location means that it still makes a good stop for pizza or pasta. Daily 9am–7pm.

Green Chilli Nampan village ⓣ095 214101. One of the best-looking restaurants around the lake, this elegant stilt house has more or less the same mainly Burmese menu as its sister venue in Nyaungshwe (see p.255), although it may not always be open during quiet periods. Daily 9am–7pm.

★**Inle Heart View** North of Myatheintan village ⓣ09 428 314 979. A *Far Side* cartoon come to life, this quirky, solar-powered restaurant is located in almost comical solitude on a shallow hillside east of the lake, and east of the main road south to Maing Thauk, so keep an eagle eye out for the sign. They serve organic dishes, most of them using veggies grown in the surrounding fields. It's one of those places where the menu rarely bears much resemblance to what's actually on offer – although whatever is available is always good, with flavoursome Burmese dishes (mains K3000–4000) including fish, stir-fries and salads. Daily 6am–10pm.

Ngwe Zin Yaw Near Phaung Daw Oo Paya ☎095 211996. A cheery-looking place with lime-green tablecloths and dangling parasols, this is the best option near the Phaung Daw Oo Paya. The menu itself holds few surprises, but simple mains are yours for around K2500, plus fruit juices and beer. It's located just over one of the several footbridges you'll see around the pagoda: just look for the sign. Daily 5am–10pm.

Taunggyi and around

တောင်ကြီး

The capital of Shan State and Myanmar's fifth-largest city, **TAUNGGYI** can come as a bit of a shock after the sleepy hinterlands of Inle Lake – at least to the few foreign tourists who make it here. Most who come do so for the spectacular **Taunggyi Fire-Balloon Festival** (see box, p.264), while the city also makes the most convenient starting point for trips to the remarkable complex of **Kakku**, with its thousands of densely massed stupas – one of Shan State's most memorable sights.

Originally a small village, Taunggyi became capital of the Southern Shan States under British rule in 1894 after they relocated their administrative headquarters from Maing Thauk (Fort Stedman as was) on the eastern shores of Inle Lake, preferring Taunggyi's more elevated and salubrious climate. The new colonial centre expanded rapidly thereafter, while more recently the city has attracted large numbers of illegal Chinese immigrants, who now mingle with the local Pa-O and Intha population.

Taunggyi's best feature is its dramatic location below a steep and rocky ridge of the Shan hills, from where the city gets its name (meaning "Huge Mountain" and pronounced, roughly, as "town-*ji*") – best appreciated during the drive down the spectacular hairpins of the main road in from Kalaw and Nyaungshwe, or from the Shwe Phone Pwint Pagoda. Down at street level the city is a mainly modern affair, with few mementos of its colonial origins in evidence, bar the eye-catching, spikily spired **St Joseph's Cathedral**. The huge, grimy and borderline anarchic central **market** is the best place to enjoy the town's enjoyably workaday atmosphere and diverse ethnic mix and also hosts a comparatively tourist-free turn on Inle's rotating **five-day market** schedule (see box, p.241).

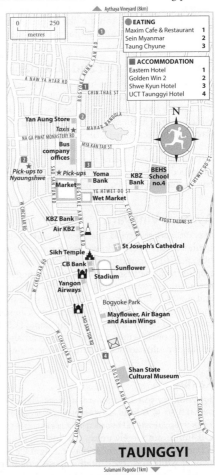

Aythaya Vineyard (8km)

● EATING	
Maxim Cafe & Restaurant	1
Sein Myanmar	2
Taung Chyune	3

■ ACCOMMODATION	
Eastern Hotel	1
Golden Win 2	2
Shwe Kyun Hotel	3
UCT Taunggyi Hotel	4

TAUNGGYI

Sulamani Pagoda (1km)

6

6

THE TAUNGGYI FIRE-BALLOON FESTIVAL

Mention Taunggyi to a Shan local, or perhaps even Burmese from other states, and they'll likely rhapsodize about the city's famed **balloon festival** – a local manifestation of the nationwide Tazaungdaing Festival of Lights, held annually over a week around the full-moon day of the lunar month of Tazaungmon (usually falling in November). Vast crowds assemble to watch thousands of unmanned hot-air balloons being launched into the sky, decorated with all manner of images and text (often made up of cleverly arranged candles), although the fire-balloons themselves aren't the safest of objects – fireworks are attached to many of them and the balloons occasionally catch fire, so it's a good idea to keep your distance. Most visit on a day-trip from Nyaungshwe, though traffic can get snarled up when heading back in the late evening, partly down to the fact that many of those on the road will be rather drunk. If staying in Taunggyi, book accommodation well in advance.

Shan State Cultural Museum

Bogyoke Aung San Rd • Tues–Sun 10am–4pm • K5000

At the southern end of town, the dusty **Shan State Cultural Museum** hosts the usual array of traditional clothes worn by local ethnic groups, assorted weapons and artefacts, musical instruments and the like – barely worth the effort of getting to, and certainly not worth the hiked-up foreigners' entrance price.

Shwe Phone Pwint and Sulamani pagodas

Sitting atop a rocky spur high above the eastern side of town, the **Shwe Phone Pwint Pagoda** offers stunning views over Taunggyi and the surrounding hills (and even, on a clear day, Lake Inle itself). The temple itself is little more than a modest cluster of gilded stupas, although it's worth hunting out the atmospheric, Buddha-filled **Ruby Cave** on the west side of the complex. It's a steep one-hour walk from town up an interminable covered staircase, or catch a taxi (around K6000).

At the southern end of the town is Taunggyi's biggest temple, the **Sulamani Pagoda**, modelled after the great Ananda Pahto in Bagan, and constructed in 1994 to commemorate the city's centenary.

Aythaya Vineyard

About 10km from Taunggyi by road, just off the main road to Kalaw • Daily 8.30am–9.30pm • ☎ 081 208653, ⓦ myanmar-vineyard.com

Undeservedly overshadowed by the much better-known Red Mountain Winery (see box, p.256) just outside nearby Nyaungshwe, the **Aythaya Vineyard** offers an idyllic respite from the rush of downtown Taunggyi. Set amid undulating hills northwest of town, the vineyard was established by German entrepreneur Bert Morsbach in 1999 and now produces around 300,000 bottles a year, sold under the Aythaya label and including Shiraz, Sauvignon Blanc and Chenin Blanc reds, whites and rosés. Daily tastings can be had of four different grapes (K2000, or K1000 if you take lunch or dinner), and tours of the vineyard and winery can also be arranged. There's also a good on-site restaurant, plus attractive bungalow accommodation if you fancy staying the night.

Kakku

မွေတော်ကက္ကူဘုရား • Around 45km south of Taunggyi • Daily 6am–6pm • K5000 or $3 • It's a 1hr 30min drive from Taunggyi (around K35,000–40,000 by taxi – ask around at the taxi stand outside the Kan-Tone Hotel in Taunggyi) • You're free to explore the site independently, although local Pa-O guides give informative tours for $5 • No footwear

Off-limits and largely unknown due to ethnic conflict until as recently as 2001, **KAKKU** is one of Shan State's most magical sights: a dense mass of well over two thousand slender white and rose-tinted stupas rising from a remote hillside some 45km south of

Taunggyi. Constructed by – and sacred to – the numerous Pa-O who live in the area, the site (according to legend) traces its roots back to a visit by missionaries despatched by the great third-century BC Indian Buddhist ruler Asoka, although its historical origins date from the reign of the pious King Alaungsithu of Bagan (ruled 1112–67), who is believed to have constructed a pagoda here. Many of the current stupas date back to the sixteenth and seventeenth centuries, although the majority have been significantly restored or rebuilt, and only a few look their true age.

Packed into an area around 300m wide and 150m long, the stupas are arranged in neat rows bisected by little brick-paved "streets", the air filled – assuming there's any breeze – with the magical tintinnabulations of innumerable tiny bells set in the stupas' *htis* (the ornate metal finials which crown the summit of each stupa spire). Most of the stupas are thin, round and rather elongated, although many of the taller structures have lost their crowning *hti* or the tops of their spires, while others wear their *htis* at a decidedly rakish angle. You'll also see other designs, including stupas built up in tiers of diminishing cubes, along with a few unusual examples designed to resemble miniature two-storey buildings, complete with quaint hipped roofs. Look out too for the small **pond** at the front right-hand side of the complex, offering marvellously photogenic reflections of the myriad spires. Food and drink can be found at a pleasant **restaurant** up the small hill opposite the main entrance.

The site hosts the annual **Kakku pagoda festival** on the full-moon day of the lunar month of Tabaung (usually falling in March), during which Pa-O from across the state come to pay their respects at the pagoda, dressed in their finest clothes and riding in on prettily decorated bullock carts.

ARRIVAL AND DEPARTURE TAUNGGYI

By plane Heho airport (see p.241) is Taunggyi's closest airport. It would be a minor miracle to find other foreigners headed to Taunggyi, rather than Inle Lake, but if you'd like to share a taxi (around K30,000–35,000) you may get some luck asking locals. Pretty much all the domestic airlines have offices in Taunggyi, although for tickets it's generally easiest to visit either Sunflower Travels & Tours (☎ 081 212 2575, ✉ sunflowertgy@gmail.com) or Mayflower Travels & Tours (☎ 081 212 2669, ⊕ mayflower-travels.com), both on Bogyoke Aung San Rd.

By bus Bus company offices are lined up in a row next to the main road right in the centre of town, although not much English is spoken and absolutely everything is signed

in Burmese only. Along with the destinations listed below there are also buses to Loikaw, but foreigners are not currently allowed on them (see p.265).
Destinations Bagan (2 daily; 8–9hr); Mandalay (6 daily; 8–10hr); Meiktila (3–4 daily; 7hr); Thazi (6 daily; 6hr); Yangon (8 daily; 12hr).

By pick-up Regular pick-ups connect Taunggyi to Nyaungshwe (6.30am–5pm; K1500), leaving from a little backstreet northwest of the market. Pick-ups to Kalaw and other destinations leave from various stops along the chaotic street running along the north side of the market.

By taxi Taxis congregate around the *Kan-Tone Hotel*, just north of the bus company offices.

ACCOMMODATION

Taunggyi isn't exactly rushing to pull in foreign tourists and there's a chronic lack of budget options, although a couple of good mid-range choices. Note that accommodation becomes scarce and prices rise during the **balloon festival** (see box, p.264). All places listed have a/c unless stated otherwise.

Eastern Hotel 27 Bogyoke Aung San Rd ☎ 081 212 2243, ✉ easternhotel.tgi@gmail.com. This old-fashioned two-star is one of the cheapest options in town, bearable for a night, although the unenthusiastic service and cramped rooms (no a/c) don't exactly encourage you to linger. $30
Golden Win 2 West Circular Rd (not to be confused with the Golden Win 1 on the main road right in the town centre) ☎ 081 200178, ✉ goldencrown.inn @gmail.com. Taunggyi's cheapest option at present, set around the back of a ramshackle block in a scuzzy part of

town. Rooms are actually better than you might expect, small but neat and reasonably equipped, with good hot showers in the tiny bathrooms and flatscreen TVs, although the thin walls mean you might end up getting to know your neighbours a bit better than you really wanted to. Friendly service, although not much English spoken. $25
Shwe Kyun Hotel Corner of Sittaung and Dhamma Rakhidha sts ☎ 081 201392, ⊕ shwekyunhotel -myanmar.com. Central Taunggyi's smartest option, with fancy rooms decorated with wood panelling and traditional

fabrics, although bathrooms are small (and the deluxe rooms aren't worth the extra $20). No bar or restaurant, although there's a small gym attached to reception if you fancy flashing your abs at your fellow guests. $63
UCT Taunggyi Hotel 4 Bogyoke Aung San Rd

☏ 081 212 5474, ⓦ facebook.com/uct.taunggyihotel. Taunggyi's stand-out accommodation option, with crisp, attractively furnished modern rooms plus a good restaurant and the town's most switched-on staff. Rates, by Taunggyi standards, are a snip. $40

EATING

Maxim Cafe & Restaurant 24 Boyoke Aung San Rd ☏ 081 212 2562. This neat little café-cum-coffee shop is a real haven, popular with young student types and Taunggyi's ladies who lunch. Food features a wildly eclectic selection of international offerings, with soups, salads, burgers and sandwiches alongside assorted Asian, European and Mexican mains (mostly K2000–4000), plus pricier pizzas (K7000–9500). Daily 10am–9pm.
Sein Myanmar 15 Bogyoke Aung San Rd ☏ 081 212 4255. Bustling local restaurant dishing up the usual curries and stir-fries accompanied by a vast spread of vegetable sides dishes and soup, rounded off with a plate of shredded

ginger, tea-leaf and peanut *digestif*. There's an English-language menu (but no prices on it). Expect to pay around K3000 for a complete meal. Daily 9am–9am.
Taung Chyune Yae Htwet Oo St ☏ 09 503 8317, ⓦ inletaungchune.com. Easily Taunggyi's best-looking place to eat, in an alluring little tree-studded garden restaurant under a bamboo pavilion. Food (most mains K2500–4000) features a good selection of local specialities, including Shan-style noodles, salads and "tapas" alongside assorted pan-Asian dishes, plus pizzas (K5000–6000) and a few other Western-style dishes. Daily 8am–9pm.

DIRECTORY

Banks and exchange There are numerous banks and ATMs all over town, including several branches of KBZ (who sponsor the local football team, Shan United FC – until

recently known as KBZ FC). Forex facilities are available at the centrally located Yoma Bank.

Kayah State

One of Myanmar's smallest states, **KAYAH** was off limits to foreign travellers until 2012 due to ongoing clashes between the government and various local ethnic groups. Now restored to peace, parts of the state remain sealed to outsiders, although considerable areas have been opened up to independent travellers and are now beginning to attract a steady stream of overseas tourists – not quite the final frontier you might imagine it to be, although still an enjoyable break from the tourist mainstream.

As its name suggests, the state's principal ethnic group is the **Kayah** (aka the Karenni or "Red Karen" – see p.383), whose subgroups include the **Kayan** (commonly known as the Padaung – see box, p.270), with their famously long-necked ladies. Laid-back **Loikaw**, the state capital, is currently the only place with foreigner-licensed accommodation, and makes a pleasant place to unwind for a couple of days; it also serves as a good base for trips into the local countryside and visits to nearby Kayah and Kayan villages.

Loikaw

လွိုင်ကော်မြို့

The laid-back little garden city of **LOIKAW** is one of Myanmar's most enjoyable state capitals, with tree-lined and relatively traffic-free streets, a clutch of eye-catching temples and a soothingly somnolent atmosphere. A largely modern creation, Loikaw was just another Burmese village until 1922, when the British arrived, using it as a base from which to administer the Karen States. The town also became a fertile ground for overseas missionaries (particularly Catholic, who first descended on the region in 1868), accounting for the unusual number of churches you'll see around the place, including the impressive **Christ the King Cathedral**, north of Loikaw Lake, the oldest Catholic place of worship in Kayah.

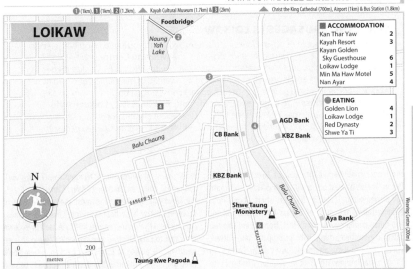

LOIKAW

■ ACCOMMODATION	
Kan Thar Yaw	2
Kayah Resort	3
Kayan Golden Sky Guesthouse	6
Loikaw Lodge	1
Min Ma Haw Motel	5
Nan Ayar	4

● EATING	
Golden Lion	4
Loikaw Lodge	1
Red Dynasty	2
Shwe Ya Ti	3

6

The compact town centre is wrapped within a bend of the serpentine **Balu Chaung River**, with the rocky **Taung Kwe Pagoda** on its southern side. North of the river (a ten-minute walk from the centre) lies pretty little **Naung Yah Lake**, surrounded by parkland and a string of restaurants. Further north is the second – larger – **Hteenhgarylar Lake**, where you'll find the town's more upmarket accommodation and the **State Cultural Museum**.

Taung Kwe Pagoda
Immediately south of the town centre • Daily 6am–6pm • Free, camera K500

Loikaw's most interesting – and certainly its most visible – sight is the wacky **Taung Kwe Pagoda**, on the south side of the town centre. This is one of Myanmar's more outlandish temples, with an impressive string of jagged limestone outcrops pin-cushioned with dozens of gilded little stupas and colourful shrines, the whole faintly kitsch-looking ensemble linked together with winding steps and staircases. There are impressive views over town and a further string of temple-topped hills nearby, and the whole thing is impressively illuminated after dark.

Kayah State Cultural Museum
North of the centre, near the Kayah Resort • Tues–Sun 9.30am–4.30pm • K5000

A couple of kilometres north of town stands Kayah State's inevitable **Cultural Museum**. Recent renovations mean it at least looks a bit fresher than other identikit museums around the country, although the exhibits – traditional dress and jewellery, musical instruments and assorted artefacts of local ethnic life – are pretty much par for the course.

ARRIVAL AND DEPARTURE   LOIKAW

Loikaw can easily be combined with a tour of Inle Lake, perhaps flying up to Loikaw from Yangon then continuing by bus or boat to Nyaungshwe (or vice versa). Frustratingly, foreigners aren't allowed to take the bus between Taunggyi and Loikaw, although you can use this route (a 3hr drive) if travelling with an authorized guide.

By plane There are regular flights from Loikaw's small airport, just north of the centre, to Yangon (1–2 daily; 50min), but nowhere else.

By bus, minibus and pick-up Given that foreigners aren't allowed to take direct services to Taunggyi, travelling north from Loikaw means you'll have to take

6

SILKS AND SAUSAGES IN LOIKAW

Loikaw boasts a couple of other low-key attractions, although you'll need a guide (see below) to visit them. Run as a training centre for local girls, the **Weaving Centre** (Mon–Fri 8.30–4.30pm; $3, plus guide fees) offers the chance to see traditional dyes being made and cotton-spinners and loom-weavers in action on a variety of mechanical and traditional wooden looms. It's also a great place to pick up inexpensive local textiles woven on site.

For a **cookery class** with a difference, try your hand at making spicy **Loikaw-style sausages** at a quaint little local cottage factory. Classes last around 1hr 30min (after which the sausages are left to cook for a further 90min) and cost $15 per group (2–6 people), plus $5 per person plus guide fees.

---

the longer route round the west of Lake Moebye via Pekon. There's at least one daily minibus along this route to Shwenyaung (see p.252), a short hop from Nyaungshwe. There services bypass Kalaw, but will set you down in nearby Aungban (4hr), from where you can catch a motorbike, minibus or pick-up to Kalaw itself. There are also two afternoon buses from Loikaw to Yangon via Taungoo (plus more regular minibuses to Taungoo), although it's a tortuously long and slow drive. Services depart from the small bus station north of the centre past the airport on National Highway 5.

Destinations Shwenyaung, for Nyaungshwe (1 daily; 6hr); Taungoo (5 daily; 7hr); Yangon (2 daily; 11hr).

By boat Far and away the most memorable way of reaching Loikaw is by boat from Inle Lake – a six-hour journey from Nyaungshwe across Inle Lake itself then down the canal to Lake Moebye, passing Sankar (see p.261) en route, before ending at the town of Pekon, where you'll need to transfer to a car for the final hour's drive to Loikaw. It's a fine (albeit slow) journey. Count on a minimum of around $75 for boat plus car, which you should be able to arrange through a tour operator in Nyaungshwe.

TOUR OPERATORS

All the following operators can arrange tours to the local villages of Pan Pet and Hta Nee La Leh (see p.269), along with various other local excursions. Count on around $110 per person for the full day-trip to Pan Pet in a group of two (falling to around $70 in a group of five or six), or $100 per person in a group of two to Hta Nee La Leh ($55 in a group of five or six).

Amazing Kayah ☎09 560 0315, ✉amazingkayah .loikaw@gmail.com.
Meticulous Myanmar ☎09 780 166 815,

✉meticulousmyanmartravel.lkw@gmail.com.
9 Generation Force ☎09 256 502 908, ✉9generation force.office@gmail.com.

ACCOMMODATION

Accommodation in Loikaw is plentiful but pricey, with lots of mid-range options but virtually nothing in the way of budget lodgings. Cheaper options are concentrated in the town centre while upmarket places are clustered around Hteenhgarylar Lake – an attractively rural area, although a bit of a hike (at least 20min) north from town. All places listed have a/c unless stated otherwise.

Kan Thar Yar U Ni St ☎083 22344, ✉kantharyarhotel @gmail.com. Super-peaceful modern hotel right next to the larger of Loikaw's two lakes, around 2km north of the centre. Rooms are bright, spacious and comfortable, and well equipped with safe, fridge, flatscreen TVs and big Kangaroo boilers, while most also come with soothing lake views through big French windows. **$45**

Kayah Resort U Kun Li St ☎08 321374, ⦿kayah resort.com. Attractive upmarket resort with spacious and stylish teak-floored rooms set in attractive gardens around a large pool around 2.5km north of the centre. The whole thing does, admittedly, appear to have been knocked up on the cheap, with comedy wi-fi and showers which alternately freeze and scald (and the derisory breakfast could do with an upgrade too), but it's

nice enough if you don't mind the rough edges, and at a reasonable price. **$100**

Kayan Golden Sky Guest House 29 Khattar St ☎083 21923, ✉kayangoldensky@gmail.com. Good mid-range modern hotel, with comfortable and well-equipped rooms at (by Loikaw standards) very competitive rates, plus great views of the Taung Kwe Pagoda from the rooftop dining terrace. **$40**

★**Loikaw Lodge** U Ni St ☎09 257 426 673, ⦿loikawlodge.com. This beautiful lakeside retreat, around 2km north of the centre, is a real labour of love, painstakingly conceived and constructed by the resident German owner Jens Uwe Parkitny. There are just twelve rooms, each a model of cool, contemporary interior design, with white walls, teak floors and finishes, beautiful wooden furniture and a water-facing balcony or terrace – even the bathrooms are miniature works of art. One corridor serves as an impromptu gallery showcasing the owner's stunning photography of the famous tattoo-faced Chin (see p.132), and there's also a great in-house restaurant (see below) and full tour and travel services. $95

Min Ma Haw Motel 120 Gangaw St ☎083 21451, ✉minmahaw96@gmail.com. One of the best of the town's cheaper options, in a central location just south of the river, with helpful English-speaking management.

Rooms are spacious and comfortable – if you don't mind the mad crazy-paving-style walls – and there are also a couple of bargain non-a/c singles ($15) with (rather knackered-looking) shared bathroom. $40

Nan Ayer Nat Shine Naung St, just north of the river opposite the town centre ☎083 21306. A real old-school Burmese guesthouse, and currently the cheapest option in town. The simple wooden-box rooms are basic and battered, although they do come with a/c, hot water and wi-fi. There's also one bargain non-a/c room at just $11 (or $6 single) with outside bathroom. $18

EATING

Golden Lion Restaurant Town centre, east side of the river ☎083 21431. Convivial local restaurant, serving mainly Chinese-style food (mains around K4000), well prepared and in generous portions – the terrace overlooking the river is a particularly nice place to hang out of an evening. An English-language menu is available, although with no prices on it. Daily 10am–9pm.

Loikaw Lodge U Ni St, around 2km north of the centre ☎09 257 426 673, 🌐loikawlodge.com. Several cuts above anywhere else to eat in town is this attractive, modern glassed-in restaurant at a lovely lakeside hotel (see p.268). The regularly changing menu features an excellent range of Burmese and European fare (mains $10–15) using quality local and imported ingredients. Also serves up excellent home-made breads, desserts and the best – indeed, pretty

much the only decent – coffee in Kayah State. Daily 11.30am–2pm & 6–9pm.

Red Dynasty Southeast corner of Loikaw Lake, near the footbridge over the lake ☎09 444 894 343. The most upscale of the various restaurants ringing the smaller of Loikaw's two lakes. Barbecued dishes are the speciality, including flambéed seafood and good Chinese-style meat mains (around K4000). There's an English menu, but no prices on it. Daily 10am–10pm.

Shwe Ya Ti Next to the bridge over the river just north of the centre. Classic Burmese teahouse, set on stilts in a pleasantly rustic location next to the river, just opposite the town centre. Good to visit at any time, but particularly at breakfast, when they serve up delicious paratha with sweet lentils and Chinese doughnuts. No English sign, although it's easy enough to spot. Daily 6am–6pm.

Around Loikaw

The wonderfully unspoilt countryside around Loikaw is slowly coming onto the tourist radar, particularly **Pan Pet**, home to the celebrated long-necked ladies of the Kayan (Padaung). Two local communities – Pan Pet itself and the Kayah village of **Hta Nee La Leh** – are now run as part of an innovative Netherlands-funded community-based tourism (CBT) scheme, aiming to ensure the best experience of tourism for villagers and visitors alike. Locals see significant economic benefits from welcoming tourists into their villages and homes, while tourists enjoy cultural insights and interactions with locals which would otherwise be unavailable. Tours (see opposite) are pricey, admittedly, although not so punitive if you can get a group together.

Pan Pet

The main attraction in the vicinity of Loikaw is the settlement of **PAN PET**, an hour and a half's drive to the south. The village is one of the heartlands of the **Kayan (Padaung)** tribe (see box, p.270), whose famous "long-necked" ladies are one of Myanmar's most emblematic and exotic sights. The area actually comprises a string of Kayan villages running west of the main road south of Loikaw, with a small **market** by the turn-off from the main road.

It's possible to arrange the trip independently by taxi from Loikaw, although this will leave you more or less stranded at the market and unable to reach any of the villages further down the (rough) track or properly meet or interact with any of the local villagers. It's far better, if you can stump up the funds, to visit with one of the recommended **tour operators** in Loikaw (see p.268). These will provide a local

> ### KAYAN OR PADAUNG?
> The people of Pan Pet are commonly referred to as the **Padaung**. This is actually a Shan name and considered pejorative by the so-called "Padaung", who actually refer to themselves as **Kayan**. However, Padaung remains by far the most commonly encountered appellation. For more on the Kayan/Padaung, see p.383.

6

interpreter and guide and give you the chance to visit and talk with the Kayan ladies in their own homes – a memorable and equitable experience, and a far cry from the touristy "giraffe lady"-style encounters you'll get around Inle Lake. Coming on a guided tour, it's also possible to combine visits to the village with a **short trek** (90min) through the beautiful surrounding countryside.

Hta Nee La Leh
Less memorable than Pan Pet but still offering an enjoyable day-trip from Loikaw is the neat Kayah village of **Hta Nee La Leh**, around a 45-minute drive southeast of Loikaw. CBT tours (see p.268) offer the chance to visit local homes of the village's Kayah residents in their traditional red garb, see local cultural artefacts including unusual totem poles and a traditional "hunting shrine", and take an ox-cart ride to the local **Seven Lakes** beauty spot (traditional Kayah-style lakeside barbecues can be arranged on request).

Kengtung
ကျိုင်းတုံ
The third-largest town in Shan State, **KENGTUNG** (also known as Kyaingtong, and in either case pronounced "Chengtong") feels both physically and culturally quite separate from the rest of Myanmar, nestled deep in the country's far east, just a few hours' drive from Thailand, China and Laos (although only the Thai border is open to foreigners). Thai baht and Chinese yuan are accepted alongside Burmese kyat, while Shan is the predominant language and the signature Burmese longyi and *thanaka* are notable by their almost complete absence. The proximity of **Thailand** is particularly in evidence, with Thai products lining the shelves of local shops and Leo and Singha beer served in the town's cafés and beer stations alongside the ubiquitous Myanmar brand. Many pagodas also show a certain Siamese influence and are named using the Thai *wat* rather than the Burmese *paya* – even the monks wear Thai-style orange robes alongside the usual Burmese red.

Kengtung was formerly the capital of the most important of the Shan States (the *saopha's* fine palace survived until 1991, when it was ignominiously destroyed by the Burmese military). The town later become a major colonial administrative centre during the British era and was occupied by Thai forces for three years during World War II. Largely neglected under military rule, it has yet to experience the creeping modernization which is changing the face of other similar-sized Burmese towns, and preserves an unhurried atmosphere, a fascinating ethnic patchwork of peoples and more pagodas than it properly knows what to do with. The bother and expense of reaching the place (see p.273) also means that it sees relatively few tourists – most of those who visit are en route to or from Thailand – although the rewarding **trekking** opportunities (see box, p.272) in the surrounding countryside and the chance to get well off the tourist trail might tempt you to splash the cash on a plane ticket here even if you're not Thailand-bound.

Kengtung Market
ကျိုင်းတုံဈေး • Just off the Taunggyi–Tachileik Rd • Daily 6am–6pm • Free
Kengtung's **market** is as colourful as any in Shan State, with a multicultural array of shoppers and stallholders including Shan, Lahu, Akha, Thai, Chinese and Indian,

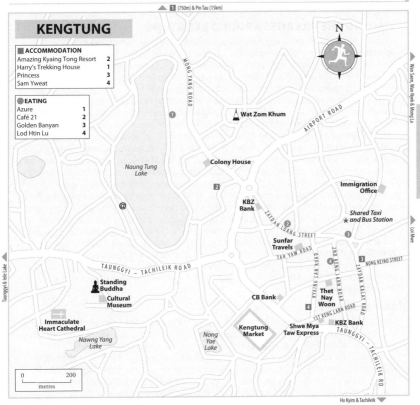

many wearing traditional clothes and headgear. Entering from the town side, you'll run the gauntlet of kitchenware, cheap clothing and other workaday fare, though before long you'll track down one of the areas with stalls selling ethnic beads and fabrics.

Naung Tung Lake

ေနာင္တုံကန္ • Best accessed from the Taunggyi–Tachileik Rd to the south, or the small road south of *Amazing Kyaing Tong* hotel to the east

At the heart of Kengtung, the small **Nang Tung Lake** is undoubtedly the prettiest place in the city. The best views are from the east side, near the *Azure* café (see p.273), from where you can make out the standing Buddha statue (see p.272), framed by the Shan mountains cascading into the distance – particularly beautiful during sunset. You can walk around the whole lake in half an hour along the small and relatively traffic-free road which circles it. Overlooking the lake from the east is the town's old **colonial quarter**, which includes several buildings surviving from the British era; best is the **Colony House** on Mong Yang Road.

Wat Zom Khum

On the hill between Mong Yang Rd and Airport Rd • Daily 4am–8pm • Free

Peeking down on Kengtung from a lofty vantage point atop a small hill above the lake, **Wat Zom Khum** (also known as Wat Jong Kham) is by far the most appealing of the

6

VISITING THE VILLAGES AROUND KENGTUNG

For most, the main reason to visit Kengtung is to take advantage of the **trekking opportunities** in the hills around town. Clutches of Akha, Eng, Lahu, Loi, Padaung and Shan live hereabouts, amid some splendid scenery. Diverse though these peoples are, most travellers feel that a single day of village-visiting suffices; things can get samey rather quickly, and overnight stays are currently forbidden by the authorities.

The most common target is the **Pin Tau** area 16km north of town, in which it's possible to visit several villages on a loop trek. It's an easy walk, though the area's popularity with foreign visitors means that you may encounter begging or over-persistent vendors. Alternatively, the lofty **Ho Kyim** area is 16km south of town; the journey up is rather beautiful, and rewarded with some pleasant Loi and Akha villages. Further south and east, on a separate mountain range around 32km from Kengtung, is the equally high **Loi Mwe** area; despite its name, most villages here are Ahka and Lahu, rather than Loi. This has the most to get one's teeth into of all the village areas around town, and also easiest to access for single travellers; the steep, luxuriantly forested drive up is smooth yet quite spectacular (look for a miniature Golden Rock on the way, opposite the hydroelectric system used to power the villages), while near the top are a small, pretty lake, a decent little market (great for lunchtime noodles) and a clutch of colonial structures dating back to the area's time as a minor hill station. Farther afield, nestled into a small valley on the way out towards Mong La (see box, p.274), are the Loi villages of **Wan Sen** and **Wan Nyek**; here, people still live in communal longhouses, which sometimes play host to more than ten families at a time. Also check out the gorgeous carved panels and doorways on Wan Nyek's beautiful *wat*; it looks like they're awaiting donations to bring the cheap roof into line.

PRACTICALITIES

Most people hit one or more of these areas as part of a day-long **tour**; most hotels will be able to organize these for you. This generally costs around $25 for the guide (which you'll need in order to be able to find most villages), plus $40 for a car or minibus, all split between the group. You'll be able to hit the Pin Tau and Ho Kyim areas in one day; if you want to head further out to the Wan Sen and Wan Nyek villages, figure on an extra $20–30 for the vehicle. Trips to Pin Tau or Ho Kyim involve a bit of walking – the going isn't too tricky on any of these trails, but it's sensible to wear decent footwear and take a bottle of water.

A cheaper option is to head to the **shared taxi** rank behind the *Golden Banyan* restaurant, where you should be able to find a motorbike driver to take you to Loi Mwe and back for around $20. This is the best area to head for if you don't want to pay for a guide-plus-car, since most of its villages and sights are directly accessible by road and reachable without a guide.

---

town's many, many religious sites. It's certainly worth the walk up for the fine views both inside and out. The interior has stencilled gold markings on a burgundy background, giving it a somewhat Vietnamese feel, along with a panoply of golden statues, no two of which are identical. From the pavilion to the rear of the complex you can see the lake, the standing Buddha statue (see below) and the mountains muscling away beyond.

West of the centre

There are a few sights located in a small huddle just west of the town centre. From the market or lake, head down the busy Taunggyi–Tachileik Road and make the steep plod west. Once over the ridge, you'll see the **Immaculate Heart Cathedral** on your left, whose attached school has been educating and assisting local orphans since the days of empire. Accessible from the rear gate of the complex, and visible from all over town, is a **Standing Buddha** statue some 18m in height. Near its foot is the local **Cultural Museum** (Tues–Sun 10am–6pm; K2000), which is barely worth the modest entrance fee (and is often locked during official opening hours, in any case), with a few moth-eaten exhibits including costumes from all the main ethnic-minority peoples hereabouts, along with assorted beads, necklaces and farming equipment.

ARRIVAL AND DEPARTURE — KENGTUNG

Foreigners are prohibited from travelling overland **between Taunggyi and Kengtung** by bus or any other form of unlicensed transport, meaning your only options are to fly or to arrange the trip using a licensed government guide and transport – for which you won't get much change out of $1000. Foreigners are, however, permitted to take the bus between **Kengtung and Tachileik**, with the correct paperwork (see below), and also to visit the notorious border town of **Mong La** – although we don't recommend that you do (see box, p.274).

By plane If you're combining Kengtung with any Myanmar destination bar Tachileik, you're going to have to make use of its tiny airport, located 3km east of the centre – within walking distance, although the route isn't terribly pleasant. It costs around K3000 for a tuk-tuk to or from town. Tickets are available from agencies dotted around the town centre; count on at least $150 for the flight to Heho or Mandalay. Given how few flights there are out of Kengtung, it pays to book as far in advance as you can – or be prepared to fly out to wherever you can get to, then take a second (and possibly a third) flight to your preferred destination.

Destinations Heho (4 weekly; 35min); Mandalay (3 weekly; 1hr); Yangon (2 weekly; 1hr 45min).

By bus and minibus The only roads unsupervised foreigners are allowed to take out of Kengtung are those south to Tachileik on the Thai border and northeast to Mong La, though you'll need to get permission from the nearby immigration office. This is free, and only takes a few minutes. You'll need to present your passport and your bus ticket, which will need to be photocopied for presentation at the three checkpoints en route. Though your bus company should take care of this before you board, it's safer to have it taken care of the day before. Several companies make the run to Tachileik, including Shwe Mya Taw Express and Thet Nay Woon, east of the market, though strangely they all make the run in near-convoy at the same times (8am & noon; 5hr).

ACCOMMODATION

Kengtung has very few decent places to stay, and most find that a couple of nights here is more than enough. Note that though the following places claim to have wi-fi, it often goes down across the whole town. All places listed have a/c unless stated otherwise.

Amazing Kyaing Tong Resort Mong Yang Rd ⓣ084 21620, ⓦamazing-hotel.com. Part of the nationwide Amazing chain, this newly renovated resort is Kengtung's most upmarket option, set in a big four-storey complex overlooking a large pool, with well-equipped, colourfully decorated rooms. Good value at current rates. $70

Harry's Trekking House Mong Yang Rd ⓣ084 21418. The only decent place at this price level, despite a far-flung location north of the lake. Rooms (more expensive ones with a/c) are set in three separate buildings and differ a fair bit: those in the main wooden house are the cheapest and most basic, while there are more modern and pricier alternatives in the two newer buildings out the back. $13

Princess Zaydan Kalay Rd ⓣ084 21319, ⓔkengtung@main4u.com.mm. Reliable mid-range choice, though overpriced for what you get, and some rooms lack windows. Rooms come with a fridge, and the location near the market is a plus point. $45

Sam Yweat Kyaing Lan Rd ⓣ084 21235. One of Kengtung's best all-round options, at least once you're past the reception area-cum-moped park, in a bright and clean modern building. Rooms are a bit bare but perfectly comfortable (albeit hot water is erratic), and staff can help arrange treks. $35

EATING

Eating options in Kengtung are decidedly thin on the ground. As well as the places listed below there are plenty of **snack-shacks** around the market and on the streets leading down to the lake from Mong Yang Road. At night, you could try to track down one of the town's many **barbecue-stick places** for some cheap, tasty snacks; there's one on the east shore of the lake, near the corner where the road descends.

Azure East side of lake. Tiny lakeside place selling tasty Shan-style noodles (mains around K2000) – the fried pork and prawns are both good – plus draught beer. They may even set up a table for you in the grassy area by the lake. Daily 10am–9pm.

Café 21 Zaydan Loang St ⓣ09 5842 1952. A sign of the

6

MONG LA

Way out near the Chinese border, around 80km northeast of Kengtung, **Mong La** (မိုင်းလား) has a bit of a reputation. The town is run as a private fiefdom of the Shan separatist National Democratic Alliance Army (NDAA) and offers a surreal splash of modernity in this remote region, with neon-lit streets and dozens of high-rises poking up from between the surrounding hills. Mong La is effectively an extension of China, using Chinese currency, electricity, phone lines and even running on Beijing time, and has long been popular with (almost exclusively male) Chinese tourists, who come across the border to throw down cash at the town's casinos. Pressure from the Chinese government forced many to close in 2005, though in the words of one local NDAA official, "we just moved them all back ten miles, and made them much larger". The town also has a flourishing drugs and prostitution scene – child prostitution is endemic, with some of the girls in the town's innumerable brothels as young as 13. The town is also a major trading centre for animals and animal parts, as a visit to the market will make clear, with live pangolins and monkeys, as well as tiger claws, elephant skin, bear paws and the like all offered for sale. There's no real reason to come here, except to experience the general weirdness of the place, and the border is closed to third-party nationals. It's also worth reflecting that every foreign dollar spent here contributes, however inadvertently, to propping up an economy whose entire rationale is based on drugs, animal cruelty and sexual abuse.

changing times in Kengtung. The almost-funky decor is certainly a change from your average teahouse, as is the menu, featuring pizza, pasta and dim sum alongside traditional Shan dishes (most mains around K3000) – plus the best coffee between Taunggyi and Thailand. Daily 7am–10pm.

Golden Banyan Zaydan Loang St ☎ 084 21421. One of the most reliable places to eat in town, serving a wide range of Chinese dishes (most mains around K3000)

including good soups, stir-fries and tofu dishes (K3000). You can eat outside under the giant banyan tree – although it's not a garden, sadly, but a sort of concrete shelf. Daily 10am–9pm.

Lod Htin Lu 2nd Keng Larn Rd. Similar to – if a bit dingier than – the *Golden Banyan*, serving up a similar array of generic Chinese-style fare (mains around K3000). Reliable, if not wildly inspiring. Daily 10am–8pm.

DIRECTORY

Banks There are ATMs at the CB and KBZ banks in the town centre.

Tachileik

တာချီလိတ်

You'll find yourself passing through the rapidly expanding little city of **TACHILEIK** if making the trip between Kengtung and northern Thailand. There's a palpable frontier atmosphere here – it's almost as if a zest for foreign currency has physically yanked the place right up to the border, with Thai baht being the main currency accepted everywhere from hotels to the tiny stores dealing in black-market goods. That said, these days Chinese is quite possibly the second language here – a sign of the times.

Although there's no reason to visit the place on its own merit, Tachileik has long been a popular visa-run destination for expats living in Thailand and travellers wanting to peek inside Myanmar without shelling out on a visa or benefiting the regime. If you find yourself here with time to kill it's worth having a look at the labyrinthine **market**, stuffed full of contraband and pirated goods, from Thai cigarettes to fake foreign liquor. Access to the surrounding countryside and hills, however, is strictly forbidden.

ARRIVAL AND DEPARTURE

TACHILEIK

By plane Tachileik's small airport is 10km northeast of the town centre, just east of the Kengtung road (around 100

baht by motorbike, or 300 baht by tuk-tuk). You can buy tickets from various agencies around the junction just up

TACHILEIK–MAE SAI BORDER CROSSING

The **immigration offices** on both sides of the border are open daily 6am–6pm. There are no restrictions on foreigners crossing the border **into Thailand** from Tachileik; citizens of most Western and many other countries are issued a free 30-day tourist visa on arrival. Travelling **into Myanmar**, various options are available. Entering Myanmar on a **full tourist visa** is straightforward (e-visas are also accepted), although you'll need official permission to make the onward journey by bus to Kengtung (see below). Full tourist visas are not issued at the border, however, so you'll need to organize one before you arrive if you intend to continue on into Myanmar beyond Kengtung. A **day pass** to visit Tachileik on its own costs 500 baht, and border officials will retain your passport for the duration of your visit. You can also **stay overnight** in Tachileik (or indeed longer if you fancy) for an additional K10,000 per day on top of the cost of a day pass. It's also possible to **travel on to Kengtung** (but no further) even if you don't have a full Burmese tourist visa, although you'll have to hire a local guide from the tourist office next to immigration (500 baht per day, plus their transport costs), as well as paying the 500 baht day-pass fee and K10,000 per day.

The pleasant Thai town of **Mae Sai** hugs up against the border. Small red buses make the trip between the border and the bus station for 15 baht, while it's more like 50 baht by motorbike, or 90 baht by taxi. Mae Sai has regular connections to and from Chiang Rai (1hr 30min), slightly less frequent ones to Chiang Mai (4–5hr), and others to destinations across Thailand.

6

from the Thai border; if you're in Thailand and intending to fly from Tachileik to other parts of Myanmar, check latest schedules before crossing the border, or you could be in for a boring few days' wait.

Destinations Heho (5 weekly; 1hr); Lashio (1–2 daily; 1hr); Yangon (3 weekly; 1hr 10min).

By bus or shared taxi Numerous companies have daily services to Kengtung (5hr), all departing at either 8am or 11am/noon. It's best to buy tickets at the town's hotels, even if you're not staying. If you arrive in the afternoon after all the buses have gone and want to travel on to Kengtung without spending a night in

Tachileik you'll need to get a seat in a shared taxi (around K15,000), or hire one outright (from around K70,000 depending on your bargaining skills). To make the journey to Kengtung you'll need official permission from the tourist office by the immigration post; take your passport and bus ticket. The permission slips must be photocopied three times for presentation at each of the checkpoints along the road – this can usually be done when buying the ticket, though you may have to pay for the copies. The bus station itself is 2km from the centre on the Kengtung road, and easily accessible by tuk-tuk (around 100 baht) or motorbike (80 baht).

ACCOMMODATION AND EATING

In general, you'll get far more bang for your baht by staying over the Thai border in Mae Sai instead. Baht's the preferred currency in Kengtung's hotels, though they'll accept kyat and (usually) dollars too.

Erawan Mahabandota Rd ☎ 012 892863. Just about the cheapest option in town, and good value for the price, with a range of clean, ample-sized rooms; you'll pay extra for a/c and a private bathroom. To get here from the Thai border, turn right at the junction, then take the first proper road on the left (after the Ayeyarwady Bank). ฿10
Golden Cherry Arrkazar Yone St ☎ 084 52517, ⓦ goldencherryhoteltachileik.com. Right in the middle of town, this newish mid-range hotel is about as good as it gets in Tachileik, albeit no bargain. Rooms are plain but

spacious and comfortable enough, with a/c, and there are good views from the rooftop breakfast area. To reach it, follow the main road as it curves to the right into town (about 1.5km from immigration), then head left down Arrkazar Yone St. ฿40
Valentine Main Rd. A nice hi-hi or bye-bye to Burmese cuisine, just around the corner from the Thai border – turn right at the junction, and it's almost immediately on your right. They sell Thai and Chinese-style mains too (K2000–2500), as well as Burmese-style tea. Daily 5am–9pm.

DIRECTORY

Banks There's a KBZ Bank, with ATM, just a short walk from the Thai border; with Thailand at your back, turn right at the junction, and you're almost there. If that one fails,

there are more banks further up the same road. The exchange rate at the time of writing was roughly 1 Thai baht to K40.

Mandalay
and around

U BEIN BRIDGE, AMARAPURA

Mandalay and around

History lies thick on the ground in and around Mandalay. Occupying a strategic location on the Ayeyarwady River almost at the exact centre of the country, the area emerged as the leading centre of political, military and religious power in Upper Burma following the collapse of Bagan in the late thirteenth century, and retained its pre-eminent position (with occasional interruptions) right up until the final overthrow of the Burmese monarchy by the British in 1885. Mandalay is still considered the de facto cultural capital of Myanmar, while the great palaces, pagodas and other monuments of Mandalay and the former royal cities of nearby Inwa (Ava), Amarapura and Sagaing provide a touchstone of national identity in a rapidly changing world, giving the area a cultural and historical lustre compared to which Yangon is a mere colonial upstart, and Naypyitaw a deranged military fantasy.

7

Mandalay city itself is a relatively recent arrival on the historical scene but boasts numerous attractions both religious and secular, despite unpromising first impressions. In many ways, however, it's the area **around Mandalay** which is the real highlight, with its myriad mementoes of former imperial glory. The slight but impressive remains of the old royal city of Ava can be seen during a horse-and-carriage tour around the enjoyably rustic village of **Inwa**, while another former capital, **Amarapura**, boasts a lovely lakeside setting, pagodas galore and the spectacular U Bein teak bridge. The stupa-studded hills of **Sagaing** are another major draw, although perhaps most enjoyable of all is the breezy boat trip down the Ayeyarwady to the little village of **Mingun**, home to the gargantuan remnants of what was intended to be the world's largest stupa, accompanied by one of its largest bells.

Mandalay

မန္တလေး

MANDALAY is one of those names – like Timbuktu, Zanzibar or Samarkand – which has long lingered in the imagination of Western travellers, thanks largely to a poem ("Mandalay") penned by a writer (Rudyard Kipling) who never actually visited the place. Redolent with images of a bygone Asia, modern Mandalay can prove a disappointing, if not downright exasperating, place at first glance, with its endless grid of largely modern, generally indistinguishable and consistently traffic-plagued streets – Kipling's "tinkly temple bells" and "spicy garlic smells" replaced with the deafening klaxons of rampaging buses and pick-up trucks belching clouds of exhaust.

WOODCARVINGS, SHWE IN BIN KYAUNG

Highlights

❶ Shwe In Bin Kyaung Flamboyant, off-the-beaten-track teak monastery, carved with a riot of intricate decoration. **See p.290**

❷ Sunset over the Ayeyarwady Myanmar's greatest waterway is at its most beautiful around sunset; take it in from the riverside road, or over cocktails on the roof of the *Ayarwaddy River View Hotel*. **See p.295**

❸ Mandalay shows Myanmar's capital of culture, Mandalay boasts a series of enjoyable shows ranging from traditional theatre and puppets through to cutting contemporary satire. **See p.297**

❹ U Bein Bridge Just south of Mandalay, this iconic teak bridge – more than 1km in

length – is one of Myanmar's most famous sights. **See p.301**

❺ Inwa Take a horse-drawn carriage around the pastoral back roads of this sleepy village, dotted with the evocative remains of one of Myanmar's greatest former royal capitals. **See p.303**

❻ Sagaing Peaceful riverside town with a stunning profusion of white and gold stupas and pagodas dotting the beautiful wooded hills above the Ayeyarwady. **See p.305**

❼ Boat trip to Mingun Slide up the Ayeyarwady River on a boat towards Mingun, a tiny village featuring the unfinished remains of what was intended to be the world's largest stupa. **See p.309**

HIGHLIGHTS ARE MARKED ON THE MAP ON P.280

It's a difficult city to love, admittedly, although there are plenty of attractions hidden away amid the metropolitan sprawl. The beautifully wooded, pagoda-strewn slopes of **Mandalay Hill** offer a blessed retreat from the city streets, as do the sylvan grounds of **Mandalay Palace** (even if most of it is off-limits, and the palace itself is actually a modern replica). Temples are another attraction, including the revered **Mahamuni Pagoda** with its memorably misshapen, gold leaf-encrusted Buddha, while the flamboyant **Shwe In Bin** and **Shwenandaw Kyaung** teak monasteries and the extraordinary massed stupas of the **Kuthodaw** and **Sandamuni pagodas** (housing what is claimed to be the world's largest book) are also essential viewing. Sunset strolls along the **Ayeyarwady** are another draw, while even the endless concrete waffle of downtown Mandalay has its compensations, including spit-and-sawdust markets, colourful mosques and Hindu temples, and the streetside food stalls which spring up after dark. There's also Myanmar's best selection of **traditional performing arts**, including puppets, music, dance and old-school *anyeint* comedy, given a contemporary satirical twist by the celebrated Moustache Brothers.

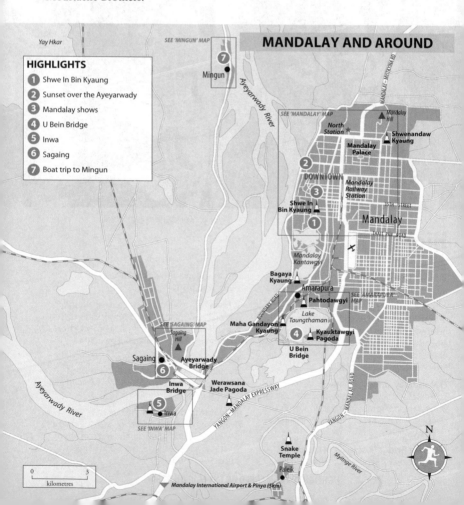

A RIGHT ROYAL MERRY-GO-ROUND

From the mid-fourteenth century until the British arrived some half a millennium later, Mandalay and its surrounding area played host to a curious travelling courtly circus, as the Burmese capital regularly shifted from one part of the region to another. The first royal capital in the area was established by King Thihathu at **Pinya**, one of the minor statelets which emerged in northern Myanmar following the collapse of Bagan. In 1315 Thihathu's son, Saw Yun, set up a rival kingdom in **Sagaing**, with the two kingdoms collectively controlling considerable parts of central and northern Myanmar.

The two kingdoms were eventually unified in 1364 by Thihathu's great-grandson, Thado Minbya, who set about building a new capital at **Ava** (or **Inwa**, as it's now known). Despite fluctuating fortunes, Ava would become the longest-lasting and, intermittently, the most important centre of political power in Myanmar right up until its final abandonment in 1838.

The kingdom of Ava survived under Thado Minbya's successors until 1527 when it fell to a Shan confederacy, continuing as capital of the north until 1555, when it was captured by the **Taungoo dynasty** (see p.362). Briefly stripped of its privileges, the city returned to pre-eminence in 1599, becoming capital of a reformed Taungoo empire until 1613, and again from 1635 to 1752, when it was sacked by forces of the Hanthawaddy Kingdom (see p.364), with a little help from the French.

A new dynasty, the Konbaung (see p.364), emerged soon afterwards at nearby **Shwebo** (see p.340) under the formidable King Alaungpaya. The Konbaung capital was moved briefly to Sagaing in 1760–63, only to be moved back to the old imperial capital of Ava and then, in 1783, moved again by the increasingly restless Konbaung royals to a new location at **Amarapura** under King Bodawpaya. Amarapura served as the seat of royal power until 1821, before Bodawpaya's grandson, King Bagyidaw, returned the capital to Ava – only for it to be devastated by an earthquake in 1838, whereupon the capital was shifted back to Amarapura. This time it lasted less than twenty years, and in 1857 King Mindon established the new city of **Mandalay**, Burma's final royal capital.

7

Brief history

Given its historic reputation, Mandalay is a surprisingly young city. Locals tell of how the Buddha climbed Mandalay Hill and prophesied that, 2400 years into the future, a grand city would be founded at its foot. The promised city was duly founded in 1857 by **King Mindon**, said to be the reincarnation of San Da Mukhi, an ogress who impressed the Buddha by lopping off her breasts and presenting them to him. Mindon named his new city **Yadanarbon**, from the Pali Ratanapura, meaning "City of Gems", a name which is still widely used by businesses around town (as well as by the local football team, Yadanarbon FC), although it subsequently become known as Mandalay, after nearby Mandalay Hill.

Politically, the founding of Mandalay was intended to impress the **British**, who had already seized control of Lower Burma, of the strength of Mindon's significantly reduced but still powerful kingdom – although this didn't stop the British from marching into the city in 1885 and sending Mindon's son and successor, Thibaw, and the rest of the royal family into exile in India. Following the British takeover, the city prospered until the Japanese occupation during **World War II**, which saw many of the old buildings levelled by Allied bombing.

Modern Mandalay is now Myanmar's second city and the economic powerhouse of the north, with a population of well over a million people. The city feels much more purely Burmese than multicultural Yangon, although large-scale Chinese immigration (and increasing economic links with that country) over recent decades has also subtly changed the city's demographic. There are also plenty of ethnic Shan, mostly concentrated in areas west of 86th Street, while the innumerable mosques and occasional Hindu temples dotted around downtown bear witness to the long-established Muslim and Indian communities which still call the city home.

7

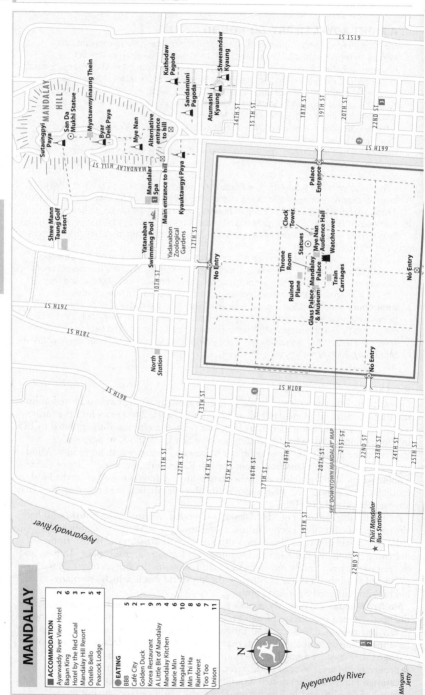

IS IS19

Kuthodaw
Pagoda

Shwenandaw
Kyaung

MANDALAY
HILL

Sandamuni
Pagoda

Myatsawnyinaung Thein

San Da
Mukhi Statue

Atumashi
Kyaung

14TH ST
15TH ST
18TH ST
19TH ST
20TH ST
22ND ST
B

Sutaungpyi
Paya

Byar
Deik Paya

Mye Nan

Alternative
entrance
to hill

IS H199

2

MANDALAY HILL ST

Mandalar
Spa

Main entrance to hill

Alternative entrance to hill

Kyauktawgyi Paya

Palace
Entrance

Shwe Mann
Taung Golf
Resort

Yatanaban
Swimming Pool

Yadanabon
Zoological
Gardens

12TH ST

Clock
Tower

Mye Nan
Audience Hall

Watchtower

No Entry

10TH ST

Throne
Room

Statues

Ruined
Plane

Glass Palace,
& Museum

Mandalay
Palace

Train
Carriages

No
Entry

79TH ST

78TH ST

76TH ST

13TH ST

North
Station

No Entry

H98 ST

80TH ST

14TH ST

15TH ST

16TH ST

17TH ST

18TH ST

20TH ST

21ST ST

22ND ST

23RD ST

24TH ST

25TH ST

11TH ST

12TH ST

SEE DOWNTOWN MANDALAY MAP

Thiri Mandalar
Bus Station

19TH ST

22ND ST

Ayeyarwady River

N

Ayeyarwady River

Mingun
Jetty

7

Mintha Theater

Mandalay Marionettes ❶

MTT ⓘ

Myanmar Upper Land ❷

Chinese Consulate

Pyi Gyi Myat Shin Bus Station

Mandalay University

ADIPADILI RD

MAHA MYAING ST

THEIK PAN ST

26TH ST
27TH ST
29TH ST
30TH ST
31ST ST
32ND ST
33RD ST
34TH ST
35TH ST
36TH ST
37TH ST

Ever Smile ❻
GGG Massage ❼

Mandalay Railway Station

CB Bank

Mandalay Yatanar Mall ❼

78TH ST
79TH ST
77TH ST
80TH ST
81ST ST
82ND ST

Myanmar Golden River Group (MGRG)

Moustache Brothers

Mahamuni Paya

38TH ST
39TH ST
40TH ST
41ST ST
42ND ST
43RD ST
44TH ST
45TH ST

Man Myoe Market

Jade Market ❺

Stone Carvers' Workshops

Eindawya Pagoda

Shwe In Bin Kyaung

86TH ST
87TH ST
88TH ST
89TH ST

Thinga Yazar Channel

STRAND ROAD

Gaweik Jetty & IWT office

Amarapura (8km), Sagaing (14km) & Inwa (14km) ▶

▶ Kwe Se Kan Bus Station, Airport & Yangon

 ⊠ Entrance

╱╲ Escarpment

0   500
metres

■ **DRINKING**

Ayar Sky Bar 1
Central Park 2

● **SHOPPING**

Jade Market 5
King Galon 3
Mandalay Yatanar Mall 2
Rocky 1
Shwe Pathein 4

Mandalay Hill and around

Rising above the northeast corner of the city – and visible from much of it – the stupa-sprinkled **Mandalay Hill** is one the city's most enjoyable sights, its endless tree-shaded stairways and tranquil pagodas offering a blissful retreat from the traffic-plagued streets of the city below, and particularly beautiful towards sunset. Further temples lie dotted around the foot of the hill, easily combined with Mandalay Hill into a half-day mini-tour. These include the spectacular **Shwenandaw Kyaung** teak monastery, while close by the **Kuthodaw** and **Sandamuni pagodas** are home to an extraordinary array of carved slabs popularly described as "the world's largest book".

Mandalay Hill

မန္တလေးတောင် • Accessible from 10th St • Daily 24hr • K1000 to enter the topmost Sutaungpyi Paya, although access to the rest of the hill is free; K200 to enter footwear at the base, or you can carry it with you for free • Motorbike taxis to the top cost around K4000–5000 including waiting time, while pick-ups cost K1000; both are available on 10th St

For many people, the 45-minute walk up **Mandalay Hill** for sunset is one of the highlights of a visit to the city. The usual starting point is the staircase between a large pair of chinthe on 10th Street; there's a second entrance a little further east. Concrete steps run uphill from both entrances before meeting at **Byar Deik Paya**, from where a large standing Buddha points back the way you came.

Further shrines punctuate the ascent. One of the first you reach is the memorably ugly **Myatsawnyinaung Thein**, looking oddly like an abandoned factory with its cracked concrete shell supported by dozens of iron pillars. Peer out of the hall's eastern flank and you'll see the walls of an old colonial-era fort to the rear. Just above here (and built into a further section of the old fort) is **Ngon Minn**, decorated with the names of hundreds of donors written on its white columns.

As you get higher the crowds become thicker, particularly towards sunset, with stalls of souvenir vendors, palmists and astrologers lining the disorienting tangle of stairways (remember the way you came up, lest you get completely lost on the way back down). After a fair few "Is *this* the top?" false dawns, the actual summit is quite obvious; the wide terrace of **Sutaungpyi Paya** ("Wish-Granting Temple") rewards the effort of climbing to the top with superb views and a colourful ensemble of yellow, green and pink shrines, glittering with glass mosaics.

At the eastern side of the first major level on the way back down, don't miss the tiny statue of **San Da Mukhi**, merrily holding her severed breasts in homage to the Buddha, an act of piety which eventually saw her reincarnated as King Mindon, creator of Mandalay (see p.281).

Yadanabon Zoological Gardens

မန္တလေးတိရစ္ဆာန်ရုံ • 10th St • Daily 9am–6pm • K2000

The city's awful **zoo** has been included here as a warning alone – even by the almost uniformly low standards of such facilities across Asia, this is a real shocker, with most of the animals kept in featureless, undersized concrete cages. Unless you fancy seeing depressed hippos standing for hours on end with their heads to the floor, bears and big cats endlessly pacing the same side of their enclosure, or monkeys making all-too-obvious calls of distress, leave this place well alone.

Kyauktawgyi Paya

ကျောက်တော်ကြီးဘုရား • Off 10th St, south of the Mandalay Hill entrance • Daily 5am–7pm • Free

Right at the foot of Mandalay Hill, the small **Kyauktawgyi Paya** is centred on a giant Buddha, hewn from a single slab of marble – no mean feat, given that the statue is 12m tall. Shiny mirrored corridors surround the statue, glittering like Santa's grotto on Christmas Eve and "enhanced" with the LED disco-Buddha lights so beloved by the Burmese; the complex also serves as a popular playground for flocks of local sparrows. Normally one of the city's more peaceful shrines, the pagoda comes dramatically to life during Mandalay celebrations of the countrywide Thadingyut festival in October (see box, p.42).

Kuthodaw Pagoda

ကုသိုလ်တော်ဘုရား• • Off 12th St • Daily 6am–9pm • Covered by the Mandalay Combination Ticket (see box, p.286)

Southeast of Mandalay Hill, the **Kuthodaw Pagoda** is home to a remarkable series of engraved marble slabs which, along with those at the nearby Sandamuni Pagoda (see below), are collectively referred to as "the world's biggest book". Commissioned by King Mindon in 1857, the 729 slabs, each housed in its own individual mini-stupa, are intricately carved with the entire fifteen books of the Tripitaka, the canonical works of the Buddhist religion. It took more than a decade to complete the work and check for errors; the creation of the complex is described on yet another slab, bringing the grand total up to 730. The complex was heavily damaged during British rule, with bricks from the stupas used for military roads, though rebuilding was swift.

Sandamuni Pagoda

စန္တာမုနိဘုရား• • Off 12th St • Daily 6am–9pm • Free

Amazingly, even the inscriptions at the Kuthodaw Pagoda are trumped by nearby **Sandamuni Pagoda**, which boasts another 1774 slabs engraved with commentaries on the Tripitaka, created in 1913. Unlike the concentric formations of Kuthodaw, here they're arrayed in an almost military-like formation, with long lines of dazzlingly whitewashed stupas framed against the tree-covered hump of Mandalay Hill. The pagoda itself dates back to the rule of King Mindon, who commissioned it in 1874 as a memorial to his younger half-brother, Crown Prince Kanaung, assassinated during an attempted palace coup in 1866 and buried here, along with three other princes killed in the rebellion. The complex is also home to the largest **solid-iron Buddha** in Myanmar (although covered in gold), commissioned by King Bodawpaya in 1802 and subsequently brought here by Mindon from Amarapura – despite weighing an estimated 20 tonnes.

Atumashi Kyaung

အတုမရှိကျောင်း• • Off 14th St • Daily 9am–5pm • Covered by the Mandalay Combination Ticket (see box, p.286)

The **Atumashi Kyaung** ("Incomparable Monastery"), built by King Mindon in 1857, was originally one of the glories of Mandalay: a huge teak monastery containing various treasures including a large lacquered Buddha with a diamond set in its forehead – although both Buddha and diamond went missing after the British took the city and the entire building burned down in 1890. The current structure is a 1990s stone reconstruction of the original, a flamboyant white-and-gold wedding cake of a building topped with an unusual stepped-platform roof and with a large but disappointingly bare hall inside.

Shwenandaw Kyaung

ရွှေနန်းတော်ကျောင်း• • Off 14th St • Daily 9am–5pm • Covered by the Mandalay Combination Ticket (see box, p.286)

An extravagant teak construction under a densely stacked four-tiered roof, the **Shwenandaw Kyaung** was originally built within the palace walls as a residence for King Mindon. The building was converted to a monastery and moved to its current site east of the palace after Mindon died in it, as this was considered bad luck by his son, Thibaw; this relocation saved it from burning alongside the palace's other buildings during World War II. Inside, elegantly carved Jataka stories decorate the raised main hall, whose atmospheric interior glows a dim gold.

Mandalay Palace

မန္တလေးနန်းတော် • Entrance on 66th St • Daily 8am–5pm • Covered by the Mandalay Combination Ticket (see box, p.286)

Hogging a huge square of land at the heart of Mandalay are the grounds of the city's erstwhile **royal palace**, constructed by King Mindon almost immediately after

7

THE MANDALAY COMBINATION TICKET

A number of sights in and around Mandalay are covered by the **Mandalay Combination Ticket** (K10,000), valid for five days – unfortunately, it's not possible to purchase individual tickets to the sights it covers. The relevant section of the ticket is stamped at each sight you visit, meaning it can't be re-used. The main attractions covered by the ticket are **Mandalay Palace** and the Maha Aungmye Bonzan and Bagaya Kyaung in **Inwa**. In theory you'll also need the ticket to visit **Kuthodaw Pagoda**, **Atumashi Kyaung**, **Shwenandaw Kyaung** and (in Amarapura) **Bagaya Kyaung** and to walk across **U Bein Bridge**, although in practice the ticket isn't always asked for at these places (and seemingly never at U Bein Bridge).

7

establishing his capital here in 1857. The palace followed a traditional design informed by links with China – much like Beijing's famed Forbidden City – with a geometrically auspicious alignment of buildings set inside crenellated walls surrounded by a broad moat. The huge walls themselves (3m thick, 7m high and 8km in length) are punctuated by 36 bastions and twelve gateways, symbolizing the signs of the zodiac. Five-tiered *pyatthat* (spire-style roofs) are placed above each of the bastions and gates, with the exception of the four main gates (one on each side), through which the king himself would have passed and which are surmounted with seven-storey *pyatthat* – the number of tiers on a roof signifying the status of the person using the building below.

Despite the effort put into building the thing, only Mindon and his successor Thibaw had the chance to rule from here before the latter was overthrown by the British (who rechristened the palace Fort Dufferin and billeted troops in its former royal quarters). Even worse was to follow in World War II, when almost the entire palace was flattened by Allied bombs. What you see today is a 1990s reconstruction carried out by the military, who have long controlled the complex.

As a military area the palace grounds are mostly off-limits to foreigners, save for the reconstructed palace and the main approach road in from the east – frustratingly, the only direction from which foreigners are allowed to enter. There are a couple of low-key shops and teashops along the approach road, but no other sources of refreshment. Above the eastern entrance a sign states: "Tatmadaw and the people, co-operate and crush all those harming the union", and the army enhance their already stellar international reputation by insisting that foreign cyclists leave their machines at the gate; tour buses, of course, get to head straight to the centre.

The palace

The palace itself is more impressive as a whole than for any particular part, and many of the smaller buildings are no more than empty shells, giving the whole place the feel of a rather opulent film set. A spine of reconstructed ceremonial halls runs down the centre of the complex, with signs stating what each was used for (complete with bombastic references to the cannons which "can crush all enemies", and other such details). Starting from the east is the **Mye Nan Audience Hall** (signed "Great Audience Hall"), which contains then-and-now pictures attesting to the accuracy of the re-created palace, along with a replica of the king's famous Lion Throne under a seven-tiered *pyatthat* roof. Another richly decorated throne stands in the impressive **Throne Room** (signed "Central Palace") slightly further along, placed beneath a high wood roof supported by soaring red columns.

At the western end of the palace is the **Glass Palace** (signed "Chief Queen's Audience Hall"), named after a glass bed brought from France by King Thibaw. The palace now houses a small **museum** (closed for renovations at the time of writing) containing the rather impressive bed itself, along with a series of elaborate traditional costumes.

On the south side of the complex, an eye-catching circular **watchtower** offers fine palace and city views from the top of the spiral staircase wrapped around its exterior.

The rest of the complex

A couple of curios dot the out-of-bounds area beyond the palace walls. Look out from the northern wall, towards the west of the complex, and you'll make out a ruined **plane**; do likewise from the south, and you'll see a rusting **railway engine** which once pulled a toy train around the ground.

Exiting the palace, you'll see a circle of nine **statues** of kings and other historical figures to your left; it's technically out of bounds to foreigners, although you're unlikely to be stopped. Slightly further east, next to the main approach road, is the palace's striking **clocktower**, an open-sided structure perched on a tall plinth, with wooden steps leading up to a platform housing the "clock" itself – actually a large drum, which was formerly beaten to mark the hours.

7

Downtown Mandalay

Sprawling away to the west of the palace, **Downtown Mandalay**'s polluted sprawl of concrete streets has few obvious attractions but provides an interesting – if sometimes exhausting – place to take the pulse of urban life in modern Myanmar, with a few pretty Buddhist and Hindu shrines tucked away here and there, along with dozens of mosques, street cafés and stray dogs, and some interesting markets.

Sri Ganesh temple and around

27th St, at the corner of 81st St • Usually open daily around 8am–noon & 5–8pm • Free

Close to one another on 27th Street, a pair of Hindu temples serve Mandalay's sizeable Indian-descended community. The richly decorated *gopuram* (tower) of the **Sri Ganesh temple** provides an unmissable landmark – and welcome splash of colour – at the junction of 81st Street, while inside an eclectic collection of icons includes a striking green Ganesh in the central shrine (often hidden behind its curtain) surrounded by other deities ranging from a black-skinned, flute-playing Krishna through to a typically seraphic Buddha. Close by, between 79th and 80th streets, is the low-slung **Sanatan Dharma** (same hours), topped by five pretty little bright red, gold-trimmed towers. Food hawkers can often be found outside both temples selling sugary Indian sweets.

The fire lookout tower and fire station

Corner of 29th and 81st sts

Now hemmed in by high-rises, Mandalay's **fire lookout tower** formerly provided a handy vantage point from which conflagrations anywhere in the city could be seen – a useful early-warning system in a metropolis whose buildings were mostly made of wood. It's no longer in use, although the city's main **fire station** can still be found alongside it on 29th Street, complete with a pair of vintage 1970s engines (although they look at least two decades older), usually to be seen parked at the front and still in occasional use.

Zegyo Market and around

ဈေးချို • Between 24th & 25th sts and 84th and 86th sts • Daily 8am–5pm

On the west side of downtown, the **Zegyo Market** dates back to the days of King Mindon and is the largest in Mandalay, a busy commercial hive with hundreds of shops selling a huge range of everyday goods. Sadly, the old colonial market of 1903 was pulled down during the 1990s and replaced with the current Chinese-style centre.

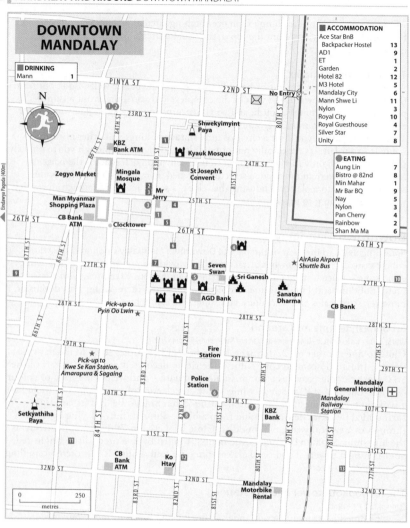

Bustling street markets spill out onto 86th Street, while immediately to the south of Zegyo, the **Man Myanmar Shopping Plaza** (84th St between 25th and 26th sts) offers more of the same, but even more hectic.

Eindawya Pagoda

အိမ်တော်ရာဘုရား • Off 28th St • Daily 24hr • Free

The most striking temple in central Mandalay, the **Eindawya Pagoda** is centred on a glittering, gold-leaf-covered stupa. The temple was constructed in 1847 on the orders of King Pagan Min, who was living in his summer house on this very site when he ascended to the throne. The temple is also remembered for its role in the cultural confrontations of the colonial era thanks to a famous incident in 1919 when a group of Burmese – increasingly infuriated (along with most of the population) at the refusal of foreigners to remove their footwear when entering local pagodas – attacked a group of shoe-wearing Europeans. Four monks were subsequently tried for the assault, with their leader being convicted of attempted murder and sentenced to life imprisonment.

If you've a little time, head out of the western entrance and cross the road to a lovely, secluded area of monastic dwellings – one of the calmest and most charming places in the entire city.

South of the centre

South of the centre, the city streets becomes more workaday, exemplified by the hectic **Jade Market** and the stone carvers near the huge **Mahamuni Paya**, the city's most revered temple. The nearby teak monastery of **Shwe In Bin** provides a haven of peace amid the bustle.

Mahamuni Paya

မဟာမုနိဘုရား• Off 82nd Rd, just east of Mandalay–Sagaing Rd • Daily 24hr; Buddha cleaning daily 4am • K1000 camera fee

The large **Mahamuni Paya** is Mandalay's most important Buddhist site, and also home to one of its biggest festivals (see box, p.298). The temple's importance derives from the presence of the revered **Mahamuni Buddha**, a 3.8m-high figure taken from Mrauk U in 1784 by the army of King Bodawpaya (see p.365) – a tale portrayed in a series of paintings lining a gallery-like wing to the northeast of the main hall.

Male devotees visit to apply ultra-thin squares of **gold leaf** (from around K2000) to the figure; women are not allowed within the inner sanctum and instead hand their gold to a male assistant. The figure itself is said to weigh six tonnes, while the gold-leaf covering adds another two tonnes. Pictures from 1901, 1935 and 1984 show just how much bling the figure has accreted over the years, and the weight has really gone to the Buddha's calves, to such a degree that he appears to have elephantiasis. In the early morning, a small crowd of early birds gathers while the face of the statue – pretty much the only part not covered in gold leaf – is tenderly washed.

Northwest of the main shrine is a cream concrete building containing Hindu figures taken originally from Angkor Wat by the Rakhine, before being appropriated by Bodawpaya at the same time as the large Buddha.

Stone carvers' workshops

Off 84nd St

Just west of the Mahamuni Paya complex is a dusty and noisy **stone-carving** district. Dozens of workshops line the road, with Buddha statues in various sizes and stages of completion spilling out onto the pavement, including rather spooky-looking unfinished figures with blank red squares where their faces will eventually be.

Jade Market

Between 86/87th and 38/41st sts • Daily 8am–5pm • K1000

The stalls in the large **Jade Market**, located in a ramshackle and borderline chaotic canal-side district southwest of downtown, sell mostly to dealers. The main trading in the market takes place in the morning, but it's possible to see jade being cut, shaped and polished at any time, both in the market itself and in the workshops outside, on the eastern side. If you're interested in buying jade here yourself (see p.298), do some research first.

Man Myoe Market

84th St, between 38th & 39th sts • Daily 8am–6pm

Two blocks east of the Jade Market is the contrastingly quiet and completely untouristed **Man Myoe Market**, offering a peaceful, almost rustic, retreat from the hectic surrounding streets, with dozens of quaint little gold and jewellery shops, plus a colourful miniature fruit and vegetable market running through the middle.

Shwe In Bin Kyaung

ရွှေအင်းပင်ကျောင်း • 89th St, between 37th & 38th sts • Daily 24hr • Free

Raised on stilts, the teak **Shwe In Bin Kyaung** is a real stunner, and surprisingly untouristy too. The monastery was built in the late nineteenth century by jade merchants from China – whose legacy lives on in the nearby Jade Market (see p.289) – and is most notable for the fantastically rich profusion of carvings covering every doorway, eave and balustrade, many of them covered in spiders' webs, and extending way up to the extravagant five-tiered roof.

ARRIVAL AND DEPARTURE   MANDALAY

BY PLANE

Mandalay International Airport Mandalay International Airport (ⓦ mandalayairport.com) is some 35km south from the city centre. There are a few ATMs at the airport.

Transport to/from the city The taxi booking desk in the airport charges a set K5000 per seat, or K12,000 for the full cab.

Tickets Plane tickets can be booked through many travel agents around town including the reliable Seven Swan (see p.292).

Destinations Bagan (1–2 daily; 30min); Bhamo (4 weekly; 50min); Heho (5 daily; 35min); Kengtung (2 weekly; 1hr); Lashio (1 daily via Heho; 2hr 30min); Myitkyina (3 daily; 1hr 10min); Putao (2 weekly via Myitkyina; 2hr); Tachileik (6 weekly; 1hr 10min); Yangon (around 10 daily; 1hr).

BY BUS

Mandalay is the transport hub of northern Myanmar and there are services to just about everywhere you might want to go. There are numerous services to Bagan, including express services, while numerous operators head to Yangon, with a mix of ordinary services and luxurious express buses run by operators including Boss, Elite, Shwe Mingalar and JJ Express. There are also a reasonable number of buses to Inle Lake, all travelling via Kalaw – some go into Nyaungshwe, others drop off in Shwenyaung on their way to Taunggyi. Heading northeast, note that if travelling to Hsipaw or Kyaukme you may have to pay the full fare to Lashio.

Bus stations Mandalay has three bus stations. The main terminus is teeming Kwe Se Kan (Main) Station, which serves destinations south and lies around 10km south of the centre. If your ticket doesn't come with a pick-up or drop-off service, a motorbike taxi will cost around K3000 and a taxi K6000. You can also catch a pick-up to the station from the stop on 84th St at the corner of 29th St, although

these can be a nightmare if you've got any amount of luggage. Pyi Gyi Mat Shin Station is 3km east of the centre and serves destinations to the northeast including Hsipaw, Kyaukme and Lashio. Finally, Thiri Mandalar Station is the most central of Mandalay's three stations, though only covers a few destinations, among them Pyin Oo Lwin, Shwebo and Monywa (buy your tickets from the windows on the south side of the station).

Booking tickets The easiest way to book bus tickets is either through your hotel, at a travel agent or at one of the bus company offices dotted around town; they'll charge commission (around K1000–3000), but this works out far cheaper and less time-consuming than taking a motorbike taxi or taxi out to the main bus station and back. There are a number of handy bus company offices along 32nd St between 84th and 82nd streets, including the well-run Ko Htay, who can arrange tickets to pretty much anywhere. More expensive tickets also include transfers from your hotel or the bus company office in town to the bus station. If travelling to the main bus station independently, ask your taxi driver to drop you at the appropriate bus office – it's a large and confusing place.

Kwe Se Kan Station destinations Bago (2 daily; 7–8hr); Kalaw (6 daily; 6hr); Meiktila (7 daily; 3hr); Naypyitaw (8 daily; 4hr); Nyaungshwe (5 daily; 8hr); Nyaung U for Bagan (16 daily; 6–8hr); Pyay (2 daily; 13hr); Taungoo (2 daily; 7–8hr); Yangon (18 daily; 8–10hr).

Pyi Gyi Mat Shin Station destinations Hsipaw (2 daily; 6–8hr); Kyaukme (3 daily; 5hr); Lashio (2 daily; 9hr).

Thiri Mandalar Station destinations Monywa (hourly until noon; 3hr 30min); Pyin Oo Lwin (hourly; 2hr); Shwebo (hourly until 4pm; 3hr).

BY PICK-UP

Pick-ups to Pyin Oo Lwin (3hr; K30,000) run between 5am and 5pm, departing when full from the corner of 28th St

---

MANDALAY ADDRESSES

Mandalay's roads are laid out along a numbered **grid system**, which makes it easy to find your way around the city. One common source of traveller confusion, however, is that streets up to 50th run west-to-east, and streets above 50th run north-to-south. Our addresses give the street on which the place sits first (81st St, for example), and then the cross streets between which it lies (eg 29th & 30th streets).

BOAT TRIPS FROM MANDALAY

Considering the wealth of destinations both up and down the **Ayeyarwady River**, it's no surprise that a fair proportion of visitors to Mandalay rock up on a boat. You're advised to book ahead; again, travel agencies will help if your accommodation can't (and may occasionally include transfers to the jetty); some companies now allow you to book online. Unless otherwise stated, all services arrive at and depart from the **Gawein jetty** area, 3km west of the centre at the end of 35th St; the exact point will depend upon the river level. Boat trips to **Mingun** are covered in the Mingun section (see p.307). A number of **luxury cruises** (see p.30) also start in, terminate at, or pass through Mandalay.

TO BAGAN

There are a number of services to Bagan. The three private companies listed below all run boats departing at 7am and arriving in Bagan around 4.30–5pm. Tickets on all three cost $42 including breakfast and lunch. The Malikha and MGRG ferries are generally reckoned a bit nicer than the slightly battered Shwe Keinnery boats.

Malikha River Cruises 4 Pearl St, between 77th and 78th sts ☎ 09 7314 5748, ⓦ malikha-rivercruises.com. Departures most days.

Myanmar Golden River Group/Pioneer (MGRG)

38th St, between 79th and 80th sts ☎ 02 66204, ⓦ mgrgexpress.com. Departures daily.

Shwe Keinnery Seinpan Rd, between 35th and 36th sts ☎ 02 63983. Departures daily.

TO THE NORTH

An **IWT government boat** runs three times weekly (in theory, on Mon, Thurs & Sat) to Bhamo (at least 30hr; $12 on deck, $80 in a cabin) via Kyaukmyaung and Katha at 6am. Faster **special Express boats** depart daily for Katha (around 16hr), travelling via Kyaukmyaung, Tagaung and Tigyaung; if heading to Bhamo, you'll need to spend the night in Katha and then catch another boat the next morning to Bhamo (around 7hr).

and 83rd St. They are most frequent early in the morning, and may not run after 3pm.

BY TRAIN

Mandalay Railway Station The main station is centrally located just off 30th St, between 78th and 79th sts. There's a tourist information office as you enter (on your left); tickets are sold upstairs, though queues get longer as departure times approach.

North Station Note that there's also a small station just off the palace's northwest corner, though the line heading north from here doesn't go anywhere of tourist

interest; services to Myitkyina and other places to the north use the main station, and actually start their journey by heading south.

Destinations Nyaung U, for Bagan (2 daily; 7–12hr); Bago (3 daily; 13hr); Hsipaw (1 daily; 11hr); Kyaukme (1 daily; 10hr); Lashio (1 daily; 16hr); Monywa (1 daily; 5hr); Myitkyina (4 daily; 18–21hr); Naba, for Katha (3 daily; 10–15hr); Nawngpeng, for Gokteik Viaduct (1 daily; 7hr); Naypyitaw (3 daily; 6hr); Pyin Oo Lwin (1 daily; 4hr); Shwebo (4 daily; 3hr); Taungoo (3 daily; 8–9hr); Thazi (3 daily; 2hr 45min); Yangon (3 daily; 15hr).

GETTING AROUND

By bicycle and motorbike Almost pancake-flat, Mandalay would be a great city in which to cycle were it not for the sometimes heavy traffic, which can make for a nerve-wracking experience. Almost everywhere in this chapter can be reached by bike (though Mingun is a bit of a stretch, and Pinya and Paleik are only for dedicated pedallers); if you fancy a fun little trip, try crossing the small bridge which starts just beyond the western end of 14th St into the pretty little village beyond. If you do decide to cycle you may want to rent a bike on your first day and keep it with you until leaving Mandalay. Renting a motorbike is another possibility, although again traffic is a concern. Bikes are available at some hotels, while both

bikes and motorbikes can be rented from Mr Jerry, just north of *Mann* bar on 83rd St, between 25th and 26th sts, and from Ever Smile at *Rainforest* restaurant (see p.296). Count on around K2000/day for bikes, and from K5000/day upwards for motorbikes. In addition, Mandalay Motorbike Rentals and Tours at 32nd St, between 79th and 80th sts (☎ 09 444 022 182, ⓦ mandalaymotorbike.com), has a wide range of quality bikes starting from K10,000 per day and also arranges guided tours around the north.

By bus and pick-up Mandalay does have a bus network of sorts, though precious few foreigners ever use it – the numbers are all in Burmese, vehicles are packed to the gills and it's simply easier to use the only slightly more expensive alternatives. There are also (equally packed) pick-ups to Amarapura (see p.300) and Sagaing (see p.305), which you can find rolling down 84th St, near the junction with 29th St, although these drop you some distance from the sights in both towns, so you'll have to find onward transport in any case.

By taxi and motorbike taxi Mandalay's many taxi and motorbike taxi drivers will take you anywhere you need to go, although taxis are relatively expensive (and significantly pricier than in Yangon). From downtown a motorbike taxi to the Mingun ferry terminal or Gawein jetty will set you back K2000–3000, and to the Kwe Se Kan bus terminal K3000–4000; you can double these fares for taxis. Hiring a motorbike taxi for the day is an inexpensive and convenient way to access the various sights around Mandalay (see p.299).

INFORMATION, TRAVEL AGENTS AND TOUR OPERATORS

Ever Smile c/o Rainforest restaurant, 27th St, between 74th and 75th sts ☎09 4316 1551. Inexpensive local tours and transport, plus tickets for buses and Bagan ferries, and motorbike and bike rental.

LM Travel ☎09 7019 8798, ⓦlmtravelmyanmar.com. Reliable local operator offering all the usual city and around Mandalay tours, including bike tours and a trip to Mingun plus village tour and lunch.

MTT 68th St, between 26th and 27th sts ☎02 60356. The government-run tourist office is a decent place to head for general local information, and they can also book ferry tickets to Bagan. Daily 9.30am–4.30pm.

Myanmar Upper Land 27th St, between 71st and 72nd sts ☎02 65011, ⓦmyanmarupperland.com. Professional tours (private and shared) of the city and surrounding sights, plus further tours across northern Myanmar.

Seven Swan Corner of 27th and 81st sts ☎09 250 200 404, ⓔsevenswanmyanmar@gmail.com. Efficient airlines agents handling tickets for all domestic airlines.

Zin Mi c/o Moustache Brothers Theatre, 39th St, between 80th and 81st sts ☎09 4315 9591, ⓔzinmehtunshinshin1987@gmail.com. Local tours and transport arranged by a daughter of Moustache Brother Lu Maw (see p.297).

ACTIVITIES

BALLOONING

Oriental Ballooning No.C1, corner of 35th & 71st sts ☎09 256 224 976, ⓦorientalballooning.com. The ultimate escape from the Mandalay crush, offering privileged bird's-eye views of the city, the Ayeyarwady and the surrounding countryside. Nov to mid-March only; 1 week advance booking required; $380pp.

GOLF

Shwe Mann Taung Golf Resort 73rd St, at the corner of Lan Thit Rd ☎02 75898. Passable eighteen-hole course with nice views of Mandalay Hill.

MASSAGES AND SPA

GGG 27th St, between 74th and 75th sts ☎09 4025 77711. A reliable place for a good Burmese-style massage; 1hr massage K8000. Daily 10am–11pm.

Mandalar Spa 10th St, Mandalay Hill Resort hotel, by Mandalay Hill ☎02 35638. Attractive spa conveniently located at the rear of the *Mandalay Hill* hotel. A good place to re-energize after climbing the hill, with a range of Burmese and international massages and treatments (from around K35,000). Daily 8am–10.30pm.

MEDITATION

Dhamma Mandala Yaytagun Hill ☎02 39694, ⓦmandala.dhamma.org. A large complex with room for 160 visitors, located on a rise around 16km from central Mandalay. Their ten-day introductory courses, which can also be conducted in English, are paid for by donations from those who've already benefited from the experience, meaning that there are no set fees.

Kyunpin Meditation Centre Kanphyu Village, Wetlet Township, Sagaing ☎09 421 018 765, ⓦkyunpin.com. Located in Sagaing, around 20km southeast of Mandalay, this centre receives good reports from foreign visitors. There are no set fees for food or accommodation, and you'll be expected to meditate for 12–14hr/day.

SWIMMING

Other than the public venue listed here, those fancying a swim can take a dip in the pools at the *Ayarwaddy River View* (see p.295), *Mandalay City* (see p.294) or *Mandalay Hill Resort* (see p.295) hotels, all of which charge around K5000 per person.

Yatanaban Swimming Pool 10th St, west of Mandalay Hill Resort hotel. Huge outdoor pool (K2000) near Mandalay Hill, kept reasonably clean and in decent shape – but avoid the diving boards. Daily 6am–6pm.

ACCOMMODATION

Accommodation in Mandalay is unlikely to set the pulse racing, although there are a few enjoyable **upmarket** options, while increasing competition means that **mid-range** and **budget** places are now more affordable (and more widely available) than a few years back. The majority of accommodation is in the downtown area **southwest**

of the palace, west of the railway lines, with dozens of largely indistinguishable two- and three-star concrete boxes. There are also further options east of the railway lines immediately **south of the palace** – a more peaceful area, and closer to the city's best selection of restaurants. All the places listed have a/c, free wi-fi and include breakfast in their rates unless otherwise stated.

DOWNTOWN

AD1 Between 27th and 28th sts, and 87th and 88th sts ☎02 34505; map p.288. One of the city's cheapest options, in a down-at-heel market area near the Eindawya Pagoda, with basic and dated rooms (fan only), although they're reasonably well maintained and bearable at the price. $\overline{\$20}$

ET 83rd St, between 23rd and 24th sts ☎02 65006, ✉ethotel129a@gmail.com; map p.288. Central, competitively priced hotel. Rooms are a bit gloomy and nothing special, but well maintained and decent value at the price. $\overline{\$20}$

Garden 83rd St, between 24th and 25th sts ☎02 31884, ✉gardenhotelmdy@gmail.com; map p.288. Cut-price if uninspiring budget choice. The whole place could use some repairs and a good clean, although rooms are comfortable enough, albeit on the small side. $\overline{\$18}$

Hotel 82 82nd St, between 31st and 32nd sts ☎02 60773, ✉hotel82mandalay@gmail.com; map p.288. Smart and modern mid-range option, looking a lot fresher than most of the competition. Rates are top value given the quality, with small but neat modern rooms equipped with flatscreen TV, kettle and fridge, backed up by very helpful service. $\overline{\$28}$

M3 Hotel 26th St, between 82nd and 83rd sts ☎02 67171, ⓦm3hotelmandalay.com; map p.288. Reliable, modern and competitively priced mid-range option, spread over eight floors. The well-equipped, wood-floored rooms come with fridge, flatscreen TV, safe and good-looking bathrooms; superior rooms ($15 extra) are fractionally larger and come with a bathtub, but aren't significantly different. $\overline{\$45}$

★Mandalay City 26th St, between 82nd and 83rd sts ☎02 61700, ⓦmandalaycityhotel.com; map p.288. The most upmarket choice in the city centre, hidden away in the middle of lush gardens off 26th St – an unexpected oasis of space amid the cramped blocks of downtown, complete with a good-sized, tree-shaded pool (also open to non-guests; see p.292). The wooden-floored rooms are very comfortably furnished, with smart modern bathrooms. $\overline{\$95}$

Mann Shwe Li 84th St, between 31st and 32nd sts ☎09 258 949 353, ✉manshwelimdy1@gmail.com; map p.288. Tricky-to-find hotel down an alley off 84th St (look for the small overhead LED sign) but well worth hunting out. The whole place is unusually spacious compared to cramped quarters typical of most city hotels, with good-sized, nicely furnished modern rooms, plus a welcome lift and some of Mandalay's jolliest staff. $\overline{\$25}$

Nylon 83rd St, at the corner of 25th St ☎02 33460, ✉nylonhotel25@gmail.com; map p.288. Sharing its lobby with an electrical equipment store, this oddly named hotel is one of the best budget options in the area, with unusually large, clean, nicely furnished and well-equipped rooms with fridge, kettle and surprisingly spacious bathrooms. $\overline{\$20}$

★Royal Guesthouse 25th St, between 82nd and 83rd sts ☎02 31400; map p.288. Intimate and homely, this is the best of the area's budget choices, and one of the cheapest too. Common areas are neatly decorated (perhaps using a Rubik's cube as a colour palette) and rooms are small but cosy, like little ships' cabins, although not all have windows and you'll pay $6 extra for an en-suite room with a/c. Non-a/c singles with shared bath go for just $8. $\overline{\$14}$

Silver Star 27th St, at the corner of 83rd St ☎02 33394, ⓦsilverstarhotelmandalay.com; map p.288. A solid mid-range city-centre option in one of downtown's taller hotels, with nicely furnished rooms spread over eight floors and offering good views from higher storeys – the corner rooms ($10 extra) with wraparound windows are particularly nice. $\overline{\$45}$

Unity 27th St, at the corner of 82nd St ☎02 66583, ⓦunityhotelmyanmar.com; map p.288. Not the cheapest beds in town, but offering excellent value for money, with a lobby that feels like that of a "real" hotel, a functional lift, and a nice little coffee bar on the ground level. The cheapest rooms lack windows, but all are well equipped with minibar, safe and kettle, and attractively furnished with modern bathrooms and fittings. $\overline{\$25}$

SOUTH OF THE PALACE

Ace Star BnB Backpacker Hostel Thazin Plaza, between 31st and 32nd sts, and 77th and 78th sts ☎09 258 411 776, ⓦacestarbnb.com; map p.288. Reliable new hostel with functional but well-equipped eight- and ten-bed dorms (including male- and female-only dorms) – although the beds are rather crammed in. Dorms $\overline{\$12}$

Bagan King Corner of 28th St and 73rd St ☎02 67123, ⓦbagankinghotel.com; map pp.282–283. One of the city's more stylish offerings, spread over six floors, with chintzy Bagan-inspired decor and a breezy rooftop restaurant offering fine views over the concrete jungle below. Rooms come with antique-style wooden beds and furnishings, traditional fabrics and cool brick bathrooms (some with tubs), while rates include afternoon tea, an evening cocktail and nightly traditional puppet show. $\overline{\$100}$

Ostello Bello 28th St, between 73rd and 74th sts ☎02 64530, ⓦostellobello.com; map pp.282–283.

Smart new hostel offering a varied selection of attractive four- to eighteen-bed dorms (rates more expensive in smaller dorms), including a four-bed female dorm, plus a few private rooms and a neat lobby café. Dorms $10, doubles $30

Royal City 27th St, between 76th and 77th sts ☎ 02 66559, ⍟royalcityhotelmandalay.com; map p.288. Old but well-maintained mid-range hotel offering comfortable, good-value accommodation in a relatively peaceful area just east of the railway tracks, conveniently close both to downtown and the clutch of good restaurants south of the palace moat. Rooms are bright and spacious (corner rooms – same price – are particularly nice) and have good views from higher floors, while breakfast is taken on the lovely rooftop terrace, with fine views. $35

OUTSIDE THE CENTRE

Ayarwaddy River View Hotel Strand Rd, at the corner of 22nd St ☎ 02 64945, ⍟ayarwaddy riverviewhotel.net; map pp.282–283. Well-run four-star very convenient for the boat jetties (albeit a bit of a way from town). Rooms are rather utilitarian, although some sport great Ayeyarwady views and there's also a swimming pool (open to non-guests; see p.292). Rates include free evening cocktail in the attractive rooftop *Ayar Sky Bar* (see p.297). $70

★ **Hotel by the Red Canal** 63rd St, at the corner of 22nd St ☎02 61177, ⍟hotelredcanal.com; map pp.282–283. Gorgeous boutique hotel lurking away by a canal in the side roads east of the palace, with smallish but very chic rooms designed in cool contemporary Burmese style, sporting lots of hardwood finishes, traditional fabrics and (in more expensive rooms) beautiful outdoor showers and water features. Rates include free afternoon tea and traditional snacks, plus evening cocktails, and there's also a small kidney-shaped pool, spa, well-equipped gym and in-house Indian restaurant. $240

Mandalay Hill Resort 10th St, by Mandalay Hill ☎02 35638, ⍟mandalayhillresorthotel.com; map pp.282–283. Luxurious hotel in a large white eyesore at the foot of Mandalay Hill. The whole place is a study in five-star bland: pleasant and totally unobjectionable, but with about as much personality as a teabag, although plus points include a lovely swimming pool (open to non-guests – see p.292), a good spa (p.292) and fine views from upper-floor rooms. $200

Peacock Lodge 60th St, between 25th and 26th sts ☎02 61429, ⍟peacocklodge.com; map pp.282–283. Soothingly peaceful guesthouse east of town. The nine rooms (reserve ahead) are modern and lovingly decorated, while the main building backs onto a pleasant, mango tree-shaded garden. It's a little hard to find; from 26th St, look for the sign heading north down a side road to *Hotel Treasure* and *Ma Ma Guesthouse*. $40

7

EATING

Mandalay has surprisingly few good restaurants for a city of its size and, although things are slowly improving, for the time being it makes even Yangon look like Paris. Western restaurants and upmarket Asian venues are still very thin on the ground, although the city preserves a lively traditional **teahouse** culture now largely vanished from Yangon, as well as plenty of no-frills buffet cafés and **streetside food stalls** – the downtown area west of the palace between 22nd, 24th, 84th and 80th streets is the best hunting ground, dotted with Shan-style buffets and Indian cafés, while the chapati snack-shacks which spring up in the evening around the junction of 27th and 82nd streets are also fun places to fill up.

DOWNTOWN

Aung Lin 30th St, between 80th and 81st sts ☎02 23151; map p.288. Simple little Chinese restaurant in an airy tiled dining room complete with lucky cats and Chinese characters and landscapes on the walls. Food comprises a good selection of meat, fish, seafood and veg Chinese standards (mains K4000–5000), with friendly service from the attentive English-speaking owners. Food can sometimes take a while to arrive, but is worth the wait. Daily 11am–10pm.

★ **Bistro @ 82nd** 82nd St, between 30th and 31st sts ☎09 250 121 280, ⍟facebook.com/Bistro82nd; map p.288. One of Mandalay's most unexpected finds, easily missed on grubby 82nd St, but serving the best food in the city in a cool modern dining room. The menu features mainstream European dishes such as Wiener Schnitzel, chicken with red-wine sauce, and salmon and seabass fillets – no culinary surprises, but beautifully prepared and

full of rich, French-influenced flavours. It's pricey, with mains around K14,000–16,000, but you'll not find this quality anywhere else in town. Daily 10am–10pm.

Min Mahar 23rd St, at the corner of 86th St ☎09 508 7882; map p.288. This large, always lively teahouse is a good place for tea and a snack and also serves up excellent Shan noodles at cut-throat prices (K1000), along with assorted other dishes including local-style banana pancakes (banana parathas, effectively) and the oddly named "nutritious meal" – a curious mix of banana, boiled egg, strawberry cream and sweetened condensed milk. Daily 5am–5.30pm.

Mr Bar BQ 31st St, between 80th and 81st sts ☎02 73920; map p.288. Cavernous place, somewhere between an upmarket beer station and a Chinese restaurant, serving up a vast selection of tasty Cantonese-style meat, veg and seafood dishes (mains around K5000) to a lively crowd of locals and tourists. Daily 9am–11pm.

Nay 27th St, at the corner of 82nd St; map p.288. The pick of this area's many street-side chapati-shacks, as evidenced by the crowd that's gathered around every single evening. They even have a menu of sorts, though there are no prices on it – ask when ordering, to avoid any unpleasant surprises. Expect to pay around K2000, perhaps a little more if you plump for the "mutton brain", which gets you a little sheep cerebellum sitting in a curry sauce – surprisingly tasty, though served lukewarm. No alcohol, though they're happy for you to bring your own. Daily 4pm–1am.

Nylon 25th St, at the corner of 83rd St ✆02 32318; map p.288. A kind of rough-and-ready Burmese ice-cream parlour, serving good ice cream (K800–1000) in myriad flavours including durian, tapioca and cream soda, along with assorted shakes (K800–1500). Daily 8am–8pm.

Pan Cherry 81st St, between 26th and 27th St ✆02 39924; map p.288. The best of the several South Indian choices in this area, this cheery restaurant serves good refillable meals (K4000) with a choice of all sorts of curries, ranging from chicken, mutton, duck and butterfish through to more off-the-wall options including liver, brain, the mysteriously named "fish heat", and of course "fighting ball" (a polite name for goats' testicles). Daily 10am–9pm.

Rainbow 84th St, between 22nd and 23rd sts ✆02 23266; map p.288. Set over three floors, the uppermost on the roof, this corner restaurant is a popular spot for cheap draught Myanmar beer. They also have a menu of snacks and a few Chinese basics (mains K4500). Daily 8am–9pm.

★**Shan Ma Ma** 81st St, between 29th and 30th sts ✆02 71858; map p.288. Usually one of the liveliest places in downtown after dark, with hordes of tourists sitting at tables spilling out into the street and tucking into delicious piles of Shan and Chinese-style food. Choose what you want from the vast array of dishes on display – a full spread usually comes in at around K3000–4000. Daily 6am–10pm.

SOUTH OF THE PALACE

★**BBB** 76th St, between 26th and 27th sts ✆02 73525, ⓦfacebook.com/bbbrestaurant; map pp.282–283. This quiet, urbane and stylish restaurant is one of Mandalay's top eating venues – pricey, but serving up a big selection of international flavours available in few other places. The menu (mains K6500–10,000) features all sorts of grilled and fried meat and seafood dishes (anything from brandy chicken, kebabs and steaks through to honey prawn, sea perch and salmon) plus excellent burgers and well-made cocktails. Daily 10am–10.30pm.

Korea Restaurant 76th St, between 28th and 29th sts ✆02 71822; map pp.282–283. Run by a Korean–Burmese couple, the pleasingly authentic Korean flavours here can come as a nice change to tired tastebuds. The menu includes favourites such as kimchi, seaweed rolls, ginseng chicken and *bibimbap* (rice topped with beef,

vegetables, egg and chilli paste, which you mix together before eating). Mains K3000–4000. Daily 9am–9.30pm.

★**Marie Min** 27th St 74th and 75th sts ✆02 36234; map pp.282–283. Cute little vegetarian café on the upstairs balcony of a neat wooden building. The good mix of Indian and Burmese cooking ranges from samosas, chapatis and curries through to noodles and salads (mains K3000–3500), plus they also serve lassis, juices and the best milkshakes in town. Daily 10am–9pm.

Mingalabar 71st St, between 28th and 29th sts ✆02 60480; map pp.282–283. Smart, modern restaurant serving up excellent and authentic Burmese curries (around K6000), including traditional dishes like pork curry with dried mango and butterfish with spicy-sour leaves, along with local ingredients ranging from fresh Ayeyarwady River prawns to wild hog. There are also a few vegetable curries, plus lots of unusual side dishes and salads (K1500–2000) – tamarind, white seaweed, smoked *gar* fish, and so on. Daily 6am–9pm.

Min Thi Ha Corner of 72nd and 28th sts; map pp.282–283. Popular teahouse, part of a small chain known for its mutton curry puffs, which you can nibble on while pondering Samuel Johnson's quote on the wall: "Great works are performed not by strength but by perseverance." Daily 5am–4pm.

Rainforest 27th St, between 74th and 75th sts ✆09 4316 1551; map pp.282–283. One of Mandalay's best-looking restaurants – choose between the lovely antique-filled downstairs dining room or the sunny terrace above – serving up good Thai food (mains K4000–6000), including classic dishes such as *larb*, tom yum and *pad thai*. Daily 8am–9pm.

Too Too 27th St, between 74th and 75th sts; map pp.282–283. A good place to fill up on some local fare, if you don't mind the rather dreary dining room, with a big buffet spread of Burmese curries (K3500–5000), all served with at least five side dishes. Daily 10am–9pm.

OUTSIDE THE CENTRE

Café City 66th St, between 20th and 22nd sts ✆09 522 4054; map pp.282–283. Precisely the same menu as you'll find at *BBB* (see opposite), though a bit further out (just east of the palace walls), and decorated more like an American bar. Daily 10am–10.30pm.

Golden Duck 80th St, at the corner of 16th St ✆09 256 378 572; map pp.282–283. This large and lively place is one of the best of Mandalay's many Chinese restaurants, popular with local middle-class types and their families. Many people opt for the signature crispy duck, although there are plenty of other authentic mains (K4000–6000) along with some Burmese dishes. The location just west of the palace walls makes it a great sunset spot. Daily 10am–10pm.

★**A Little Bit of Mandalay** 28th St, between 52nd and 53rd sts ✆09 797 735 545; map pp.282–283. Way out east in a delightfully secluded location, this is a great place in which to sample Burmese food (mains K5000–6000), prepared with below-average levels of oil and spice, and with good vegetarian options as well. The extensive drinks list includes local Red Mountain wine from Inle Lake (see box, p.256). Bring mosquito repellent after dark. Daily 11am–2pm & 5–9pm.

Mandalay Kitchen (formerly Mya Nandar) Strand Rd ☎09 444 977 971, ☻amazing-hotel.com/mandalay kitchen; map pp.282–283. In a prime position by the Ayeyarwady, this vast tour-party favourite (seating well over five hundred people) in an ersatz Burmese wooden complex has about as much traditional atmosphere as an airport terminal. The river views, however, are superb (assuming you can bag a table with a view – arrive very early or book), and the food, featuring a mix of Thai, Chinese and Burmese dishes, isn't bad, albeit overpriced (mains K10,000–14,000). Traditional puppet and dance performances are staged every evening. Daily 11am–3pm & 5.30–9.30pm.

Unison 38th St, at the corner of 87th St; map pp.282–283. This round-the-clock operation is surely the largest teahouse in Mandalay, housed in an octagonal thatched pavilion and serving up a good range of salads plus a few noodle and rice dishes (K1500–2000), along with French fires, grate fruit and coat (we think they mean coke) – although tea and coffee is a rip-off at K600 per not-very-generously-sized cup. Daily 24hr.

DRINKING

Don't expect nightclubs (or, indeed, anything with a dancefloor), but Mandalay does have its fair share of decent, low-key places to drink. As well as the following, most of the restaurants listed in the Eating section (see p.295) serve alcohol; you could also make use of any number of identikit beer stations dotted liberally around the city.

Ayar Sky Bar Ayarwaddy River View Hotel, Strand Rd, at the corner of 22nd St ☎02 64945; map pp.282–283. Open-air rooftop bar with gorgeous views out over the river serving up (given the location) reasonably priced drinks, with cocktails from around K6000 and beers for K3000. Daily 5.30–10pm.

Central Park 27th St, between 68th and 69th sts; map pp.282–283. Looking a bit like a beach bar without the sand, this place draws a crowd of young locals and expats. They tend to show up in time for happy hour (6–7.30pm), when draught beer is three-for-two and cocktails are two-for-one. The soundtrack is Western and chilled out, and the food includes pizzas (K4000–6000), burgers and barbecue. Daily 3–11.30pm.

Mann 83rd St, between 25th and 26th sts ☎02 66025; map p.288. Spit-and-sawdust drinking hole attracting an eclectic mix of locals and tourists with cheap beer, Mandalay rum and other cut-price tipples – although the food is best avoided. Daily 10am–10pm.

ENTERTAINMENT

There are a few great shows to catch in Mandalay, with all of the acts listed below having found fame – or actually performed – overseas. It's just a pity that they all take place at precisely the same time.

Mandalay Marionettes 66th St, between 26th and 27th sts ☎02 34446, ☻mandalaymarionettes.com. Controlled from behind the tiniest stage imaginable (though the one in Nyaungshwe is smaller still), colourful puppets re-create scenes from the life of the Buddha. Given the subject, the hour-long show is actually quite

---

THE MOUSTACHE BROTHERS

It's not easy to criticize the military authorities in Myanmar, especially in public – but this is precisely what the internationally famed **Moustache Brothers** (see p.298) have been doing for decades, playing on the edge of what was acceptable to the former regime and now, post-democracy, to their army successors and business cronies. This comic dissidence has, inevitably, landed them in trouble – in 1996 the three brothers performed at Aung San Suu Kyi's compound in Yangon, after which two of them (Par Par Lay and Lu Zaw) were sentenced to six years of hard labour. Undeterred, they resumed their show in 2002; barred from performing in any public area, they decided to do so at their Mandalay home instead, satirizing national politics under the watchful gaze of the authorities. Officialdom then decreed that they weren't allowed to perform either; the brothers then decided to do the same act without costumes and make-up, since it then couldn't be called a "show". Somehow, this ruse worked, and they've been performing ever since. Sadly, Par Par Lay died in 2013, but the two remaining performers have carried on. Lu Maw (the only English-speaker) is always happy to chat to those who pop by during the day.

7

FESTIVALS IN AND AROUND MANDALAY

Traditional **festivals**, known as *pwè*, take place throughout the year in Mandalay. The dates of most *pwè* follow the lunar calendar, with exact dates varying from year to year – ask staff at your hotel or guesthouse, or one of the city's many motorbike taxi drivers, if there are any happening during your stay. *Pwè* are incredibly noisy affairs, and some go on well into the night – people have reported having to change hotels to get away from the din.

Mahamuni Paya Pwè Villagers from across the region descend in their thousands on the Mahamuni Paya for this two-week festival, with umpteen shows every evening, including music, dance and traditional *anyeint*. Usually early Feb.

Thingyan Water Festival Mandalay celebrations of this countrywide festival (see p.42) are as riotous as you'd expect – expect to get totally drenched. Mid-April.

Sand Stupa Festival Large sand stupas are erected over the course of a single night in three different locations around Mandalay. Usually May.

Shwe Kyun Pin Nat Pwè Hundreds of colourfully dressed farmers driving elaborately decorated bullock carts congregate at nearby Mingun (see p.307) to celebrate a brother and sister who drowned in the river and were transformed into *nats*. Usually July.

Taungbyone Nat Pwè Held in the town of Taungbyone, around 18km north of Mandalay, this huge event is one of Myanmar's most famous *nat pwè* (see box, p.41). The *nat pwè* honours two brothers, Min Gyi and Min Lay (see p.230), who assumed supernatural powers after eating the body of a dead *zawgyi* (magician) – although for most of the thousands attending it's mainly an excuse for manic eating, dancing and partying. July/Aug.

Yadanagu Nat Pwè The week after Taungbyone's *pwè*, the circus moves south to Amarapura to honour Mai Wunna, the brothers' mother (see box, p.230). Usually Aug.

Thadingyut Festival Central Mandalay's largest festival, part of the countrywide celebrations marking the end of Buddhist Lent. One week, usually early Oct.

Irrawaddy Literary Festival ⓦ irrawaddylitfest.com. Myanmar's leading literary festival, established in 2013 and attracting leading local and international authors. Three days in Nov.

---

light-hearted, and even rather funny in places. Do, however, try to read the programme before the lights go down – you'll be a little lost otherwise. Daily 8.30pm; tickets $8.

Mintha Theater 58th St, between 29th and 30th sts ⓣ09 680 3607, ⓦminthatheater.com. A great opportunity to see traditional dance with extravagant costumes, accompanied by live music, with ten different performances packed into the show. Daily 8.30pm; tickets K14,000.

Moustache Brothers 39th St, between 80th and 81st sts ⓣ09 4303 4220, ⓔbosoeoo@gmail.com. The only chance you're likely to get to experience *anyeint*, a traditional form of comedy combining political satire and broad slapstick, delivered in a mix of Burmese and English. Two of the brothers, Par Par Lay and Lu Zaw, served six years' hard labour after making jokes about the regime in 1996 (see box, p.297), and this context is reason enough to attend even if the jokes don't always hit the mark. Daily 8.30pm; tickets K10,000.

SHOPPING

Pretty much all of the **gold leaf** applied to Buddha images by devotees in Myanmar comes from a small area of Mandalay. There are about fifty gold-leaf workshops across the city, many of them based in homes in the blocks around 36th St, just east of the railway line. Mandalay is also famed for the production of wonderful **tapestries**, most of which depict scenes from the Jataka stories. Sadly, despite the many handicrafts produced in the city, there are very few places to buy them, and you're much better off shopping for souvenirs in Yangon or Bagan.

Jade Market Between 86/87th and 38/41st sts; map pp.282–283. Myanmar's jade-mining industry has long-standing ties with the military regime and is responsible for widespread exploitation, corruption and other abuses, meaning that this is one local trade you might prefer not to support. If you do decide to buy, the first prices quoted are likely to be rip-offs, although you should be able to haggle these down as part of a "look, I'm *really* walking away"

strategy. It also helps to do some research first if you're a jade novice so you know what you're looking for. Daily 8.30am–5.30pm.

★**King Galon** 36th St, between 77th and 78th sts ⓣ02 32135; map pp.282–283. The most tourist-friendly of the various gold-pounders' workshops on 36th St, with visitors welcome to look around and no pressure to buy. The shop stocks a wide selection of Bagan lacquerware with gold decoration applied in-house, and is also a good place to stock up on gold leaf (from K5000 for a packet of ten pieces) for putting onto an appropriate Buddha image (see p.289). The sight (and sound) of the workmen beating the gold into super-fine thickness is oddly hypnotic, almost musical, and there's also a small display on the making of bamboo paper. Daily 8am–6pm.

Mandalay Yatanar Mall 34th St, at the corner of 78th St; map pp.282–283. This huge shiny new mall is the latest word in Mandalay retail, with a range of international designer outlets and a top floor stuffed full of jewellery and gem shops – although many of the outlets hadn't yet opened at the time of writing. Daily 8am–6pm.

Rocky 27th St, between 62nd and 63rd sts ☎02 74106; map pp.282–283. This shop-in-a-house is a good place to pick up all sorts of local crafts. They're currently repurposing the business to focus exclusively on gems and stones (jade in particular) and running down their other stock, although at the time of writing they still had big piles of interesting traditional merchandise including marionettes, Jataka tapestries and woodcarvings (cleverly aged to look like antiques). Daily 8.30am–8.30pm.

Shwe Pathein 36th St, between 77th and 78th sts ☎09 504 3067; map pp.282–283. This tiny store (also known as *Zaw Man Khaing*) sells gorgeous paper parasols from Pathein in a range of sizes, from miniature kid-sized umbrellas to huge creations big enough to shade an elephant. The cheapest cost just K8000 – just a pity that the staff are usually so grumpy. Daily 6am–6pm.

DIRECTORY

Banks There are foreign exchange counters and ATMs in the arrivals section at the airport and lots of banks around the city with ATMs accepting foreign Visa and MasterCards; many banks also have Forex facilities.

Hospital Mandalay General Hospital is on 30th St, between 74th and 77th sts (☎02 21041; call ☎192 in an emergency).

Police There are many police offices around town, with even the far-flung ones often featuring an English-language "How may I help you?" sign outside. The main office is on 81st St, between 29th and 30th sts (☎02 36869).

Post office The main post office is at 22nd St, between 80th and 81st sts. There's also a DHL office on 78th St, between 37th and 38th sts, outside the *Hotel Mandalay*.

Around Mandalay

In many ways the myriad sights scattered across the countryside around Mandalay – including a trio of former royal capitals and a gigantic, although unfinished, stupa – are more interesting, and enjoyable, than the city itself. Now virtually a suburb of Mandalay, the sleepy former royal capital of **Amarapura** has dozens of temples surrounding a tranquil lake, plus the famed teak footbridge of U Bein. Further myriad pagodas dot the beautiful hills of **Sagaing**, while the nearby village of **Inwa** preserves a few reminders of its royal heritage, plus fun horse-and-carriage rides through its syvlan country lanes. All of these former capitals are tethered together by the mighty Ayeyarwady, a river which – as elsewhere in the country – functions as the lifeblood of the region; the Ayeyarwady also slides quietly by the village of **Mingun**, which never functioned as a capital but boasts a building which (had it been completed) would have beaten any in the area for size.

Most people combine Sagaing, Inwa and Amarapura in a single day's excursion, although this is a lot to take in at one go and you might prefer to spread them over two days; this would give you the chance to explore some lesser-known and less-touristed attractions, and allow you to combine a visit to Amarapura with a trip to the interesting "**snake temple**" at Paleik.

GETTING AROUND   AROUND MANDALAY

By pick-up It's possible to reach Inwa from Mandalay by pick-up (see p.305). There are also pick-ups in the direction of Amarapura and Sagaing, though since they don't go anywhere near any of the sights in those cities, they're barely worth bothering with – you'd have to get a taxi in any case.

By taxi/motorbike taxi Most people choose to hire a motorbike driver or taxi for a day or half-day; a motorbike taxi will ask for around K8000 to Amarapura, K12,000 to Amarapura plus Sagaing, and around K18,000 for these two plus Inwa. By taxi it'll be more like K40,000 to visit all three, though you can split this between up to four people. To add Paleik onto these itineraries will cost an additional K10,000 or so, or

K15,000 as a stand-alone trip. A motorbike taxi to Mingun will cost around K20,000 return, or double that in a taxi.

By bike It's possible to visit all the sights around Mandalay by bike, though you'll be sharing the main road from Mandalay to Sagaing with plenty of buses, lorries and the like – it's not terribly pleasant. However, having a bike certainly makes a visit to Inwa a lot more interesting; rather than sitting in a cart and following all the other carts around, you can plot your own course, and even take off into the countryside. Mingun is a long return trip by bike, though you can always take your bike on the ferry one-way (see p.309) and cycle back via Sagaing.

By ferry Both private and government boats operate to Mingun (see p.309).

Amarapura

အမရပူရ

Just 11km south of central Mandalay is the small town of **AMARAPURA** (from the Pali, meaning "City of Immortality", and pronounced with the stress on the first "ra"). Nowadays a rather sleepy suburb of Mandalay, the area has substantial historical pedigree, having twice served as Myanmar's royal capital (see box, p.281). The town is a major religious centre, with numerous temples dotted around the lake, although it's best known for the remarkable **U Bein Bridge**, a lengthy teak construction that's up there with Myanmar's most photogenic sights.

The bridge stretches across pretty **Lake Taungthaman**, named after an ogre who came here in pursuit of the Buddha, and ringed with an impressive series of stupas. **Paddle boats** (around K10,000/45min) can be rented for short trips around the lake from the western end of the bridge. Hunt around the maze of lanes inland from the bridge's western end (beyond the umpteen trinket stalls by the bridge itself) and you'll see plenty of villagers making longyi and other garments – despite the horde of tourists padding along the bridge nearby, this is up there with Myanmar's cheapest places in which to shop for **fabrics**. If coming here on a tour, your driver might take you to **Shwe Sin Tai Silkwear**, just west of the lake, where there's an interesting traditional silk-weaving workshop, plus attached shop.

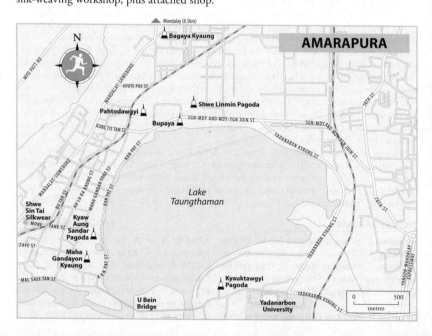

U Bein Bridge

ဦးပိန်တံတား • Daily 24hr • In theory part of the Mandalay Combination Ticket (see box, p.286), although it's highly unlikely you'll be asked to produce it

The world's longest teak footbridge, the spectacular **U Bein Bridge** stretches more than 1200m across Lake Taungthaman. Most evenings it probably also hosts the world's longest unbroken line of tourists: no bad thing, and in fact quite a spectacle when the colours of everyone's shirts flare up in the sun's last rays. Though most visit at this time, early birds can catch something similar with far fewer people at daybreak.

The bridge's existence stems from a salvage job that took place following one of Myanmar's many changes of regal power: after the palace was shifted north to Mandalay in 1859, Amarapura's mayor **U Bein** decided to create a bridge using the teak support columns left behind. There are, today, just over a thousand pillars along the course of the bridge, some of which have been replaced with concrete poles. If you're wondering why the thing was built so high above the lake, you're obviously visiting in the dry season – the water level rises considerably after the rains.

Most visitors like to walk the length of the bridge, so unless you want to walk it twice, ask your driver to pick you up from the other end.

7

Kyauktawgyi Pagoda

ကျောက်တော်ကြီးဘုရား • Daily 6am–6pm • Free

A short walk from the eastern end of U Bein Bridge, the **Kyauktawgyi Pagoda** (also known as the Taungthaman Pagoda) was commissioned in 1847 by King Pagan Min to a design based on the great Ananda Paya at Bagan. It's a somewhat smaller and dumpier affair than its older relative, but still impressive enough, as are its extensive, intricately detailed paintings showing assorted religious buildings across the country either built or restored by Pagan Min, plus various astrological symbols and pictures of nineteenth-century Burmese at work and play.

Maha Gandayon Kyaung

မဟာဂန္ဓရုံကျောင်း • Entrance on Maha Gandar Yone St • Daily 24hr • Free

Home to hundreds of monks, the huge, nationally renowned **Maha Gandayon Kyaung** sprawls across the area to the west of the U Bein Bridge. The monastery is best avoided during the mornings from around 10am to 11.30am, when swarms of tour groups arrive to stare at the monks eating lunch – a lot like feeding time at a human zoo. At other times it's an enjoyable place for aimless wandering, with a tree-shaded and wonderfully peaceful sprawl of monastic halls, although surprisingly few religious buildings or Buddhist iconography on display, giving the place the look and feel of a rather idyllic university campus.

Kyaw Aung Sandar Pagoda

Daily 24hr • Free

On the north side of the Maha Gandayon Kyaung, the **Kyaw Aung Sandar Pagoda** sees few foreign visitors but is well worth a look for its seriously wacky array of statues. These include a pair of absolutely gargantuan Buddhas, one sitting and one reclining; a golden hall full of seated and standing Buddhas, with assorted animals outside; and a large green circular shrine guarded by a pair of giant owls.

Pahtodawgyi and around

ပုထိုးတော်ကြီး • Entrance to south of complex • Daily 24hr • Free

If cycling south from Mandalay, **Pahtodawgyi** will be the first hint that you're nearing Amarapura – a giant white, bell-shaped stupa protruding from the flatlands, completed in 1819 at the beginning of King Bagyidaw's reign. Male visitors can get a great view of the surrounding countryside by walking up to the stupa's upper level – sadly, women are not allowed.

A couple of further large and eye-catching stupas stand close to the lake just west of the Pahtodawgyi: the boxy-looking **Bupaya**, right on the water's edge and, slightly further west and away from the lake, the large **Shwe Linmin Pagoda**, with its golden spire poking up out of the trees.

Bagaya Kyaung

ဘာ:ကရာကျောင်း · Just east of Mandalay–Sagaing road · Daily 9am–5pm · Covered by the Mandalay Combination Ticket (see box, p.286)

Around 2km north of the lake, the **Bagaya Kyaung** is a modern reconstruction of a monastery built here during Amarapura's first stint as royal capital. The averagely pretty wooden exterior features a couple of steeply tapering towers, although otherwise there's not a great deal to see.

ARRIVAL AND DEPARTURE · AMARAPURA

By pick-up It is possible to get to Amarapura by pick-up from Mandalay (see p.291), though these drop off nowhere near the sights, which are also rather distant from each other – far more trouble than it's worth.

By taxi or motorbike tour Most visit Amarapura as part of a motorbike or taxi tour (see p.299); your driver is certain to stop by the bridge, but let them know if you'd like to add other sights to your itinerary.

By bike You can cycle to Amarapura from Mandalay in well under an hour; use the tall Pahtodawgyi stupa (see p.301) as a reference point for when to turn off the main road.

Werawsana Jade Pagoda

Just off the Yangon–Mandalay Expressway, 6km by road from Amarapura (easily visited en route between Sagaing/Inwa and Amarapura) · 24hr · Free

Completed in late 2015, the kitsch **Werawsana Jade Pagoda** was the brainchild of gem dealer U Soe Naing, who spent 25 years amassing over a thousand tonnes of the precious stone in order to build what is claimed to be the world's only Buddhist temple constructed entirely out of jade. The sickly-green structure is perhaps stronger on novelty value than aesthetic merit, by day at least; when illuminated after dark it's weirdly impressive, its 22m-high stupa (decorated with around thirty thousand miniature jade Buddhas plus Jataka carvings) glowing luminously beneath the lights.

Snake Temple, Paleik

18km south of Mandalay; most visit the temple as part of a motorbike or taxi tour (see p.299), but with an early start and a good breakfast it's quite possible to cycle here and back in a day

The village of **PALEIK**, around 18km south of Mandalay, is famous for one thing and one thing only – the "**Snake Temple**" (Hmwe Paya) at its centre. An unassuming little place, it has earned fame thanks to a clutch of resident pythons – some made the temple their home in 1974, and despite efforts from the monks to keep them out, the serpents kept on coming back. The monks decided that the snakes were probably holy, and allowed them to settle here. There are usually two or three pythons in residence at any one time, coiled in corners or wrapped around pillars. Most people visit at 11am, when the snakes are washed in a bath filled with petals and then fed a mixture of milk and raw egg. A cluster of several hundred **stupas**, some of them ruined and covered in picturesque layers of vegetation, stands a few minutes' walk south of the temple.

Pinya

ပင်:ယ · About 26km from Mandalay Palace along the expressway · Daily 24hr · Free

Southwest of Mandalay, a few kilometres from the international airport, **PINYA** is the oldest and most obscure of the Mandalay region's former royal capitals (see box, p.281).

The city was founded in 1313 by **King Thihathu**, youngest of the three brothers who had previously established the Myinsaing Kingdom (see p.361), perhaps the most significant of the various mini-states which emerged following the collapse of Bagan. From Pinya, Thihathu and his successors controlled a sizeable swathe of central Myanmar between 1313 and 1364, when the kingdom was merged with that of nearby Sagaing (see box, p.281).

The small but modestly interesting sight sees few visitors but is an easy stop-off while travelling to or from the airport. Little remains of Thihathu's former capital, once covering over a square kilometre, save a brooding trio of almost windowless Bagan-style **temples** (currently under restoration, although you can still visit), built of red brick and still preserving traces of old murals and glazed tiles decorated with Jataka scenes.

Inwa

အင်းဝ

Now a sleepy rural village, **INWA** was once a place of great importance. Originally known as **Ava**, it served as the capital of Myanmar on four separate occasions, totalling over three hundred years (see box, p.281) – almost impossible to imagine today while you're rumbling between fields along the dusty lanes.

Scattered in and around the ancient **city walls**, sections of which remain visible (as do the ditches which once formed the surrounding moats), the various sights dating from Inwa's regal era are quite spread out; the vast majority of visitors chalk them off as part of a **horse-drawn carriage** tour (see p.305). A pleasant alternative is to make the rounds yourself on a **bicycle**, though you'll have to ride this down from Mandalay (see p.291). Cycling here also gives you the chance to strike off along roads left alone by the horse-and-cart drivers.

Maha Aungmye Bonzan and around

မဟာအောင်မြေဘုံစံ • Daily 6am–7pm • Covered by Mandalay Combination Ticket (see box, p.286)

The first sight you'll reach approaching from the ferry is the imposing **Maha Aungmye Bonzan** (also known as Me Nu Ok Kyaung – "Me Nu's Brick Monastery"),

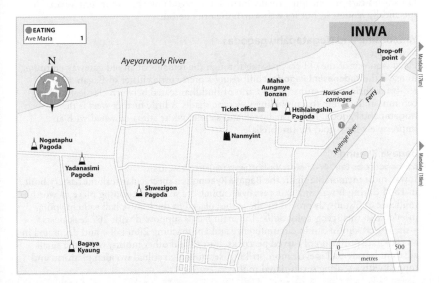

> ### THE MANDALAY COMBINATION TICKET AT INWA
>
> A **Mandalay Combination Ticket** (see box, p.286) is needed for entry to Inwa's two main sights, the Maha Aungmye Bonzan and Bagaya Kyaung. Tickets (K10,000, valid for 5 days) can be purchased from the office next to the Maha Aungmye Bonzan.

commissioned in 1818 by the chief consort of King Bagyidaw for her religious instructor. The monastery is unusual in being built of stuccoed brick, rather than the wood usually used for such structures, with a rectangular building topped by three diminishing tiers of roofs set on a huge base. The interior is largely bare and somewhat dilapidated, with a split-level wood-floored hall and a musty (but pleasantly cool) cellar below, whose thick pillars provide useful cover for love-struck local couples.

Immediately east of the monastery rise the clustered stupas of the **Htihlaingshin Pagoda**, parts of which date back to the era of King Kyansittha (r.1084–1112) of Bagan. Alternatively, walking out of the rear of the complex takes you down to the **river**, with the golden spires of Sagaing (see opposite) glistening on the opposite bank.

Nanmyint

နန်းမြင့် · Daily 6am–7pm

The "Leaning Tower of Inwa", as it's inevitably known, the wonky **Nanmyint** tower is the only surviving section of the palace which King Bagyidaw built here in 1822. Originally a watchtower, the building acquired its distinctive tilt during the series of earthquakes in 1838–39 which eventually led to Inwa losing its status as capital forever, although safety concerns mean that you can no longer climb it yourself.

Shwezigon Pagoda

ရွှေစည်းခုံ · Daily 24hr · Free

Marking the southwestern corner of the ancient city walls, the gleaming golden stupa of the hefty **Shwezigon Pagoda** is unmissable when heading west to Bagaya Kyaung. Horse-and-cart drivers don't usually include the pagoda on their tours unless you specifically request it, but it's well worth the brief detour.

Yadanasimi and Nogatapahu pagodas

Daily 24hr · Free

Head west out of the old city, passing through the remains of an old gateway en route, to reach the **Yadanasimi Pagoda**, comprising a pretty little cluster of Bagan-style red-brick shrines and stupas, with a trio of Buddhas seated between classical-looking columns and a flame tree providing welcome shade. A little further west is the **Nogatapahu Pagoda**, its unusually tall and slender white stupa crowned with an impressively large gold *hti* (umbrella).

Bagaya Kyaung

ဘားကရာကျောင်း · Daily 24hr · Covered by Mandalay Combination Ticket (see box, p.286)

Inwa's most memorable sight, the **Bagaya Kyaung** is a spectacular teak monastery built in 1834 during Inwa's final stint as royal capital. It's still a functioning place of worship, residence and study, as proved by the globes placed in the lecture hall to help young monks with their geography skills. The main hall is supported with 267 teak posts – the largest almost 3m in circumference and approaching 20m tall – and decorated in an elaborate profusion of carved peacocks, lotuses and other motifs, while the small adjacent lecture hall is even more striking, set on a high stilted wooden platform and topped with a soaring seven-tiered roof.

ARRIVAL AND DEPARTURE

You can visit Inwa as part of a **motorbike** or **taxi tour** (see p.299), or on a **bicycle** (just over 1hr from central Mandalay). By public transport you'll need to catch a **pick-up** from Mandalay (corner of 29th St and 84th St; 30min) and get off as the road curves around just before crossing the Inwa Bridge into Sagaing; from here it's a 10min walk southwest down a long, straight road to the jetty. Whichever way you arrive, you'll have to take a very short **ferry** ride (regular departures daily 6am–6pm; K1200 return, bikes free) across the river.

GETTING AROUND

By horse-drawn carriage The easiest way to get around Inwa's scattered sights is on a horse-and-cart tour – for some it's this experience that sticks in the memory, rather than any of the sights in particular. The going rate is K10,000 for a 2–3hr tour, although you might be able to haggle this down slightly if business is slow.

EATING

Ave Maria 09 471 20773. The best, and most reasonably priced, of the trio of overpriced, tour party-oriented restaurants near the ferry landing stage (Inwa's only eating options). The calm riverside setting slightly away from the horse-and-cart madness is a major bonus, while food features a well-prepared selection of dishes from a mainly Chinese menu (mains K5000–6000). Daily 9am–5pm.

Sagaing
စစ်ကိုင်း

The low-key city of **SAGAING** sits just 25km south of Mandalay on the opposite side of the Ayeyarwady River. As with nearby Inwa and Amarapura, Sagaing formerly served as the country's royal capital, though its stint was by far the shortest of the three, lasting just four years (see box, p.281). The town was also the centre of a Shan kingdom during the fourteenth century and is now capital of **Sagaing Region**, which stretches way up north, almost to Tibet.

The main reason to come here is **Sagaing Hill**, a modest rise bristling with so many Buddhist spires that it resembles some sort of Burmese pin cushion, while numerous further pagodas and stupas dot the surrounding area. The view from either of the **bridges** into Sagaing (one built by the British in 1934, the other in 2005) is among the most magical in Myanmar, with rolling lines of tree-shrouded hills dotted in an extraordinary profusion of snowy-white, gold-tipped stupas, and the boat-strewn Ayeyarwady sliding lazily between.

If you fancy a break from Mandalay while remaining in the area, Sagaing is also the only one of the city's satellite towns with foreigner-licensed **accommodation**.

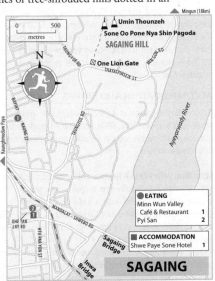

EATING
Minn Wun Valley
Café & Restaurant 1
Pyi San 2

ACCOMMODATION
Shwe Paye Sone Hotel 1

SAGAING

Sagaing Hill
စစ်ကိုင်းတောင် • Access from One Lion Gate on Ta Yat Pin Seik St • Daily 24hr • Covered by Sagaing-Mingun Combination Ticket (see box, p.306); K300 fee for camera or video, usually only collected from road entrance

Around 250m high, splendid **Sagaing Hill** pokes its omni-spired head out just north of the city centre. The views from the top are predictably fantastic, though for some the walk up the hill (around 25min) is the best part of the experience. The covered pathway starts from **One Lion Gate** (boasting a single

> ### THE SAGAING–MINGUN COMBINATION TICKET
>
> In theory, to enter Sagaing or Mingun you'll need to buy or show a **Combination Ticket** (K5000), valid for both towns. At the time of writing ticket checks were being rigorously enforced at Mingun but not at all in Sagaing – although don't be surprised if the situation has changed by the time you read this.

7

chinthe rather than the customary pair) and gets steeper as you go – if you can make it to the top without pausing for a breather you're officially in decent shape.

The **Sone Oo Pone Nya Shin Pagoda** crowns the summit of the hill, its 30m stupa fancily decorated with colourful tiling and rich turquoise-and-green tessellated glass. A pair of large seated Buddhas sit in shrines inside – note the quirky donation boxes next to the Buddhas, including two in the form of a frog, plus another of a carrot-munching rabbit. In addition, the views of the river are quite superb from here, and in clear weather you'll see Mandalay's grey sprawl way to the north.

There are several other religious structures on the hill, the most interesting of which is **Umin Thounzeh**, a curved chamber containing 43 seated and two standing Buddha images, a twenty-minute walk from the Sone Oo Pone Nya Shin Pagoda.

Kaunghmudaw Paya

ကောင်းမှုတော်ဘုရား • 7km northwest of central Sagaing • Daily 24hr • Covered by Sagaing-Mingun Combination Ticket (see box above) • Motorbike taxis charge K6000–8000 return from Sagaing Hill

Some way to the northwest of Sagaing but easily visible from a distance, **Kaunghmudaw Paya** is the town's most interesting religious monument. Looking somewhat like a whitewashed, 50m-tall mammary gland, it was completed in 1648, its decidedly non-Burmese design based on the Ruvanvalisaya stupa in Anuradhapura, Sri Lanka. Like its counterpart, it is said to house a number of relics of the Buddha, including a tooth – actually an ox-bone fake – and several strands of hair.

ARRIVAL AND DEPARTURE
                                                                              SAGAING

By pick-up It's possible to get to Sagaing on one of the smoke-belching pick-ups from Mandalay (see p.299), but these drop off near the market – nowhere near Sagaing Hill, but fine if you're planning to stay in or otherwise make use of the town itself. It's a 2km climb from the market to the hill – walkable, though it's far easier to hop on a motorbike taxi.

By taxi or motorbike tour Most travellers arrive in Sagaing on a motorbike or taxi tour (see p.299). Some drivers will take you to the base of Sagaing Hill, and others to the top – ask about this when arranging your trip, since you might be asked extra for the latter, unless your driver is also planning to visit a commission-friendly silversmith on the way down.

ACCOMMODATION AND EATING

Outside Mandalay, Sagaing is the only place in the area with foreigner-licensed **accommodation** – and there's one whole hotel to choose from. While a day-trip is enough for some, staying the night gives you the chance to soak up the atmosphere and explore some of the many other pagodas dotting the riverside, and come nightfall you may well be the only foreigner in town.

Minn Wun Valley Café & Restaurant Bayint Naung St ☎09 252 444 229. Popular drop-in spot for tour groups buzzing through Sagaing, with a wide range of well-prepared Asian food plus a few Western dishes (mains around K5000). Service can be slow. Daily 10am–8pm.

Pyi San One road north of Ohe Tan Lay Rd ☎072 34505. A passable place to eat, located one street parallel to the *Shwe Pyae Sone* hotel, serving hefty-sized Chinese staples (from K2000) and draught Dagon beer,

although – as with most restaurants in Sagaing – you'll have curious locals gazing at you throughout your meal. Daily 8am–9pm.

Shwe Pyae Sone Ohe Tan Lay Rd ☎072 22781. If you feel like staying in the Mandalay area but not in Mandalay itself, here's your only option. It's actually a very nice little place, with courteous staff and presentable a/c rooms with flatscreen TVs and minibar. They also rent out bicycles (K3000/day). $30

Mingun

မင်းကွန်း • Entrance to the village costs K5000 with the Sagaing-Mingun Combination Ticket (see box opposite)

The village of **MINGUN** would be largely unknown today were it not for King Bodawpaya, who in 1790 chose it as the site of the gigantic **Mingun Pagoda**, intended to be the world's largest stupa, although all that was completed by the time of his death, 29 years later, was the bottom portion – a stupendous cube of bricks on top of a huge terrace. The village is around 10km northwest of Mandalay on the opposite side of the Ayeyarwady (most visitors arrive by boat from the city), with a trip here offering a mix of historical attractions, a taste of rural life and an interesting river excursion all rolled into one. The vast flocks of tourists who descend on the place when the government ferries arrive in the morning have somewhat dented its former sylvan charms, admittedly, but visit after midday – either by road or on the afternoon MRGR ferry (see p.309) – and you'll have the place largely to yourself.

MINGUN

Hsinbyume Pagoda

Mingun Buddhist Home for the Aged ①

Mingun Bell

Mingun Sayadaw Memorial

Mingun Pagoda

Chinthe

Settaya Pagoda ②

Ticket booth

Pondaw Pagoda

Ayeyarwady River

N

EATING
| The Garden Café | 1 |
| Point | 2 |

0 — 200 metres

Boat jetty

Sagaing (18km)

7

Pondaw Pagoda

ပုံတော်ဘုရား • Daily 24hr • Free

On your right just before you reach the ticket booth and enter the village, look out for the small **Pondaw Pagoda**, a scale model of what the Mingun Pagoda was intended to look like when finished. The model gives a striking sense of how absurdly huge the actual stupa would have been had it ever been completed, with even the gargantuan base of the monument (which did get built) dwarfed by the huge stupa (which didn't) sitting on top of it.

Settaya Pagoda

စက်တော်ရာဘုရား • Daily 24hr • Free

Just north of the ticket booth is the **Settaya Pagoda**, a bright-white cube in quasi Bagan style, with steps leading down to the river beside it. Inside is a representation of the **Buddha's footprint**, a metre-long indentation decorated with shells on the toes and a flower on the heel.

Mingun chinthe

Standing opposite the steps up to the Mingun Pagoda is a pair of huge, semi-ruined **chinthe** – the mythical creatures, part lion with a hint of dragon, which can be found symbolically guarding the gates of pagodas across the country. The two here were constructed on an appropriately grand scale, given the size of the shrine they protect, and are still impressively huge, despite having lost their heads.

7

KING BODAWPAYA AND THE MINGUN PAGODA

Creator of the Mingun Pagoda, **King Bodawpaya** (ruled 1782–1819) was one of the most powerful and longest-serving monarchs in Myanmar's history, popularly known as the "Grandfather King" – perhaps on account of his 200-odd wives and concubines, and 120 children. Bodawpaya's lusty appetites didn't prevent him from proclaiming himself the next Buddha-in-waiting (a claim politely rejected by the *Sangha*) or from taking a keen interest in religious affairs, as well as setting up an observation post on an island near Mingun from which to personally supervise the construction of his great pagoda.

Various legends purport to explain why Bodawpaya's supersized monument never actually got finished. One story claims that construction work was taking such a heavy toll on the state that a fake prophecy was concocted in order to halt the project, alleging that as soon as the stupa was finished, the kingdom would fall or the king would die (or possibly both). Much affected by this prediction, Bodawpaya ordered a deliberate go-slow. Work continued, but only at a snail's pace, and was abandoned entirely as soon as the king expired, never to be resumed – although given the vastness of the undertaking it seems difficult to believe it could ever have been completed, whatever the circumstances.

Mingun Pagoda

မင်းကွန်းဘုရား

The world's largest pile of bricks (as it's often described), it's hard to imagine how majestic a sight **Mingun Pagoda** would have been if finished (although the Pondaw Pagoda – see p.307 – gives an approximate idea). Constructed using thousands of prisoners of war and other slave labour, the project was originally intended to reach -a final height of around 150m.

Though only one-third was completed, it's still an astonishing sight, made more dramatic by the jagged, lightning-like fissures created when earthquakes hit in 1819 and 2012. A staircase on the right-hand side of the pagoda leads up to the summit of the monument; although visitors can at present only go about two-thirds of the way up, the views over Mingun and the Ayeyarwady are still worth the climb.

Mingun Bell

မင်းကွန်းခေါင်းလောင်း • Daily 5.30am–5.30pm

As well as the planet's biggest pile of bricks, Mingun also boasts one of the world's largest functioning **bells**. Like its fellow record-breaker, this was commissioned by King Bodawpaya, to whom size clearly did matter: it's around 5m wide at the base and weighs 55,555 viss (corresponding to around 97 tonnes) – formerly the world's heaviest bell until being surpassed in 2000 by the 126-tonne Bell of Good Luck in Henan, China – although both pale in comparison to the mother of all bells, the 327-tonne Great Bell of Dhammazedi (see p.74), lost in the Yangon River after being looted by Filipe de Brito e Nicote in 1608. The done thing here is to duck inside, then get someone to clang the bell with a wooden beater. Despite the bell's size, it's not particularly sonorous, and the layers of graffiti scribbled inside don't much add to the experience. Pray the bell doesn't fall off its supports while you're underneath it either – the last time it was knocked off its perch (by the 1839 earthquake) it took 57 years before being finally re-hung.

Hsinbyume Pagoda

ဆင်ဖြူမယ်ဘုရား • Daily 24hr

Just north of the Mingun Bell is the whitewashed **Hsinbyume Pagoda**. Its extravagant wavy design is said to represent Mount Sumeru – the mountain at the centre of the Buddhist cosmos – and the seas that surround it, represented by the central stupa and the seven terraces on which it's placed. Climb to the top for superlative views over Mingun, the river and the countryside beyond.

ARRIVAL AND DEPARTURE

By ferry Far and away the nicest way to reach Mingun is by ferry – the trip from Mandalay takes about 1hr, slightly faster when travelling downstream on the way back. Government boats (K5000) leave from the pier on 26th St in Mandalay at 9am, returning at 12.30pm. You'll need to show your passport (or some of form of ID) when buying a ticket. The alternative is to take one of the boats operated by MGRG/Pioneer (38th St, between 79th and 80th sts; ☎ 02 66204, ⓦ mgrgexpress.com), which depart Mandalay at 9.30am and 2.30pm, and stay in Mingun for 3hr (K8000

return); these depart from Gawein Jetty, not the Mingun Jetty, and run Jan–April only. Bikes can be taken aboard for a small additional charge.

By taxi or motorbike tour It's possible to combine Mingun with Sagaing and other destinations on a motorbike or taxi day-trip, though this will add two hours of travel to the day, and a fair bit more to the price. It does, however, give you the chance to see the village during the peaceful afternoon hours after the ferries have left.

EATING

The Garden Cafe On the riverbank opposite the Mingun Bell ☎ 09 773 077 933. An unexpected find, this idyllic French-owned garden café has a lovely riverside location and serves up sandwiches (with proper baguettes), salads and a few grilled dishes (mains K5000–6000), as well as Myanmar set lunches

(K12,000), good juices and real coffee. Daily 9am–5pm.
Point Behind Settaya Paya. This riverside establishment is one of the nicest of the various low-key teahouse dotting Mingun, set slightly away from the busy village centre. It serves up simple noodle and rice dishes (K2000–3000), plus beer. Daily 8am–10pm.

7

Northern Myanmar

KACHIN FESTIVAL, MYITKYINA

Northern Myanmar

With its dense jungles, ice-capped mountains, fiercely independent people and outstanding natural resources, northern Myanmar fuels the imagination like few other places. This fascinating land has been crisscrossed by armies and explorers for centuries, yet it remains one of the least-known places in Asia. Overland travel is still controlled across much of the region, but it is currently possible to travel on most of the major rail and river routes without permits.

The most accessible part of **northern Myanmar** lies in the hills east of Mandalay, between balmy **Pyin Oo Lwin** and the modern town of **Lashio**. Once the summer capital of British Burma, Pyin Oo Lwin is still redolent of the Raj, with colonial piles dotting its leafy suburbs. To the east, train enthusiasts and those with a head for heights will appreciate the monumental **Gokteik Viaduct**, constructed in 1901 and made famous by Paul Theroux in *The Great Railway Bazaar*. Further on, **Kyaukme** and **Hsipaw** are both excellent bases from which to trek into the tea-swathed hills and explore the villages of northern Shan State.

In northern Myanmar, as elsewhere in the country, the **Ayeyarwady River** is a major transport artery. It's possible for foreigners to travel upstream as far as **Bhamo**, a pleasant riverside town with a long history as a trading post. Downstream, there are interesting stops at **Shwegu** with its overgrown, island-bound pagodas, and **Katha**, the inspiration for "Kyauktada" in George Orwell's must-read novel, *Burmese Days*. Further south, the river flows through the Sagaing Region past the riverside potteries of **Kyaukmyaung**, not far from **Shwebo**, a one-time Burmese capital, and the remains of ancient **Hanlin**, today a major archeological site. Further into Sagaing Region on the bank of the Chindwin River, Myanmar's little-visited fourth city of **Monywa** is a base for visiting unusual temples and the world's tallest Buddha statue.

In the far north, the modern town of **Myitkyina** is a springboard into the wilds of northern **Kachin State**. The journey to **Indawgyi Lake** is a permit-free way to experience the region's serene natural environment. However, to find true wilderness, try to get as far as **Putao** and the national parks that line Myanmar's Himalayan border, for which you'll need to sign up for a tour.

Much of vast **Sagaing Region** is closed to foreign travellers without permits – particularly along the Indian border in the state's mountainous northwest. Further south, it's possible to cruise along the Chindwin River (see box, p.345) north to **Kalewa**, with occasional boats all the way up to **Khamti**, and the southeast of the state – between Sagaing and Shwebo – is completely open.

GOKTEIK VIADUCT

Highlights

❶ Pyin Oo Lwin With its horse-drawn carriages and strawberry fields, colonial hill station spirit lives on in British Burma's former summer capital. **See p.314**

❷ Gokteik Viaduct A century after its construction, trains still cross this latticework bridge at a crawl on one of Myanmar's incomparable rail journeys. **See p.320**

❸ Shan State treks Hike across hillsides lined with tea plantations and stay in remote Palaung villages around Hsipaw and Kyaukme. **See p.321 & p.327**

❹ Ayeyarwady River trips Float past waterside pagodas and watch for dolphins on Myanmar's most important river. **See box, p.334**

❺ Katha Hunt down locations from George Orwell's novel *Burmese Days* in this quaint riverside town. **See p.337**

❻ Myitkyina Time your visit to Kachin State's capital to coincide with one of its colourful festivals, or console yourself with a Kachin feast if you miss them. **See p.346**

❼ Indawgyi Lake Kayak to the beautiful Shwe Myitzu Pagoda, or hike in the forested hills to the east of Myanmar's placid largest lake. **See p.351**

HIGHLIGHTS ARE MARKED ON THE MAP ON P.314

Pyin Oo Lwin and around

ပြင်ဦးလွင်မြို့

Situated on a lush plateau 65km east of Mandalay, **PYIN OO LWIN** sits far above the dust of central Myanmar. At an elevation of 1070m, the town is famed for its pleasant climate, with temperatures seldom creeping above 30°C, even in summer. It was established formally only in 1896, on the site of a British army camp near a small Shan village named Pyin Oo Lwin, and renamed **Maymyo**, or "May Town", after a Colonel James May who was stationed here (the name was changed back after independence). After the construction of the railway from Mandalay reduced the journey time from two days in a bullock cart to a mere five hours, it developed rapidly as a hill station, providing refuge from the heat of lower Burma. From the turn of the twentieth century, the entire British establishment decamped here at the start of each summer,

NORTHERN MYANMAR

HIGHLIGHTS

1. Pyin Oo Lwin
2. Gokteik Viaduct
3. Shan State treks
4. Ayeyarwady River trips
5. Katha
6. Myitkyina
7. Indawgyi Lake

TRAVEL RESTRICTIONS

Travelling in northern Myanmar is made considerably slower and more complicated by a changing array of travel restrictions. A consequence of the north's numerous ethnic insurgencies, restricted areas (see map, p.27) may be completely closed (the jade mining town of **Hpakant**), or accessible only with a pricey permit (the area surrounding **Putao**). Even in open areas, overland travel is frequently limited – **Myitkyina** can be reached by rail but not by boat or road, while **Bhamo** can only be approached by boat or plane, and the latter is sometimes the best option. To visit Putao, it's the only option.

If you do want to visit a no-go zone, you'll need to contact MTT (see p.28) or a tour operator well in advance of your trip – permit applications can take upwards of a month. For the latest on local restrictions, foreigner-oriented hotels and guesthouses are the best places for up-to-date information.

gradually covering the town's gently rolling hills with half-timbered government offices and graceful brick villas.

Pyin Oo Lwin's history still shows today in the horse-drawn carriages clip-clopping past its colonial mansions, the chiming of **Purcell Tower**'s bells – cast in London in 1935 for King George V's Silver Jubilee – and in the strawberries nestling alongside tropical fruit in the **Shan Market**. Another British leftover is the **National Kandawgyi Gardens**, a huge botanic garden where neat tulip beds thrive alongside half-wild groves of teak trees.

Further afield, the rolling countryside outside the town is peppered with sights. Most are withing a few kilometres of the Mandalay–Lashio Road, making them straightforward to reach, especially if you have your own transport. Between picking your way through **Peik Chin Myaung**'s humid cavern, trekking to nearby Shan villages, or floating away in the plunge pools of the **Anisakan Falls**, Pyin Oo Lwin is an excellent place to linger.

The town centre

The 1936 **Purcell Tower** marks Pyin Oo Lwin's compact town centre, home to large ethnic Indian and Nepali communities, the descendants of soldiers and labourers who moved here under British rule. Today, many run shops selling the fruit wine, jam and woolly jumpers for which the town is known, and mosques and Hindu temples abound.

Not far away, the **Central Market**, selling fruit, tea, clothing and household goods, is a warren of dark passages broken up by pools of light. In the evenings, the roads around here start to fill with the food stalls of the night market. On the other side of the market is the **Shwe Daung Kyaung Gyi**, which pre-dates the town, and across the road the old Whiteway department store is now the Cherry Cinema, the last in Pyin Oo Lwin, with seats from K1000.

As Maymyo, the town was an important **military cantonment** on the edge of the Shan plateau and today the military connection remains – the Defence Services Academy occupies a vast site just west of the centre.

Governor's House

ဘုရင်ခံအိမ်မြတော် • 1km southwest of Purcell Tower, Mandalay–Lashio Rd • Daily 8am–6pm • $3 or K4200 • ☎ 085 21901, Ⓦ aureumpalacehotel.com

Built in 1903 as the British governor's summer residence, **Government House** stood for just forty years before it was destroyed in World War II. Rebuilt in 2005, today it is part of the *Governor's House Hotel*. A small **museum** has been set up in the mansion and the adjoining office building, which is filled with greenish waxworks of colonial personalities and decorated with sepia photographs of the original house – it's not terribly exciting, but it's one of the few colonial-style buildings open to visitors and

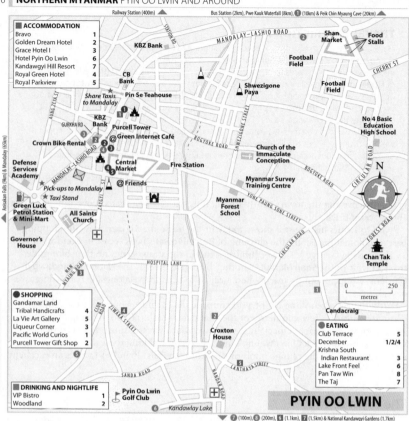

Railway Station (400m) ▲   Bus Station (2km), Pwe Kauk Waterfall (8km), ❶ (10km) & Peik Chin Myaung Cave (20km) ▲

■ **ACCOMMODATION**
Bravo	1
Golden Dream Hotel	2
Grace Hotel I	3
Hotel Pyin Oo Lwin	6
Kandawgyi Hill Resort	7
Royal Green Hotel	4
Royal Parkview	5

KBZ Bank

MANDALAY–LASHIO ROAD

CB Bank

Share Taxis to Mandalay   Pin Se Teahouse

KBZ Bank

GURKHA RD

Purcell Tower

Crown Bike Rental   @ Green Internet Café

BOGYOKE ROAD

Defense Services Academy

MANDALAY–LASHIO ROAD

Central Market   Fire Station

Pick-ups to Mandalay

@ Friends

Taxi Stand

Green Luck Petrol Station & Mini-Mart   All Saints Church

Governor's House

MAN MYAING ROAD

HOSPITAL LANE

Shan Market   Food Stalls

Football Field

Shwezigone Paya

Football Field

CHERRY ST

No 4 Basic Education High School

Church of the Immaculate Conception

BOGYOKE ROAD

Myanmar Survey Training Centre

Myanmar Forest School

YONE PAUNG SONE STREET

CIRCULAR ROAD

FOREST ROAD

Chan Tak Temple

N

0   250
metres

8

● **SHOPPING**
Gandamar Land	
Tribal Handicrafts	4
La Vie Art Gallery	5
Liqueur Corner	3
Pacific World Curios	1
Purcell Tower Gift Shop	2

CLUB ROAD

ZIWAKA STREET

Croxton House

Candacraig

● **EATING**
Club Terrace	5
December	1/2/4
Krishna South Indian Restaurant	3
Lake Front Feel	6
Pan Taw Win	8
The Taj	7

SANDA ROAD

LANTHAYA STREET

■ **DRINKING AND NIGHTLIFE**
VIP Bistro	1
Woodland	2

Pyin Oo Lwin Golf Club

Kandawlay Lake

MANDA ROAD

PYIN OO LWIN

Amarkan Falls (9km) & Mandalay (65km)

CIRCULAR ROAD

▼ ❼ (100m), ❽ (200m), ⑥ (1.1km), ❼ (1.5km) & National Kandawgyi Gardens (1.7km)

a favourite with domestic film-makers. If you're feeling seriously flush, the five-bedroom house can be yours for $1950 a night. If you book it they'll close the museum and shoo away the day-trippers for the duration of your stay. Downhill is a discreet cluster of more affordable bungalows.

Shan Market and around

ရှမ်းဈေး • 2km northeast of Purcell Tower, Mandalay–Lashio Rd • Daily 6am–4pm

Start the morning at the bustling **Shan Market** on the eastern side of town, which is at its busiest between 6.30am and 8am. Originally, Shan farmers gathered here to sell their produce because of the market's proximity to their villages east of Pyin Oo Lwin, and while it's still a great place to visit, nowadays the full-time Chinese, Shan and Burmese stallholders favour imported and generic goods. To find the farmers who come by in the mornings, you may have more luck heading 600m further east along the Mandalay–Lashio Road, to Zayad Kadone street market.

Circular Road and the suburbs

မြို့ပတ်လမ်း

Circular Road started life as a forest ride for British officers. Today, the leafy thoroughfare follows a semicircle around the eastern half of Pyin Oo Lwin, leading south from the Mandalay–Lashio Road into the wealthier suburbs and the richest seams of colonial buildings. Of note is the half-timbered **No. 4 Basic Education High School** (formerly St Michael's, a missionary school for Anglo-Burmese students).

Colonial government buildings were clustered on **Yone Paung Sone Street**. Several fulfil similar functions today – the imposing pink brick and teak structure of the former Survey Office is now the Myanmar Survey Training Centre, and across the road the old Forestry Department is today's Myanmar Forest School.

It's also worth seeking out **Candacraig** and **Croxton House**, built in 1904 for the Bombay Burmah Trading Company. After independence, they operated as state-run hotels, and now they've been privatized they are currently closed for renovation. Candacraig, now known as Thiri Myaing, is set in expansive grounds and expected to re-open in 2018, and was once the "chummery" or residence for unmarried company staff. Croxton, now Gandamar Myaing, was the manager's home.

Chan Tak Temple

ချန် တက် ဘုရား• Forest Rd • Daily 6am–6pm • Free; $1 to climb pagoda • ☎ 09 204 5570

Despite its relative newness, **Chan Tak Temple** is a classically styled Chinese complex, its ornate halls and pagoda set among formal gardens and replete with flying eaves and concrete dragons. The dining hall serves a vegetarian buffet at lunchtime (10am–1pm) and serves drinks all day.

National Kandawgyi Gardens

အမျိုးသားကန်တော်ကြီးဥယျာဉ် • Nanda Rd, 4km southeast of Purcell Tower • Daily 8am–6pm (some attractions close at 5.30pm, and staff may be reluctant to let you in after 5pm) • $5 or K6000 • ☎ 085 22497

Pyin Oo Lwin's major attraction, the **National Kandawgyi Gardens** were established between 1915–17, when hundreds of Turkish prisoners of war were put to work excavating **Kandawgyi Lake** and landscaping its surroundings. After independence the park gradually deteriorated, until the Htoo Group took over in 2000 and redeveloped it as a scenic spot.

Today, the pretty lakeside area, filled with pansies and tulips, is popular for photo opportunities, while further on the gardens are more interesting and unkempt, with exotic orchards, a jungly swamp walkway and behind it all a stretch of undeveloped forest crossed by a few rough paths. The 380-acre gardens take at least two hours to explore, and with attractions including a walk-through aviary, a large orchid nursery, a swimming pool and an airy café overlooking the lake (coffee from K1000, juice K1500, dishes from around K3000), it's easy to spend half a day here. Overlooking it all is the distinctive **Nan Myint Tower**, which looks a bit like an ancient oriental helter-skelter. Go up in the lift and down by the external staircase to see the view over Pyin Oo Lwin's suburbs – it's free to climb. The garden hosts a flower festival each December.

Anisakan Falls

အနီးစခန်း ရေတံခွန် • Near Anisakan, 9km southwest of Pyin Oo Lwin • Free • Motorbike taxis (K5000 return) depart from the roundabout near the Green Luck Petrol Station, or you can take a Mandalay-bound pick-up (K300) to Anisakan and walk the remaining 2km

Just outside the village of Anisakan, the plateau on which Pyin Oo Lwin sits drops away dramatically into a forested canyon, carved out by a tributary of the Dokhtawady River as it plunges down **Anisakan Falls** (also known as the Dat Taw Gyaint waterfall) to the valley floor. It takes 45 minutes to walk down from the road to the foot of the falls, and a sweaty hour to hike back to the car park, but the scenery and the chance to cool off in the jade-green plunge pools make it worthwhile.

8

There is an alternative route up the opposite side of the falls to **The View Resort** (☎085 50262, ⊛theviewpyinoolwin.com), from where it's a 2.5km walk back to the main road. The luxurious hotel itself is not open to walk-in guests, but there's a restaurant on site where you may have better luck – call ahead to check it's open.

Maha An Htu Kan Tha Paya

မဟာအံ့ထူးကံသာဘုရား • 8km northeast of Pyin Oo Lwin • Daily 5am–7pm • Free • K3000 (return) by motorbike taxi

The main reason to visit the **Maha An Htu Kan Tha Paya** ("Reluctant Buddha Paya"), completed in 2000, is for its backstory. In 1997, a temple in China commissioned three marble Buddha statues from Mandalay. When the statues came to be delivered, one fell off the truck just outside Pyin Oo Lwin, and after several attempts to reload it, the head of a nearby village claimed that the Buddha visited him in a dream to tell him the 17-tonne statue wished to stay where it was. A **festival** takes place here around the Tazaung full moon in November each year, when locals gather on the hillside to release huge bamboo and paper hot-air balloons shaped like animals.

Pwe Kauk Waterfall

ပွဲကောက်ရေတံခွန် • Pwe Kauk, 8km northeast of Pyin Oo Lwin • K500; camera fee K300, video fee K500 • Turn north opposite the Maha An Htu Kan Tha Paya entrance

Then known as Hampshire Falls, **Pwe Kauk Waterfall** was a favourite picnic spot for the British. The series of short, wide falls in a woodland dell occupies a setting that's pretty rather than dramatic, with some man-made attractions along the riverbank, including a water-powered merry-go-round. It's hardly worth the trouble of visiting, but if you're passing you could drop in for some people-watching.

Peik Chin Myaung Cave and around

ပိတ်ချင်းမြောင်ဂူ • Near Wet Wun village, 20km northeast of Pyin Oo Lwin • Daily 6.30am–5pm • Free; camera fee K300, video fee K1000 • K5000 by motorbike taxi from central Pyin Oo Lwin

Peik Chin Myaung Cave snakes into a hillside some 3km east of the village of Wet Wun. The humid cavern is filled with gold-coated Buddha statues, large concrete alligators and Jataka dioramas, and an underground stream gushes alongside the concrete path. While you'll need to stoop in places, the cave is open and well lit. It takes around fifteen minutes to reach the end, and no socks or shoes are allowed – although there are mats laid out in some places, the path can be slippery and your feet will get wet. At the entrance to the cave is a large parking area with a few shops and restaurants.

WET WUN (pronounced more like Woon than One) itself is worth a brief stop. Ancient Banyan trees line the road, and you'll find **Wet Wun Zeiguan** monastery through a gate on the right as you travel away from Pyin Oo Lwin, where some of the monks speak English. Join them playing football in the yard between the low hall and the side buildings with their steeply tiered roofs.

ARRIVAL AND DEPARTURE

By bus Buses and minibuses to Hsipaw leave from *San Pya* restaurant, 3km northeast of the Purcell Tower on the main road. Buses to most other destinations leave from the Thiri Mandalar Bus Station just southeast of *San Pya*.

Destinations Hsipaw (6 daily; 4hr); Kyaukme (6 daily; 3hr); Lashio (3 daily; 6hr); Mandalay (hourly; 2hr 30min); Monywa (3 daily; 7hr); Naypyitaw (2 daily; 8hr); Taungoo (daily; 10hr); Yangon (daily; 12hr).

By pick-up Pick-ups to Mandalay (3hr; K2500) leave when full from just north of the first roundabout southwest of the Purcell Tower. Services start around first light, petering out in the afternoon.

By shared taxi The fastest way to get to Mandalay (2hr), Kyaukme (2hr 30min), Hsipaw (3hr 30min) and Lashio (5hr 30min) is by shared taxi. Mandalay-bound taxis (K7000) depart when full from behind the *Pin Se Teahouse*, from

6am until they run out of passengers. Shared taxis to Kyaukme, Hsipaw and Lashio leave from near the Shan Market from 8am onwards – regardless of your destination, you'll need to pay the full fare to Lashio (K14,000, or K15,000 in the front seat). It's easiest to book shared taxis through your accommodation the day before; the car will pick you up from there in the morning, and the price should be the same.

By train Pyin Oo Lwin's small railway station is north of the town centre, 600m north of Mandalay–Lashio Road. There's one train a day each way, nominally departing for Mandalay just after 5pm and for destinations east of Pwin Oo Lwin before 8.30am. A blackboard in the station is updated each day with the actual expected times.
Destinations Hsipaw (daily; 6hr 30min); Kyaukme (daily; 5hr); Lashio (daily; 11hr); Mandalay (daily; 5hr).

GETTING AROUND AND TOURS

By motorbike taxi A short journey around town ought to cost K1000. Andrew (☎ 09 4316 7181), based at the *Pin Se Teahouse* near the *Bravo* hotel, speaks excellent English and charges K25,000 per day for guided tours. If he's busy, he can find you another guide, or arrange a car, tuk-tuk or motorbike taxi for shorter trips. Alternatively, motorbike riders congregate near Liqueur Corner by the Central Market.

By bicycle Bikes are available to rent from most hotels as well as Crown Bicycle Rental (daily 7.30am–6pm) on Mandalay–Lashio Road near the Purcell Tower – they cost K2000 to rent until 6pm, or K2500 for a full 24 hours.

By motorbike Crown Bicycle Rental have motorbikes for K8000/day. Some guesthouses and hotels also have motorbikes, though they tend to be more expensive.

By horse-drawn carriage Pyin Oo Lwin's iconic horse-drawn carriages (gharries) cost around K8000/hr, or K15,000 for a trip to the Kandawgyi Gardens including waiting time. If you're tall, they can feel cramped inside.

Tours Trekking Kyaw Kyaw Oo (☎ 09 797 781 778, ✉ kyawkyawoo123pol@gmail.com) leads treks in the Pyin Oo Lwin area. All-inclusive fees range from $25 to $40 per person per day.

ACCOMMODATION

8

Bravo Mandalay–Lashio Rd ☎ 085 21223, ✉ bravo hotel.pol@gmail.com. Although some of the rooms are a little shabby around the edges at this centrally located hotel, all of them are clean and neat, and the staff are friendly. Singles from $20. **$30**

Golden Dream Hotel 64 Mandalay–Lashio Rd ☎ 085 21302, ✉ goldendreamhotel@gmail.com. This is still the cheapest place in Pyin Oo Lwin, with single rooms with fans and shared bathrooms from $5, and $24 doubles with a/c, bathtubs and TVs. Breakfast is only included for the better rooms; if you stay in the cheapest ones, you'll need to pay $1 extra. Not much English is spoken, but the receptionist is friendly. Single guests pay half in the double rooms. **$14**

Grace Hotel I 114 Nan Myaing Rd ☎ 085 21230. The only budget hotel in the leafy suburbs, *Grace I* is set in spacious grounds and offers basic, fan-cooled two- to four-bed en suites for $10 per person, or $15 for single guests. There's plenty of outdoor space for lounging in the sun. Bike rental is K3000/day, motorbike rental K10,000. **$20**

Hotel Pyin Oo Lwin 9 Nanda Rd ☎ 085 21226, ⓦ hotelpyinoolwin.com. Not far from the Kandawgyi Gardens, this luxurious hotel opened in 2011. The 36 rooms and suites, spread between 18 bungalows on a gentle slope, are beautiful and spacious, with dark wood panelling and private verandas, and the service is impeccable

– though the large pool is unheated. Prices fall sharply out of season. **$150**

Kandawgyi Hill Resort Nanda Rd ☎ 085 21839, ⓦ myanmartreasureresorts.com. Housed in a historic brick mansion and five newer bungalows, just above sweeping lawns overlooking Kandawgyi Lake, this is one of the few genuine colonial-house hotels in operation. The reception area is unimpressive, but the rooms are well appointed, especially in the main house. **$75**

Royal Green Hotel 17 Ziwaka St ☎ 085 28411, ✉ royalgreenhotel.pol@gmail.com. The comfortable standard rooms with satellite TVs are good value in expensive Pyin Oo Lwin. For $45, you can have a room with a balcony and bathtub, while the $55 corner rooms are beautiful and airy. Try to get a room upstairs. **$35**

Royal Parkview 107 Lanthaya St ☎ 085 22641, ✉ royalparkview107@gmail.com. In a quiet spot 2km southeast of the centre, this hotel's rooms are tastefully decorated with parquet floors. The cheapest, based in bungalows in front of the main building, are a little dark, but the $50 rooms behind reception are spacious, comfortable and pleasant. Some are set alongside the path with their own semi-private gardens (though staff sometimes walk along the fence in the mornings), and others are in a block with views over the parkland behind the hotel. All rooms have a/c. **$35**

EATING

Club Terrace 25 Club Rd ☎ 085 23311. In a red-brick building set back from the road near the golf club, this

restaurant has a pretty patio and polished service. There's Thai and Chinese food (most dishes around

THE MANDALAY–LASHIO RAILWAY

The 280km railway between Mandalay and Lashio took eight years to complete, thanks to a series of major geographical challenges en route. First, between Mandalay and Pyin Oo Lwin, it relies on a series of zigzags and reverses to climb a steep escarpment onto the Shan Plateau. More dramatically, near Nawnghkio the single strand of track soars 102m above the Dokhtawady River on the famous **Gokteik Viaduct**.

Still Myanmar's highest bridge today, the viaduct was completed in 1901, built by a US contractor using parts cast by the Pennsylvania Steel Company and shipped from the United States. The viaduct has been regularly renovated, but trains still cross at a crawl – leaving those unafraid of heights with plenty of time to lean out of the windows and enjoy the view.

Gokteik Station is on the Mandalay side of the viaduct. If you wish to cross the bridge and catch the train back to Mandalay in a single day, you'll need a ticket to Nawngpeng, fifty minutes beyond Gokteik Station, where the train arrives around noon. The train back departs at 12.30pm – in theory, at least.

K5000), and a few Burmese and Western options are also available. Make sure you try the excellent local coffee. Daily 10am–10pm.

December Mandalay–Lashio Rd ☎ 085 21053. This small local chain started life as a rest stop on the Mandalay–Lashio Road, serving fresh juice (from K1000), yoghurt (K800) and ice cream (from K800; elaborate sundaes from K1800) to passing travellers. While there are now two small additional branches near the Central Market, the original roadside store is set on a large site with a petting zoo and strawberry fields. You can ride horses around the estate, and in season pick your own strawberries and have them turned into milkshake in front of your eyes. Turn off when you see a black-and-white cut-out cow beside the road. Daily 7am–9pm.

Krishna South Indian Restaurant Gurkha Rd. Of the many Indian restaurants in town that seem to have been set up in someone's front room, *Krishna* has among the best and the most authentically Indian food. A meal with curry and chapati will set you back K3000. Vegetarian options available. Daily 10am–9.30pm.

Lake Front Feel Off Nanda Rd ☎ 085 22083. The kitchen here copes well with the restaurant's ridiculously extensive menus (plural), which cover everything from sushi to hamburgers and hotpots, and there's a good range of cakes, too. The pretty lakeside deck is popular with visitors and locals alike. Fried rice from K3000. There's another *Feel* near the Golf Club, but the lake makes this one extra special. Daily 9.30am–9pm.

Pan Taw Win Nanda Rd ☎ 09 853 0186. Just down the road from *The Taj*, this is the place to drink locally grown coffee (from K1200). The polite, professional staff here also serve cocktails (from K2500) and Korean, Thai, Japanese and local cuisine. A typical dish is around K5000. Coffee beans are also on sale. Daily 7am–10pm.

★**The Taj** 26 Nanda Rd ☎ 09 784 049 880. This is the best Indian restaurant in town, and probably the best restaurant of any sort in Pyin Oo Lwin, under the same management as *Hotel Pyin Oo Lwin*. This large lakeside hall, with picture windows and tables neatly divided by screens, offers meticulously prepared and presented dishes served by well-trained, English-speaking staff. A full meal with dessert and drink will cost around K12,000. Daily 10am–10pm.

DRINKING AND NIGHTLIFE

Very few places in Pyin Oo Lwin stay open after 10pm. The places listed here are restaurants that close later than most and offer a good selection of drinks – there's no need to eat if you don't want to.

VIP Bistro Forest Rd and Kan Thar Yar St ☎ 09 797 355 777, ⓦ facebook.com/viphouserestaurant. Between Candacraig and Circular Rd you'll see a roadside sign for this cocktail bar and restaurant in the grounds of a white colonial house. Cocktails cost from K2500, and there's another branch out of town on the Lashio Rd. Daily 6.30am–10pm.

Woodland 53 Circular Rd ☎ 085 22713, ⓦ woodlandtk .com. This is the closest Pyin Oo Lwin gets to nightlife, with a blue-lit, open-air cocktail bar and a good restaurant with European, Thai, Chinese and local food. Cocktails start from K3500, and on the menu you can expect to see usual suspects like the "Blue Hawaiian" as well as more imaginative options like the "Human Brain". Daily 10am–11pm.

SHOPPING

Gandamar Land Tribal Handicrafts Zaygyi St ☎ 09 4315 2931. Set in the outside of the central market building, this antique and curio shop sells colonial relics and vintage goods such as traditional costumes. Daily 8am–6.30pm.

La Vie Art Gallery Central Market, just around the corner from Gandamar Land ☏09 402 628 735, ✉friendly.mi@gmail.com. This gallery, open since 1984, displays works by award-winning local artist Muu Muu. Prices range from $50 to $700; his ink on mulberry paper drawings of the views of Pyin Oo Lwin make extravagant souvenirs. Occasionally flexible hours. Daily 9am–5pm.

Liqueur Corner Zaygyi St. There's no shortage of shops selling local fruit wines – this one is centrally located and has a well-presented selection. Daily 8.30am–8pm.

Pacific World Curios Off Mandalay–Lashio Rd. Owned by the manager of the *Bravo* hotel just around the corner, this well-signposted shop sells mostly Palaung and Shan artefacts. Daily 9am–7pm.

Purcell Tower Gift Shop Under the Purcell Tower ✉purcelltowersouvenirs@gmail.com. If you absolutely must have an "I heart Pyin Oo Lwin" keyring, this tiny shop is your best bet. The shop next door with sewing machines on display is also useful if you need to get your bag fixed. Daily 9am–6pm.

DIRECTORY

Banks Most banks have ATMs and exchange facilities, including KBZ Bank, opposite the Purcell Tower, and CB Bank, further down Mandalay–Lashio Rd.

Golf Once the site of a colonial-era polo field, the eighteen-hole Pyin Oo Lwin Golf Club on Sanda Rd (daily 6am–6pm; ☏085 22382) is one of Myanmar's more popular courses – perhaps because the ball flies further at this altitude. No jeans or T-shirts allowed. Green fees $10, caddy $5, club and shoe rental also available.

Internet Access costs K400/hr at Green on Zaygyi St (daily 8am–8pm), directly across from the Purcell Tower, and K300/hr at Friends Net Game & Internet near the Central Market (daily 24hr; ☏09 4319 5387).

Kyaukme and around

ကျောက်မဲမြို့

8

A major tea- and gem-dealing town for many years, **KYAUKME** is today a relatively wealthy little place. The government selected it to be the local administrative centre in preference to nearby Hsipaw, and as a result it's grown both larger and livelier. The surrounding countryside where the tea is grown sees far fewer foreigners than Hsipaw, and offers plenty of opportunities to trek and ride motorbikes to secluded

HIKING AROUND KYAUKME

Although Hsipaw is better known, Kyaukme is the more rewarding centre for **treks** and **motorbike tours**. Far less busy and with some quite exceptional local guides, the area offers the chance to see unspoiled Shan and Palaung villages set amid beautiful landscapes, whose friendly inhabitants are as interested as you to encounter another culture. On top of this, there are hot springs, temples and even a ruined hilltop palace. Treks can last one day or up to a week or more, and the pace will be adjusted to suit – typically you might be walking four to five hours a day to cover around 15km.

Keep in mind that conflict occasionally breaks out in the area, so if you want to go off the beaten track it's strongly recommended that you take a **local guide**, who will have up-to-the-minute information and will know where it's safe to go. Kyaukme guides charge a sliding scale depending on the size of the group. For two people, a typical guide would charge around K30,000 per person per day, all-inclusive. Motorbike tours cost K13,000 extra for each bike on the trip, including the guide's.

LOCAL GUIDES

Naing Naing ☏09 4730 7622, ✉naingninenine @gmail.com. An ethnic Palaung who speaks excellent self-taught English, Naing Naing takes groups on adventurous treks deep into the hills. His daughter, Han Ni Soe, also works as a guide and speaks fluent English.

Sai Kyaw Hlaing ☏09 403 706 076, ✉shanprinces .webs.com. This young English graduate, who goes by the English name Joy, has been a guide in Kyaukme for ten years. He works with a group of friends who all speak preposterously good English. Joy's speciality is motorbike tours – he'll take you on the back of his bike or rent you a bike to ride, and his colleagues also lead walking treks. Joy's website is worth checking out even if you're just passing through Kyaukme.

Palaung villages, where you can stay overnight in a bamboo house. You can also make the short trip to the picturesque ruin of **Sakandar**, which was the summer palace of the *saopha* of Hsipaw, until it was damaged during World War II and eventually destroyed by the government, who were fearful it would become a symbol of Shan autonomy.

Kyaukme was an established tea-dealing centre well before the arrival of the British in the 1890s (see box, p.324), and today the tea warehouses are concentrated in a block southeast of the railway station. The area beyond is dotted with characterful old buildings, while the **central market** between Pinlon Street and Aung San Road attracts a mix of Shan, Bamar and Palaung customers.

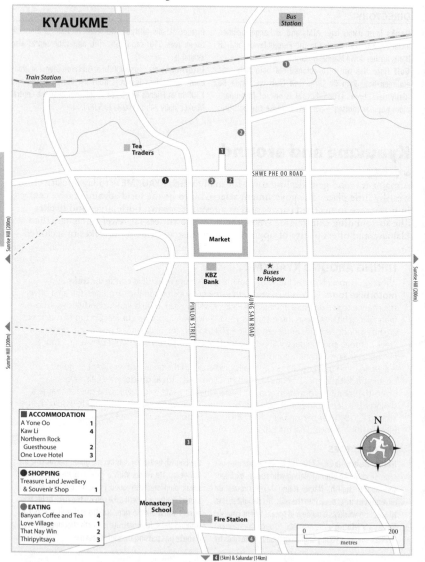

KYAUKME

Bus Station

Train Station

Tea Traders

SHWE PHE OO ROAD

Market

KBZ Bank

★ Buses to Hsipaw

Sunrise Hill (200m)

Sunrise Hill (200m)

Sunrise Hill (200m)

PINLON STREET

AUNG SAN ROAD

■ ACCOMMODATION
A Yone Oo	1
Kaw Li	4
Northern Rock Guesthouse	2
One Love Hotel	3

● SHOPPING
| Treasure Land Jewellery & Souvenir Shop | 1 |

● EATING
Banyan Coffee and Tea	4
Love Village	1
That Nay Win	2
Thiripyitsaya	3

Monastery School

Fire Station

N

0 — 200
metres

4 (5km) & Sakandar (14km)

8

Kyaukme is flanked to the east and west by pagoda-topped hills. In the west, **Sunrise Hill** can be climbed via covered staircases leading from the town, and holds a small monastery set around the Loi Kaun pagoda, while **Sunset Hill** on the east side of town has excellent open views.

ARRIVAL AND DEPARTURE

KYAUKME

By bus Buses to most destinations leave from the bus station on Aung San Rd, just north of the railway line. Hsipaw-bound buses leave from the southwest corner of the central market each morning at 7am, and a few buses to Lashio leave from here as well. Your hotel can help book tickets, as can the friendly Kyaw Swar – also known as "Mr Ticket" – who works at the bus station (☏ 09 403 719 692).

Destinations Hsipaw (6 daily; 1hr); Kalaw (2 daily; 12hr);

Lashio (3 daily; 3hr); Mandalay (daily; 5hr); Pyin Oo Lwin (6 daily; 3hr); Yangon (daily; 13hr).

By train Kyaukme's railway station is slightly northwest of the town centre, about a 10min walk from *Northern Rock Guesthouse* (see below). There's a popular teahouse in the station, which is handy if your train is running late.

Destinations Hsipaw (daily; 1hr 30min); Lashio (daily; 7hr); Mandalay (daily; 11hr); Pyin Oo Lwin (daily; 5hr).

GETTING AROUND

By motorbike Motorbikes can be rented from *One Love Hotel* for K10,000/day or K5000/half day, and from Joy (☏ 09 403 706 076), who charges K10,000/day for scooters and K15,000/day for dirt bikes

– he'll also deliver them to your hotel.

By bike Bikes can be rented from *Northern Rock Guesthouse* for K2000 if you're staying there – though it's still worth asking if you're not.

ACCOMMODATION

A Yone Oo Shwe Phe Oo Rd ☏ 082 40669. Until 2015, this hotel – owned by a well-connected local tea trader – was the only option for foreigners. There's a wide variety of basic rooms arranged around a large courtyard, with prices for doubles ranging from $18 (fan, shared bath) to $32 (a/c, en-suite bathroom). If you can, opt for one of the rooms in the 1940s building out front. Larger rooms are also available, for up to five people, and there are also some spartan, cell-like rooms – though you probably won't even be offered them. **$18**

Kaw Li Lashio–Mandalay Rd ☏ 09 9724 5100. This ambitious hotel is the brainchild of Nelson, the owner of *A Yone Oo*, and it's based a few kilometres along the road to Mandalay. On site there's a large dining hall, a swimming pool and a spa/beauty salon/foot massage parlour, overlooked by a terrace bar, and rooms come in all shapes and sizes – right up to a monstrous $150 suite overlooking farmland. However, the whole thing seems cheaply constructed – and although it's not quite finished, it's already starting to crumble. The owner's collection of worldly goods

(including, bizarrely, a German Iron Cross) is displayed in a cabinet in reception. **$18**

Northern Rock Guesthouse 4/52 Shwe Phe Oo Rd ☏ 082 40660, ✉ northernrock.kme@gmail.com. Run by the friendly family of Dr Khin Mg Nyo (who also runs a small clinic here when he's in town), this rambling wooden house has small partitioned rooms with fans and basic shared bathrooms from $6 per person, as well as two rooms with a/c and en-suite bathrooms in a newer building behind (from $20). Bikes for rent at K2000, or free if you're staying in the better rooms. Their hand-drawn photocopied map is crammed with detail. Breakfast K3000. **$12**

★ **One Love Hotel** 1/139 Pinlon St ☏ 082 40943, ✉ one lovehotel.kme@gmail.com. This clean, modern building is already the best hotel in town, and the new block that's almost complete behind it is slated to be even better. Twin rooms have balconies, and doubles don't but are a bit larger. Family rooms sleep three and have bathtubs. All rooms have en-suite bathrooms and a/c, TVs and fridges. The receptionist speaks good English. Motorbikes can be rented for K10,000/day or K5000/half day. **$30**

EATING

During the day, stalls inside the **covered market** serve *moun-di* and *mi-shay* noodles. If this doesn't appeal, there are also several restaurants on the street one block south.

Banyan Coffee and Tea 2/418 Aung San Rd ☏ 09 960 615 962. Run by David, an expat Texan, this little coffee shop is building a strong local fanbase with its tea, coffee (from K2000) and Western food – doughnuts, pancakes, burgers and a K3500 American breakfast. This is also a good

place to ask for local advice. Mon–Sat 7am–7pm.

Love Village Head north up Aung San Rd and turn right after the stream. This little place serves good authentic Shan food, including some pretty exotic things – though you may have to point to order. Try the

8

hot-and-sour mushroom soup for K1000. If you can't find it, look for the bamboo building with open-air seating under a corrugated-iron roof. Daily 11am–5pm.

That Nay Win Aung San Rd. Also known as "Chapati Place", this Indian restaurant serves only three things – and it does a roaring trade. The chapati and curry sauce (K300) and fried rice (K700) are both good, but best of all is the milk tea with a touch of ginger (K300). Chapati Place is open later than anywhere else in town. Daily 6–11pm.

Thiripyitsaya 4/54 Shwe Phe Oo Rd ☎082 40340. Opposite *A Yone Oo*, this little place has an English-speaking owner and an English menu, and serves simple food like omelettes, toast, juices and Shan noodles (K500–K1000). Daily 7am–9pm.

SHOPPING

Treasure Land Jewellery & Souvenir Shop 5/26 Shwe Phe Oo Rd ☎09 5824 0190, ✉phyusinwin @gmail.com. One block west of *Northern Rock Guesthouse*, this place sells local souvenirs and simple jewellery. If you're looking for something more serious, the friendly owner also sets and sells rubies and sapphires from nearby Mogok, along with Indian diamonds and other precious stones. She's happy to show you her work and talk about the gems, even if you don't want to buy. Best to call ahead.

DIRECTORY

Bank KBZ Bank on the south side of the market has an ATM and offers currency exchange.

Hsipaw and around

သီပေါမြို့

8

HSIPAW (sometimes called Thibaw) is the former seat of an independent Shan state. Today, the small, dusty town has an attractive air of tranquillity – venerable tamarind and rain trees line the main street, the **Dokhtawady** (or Namtu) River flows languidly to the east and the nearby hills conceal thatch-roofed Palaung and Lisu villages. Add to this a good range of accommodation and some excellent cafés, and it's unsurprising that Hsipaw is a popular base for trekking into the surrounding countryside (see box, p.327).

The town rewards detailed exploration, with a candle-lit **morning market** near the river and small workshops around town, where it's possible to watch tea being sorted and cheroots being rolled. The most interesting sights, including the crumbling pagodas of Little Bagan, the shrine to Hsipaw's local *nat*, and the former palace, all lie on the outskirts of town, a short bike ride away.

Brief history

The Shan *saophas*, or "sky lords", of Hsipaw were among the most powerful leaders in the Shan States, thanks to Hsipaw's strategic location at the edge of the Shan Plateau, above the Bamar-dominated lowlands. In 1886, **Sao Hkun Hseng** was among the first

---

PLATE OF TEA, VICAR?

Northern Shan State is one of the original homes of the tea plant, **Camellia sinensis**, which originated somewhere in the hills that range between northeast India, northern Myanmar and southwest China. When the British first surveyed the Shan States in the nineteenth century, Palaung and Shan villagers had already been cultivating tea for centuries. In 1855, Burmese officials told a visiting British delegation that the idea that the Chinese grew their own tea was "preposterous", so great was their neighbour's demand for Burmese exports.

Tawngpeng, a largely Palaung district that surrounds the (currently off-limits) hill town of Namhsan, is Myanmar's main tea-growing region, with much of the harvest being reserved for the production of **lahpet** (fermented tea leaves). The fresh leaves are lightly steamed and then packed into lengths of bamboo, buried and left to ferment for up to a year, before they're ready to be eaten as **lahpet thouq** (tea-leaf salad), which is served as a snack everywhere from Yangon's *Strand Hotel* to the hawkers on Myanmar's trains.

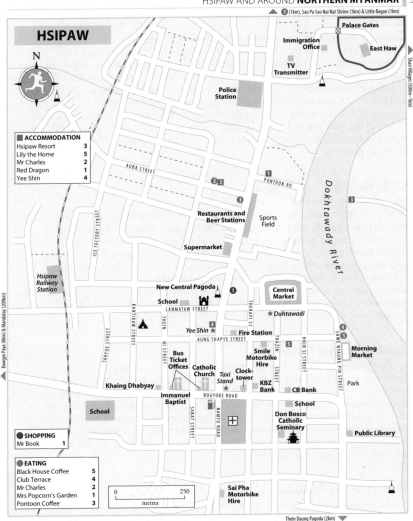

HSIPAW

N

(1km), Sao Pu Sao Nai Nat Shrine (1km) & Little Bagan (1km)

Palace Gates

Immigration Office

East Haw

TV Transmitter

Shan Villages (500m–1km)

Police Station

AUBA STREET

PONTOON RD

ICE FACTORY STREET

Dokhtawady River

ACCOMMODATION
Hsipaw Resort	3
Lily the Home	5
Mr Charles	2
Red Dragon	1
Yee Shin	4

Restaurants and Beer Stations

Sports Field

Supermarket

Hsipaw Railway Station

Bawgyo Paya (8km) & Mandalay (200km)

New Central Pagoda

School

LANMATAW STREET

Central Market

KANTIKAW STREET

THEIN STREET

NI STREET

TARYOE STREET

★Duhtawadi

Yee Shin ★

Fire Station

AUNG THAPYE STREET

THERAPI ST

Bus Ticket Offices

Catholic Church

Taxi Stand

Clock-tower

Smile Motorbike Hire

KBZ Bank

THAZIN STREET

HNIN SI STREET

SHWE NYAUNG PIN STREET

Morning Market

Park

Khaing Dhabyay

Immanuel Baptist

BOGYOKE ROAD

NAMTU ROAD

CB Bank

School

School

SABAT STREET

Don Bosco Catholic Seminary

Public Library

SHOPPING
| Mr Book | 1 |

EATING
Black House Coffee	5
Club Terrace	4
Mr Charles	2
Mrs Popcorn's Garden	1
Pontoon Coffee	3

0   250
metres

Sai Pha Motorbike Hire

Thein Daung Pagoda (2km)

8

Shan *saophas* to submit to British rule, and the first to meet Queen Victoria. His English-educated son, Sao Hke (later **Sir Sao Hke**), took forty wives and ruled from a jewel-encrusted throne in his magnificent court at Sakandar, which now lies in ruins outside Kyaukme (see p.322).

The most well-known of Hsipaw's *saophas*, however, was **Sao Kya Seng**, who ruled Hsipaw with his Austrian *mahadevi*, Inge Sargent, from 1954. Hsipaw flourished under their command, until Sao Kya Seng disappeared in 1962 on his way home from a political conference in the immediate aftermath of Ne Win's coup. Save for two letters smuggled to his wife from a military camp near Taunggyi, Hsipaw's last *saopha* was never heard from again, and the authorities never acknowledged his death – a story told in Inge Sargent's book *Twilight over Burma*, written after she and the couple's two daughters had left Burma for the US. Kya Seng and Inge's enthronement portrait can be seen around Hsipaw today, a testament to their lasting popularity.

East Haw

သီပေါဟော် • 1km northeast of the town centre • Daily 3–5pm • Free (voluntary donation)

While Sakandar, the Neoclassical summer palace of the Hsipaw *saophas*, was abandoned after it was damaged in World War II, the 1924 **East Haw** still stands, and it was here that Sao Kya Seng and Inge Sargent lived in the 1950s (see p.325). Today, the last *saopha*'s niece (who uses the English name Fern) opens the palace gates and receives visitors each afternoon in what used to be the throne room. Herself a princess by birth, she refuses to charge an entrance fee, and does what she can to maintain the building and grounds while hoping to regain contact with Sao Kya Seng's family in exile. It's a rare opportunity to hear first-hand stories of Hsipaw's colourful recent history.

Little Bagan

500m west of Namtu Rd, 1.5km northwest of Hsipaw • Free

Northwest of Hsipaw, a handful of crumbling and overgrown brick pagodas has earned this area the jokingly overblown name of **Little Bagan**. While it may be a fraction of its namesake's size, it's still an appealing place to explore. At the eastern extremity is **Kotaun Kyaung**, which is marked by a dramatically cracked pagoda with a tree sprouting from its crown. As you continue to make your way along, you'll pass **Madhaya Shwe Kyaung** and **Maha Nanda Kantha Kyaung**, a pair of 150-year-old teak monasteries that flank the road – the latter in particular is worth seeing for its Buddha figure woven from bamboo and covered with gold leaf. A few further groups of pagodas lie northwest of here.

Sao Pu Sao Nai Nat Shrine

ဘိုးဘိုးကြီးနတ်နန်း• 100m west of Namtu Rd, 1.5km north of Hsipaw • Daily dawn–dusk • Free

Between Namtu Road and Little Bagan is **Sao Pu Sao Nai Nat Shrine**, filled with picturesque statues of animals and dedicated to Hsipaw's guardian *nat*, Tong Sunt Bo Bo Gyi, whose effigy stands in the main hall. The compound is also home to several smaller pavilions furnished with miniature beds, covered with pink satin sheets – the last word in *nat* hospitality. Towards the rear of the complex, a green-canopied shrine holds two swings; local people push the (empty) swings to please the female *nat* depicted behind and gain her blessing.

Thein Daung Pagoda

သိမ်တောင်ဘုရား• 2.5km south of Hsipaw • Daily dawn–dusk • Free

Also known as Sunset Pagoda, **Thein Daung Pagoda** offers views over Hsipaw and the hills that bracket the town. To get here, head south along the Mandalay–Lashio Road and cross the Dokhtawady River. Just beyond the bridge, there's a decorative gateway by the roadside – the pagoda is a thirty-minute walk uphill.

Bawgyo Paya

ဘော်ကြိုဘုရား• 9km west of Hsipaw • Daily dawn–dusk • Free

A twenty-minute drive west of Hsipaw, **Bawgyo Paya**'s strikingly tiered central shrine contains four wooden Buddha statues, believed to date from the thirteenth century when they were carved from a piece of wood given to King Narapatisithu by an immortal. The leftovers were buried in the temple complex, where they miraculously took root, growing into a tree that still thrives today. The Buddha images are shown publicly once a year, during a festival that takes place around the Tabaung (February or March) full moon.

HIKING AROUND HSIPAW

Trekking is firmly established in Hsipaw; almost every hotel or guesthouse has English-speaking guides on hand (*Mr Charles* has over 20; see p.328). Some agencies produce brochures listing ten or eleven itineraries, ranging from a half-day boat trip with an hour-long walk to a mountain monastery, up to strenuous treks of three or more nights. That said, guides are always willing to adapt to your timetable and interests.

ROUTES

A popular hike from Hsipaw is the five-hour trip to **Pan Kam** village, where it's possible to stay overnight. The trail starts at the Muslim cemetery on the western edge of Hsipaw, and soon passes a hot spring and winds uphill through farming villages and fields. While Pan Kam can feel a little touristy at times, it's also possible to stay in **Htan Sant**, which is just an hour and fifteen minutes further along the picturesque mountain paths. The standard route involves taking the left-hand path at a fork just after you leave Pan Kam, but the longer right-hand path has exceptional views of the valley. The following day, you can retrace your steps or choose between several routes further into the mountains. One leads to **Sar Maw** village and thence to Bawgyo Paya (see p.326), from where it's 8km back to Hsipaw; your guide can call a motorbike from Hsipaw to pick you up. Another route passes through **Man Loi** village, from where you can again branch off to the Mandalay–Lashio Rd, or continue towards Kyaukme. Bear in mind, though, that Hsipaw guides may not be *au fait* with the Kyaukme security situation (or vice versa).

PRACTICALITIES

Although it's usually peaceful around Hsipaw, skirmishes do occasionally break out between Shan and Palaung militias, so it's not advisable to set off into the mountains without a **guide**, or at least without getting up-to-the-minute information before you go. The local guides have well-established lines of communication, both with the villages and with the militias themselves.

   Prices are fairly standard among Hsipaw guides, and vary mainly with the size of your group – a couple might pay K20,000 each per day, while in a group of four or more you may only need K15,000. This will usually include food and accommodation. You can find a guide through your hotel, or go direct by contacting either Kham Lu (☎09 250 693 985, ✉kyawmoonoo @gmail.com) or Than Htike (☎09 3618 6646, ✉lionmanhpw@gmail.com).

8

ARRIVAL AND DEPARTURE

HSIPAW AND AROUND

By bus There is no bus station in Hsipaw, but buses and minibuses depart from restaurants and guesthouses that double as ticket offices, including *Yee Shin* guesthouse, *Duhtawadi Café* on Lanmataw St and *Khaing Dhabyay* on Bogyoke Rd.
Destinations Kyaukme (6 daily; 1hr); Lashio (3 daily; 2hr); Mandalay (6 daily; 6hr); Monywa (daily; 11hr); Naypyitaw (3 daily; 12hr); Nyaungshwe (for Inle Lake, 3 daily; 15hr); Pyin Oo Lwin (6 daily; 4hr); Yangon (3 daily; 16hr).
By shared taxi Shared taxis east to Lashio (2hr; K6000/person) and west to Kyaukme (1hr), Pyin Oo Lwin (3hr 30min) and Mandalay (5hr 30min) depart Hsipaw around 6–7am. Westbound you will pay the same fare (K15,000)

regardless of your destination. Book a seat through your accommodation or through *Khaing Dhabyay* on Bogyoke Rd.
By train Hsipaw's railway station is west of the town centre, 500m west of Namtu Rd. There's one train in each direction each day, and tickets only go on sale 30min before each train arrives. If you are heading for Mandalay, you can knock 3hr off the journey by getting off the train in Pyin Oo Lwin and taking a bus or shared taxi (K7000) for the remaining distance.
Destinations Lashio (daily; 4hr 20min); Kyaukme (daily; 1hr 25min); Pyin Oo Lwin (daily; 6hr 25min); Mandalay (daily; 13hr).

GETTING AROUND

By tuk-tuk A short journey around town ought to cost no more than K1000.
By bicycle Most of Hsipaw's sights are within easy cycling distance of the town centre. Bikes are available to rent from most hotels for K2000/day.
By motorbike Since a couple of tourists were involved in

minor accidents, the local government discourages guesthouses from renting motorbikes to foreigners. However, it's still possible to find them in a couple of places: try *Smile* (no English sign, but lots of motorbikes) just up the road from *Lily the Home*, or Sai Pha a bit further out of town at the southern end of Namtu Rd (both daily 7am–7pm; K8000/day).

ACCOMMODATION

Hsipaw Resort 29/30 Myohaung Village ☎082 80721, ⓦhsipawresort.com. Hsipaw's most upmarket hotel offers 28 classy rooms in pretty bungalows with wonderfully comfortable beds. Each room has a terrace with a bench looking over the gardens to the river. Based on the opposite bank of the Dokhtawady River from the town, next to a small agricultural village, the hotel operates a free boat service and also has a good restaurant. While the wi-fi is good in the reception, it's much weaker in the rooms. $90

Lily the Home 108 Aung Thapye St ☎082 80318, ⓦlilythehome.com. This family-run hotel's new block has a range of comfortable en-suite rooms starting at $30 (some with balconies), as well as a top-floor terrace for breakfast. Behind, the two-storey older building has cheaper rooms, though they're rather dark on the ground floor. Another building has "backpacker" rooms with shared bathrooms, which sell out quickly at $8/person. There's a computer in the reception for guests to use. Bikes can be rented for K2000/day, and treks can be arranged. $20

Mr Charles 105 Auba St ☎082 80105, ⓦmrcharles hotel.com. The most established accommodation option in town, *Mr Charles* is divided into two sections: on the right, a pleasant but cramped wooden guesthouse has a range of dorms from $7 (some with a/c) as well as some $16 twin rooms with shared facilities; and on the left there's a hotel with en-suite rooms with a/c from $22 (or $18 if you're on your own). In the guesthouse, the wi-fi doesn't extend beyond the reception area. $16

Red Dragon Mahaw Gani St ☎082 80740, ⓔreddragonhotel.hsipaw@gmail.com. This newly built block stands above the surrounding buildings, just north of the town centre. One of the best-value places in Hsipaw, especially for single guests, its high-ceilinged rooms are perhaps a little impersonal and there are odd quirks like bolts on the outside of the rooms. That said, the hot water is reliable and you get a lot of space for your money. The $20 standard rooms face the street and the $24 superiors have river views, and both come with a/c and en-suite bathrooms. Single travellers pay half, except in the cheapest rooms where they pay $7. $12

Yee Shin Namtu Rd ☎082 80711, ⓔyee.shin2012 @gmail.com. This small, central guesthouse has fourteen tiny rooms, ranging from $6 singles with fans and shared bathrooms to $20 en-suite doubles with a/c. The cheaper rooms are divided with plywood partitions. $12

EATING

North of the bridge, Namtu Road is lined with inexpensive teahouses and small restaurants.

★**Black House Coffee** Shwe Nyaung Pin St. You can relax in the reclining chairs on the peaceful riverside terrace at *Black House Coffee*, based in an old wooden house and owned by a friendly Shan family. Hot drinks including coffee start from K1000, and cake costs around K700. Daily 7am–6pm.

Club Terrace 35 Shwe Nyaung Pin St ☎09 4924 2416. With something of the understated style of its namesake in Pyin Oo Lwin, this restaurant has a pretty wooden deck overlooking the river and a menu that covers the usual bases – Thai, Chinese and Burmese. It's pricier than most other restaurants in Hsipaw (K2500 for a bottle of Myanmar Beer, K3500 for meat and fish dishes), but the food, service and environment all make it worth visiting. Daily 10am–10pm.

Mr Charles 105 Auba St ☎082 80105. The dining room at *Mr Charles* serves a range of Asian dishes, along with a few Western favourites like burgers starting from around K3000. The delicious Shan set menu, K20,000 for 2–4 diners, needs to be ordered in advance. Daily noon–9pm.

Mrs Popcorn's Garden Near Little Bagan ☎09 402 664 925. In a lovely garden on the road between Little Bagan and the *nat* shrine, the cheerful Mrs Popcorn and her daughter serve locally grown tea and coffee, plus simple snacks – no popcorn, though. This is the perfect place to spend the afternoon lazing in the sun. Cooked meals are available if you order in advance. Daily 9am–dusk.

Pontoon Coffee Namtu Rd. Run by an Australian expat called Maureen, this café has moved from the riverside and now occupies an airy two-storey building on a quiet corner of the main road. Serves coffee (from K1500) and a small range of snacks like pancakes, sandwiches and guacamole. Daily 9am–9pm.

SHOPPING

Mr Book Namtu Rd. The kindly Ko Zaw Tin, aka "Mr Book", runs a small bookshop from a dusty shack on Namtu Rd, which has an interesting selection of English books on sale. He's also involved with several charitable projects and often donates school supplies and funds to village schools near Hsipaw – donations of any kind are gratefully received. Daily 6am–9pm.

DIRECTORY

Banks Hsipaw's banks are clustered around the clocktower on Bogyoke Rd, with branches of KBZ Bank and CB Bank offering currency exchange and ATMs.

Lashio

လားရှိုးမြို့

The last major town before the Chinese border, **LASHIO** sprawls over a series of hillsides 170km south of the Muse–Ruili border crossing (see box, p.331) and has a large Chinese population. The town itself has repeatedly risen from its own ashes like an ungainly phoenix, most recently after a 1988 fire ripped through many of its old wooden houses. Formerly the seat of a Shan *saopha*, Lashio is today an important regional hub, sitting between the **Burma Road** (see box, p.330) leading east, and the Mandalay–Lashio railway heading west.

There's little reason to visit Lashio unless you're heading on to Hsipaw or to China (though the border was closed at the time of research; see box, p.331). If you find yourself here, you'll still find plenty to keep you occupied, with a few temples and several thronging markets to explore.

The markets and around

The closest thing to a town centre in Lashio is the area around the covered **Myoma Market** between Lanmadaw Street and Thukha Road. A morning **vegetable market** spreads out before dawn along Bogyoke Road (sadly no longer lit by candles), before the action moves inside around 7am. To end the day, a lively **night market** sets up each evening along Bogyoke and Thiri roads, selling food and Chinese clothes. Just next to all the market action is Lashio's pretty central mosque, which was rebuilt after its predecessor was torched during anti-Muslim riots in May 2013.

8

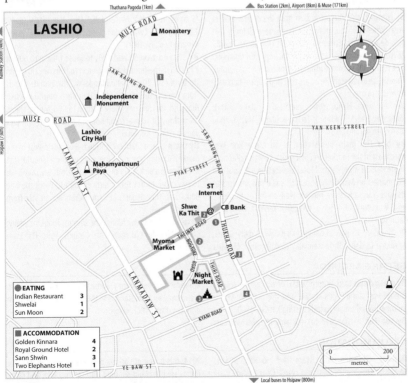

THE BURMA ROAD

In November 1937, when the Japanese Imperial Army took control of Shanghai after a savage three-month battle, China lost its largest port and the last obstacle between the Japanese forces and the Chinese capital, Nanjing. The government scrambled to relocate to a provisional capital in Chongqing, deep in the interior, and alternative supply routes were urgently needed. As a result, work began on the **Burma Road**, linking the Chinese city of Kunming to the Burmese railhead at Lashio.

A rough, cobbled track that crossed countless jungle-covered hills and the Mekong and Salween rivers, built by an estimated 200,000 Burmese and Chinese labourers, the road was 1150km long at its completion in 1939. This vital supply route functioned for just three years until the Japanese overran Lashio in April 1942 and closed the road. After months of airlifting supplies from Assam to Kunming – over the infamous "Hump" at the eastern end of the Himalayas – the Allies began construction of an arduous alternative route, the **Ledo Road** between Ledo in Assam and Kunming, which finished construction early in 1945, just months before the Japanese surrender.

Thathana Pagoda

သာသနာ ၂၅၀၀ ဘုရား • Thathana Pagoda Hill, off the Mandalay–Muse road, 2km north of the market

A gilded octagonal pagoda, **Thathana Pagoda** sits on a ridge surrounded by wooded slopes offering views over Lashio to the rounded hills beyond. The most interesting way to reach it is along a steep staircase that leads from the Muse road uphill to an unusual monument on stilts, before turning north to the pagoda.

8

ARRIVAL AND DEPARTURE   LASHIO

By plane Lashio Airport is 8km from the central market area. When arriving, note that baggage reclaim is just outside the gates. Shwe Ka Thit at 34 Theinni Rd (☎082 25702), immediately to the left of the *Royal Ground* hotel (see p.331), offers competitive ticket prices and has helpful, English-speaking staff. Be aware that flight prices fluctuate from day to day.
Destinations Heho (for Inle Lake; daily; 1hr); Mandalay (weekly; 45min); Tachileik (daily; 1hr); Yangon (daily; 1hr 45min).

By bus The main bus station is on Muse Rd, 3km northeast of the market and just south of Mansu Pagoda. There's also a more central local bus station just south of the market on Mandalay St, which has a few services to Hsipaw. Foreigners are not allowed on buses to Muse, and you may also have difficulty buying tickets to Taunggyi.
Destinations Hsipaw (3 daily; 2hr); Kalaw (3 daily; 15hr); Kyaukme (3 daily; 3hr); Mandalay (3 daily; 9hr); Meiktila

(5 daily; 10–11hr); Muse (daily; 4hr); Naypyitaw (daily; 13hr); Pyin Oo Lwin (3 daily; 6hr); Taunggyi (daily; 15hr); Yangon (2 daily; 18hr).

By shared taxi Shared taxis to Muse (4hr; K10,000 or K12,000 in the front seat) and west to Hsipaw (2hr), Pyin Oo Lwin (5hr 30min) and Mandalay (7hr 30min) depart from around the main bus station each morning when full, and the journey there costs K15,000 for all three. Book through your accommodation and the car will pick you up from your hotel.

By train Lashio's railway station is 5km northwest of the market. During the day, the journey there should cost K1500 with a pick-up or motorbike taxi, but you may have to pay more to get there early enough to catch the one daily train that departs at 5am. Tickets are on sale from around 4am.
Destinations Hsipaw (daily; 4hr 25min); Kyaukme (daily; 6hr); Mandalay (daily; 17hr 40min); Pyin Oo Lwin (daily; 11hr).

GETTING AROUND

By motorbike taxi Motorbike taxi drivers gather around the railway station, bus station and the market, with a journey around town typically costing K1000–1500.
By tuk-tuk A chartered tuk-tuk around town will cost

around K1500 per journey. Some shared tuk-tuks run from the railway and bus stations to the market, with a trip from either costing K300/person.

ACCOMMODATION

Golden Kinnara 86 Kyani Rd ☎082 30891, ✉goldenkinnarahotel@gmail.com. Opened in early

2014, this is one of Lashio's better mid-range hotels. The rooms are bland but spacious and comfortable, and come with fridges, kettles, hairdryers and a/c. The $70 family rooms also have bathtubs. This place is centrally located and has friendly staff, but it's still not quite as good as the *Two Elephants*. $50

Royal Ground 34 Theinni Rd ☎082 25516. Just downhill from the market, this place is larger than it looks from the street and has a good collection of reasonably priced rooms, which all come with a/c and private bathrooms – some with bathtubs. $25

Sann Shwin Thukha Rd ☎082 25290. This extra-friendly, family-run place is one of Lashio's cheaper options. It has three sizes of rooms with high ceilings, bathrooms and a/c; some of the K25,000 options have bathtubs and pleasant views. All but the cheapest have fridges. K21,000

Two Elephants 36 Bogyoke Rd ☎082 220 4112, ⓦtwoelephantshotel.com. Lashio's first international-standard hotel opened in January 2017, and it has a panoramic roof terrace with bar (though this wasn't finished at the time of research) and modern rooms that are well decorated. Suites ($65–75) and deluxe rooms ($55) are particularly large, though only the former have bathtubs – much to the chagrin of the manager. The prices are likely to rise, given the quality of the competition. $45

EATING

The **market** area is a good place to try chewy Chinese *ersi* noodles, while the **night market** (daily 5–9pm) along Bogyoke Rd has several stalls selling Shan noodle soup and Burmese curries as well as cheap clothes and cosmetics.

Indian Restaurant Just south of the night market. Up a short alley next to a Sikh temple (look for the "Indian Restaurant" sign) is this tiny restaurant, which serves excellent Indian cuisine. Rice, dhal and a curry will cost K3000, accompanied by a delicious tamarind pickle. Best to place your order before 7pm. Daily 10am–8pm.

★**Shwelai** Thukha Rd. This Chinese-Burmese restaurant doesn't have an English sign, so keep your eyes peeled for its yellow-painted woodwork and the large red Burmese menu on the wall. Some of the staff speak enough English for you to place an order, though you can also take your pick from the weird and wonderful array of bubbling pots on display. Fried rice K2000, large Myanmar Beer K2000. Daily 10am–8.30pm.

Sun Moon Bogyoke Rd ☎082 30606. With several branches around town, this bakery sells bread and cakes in cardboard boxes – perfect if you have a long train ride ahead of you. Their K500 iced coffee is so rich and sweet it seems like melted ice cream. Daily 8am–9pm.

DIRECTORY

Banks CB Bank on Theinni Rd and KBZ Bank on Bogyoke Rd have ATMs and currency exchange.

Internet ST Internet (daily 8am–10pm), next to the *Royal Ground Hotel* on Theinni Rd, charges K500/hr.

MUSE AND THE CHINESE BORDER

The small town of **Muse** (pronounced Mu-say) sits just across the Shweli River from the high-rises of **Ruili** on the Chinese side of the border. Until recently the border was nominally open to foreigners, though a permit and an official guide from Lashio were required. However, in November 2016 the Northern Alliance, a grouping of four rebel armies, seized the nearby village of Mong Koe from government forces, and the subsequent fighting escalated to the point of air strikes and heavy artillery fire. At the time of writing, the border area was closed to foreigners and permits were no longer being issued.

PERMITS

If the situation improves and you're interested in crossing here, check with a Yangon- or Kunming-based tour operator, as **permits** can take up to a month to process and the whole package (including guide and transport) usually costs $200–250 for a single day from Ruili to Lashio or vice versa.

VISAS

There is a Myanmar consulate-general in Kunming (☎+86 871 6816 2804, ⓦmcgkunming.org), where visas take three days to process. **Chinese visas** are available from the embassy in Yangon (see p.97) and the consulate-general in Mandalay (35th St, between 65th and 66th Sts; ☎02 35937, ⓦmandalay.china-consulate.org/eng).

Bhamo and around

ဗန်းမော်မြို့

For centuries, caravans carrying jade and tea passed through **BHAMO** (also spelt Bamaw and Banmaw) on their way to the markets of southwest China. Today, this small town on the eastern bank of the Ayeyarwady is a pleasantly relaxed place, punctuated with aged rain trees, dark teak houses and busy markets.

The town certainly doesn't make much of its waterfront, with busy Strand Road mostly home to shops catering to farmers heading to the **vegetable market** that sets up here each morning (Mon–Sat 6.30–8am). The **main market**, hidden away one block east of the river, is also worth a look – though more for the quaint building, surrounded by a small moat, than for the goods on sale.

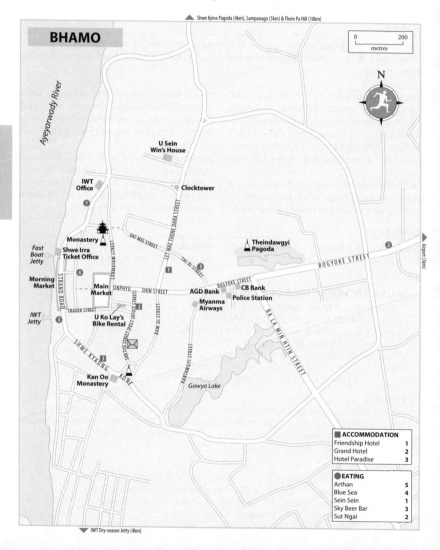

■ ACCOMMODATION	
Friendship Hotel	1
Grand Hotel	2
Hotel Paradise	3

● EATING	
Arthan	5
Blue Sea	4
Sein Sein	1
Sky Beer Bar	3
Sut Ngai	2

Pagodas and temples pepper the town, the most notable being **Theindawgyi Pagoda**, 500m east of the river on Bogyoke Street – look for the photogenic procession of larger-than-life concrete monks queuing along its western side. In the evenings, Bhamo's trendy young people and students congregate in the small park between the road and the pagoda precincts.

Out of town, you can cycle across a wonderfully rickety bamboo bridge and along the river to **Thein Pa Hill**, or hop on a boat and sail down the Ayeyarwady to Shwegu and beyond (see box, p.334).

Sampanago

စမ္ပာနဂိုရ် • 5km north of Bhamo • Daily dawn–dusk • Free • From Bhamo, cycle north to the prison, turn left shortly after and follow this road for 1.5km to Shwe Kyina Pagoda; Sampanago's remains are on the left-hand side of the road 200m southwest of the pagoda

The plains around Bhamo were once part of Manmaw, an independent Shan kingdom that ruled the area between the Ayeyarwady and the Chinese border. The remains of Manmaw's capital, **Sampanago** (locally known as "Old Bhamo" or *Bhamo myo haung*), lie 5km north of town hidden among the houses and fields near the modern **Shwe Kyina Pagoda**. All that can be seen today is a raised embankment and a ditch alongside it – fragments of the city walls and moat, with occasional rammed earth hillocks that are thought to have been watchtowers.

Thein Pa Hill

တိမ်း ပါတောင် • 10km north of Bhamo • Daily dawn–dusk • Free

A ninety-minute bike ride north, the path up **Thein Pa Hill** is lined with monastery buildings and small pagodas, and the hilltop looks out over the Ayeyarwady's midstream islands. The real attraction, though, is the trip out here, as the path winds along sandy riverbanks and across a **400m-long bamboo bridge**, which is swept away by the monsoon each year. Each December, hundreds of villagers get together to rebuild the bridge over just two days.

To get there, cycle north towards Sampanago (see above), turn left just before you reach Shwe Kyina Pagoda and continue to the bamboo bridge (December–June only; K300 per person). When the bridge is out of service, a long-tail boat (K300 per person; K200 per bike) ferries people across. Beyond the river, go straight until you reach the second village, where a small turning leads back to the river – Thein Pa is a few kilometres further north. It's also possible to take a boat here from Bhamo (see p.334).

ARRIVAL AND DEPARTURE   BHAMO

For years, foreigners have not been allowed to travel in or out of Bhamo by road, and though there are rumours of a possible railway linking Katha and Bhamo, this is not expected to be completed any time soon.

By plane Originally built as a Japanese Air Force base in World War II, Bhamo's airport is 3km east of town. Purchase tickets through your hotel, or through Kong Tong travel agent, attached to the *Friendship Hotel* (☎ 074 50095). The Myanmar National Airlines office (☎ 074 50269) is on Kantawgyi St.

Destinations Mandalay (4 weekly; 45min); Myitkyina (2 weekly; 30min); Yangon (6 weekly; 2hr 30min).

By boat As river travel to Sinbo and Myitkyina is forbidden, foreigners travelling by boat are only permitted to depart by going downstream. Daily fast boats to Shwegu (4hr;

K6000) and Katha (8hr; K12,000) leave at 8.30am from the riverside by Strand Rd; if you're travelling on to Mandalay, you'll need to spend the night in Katha before continuing your journey. Slower IWT ferries depart Bhamo at 7am on Mon, Wed and Fri for Shwegu (5hr), Katha (9hr) and Mandalay (30hr) in theory, but the schedule varies with river conditions. During the dry season, IWT boats leave from a jetty 4km south of Bhamo. You can buy tickets on the boat, or from the IWT office (☎ 074 50117; daily 9am–5pm) in a colonial building set back from Strand Rd just north of the main waterfront.

AYEYARWADY RIVER TRIPS

The **Ayeyarwady River** north of Mandalay sees far fewer visitors than the stretch to Bagan. Although the scenery is largely flat – save for the brief drama of the "second defile", where the hills close in and the river deepens and narrows (see p.335) – the journey between Bhamo and Mandalay offers more scope for interacting with local people, as well as the opportunity to jump ship at some interesting and little-visited spots en route.

The river **north of Bhamo** has been closed to foreigners since fighting between the government and the Kachin Independence Army flared up in 2011. Since you aren't allowed to get to Bhamo by road (see p.333), the easiest way to do the whole available route is to fly into Bhamo then take the boat downriver; the cheapest is to take a train to Katha (via Naba – pronounced "na-bar"), then travel upriver to Bhamo and back again by boat.

Three types of boat ply this stretch of the river: government-run IWT ferries, privately operated fast boats (both of which run regularly year-round), and a handful of luxury riverboats organized by upmarket tour operators (see p.30).

IWT FERRIES

The journey by **IWT ferry** from Bhamo to Mandalay ($12 on deck, $60 in a cabin) takes around thirty hours when water levels are high – during the dry season, the boats moor each night to avoid hitting the sandbanks and the journey will take longer. Shwegu, Katha and Kyaukmyaung are the main stops of interest to visitors. There are three departures each week in either direction, though the schedule can be erratic – as long as you have plenty of time, these boats are a great way to experience the river. The cabins, which are small rooms with two bed-like platforms and a small table, offer more privacy and a little more comfort, but restrict both your view and your opportunities to mingle with locals.

FAST BOATS

Special Express boats depart Bhamo every morning for Katha, stopping at Shwegu en route. Between Katha and Mandalay the boats stop at Tigyaing, Tagaung and Kyaukmyaung. Seating is usually on hard wooden benches under an awning, where you may be subjected to a Burmese pop music marathon. Food is available at most stops, and while the service is faster than the IWT boats, it's good to be prepared for delays.

GETTING AROUND AND TOURS

By tuk-tuk A tuk-tuk to the IWT dry-season jetty or to the airport costs K2000.

By bicycle Bikes (K2000/day) are available to rent from U Ko Lay's shop (☎ 09 4701 7296), which is down the alley opposite the *Grand Hotel*.

Tours U Sein Win (☎ 09 256 350 518) speaks excellent English and can guide you around Bhamo for K10,000/day.

To find him, walk north from the clocktower and you'll soon see an English sign pointing down a side road to the left. Sein Win's house is a short way down this road. With a little notice, between November and February he can arrange boat trips to Thein Pa Hill – and there's a chance of seeing dolphins on the way.

ACCOMMODATION

Bhamo's three **hotels** offer a wide selection of rooms and are all reasonably comfortable – good news if you've just disembarked from a long boat journey.

★**Friendship Hotel** Let Wae Thone Dara St ☎074 50095, ✉khinhtwemon@gmail.com. The most basic rooms here cost $10 per person, have a/c and shared bathrooms and sell out quickly; all other categories are en suite. Standard rooms have showers, but you can upgrade if you'd rather have a bathtub. There's a karaoke lounge downstairs, but thankfully the noise from this doesn't reach the upper floors. In the morning, make sure you take advantage of the breakfast buffet on the top-floor terrace, as it's astonishingly varied and extensive. $20

Grand Hotel Sar Tite St (sometimes called Post Office St) ☎074 50317. Unusually for Bhamo, the *Grand* has only three types of room: standard twins come with a/c and bathrooms; the next best cost $5 more but don't seem to offer any advantage; and the upgraded $40 suites come with nice bathtubs. No discount for single occupancy. $25

Hotel Paradise 36 Shwe Kyaung Kone ☎074 50136, ✉hotelparadisebanmaw@gmail.com. The newest hotel in town has a range of clean, comfortable rooms and is based a short walk south of the town centre. The spacious $15 singles and $25 twins and doubles (with king-size beds) offer good value. All are en suite, apart from the very cheapest rooms that share bucket showers (from $7). All rooms are equipped with a/c. $14

EATING

After dark, Bhamo's centre of gravity shifts from the waterfront to the food stalls on Bogyoke Street, but across town most places close down by 9.30pm.

Arthan Strand Rd. This airy teahouse is the only place in Bhamo with views over the river. The kitchen serves up the usual teahouse menu: noodles, fried things and endless cups of tea and coffee. Any attempt to speak English causes more than the usual confusion, so you may have to point at what other tables have to order. Daily 6am–7pm.

Blue Sea Near Strand Rd ☎09 650 4090. Housed in a grand colonnaded building that's clearly visible at the end of a short road, this Chinese and Kachin restaurant is a reliable place, with most dishes around the K3000 mark. The draught beer (K750) and stout (K950) don't hurt, either. Daily 7am–9pm.

Sein Sein Strand Rd ☎074 50031. With Myanmar Beer on tap and an extensive menu of stir-fried dishes (from K2500), this is one of the best Chinese restaurants in town – even if the chef shows a rather Burmese enthusiasm for oil. Unfortunately, despite its location, there's no view of the river from the dining room. Daily 9am–9pm.

★Sky Beer Bar Thi Ri St ☎074 50727. Around the corner from the *Friendship Hotel*, this cavernous and popular Sagaing restaurant-cum-beer-hall has barbecued skewers at K300–1000, dishes from K2000 (meat dishes mostly K3500) and Western favourites like chips, along with draught beer and stout to wash them down. Daily 9am–9pm.

Sut Ngai Bogyoke St. A few blocks east of Theindawgyi Pagoda, this Kachin restaurant serves traditional dishes including *sipa* (steamed vegetables with herbs) and chicken and pork steamed in banana leaves. Daily 9am–9pm.

DIRECTORY

Banks There are several banks with ATMs and exchange facilities on Sinphu Shin and Bogyoke streets, including AGD Bank and CB Bank opposite Theindawgyi Pagoda.

Bhamo to Katha

The main spectacle along the Ayeyarwady between Bhamo and Katha is the **second defile**, where the river narrows to just 90m across and flows through a tight S-bend. Towards the western end of the defile, a **parrot's head** is painted on the cliffs – when the water rises to touch the bird's beak, the river currents are judged to be too strong for certain craft to continue upstream. The three Ayeyarwady defiles are extremely deep, and *naga* – the local equivalent of Scotland's Loch Ness monster – are said to lurk in the river's depths.

The most interesting place to stop along this stretch of the river is **Shwegu**, where there is a mysterious island pagoda complex.

Shwegu

ေရႊကူျမိဳ့

Spread along the Ayeyarwady River's southern bank, **SHWEGU** sees few foreign visitors. Those who do disembark here are either on their way to **Shwe Baw Kyun** on the island of **Kyun Daw**, where hundreds of pagodas in varying states of decay picturesquely cover the island's southeastern tip, or they are searching for **pottery workshops** in the town's dusty backstreets.

The main road runs a block inland of the river, and the main pottery district is further inland again, although most activity takes place behind fences and in backyards. The pots, some painted with colourful flower designs, are displayed in shops on the main road.

8

Shwe Baw Kyun Pagoda

ေရွေေပၚကျွန်းဘုရား•• Kyun Daw Island, 2.5km southwest of Shwegu's harbour • Daily dawn–dusk • Free • Take a boat from near Shwe Andaw; K500 one-way

Hidden away above the wide sandy shores of **Kyun Daw** ("Royal Island") is **Shwe Baw Kyun** (also spelt Shwe Paw Kyawn). An estimated seven thousand pagodas cover the island's eastern end, some gleaming with new gold leaf while others are just barely recognizable piles of bricks. The site's origins are murky, but it was apparently already in need of renovation by the mid-eleventh century, when King Anawrahta (see p.359) perked it up and gave the central pagoda a new *hti*.

Today, it makes an intriguing – if somewhat uncomfortable – place to wander barefoot for an hour or two (you'll need to carry your shoes). Whitewashed corridors radiate outwards from the main shrine; shy cows graze nearby while birds sing from the undergrowth that blankets many of the older stupas, and fragments of stucco decoration cling to exposed brickwork.

Bordering Shwe Baw Kyun is a pleasingly bucolic village, and on the riverbank opposite there's the small monastery of **Shwe Andaw**, which is the site of a festival around the time of the Tabaung (February/March) full moon.

ARRIVAL AND DEPARTURE SHWEGU

By boat For foreigners, the only way to get to Shwegu is by boat – and catching one out requires a willingness to lurk around the jetty and wait. Fast boats to Katha pass through around 11.30am, and ones headed for Bhamo leave around 1.30pm. Each journey lasts about 4 hours – pay on board. The IWT ferries to Mandalay theoretically stop at Shwegu just after noon on Mon, Wed and Fri, though delays are frequent and you can't rely on them. If you find you're ready to leave earlier, it's worth asking when the next boat leaves – sometimes other, less official, passenger services pass by.

GETTING AROUND

By boat Long-tail boats (K500 one-way) crossing to Shwe Baw Kyun can be found 300m north of Shwe Andaw – they generally start running from 8am and disappear entirely after 6pm. Boats can also be found at other points along the river, including just below another pagoda on the way to Shwe Andaw – they'll agree to take you, but the journey will be longer and more expensive. Look out for the pagodas among the greenery on the opposite bank to your right, and a low staircase rising from the sand – if you see them, you're in the right place. It's also possible to charter a boat from the main harbour, though this costs K10,000 for the return trip including waiting time.

By tuk-tuk and motorbike taxi Tuk-tuks and motorbike taxis are often hard to find in Shwegu, though there will usually be at least one waiting at the harbour when the boat comes in, and you'll occasionally be offered a ride as you walk around town. The 15min drive from one end of Shwegu to the other usually costs K2000; from the jetty to the guesthouse should set you back around K1000.

ACCOMMODATION AND EATING

Shwegu has only one guesthouse licensed for foreigners, around 1km from the harbour. Scattered restaurants, teahouses and beer stations can be found along the main road nearby.

Dagon Station Main St. If you're heading out from *SAG Guesthouse*, walk back to the main road and a couple of blocks towards the harbour, and you can't miss this green-fronted beer station. The super-friendly owner speaks a few words of English and serves a mean chicken fried rice for K2000. And plenty of draught beer, of course.

SAG Guesthouse 3 Saigon Quarter ☎074 52647. A 15min walk west of the harbour (turn right once you reach the road), and tucked away one block south of the main street, Shwegu's only guesthouse is set in a wooden building. The fan-cooled rooms have large shuttered windows and shared bathrooms, and more expensive rooms have a/c and en-suite bathrooms (K18,000). Some rooms also have balconies. It's worth checking all the rooms on offer, as the basic ones are usually brighter and airier. Staff are friendly and can give you an excessively detailed map of town. Downsides here are that there is no breakfast on offer, and no wi-fi. However, a collection of low key, outdoor cafés offering light meals and snacks is just metres away. If you can't find the guesthouse, ask anyone for "S-A-G"(not "sag"). **K15,000**

Katha

ကသာၿမ္မ့

For travellers, **KATHA** would have been just another quaint riverside town of teak houses, monks and mud – had one Eric Blair (later known as **George Orwell**; see box below) not served his last posting as a colonial policeman here in 1926–27. Orwell used the town as the setting for his novel *Burmese Days*, and though it was renamed "Kyauktada" and the layout was disguised (Orwell's publisher was concerned about libel), several of the colonial buildings that played a part either in the novel or in Orwell's life are identifiable today.

Katha lies on the western bank of the Ayeyarwady River. **Riverside Road** (also known as Strand Road) is lined with dark teak houses, the town's cheapest accommodation and several pagodas – the largest of which stands at its southern end, near the menacing British-built **jail** that is still in use. The town is usually liveliest around the busy **market** (daily 6.30am–4pm), a few blocks in from the river.

Orwell-era buildings

The most interesting Orwell-era buildings are north of the town centre on **Club Street**, although they are neither signposted as such nor formally open to visitors – do bear this in mind before you invite yourself in for a look around. The easiest to find is the 1924 **tennis club**, with its tiny mint-green clubhouse. Just behind the tennis court is the half-timbered former **British Club**, still much as Orwell described it – "a dumpy one-storey building with a tin roof" – now housing a local co-operative. It's usually locked, but the caretaker may unlock the door and produce the visitors' book for you. One block north of the tennis club, on the other side of the street, the **District Commissioners' House** stands alone in a huge lot. It's being renovated by the Katha Heritage Trust, founded in 2012 by local artist Nyo Ko Naing (✉nyokonaing@gmail .com), who hopes to open it as a **George Orwell Museum**. Orwell's own house, the Deputy Superintendent's house in the novel, stands just off the main road, halfway between the market and *Hotel Katha*. Admire it from the street – it's now the residence of the Chief of Police.

8

ARRIVAL AND DEPARTURE

KATHA

By train Katha lies 20km from the station at Naba, which is on the Mandalay–Myitkyina line. Although there is a line from Naba to Katha, there is only one train a day and the journey is very slow (3hr); instead, most people bound for Katha continue their journeys using the pick-up trucks (1hr; K1000) that wait in the station yard to meet each train. Ignore touts, who may approach you inside the station. Returning to Naba, pick-ups leave

---

GEORGE ORWELL IN BURMA

Eric Blair (1903–50), who would later find fame under the nom de plume **George Orwell**, arrived in Burma in November 1922 as a youthful officer of the Indian Imperial Police. Sent to Mandalay for training and then to Pyin Oo Lwin, he also spent time in the Ayeyarwady Delta and Mawlamyine, where his mother had grown up, before being posted to Katha.

Orwell's experiences in Burma convinced him of the wrongs of imperialism, and he acquired tattoos and a reputation as an outsider more interested in spending time with the Burmese than in more "pukka" (appropriate) pursuits. In this he resembled **John Flory**, the protagonist of his first novel *Burmese Days* (1934), which was set in a thinly disguised Katha. Orwell also wrote about Burma in his essays *A Hanging* (1931) and *Shooting an Elephant* (1936).

There's a long-standing joke that Orwell actually wrote three books about Burma, including his denunciations of totalitarianism in *Animal Farm* (1945) and *Nineteen Eighty-Four* (1949); unlike the anti-imperialist *Burmese Days*, both of these later works were banned by the authorities until recently.

from the roadside north of Katha's market. Your hotel can confirm departure times, or alternatively arrange a taxi (40min; K18,000). Naba is served by three trains in each direction each day, with services to Myitkyina (12hr) leaving at 1am, 4am and 9am. Train times towards Mandalay (12hr) are slightly better, departing in the late afternoon and evening.

By boat Fast boats depart daily at 5am for Mandalay (14hr; K25,000) and 9am for Bhamo (8hr; K12,000) via Shwegu (4hr; K6000), with tickets for both services available shortly before departure from the Special Express ticket booth (☎ 09 250 559 104) on Riverside Rd. Tickets for IWT ferries are available an hour before departure from the IWT office (☎ 074 25057) on Riverside Rd, a little north of the fast ferry ticket office – look for the Myanmar flag outside. Tickets can also be purchased on board. The IWT ferries themselves depart 600m south of the office, just past a large pagoda.

ACCOMMODATION

Along the waterfront are basic guesthouses with plywood partitions, some of which no longer accept foreign guests.

Ayarwaddy Guesthouse Riverside Rd ☎ 075 25140. This old-school guesthouse has small rooms upstairs with shared bucket showers, and a few en-suite rooms downstairs. The walls are so thin you'll hear every time your fellow guests yawn, snore or play tinny muzak on their phones. Try to get one of the double rooms with river views at the front of the building. No breakfast, no wi-fi. Single rooms K8000. **K16,000**

★**Hotel Katha** Lanmadaw Rd ☎ 075 25390, ⓦ hotelkatha.com. This friendly hotel in a colonial-style building opened in 2015. It has a wide selection of rooms, from $18 singles to $50 VIP rooms, all with their own bathrooms and a/c. The hotel brochure includes a very useful illustrated map of Katha in Orwell's time. **$25**

EATING AND DRINKING

Katha has an interesting **night market** (daily 5–9pm) offering various options beyond the usual noodles, including fresh fruit lassis and good curry-and-rice combos. The market is on a street running away from the river, just south of the fast boat office – it's known locally as "Night Market Street".

Jet Sun Night Market St. One of the few places open early in the morning, this small teahouse is a good choice for a hearty breakfast of sweet tea and hot paratha. Daily 5am–6pm.

Shwe Sisa Riverside Rd. This restaurant offers grills and stir-fries (from K2000), draught beer, Premiership football and a balcony overlooking the river. Barbecued fish is their speciality. Daily 9am–10pm.

Zone Café Lanmadaw Rd. On Katha's main road, south of the market and near AYA Bank, this café is owned by local artist and Orwell enthusiast Nyo Ko Naing. Serves tea, coffee (K300 each), cold drinks and snacks including tea-leaf salad (K500) and some fried dishes (K1000). Daily 7am–10pm.

DIRECTORY

Bank There are two or three banks with ATMs in the vicinity of the market.

Katha to Mandalay

The broad ribbon of the Ayeyarwady flows almost due south between Katha and Mandalay, through low hills that have been intensively logged for teak – elephants hauling tree trunks and barges loaded with logs can still be spotted along the river. Just before the town of **Inywa**, the river traffic negotiates its way around wthe **Shweli sandbar**, where the Shweli River dumps silt at its confluence with the Ayeyarwady.

Fast and slow boats alike stop at Tigyaing and Tagaung, but the place most likely to interest travellers is **Kyaukmyaung** where potters produce huge **Martaban jars**, using techniques that have been unchanged since King Alaungpaya forcibly relocated thousands of Mon captives from Mottama (formerly Martaban) near Mawlamyine in the eighteenth century. Alaungpaya also left his mark on his birthplace, **Shwebo**, where he established his capital between 1752 and 1760. Outside Shwebo are the ruins of a far more ancient city, **Hanlin**.

IRRAWADDY DOLPHINS

Despite its name, the **Irrawaddy dolphin** can be found in estuaries, rivers and coastal waters from the Bay of Bengal to the Great Barrier Reef. Although not a true river dolphin – they're related to killer whales – subpopulations do live in several Southeast Asian rivers, with one group eking out an existence in the turbid waters of the Ayeyarwady.

While there are many stories of the dolphins cooperating with fishermen, the use of gill- and drag-nets – and even illegal electro-fishing by rogue fishermen using car batteries – has seen Myanmar's dolphin population drop alarmingly, and CITES lists the Ayeyarwady's dolphins as critically endangered.

In 2005, the government established a protected area for the dolphins in a 68km stretch of the river between Kyaukmyaung and Mingun, banning certain types of fishing nets and the use of mercury in riverside gold mines. While Irrawaddy dolphin numbers initially showed a slight recovery, they're now facing a new threat due to overfishing, with just an estimated 62 individuals left in 2017. Nonetheless, if you spend much time on the Ayeyarwady ferries you may occasionally see a rounded grey head poking above the water, and you'll know they're still holding on against the odds.

Kyaukmyaung

ကျောက်မြောင်း

74km north of Mandalay, **KYAUKMYAUNG** is the last major stop on the way south. From the jetty, the main pottery area of **Ngwe Ngein** is 1.5km south along the riverside, just north of the Radana Thinga Bridge. Kyaukmyaung is a sleepy little place, and save for the potteries and a few pagodas that were badly cracked in a 2012 **earthquake**, there's little to occupy you – which is just as well, as the nearest accommodation for foreigners is 17km west in Shwebo (see below).

While Kyaukmyaung's workshops produce a variety of earthenware jars, the most recognizable are the large Martaban jars that were used for centuries by Mon merchants in their Indian Ocean trade – also known as "Ali Baba jars" after their cameo in *Ali Baba and the Forty Thieves*. In shady huts set back from the riverside, potters can be seen shaping the jars using foot-turned wheels, later firing them in low brick kilns fuelled by rice husks.

ARRIVAL AND DEPARTURE   KYAUKMYAUNG

By bus Buses for Shwebo (1hr) and Mandalay (3hr) depart until mid-afternoon from near the market.

By motorbike taxi A motorbike taxi to Shwebo will cost K3000–5000, depending on how late you arrive in Kyaukmyaung and how much luggage you have.

By tuk-tuk Tuk-tuks to Shwebo (1hr; K700) leave hourly until 3pm, and drivers usually wait to meet each boat.

By boat Slow boats pull in at Kyaukmyaung (northbound on Mon, Thurs and Sat; southbound on Sat, Tues and Thurs) – ask at the IWT office opposite the jetty for times. Southbound fast boats pass through Kyaukmyaung around 2–4pm, but don't always pull in – you may need to take a long-tail out to join the boat midstream. Northbound fast boats pass through at around 7–9am. On all services, it's possible to buy tickets on board.

Shwebo and around

ရွှေဘိုမြို့

SHWEBO ("Golden Leader") was a village known as Moksobo ("Leader of Hunters") until 1752. Following the collapse of the Taungoo dynasty, the village chief Alaungpaya established Burma's final Konbaung dynasty, with himself as king and the renamed Shwebo as his capital. The dynasty survived until 1885, but the capital moved to Sagaing on Alaungpaya's death in 1760. Today, only a concrete reproduction of the palace at **Shwebon Yadana** and a wide moat almost surrounding the town centre hint at its glorious past.

Best known for its *thanaka*, said to be the best in the country, Shwebo is rarely visited by foreigners. When leaving the station, you may not find a crowd of motorcycle taxis jostling for your business (don't worry, one will turn up), but everywhere you will encounter the sort of charming friendliness and shy curiosity you find only when discovering a new destination.

Shwebo makes a good base for exploring the ruins of the ancient Pyu city of **Hanlin**, 20km to the southeast, and it's also possible to make a day-trip to the potteries in Kyaukmyaung (see opposite). The town is also a useful stop if you want to travel from the river at Kyaukmyaung to Bagan, with transport on to Monywa and Pakokku.

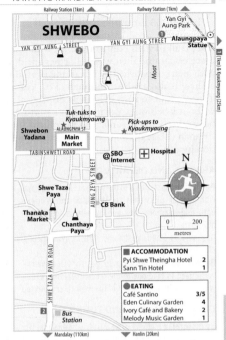

Shwe Taza Paya
ရွှေတာန်ဆာဘုရား• Shwe Taza Paya Rd • Daily 5am–7pm
• Free

Just off the main north–south road, an alluring array of golden spires punctuates the skyline – they belong to **Shwe Taza Paya**, one of Shwebo's most important religious complexes.

Established in the eleventh century, the *paya*'s main treasure is a small golden **Buddha statue** in the main hall, which is said to emit rays of light from its head and is paraded around Shwebo to hasten the rains each year around the Waso (July) full moon. Keep an eye out for the *nat* shrine on the southern side of the *paya*, where you can see Shwebo's council of nine guardian *nats* with offerings piled in front of each.

The main shrine can be reached from several directions; the covered corridor from the south hosts Shwebo's principal *thanaka* market, lined with stacks of sawn branches and vendors grinding the bark into a paste for customers to sample. If you want some for yourself, the older, thicker branches are the best quality.

Shwebon Yadana
ထန်လင်း• Alaungpaya St • Daily 8am–5pm • K2000

After King Alaungpaya founded the Konbaung dynasty in 1752, he built his palace at **Shwebon Yadana**, where he ruled until his death in 1760 – whereupon his successor moved the capital to Sagaing (see p.305).

The original palace buildings were destroyed by the British after the annexation of Upper Burma, and the site was used as a **prison** until 1994 (the colonial-era courthouse still stands just inside the gates), when two of the halls were reconstructed.

Hanlin
ထန်လင်း• 20km southeast of Shwebo • Motorbike taxis from K10,000 return

Between the first and ninth centuries AD, the walled city of **HANLIN**, one of the most important Pyu city-states, flourished to the southeast of Shwebo. Archeologists have been excavating the area enclosed by Hanlin's rectangular brick walls since 1962, uncovering inscribed stones, coins and jewellery made from gold and semi-precious stones – examples of which are on display in the informative **museum** in Hanlin village (Tues–Sun 9.30am–4.30pm; K5000). The dig has also exposed several of the city's curved gates and burial sites. As the latter are covered by locked huts, it's best to visit the museum first; they will sell you a ticket and tell you which sites can be visited that day.

There are 33 excavation sites scattered across the countryside. While they're signed in English, it's a good idea to have a local driver or guide to show you the way. Pits 26, 29 and 30 all contain human remains, with some of the skeletons in Pit 29 still wearing bracelets around their wrists. Further afield, site 22 is an interesting religious building with altars of polished stones arranged on three sides.

There is also a **private museum** ($10; kyat not accepted), run by a supercilious monk. The museum consists of a single display cabinet containing pots, stones and coins without labels or explanations. To a non-specialist, there is nothing here that cannot be seen to better advantage in the official museum.

Hanlin village itself has hot springs, salt wells and a host of crumbling stupas to occupy you.

ARRIVAL AND DEPARTURE

By bus The bus station is to the south of Shwe Taza Paya, with regular departures to Mandalay and Monywa until mid-afternoon and a daily service to Pakokku at 7.30am.

Destinations Mandalay (hourly; 3hr); Monywa (hourly; 3hr); Pakokku (daily; 6hr).

By tuk-tuk and pick-up To get to Kyaukmyaung, you'll need to take one of the regular tuk-tuks (K700), which leave from just north of the market, or a pick-up

SHWEBO AND AROUND

(K500) departing when full from a side street 100m further east.

Destinations Kyaukmyaung (daily; 1hr).

By train Shwebo's railway station is 1.5km north of the market, just within the northeastern corner of the city moat. The town is on the main line between Mandalay and Myitkyina, with three "up" and three "down" trains daily.

Destinations Mandalay (3 daily; 3hr); Myitkyina (3 daily; 16–18hr); Naba (3 daily; 7–10hr).

GETTING AROUND AND TOURS

By motorbike Motorbikes are usually available from *Win Guesthouse*, just south of the main market on Aung Zeya St (K10,000). Motorbike taxis can be found outside the bus station, and may offer slightly cheaper rates for simple transportation – but they won't allow as much time or offer

the same thorough explanations as on organized tours.

Tours Friendly, English-speaking motorcycle taxi driver Kyaw Soe (❶ 09 974 604 545, ✉ kyawsoe040@gmail.com) can organize various tours of Shwebo, Hanlin (K15,000) and Kyaukmyaung (K13,000).

ACCOMMODATION

There are only two accommodation options in Shwebo, and only one is based near the town centre.

Pyi Shwe Theingha Hotel Shwe Taza Paya Rd ❶ 075 22949, ✉ pyishwetheingha@gmail.com. One of Myanmar's fancier bus station hotels, with the only elevator in Shwebo and a range of rooms all with private bathrooms and a/c. The hot water is unreliable. Staff are charming and friendly, but some rather grim rooms face only an internal wall – try to get one with an outward-facing window. K28,350

Sann Tin Hotel Kyaukmyaung Rd ❶ 075 22128, ✉ santinhotel@gmail.com. This new hotel, about 1.5km east of the moat, isn't particularly characterful – but with individual water heaters in each room, it's probably your best chance of a hot shower in Shwebo. For single travellers it's also the cheapest option, starting at K20,000. All rooms en suite, with a/c. K30,000

EATING

Café Santino Aung Zeya St ❶ 09 400 425 714. With two cavernous teashops on Aung Zeya St, *Café Santino* is popular all day long, offering everything from breakfast-time fried rice and *moun-di* to late-night football matches, with plenty of coffee and tea in between. Daily 6am–8.30pm.

Eden Culinary Garden Near Aung Zeya St ❶ 075 21651. With a dining room and some tables set around a little courtyard, *Eden* serves Burmese and Chinese standards, with a few Western dishes to boot. Check the prices before you order – while it's not an expensive place overall (a meal for two costs from K4000), there are a few unwelcome surprises, like a K7000 omelette.

Breakfast served until 10am. Daily 5.30am–9.30pm.

Ivory Café and Bakery Yan Gyi Aung St ❶ 09 774 458 008, ✉ ivory.sbo@gmail.com. This newly opened coffee shop has a wide selection of cakes and pastries, and an espresso machine producing real coffee from K1000. Daily 7am–9pm.

★**Melody Music Garden** Yan Gyi Aung St ❶ 075 22011. One of the few places in town that takes advantage of the city moat, with a veranda that's a great spot for sitting and enjoying the view with a glass of beer (K750) or a meal (dishes from K1500). Don't forget your mosquito repellent. Daily 9am–10pm.

DIRECTORY

Banks There are branches of the main banks on Aung Zeya St, most with ATMs.

Internet SBO Internet (daily 9am–10pm) on Tabinshweti Rd has a good connection for K300/hr.

Monywa and around

မုံရွာမြို့

Sitting on the Chindwin River around 130km west of Mandalay and a similar distance north of Bagan, the large town of **MONYWA** (pronounced as two syllables something like "Moan-ywa") is of minimal interest in itself but makes a handy base for visits to several fine attractions in the surrounding countryside. These include the gigantic Buddha figures at **Maha Bodhi Tataung**, the quirky **Thanboddhay Pagoda** and the hillside cave shrines of **Pho Win Taung**.

Thanboddhay Pagoda

သမ္ဗုဒ္ဓေဘုရား• 11km southeast of Monywa, 1.5km northeast off the Mandalay road • **Temple complex** Daily 24hr • Free • **Main shrine** Daily 6am–5pm • $3

Built between 1939 and 1952, the zany **Thanboddhay Pagoda** is one of Myanmar's wackiest temple complexes: a technicolour riot of cartoon shrines, fairy-tale pagodas and shameless super-kitsch, enough to make even the most lavish Hollywood film set blush with embarrassment. Two huge white stone elephants, each with a small temple on its back, flank the entrance, setting the tone for what lies inside.

The **main shrine** is an eye-popping, blood-red affair, surrounded by a riot of obelisks, lion statues, sphinxes and shrines, its roofs spiked with 864 needle-thin mini-stupas, like an architectural pincushion. Its vaguely Neoclassical-looking **interior** is a maze of dark-red arches, with walls covered in a dense mosaic of (it's claimed) over five hundred thousand tiny Buddha statues.

Further shrines and structures surround the main building on all sides, including a pea-green bathing pool surrounded by elephant carvings; a string of monastic buildings painted in vivid pastel blues, reds, pinks and greens; and a truly bizarre tower, looking like a cross between a minaret and a helter-skelter, with a small stupa on top.

Maha Bodhi Tataung

မဟာဗောဓိတစ်ထောင်• 8km east of Thanboddhay Pagoda • Daily 6am–5pm • Free

Even more surreal than the Thanboddhay Pagoda is the nearby **Maha Bodhi Tataung**, a sprawling religious complex founded in 1960 and dominated by two of the world's biggest Buddha statues. The name Maha Bodhi Tataung translates as "One Thousand Bodhi [Bo] Trees" (although there are now over nine thousand in total), and approaching the complex you'll pass swathes of these trees, each with a seated Buddha below.

It's the two giant Buddhas that really hog the attention, however, particularly the superhuman **Laykyun Setkyar** standing Buddha image, bestriding the landscape like some Brobdingnagian colossus and visible for many kilometres in every direction. Built between 1996 and 2008, this is the world's second-tallest statue, rising a massive 116m (or 130m if you include the base) – getting on for three times the height of Nelson's Column in London and outstripped only by the 128m-tall Spring Temple Buddha in Henan, China (which is 153m tall with its pedestal). The statue is actually hollow, with a 25-storey building concealed inside, each floor decorated with vivid murals. The bottom five or so storeys show the gruesome punishments awaiting sinners in hell, while paintings on higher levels become gradually more exalted in subject matter, with depictions of the various Buddhist heavens at the top of the

8

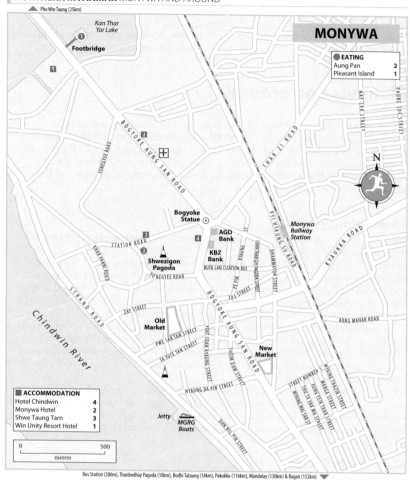

Pho Win Taung (25km)

MONYWA

Kan Thar Yar Lake

Footbridge

BOGYOKE AUNG SAN ROAD

YONEGYEE ROAD

THAR ZI ROAD

NAY TAR STREET

PHONE SOE STREET

N

Bogyoke Statue ⊙

AGD Bank

KBZ Bank

BUTA LAN (STATION RD)

STATION ROAD

KHAR PANN ROAD

Shwezigon Pagoda

YO NEGYEE ROAD

Monywa Railway Station

PYI HTAUNG SU ROAD

CHAN THAR GYI PAGODA STREET

DHAMMA YON STREET

KYAUKKA ROAD

STRAND ROAD

Chindwin River

ZAY STREET

PE ZIN STREET

ZAE STREET

Old Market

PWE SAR TAN STREET

TA YOTE TAN STREET

YOAT SOUN KYAUNG STREET

HEIM ZAN STREET

BOGYOKE AUNG SAN ROAD

New Market

AUNG MAHAR ROAD

STREET NUMBER 3

MYAING THAZIN STREET

MARGA STREET

AUNG YEIK THAR STREET

THUTA TAY MA STREET

MYAING WAI SAR ST

NYAUNG DA PIN STREET

Jetty
MGRG Boats

OHN WEL PIN STREET

0   500
metres

Bus Station (500m), Thanbodhay Pagoda (10km), Bodhi Tataung (18km), Pakokku (116km), Mandalay (130km) & Bagan (152km) ▼

8

statue – although visitors are allowed only as far as the sixteenth floor, some way short of nirvana (and slightly below where the Buddha's belly button would be). There's no lift, either, so it's a bit of a climb.

The **reclining Buddha** (completed in 1991) directly in front is only a little less huge, measuring 95m in length. It's also hollow, with entrance via the Buddha's rear (as it were), although there's not much to see inside the gloomy interior bar a hall full of rather battered-looking Buddhist bas-reliefs. Nearby is the huge gilded **Aung Sakkya Pagoda** (1979), with fine views of the two statues and surrounding countryside from its terrace.

Two further supersized Buddha statues – one seated on a nearby hillside and the other sprawled out asleep (below the reclining Buddha) – are also under construction.

Pho Win Taung and around

ဖိုဝင်တောင် • Daily 24hr • $2

Buried deep in the countryside around 25km west of Monywa, **Pho Win Taung** (also transliterated as "Hpo Wing Daung") displays Burmese piety at work upon the landscape – it's more understated than the nearby Maha Bodhi Tataung, but equally memorable. Hundreds of cave-shrines were cut into the hillside here between the fourteenth and eighteenth centuries – some sources put the number of shrines at exactly 492, although others claim there are actually more than double that. Many of the "caves" are tiny, with room for just a single Buddha image; others are larger, decorated with fine Jataka murals (bring a torch) rivalling anything in Bagan, and still retaining much of their original colour after two hundred-plus years.

Getting to the caves is part of the fun. Visiting by hired car from Monywa (around K50,000), you'll pass the chintzy **Shwetaung U Pagoda**, worth a stop for its sweeping river and countryside views. Alternatively, hire a boat from the jetty on Strand Rd (K3000 one-way) to cross the Chindwin to bustling **Nyaungbin** village, from where you can pick up a jeep to take you to the caves ($20 including wait time).

ARRIVAL AND TOURS   MONYWA AND AROUND

Monywa is easy enough to get to. Some people choose to visit it as a day-trip from Bagan, but in truth it's a bit too far out to make the journey worthwhile.

By bus The bus station is about 1km south of the centre, and you can count on around K1000 for the ride by motorbike taxi from here into town. Heading to Pakokku (3hr) and Nyaung U (4hr), there are a couple of daily minibuses plus regular but slower and uncomfortable pick-ups.

Destinations Homalin (daily; 9hr); Hsipaw (3 daily; 11hr); Mandalay (hourly; 3hr 30min); Pyin Oo Lwin (4 daily; 7hr); Shwebo (hourly; 3hr).

CHINDWIN RIVER TRIPS

8

Monywa is the major port on the **Chindwin River**, the main tributary of the Ayeyarwady that runs north from here for almost 1000km. Cruises along the Chindwin offer a chance to see a part of Myanmar still virtually untouched by tourism, striking deep into the Sagaing Region and following the river as it runs close to the Indian border.

A number of **luxury cruises** run regularly along the Chindwin, particularly in later July/August directly after the monsoon, when water levels are high. The main vessel is the **RV Pandaw** (ⓦpandaw.com), a luxury colonial-style vessel; seven-day cruises are run year-round between Monywa and Homalin, flying into Homalin and then heading back downriver. It's a memorable experience, although expensive, with prices starting at around $2800 per person (including flight). Longer (ten- to eleven-night) and even pricier cruises are also available on other vessels – such as the *Orcaella* (ⓦbelmond.com), *Paukan* (ⓦpaukan.com) and *Ananda* (ⓦsanctuaryretreats.com), which start from Mandalay and include a trip up and down the Chindwin before depositing passengers at Bagan. Cruises typically stop at (heading north) the riverside towns of Kani, Mingin, Moktaw, Kalewa (Kalay), Mawleik and Sittaung before reaching Homalin; journeys ending in Bagan usually visit Kani and Mingin on their way back down the river.

An alternative to an organized cruise is to arrange an **independent trip**, staying in guesthouses and travelling on local cargo boats, which stop at all the main riverside settlements. Travel permits are no longer required, but it's possible that officials in remote upriver towns might not be aware of this.

Cargo ferries chug up the Chindwin River as far as Homalin, with occasional ferries all the way up to Khamti in Kachin State – an adventurous journey with minimal facilities. You will sleep on the deck and must bring your own food and drink. Boats dock in Monywa on the river at the jetty, a short walk southwest of the centre, and you can buy tickets from the tables set up along Strand Road. MGRG (☎09 3333 2581) is a good operator. Their "ticket office" is the table with the rainbow-coloured umbrella, located under a tree covered in creepers and with a few little Buddha shrines.

Departure times are very flexible, but in general boats leave Monywa for Homalin daily at 4am. The journey takes around two days and costs K36,000. In Homalin you can change for Khamti (K20,000), which is another day's travel upriver. Journey times are always quicker coming back downriver, but even so you should always be prepared for it to take longer than expected due to delays. Simple accommodation is available in both Homalin and Khamti.

By train The railway station is just east of the centre, though there's only one slow service each day from Mandalay (6hr) and Pakokku (5hr).

Tours A half-day trip combining Thanboddhay Pagoda and Maha Bodhi Tataung by motorbike taxi costs around K20,000.

Alternatively, your hotel may be able to arrange a car – the *Win Unity* hotel (see below) can arrange these and other local trips, including taxis to Pho Win Taung, Maha Bodhi Tataung and Thanboddhay for around $30 each – although you might be able to find a cheaper deal elsewhere.

ACCOMMODATION

Hotel Chindwin Bogyoke Aung San Rd ☎071 26150, Ⓦhotelchindwinmonywa.com. The smartest hotel in the town centre is this large glass block that towers above all else. The cheapest rooms are dark and cramped, so opt for the next level up ($50), which has more space, more light and better decorations. **$31**

Monywa Hotel Bogyoke Aung San Rd ☎071 21581, Ⓔmonywahotel071@gmail.com. The standard rooms here, which are in some rather grubby-looking chalets, are definitely past their best, but the large and bright (if rather bare) superior rooms are based in a separate modern block and are much nicer – and cost just $5 extra. All rooms come with a/c and hot water. **$40**

Shwe Taung Tarn Station Rd ☎071 21478. This is a centrally located cheapie on a quiet side road, with basic

but bearable rooms in the main building, plus so-called "bungalows" (although they're actually just bog-standard rooms) for $5 extra in a two-storey block behind – fractionally nicer if you can ignore the grimy exterior and faint smell of sewage outside. All rooms come with a/c and attached bathroom. **$20**

Win Unity Resort Hotel Bogyoke Aung San Rd ☎071 22438, Ⓦwinunityhotels.com. Monywa's top option is set in spacious grounds with a fantastic pool, and offers a particularly impressive breakfast spread each morning. Rooms come in a bewildering variety of styles, with the cheapest being fairly plain but acceptable. There's also a small spa offering inexpensive traditional massages (from $15). **$75**

EATING

Aung Pan Just off Station Rd. Popular local café dishing up reasonable curries (around K2500) served with an above-average spread of side dishes and accompaniments, although there's no English menu so you'll have to point. Daily 10am–9pm.

Pleasant Island Bogyoke Aung San Rd ☎09 681 8162.

Directly opposite the *Win Unity Resort*, this attractively rustic garden restaurant is set on its own tiny island, reached via a small rickety footbridge. The exclusively Chinese menu is good, if pricey, with most mains at around K6000–9000, plus more expensive seafood dishes. Daily 7am–10pm.

DIRECTORY

Banks The ATM at the AGD Bank accepts foreign cards, and there's a money exchange counter at the KBZ Bank.

Myitkyina and the far north

Despite the allure of its jungles and hill tribes, Myanmar's **far north** – where the country forms a wedge between China and India – sees few foreign visitors. In part this is down to the byzantine **travel restrictions** that govern much of the region, but the north's dated infrastructure and damp, steamy climate both also play their parts.

However, for those who are willing to stump up the cash for permits or happy to brave long, sometimes uncomfortable, journeys, Myanmar's northern tip has plenty to offer. The main town, **Myitkyina**, is the best place to get a taste of Kachin culture, while the peaceful **Indawgyi Lake Wildlife Sanctuary** is the most accessible of the region's nature reserves. Further north, the small town of **Putao** is a useful base for adventurous expeditions into the surrounding jungle-clad mountains.

Myitkyina and around

မြစ်ကြီးနားမြို့

Capital of Kachin State, **MYITKYINA** was largely destroyed in the three-month **Battle for Myitkyina** during World War II, and just a few old buildings survive – but what it lacks

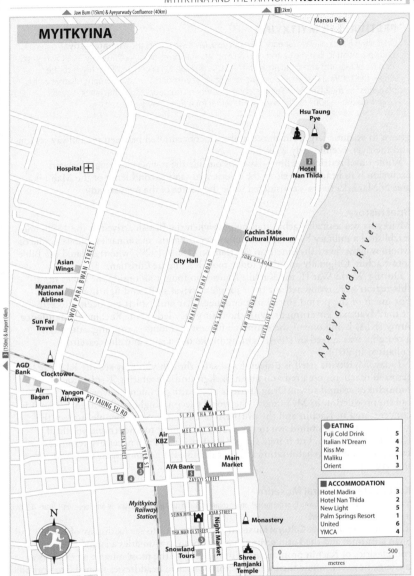

Jaw Bum (15km) & Ayeyarwady Confluence (40km)

(2km)

Manau Park

MYITKYINA

Hsu Taung
Pye

Hospital

Hotel
Nan Thida

Kachin State
Cultural Museum

Asian
Wings

City Hall

YONE GYI ROAD

SWON PARA BWAN STREET

THAKIN NET PHAY ROAD

AUNG SAN ROAD

ZAW JUN ROAD

RIVERSIDE STREET

A y e y a r w a d y   R i v e r

Myanmar
National
Airlines

Sun Far
Travel

AGD
Bank

Clocktower

Air
Bagan

Yangon
Airways

PYI TAUNG SU RD

THITSA STREET

N YER ST

SI PIN THA YAR ST

MEE THAT STREET

KHYAY PIN STREET

Air
KBZ

AYA BANK

Main
Market

ZAYGYI STREET

Myitkyina
Railway
Station

SEINN MYA

AYAR STREET

Monastery

THA MAR DI STREET

Night Market

Snowland
Tours

Shree
Ramjanki
Temple

N

● EATING	
Fuji Cold Drink	5
Italian N'Dream	4
Kiss Me	2
Maliku	1
Orient	3

■ ACCOMMODATION	
Hotel Madira	3
Hotel Nan Thida	2
New Light	5
Palm Springs Resort	1
United	6
YMCA	4

0   500
metres

8

in architectural history, it makes up for in cultural variety and bustling commerce.
Spreading out from the western bank of the Ayeyarwady, it's a centre for the six ethnic
groups that comprise the Kachin (see p.383), and home to substantial communities
from the Indian subcontinent – churches decorated with geometric Kachin patterns
stand alongside mosques and Sikh gurdwara – with everyone speaking Burmese as the
lingua franca.

Thanks to its proximity to the **jade mines** of Hpakant (see box, p.352), Myitkyina is
a major jade trading centre, bringing a steady stream of Chinese buyers. The town has

---

FESTIVALS IN MYITKYINA

On Kachin National Day (January 10) each year, Myitkyina hosts the **Manau Festival**, originally a *nat*-propitiating ceremony and now an important expression of Kachin unity. The town stops for days of feasting and dancing, with the focus on Manau Park north of the town centre, where the totem-like Manau poles are on display year-round. In early February, Myitkyina also plays host to the **Lisu New Year** celebrations, when Lisu people from Kachin State and neighbouring regions of China gather together for a three-day party.

---

grown to be quite large, but the central area, concentrated between the railway station and the river, is eminently walkable.

While travel restrictions limit day-trips outside the town, one straightforward excursion is to head north along the Ayeyarwady to the confluence of the Mali Hka and N'Mai Hka rivers – considered to be the **source of the Ayeyarwady**.

Brief history

Myitkyina was a small Kachin trading post when the British arrived in the 1890s and established a military base. Roman Catholic and Baptist missionaries followed, one of whom was the Swedish–American **Ola Hanson** (1864–1927), who translated the Bible into Kachin. Originally animists, today most Kachin are **Christian**.

During World War II, the Kachin levies who fought alongside the Allies in this region were renowned for their jungle survival skills and fighting spirit. For much of the period since independence, that same spirit has been directed at the Myanmar government, with the insurgency led by the **Kachin Independence Army** (KIA) being one of the country's fiercest and longest running. Although a ceasefire was agreed in 1994, fighting broke out again, and the ceasefire collapsed in 2011.

Today, Myitkyina itself is peaceful and safe, though you may see the KIA flag (crossed machetes on a red and green background) decorating T-shirts and motorbikes around town. Drug abuse is also quite prevalent in Myitkyina, as opium production in Myanmar – the world's second highest after Afghanistan – is concentrated in Kachin and the northern Shan States. Some people suspect the government turns a blind eye to the problem, hoping to undermine youthful Kachin nationalism, but it may simply be that it lacks the necessary resources to tackle it – and the rehabilitation efforts that do exist are mostly in the hands of the church.

Kachin State Cultural Museum

ကချင်ယဉ်ကျေးမှုပြတိုက် • 1km north of the market, on the corner of Thakin Net Phay Rd and Yone Gyi Rd • Tues–Sun 9.30am–4.30pm; closed on national holidays • K5000

The small **Kachin State Cultural Museum** is worth a visit to see its display of Kachin and Shan costumes and the Latin scripts that European missionaries adapted to express the complexities of Kachin pronunciation in the 1890s. The most interesting exhibits are upstairs, however, where there's a collection of Manau headdresses shaped like hornbills and a wide selection of everyday items made out of bamboo and rattan.

Hsu Taung Pye

ဆုတောင်းပြည့် • Northern end of Zaw Jun and Aung San roads • Daily dawn–dusk • Free

Although **Hsu Taung Pye** (its name meaning "wish fulfilling") is one of the main Buddhist temples in Myitkyina, with its golden pagoda right on the riverbank, your attention is more likely to be captured by the 30m-long **reclining Buddha** opposite (look at the designs on the soles of his feet). A former Japanese soldier donated the main Buddha statue in memory of 1280 of his countrymen, who died in the 1944 Battle for Myitkyina.

The Ayeyarwady confluence

မြစ်ဆုံ • 40km north of Myitkyina • Daily during daylight hours • Free; camera fee K1000, parking K300 • A motorbike taxi from Myitkyina (1hr 30min each way) costs K15,000

North of Myitkyina, a good road winds for around 30km through a series of modern Kachin villages. The road then branches: the right fork, closed to the public, leads to the site of the **Myitsone Dam** (see box below); the left road leads a few kilometres further north to the **Ayeyarwady confluence**, where the Mali Kha and N'mai Kha rivers meet to form Myanmar's most important artery. Despite the site's geographical importance, it is a fairly low-key spot with simple restaurants set up on the silt beach overlooking the confluence.

On top of the riverbank is a reproduction Kachin **longhouse**, and around the bend are the ravaged remains of an artisanal **gold-panning** operation. When the dam project was confirmed, locals flocked here to extract all the precious metals they could before the area was flooded. The minor gold rush has now subsided, leaving the bank pocked with deep holes.

On the way to the confluence, your driver may suggest a brief diversion to **Jaw Bum** (pronounced "boom"), a hill with a concrete tower on top from which you can look out over the trees. It's not the most exciting sight, but it's close to the route and it's free.

ARRIVAL AND DEPARTURE	MYITKYINA AND AROUND

At the time of research, foreigners were only allowed to travel in and out of Myitkyina by plane or train. Following weather damage in 2016, the authorities were obliged to repair parts of the existing railway line, and train journeys are now smoother and faster than they used to be – though they're still quite slow and bumpy overall.

By plane Myitkyina's airport is 5km west of the town centre. On arrival, don't worry if you're herded out without your bags – luggage reclaim is in a shed outside the gates. Most airline offices are on Pyi Taung Su Rd and Swon Para Bwan St, as are travel agencies such as Sun Far (daily 9am–5pm; ☎ 074 23392).
Destinations Bhamo (2 weekly; 30min); Mandalay (8 weekly; 45min–2hr); Putao (5 weekly; 50min); Yangon (7 weekly; 2hr 20min).

By train Myitkyina's railway station is right in the centre of town. The ticket office is open from 7am to 9.30pm, and it's possible to buy tickets one day in advance. While basic English is spoken at the station, the timetables are all in Burmese. There are three or four services a day.
Destinations Hopin (4hr); Mandalay (16–22hr); Naba (9hr 30min); Shwebo (19hr).

DAM NATION: THE MYITSONE DAM PROJECT

The **Myitsone Dam** on the Ayeyarwady is one of Myanmar's most controversial engineering projects. When completed, the 140m-high dam is expected to flood 447sq km and force the relocation of 11,800 local people, and prevent fertile sediment from washing down the river to Myanmar's "rice bowl", the Ayeyarwady Delta. Critics also point out that the site sits upon the unstable Sagaing fault line, and that, as with many of Myanmar's mooted mega-projects, a foreign nation will reap the benefits while leaving Myanmar to deal with the environmental and social costs – in return for Chinese finance, much of the electricity generated will be exported to Yunnan province.

In 2011, President Thein Sein announced that the project would be suspended for his term of office, but his successor has since not renewed that commitment. For now the site is sealed off from view, and locals fear that construction is continuing in secret using Chinese workers. Opposition to the dam has led to skirmishes between the KIA and government troops.

The road from Myitkyina to the Ayeyarwady confluence passes **Aung Myint Tha**, a new village with eerie rows of suburban-style housing that was constructed for local people who will be displaced by the dam. The village has not been a notable success – today, most inhabitants continue to work the fields near their old village, where the land is more fertile.

KACHIN CUISINE

Kachin cooking places a greater emphasis on fresh herbs and spices than Bamar cuisine, generally to delicious effect. Dishes to try include *chekachin* (chicken steamed with herbs in a banana leaf), *amedha thouq* (a spicy salad made with pounded dried beef) and pretty much anything on a skewer – barbecue dishes being a particular highlight.

GETTING AROUND AND TOURS

By motorbike taxi A motorbike taxi around town will cost K500–1000, while a trip up to the area around Manau Park is K2000 and the journey to the airport is K5000. The drivers wait at designated spots on the streets, marked "Taxi".

By cycle rickshaw A cycle rickshaw around downtown Myitkyina will cost K1000.

By bike and motorbike The *YMCA* (see below) rents out bicycles for K3000/day and motorbikes for a steep K20,000/day.

Tours The staff at the *YMCA* can arrange day-trips by motorbike to the sights around Myitkyina with one of their English-speaking staff for around K25,000/day – pretty reasonable, considering the cost of renting a motorbike through them alone. Myanmar Snowland Travels & Tours – based in an upstairs office at 79 Shansu North – can also arrange tours further afield into Kachin State (☎074 1618, ✉yawsepaww @gmail.com).

ACCOMMODATION

Hotel Madira 510 Pyi Taung Su Rd ☎074 29455, ⓦhotelmadira.com. Although its location (1.5km northwest of the railway station towards the airport) is a little inconvenient, the clean, bright rooms here are a cut above its town-centre competition, with international channels on the TV. $80

Hotel Nan Thida Zaw Jun Rd ☎074 22362. Overlooking the river, this old-school hotel is set in its own grounds in a slightly awkward location at the northern end of Zaw Jun Rd, just south of Hsu Taung Pye. Avoid the rather dark bungalows, and opt instead for one of the spacious, colourful $60 rooms in the main building, which come with large beds, high ceilings, big bathrooms and river views. $40

New Light 70 Zaygyi St ☎074 23576, ✉snghskng 958@gmail.com. The cheapest of the basic white-tiled rooms here are small and neat with fans and shared bathrooms, while their pricier (K32,000–42,000) counterparts have a/c and en suites – most also have small balconies. Single travellers pay K10,000 less per room. Not to be confused with the *New Light Guesthouse* near the *YMCA*. **K27,000**

Palm Springs Resort 7/8 Sitarpu Quarter ☎074 22828. Around 4km north of town, this luxurious

hotel has wonderfully comfortable rooms set in bungalows around nicely landscaped gardens and a tiny infinity pool overlooking the river. $120

★**United** 38 Thitsa St ☎074 22085, ✉hotelunited myitkyina@gmail.com. The friendly staff here offer pleasant rooms ranging from $30–45, some of which have balconies facing the street. Those on one side of the hotel look directly into the neighbouring building a few metres away, so do check before you pay up. All rooms have a/c and bathrooms with hot water. A redecoration was planned at the time of research, which may lead to price increases. $30

YMCA Ayer St ☎074 23010, ✉shkawnmai2012 @gmail.com. A favourite with the few backpackers who make it to Myitkyina, the *YMCA* (women welcome) has accommodation ranging from fan-cooled rooms with shared cold-water bathrooms, to slightly nicer en-suite rooms with hot water ($24) – some with a/c ($28). If you're on your own, prices are around $10 less. The saving grace here are the Kachin staff, who are friendly and knowledgeable about everything from local restaurants to national politics. They also produce a rather small-scale photocopied map of Myitkyina and its outskirts. No breakfast. $20

EATING

Each evening a brightly lit **night market** sets up on Aung San Rd, south of Zaygyi St. The varied food stalls are concentrated at the southern end of the market area, and at the northern end of town around Manau Park the backstreets are full of Kachin restaurants – usually indicated by the word *luseng* on their sign in Latin letters.

Fuji Cold Drink Aung San Rd. This street-side store whisks up delicious seasonal fruit juices and cold drinks without tooth-rotting amounts of sugar. Locals come here for *falooda*, but their lassis are also among the best in town. Daily 9am–5pm.

★**Italian N'Dream** Myo That ☎09 793 608 656. Around the corner from the *YMCA*, this new coffee and ice-cream bar has friendly staff, comfortable chairs and even a few English books to read. The cake is a bargain at only K500. Real coffee from K1500. Daily 7.30am–9pm.

JUNGLE FEVER

Hundreds of rare and endemic species inhabit the mist-cloaked hills of northern Myanmar, where the humid jungles of the Indian subcontinent meet the southern slopes of the Himalayas. The same geographic and political factors that have prevented commercial exploitation have also hampered attempts to catalogue and protect what's out there, so Myanmar in the early twenty-first century finds itself home to some of the best preserved, most extensive, and least understood wilderness areas in Southeast Asia. Despite the challenges, a select few scientists have managed to get in since the first British surveys in the late nineteenth century.

Botanist and spy **Frank Kingdon Ward** made ten epic journeys across northern Burma (as it was then known) between 1914 and 1956, collecting seeds from unknown plants as he went. He survived multiple bouts of malaria, "hordes of famished leeches", and impalement on a bamboo spike in his hunt for new species.

American zoologist **Alan Rabinowitz** also travelled widely through Kachin State and Sagaing Division in the 1990s to establish a series of nature reserves, including the Hkakabo Razi National Park, the country's largest. His main objective has been to preserve the habitat of Myanmar's vanishing tigers.

Myanmar's recent political and economic opening has led to renewed fears that commercial interests may trump environmental concerns. In 2013, a joint BBC-Smithsonian team led by **Chris Wemmer** undertook a series of televised expeditions to document the wildlife in remote areas, hoping to persuade Myanmar's government to establish further reserves before logging, mining or agricultural interests move in. Although they encountered a wide range of species, some new to science, things happen slowly in Myanmar and it remains to be seen whether their work will bear fruit. Setting up a new reserve is also only the start – lax enforcement has sometimes seen miners and hunters encroaching on supposedly protected areas with impunity.

8

★**Kiss Me** Zaw Jun Rd ☎074 20621. Hidden between Hsu Taung Pye and the river, *Kiss Me* has a great terrace and some extra-enthusiastic tea boys. The menu covers everything from Kachin to Malaysian dishes, with some delicious snacks as well – their "rolls" (paratha with various stuffings, from K1000) are particularly good. Daily 6am–9pm.

Maliku South of Manau Park. You'll need some help both finding this place and ordering once you get here (ask someone to write down a few dishes in advance), but it's said to be the best Kachin restaurant in town. Daily lunch and dinner.

Orient Ayer Rd ☎09 420 184 941. Next to the *YMCA*, this friendly little restaurant has a fairly broad menu – the Kachin owner worked in Japan for some years – with good kimchi fried rice (K2000) and a range of other dishes at similar prices. Takeaway lunchboxes can be ordered for K3500. Mon–Sat 7am–9pm, Sun noon–9pm.

DIRECTORY

Bank The usual suspects are scattered around town. One of the most central is AYA Bank on Aung San Road, which has an ATM.

Indawgyi Lake

အင်းတော်ကြီးကန်

Myanmar's largest lake, beautiful but remote **Indawgyi** is well off the tourist trail. The few travellers who do make the long journey find a peaceful natural environment, with opportunities for hiking in the hills to the east, kayaking across the lake and cycling to several small villages. At the time of research, work to resurface the road from the railhead town of **HOPIN** was also almost complete.

The lake is part of the 736-square-kilometre **Indawgyi Lake Wildlife Sanctuary**, established in 1999 to protect the area's birds and animals, which include several **endangered species** as well as gibbons, gaur, elephants and clouded leopards. At certain times of year your fellow visitors are as likely to be birdwatchers and field biologists as backpackers (December to March is the main birdwatching season).

The only accommodation nearby is in the village of **LONTON** (pronounced and sometimes spelled "Lone Ton"), which sits on the southwestern shore of the lake.

Shwe Myitzu Pagoda

ရွှေမြို့ဘုရား· • 10km north of Lonton • Daily during daylight hours • Free • Shwe Myitzu can be reached from the village of Namde, halfway up Indawgyi's western shore and 8km north of Lonton, from where the pagoda is 2km down an access road, with the turning signed in English

Dating from the mid-nineteenth century, the picturesque **Shwe Myitzu Pagoda** is built on a low island off the western shore. From a distance, it seems to float above the lake's surface, and around the time of the annual **festival** (a week before the Tabaung full moon, usually in March) the waters recede to reveal two sandy causeways – one for humans and one for *nats*. At other times, the pagoda is reached by a boat service, or you can make your own way by kayak from Lonton.

Lwemon and Nammilaung

Two interesting places to stop on the western side of Indawgyi Lake are the villages of **LWEMON** and **NAMMILAUNG**. Both are filled with weathered teak houses and have basic snacks on sale. According to legend, Indawgyi was once the site of a thriving city that was flooded by two *nagas*. Only a solitary widow escaped, and she settled in Lwemon – there's a shrine telling the full story in the village, 11km north of Lonton. On full-moon nights, locals claim to hear the sounds of the drowned city coming from below the water. Around 4km further north, Nammilaung is home to a cane Buddha image and a family of working **elephants**.

ARRIVAL AND DEPARTURE | INDAWGYI LAKE

By train and pick-up To reach Indawgyi Lake, take a train to Hopin on the Mandalay–Myitkyina line (16hr from Mandalay, 4hr from Myitkyina). From Hopin, you'll need to clamber on a pick-up to Lonton, 40km away (1hr; K5000), or find a motorcycle taxi (K15,000). The trucks leave when full from a street corner outside the station. Beware – if your truck is empty or near empty, it'll probably spend an hour or two driving slowly around Hopin picking up passengers before it departs. Pick-ups in the opposite direction leave from Lonton's main street between 7am and 2pm – book through your accommodation and the truck will pick you up first.

ACTIVITIES

Inn Chit Thu A few metres north of Indaw Mahar Guesthouse ☏ 09 451 511 823. Established in 2013, this small local organization works with Fauna & Flora International (⊛ fauna-flora.org) to develop

---

HPAKANT: MYANMAR'S WILD NORTHWEST

More than seventy percent of the world's jadeite is mined in Myanmar, most of it around **Hpakant** in Kachin State, 70km north of Indawgyi Lake. This semi-precious stone has been exported to China since the thirteenth century, after its presence was supposedly discovered by a Chinese merchant picking a stone from the roadside to balance his donkey's load, but after a 1994 ceasefire between the KIA and the Myanmar government (see p.348) paved the way for both sides to extract Hpakant's jade, mining practices have become increasingly destructive.

Today, the countryside around Hpakant has been reduced to a hellish moonscape that's best seen on satellite pictures, and in the town itself it's said heroin is as easy to buy as soap. While Chinese- and military-backed mining conglomerates evade taxes and export duties on a trade whose true value is estimated at nearly half Myanmar's legitimate GDP, desperate junkies spend their lives searching through unstable slag heaps for overlooked rocks to sell. **Landslides** are common, as are fatalities. The new government has promised to reform the industry, and has refused to renew licences for some mines. Success would mean a boost for the national economy, as well as the environment and local livelihoods – but given the powerful interests involved, it remains to be seen how this will play out.

community-based tourism, with the profits ploughed back into conservation projects. They offer kayak (K15,000/day), bicycle (K7000/day) and motorbike (K15,000/day) rental, have good maps of the lake and can provide guides for day-treks for K10,000 per person and specialist birdwatching guides for K15,000. They can also arrange motorbike taxis back to Hopin (K15,000). Most of their staff speak good English.

ACCOMMODATION AND EATING

Lonton has one guesthouse as well as two or three "**homestays**" (although they're actually small licensed guesthouses rather than private homes). They're all fairly basic, with bucket showers and mosquito nets over the beds, and none of them provides breakfast. None of the homestays has an official name, so they're listed here under their owners' names. All accommodation in Lonton charges the same price of K10,000 per person, and they work cooperatively – if one is full, they'll direct you to another. Lonton also has a few simple **restaurants**, while cheap and generous bowls of noodles can also be found in many of the other lakeside villages.

HOPIN

Hopin Star Pyay Doung Su Rd ☎ 074 62261. Very little English is spoken here, but the owners are friendly and the simple rooms with shared bathrooms are perfectly adequate. There are also a few en-suite rooms (K15,000). It's based in a green three-storey building not far from the station, but it isn't well signposted – to find it, you'll have to ask locals. No breakfast. **K20,000**

LONTON

Indaw Mahar Guesthouse Lake side of the road ☎ 09 7325 1692. Trucks from Hopin will drop you outside this striking white lakeside guesthouse, which is reached by a wooden walkway from the roadside. It has six simple rooms and a pleasant open veranda overlooking the lake. **K20,000**

★**Shwe Toe** South of Indaw Mahar Guesthouse ☎ 09 7827 3313. This is the most attractive homestay, and the only one on the lake side of the road. Its six rooms are spread over a series of wooden buildings connected by raised walkways. To find it, walk back south from *Indaw Mahar Guesthouse*; after you've passed the third building, you'll see a gate in a white fence, and through it a small arched bridge lined with flowerpots. **K20,000**

Tha Zin Phyu & Su Hla Phyu Opposite Indaw Mahar Guesthouse ☎ 09 254 010 431, ☎ 09 421 144 061. This newly built house appears larger and more solid than its neighbours. Still unfinished at the time of research, this homestay will be up and running by the time you read this. The staff here speak excellent English, and they also work for Inn Chit Thu (see opposite). **K20,000**

The far north

Located at the point where the subtropical rainforests of Southeast Asia abut the Himalayas, Myanmar's thickly forested northern tip is a hotspot of biodiversity – a treasure-trove of endangered and endemic species. At the far northern point, Southeast Asia's tallest mountain, **Hkakabo Razi** (5881m), was only climbed for the first time in 1996, by a Burmese–Japanese team.

The far north is home to a number of wildlife sanctuaries and national parks, including the world's largest tiger reserve in the **Hukaung Valley**. Unfortunately, in the latter case, the sanctuary's creation doesn't seem to have stopped logging companies and gold-miners from encroaching on the natural environment. Happily, ecosystems elsewhere are more intact, making this area still your best chance of spotting exotic wildlife.

Putao

ပုတာအိုမြို့

The small town of **PUTAO** (pronounced "Pu-Ta-O") is the gateway to this region, but while you can fly into the town without a permit, travelling beyond its borders is only possible as a guest of the eye-wateringly expensive *Malikha Lodge* or a paid member of a tour (with permits taking three weeks or more to process; see box, p.384). Once a Shan stronghold, and subsequently known by the British as **Fort Hertz**, Putao was spared Japanese occupation during the war.

This quiet and rather spread-out town has a central market, a sprinkling of pagodas and enticing views of distant mountains. Because of its remoteness,

TREKKING FROM PUTAO

Once you get to Putao, you can only travel outside town with a permit, as a member of an **organized tour**. The tour company will arrange the permit, but it may take a few weeks. In extreme cases, the government may stop issuing permits for a time due to ethnic conflicts in the region.

The local tour guides work for independent organizations or in branches of Yangon-based trekking companies. You can typically choose between a clutch of relatively gentle two-day hikes to stay overnight in Rawang and Lisu villages, go rafting on the Malikha River or head for the summits of mountains such as Phongun Razi, Phangran Razi or the base camp of Myanmar's tallest mountain, Hkakabo Razi. The difficulty of these treks varies considerably – consult the tour operator before deciding.

One of the **most popular treks** is to Phongun Razi (3635m), the most accessible of the mountains. It takes around five days (walking six hours per day) to reach the summit as part of a twelve-day package, with a day in Putao at either end. This trek will cost around $1900 per person for a group of four, all-inclusive. You'll be walking through primeval forests, staying in village houses at first and then camping as you approach the mountain. On all of these treks, you'll have the opportunity to see the indigenous wildlife and plants, including (with luck) some endangered species.

LOCAL GUIDES

Myanmar Trekking ☎01 667948, ⊛myanmar trekking.com. This Yangon-based company has branches nationwide. Their Putao branch offers treks ranging from a four-day walking tour or "soft trek" ($830 per person in a group of four) right up to a 33-day adventure trek to the base camp of Hkakabo Razi ($8500 per person in a group of four). They can also design trips to your own specifications.

Putao Trekking House ☎09 840 0138, ⊛putaotrekkinghouse.com. These local specialists operate from their own hotel in Putao. The team leads day-trips, cycling and rafting expeditions and treks ranging from four-day trips to visit minority villages ($805 each in a group of four) up to an epic 26-day mountain hike.

prices of some goods are higher than elsewhere in Myanmar, though locally produced items such as tribal costumes and fabrics in the market can be a real bargain.

Excursions out of Putao range from two-day trips to nearby Kachin villages to multi-day whitewater rafting excursions and a twelve-day round-trip hike to **Phongun Razi** (3635m), the region's most accessible trekking peak. Once out of Putao, the only accommodation options are wild camping and the occasional village house. You can forget about camping independently, though – you'll be stopped as soon as you try to get out of town by yourself.

ARRIVAL AND DEPARTURE   PUTAO

By air The only way for foreigners to get to Putao is by air, and flights can be booked up weeks in advance in high season. If you're having trouble finding available flights and agencies are unable to help, try visiting airlines' websites and offices directly, as they sometimes keep seats back. Putao is currently served by Myanmar National Airlines (⊛flymna.com), Yangon Airways (⊛yangonair.com) and Air Bagan (⊛airbagan.com). The airport is a few kilometres north of the town; if you've booked accommodation in advance, hotel staff will normally come to the airport to meet you.

Destinations Mandalay (3 weekly; 2hr 20min); Myitkyina (5 weekly; 50min).

ACCOMMODATION

Kham Su Ko Near the market ☎09 840 1082. This is owned by a Kachin family, who converted their wooden family home to make a simple guesthouse and restaurant. K40,000

Malikha Lodge Mulashidi Village ☎09 860 0659, ⊛malikhalodge.net. Set on a large site next to a Lisu village around 12km from Putao, this Jean-Michel Gathy-designed lodge has ten high-roofed thatched bungalows complete with log fires and round teak bathtubs. Room rates (minimum two nights; longer stays are slightly cheaper) include hotel transfers, day-trips and activities (including rafting and elephant trekking) and all meals. Some guests find the meals a bit monotonous. Open Oct–April. $1250

Hotel Putao Putao Airport Market St ☎ 09 5965 5777, ⓦ hotelputao.com. A comfortable, modern hotel, set in its own compound with a full range of amenities. The downside is its location, three minutes from the airport – great for arrival and departure, but quite a trek down into the town. $70

Putao Trekking House 424/425 Htwe San Lane ☎ 09 840 0138, ⓦ putaotrekkinghouse.com. Tastefully decorated wooden bungalows with small verandas, private bathrooms and fireplaces both in the dining room and on the outdoor deck. The largely Kachin staff also organize a good range of treks – full details are listed on their website. Closed June–Oct. $120

Thawan Razi Near the market ☎ 09 840 0186. The second of Putao's two guesthouses is owned by a Rawang family. The rooms are airy, and some come with en-suite facilities. K40,000

8

BURMESE SCRIPT

Contexts

History

Myanmar's past reflects its unique geographical location at the cultural watershed between China, Southeast Asia and the Indian subcontinent, and the country has been buffeted throughout its history by the rival claims of competing kingdoms and cultures – not to mention the conflicting demands of its numerous ethnic groups and the traumatic effects of colonial occupation. Myanmar's tendency to disintegrate into competing kingdoms (often divided along ethnic lines) has been a repeated feature of its history, like a kind of tropical Yugoslavia, and the threat of imminent Balkanization continues to hang over the country right up to the present day.

Physically, Myanmar grew up around its great river valleys, particularly the mighty **Ayeyarwady** – a cradle of civilization every bit as impressive as the Ganges, Indus or Nile. Culturally, the unifying effect of **Theravada Buddhism** has played a major role in uniting Bamar, Mon and other Burmese peoples throughout their history, although significant Christian and Muslim minorities remain.

Written **records** of early Burmese history are slight: much of what is known about the Pyu – the first recorded settlers – for example, comes from Chinese annals (and the now extinct Pyu language itself wasn't deciphered until the early twentieth century), while even some quite basic assumptions about Burmese history have been repeatedly questioned. Many details remain politically charged to this day (the exact role of the Mon in the development of the Bagan Empire, for example). Early **dates** can also be problematic – two different dating systems exist for the rulers of Bagan, for instance, meaning that sources don't always agree.

Prehistory

The first modern humans, **Homo erectus**, are thought to have arrived in Myanmar as early as 750,000 BC, settling around the Ayeyarwady River. **Homo sapiens** appear to have been present in Myanmar since at least 11,000 BC, judging by archeological finds from the Padah-Lin Caves near Taunggyi, including pieces of charcoal, stone tools, fragments of bone and simple cave paintings in red ochre.

By 1500 BC, the inhabitants of Myanmar had spread along the Ayeyarwady and Chindwin rivers and out into the areas that now form Shan and Kachin states. Inhabitants of the copper-rich Shan hills had begun to smelt **bronze**, while in the river valleys the art of growing rice had also been mastered – although perhaps the most notable achievement of the early Burmese is to have been among the first people in the world to domesticate the chicken. By 500 BC, villages in the vicinity of modern Mandalay were producing **iron**, while there is also evidence of trade both locally and as far afield as China – a precursor of the human migrations from southern China into Myanmar that were to prove so crucial in the country's early development.

750,000 BC	11,000 BC	1500 BC	c.200 BC
Arrival of *Homo erectus* in Myanmar	Evidence of prehistoric settlement at Padah-Lin Caves	Early human settlement of the Ayeyarwady River valley	Development of the early Pyu city-states along the northern Ayeyarwady River

HISTORY AND POLITICS IN MODERN MYANMAR

The history of Myanmar is a multifaceted, complex and frequently controversial subject. The official government-sponsored narrative emphasizes Myanmar's status as a country forged out of a patchwork of disparate peoples joined together in the glorious cause of national unity, sovereignty and the greater good, while travelling around the country you'll probably notice posters and displays promulgating the "Three Main National Causes" promoted by the military: "Non-disintegration of the Union/Non-disintegration of national solidarity/Perpetuation of Sovereignty".

Not surprisingly, official history tends to focus on the primacy of the country's Bamar majority and their role in building the modern nation-state of Myanmar, while huge statues of the country's three great Bamar unifiers and nation-builders – Anawrahta, Bayinnaung and Alaungpaya – tower symbolically over the new capital of Naypyitaw. Such history inevitably tends to be written at the expense of smaller ethnic groups – the Mon, Shan, Rakhine, Kayin and many others – who have found themselves at the margins of the majority Bamar world-view, and whose cultures, languages and identities have been progressively swamped and suppressed.

Pyu city-states

Myanmar's recorded history begins with the arrival of the **Pyu** in the second century BC. Migrating south from Yunnan in southern China, the Pyu gradually settled along the northern Ayeyarwady valley, establishing a string of independent city-states along local trade routes between China and India. Tang-dynasty Chinese annals record eighteen Pyu statelets, including eight walled cities (each with twelve gates – one for each sign of the zodiac). The largest early Pyu city was at **Hanlin** (see p.341), although as the Pyu migrated south down the Ayeyarwady this was eventually eclipsed, in around the seventh or eight century, by **Sri Ksetra** (aka Thayekhittaya; see p.193).

Pyu civilization lasted roughly a thousand years – the "Pyu Millennium", as it's sometimes described – laying the foundations for the great Bagan Empire that would eventually succeed it and, by extension, much of the basis of modern Burmese culture. Religious and cultural ideas travelling north from India played a profound role in Pyu society. By the fourth century most Pyu had converted to a local form of "Ari Buddhism" (see p.385), while they also developed an alphabet based on the Indian Brahmi script and adapted architectural ideas from the subcontinent – Myanmar's first stupas, later to become the country's defining architectural and religious symbol, made their first appearance at Sri Ksetra.

Mon kingdoms

Meanwhile, the second of Myanmar's two major early civilizations was taking root in the south of the country. The first **Mon** peoples began to migrate into Lower Burma from the kingdom of Dvaravati (roughly equivalent to present-day Thailand) from the sixth century onwards (although some studies, particularly by Mon historians, claim that they arrived much earlier). Like the Pyu, the Mon established a series of miniature kingdoms and city-states, the most notable being at **Thaton** and **Bago** (aka Pegu), both founded in the ninth century.

c.700 AD	c. 825	832 & 835
Sri Ksetra (Thayekhittaya) emerges as the main Pyu city in the Ayeyarwady valley	Foundation of the Mon cities of Thaton and Bago in southern Myanmar	Bamar raiders from Yunnan attack Pyu settlements in the northern Ayeyarwady valley

As in the Pyu city-states, the Mon traded extensively with India, and were strongly influenced by Indian culture and ideas. They were among the first peoples to convert to **Theravada Buddhism** and followed (at least to begin with) a relatively pure form of the religion – unlike the heterogeneous Ari Buddhism practised further north by the Pyu.

Bagan and the Bamars

The beginning of the end of the Pyu Millennium came in 832 with the arrival of a new wave of invaders and settlers who would subsequently become the nation's dominant ethnic group: the **Bamar** (see p.381). Following migratory routes first taken by the Pyu a thousand years previously, Bamar raiders descended upon the Ayeyarwady valley from the Nanzhao Kingdom in Yunnan, sacking the major Pyu city of Hanlin in 832 before returning in 835, raiding and pillaging further Pyu towns. Some of the invading Bamar appear to have brought their families with them and to have settled in the region. The exact details are vague, although what is known is that sometime in the mid-ninth century – the traditional date given is 849 – the Bamar settled and fortified the small town of **Bagan** (aka Pagan), located in a strategic location close to the confluence of the Ayeyarwady and Chindwin rivers in the middle of the old Pyu heartlands.

After their initial raids, the migration of the Bamar appears to have been a relatively peaceful affair – not so much an apocalyptic clash of cultures as a gradual merging of two related ethnic groups, Pyu and Bamar, both originally hailing from southern China and speaking similar Sino-Tibetan languages. Further Bamar from Nanzhao continued to arrive in the region during the ninth and tenth centuries, assimilating many aspects of the already thousand-year-old Pyu civilization. Bagan, meanwhile, gradually extended its authority over the surrounding plains and by 1044 had expanded to become the centre of its own sizeable statelet, covering an area stretching across the central plains as far as modern Mandalay, Meiktila and Magwe.

King Anawrahta and the rise of Bagan

The history of the Bagan Empire began in 1044 with the accession of **King Anawrahta** (aka Aniruddha; ruled 1044–78), who transformed Bagan from one of several minor kingdoms in Upper Burma into the pre-eminent power in the land. In doing so, he united most of the territories now comprising modern Myanmar into a single state and laid the foundations of the modern nation, at the same time establishing the primacy of the Bamar people within it.

Anawrahta began by strengthening Bagan's economic base, launching ambitious irrigation schemes whereby large swathes of formerly arid land were opened to new settlers. Canals were constructed and villages created, establishing the Bagan area as the rice bowl and commercial powerhouse of Upper Burma. Having consolidated Bagan's wealth and influence, Anawrahta gradually expanded the territory under his control. Formerly independent Pyu towns were taken under Bagan's rule, while expeditions were also sent south into Mon territories. The ruler of **Bago** submitted to Bagan's authority, while in 1057 the kingdom of **Thaton** (which had resisted Anawrahta's demands for tribute) was conquered, and its king, Manuha, taken back to Bagan as a captive.

The conquest of Thaton is traditionally seen as pivotal in the history of Bagan. Anawrahta, it is said, returned to Bagan with over 30,000 Mon slaves, including many

849	**1044–77**	**1057**
Bamar settlers establish Bagan	Bagan emerges as a major power during the rule of King Anawrahta; Theravada Buddhism is established as the state religion of the expanding Bagan Empire	Thaton falls to Bagan forces under King Anawrahta

craftsmen and artists, who would subsequently play a key role in helping create the thousands of flamboyant temples that survive to this day. Anawrahta's conversion to Theravada Buddhism by the Thaton-born monk **Shin Arahan** (see p.385) also proved crucial in establishing this branch of Buddhism as the country's dominant faith, as it continues to this day. Anawrahta also safeguarded the religion elsewhere in Southeast Asia by stopping the advance of the (then) Hindu Khmer, and helped to restart Theravada ordinations in Sri Lanka, whose Buddhist monasteries had been destroyed by the Indian Cholas.

Age of empire

The following two centuries marked the golden age of Bagan, led by a succession of capable rulers who continued Anawrahta's grandiose building works at home and conquests abroad, establishing the Bagan dynasty as one of the two great Southeast Asian powers, rivalled only by the Khmer Empire of Angkor.

Anawrahta was succeeded by his eldest son, **Sawlu** (ruled 1078–84), whose brief reign ended when he was killed during a rebellion in the south. Sawlu was succeeded in turn by Anawrahta's second son, **Kyansittha** (ruled 1084–1112), and Kyansittha's grandson, **Alaungsithu** (aka Sithu I; ruled 1112–67), both of whom continued to push back the frontiers of the Bagan Empire while launching into ever more spectacular temple-building projects at home. Alaungsithu was murdered by his homicidal son, **Narathu** (ruled 1167–71; see box, p.213), who was himself assassinated shortly afterwards. Order was restored under **Narapatisithu** (ruled 1174–1211), under whom the empire reached its greatest geographical extent, stretching south to the Malay peninsula and east into present-day Thailand.

The period also saw the emergence of a new and distinctive **Bamar culture**. Bagan's temple architecture began to develop its own unique flavour, transcending earlier Mon and Pyu models, while Burmese script became the primary vehicle for the written language, displacing Mon and Pyu scripts. The region's ethnic Pyu increasingly merged with the Bamar majority, while their language died out and their legends and histories were appropriated by the rulers of Bagan.

Decline and fall

A further four decades of peace and stability followed under Narapatisithu's successors, the devout but ineffectual **Htilominlo** (ruled 1211–35), the last of Bagan's great temple builders, and his successor **Kyazwa** (ruled 1235–50). The empire's former dynamism had been lost, however. Revenues remained static, while expenses continued to rise, as kings and nobles continued their attempts to accrue religious merit by endowing yet more temples and monastic foundations – by 1280, it's estimated, as much as two-thirds of Upper Burma's available agricultural land had been donated to the Buddhist clergy, effectively destroying the rulers' own revenues.

The agents of change came, once more, from the northeast. In 1271, and again in 1273, the **Mongol** armies of Kublai Khan demanded tribute of King **Narathihapate** (ruled 1256–87; see p.219), and, when this was refused, launched a series of attacks against the northern Bagan provinces in 1277, 1283 and 1287, moving progressively southwards on each occasion, eventually reaching Bhamo. Narathihapate fled south and was subsequently murdered, at which point many of the empire's tributary states,

1174–1211	1287	1300 onwards
Bagan Empire reaches its apogee under King Narapatisithu	Mongol invasion leads to the collapse of the Bagan Empire	Emergence of the independent Shan States in northeastern Myanmar, and the Hanthawaddy Kingdom in the south

including Arakan and the southern Mon territories, rebelled and declared independence. Almost overnight, the great empire of Bagan had ceased to exist.

A period of confusion ensued. The Mongols moved still further south into Tagaung, north of Mandalay (although it appears they possibly never reached Bagan itself), but showed no signs of wishing to permanently occupy the lands of the empire whose demise they had just precipitated. A new king, **Kyawswa** (ruled 1289–97), appeared in Bagan, although real power was held by three local brothers and former military commanders – Athinhkaya, Yazathingyan and Thihathu. Kyawswa submitted to Mongol authority and was recognized as governor of Bagan in 1297, only to be promptly overthrown by the three brothers, who proceeded to found the short-lived **Myinsaing Kingdom**. The Mongols despatched yet another force to reinstate Kyawswa, but this was beaten back, and Mongol forces finally left Myanmar for the final time in 1303, never to return.

Bagan, meanwhile, had been reduced from a once flourishing city of 200,000 people to an unimportant town. Further descendants of Anawrahta continued to rule as local governors owing allegiance to subsequent kingdoms until 1369, but the town itself would never regain its former political pre-eminence.

After Bagan: the successor kingdoms

The collapse of Bagan left a power vacuum in Myanmar, during which a series of smaller successor kingdoms – **Ava**, the **Shan States**, the **Mon** territories and **Arakan** – jostled for pre-eminence over a period of almost three centuries before the rise of the next great Burmese dynasty, the kingdom of Taungoo.

Ava

The remains of Bagan itself mutated, via the Myinsaing Kingdom and other local fiefdoms (including the Pinya and Sagaing statelets, which had emerged following the collapse of Bagan), into the **Kingdom of Ava**, the dominant power in Upper Burma for almost two centuries. Based in the city of Ava (at Inwa, near Mandalay; see p.303), the dynasty was founded by King Thadominbya, an ethnic Shan, in 1364. Despite their non-Bamar origins, Thadominbya and his successors regarded themselves as descendants and rightful heirs to the kings of Bagan and fought a series of wars in an attempt to reconquer former Bagan territories, although with only partial success. Long battles against the Mon, in particular, exhausted and impoverished the kingdom. The **Forty Years' War** (1385–1424) against the southern kingdom of Hanthawaddy (see p.362) took a particular toll, as did attacks on Ava by the Shan States, which succeeded in conquering Ava itself in 1527. The enfeebled kingdom never recovered, and in 1555 was toppled once again by the armies of the emerging Taungoo dynasty.

The Shan States

Yet another people from Yunnan in southern China, the **Shan** had been moving down into northern Myanmar from at least the tenth century, establishing a series of minor kingdoms, at first under the authority of Bagan, and then, following the Mongol invasion of 1287, independently. Shan rulers gained increasing power during the two centuries after the fall of Bagan, establishing the Kingdom of Ava (see above) as well as a series of

1364	1369	1385–1424
Foundation of the Kingdom of Ava	The Hanthawaddy Kingdom establishes its new capital at Bago	Repeated clashes between the Ava and Hanthawaddy kingdoms during the Forty Years' War

other Shan states including Mohnyin (Mong Yang) and Mogaung (Mong Kawng) in present-day Kachin State, along with Thibaw (Hsipaw), Theinni (Hsenwi), Momeik (Mong Mit) and Kyaingtong (Kengtung) in what is now Myanmar's northern Shan State.

Hanthawaddy

Meanwhile in the south, the Mon territories had reasserted their independence immediately after the fall of Bagan, establishing the **Hanthawaddy Kingdom** (aka "Hanthawaddy Bago" or "Ramannadesa"), a loose confederation of three semi-independent statelets – **Bago**, **Mottama** (formerly known as Martaban), near present-day Mawlamyine, and the **Ayeyarwady Delta**. The kingdom's first capital was at Mottama, but was moved to Bago in 1369. After repulsing Ava in the Forty Years' War, the Hanthawaddy enjoyed a miniature golden age, growing rich from trade with India and becoming a major centre of Mon language and literature, and also Theravada Buddhism – as witnessed by the numerous pagodas which still dot Bago to this day.

Arakan

In the far west of the Myanmar, the kingdom of **Arakan** (modern-day Rakhine State) had already been in existence for centuries (see box, p.120), squeezed between the Bagan Empire on one side and the Bengal Sultans on the other. Arakan suffered repeated attacks by the rulers of Ava following the collapse of Bagan, finally repulsing them only during the reign of King Narameikhla (aka Min Saw Mon; ruled 1429–33), who established a new Arakanese capital at **Mrauk U** in 1430 with military assistance from the Sultanate of Bengal. Indian influence was strong: in return for their help, Narameikhla recognized Bengali sovereignty over the kingdom and also ceded territory to the sultan. Close links with Bengal also led to the arrival of many Indian Muslims, perhaps the ancestors of the modern **Rohingya** (see box, p.121).

The first Taungoo empire

In the end, the second great pan-Burmese empire came from an unexpected direction. The kingdom of Ava was gradually crumbling in the face of repeated Shan attacks, and in 1510 the minor statelet of **Taungoo** (often spelled "Toungoo") in the far south of the Ava kingdom rebelled against its Ava rulers under the leadership of King Mingyinyo (ruled 1510–30), inaugurating the first Taungoo dynasty. Following the Shan conquest of Ava in 1527, many ethnic Bamar fled to Taungoo, now the only independent kingdom under Bamar rule, but menaced by much larger and more powerful states – Shan, Arakanese and Mon – on all sides.

Nothing daunted, Taungoo ruler **King Tabinshwehti** (ruled 1530–50) set out to expand his territories, taking on and eventually defeating his southern neighbours in the Taungoo–Hanthawaddy War (1535–41) and subsequently moving his capital to newly conquered Bago in 1539. By 1544 Taungoo forces had taken control of the country as far north as Bagan, but failed in later campaigns against Arakan and the Thai city of Ayutthaya, leading to Tabinshwehti's assassination in 1550.

It was left to Tabinshwehti's former military commander and successor, the legendary **King Bayinnaung** (ruled 1550–81), to restore the fortunes of the struggling kingdom. Born (it's said) the son of a lowly toddy-tapper, Bayinnaung succeeded by force of

1430	1510	1527	1531–54
Foundation of the kingdom of Mrauk U	Foundation of the first Taungoo dynasty	Shan forces capture the city of Ava	The Kingdom of Mrauk U reaches its apogee under King Minbin

character and military prowess in rising through the ranks. Following the assassination of the former king, he succeeded in beating off a series of rivals, laying siege to Taungoo and ultimately claiming the throne.

Having quelled dissension at home, Bayinnaung set out on a series of ambitious campaigns that brought a swathe of far-flung regions under the rule of Taungoo. Ava and the Shan States were conquered, along with further-flung territories including Ayutthaya, Manipur (in what is now northeastern India) and the Lao state of Lan Xang – establishing the largest and most powerful kingdom in Southeast Asia of its time.

Not surprisingly, the kingdom struggled to outlast the death of Bayinnaung, and by 1597 all the Taungoo dynasty's former possessions (including, ironically, their former home city of Taungoo itself) had rebelled, while in 1599 Arakanese soldiers sacked Bago.

Back in Arakan: the rise of Mrauk U

Meanwhile, back in the west, **Arakan** had remained subordinate to Bengal until 1531 and the arrival of Mrauk U's greatest king, **Minbin** (aka Min Pa Gyi; ruled 1531–54). After seizing the throne, Minbin took advantage of a weakened Bengal Sultanate, sending an army of 12,000 to claim large swathes of what is now Bangladesh and celebrating his victory with the construction of the landmark Shittaung Paya, the first of Mrauk U's great temples.

Even after recovering their independence, Arakanese Buddhist rulers continued to style themselves as "sultan", and court fashions were widely modelled on those at the Islamic Sultanate of Bengal. Mrauk U's uniquely multicultural kingdom was also the first part of Myanmar to experience the full impact of Western traders and invaders, suffering repeated attacks from Portuguese mercenaries as well as hosting a large community of Arab and European merchants.

Threats from the Portuguese and from the emerging Kingdom of Taungoo remained an ever-present danger during the reigns of Minbin's successors. Min Phalaung (ruled 1572–93) was obliged to fight off a major invasion by Taungoo in 1580–81, while his successor Min Razagyi (ruled 1593–1612) managed to defeat Taungoo forces in 1599 and even succeeded in sacking the Taungoo capital of Bago itself.

The empire strikes back

Reports of the demise of the Taungoo dynasty turned out to be somewhat premature. Following Arakan's sack of Bago in 1599, the empire revived dramatically under Bayinnaung's son, **Nyaungyan** (ruled 1599–1606), who by the end of his reign had regained control of much of northern Myanmar and the Shan States, ushering in the so-called **Restored Taungoo Dynasty** (aka the Nyaungyan dynasty). His son and successor, **Anaukpetlun** (ruled 1606–28), further reasserted Taungoo's control over large parts of Myanmar as well as defeating the army of Filipe de Brito e Nicote, the rogue Portuguese ruler of Thanylin (see p.84), in 1613. The old city of Ava became the capital of the kingdom from 1599 to 1613, after which it was returned to Bago until 1635 before once again returning to Ava, where it remained.

Almost a century of relative peace and stability followed until the 1720s and 1730s, during which period growing external pressures led to the empire's slow disintegration.

1535–41	**1550–81**
Taungoo forces overrun the Mon territory during the Taungoo–Hanthawaddy War, moving their capital to Bago in 1539	The Taungoo Empire reaches its apogee during the reign of King Bayinnaung

Raiders from Manipur began encroaching along the Upper Chindwin valley, while Taungoo's Thai provinces in Lan Na (Chiang Mai) also rebelled, and Qing-dynasty forces from China seized parts of Shan and Kachin states. Then, in 1740, the Mon also cast off the Taungoo yoke, founding the **Restored Hanthawaddy Kingdom** (with the support of the French). Not content with reasserting their own independence, Mon forces invaded northern Myanmar in 1751, assisted by Portuguese and Dutch mercenaries and using weapons supplied by the French. In 1752 they captured Ava itself, ending two and a half centuries of Taungoo rule.

The Konbaung dynasty

Scarcely had the Taungoo dynasty been erased from the face of Myanmar when the last of Myanmar's three great pre-colonial empires appeared in the shape of the **Konbaung dynasty** – which would eventually go on to wield control of the second-largest empire in Burmese history. The dynasty was founded in Shwebo, northwest of Mandalay, in 1752 by one Aung Zeya, a village chief who refused to accept the authority of the new Restored Hanthawaddy rulers in Ava. His initial territory was small – just 46 villages – but Aung Zeya had himself crowned nonetheless, taking the name **King Alaungpaya** (ruled 1752–60). Three attempts by Hanthawaddy forces to capture Shwebo were repulsed and growing numbers of recruits arrived to fight for Alaungpaya's anti-Hanthawaddy cause. By early 1754 he had acquired sufficient forces to recapture Ava and to drive out all Hanthawaddy forces from northern Myanmar.

The conflict had by now acquired an increasingly ethnic dimension: a possibly decisive battle between the Mon south and the Bamar north. Hanthawaddy persecution of Bamar living in Mon lands played directly into Alaungpaya's hands, and in 1755 he struck south, taking control of the Ayeyarwady all the way down to the small town of Dagon, which he renamed **Yangon** – only to be brought to a halt by French forces defending the port city of Thanlyin. A fourteen-month siege ensued before the city finally capitulated, after which Konbaung forces marched to Bago, capturing and sacking the city in 1757, signalling the demise of the Hanthawaddy dynasty – and, indeed, the end of the very last independent Mon kingdom in Myanmar, a blow from which the Mon people, culture and language have yet to recover.

Following the capture of Bago, various territories including Chiang Mai and other Thai provinces that had once formed part of the Taungoo Empire sent tribute to Alaungpaya, as did the governor of Mottama in the south. Konbaung forces also recaptured former Taungoo territory in the northern Shan and eastern Kachin states taken by the Qing dynasty in the 1730s, while Manipur was overrun in 1756. Scarcely had Alaungpaya finished fighting in the north, however, when a Mon rebellion broke out in the south, with Thai backing. In 1759 Alaungpaya led an army of forty thousand men into southern Myanmar before heading east, eventually reaching and laying siege to the Thai capital at Ayutthaya in April 1760. Just a few days into the siege, however, Alaungpaya suddenly fell ill and died, and Konbaung forces retreated back into Myanmar.

Ayutthaya again

The brief reign of Alaungpaya's son and successor **Naungdawgyi** (ruled 1760–63) was plagued by further rebellions – in Ava, Taungoo, Mottama and Chiang Mai – and it

1555	1599	1606–28
Taungoo dynasty forces conquer and destroy the Kingdom of Ava	King Min Razagyi of Mrauk U sacks the Taungoo Empire capital of Bago; the Taungoo dynasty establishes a new capital at Ava	Armies of the Restored Taungoo Dynasty under King Anaukpetlun reconquer large areas of the former Taungoo Empire

was left to his younger brother, the formidable **Hsinbyushin** (ruled 1763–76), to complete Alaungpaya's expansionist work. Having moved the Konbaung capital to a newly rebuilt Ava in 1765, Hsinbyushin conquered the Lao kingdoms of Vientiane and Luang Prabang and then led his armies east, slowly fighting his way south to the Thai capital of **Ayutthaya** in 1766. A fourteen-month siege ensued before the city finally fell. Kongbaung forces proceeded to devastate what was then one of Asia's largest and most magnificent cities, taking thousands of captives back to Myanmar.

Thai forces succeeded in recapturing most of their lost territory over the next few years. Ayutthaya, however, never recovered, and the Thai capital was subsequently moved to a new location, later to become known as Bangkok.

The return of the Chinese

Meanwhile, just as Konbaung forces were marching towards Ayutthaya, the Chinese launched successive invasions of their own into northeastern Myanmar. The first two were repulsed, but in late 1767 a Chinese army of fifty thousand defeated Konbaung forces at the **Battle of Goteik Gorge** and marched south to within 50km of Ava. Stretched perilously thin, Hsinbyushin finally recalled his armies from Thailand, eventually beating off the Chinese at the **Battle of Maymyo** in 1768 and repulsing yet another invasion the following year.

Hsinbyushin's achievement in simultaneously taking Ayutthaya while holding off the Chinese is often considered one of the greatest strategic feats in Burmese history, although the increasingly militarized nature of the Konbaung state and the cost of endless wars had its inevitable effect. The now ever-present Chinese threat, a resurgent Thailand, endless rebellions in Manipur and (in 1773) another Mon rebellion all conspired to cast a major shadow over the king's achievements, as did the wanton destruction of Ayutthaya, the root of widespread anti-Burmese sentiments which persist in Thailand right up to the present day.

Bodawpaya and the fall of Mrauk U

Hsinbyushin's successor, **King Singu** (aka Singu Min; ruled 1776–82), largely put an end to his father's endless wars, ceding Chiang Mai province (which had by then been a Burmese possession for most of the past two centuries) to Thailand in 1776. He was succeeded by his uncle (and King Alaungpaya's fourth son), **Bodawpaya** (ruled 1782–1819), who moved the capital to Amarapura (see p.300) and also commissioned the lunatic Mingun Pagoda, which would have been the world's largest stupa had it ever been finished (see p.308). Bodawpaya launched two further (unsuccessful) attacks against Thailand, although it was in the west that his forces had their most notable success, particularly in 1784, when a Konbaung army captured the great city of **Mrauk U** – ending the golden age of Arakan, and also bringing Konbaung rulers, for the first time, into direct contact with the British in neighbouring India.

The arrival of the British

By the beginning of the nineteenth century, European adventurers and traders had already been sniffing around Myanmar for over two centuries. Portuguese mercenary Filipe de Brito e Nicote (see p.84) had carved out his own personal fiefdom back in

1635	1740	1752
The Dutch East India Company establishes a trading base at Mrauk U	The Mon rebel against their Taungoo rulers, founding the Restored Hanthawaddy Kingdom	Mon armies of the Hanthawaddy Kingdom capture Ava, signalling the end for the Taungoo dynasty; King Alaungpaya founds the Konbaung dynasty

1603 in the port of Thanlyin, while the **Dutch East India Company** had established a trading base in Mrauk U in 1635. Later, in the 1740s, the **French East India Company** established their own HQ in Thanlyin, supplying arms to the local Mon during their rebellion against the Taungoo Empire.

The first **British** presence in Myanmar was the small colony of **Cape Negrais**, at the far southwestern corner of the Ayeyarwady Delta, established in 1753 following the collapse of the Taungoo Empire – although it was destroyed by Konbaung soldiers in 1759, after which relations between the two nations remained strained.

The First Anglo-Burmese War

Bodawpaya's capture of Mrauk U in 1784, and his subsequent seizure of Assam in 1816, created a long and only vaguely defined border between Konbaung territories and British India. Clashes were inevitable, given the British desire to neutralize what was seen as growing French influence at the Konbaung court, and also to seize more of the border territories for themselves. After some preliminary skirmishes, war – the **First Anglo-Burmese War**, as it's now known – was officially declared in March 1824.

Led by **General Mahabandoola**, Burmese forces enjoyed some spectacular early successes in Arakan thanks to their greater experience of jungle warfare. The British countered by sending a large naval division to attack Yangon, causing the local population to flee. Eventually, in November, the rival armies met outside Yangon. British forces resisted repeated attacks by the numerically superior but poorly armed Burmese, who were cut down in their thousands and then forced back into the small town of Danubyu. At the same time, a counteroffensive was launched against Konbaung troops still in Arakan. On March 29, 1825, British forces simultaneously attacked Danubyu, killing Mahabandoola, and captured the Arakan capital, Mrauk U. The war was effectively over. An armistice was subsequently declared, and although Konbaung troops attempted a daring counterattack against British troops in Pyay in November, they too were defeated and forced to sign the humiliating **Treaty of Yandabo** (1826). Under this, the Konbaung were obliged to cede Arakan, Manipur and Assam in the west and a large slice of territory in Tenasserim (modern Tanintharyi) in the far south, as well as paying a colossal indemnity of £1 million.

The Second Anglo-Burmese War

The effect of the conflict on both Konbaung finances and morale was devastating, with the empire left economically crippled and its leaders in disarray. **King Bagyidaw** (ruled 1819–37) relocated the capital to Ava in 1823, but became increasingly reclusive and ineffectual following the disastrous war. He was overthrown by **Tharrawaddy** (ruled 1837–46) who continued to plot fruitlessly against the British, and then by his son **Pagan Min** (ruled 1848–53).

The origins of the **Second Anglo-Burmese War** (1852) were little more than a minor diplomatic squabble after the captains of two British merchant ships were detained in Bago on charges of customs violations. The British, seeing a chance of making further inroads into Burmese territory, blew the incident up out of all reasonable proportion, demanding a staggering £100,000 in compensation, blockading Yangon harbour, shelling the city and provoking a conflict in which the odds were stacked very heavily in their favour.

1754	1755	1757
Konbaung forces under Alaungpaya capture Ava and drive Mon armies out of northern Myanmar	Konbaung forces take the town of Dagon, which is renamed Yangon	Hanthawaddy, capital of Bago, falls to Konbaung armies, marking the end of Myanmar's last independent Mon kingdom

A very one-sided war ensued, with overwhelmingly superior British forces encountering only modest Burmese resistance. Mottama, Yangon and Pathein were all seized within less than a fortnight in April, with Bago following in June and Pyay in October. The British issued a "Proclamation of Annexation" stating that it was taking possession of Bago and the lower half of the country up to Pyay. Konbaung humiliation was complete.

King Mindon

The Second Anglo-Burmese War had at least one positive side effect for the Konbaung dynasty. Following the conclusion of hostilities, King Pagan Min was dethroned in favour of his half brother **Mindon** (ruled 1853–78). The most progressive of all Konbaung rulers, Mindon saw the urgent need to modernize what was left of his country, sending envoys to Europe and the US to learn about technological developments while enacting numerous reforms at home aimed at reducing corruption and modernizing the national army. He also founded a new royal capital at **Mandalay** in 1857, introduced Myanmar's first machine-made currency and encouraged trade with Britain by acquiring steamers after the opening of the Suez Canal.

The Third Anglo-Burmese War

Mindon died in 1878 and was succeeded by his son, **Thibaw** (ruled 1878–85). The British soon became concerned at Thibaw's attempts to ally himself with the French, while relations were further strained following the so-called "Great Shoe Question", when British officials who refused to remove their shoes before entering the royal palace were banished from Mandalay.

The tipping point arrived in 1885, when a dispute over logging rights was used as an excuse by the British to insist on further concessions from King Thibaw – demanding not only that they to all intents be given a free commercial hand throughout Myanmar, but also that Britain take control of all Burmese foreign policy decisions, effectively surrendering national sovereignty and making Burma a British colony. Faced with an impossible situation, King Thibaw granted all British demands bar the surrender of sovereignty.

Thibaw's many concessions notwithstanding, the British parliament decided that the moment for the annexation of the last remaining piece of independent Myanmar had finally arrived. The resultant **Third Anglo-Burmese War** was even shorter and more one-sided than the second. British troops advanced on Mandalay virtually unopposed, seized the palace and despatched Thibaw into exile in India (just as the last Mughal emperor of India had been sent by the British into exile in the opposite direction; see p.72).

Colonial Burma

Now in complete and undisputed control of the country, the British set about remodelling their new possession in their own image, with **Burma** (as it was now known) being administered – rather insultingly – as a province of British India. **Rangoon** (as Yangon, already the principal city of British southern Burma, had become known) became the new national capital, developing into one of the British Empire's

1760	1766	1783
Death of Alaungpaya during the siege of Ayutthaya	Siege and sack of Ayutthaya by Konbaung armies under King Hsinbyushin	King Bodawpaya establishes a new Konbaung capital at Amarapura

great imperial showcases with its alien, European-style courthouses, clocktowers and doughty red-brick edifices.

The opening of the Suez Canal in 1869 had greatly increased the demand for Burmese rice, and large new areas of countryside were reclaimed and opened up for cultivation, particularly in the formerly swampy, disease-ridden and mangrove-choked lowlands of the Ayeyarwady Delta. Relatively little of the country's burgeoning wealth found its way to the Burmese themselves, however. British firms controlled much of the nation's economy, while the plight of the country's native Burmese was further exacerbated by a massive influx of Indian merchants and labourers. Secular schools were established and Christian missionary activity encouraged. Improvements to the country's infrastructure also followed. Railways were built and the Irrawaddy Flotilla Company (see p.63) launched. Meanwhile, all signs of opposition to British rule were suppressed, with rebellious villages being razed to the ground and their leaders exiled, forcing many Burmese into banditry and other criminal activities.

The nationalist movement

By the turn of the twentieth century, the first signs of organized nationalist resistance had already begun to emerge. As elsewhere in Asia, many leading anti-colonialists were young people educated in Europe, who returned home demanding change through constitutional reform, rather than by taking up arms. In 1920, university students went on strike in protest at the new University Act (seen as privileging Myanmar's western-leaning, European-educated elite), while locally sponsored "National Schools" were created to counterbalance the colonial education system. The Buddhist clergy also played a leading role in anti-British protests – one of the first to speak out against colonial rule (particularly Christian missionary activity) was the remarkable Irish-born monk known as U Dhammaloka, while other prominent figures included U Ottama in Sittwe and U Wisara, who died in prison after a lengthy hunger strike.

The first major uprising was the **Saya San Rebellion** (1930–32), named after its leader, Saya San, who organized mass peasant protests, vowed to expel the British and had himself crowned king. The popular uprising was put down with considerable difficulty, after which Saya San and over a hundred other rebels were hanged.

The year 1930 also saw the creation of the **Thakin** movement (also known as the **Dobama Asiayone**, or "Our Burma", movement) – a nationalist group formed largely of students and operating mainly out of Rangoon University. The Thakins were instrumental in organizing a second university students' strike in 1936 to protest the expulsion from Rangoon University of a certain young **Aung San** and his colleague **U Nu**, both of whom would go on to play seminal roles in the history of the country.

Burma was uncoupled from India in 1937 and given a new constitution, including its own elected assembly and prime minister (although with limited actual powers). Despite these concessions, major protests erupted in 1938–39, leading to the so-called **1300 Revolution** (1300 being the Buddhist calendar equivalent to 1939). Strikes by employees of the Burmah Oil Company in the centre of the country developed into nationwide protests. The subsequent crackdown claimed 33 lives including thirteen unarmed protesters shot dead in Mandalay – a small but chilling foretaste of atrocities yet to come.

1784	1824–25
Konbaung forces sack the city of Mrauk U and take possession of Arakan	First Anglo-Burmese War: the British seize Arakan, Manipur, Assam and much of southern Myanmar

World War II

Agitations for independence took a back seat, however, with the outbreak of **World War II**, during which Burma would become a pivotal region in the fight between Japanese, Allied and Chinese forces. Many nationalists saw the war as a chance to wring further concessions out of the British in return for Burmese help; others, including the Thakins, were resolutely opposed to any form of involvement in the fighting.

The rebellious young student **Aung San**, meanwhile, had given up his university studies in order to devote himself to the anti-colonial struggle, and in 1940 was forced to flee Burma after the British issued a warrant for his arrest. He travelled to China, hoping to gain assistance from the Kuomintang government, but was intercepted by the Japanese authorities in Amoy, who offered their help instead. Aung San and 29 fellow nationalists – the so-called "**Thirty Comrades**" (whose number also included future dictator Ne Win) – were subsequently taken by the Japanese to Hainan Island and given military training.

The Japanese occupation

Meanwhile, in Southeast Asia the war was advancing steadily closer to Burma. In November 1941 the Japanese forces invaded British-ruled Malaya and began moving into Thailand (which had signed a military alliance with Japan). Two months later, further Japanese forces (accompanied by the Thirty Comrades, including Aung San) moved through northern Thailand and into Tenasserim (Tanintharyi) in southern Burma, capturing Moulmein (Mawlamyine) after fierce fighting. Rangoon was evacuated in March 1942, there being insufficient troops available to defend the city, leaving the Japanese to enter unopposed. Allied troops retreated northwards and, after further fighting, were ordered to leave Burma for India. The Thai army, meanwhile, occupied Kayah and Shan states, as previously agreed in their treaty with the Japanese.

Many Burmese initially saw the Japanese – fellow Asians and Buddhists alike – as liberators come to help them shake off British rule, although it soon became obvious that life under the Japanese was no better than it had been under the British – in fact quite possibly the opposite. The country was renamed the State of Burma and a puppet government installed, but real independence remained as distant as ever. Increasingly disgruntled, Aung San (who had served as war minister and head of the army in the Japanese-sponsored government) put himself and the Burmese National Army (of which he was now commander) at the service of the British.

The Allied counterattack

Allied attempts to retake Burma following the Japanese occupation were put on hold, the battles in Europe and the Middle East being considered of more pressing importance, while political disturbances and famine in Bengal were also tying up large numbers of troops. It was not until October 1943 that a combined force of British, Indian, African, American and Chinese soldiers began moving back into northern Burma. Progress through the jungles was slow and difficult, but by May 1944 the airfield at Myitkyina had been taken, establishing an air link with India and China. At the same time the Japanese launched a counterattack, attempting to drive through to Imphal, the capital of Manipur in British India, but their advance was halted at

1852	1853
Second Anglo-Burmese War: the whole of southern Myanmar falls to the British, who establish a new capital at Yangon (Rangoon)	King Mindon assumes power, initiating wide-reaching reforms in an attempt to modernize the country

Kohima, and they were forced to retreat with heavy losses – most caused by disease, starvation and exhaustion.

The tide slowly turned. Japanese forces fell back from the Chindwin to the Ayeyarwady. Allied troops were sent into Rakhine while Chinese forces moved south to Bhamo, followed by a decisive push into central Burma, with the Allies now able to make the most of their superior numbers and air power in the flat central plains. **Meiktila** fell in March 1945 after a devastating battle during which most of the town was destroyed and almost every member of the Japanese garrison killed, while **Mandalay** was captured shortly afterwards, following further fierce fighting that left much of the historic old town in ruins. Simultaneously, the Burmese National Army led by Aung San rose up against the Japanese. Allied forces now proceeded with increasing speed towards **Rangoon**, following the rapidly retreating Japanese. Gurkha and Indian forces arriving in Rangoon on May 1 discovered that the Japanese had already abandoned the city and fled.

To independence

Four years of fighting had left the country in physical and economic tatters, with estimates of the number of civilians who died during the Japanese occupation ranging from 170,000 up to a quarter of a million. Following the Japanese surrender, the **Anti-Fascist Organisation (AFO)** – which Aung San had founded in 1944 along with others including future prime minister Ba Swe, socialist leader Thakin Soe, communist leader Than Tun and old student comrade U Nu – emerged as the leading mouthpiece for Burmese nationalist aspirations.

Two years of uncertainty followed, as the British attempted to stall demands for immediate independence and Burmese communists, socialists and conservatives manoeuvred for position. In January 1947 Aung San led an AFO team to London, signing an agreement with British prime minister Clement Attlee guaranteeing Burma independence within a year, while in February he convened the Panglong Conference, during which leaders of the Shan, Kachin and Chin (but not, notably, Kayin) agreed to form part of a future unified Burma. In general elections in April 1947, Aung San's **Anti-Fascist People's Freedom League** (AFPFL), as the AFO had now been renamed, won 176 out of 210 seats.

Aung San was by now firmly established as Burma's post-independence leader in waiting. Or would have been. On July 19, 1947, Aung San and the Executive Council of his provisional government were in a meeting at Rangoon's Secretariat when a group of gunmen stormed the rooms and **assassinated Aung San** along with six of his ministers. The attack was eventually traced to former colonial-era prime minister U Saw, who was subsequently hanged (although, as with the assassination of another national political hero, American John F. Kennedy, conspiracy theories continue to abound; many suggest British involvement, while others point to the hand of future military ruler Ne Win).

The catastrophic effect of Aung San's death on Burma can hardly be overestimated, given his status as the one leader who might have been capable of uniting the country's widely divergent peoples, and it's often speculated how much more peaceful the country's subsequent history might have been, had he lived.

1885	1920	1930
Third Anglo-Burmese War: British forces seize the whole of Myanmar, which is now administered as a province of British India	University students strike in Rangoon in protest at colonial educational policies	Establishment of the nationalist Thakin movement by students at Rangoon University

Independence and after

It was left to socialist leader (and Aung San's old university friend) **U Nu** to oversee **independence** on January 4, 1948, becoming post-colonial Burma's first prime minister. The country was immediately wracked by a series of armed insurgencies featuring a wide-ranging cast of communists, army rebels, Arakanese Muslims and Kayin militia. Then, from 1949, fleeing Kuomintang forces, recently driven out of China by Mao Zedong's communists, took over remote areas of the north (covertly supported by the US). Physical and economic reconstruction of the ravaged country continued apace, even so. Regular elections were held, with U Nu continuing as prime minister except for a brief period in 1956–57 when he was replaced by his communist-leaning AFPFL colleague, Ba Swe.

In 1958, the ruling AFPFL split into two factions led by U Nu and Ba Swe respectively, during which U Nu narrowly survived a vote of no confidence brought by Ba Swe. U Nu subsequently "invited" army chief of staff General **Ne Win** to take over the country (some say he was coerced) until fresh elections were held. Ne Win duly obliged, taking the opportunity to arrest over four hundred alleged communist sympathizers and close three daily newspapers – a very modest taste of things to come.

Fresh elections in 1960 returned U Nu's faction of the AFPFL with a large majority, although Shan separatists almost immediately commenced agitating for independence. Faced with bickering politicians, closet communists and endless separatist uprisings by Myanmar's ethnic minorities, the army appears to have come to the conclusion that only strong leadership could save the country from disintegration. On March 2, 1962 Ne Win, along with sixteen other senior army officers, staged a **coup**, arresting U Nu and others and proclaiming the establishment of a socialist state to be run by a military-led revolutionary council, initiating a period of army rule that would last, in one form or another, until 2015. Myanmar's age of the generals had begun.

Ne Win and military rule

The coup itself was almost completely bloodless, while protests following the announcement of military rule were allowed to run their course until July 1962, when soldiers fired into a student protest at Rangoon University, killing over a hundred people. In March 1964 all opposition political parties were banned, and hundreds of activists arrested. Meanwhile, there were ongoing insurgencies by the **Kachin Independence Organization** (from 1961), and in 1964 a rebellion by the Shan State Army.

In response, Ne Win commenced slamming all Myanmar's doors on the rest of the world firmly shut. Around 15,000 private firms were nationalized, causing the economy to stagnate; foreign aid agencies and the World Bank were expelled; the study of English was cut back in schools; and visitors limited to 24-hour visas. The few Burmese who were allowed to travel were sent mainly to the Soviet Union for training; mass press censorship was put in place and foreign-language publications and privately owned newspapers banned. Over 200,000 expat Chinese, Indians and Westerners quit the country, along with almost the whole of the country's remaining Jewish population (see p.69).

More than a decade of isolation and underachievement passed. Ne Win retired from the army in 1974 but continued to run the country through the **Burma Socialist**

1930–32	1939	1940
The Saya San Rebellion sees mass popular protests against colonial rule	Outbreak of World War II	Nationalist leader Aung San and the rest of the "Thirty Comrades" are given military training by the Japanese in preparation for the overthrow of British rule

GENERAL MADNESS

The despotic excesses of modern Myanmar's two leading generals, Ne Win and Than Shwe, have been widely reported. What is less well known is their quaint shared beliefs in antique superstitions and old wives' tales – some of which appear to have played a major role in shaping huge national policy decisions and other affairs of state.

Rumours abound concerning **Ne Win**'s penchant for numerology and *yadaya* (see p.388). Warned by his astrologer of potential assassination attempts, the great dictator is said to have stood in front of a mirror, stamping on a piece of meat, and then shot himself in the mirror in order to deflect the anticipated bloodshed. In 1987 he was also responsible for disastrous currency reforms during which new K45 and K90 notes (both divisible by nine, and said to be numerologically auspicious) replaced former high-denomination notes, wiping out the lifetime savings of many Burmese at a stroke – a decision which played a major role in the 8888 Uprising that erupted the following year.

Ne Win's successor **Than Shwe** was no less superstitious. The grandiose new multi-billion capital of Naypyitaw was established, it's rumoured, largely at his astrologers' say-so, while he is also thought to have indulged a weakness for many other forms of almost cabalistic superstition. On one occasion following the Saffron Revolution in 2007 – an incident entertainingly related in Emma Larkin's *Everything is Broken* (see p.393) – his wife Kyaing Kyaing is reported to have walked a pig and a dog counterclockwise around the Shwedagon Pagoda in a *yadaya* ritual aimed either at breaking the power of Aung San Suu Kyi and/or protecting Than Shwe's own family from cowardly people (with pig and dog symbolizing either Aung San Suu Kyi or the backsliding Burmese populace – or possibly both). Whatever its intentions, Kyaing Kyaing's attempt at Buddhist black magic had little influence on subsequent events – although at least no animals appear to have been harmed in the making of this particular military fable.

Programme Party (BSPP), the nation's one and only officially recognized political organization. Further strikes and demonstrations took place in 1974, during which a further hundred-odd students and workers were shot, while in 1978 the army drove a quarter of a million Rohingya Muslims (see box, p.121) into Bangladesh.

Ne Win's disastrous currency reforms (see box above) in 1987 caused further suffering and provoked a further round of protests and riots, while new government policy forcing farmers to sell produce below market values (following on from the UN's decision in late 1987 to downgrade Myanmar to "Least Developed Country" status) led to further violent rural protests. Public letters written by Ne Win's former second in command General Brigadier Aung Gyi described Burma as "almost a joke" compared to other Southeast Asian countries. Not surprisingly, he was arrested soon afterwards.

The 8888 Uprising

Popular discontent at military rule finally erupted during the **8888 Uprising** (named after the key events which occurred on August 8, 1988). The initial spark for the uprising occurred in March 1988, when a student was shot dead by police following a trivial after-dark altercation in Yangon. Protests rapidly spread across the city's universities and several more students were killed during a protest at Inya Lake. By June, demonstrations had spread nationwide, with widescale unrest and numerous deaths in cities across the country.

1941	1943	1947
Japanese forces invade and capture Myanmar	Allied forces reconquer Myanmar, aided by Aung San and other nationalist leaders disillusioned with Japanese rule	Aung San signs an agreement with British authorities guaranteeing Burmese independence within a year, but is assassinated shortly afterwards

Then, at the height of the crisis, Ne Win unexpectedly announced his retirement, promising a multi-party democracy in the near future but also stating, ominously, that "If the army shoots, it has no tradition of shooting into the air. It shoots straight to kill." Further protests ensued, including a huge nationwide demonstration and general strike starting on August 8, 1988, a day of numerological auspiciousness. Entire neighbourhoods of Yangon were taken over by demonstrators, which now included people from all realms of Burmese society including doctors, monks, lawyers, army veterans and government workers, causing police and army to retreat in the face of the sheer scale of the protests.

On August 26, Aung San's daughter, **Aung San Suu Kyi**, made her first public speech, addressing half a million people at the Shwedagon Pagoda, urging the people and army to work together peacefully and becoming, almost overnight, the defining symbol of the nation's struggle for democracy in Myanmar. Events seemed to be moving definitively in the protesters' favour. Dr Maung Maung, a legal scholar and the only non-military member of the junta's political mouthpiece, the BSPP, was appointed as head of government, offering the promise of imminent elections.

Then, on September 18, 1988, the military suddenly and decisively struck back, imposing martial law and breaking up protests with new and unprecedented brutality in the name of the newly established **State Law and Order Restoration Council (SLORC)**. The military once again assumed total control of the country, under the leadership of Ne Win protégé **General Saw Maung**. Troops roamed through cities nationwide, shooting randomly at protesters: over 1500 were murdered in the first week of SLORC rule alone. Aung San Suu Kyi appealed for international help, but within a few days the protests had been effectively crushed. As many as ten thousand Burmese are thought to have died in the uprising, with many more missing or fled. The prospect of a democratic Myanmar – which had seemed so tantalizingly close for one heady month in August – was now as far away as ever.

The rule of SLORC

The new SLORC leadership was widely condemned by international leaders for its role in crushing the demonstrations – the military responded by more than doubling the size of the army (from 180,000 to 400,000). Aung San Suu Kyi, meanwhile, responded to the failure of the uprising by founding the **National League for Democracy (NLD)**, which would thenceforth serve as the principal vehicle for all anti-government protests. Offers by SLORC to hold elections were rejected by Aung San Suu Kyi on the grounds that they could not be held freely and fairly so long as the generals remained in power.

One of SLORC's first major acts after crushing the 8888 Uprising was to officially change the name of the country from Burma to **Myanmar** (see box, p.380). It also, surprisingly, announced the first elections in the country since 1960, designed to elect a quasi-parliamentary body that would draft a new constitution and provide a semblance of democracy. The generals, having indulged in widespread electoral manipulation and media control and placed all major opposition leaders (including Aung San Suu Kyi) under arrest, were thus horribly surprised when the **elections of May 1990** provided a landslide victory for Aung San Suu Kyi's NLD, winning 392 of the 492 seats available and trouncing the SLORC-sponsored National Unity Party (the successor to the BSPP). The SLORC refused to recognize the election result.

1948	1958	1960
Myanmar gains independence; U Nu becomes the country's first post-colonial leader	Faced with growing disorder, U Nu "invites" military leader Ne Win to take charge of the country pending fresh elections	U Nu wins the general election, but is unable to bring stability to country

AUNG SAN SUU KYI

The world's most famous former prisoner of conscience, **Aung San Suu Kyi** has for many years served as the human face of the Burmese freedom struggle – as synonymous with her country's democratic aspirations as Nelson Mandela was with the anti-Apartheid movement in South Africa.

Much of Aung San Suu Kyi's standing undoubtedly derives from her status as the daughter of the revered **Aung San** (1915–47), father of modern Myanmar, although despite her illustrious parentage there was little in her early life to suggest the path she would later follow. Born in Yangon in 1945, Aung San Suu Kyi was just two when her father was assassinated and subsequently spent many of her younger years abroad, first in Delhi (where her mother, **Khin Kyi**, served as Burmese ambassador to India and Nepal) before studying at Oxford University, where she met her future husband, the late distinguished Asian scholar **Dr Michael Aris**. She subsequently worked for the UN in New York before marrying Aris in 1971. They spent their first year of married life in Bhutan (where Aris was tutor to the royal family), after which they returned to England, living in Oxford where Aris had been made a university lecturer. Meanwhile, Aung San Suu Kyi continued her studies at London University's School of Oriental and African Studies and also became the mother of two sons.

THE STRUGGLE BEGINS

The spectacular rise to global prominence of the formerly bookish and retiring wife of an Oxford don followed a remarkably serendipitous chain of events. In 1988, Aung San Suu Kyi returned to Yangon to care for her sick mother, who had been admitted to the Rangoon General Hospital. Within weeks of her return, Aung San Suu Kyi found herself caught up in the greatest popular uprising in modern Burmese history (see p.373), with the hospital itself at the epicentre of events. Swept along in the sudden political upheavals, she determined to devote herself to the fight for democracy, espousing **political beliefs** rooted in non-violent resistance, dialogue, reconciliation and inclusivity, which owed much to the ideas of Mahatma Gandhi as well as her own Buddhist faith. Her first official **public speech**, at the Shwedagon Pagoda, was attended by thousands of Burmese whose imaginations had been fired by the unexpected return of Aung San's own daughter at the hour of their greatest need, while opposition activists began to see in Aung San Suu Kyi the perfect figurehead for their aspirations – the daughter of the country's greatest national hero, and someone entirely untainted by former political or military connections.

Than Shwe

In April 1992 SLORC leader General Saw Maung "resigned" for health reasons – although rumours suggest he was effectively deposed by rival generals worried by his apparent willingness to hand over power to the NLD – and was succeeded by the second of Myanmar's two infamous military despots, **Than Shwe**. Than Shwe proved an apt successor to Ne Win – similarly ruthless and repressive, and totally lacking in personal charisma. A reclusive leader, he rarely made public appearances or spoke to the press and was believed to take many major decisions based on the advice of his astrologers (see box, p.372). He also enjoyed the trappings of wealth – a leaked video of his daughter Thandar Shwe's wedding in 2006 caused widespread outrage due to its ostentatious extravagance, with Thandar Shwe herself wearing diamonds worth millions of dollars at a time when most Burmese were living in abject poverty.

1962	1962 onwards
Ne Win leads a military coup and seizes power, announcing a new policy dubbed the "Burmese Way to Socialism"	Myanmar becomes increasingly impoverished and isolated under Ne Win's leadership

HOUSE ARREST

The 8888 Uprising itself was soon brutally crushed. Undeterred, Aung San Suu Kyi established the **National League for Democracy** (NLD) in September 1988 with former eminent generals turned regime opponents Aung Gyi and Tin Oo. Her newly launched political career was brought to an abrupt halt in July 1989, however, when she was placed under **house arrest** – the first in a long sequence of home detentions which would last for fifteen of the next 21 years. Her international profile, meanwhile, rose ever higher, cemented by the award of the Nobel Peace Prize in 1991. This Mother Teresa-like status in the West largely insulated her from criticism – and continues to do so to this day – although some questioned both the usefulness of Gandhian passive resistance in the face of brutal military rule and the NLD's isolationist stance, with its self-declared **tourism boycott** and support of ineffectual Western sanctions which (it's argued) served to plunge the country into further atrophy.

Brief periods of release from house arrest and attempts to travel the country were met with repeated military intimidation, most notably in 2003 when at least seventy NLD supporters travelling with Aung San Suu Kyi were killed in the **Depayin Massacre** in Sagaing State. Meanwhile Aung San Suu Kyi herself was repeatedly caricatured in government media as a "Western poster girl" and "foreigner" thanks to her years abroad and UK-based family.

RELEASE – AND INTO POWER

Aung San Suu Kyi was finally freed from house arrest in **November 2010** and immediately threw herself back into the political fray. However, she began to show notable signs of entering into an increasingly murky sort of *Realpolitik*, meeting with government cronies and being careful not to say anything that might antagonize her mainly Buddhist voting-base – her repeated failure to speak up for the horribly oppressed Rohingya during a wave of communal clashes in 2012–2014 was particularly widely criticized.

Supporters argued that she was doing what was necessary in order to secure democracy for her country, which duly arrived with the NLD's landslide electoral victory in 2015. Aung San Suu Kyi was appointed to the specially created post of State Counsellor – the de facto head of the country in all but name. What has followed (see pp.378–380) has been a disappointment even to her most ardent former supporters, with political critics jailed, the Rohingya brutalized as never before, fighting continuing in Shan and Kachin states and the lady herself becoming an increasingly remote figure in far-off Naypyitaw, now behaving increasingly like the generals she fought so long to replace.

Than Shwe relaxed some state controls on the economy (although without any significant beneficial effect), cracked down on corruption and, in 1997, led Myanmar into ASEAN (the Association of Southeast Asian Nations). Ceasefires were also negotiated with Kachin and Shan rebels (although fighting against the Kayin would continue until 2012). Despite these modest reforms, spending on the army continued to soar even while investment in health and education remained among the lowest in the world. The junta was also accused of increasingly widespread and serious **human rights abuses**: as many as a million Burmese were shipped off to rural labour camps and forced to work unpaid on government projects, while there are also reports of hundreds, possibly thousands, of summary executions.

In 2003, **Kyin Nyunt**, the (relatively) moderate prime minister of the regime – now renamed the **State Peace and Development Council (SPDC)** – announced a seven-step "roadmap to democracy". A subsequent power struggle with Than Shwe saw him

1974	1987	August 1988
The first widespread protests against the military regime are brutally suppressed	Ne Win's numerologically inspired currency reforms wipe out the life savings of many Burmese	The 8888 Uprising sees mass nationwide protests against military regime; Ne Win resigns and Aung San Suu Kyi emerges as the figurehead of the democracy movement

arrested – possibly on account of his apparent willingness to reach an agreement with the NLD – and stripped of power. Most surprising was the sudden announcement, in November 2005, that the national capital was to be moved to **Naypyitaw** – a huge new project dreamt up by Than Shwe, costing billions of dollars and confirming, in the eyes of many observers, the true scale of the generals' out-of-control megalomania.

The Saffron Revolution

The next major upheaval in Burmese society – the **Saffron Revolution** (as it has been named in honour of the monks who played a leading part in it) – was in some ways a rerun of the previous protests of 1988. After a decade during which anti-government protests had been virtually unknown, simmering popular discontent with military rule once again abruptly boiled over in August 2007 following the junta's decision to suddenly remove fuel subsidies, causing petrol prices to rise by two-thirds overnight.

The first protests were held by monks in the town of **Pakokku**, from where public shows of dissent rapidly spread nationwide. By September, thousands of monks and other demonstrators were marching daily through Yangon and Mandalay (on September 24 as many as 100,000 are estimated to have taken to the streets in Yangon alone).

Then, just as in 1988, the military hit back with their customary brutality – Than Shwe was rumoured to have taken personal charge of the army after senior commanders had refused to use force against the demonstrations. Rumours circulated that the military had purchased large quantities of monastic robes and were busily shaving their heads in order to penetrate the ranks of the protesting monks; convicted criminals were also released, and being ordered to do the same. Starting in late September, soldiers began attacking and tear-gassing protesters. Thousands were beaten and dozens shot, while reports of monks being abducted, beaten and possibly murdered were widely circulated. Protesters were arrested and sentenced, usually to many years of hard labour. Although the level of killing seen in 1988 was not repeated, the crackdown was sufficient to eventually quell the uprising.

Further international sanctions and trade restrictions ensued. Rumours of dissension within the ranks of the generals, however, and reports that many soldiers and army officers had refused orders to take violent action against demonstrators, particularly monks, suggested that the tide might finally be turning against the regime, who subsequently announced that nationwide elections would be held in 2010.

Cyclone Nargis

Then, just as it seemed there might finally be light at the end of the tunnel, Myanmar suffered the greatest natural disaster in its entire recorded history. On May 3, 2008, **Cyclone Nargis** swept in from the Bay of Bengal, hitting the Delta region with little warning and unprecedented force. Large swathes of the densely populated, low-lying region were erased from the map in a matter of hours, with an estimated 130,000 dead, and a million left homeless and without food or water.

The biblical scale of the cyclone's devastation was impossible to grasp. Even more shocking, however, was the response of the embattled junta, who over the following month systematically blocked all offers of international aid, while doing almost

September 1988	1989
Founding of the National League for Democracy; protests are violently suppressed, with thousands killed by the military, who re-establish control under the newly established State Law and Order Restoration Council (SLORC)	The country's colonial-era name, Burma, is changed by the military government to Myanmar

nothing themselves to assist the survivors of the tragedy. International aid supplies and disaster experts were kept waiting in Yangon while the generals dithered in far-off Naypyitaw, and European and US naval ships stood waiting off the coast of the Delta, primed to provide relief but denied access. Hundreds of thousands of cyclone survivors are thought to have perished due to starvation, dehydration and disease thanks to the regime's paranoia and incompetence – perhaps the most damning indictment of the entire period of military rule, and certainly the most disastrous.

Towards democracy

The **elections** announced by the military in 2008 were held as promised in November 2010, although they were boycotted by the NLD since many of its most prominent members were banned from running. These included Aung San Suu Kyi herself, whose period under house arrest had been conveniently (from a military standpoint) extended after she had reluctantly given shelter to US citizen **John Yettaw**, who had swum across Inya Lake to her house in order to gain an audience. Given the non-participation of the NLD, widespread allegations of electoral intimidation and other irregularities, and the fact that a quarter of all seats were reserved for the military, the subsequent landslide victory for the government-backed **Union Solidarity and Development Party (USDP)** was therefore largely inevitable – though on a more positive note, a few days after the election Aung San Suu Kyi was finally released from house arrest, apparently this time for good.

The SPDC was officially dissolved on March 30, 2011 and replaced by the newly elected (or, at least, "elected") USDP government led by former general and junta prime minister **Thein Sein** – 77-year-old Than Shwe having decided to stand down from politics. The new leader was widely seen as a moderate and reformist – although he was also known for his key role in blocking relief efforts following Cyclone Nargis, as well as his anti-Rohingya policies (see box, p.121).

Despite its military background, the new government set about initiating a series of landmark **reforms**. Anti-corruption legislation was passed, hundreds of political prisoners released, strike laws eased and the formerly stifling press censorship significantly reduced – with images of Aung San Suu Kyi, banned just a few years previously, now seen everywhere from newspapers to T-shirts. Signs of economic reform could also be seen – a normalization of government-fixed currency exchange rates led to a virtual disappearance of the formerly ubiquitous black market, while foreign companies were allowed to do business in Myanmar for the first time in half a century, with Ford, Nissan, Suzuki and Coca-Cola among the first arrivals.

Political progress also followed, with the NLD participating in 2012 **by-elections**, winning 43 out of the 44 seats they contested. Aung San Suu Kyi herself won the seat of Kawhmu township in Yangon and was allowed to travel freely around the country. Thein Sein, meanwhile, promised that free democratic elections would be held in 2015, although it was made clear that Aung San Suu Kyi herself would be unable to head any new government thanks to a clause inserted into a new military-sponsored 2008 constitution, which bans those with foreign next of kin (such as Aung San Suu Kyi, at whom the amendment was specifically targeted) from serving as president.

1990	**1991**	**1992**
The National League for Democracy wins a landslide victory in general elections; the military refuse to recognize the results and confine Aung San Suu Kyi to house arrest	Aung San Suu Kyi is awarded the Nobel Peace Prize	Hardline general Than Shwe assumes leadership of the military government

The landmark elections were duly held on **8 November, 2015** – the first properly democratic (or nearly) elections in Myanmar for nearly sixty years. The NLD, as expected, won a huge majority, taking 390 of the 498 available seats. While the result itself was never really in doubt, lingering fears that the military would once again renege on its promises continued to persist. In the event, the government of Thein Sein stepped aside gracefully, allowing an orderly shift to civilian government – a stunningly swift and peaceful transition to majority rule for a country that had only six years earlier still been firmly in the grip of the generals.

The NLD era

Myanmar therefore became a democratic country once again – sort of – although the military remains a powerful presence to this day, with 166 of the 664 parliamentary seats reserved for their representatives. They also retain complete control of the country's armed forces, over whom the NLD government has no jurisdiction.

There was also the question of Aung San Su Kyi, who was barred by the constitution from running for president – although The Lady herself had made it clear that she would lead the new government irrespective of her position, or lack of. Attempts to have the constitution amended to allow her to serve as president continued into 2016, but were eventually abandoned; a new post was created specifically for her instead, as so-called **State Counsellor**. The role, as Aung San Suu Kyi herself has put it, is "above the president", allowing her a free-ranging remit throughout the adminstration. Irrespective of the political niceties, there was no real question of who was in charge.

The NLD took office on 1 April, 2016. Thirteen days later, the country was rocked by an **earthquake** of magnitude 6.9 northwest of Mandalay (although fortunately causing little damage), and in August that year a second earthquake of magnitude 6.8 rocked central Myanmar, damaging dozens of stupas in Bagan – a natural portent, perhaps, of further upheavals to come.

Inevitably, the new NLD government was always going to struggle to manage the sky-high expectations unleashed by its sudden rise to power. Early moves included the release of dozens of political prisoners, while in August 2016 the landmark **Union Peace Conference** – dubbed the "21st Century Panglong Conference" – staged the first in a proposed series of regular meetings between the government, military and most of the country's armed ethnic groups in an attempt to secure lasting peace for the country – even as fighting continued in three states. In October 2016, the USA also lifted most of its remaining economic sanctions against the country. Pre-election pledges to curb the political power of the armed forces were, however, quietly set aside, while outbreaks of communal violence including the destruction by mobs of two mosques in mid-2016 passed by without comment or censure from Aung San Suu Kyi herself (who had also previously been criticized for failing to field even a single Muslim candidate during the 2015 elections). Hopes that the new government would inspire nationwide peace were also thwarted. Fresh fighting in Shan and Kachin states erupted in March 2016 and was ongoing at the time of research, with conflicts between government forces and the Kachin Independence Army (KIA), the Ta'ang National Liberation Army (TNLA) and Kokang's Myanmar National Democratic Alliance Army (MNDAA).

1992 onwards	2005	2007
Than Shwe initiates modest economic reforms accompanied by widespread political repression and human rights abuses	The military government establishes a multi-billion-dollar new capital at Naypyitaw	The Saffron Revolution sees further nationwide protests, again brutally suppressed by the military

Back in Rakhine

Meanwhile, the plight of the long-suffering **Rohingya** remained as bad as ever. Simmering tensions in Rakhine, which had been bubbling up throughout 2012–14, erupted once again in October 2016 after the killing of nine border police officers by Rohingya militants. The military response was swift and brutal, with widespread reports of grotesque human-rights violations at the hands of security forces – although given that all reporters were excluded from the region, precise details are difficult to obtain. Hundreds of eyewitnesses have testified to innumerable atrocities, including the murder of civilians (many children among them) and the widespread rape of Rohingya women, while satellite imagery published by Human Rights Watch showed around 1250 Rohingya houses burned to the ground. The military are also said to have used helicopter gunships against unarmed villagers, while refugees fleeing on boats were also shot at. Nearly 70,000 Rohingya fled to Bangladesh with a further 23,000 internally displaced. The exact number of those killed remains unclear, although many fleeing Rohingya stated that they had lost at least one family member. Following a prolonged international outcry, in March 2017 the UN Human Rights Council voted to investigate alleged human rights abuses by Myanmar's army – although whether this will help improve the lot of the Rohingya themselves seems unlikely, and Aung San Suu Kyi herself has already spoken out against the investigation.

The sense of national unease was further intensified by the assassination of leading lawyer and NLD advisor **Ko Ni** by a hired gunman in broad daylight at Yangon Airport in January 2017 – one of the few prominent Muslim public figures in the country, and widely credited with masterminding the creation of the post State Counsellor for Aung San Suu Kyi the previous year. His funeral attracted thousands of mourners from across the religious spectrum – although not the person he had helped to ease into power, Aung San Suu Kyi herself. Exactly who ordered the murder remains unclear, although widespread rumours have hinted at complicit military involvement, with the killing intended, it's been suggested, to warn those who might attempt to curtail the armed forces' still immense powers.

Towards 2020

Not surprisingly, the NLD government has been able to call on deep reserves of national and international goodwill, while there is also considerable sympathy for the unrealistic expectations it must attempt to manage in the face of huge political and economic challenges. In addition, the government is also hamstrung by its lack of any control over the armed forces and by the still shadowy sense (exacerbated by the killing of Ko Ni) that the military may yet seize back control should their power be seriously challenged or the integrity of the nation threatened by ethnic unrest, as it was in 1962.

Positives are becoming increasingly difficult to find. Ethnic conflict, Rohingya repression and anti-Muslim discrimination continue, while **freedom of the press** (see p.40) – expected to flourish under the NLD – has in fact been curtailed, with restraints now allegedly worse than they were under Thein Sein, and critics of the NLD regularly thrown into jail on the flimsiest pretexts. Meanwhile, state-run newspapers continue to publish laboriously pro-government propaganda, with distorted coverage of events in Rakhine particularly. Aung San Suu Kyi herself, who once spoke weekly from the gates

2008	2010
Cyclone Nargis devastates the Delta, killing around 130,000 people; the government leaves many survivors to die, while blocking all offers of international assistance	First general elections in twenty years are won by military-backed USDP; Thein Sein becomes Myanmar's new leader; Aung San Suu Kyi is released from house arrest

THE NAMING DEBATE

Controversy has long surrounded the use of the names Myanmar versus Burma, starting in 1989 when the military government renamed the country **Myanmar**. The military argued – albeit on rather shaky linguistic and historical grounds – that **Burma** was an inaccurate name foisted on the country during colonial times, deriving from "Bamar" (the name of the majority ethnic group). They contended that "Myanmar" was not only historically and culturally more accurate, but also more politically inclusive as well.

Aung San Suu Kyi's NLD steadfastly opposed the change, however, arguing that the unelected military regime had no right to unilaterally rechristen the entire country. The UN (along with many countries including France and Japan) recognized the new name, although some governments (including the UK and USA) followed the NLD's lead and continued to refer to the country as Burma. As such, the use of either Myanmar or Burma was based less on reasoned historical, linguistic and cultural grounds than as a badge of support for either the military or their NLD adversaries.

Emotions surrounding the competing names have cooled significantly since the democratic elections of 2015, with entrenched resistance to the name Myanmar fading rapidly. The USA (for example) have now recognized the name change (Barack Obama diplomatically referred to the country as both Burma and Myanmar during his historic 2016 visit), while Aung San Suu Kyi herself has begun using the name Myanmar in public speeches.

As such, the whole Myanmar-versus-Burma debate is beginning to feel a bit like yesterday's news, especially when you realize that the two names actually spring from the same etymological roots.

of her Yangon house to anyone who would listen, is now an increasingly reclusive and authoritarian presence from her new home in the generals' city of Naypyitaw, never giving interviews to the Burmese press, and only rarely speaking to carefully selected international media.

Economically, the country continues to boom. Foreign investment reached almost $10 billion in the year ending in March 2016, while national growth is predicted to rise at over eight percent over the coming year or two, with Myanmar's per capita GDP ($5480) now above those of Laos and Cambodia – although still way behind neighbouring Thailand ($16,130), despite the country's plentiful natural resources. Needless to say, much wealth remains concentrated in the hands of a few, particularly businessmen associated with the former military regime, and rural poverty remains widespread. Life expectancy (just over 66 years) is also higher than in Cambodia and Laos, although again the average Burmese dies eight years younger than their Thai counterparts, while a fifth of the population still lacks adequate drinking water and sanitation. **Tourism** is also booming, bringing millions of dollars into the country, although visitor numbers remain concentrated in a disproportionately small number of areas, with economic benefits yet to be felt by the population at large. The still-unresolved future of the hugely controversial **Myitsone Dam** (see p.349) – and, indeed, general relations with China (which, during the days of the generals, tended to regard Myanmar as a convenient natural resource) – is another of the major issues to be faced in the coming years. To what extent a booming economy and the cult of The Lady herself succeed in masking deeper economic, democratic and humanitarian ills remains to be seen – and with elections not due until 2020, the NLD at least have time on their side.

2010 onwards	**2012–13**	**2015**
USDP introduces wide-ranging economic and political reforms	Anti-Rohingya riots in Rakhine and anti-Muslim riots in Meiktila and elsewhere	NLD wins landmark democratic elections

Myanmar's ethnic groups

Myanmar is home to an extraordinary patchwork of peoples. No fewer than 135 different ethnic groups are officially recognized by the government, arranged into eight "major national ethnic races": Bamar, Chin, Kachin, Kayah, Kayin, Mon, Rakhine and Shan. There are also some major ethnic groups not officially recognized, including the Burmese Chinese (three percent of the population), Burmese Indians (two percent of the population) and the embattled Rohingya (see box, p.121), not to mention the mixed-race Anglo-Burmese. Most ethnic groups speak their own language, with Burmese as a second language – although some (such as the Rakhine) speak a dialect of Burmese as their first language.

Ethnically, Myanmar is dominated by the **Bamar**, who have occupied the fertile Ayeyarwady valley and central plains for the past thousand years. Other ethnic groups tend to inhabit the country's mountainous margins, battling inhospitable terrain and (in recent decades) widespread military repression and human-rights abuses – every single major ethnic group in the country has been at war with the central government at some point since independence, with most insurgencies dragging on into the 1990s, while those in parts of Shan and Kachin states continue to this day.

Bamar

Far and away Myanmar's largest ethnic group are the **Bamar** (still occasionally referred to by their old colonial-era name, "Burmans", or, less accurately, as the "Burmese", although properly speaking this adjective refers to all citizens of Myanmar rather than the Bamar alone). The Bamar now make up over two-thirds of the national population – around 38 million people – and have largely assimilated formerly distinct ethnic groups including the now vanished Pyu people (see p.358) as well as large numbers of formerly independent Mon and other minorities who have been steadily "Burmanized" over the past centuries.

Originally hailing from Yunnan in southern China, the Bamar's traditional heartlands were the fertile Ayeyarwady River valley and surrounding plains, where they first settled in around 1000 AD, establishing the kingdom of Bagan. Bamar culture and language are now inextricably bound with that of the nation as a whole – the Bamar language, Burmese, is now Myanmar's official mother tongue, and many other marks of Bamar identity (the wearing of longyi and *thanaka*, for example; see box, p.7) have become synonymous with the country as a whole.

Shan

Myanmar's second-largest ethnic group – roughly nine percent of the population (around five million people) – the **Shan** live mainly in eastern Myanmar (as well as across the border in northern Thailand), where they have given their name to the country's largest state. Culturally and linguistically the Shan are closely related to the Tai peoples of Thailand and Laos – indeed, the Shan refer to themselves as "Tai", the name "Shan" being a Burmese corruption of "Siam". Originating, like the Bamar, from Yunnan in southern China, the Shan have inhabited eastern Myanmar since at least the tenth century, playing a major role in the country's history. Most are Buddhist and speak the Shan language, closely related to Thai and Lao.

Though the Shan are the most populous group in the east, you may not actually see many of them – the main Shan heartlands lie east of Taunggyi, an area off limits to foreign travellers due to the civil conflict that has been rumbling on for decades between the national government and various militias. Hopes that peace would finally return to Shan State were raised following the signing of a peace deal between the government and the large Shan State Army in 2011, although fighting broke out again in early 2016 between government forces and local militias including the Ta'ang National Liberation Army (TNLA) and Kokang's Myanmar National Democratic Alliance Army (MNDAA) – calls by many Shan for the creation of an independent Shan nation persist.

There are myriad other different hill tribes in eastern Myanmar, nominally classified as subgroups of the Shan and including the **Intha** (see below), the **Palaung, Pa-O, Eng, Danu, Akha, Lahu** and **Loi**. Many of these tribes have villages in both Myanmar and Thailand, and some of them, such as the Akha and Lahu, are more easily visited on hill-tribe treks on the Thai side of the border.

Intha

One of the country's more visible minorities, the **Intha** ("sons of the lake"; see box, p.259) number approximately 70,000 people and live mainly around Inle Lake where they eke out a living cultivating small plots and floating gardens on and around the water. They are believed to have originally come from Dawei in southern Myanmar and still speak their own distinctive Burmese dialect. They're best known for their unusual style of leg-rowing, as featured in innumerable tourist literature.

Kayin (Karen)

The **Kayin** – aka **Karen** – are Myanmar's third-biggest ethnic group, with around 3.5 million people, who live mainly in Kayin State in the south of the country (seven percent of the national population), while many more have fled to Thailand. The Kayin are the most heterogeneous of Myanmar's ethnic groups, comprising a disparate collection of hill tribes speaking various languages, most of them mutually unintelligible. They were first grouped together under the umbrella term "Kayin" in the 1800s by Baptist missionaries who had considerable success converting the region's Buddhist natives. Today, a quarter of all Kayin in Myanmar are Christian, with the rest professing Buddhism, sometimes with strong animist elements.

Strongly favoured under British rule thanks to their Christian leanings, the Kayin have suffered even more than most other Burmese ethnic minorities in the decades since independence. The separatist **Karen National Union (KNU)** was founded in 1947 to push the case for their own independence, although peaceable efforts to create a Kayin sovereign nation (provisionally named Kawthoolei) collapsed just two years later when government troops slaughtered eighty Kayin villagers in Palaw, Tanintharyi. The resultant conflict, fought between the KNU's military arm, the **Karen National Liberation Army**, and government troops, was the longest running of Myanmar's many ethnic insurgencies, displacing as many as 200,000 people before a formal ceasefire was signed in 2012. Save for the occasional KNU truck rumbling down the streets of Hpa-An, visitors to the Karen heartlands of Myanmar will see little sign of the conflict's impact, although an estimated 140,000 Kayin people still live in refugee camps along the Thai–Myanmar border.

Rakhine

Living mainly in Rakhine State, in the west of the country, and in neighbouring Bangladesh, the **Rakhine** (also spelt "Rakhaing", and previously known as the Arakanese) share much in common with the Bamar but have also been significantly influenced by their proximity to the Indian subcontinent, claiming to have been among the first converts to Buddhism in Southeast Asia as the new religion spread east from India. Comprising around four percent of the national population (a little over two million people), the Rakhine speak a distinctive form of Burmese (considered a dialect by some, a separate language by others). A brief account of Rakhine history is given in chapter 2 (see box, p.120).

Mon

Formerly the largest and most powerful ethnic group in southern Myanmar, the **Mon** people have now been relegated to the status of an embattled minority. The last independent Mon kingdom was toppled in 1757 (see p.364), and since then they have been largely assimilated into the Bamar mainstream – only around two percent of Burmese (roughly a million people) now class themselves as Mon, living mainly in the south of the country, particularly in Mon and Bago states and the Delta region. As with many other ethnic minorities, the Mon have periodically rebelled against the central government in an attempt to gain independence – a series of insurgencies ended only by a general ceasefire agreement of 1995.

Kachin

"**Kachin**" is an umbrella term used to describe some six ethnic groups living in far northern Kachin State, with a total of just under a million people; the **Jinpo** are the major subgroup. Core Burmese beliefs are less in evidence here – most Kachin are Christian, and animist beliefs remain strong too – while traditional styles of Kachin dress (although now rarely worn except on festive occasions; see box, p.348) are among the most flamboyant in the country. The **Kachin Independence Army** (KIA) has been involved in a long-running conflict with the government (see p.348), with hostilities recommencing in 2011 following the collapse of a previous ceasefire and continuing to the present.

Kayah

Living in the remote hills of Kayah State are the **Kayah** people, also known as the Red Karen or the Karenni (and sometimes classified as a subgroup of the Karen) – the name "Red Karen" derives from their fondness for red clothing. Now numbering fewer than half a million (with more over the border in Thailand), the Kayah can be divided into numerous subgroups including the famous **Kayan (Padaung)** (see box, p.384). As with other minorities, the Kayah have suffered repeated military persecution and human rights abuses, which led to clashes between the Burmese army and the **Karenni People's Liberation Front** until the agreement of a ceasefire of 1995.

Chin

Forming the majority of the half-million inhabitants of remote Chin State in Myanmar's far west, the **Chin** people share many ethnic links with the Zo (aka Mizo) people in the adjacent Indian state of Mizoram. Always remote from the Burmese mainstream, the majority of Chin converted to Christianity during the colonial period – and have suffered significantly for their beliefs since independence (see p.135). They are perhaps best known to outsiders for their curious practice of tattooing the faces of their women (see box, p.132).

Wa

Myanmar's million or so **Wa** people (descended, according to one legend, from two female tadpoles) live mainly in northern Shan and eastern Kachin states along the

THE LONG-NECKED WOMEN OF THE KAYAN

The long-necked women of the **Kayan** tribe are without doubt the most startling of all Myanmar's ethnic minorities (often referred to as the "Padaung" – although this is actually a Shan name and considered perjorative by the Kayan themselves). From the age of around five, Kayan girls are fitted with heavy brass **neck rings**, with more being added as they grow, causing their collarbones to sink. No one knows exactly why the practice began. One theory claims that it started as a means of making local girls less appealing to raiders from neighbouring tribes; another legend suggests that the neck rings were designed to protect against biting tigers – although quite possibly it simply originated as a fashion statement and marker of cultural identity. The rings are only rarely removed and it's popularly believed that the ladies would not be able to support the weight of their own heads without them, although in fact a number of women have jettisoned their rings safely in recent years and reported nothing but passing discomfort.

These days, the practice is a moneymaker. A number of long-necked ladies have left their homes in Kayah State to set themselves up around touristy Inle Lake; their houses are free to visit, but they're basically all souvenir shops. Though the women are undeniably photogenic, many visitors feel uncomfortable given that the women themselves are treated almost like zoo animals. Much more rewarding visits to Kayan villages can also be arranged in Loikaw (see p.268), where you will have the chance to interact with the long-necked ladies in their own homes using the services of a local interpreter.

Chinese border and around Kengtung. Left largely alone by the British thanks to their wild reputation (including a fondness for animal sacrifice and headhunting), the Wa retained considerable autonomy following independence and were often in armed conflict with the government until the signing of a ceasefire in 1989. Their heartlands comprise one of the country's major drug-producing areas (originally opium, more recently heroin and methamphetamine), with the lucrative trade policed and protected by the **United Wa State Army**, formerly one of the world's largest drug militias, with as many as ten thousand men under arms.

Naga

Perhaps Myanmar's most truly remote people, the **Naga** tribes are spread across northwestern Myanmar and northeastern India, living mainly – on the Burmese side of the border – around the Chindwin River and in the hills of western Sagaing Region. A patchwork of tribes, all speaking different languages, the Naga had little contact with the outside world under the British colonial era. Headhunting was formerly a popular pastime, although the practice largely died out following widespread conversion by Christian missionaries (rumour has it, however, that the practice continued into modern times). The Naga people are now increasingly "Burmanized", although some traditional settlements and customs remain. Naga men traditionally wear few clothes but many tattoos, while the Naga are also known for their exuberant dancing, drumming and singing, at its most flamboyant during the Naga New Year celebrations, when the men also don their extraordinary traditional headdresses.

Burmese Buddhism and traditional beliefs

Almost ninety percent of all Burmese people classify themselves as Buddhist. Buddhism permeates every aspect of Burmese life, with Myanmar often claimed to be the world's most devout Buddhist nation, both in terms of the amount of money dedicated to religious expenses and judged by the proportion of monks relative to the overall population – easy to believe when you've seen quite how many red-robed clergy there are in virtually every corner of the country.

There are also significant numbers of **Christians**, **Muslims** and other religious groups, although these are found mainly among ethnic minorities and exist very much at the margins of Burmese society – particularly given the prolonged discrimination against non-Buddhist individuals and groups, which has been a feature of the years since independence.

History of Burmese Buddhism

Buddhism arrived early in Myanmar, although exactly who converted to the religion and when remains conjectural. According to one tradition, the religion was introduced by two monks despatched by the great Indian Buddhist emperor Ashoka (ruled 268–232 BC), although its arrival was most likely a piecemeal affair, as the new religion travelled east from India, mingling with existing beliefs and religious practices. The Rakhine, living close to the subcontinent, claim to have been among the first to convert, while the Mon were also early adherents. Further north, the Bamar adopted an eclectic version of the faith known as **Ari Buddhism** including *nat* worship (see p.386) alongside elements drawn from Hinduism and Mahayana and Tantric Buddhism, as well as other magical astrological and alchemical beliefs.

The establishment of a relatively orthodox form of **Theravada Buddhism** as the dominant religion came in the eleventh century during the reign of the great King Anawrahta of Bagan (see p.359). Much of the credit for Anawrahta's reforming zeal goes to the legendary Mon monk, **Shin Arahan**, who persuaded the king to abandon the heterogeneous Ari faith in favour of the more conservative Theravada form – although Anawrahta made the concession of installing images of the traditional *nats* on the stupa of his great Shwezigon Pagoda (see p.203), and *nat* worship remains very much alive to this day.

Myanmar subsequently became one of the main strongholds of the Theravada faith, surviving the resurgence of Hinduism in India (which virtually wiped out the religion in the country of its birth), as well as the arrival of Islam and the onslaught of colonial-era Christianity – although missionaries had considerable success among some of the country's ethnic minorities, and significant numbers of Kayin, Kachin, Chin and Naga still profess Christianity to this day.

Surprisingly, Buddhism has never been the official state religion of Myanmar except for a brief period in 1961–62. Nonetheless, the identification between state and Buddhism has always been strong. Early Burmese kings traditionally saw themselves as patrons and upholders of the faith, while in more recent years Myanmar's ruling generals traditionally made much of their temple-building projects and other religious activities in an effort to distract attention from their murderous rule.

Theravada Buddhism

Myanmar follows the **Theravada** (the "Law of the Elders") school of Buddhism, the older and more conservative version of the religion, which also predominates in Sri Lanka, Thailand, Cambodia and Laos (in contrast to the later and more eclectic Mahayana Buddhism followed in China, Japan, Korea, Vietnam and elsewhere). As the older of the two main schools, Theravada claims to embody the Buddha's teachings in their original form. These teachings emphasize that all individuals are responsible for their own spiritual welfare, and that any person who wishes to achieve enlightenment must pursue the same path trodden by the Buddha himself, giving up worldly concerns and developing spiritual attainments through meditation and self-sacrifice. This path of renunciation is, of course, impossible for most members of the Theravada community to follow, which explains the importance of **monks** in Myanmar (and in other Theravada countries), since only members of the Sangha (see opposite) are considered fully committed to the Theravada path.

Nats

Despite its adherence to the "pure" form of Buddhism, the religion in Myanmar still shows the influence of other eclectic beliefs pre-dating the arrival of the Theravada faith. Most notable is the countrywide practice of **nat** (spirit) worship, still particularly prevalent in rural areas (although educated urban Burmese often dismiss the tradition as folk superstition). Burmese *nats* come from a variety of sources including local animist nature spirits, folk deities (such as Mai Wunna, the flower-eating ogress of Mount Popa; see box, p.230), "Burmanized" versions of major Hindu gods and *nats* related to real-life historical figures (such as Min Situ, the *nat* spirit of Bagan's King Alaungsittu) – all of whom merge in a bewildering historical and mythological melange. Some have followers nationwide; others may be linked to a single area, or even a single village.

The survival of the *nats* as an essential element in modern Burmese Buddhism owes much to King Anawrahta, the great religious reformer of Bagan, who first established Theravada Buddhism as the national religion. Realizing the hold that the *nats* had over his people, Anawrahta chose to incorporate them into his new-look Buddhist faith in an attempt to encourage the Burmese to follow the new Theravada doctrines. Some of the most important of Myanmar's myriad *nats* were chosen to form a royally sanctioned pantheon known as the **37 Nats** (see box, p.207) under the leadership of Thagyamin (a Burmanized version of the Hindu god Indra, often portrayed, like Indra himself, seated on top of a three-headed elephant). Thaygamin aside, every one of the 37 *nats* died a violent death, lending them something of the character of Christian martyrs. At the same time, they're also an engagingly humanized bunch, in stark contrast to the exalted qualities of the Buddha himself. Popular *nats* include some decidedly raffish characters with very recognizable personal flaws and earthly failings, such as Min Kyawzwa, the "Drunken Nat", whose image at Mount Popa is draped with offerings of whisky bottles and cigarettes in homage to his life spent boozing, cockfighting and hunting.

Nats have been thoroughly integrated into Burmese Buddhism, and *nat* shrines or images can be found in most temples in the country. All pagodas have a resident guardian *nat* spirit, or **Bo Bo Gyi**, typically shown as a man dressed in pink robes with a white turban. In addition, you'll also see many shrines dedicated to **Shin Upagot** (or Upagutta), a much-venerated figure who is believed to protect worshippers against watery perils such as floods and storms. He's easily recognizable thanks to his distinctive pose, seated, with one hand dipping into an alms bowl on his lap, and his head tilted upwards, gazing towards the sky as if in search of rain.

Myanmar's main centre of *nat* worship is Mount Popa, while there are also several important *nat* shrines around Mandalay. All of these places host raucous **nat pwè** festivals (see p.41) with celebrations led by spirit mediums know as **nat kadaw** (see box, p.49).

The Sangha

Myanmar's community of Buddhist monks, the **Sangha**, is one of the world's largest – the sight of monks (and also nuns) doing their daily morning rounds, bearing alms bowls and possibly a brightly coloured umbrella, is one of the country's most emblematic sights. Exact figures are hard to come by, although there are probably between 300,000 and half a million monks (plus at least fifty thousand nuns) in the country at any one time.

Burmese monks usually wear maroon-coloured robes rather than the orange robes worn in countries like Sri Lanka and Thailand. There are nine officially recognized **monastic orders** (*nikaya*); easily the largest is the Thudhamma Nikaya, followed by the more conservative Shwegyin Nikaya. All Burmese Buddhist men are expected to experience monastic life at least once. This often happens as a child – anytime after the age of seven. Young boys are entered into the monastery during an elaborate **shinbyu** ceremony, a major Burmese rite of passage during which their heads are shaved and normal clothes exchanged for robes; better-off parents may also arrange a *shinbyu* procession for their offspring, providing a symbolic re-enactment of the Buddha's own renunciation of royal life. Most boys enter a monastery for a short period only, perhaps as little as a week, although poorer children may become novices and be educated at the monastery. Full ordination (*upasampada*), for those who choose to enter the Sangha for life, follows at the age of twenty or later.

Buddhism in daily life

Daily religious life for the Burmese laypeople is mainly concerned with observing the religion's Five Precepts (a kind of Buddhist five commandments) and accumulating spiritual **merit** through good deeds and alms-giving (*dana*) – all of which, it is hoped, will ensure a favourable rebirth in the next life. **Meditation**, particularly Vipassana meditation, is also popular among both monks and laity.

Many Burmese homes have their own small Buddhist shrine, but local **temples** remain very much at the heart of religious, and indeed social, life – larger places come equipped with their own shops, resident palmists and astrologers, food vendors, flower shops (and, nowadays, ATMs, wi-fi zones and lifts). There is no congregational worship

---

BUDDHISM AND POLITICS

Myanmar's monks play an important role in Burmese life as spiritual leaders and have also assumed an important role in many of the last century's political struggles. **U Ottama** and **U Wisara** (both of whom starved themselves to death while in British prisons) were two leading figures in the anti-colonial movement. The Sangha also played a leading part during the **1988 and 2007 uprisings** (see p.372 & p.376) – despite their revered status they suffered particularly badly from military brutality, with hundreds, perhaps thousands, of monks being murdered during the 1988 uprising (during which numerous government informers reportedly shaved their heads and donned robes in an attempt to infiltrate the monastic orders and identify protesters). Their decision during the 2007 uprising to "overturn the alms bowl" (*thabeik hmauk*) and refuse all offerings from the military – a kind of Buddhist version of excommunication – served as a powerful, if ultimately unsuccessful, symbolic statement against military rule.

Not all members of the Sangha are irreproachably peaceful, however, as proved by the influential **969 Movement** and the more recently established **Ma Ba Tha** (Patriotic Association of Myanmar), both of which have done their best to stoke Burmese Islamophobia and inflame anti-Rohingya sentiment. The most prominent member of both groups is controversial monk Ashin Wirathu – dubbed the "Buddhist Bin Laden" – who has been accused of inciting anti-Muslim riots and whipping up communal hatred, declaring (with reference to his Muslim fellow nationals) that "You can be full of kindness and love, but you cannot sleep next to a mad dog". Wirathu's political clout was considered such that even the all-conquering NLD courted his support during the 2015 elections, with 88-year-old party chairman and distingushed pro-democracy activist Tin Oo himself kneeling in submission at the feet of the monk.

in Buddhism, meaning that people come to pay their respects at all times of the day and night – early evening after work is particularly popular.

Worshippers often come bearing **offerings** of flowers, money and quaint paper umbrellas, while also popular is the practice of rubbing fine slivers of gold leaf on particularly revered Buddha images (the statue at the Mahamuni Paya in Mandalay, for example, whose nether regions have now largely been buried under an estimated two tonnes of additional gold applied by visiting devotees). Inside the temple the devout will offer prayers, perhaps ringing one of the gongs with which all temples are equipped in the hope that their prayer will be answered. Depending on which day of the week they were born on, they will visit the relevant planetary post (see box, p.74) and wash its Buddha image, dousing it in water once for every year of their age, plus once more for luck.

Burmese Buddhism and the occult

Running alongside the country's orthodox Buddhist faith is a string of arcane and outlandish beliefs. First and foremost is a strong belief in **astrology**: many Burmese will consult an astrologer when planning, say, a new business or preparing to sit an exam. The day of the week on which one is born is considered especially important.

Numerology is considered particularly significant. Ne Win's disastrous 1987 currency reforms (see box, p.372) can be blamed on numerology, while the ultra-auspicious date of August 8, 1988 was chosen for the day on which the main thrust of the 8888 Uprising (see p.372) was launched; another rebellion was later planned for September 9, 1999, but failed to materialize. More recently, the 969 Movement (see box, p.387) chose its name (whose three digits "symbolize the virtues of the Buddha, Buddhist practices and the Buddhist community") in overt numerological opposition to the popular Islamic cipher 786, corresponding to the opening phrase of the Koran (the fact that 7 + 8 + 6 = 21 being seen as proof by the 969 Movement that Muslims intend to take over Myanmar during the current century).

Linked to numerology and also popular among many Burmese – including past rulers Ne Win and Than Shwe – is **yadaya**, the practice of quasi-magical Burmese rituals, prescribed by astrologers in order to ward off possible misfortune. Most *yadaya* rituals simply involve a visit to the temple and making certain specific offerings and prayers outlined by an astrologer, although some rituals can be considerably stranger – as when Ne Win elected to shoot himself in a mirror in order to avert a possible assassination attempt (see box, p.372). *Yadaya* is also said to have influenced affairs of state, both major and minor. The decision in 1970 to change the side of the road on which traffic drives from left to right, for example, is rumoured to have been taken to ward off political or military attack from right-wing groups – even though this means that large numbers of vehicles in Myanmar have their steering wheels on the wrong side right up to the present day. Likewise, in 2010 when the country's military leaders greeted the Thai prime minister at Yangon airport dressed in women's longyi, the influence of *yadaya* – in this case an attempt to harness the distaff power of Aung San Suu Kyi – was again suspected.

Combining many of Myanmar's weirder and more wonderful occult traditions is the practice of **weizza**. A uniquely Burmese Buddhist cult, *weizza* (also spelled "*weikza*") attempts to evade the usual laws of karma through rituals including magic, meditation and alchemy. Powerful practitioners of *weizza*, it is said, can live for centuries and choose the exact moment of their next reincarnation, among other supernatural powers.

Weizza incorporates many traditional beliefs, including a local fascination with *zawgyi* (wizards and alchemists) as well as elements dating perhaps all the way back to Ari Buddhism. The modern form of the tradition emerged in the late seventeenth century when **Bo Bo Aung**, a monk in Sagaing, discovered manuscripts revealing the secrets of *weizza*. Bo Bo Aung's image, traditionally dressed in an all-white robe and turban, can still be found in many temples and homes, with devotees believing he has the power to assist all those who pray to him with a pure heart.

Burmese architecture

Few countries are as abundantly endowed with religious architecture as Myanmar, from the thousands of ancient brick temples blanketing the plains of Bagan through to the huge gilded pagodas rising up above the bustling modern streets of Yangon, Mandalay, Bago, Pyay, Mawlamyine and pretty much every other city in the country. By contrast, relatively little secular architecture survives from the past, excepting the magnificent European-style colonial streetscapes of Yangon (see box, p.63).

Temple names

Temple names in Myanmar can be confusing. Buddhist temples are generally named using either the English **pagoda** or its Burmese equivalent, **paya**, with the two words being used more or less interchangeably – the Shwedagon in Yangon, for example, is widely referred to as both the Shwedagon Pagoda and Shwedagon Paya. In Bagan the word **pahto** is also sometimes used, generally when referring to "hollow" temples such as the Ananda or Sulamani, rather than solid stupas. Bagan's hollow temples can also sometimes be identified by the fact that they have the word **gu** (meaning "cave") in their name – the Gubyaukgyi, Alotawpyi-gu-hpaya and Shwegugyi temples, for example. The Burmese word for stupa is **zedi**, as in Bagan's Mingalazedi and elsewhere.

Pagoda architecture

The sheer number and size of Buddhist pagodas in Myanmar owes much to the Burmese obsession with **merit-making** – doing good works in this life in order to secure a favourable rebirth in one's future reincarnations. The rulers and nobles of Bagan virtually bankrupted their own kingdom thanks to their obsession with temple-building, while modern rulers have also left a string of pagodas in their wake, including Ne Win and Than Shwe, who sought to atone for their lifetimes of greed, repression and murder by raising (respectively) the Maha Wizaya Pagoda in Yangon and the huge Uppatasanti Pagoda in Naypyitaw. Such edifices also serve as notable memorials to their creators, handily combining religious good works and self-glorification in a single architectural package.

The vast majority of Burmese pagodas remain very much living places of worship rather than historic monuments. Many date back hundreds of years, although most have been repeatedly refurbished, remodelled – and sometimes completely rebuilt – many times over the centuries, making it difficult to get a sense of the antiquity of the country's major shrines. Even many of the seemingly ancient-looking temples at Bagan have actually been reconstructed over the past few decades according to local aesthetic whim rather than sound archeological principles, which is why UNESCO has so far refused to inscribe it on the list of global World Heritage Sites. The general sense of timelessness is also exacerbated by the fact that new pagodas being constructed today are essentially not that much different in style from those erected a thousand years ago, tradition rather than innovation being of the essence.

Parts of a pagoda

The typical Buddhist pagoda follows a basic plan that you'll see repeated all over the country. The vast majority are arranged around a central **stupa**; these are usually solid, although there are a few hollow modern pagodas with shrines inside (notable examples include the Botataung Pagoda in Yangon, the Uppatasanti Pagoda in Naypyitaw and the Lawkananda Pagoda in Sittwe). Surrounding the stupa there's usually a **terrace** ringed with subsidiary **shrines** containing assorted Buddha images, along with the occasional *nat* (see p.386). Pagodas are often built in raised positions, with **stairways** (often covered and lined with shops in larger pagodas) leading up from the streets below – grander temples typically have four entrances, one at each of the cardinal points. Larger temples often have a **monastery** (*kyaung*) attached.

Stupas

The soaring gilded **stupas** that dot Myanmar's towns and countryside are the country's most emblematic and memorable sight – vast masses of shimmering gold, dazzling by day, mysteriously glowing in the half-light of dusk, magnificently illuminated after dark. The classic Burmese-style stupa is perhaps the most beautiful in Asia: tall and slender, with a distinctive shape that seems to blend monumental size and presence with an elegantly simple outline, softened with organic, almost feminine, curves.

The country's first stupas, at Thayekhittaya (Sri Ksetra; see p.193), are little more than massive but rather crude cylindrical towers. These gradually developed at Bagan into

THE ARCHITECTURE OF BAGAN

Much of the history of Burmese temple architecture can be seen at **Bagan**. The buildings of Bagan divide into two periods: early and late. Temples of the **early period** (roughly 850–1120), such as the Pahthothamya Paya, are heavily influenced by early Pyu and Mon architectural styles – typically low and heavy one-storey structures topped by a small and rather cursory stupa. Interiors are kept deliberately dark in order to create a sense of mystery: most early shrines have just a single door and small windows with tiny latticework openings. Inside, there's usually a central shrine plus antechamber, with perhaps an ambulatory around the central shrine. Stupas, like the Bupaya and that at the Lawkananda Pagoda, are modelled on earlier Pyu examples at, for example, Thayekhittaya (Sri Ksetra): cyclindrical or slightly bulbous in outline, with little of the shapely finesse of later examples.

The city's **late period** architecture (roughly 1120–1300) shows the emergence of the unique Bagan style. Temples become taller, with the addition of a second shrine (often the main shrine) on the upper storey. Windows become much larger and interiors much lighter; many later temples also have four entrances ("four-faced" temples, as they're sometimes called) rather than the previous single entrance, also admitting more light. The rooftop stupa grows in size, ultimately developing into the soaring stupa-spires which top many temples, usually combining a rather Indian-looking tower with curved sides (known as a shikhara) with a stupa on top. Tiers of gradually smaller terraces connect the three parts of the structure – the two shrines and the stupa-spire – their corners decorated with miniature stupas or Indian-style *kalasa* (nectar pots), while many also have educational carvings showing scenes from the Buddhist Jataka tales. The earlier central shrine is now filled in to support the weight of the superstructure above, and an ambulatory (occasionally a double ambulatory) built around this solid central core, with a Buddha standing at each of its four sides.

Builders also achieved a remarkable mastery in the art of **brick vaulting**, at least a century in advance of anything else achieved in Asia at that time (the expertise proved by the fact that most temples survived the massive earthquake that hit Bagan in 1975). These skills were lost after the fall of Bagan, as demonstrated by the failed Mingun Pagoda project initiated by King Bodawpaya near Mandalay in 1790.

Late-period **stupas**, like the Mingalazedi and those at the Shwesandaw and Shwezigon pagodas, are also dramatically different from earlier models, typically much taller and more slender in outline, with a bell-shaped body set on an octagonal base and surmounted by a tall spire, with the whole structure set upon a huge square plinth. This design set the prototype for most subsequent stupas built across the country. There are also a couple of rare examples of stupas set upon **pentagonal** bases (the Dhammayazika is the best example) in order to accommodate a fifth shrine to the future Buddha Maitreya – a design feature unique in the Buddhist world.

the classic design – typified by the stupas at pagodas such as the Shwezigon and Shwesandaw – with their bell-shaped bodies rising to a delicately tapering spire above.

The massive Shwedagon Pagoda in Yangon is perhaps the ultimate Burmese stupa, and typifies many standard design elements found across the country, albeit on an unusually grand scale. The entire stupa sits on a massive square **base**, surrounded by miniature stupas, and with shrines to the four Buddhas (see box, p.74) at each of the cardinal points. Above the base rises a series of octagonal **terraces** (*pyissaya*) – access to these is restricted to monks. Surmounting this is the main body of the stupa, shaped like an inverted **almsbowl** (*thabeik*), its top decorated with lotus petals. This provides a base for the stupa spire, culminating in the distinctive "**banana bud**" (*nga pyaw bu*). At the very top, the stupa is crowned by a latticework **umbrella** (*hti*), typically decorated with precious stones, hung with bells and topped with a gilded flag.

Shrines

Surrounding the central stupa you'll usually find a ring of **shrines** (*tazaung*), typically decorated in a riot of colour and ornamentation. Most shrines are topped by a gilded **pyatthat**, a kind of cross between a roof and a spire, with tiers of flamboyantly carved, superimposed flying eaves rising to a needle-thin finial – a symbolic representation of the Buddhist cosmos, with the different tiers standing for the various realms of human and celestial beings rising to the mythical Mount Meru, home of the gods, above. *Pyatthat* were also a common feature of royal palace complexes – the higher one's status at court, the more tiers the *pyatthat* over one's residence were permitted.

Inside, walls and pillars are often decorated in dazzlingly intricate **glass mosaics**, another Burmese speciality. Virtually every shrine will have a Buddha image inside, often several. Some will also house images of *nats*, while in bigger shrines you'll find additional objects of veneration such as symbolic **Buddha footprints**, decorated with arcane symbols, or **reliquaries** containing sacred objects – typically replicas of the Buddha's Tooth or other bodily remains.

Benign Buddhas

Burmese Buddhas are everywhere, from the supersized colossi in Yangon, Monywa, Bago and elsewhere through to the myriad smaller images which can be found in every temple. The array of styles is strikingly wide, ranging from manneristic, slightly extraterrestrial-looking Shan- and Thai-influenced figures through to more realistic images such as the square-faced and rather portly-looking images that were the speciality of the Rakhine (such as the revered Mahamuni Buddha, now in Mandalay). Most images show the Buddha clad in simple monk's robes, although in later images (particularly Mandalay-style statues) these are often replaced with sumptuous royal regalia, including lavish sculpted robes and extravagant crowns.

The **Mandalay-style Buddha**, which developed during the Konbaung era, is particularly popular, showing the Buddha with a round and realistic-looking face, and a full head of closely cropped hair with a hair-bun looking slightly like a woollen cap. Most Mandalay-style seated images are shown in the *bhumisparsha* mudra (see box, p.392) with the robe tied over the left shoulder (the right shoulder is left bare).

Magical animals and mythical monsters

Mythical **beasts** are another essential feature of Burmese temple architecture, their fearsome features designed to offer supernatural protection to the building they guard. The entrances to many temples are protected by huge pairs of **chinthe**, lion-like figures (with a hint of dragon), while **sphinx**-like creatures (basically chinthe with human heads) are often placed at the corners of stupas. Grotesque **kirtimukha** (aka *kala*) – pop-eyed ogre heads swallowing chains of garlands or pearls – decorate the walls of many Bagan temples, referring to an old Hindu legend in which Shiva accidentally creates a ravenous monster and then orders it to eat his own body. Other mythological

BUDDHIST MUDRAS AND THEIR MEANINGS

Buddha images are traditionally shown in one of various iconic poses, known as **mudras**, whether standing, sitting or reclining.

Abhaya mudra The "Have No Fear" pose shows the Buddha standing with his right hand raised, the palm facing the viewer.

Bhumisparsha mudra The "Earth-Witness" pose shows the seated Buddha touching the ground with the tips of the fingers of his left hand, commemorating the moment during his enlightenment when the demon Mara, attempting to break his concentration, caused the Earth to shake beneath him, and the Buddha stilled the ground by touching it.

Dana or **varada mudra** The "offering" pose, with the Buddha seated and his right hand placed palm upwards signifying the act of giving and compassion.

Dhyani or **samadhi mudra** Shows the Buddha in meditation, seated in the lotus or half-lotus position, with his hands placed together in his lap.

Namaskara mudra Shows the Buddha (or other devotee) with hands placed together in a gesture of prayer.

Parinirvana mudra Shows the Buddha in a reclining pose to represent the moment of his death and entrance into nirvana.

Vitarka mudra ("Gesture of Explanation") and **dharmachakra mudra** ("Gesture of the Turning of the Wheel of the Law"). In both positions the Buddha forms a circle with his thumb and one finger, representing the "wheel of dharma" (dharmachakra), which symbolizes the Buddhist route to nirvana. Used in both standing and sitting poses.

monsters commonly encountered include the bird-like **garuda** and the snake-like **naga**, half-animal and half-human creatures with god-like powers. Another bird, the **hamsa** (translated either as "goose" or "swan"), is also commonly found as a decorative element and is strongly associated with the Hindu god Brahma, who also appears in some Buddhist temples as a protector of the faith.

Secular architecture

Temples apart, traditional Burmese buildings were constructed entirely of wood and have almost entirely vanished as a result of fire, earthquakes, World War II and the depredations of time – the now empty plains surrounding the temples of Bagan, for example, would once have been filled with wooden houses, palaces and monastic and administrative buildings. The reconstructed royal palace at Mandalay gives a slight (if not massively inspiring) sense of what old Myanmar looked like. More authentic are the few surviving wooden religious buildings, such as the Yoke Sone Kyaung monastery in Salay (see p.231).

Books

Myanmar has a rich English-language literary heritage dating back to colonial times, when authors from quintessential Empire tub-thumper Rudyard Kipling through to anti-imperialist freethinker George Orwell penned various poems, essays, travelogues and novels about the country. Post-independence literature largely focuses on the desperate plight of the country under military rule – often sombre reading, but offering unparalleled insights into life under the generals. Sadly, there's virtually no Burmese literature available in translation, although Burmese authors writing in English have provided a handful of excellent memoirs, histories and other works. All the following titles are widely available overseas, although less easily obtainable in Myanmar itself. Particularly recommended titles are marked with a ★ symbol.

LITERATURE

★**Amitav Ghosh** *The Glass Palace*. Set in Burma, India and Malaya, this acclaimed historical novel follows the fortunes of four Indian and Burmese families (including that of the exiled King Thibaw) during the six tumultuous decades between the fall of Mandalay in 1885 and the end of World War II. Essential Burmese reading.

Rudyard Kipling *Barrack-Room Ballads; From Sea to Sea*. Rudyard Kipling's entire experience of Burma consisted of brief visits to Rangoon (Yangon) and Moulmein (Mawlamyine) during a sea journey from India to the US in 1889 – which didn't stop him from leaving a heavy literary mark on the land. Originally published in *Barrack-Room Ballads*, "Mandalay" (which he never visited) remains the most famous poem ever written about the country, though Burma appears in several other poems and short stories. An account of his 1889 visit can be found in *From Sea to Sea*, which is also the source of his endlessly repeated quote: "This is Burma, and it will be quite unlike any land you know".

Daniel Mason *The Piano Tuner*. Bestselling novel by American writer Daniel Mason, set in 1886 and telling the story of piano tuner Edgar Drake, despatched to the remote Shan States to repair the Érard grand of an eccentric army doctor – full of convincing historical detail, and a very enjoyable read.

George Orwell *Burmese Days*. Orwell's classic critique of British colonialism has its moments, although it's a turgid read at times, with heavy-handed satire and a cast of profoundly unsympathetic and largely one-dimensional characters who are little more than mouthpieces for Orwell's anti-imperialistic screed. Burma also appears in two of Orwell's most celebrated essays, "A Hanging" and "Shooting an Elephant", both of which say more about the canker of empire in just a few pages than *Burmese Days* manages in its entire length.

Amy Tan *Saving Fish From Drowning*. This is a richly comic depiction of modern tourism following a group of bumbling American visitors who go missing near Inle Lake – with memorable consequences.

TRAVELOGUE AND REPORTAGE

★**Emma Larkin** *Everything is Broken: Life Inside Burma*. Even better than Larkin's earlier Burmese book (see below), *Everything is Broken* provides a harrowing portrait of Myanmar in the aftermath of Cyclone Nargis and a damning indictment of the ruling junta's spectacular inaction in the face of the country's greatest ever natural disaster.

Emma Larkin *Finding George Orwell in Burma*. Enjoyable and insightful mix of travel writing and reportage: part travelogue, following in the footsteps of Orwell during his stint as a colonial police officer in Burma; part examination of the state of Myanmar under the generals – and its uncanny resemblance to the Orwellian dystopias of *Animal Farm* and *Nineteen Eighty-Four*.

★**Norman Lewis** *Golden Earth: Travels in Burma*. Classic tome by one of the twentieth century's finest travel writers, describing a 1951 journey the length of the country from Myeik to Myitkyina during the turbulent early years after independence, all narrated with Lewis's characteristic insight and wit.

Rory Maclean *Under the Dragon: A Journey Through Burma*. Genre-bending book cross-cutting an account of

Maclean's travels in the footsteps of Sir George Scott with a series of novel-like episodes portraying the lives of ordinary Burmese in the shadow of the 8888 Uprising. It's somewhat uneven, although a couple of the novelistic interpolations are very fine.

★ **Andrew Marshall** *The Trouser People*. Inspired by the diaries of colonial empire-builder Sir George Scott – who also appears in Rory Maclean's *Under the Dragon* (see p.393) – *The Trouser People* serves up a compelling mix of travelogue and reportage as Marshall ventures into some of Myanmar's remotest ethnic minority areas. Brave, black and savagely funny.

W. Somerset Maugham *The Gentleman in the Parlour*.

Travel-diary-style jottings describing journeys up the Ayeyarwady to Mandalay and into the Shan hills (plus a voyage down the Mekong to Saigon), with plenty of quaint characters and exotic scenery on the way. A good record of 1930s travel in the grand style.

Rosalind Russell *Burma's Spring: Real Lives in Turbulent Times*. The recent, decisive years in Burmese history explored through a series of insightful encounters with a diverse cast of characters ranging from an illegal Burmese immigrant maid in Thailand, an astrologer, girl band, punk rocker, freedom-fighting monk and aspiring journalist (among others) through to NLD luminary Win Tin and Aung San Suu Kyi herself.

POLITICS AND CURRENT EVENTS

Maggie Lemere & Zoe West *Nowhere to Be Home: Narratives from Survivors of Burma's Military Regime*. Interviews with 22 persecuted Burmese including child conscripts, sex workers, refugee monks and representatives from ethnic minorities forced to labour for the regime – a simple but eloquent indictment of life under the generals.

David I. Steinberg *Burma/Myanmar: What Everyone Needs to Know*. A perceptive introduction to the history and

politics of Myanmar, covering all the major issues affecting the country today in handy, bite-sized chapters.

Thant Myint-U *Where China Meets India: Burma and the New Crossroads of Asia*. Wide-ranging analysis of Myanmar's possible future role as the geographical and economic conduit between the two great Asian superpowers. Mixing history, travelogue and reportage, it has thought-provoking nuggets of information and insight on virtually every page.

AUNG SAN SUU KYI

Aung San Suu Kyi *Freedom from Fear and Other Writings*. This varied collection of essays, speeches and open letters serves as a useful introduction to Aung San Suu Kyi's political credo, and includes her Nobel Prize acceptance speech and her famous address at the Shwedagon Pagoda in 1988 (see p.373).

Aung San Suu Kyi *Letters from Burma*. Rather less interesting than *Freedom from Fear*, this second collection of essays on assorted aspects of Burmese politics and culture gives the distinct sensation of a barrel being rather thoroughly scraped.

Aung Zaw *The Face of Resistance: Aung San Suu Kyi and Burma's Fight for Freedom*, o/p. Interesting short book by former political prisoner Aung Zaw, founder and editor of the ground-breaking *Irrawaddy* magazine (see p.41). It focuses not just on Aung San Suu Kyi herself but also on the rainbow tapestry of other organizations and individuals working towards a free Myanmar.

Bertil Lintner *Aung San Suu Kyi and Burma's Struggle for*

Democracy. Concise and balanced survey of Aung San Suu Kyi's life and politics – and refreshingly free of the sycophantic hagiography that colours most writing about The Lady.

Peter Popham *The Lady And The Peacock: The Life of Aung San Suu Kyi of Burma*. The blockbuster biography is more up to date (2012) than Wintle's book (see below) but not its equal in other respects, leaning towards biopic cliché in places and haphazardly organized in others – although worth a look if you want to read up on events of recent years.

Justin Wintle *Perfect Hostage: Aung San Suu Kyi, Burma and the Generals*. The first major study of Aung San Suu Kyi (originally published in 2007) and still the best of the English-language biographies currently available, combining heaps of detail with a well-structured and very readable narrative. Wintle's also not afraid to ask some hard questions about the effectiveness (or otherwise) of Gandhian-style non-violent protest against a brutal military regime.

HISTORY

Michael Aung-Thwin and Maitrii Aung-Thwin *A History of Myanmar Since Ancient Times*. The only complete scholarly history of Myanmar in English currently available – although it's far from your average academic tome. A strong polemic element runs through the entire book, with the authors launching a series of broadsides against a wide range of received historical and political opinions

– everything from Mon influence at Bagan through to the military's renaming of the country and transfer of the capital to Naypyitaw. An often interesting read, although the final chapter is little more than government propaganda.

Michael W. Charney *A History of Modern Burma*. Covering the period from 1886 to 2008, this book provides a useful continuation to Thant Myint-U's history (see below). Full of interesting detail, and particularly good on the post-1962 period.

Richard Cockett *Blood, Dreams and Gold: The Changing Face of Burma*. A detailed look into Mynamar's history, politics and culture over the past century, from the British colonial period (including particularly good coverage of colonial Rangoon) through to military rule and the pro-democracy movement.

Thant Myint-U *The Making of Modern Burma*. Microscopic examination of the history of Myanmar between the latter days of the Konbaung dynasty and the establishment of nationwide British rule. Thant Myint-U's unravelling of the intricate social and economic structures of Myanmar under kings Mindon and Thibaw is an academic *tour de force*, while accounts of the Machiavellian intrigues, infighting and palace coups at the royal court add welcome spice.

★ **Thant Myint-U** *The River of Lost Footsteps: A Personal History of Burma*. Easily the best general introduction to the history of Myanmar, Thant Myint-U's superb "personal history" covers the country from ancient times to the present, combining exemplary scholarship, vivid prose and razor-sharp insights into a superbly readable and informative whole.

MEMOIRS

David V. Donnison *Last of the Guardians: A Story of Burma, Britain and a Family*. Enjoyable portrait of life in colonial Burma between 1923 and World War II, based on the memoirs of Donnison's parents.

James Mawdsley *The Heart Must Break: The Fight for Democracy and Truth in Burma*. Gripping account of British activist James Mawdsley's fight for democracy in Myanmar and his fourteen months spent in jail there in 1999–2000.

Pascal Khoo Thwe *From The Land of Green Ghosts: A Burmese Odyssey*. Lyrical memoir describing the author's boyhood in a remote Padaung village, his years as a rebel guerrilla fighter in the 1990s and, eventually, his escape to Europe and graduation from the University of Cambridge. An unrivalled portrait of life among Myanmar's repressed minorities.

Zoya Phan *Little Daughter: A Memoir of Survival in Burma and the West*. Simple but affecting memoir by Kayin refugee Zoya Phan, describing her family's flight from their native village in 1994 and the following two years spent dodging Burmese armed forces, before her eventual escape to Thailand and the West.

CULTURE AND COOKERY

Naomi Duguid *Burma: River of Flavors*. This attractive cookbook provides a good introduction to Burmese cuisine, with solid coverage of basic ingredients and cooking techniques as well as recipes, plus lovely photos of the country to boot.

Myat Yin Saw *CultureShock! Myanmar: A Survival Guide to Customs and Etiquette*. Handy introduction to Burmese culture, customs and manners, plus plenty of general background on the country.

Robert Carmack & Morrison Polkinghorne *The Burma Cookbook: Recipes from the Land of a Million Pagodas*. Original and enjoyable cookery book featuring dozens of colonial-era recipes alongside good coverage of contemporary dishes and cooking techniques, all lavishly illustrated with a mix of modern photographs and colonial prints.

Language

Around a hundred different languages are spoken in Myanmar. Far and away the most widely used is Burmese, or "Myanmar Language" (*myanma bhasa*) as it's officially called, the native language of the country's Bamar majority as well as many other ethnic groups including the Mon. Burmese is spoken by around two-thirds of the population (37 million) as their first language and a further ten million as their second language. As well as Burmese proper, there are also several major regional dialects spoken in different parts of the country such as Intha, Danu, Yaw and Taungyo, not to mention Arakanese, spoken in Rakhine State, which is sometimes considered a dialect, and sometimes as a separate language. English is taught in schools and quite widely spoken in larger towns and cities, less so out in the countryside.

Part of the Tibeto-Burman group of tongues, Burmese is a tricky language for Westerners, although locals will appreciate any effort you make to speak it. The major difficulty derives from its **tonal** system (see p.397). Most words are monosyllabic, but word order and many other basic linguistic features of the language are also quite different to English.

There aren't many **study resources** available for learning Burmese. The best is *Burmese By Ear* by John Okell of the University of London's School of Oriental and African Studies, comprising a series of audio recordings plus accompanying book in PDF format, all of which can be downloaded for free at ⓦsoas.ac.uk/bbe. The audio files can be loaded onto a tablet or MP3 player and make for educational listening during long bus journeys and suchlike. Lonely Planet's pocket-sized *Burmese Phrasebook* is also a useful travelling companion.

Transliteration

There's no universally agreed way to show Burmese in Roman script – the same Burmese sound might be transliterated as *me*, *may*, *mei*, *mey* or *mae*, for example, while place names are similarly subject to random variation (the national capital, for example, is known variously as Naypyitaw, Naypyidaw, Nay Pyi Taw and Nay Pyi Daw). The difficulty of representing Burmese sounds in Roman script can lead to a degree of confusion, given how some Roman letters are commonly used to represent Burmese sounds with a notably different pronunciation. The only real way to grasp the language's pronunciation is to listen to Burmese-speakers themselves.

THE BURMESE ALPHABET

The Burmese alphabet's distinctively rounded appearance ("bubble writing", as some people describe it) derives from the fact that palm leaves inscribed with a stylus were historically used as the main material for writing upon, rather than paper and ink, with circular characters preferred given that numerous straight lines would have torn the leaves being used.

Like many other Southeast and South Asian languages, Burmese is written in a **consonant**-based script – **vowels** and **tones** are signified by adding additional accents and symbols to the basic consonant, rather than written separately, as in Western languages. There are 33 basic Burmese **consonants**, with distinctions made between unaspirated and aspirated consonants (see p.397). The script is written from left to right with no spaces between words, although modern written Burmese usually inserts spaces after each clause to enhance readability.

Pronunciation

There are five **tones** in Burmese – three main tones plus two additional modifiers:

Creaky high tone High, short pronunciation with tightened throat (akin to the pronunciation of the English word "squeak"). Transliterated using an acute accent, eg **á**.

Plain high tone Longer pronunciation, starting high and falling (like the English "fall" pronounced with a falling intonation). Transliterated using a grave accent, eg **à**.

Low tone Starts and stays low. Transliterated with no additional symbol.

Stopped syllable High sound cut short with a glottal stop at the end (like the first syllable of "bot-tle" spoken in a Cockney accent). Transliterated with a -q, eg **aq**.

Reduced (or "weak") syllable Usually applied to the first syllable of a two-syllable word where the first syllable is short and unstressed (as in the English "beneath", or for that matter, "reduced"). Transliterated with a breve accent, eg **ă**.

Burmese also distinguishes between **aspirated** and **unaspirated** consonants, the latter pronounced with a slight puff of air (put your hand in front of your mouth and say the English words "bin" and then "pin" to get a clear idea of the difference). Aspirated consonants are transliterated by placing an apostrophe after them (eg **k'**); those in the following section marked "whispered" begin with a sound similar to the start of the English "hmm".

ă as in "**about**"
a as in "**car**"
a in aq and an as in "**cat**"
ai in aiq and ain as in "**site**"
au in auq and aun "ou" as in "**lounge**"
aw as in "**saw**"
e as in French "**café**"
e in eh as in "**sell**"
e in eq as in "**set**"
ei in eiq and ein "a" as in "**late**"
i as in "**ravine**"
i in iq and in as in "**sit**"
o as in the French "**eau**"
ou in ouq and oun "o" as in "**tone**"
u as in "**Susan**"
u in uq and un "oo" as in "**foot**"
b as in "**bore**"
ch same as "ky" but aspirated
d as in "**door**"
dh "th" as in "**this**"
g as in "**gore**"
gy as in "**judge**"
h as in "**hot**"
hl same as "l" but whispered
hm same as "m" but whispered

hn same as "n" but whispered
hng same as "ng" but whispered
hny same as "ny" but aspirated
hw same as "w" but whispered
k as in French "**corps**"
k' as in "**core**" (aspirated)
ky "ch" as in "**cello**"
l as in "**law**"
m as in "**more**"
n as in "**nor**"
ng as in "**long**"
ny "gn" as in Italian "**gn**occhi"
p as in French "**port**"
p' as in "**pore**" (aspirated)
q glottal stop
r as in "**raw**"
s as in "**soar**"
s' same as "s" but aspirated
sh as in "**shore**"
t as in French "**tour**"
t' as in "**tore**" (aspirated)
th as in "**thaw**"
w as in "**war**"
y as in "**your**"
z as in "**zone**"

USEFUL WORDS AND PHRASES

GREETINGS AND BASIC PHRASES

Goodbye	thwà-meh-naw?
Excuse me (to get past)	nèh-nèh-lauq
Sorry	sàw-ri-naw
Please	kyè-zù pyú-bì
Thank you	kyè-zù tin-ba-deh
Thanks (less formal)	kyè-zù-bèh
Yes	houq-kéh
No	hín-ìn
Do you speak English?	ìn-găleiq sagà pyàw-daq-thălà?
What's that called in Burmese?	èh-da Băma-lo beh-lo k'aw-dhălèh?
Could you repeat that?	pyan-pyàw-ba-oùn?
I don't understand	nà măleh-ba-bù
Can you help me?	k'ăná-lauq louq-pè-ba?

There is no word for a simple "**hello**" – rather, greetings are nonverbal or based on the situation (e.g. "Where have you been?"). Locals greet foreigners with the very formal *min-găla-ba* (see p.44)

Good/bad	kaùn-deh/s'ò-deh
Hot/cold (weather)	pu-deh/è-deh
When (in the future)?	beh-dáw-lèh?
Who?	bădhu-lèh?
Where?	beh-hma-lèh?
Why?	ba-p'yiq-ló-lèh?
Open/closed	pwín-deh/peiq-t'à-deh
Bank	ban
Post office	sa-daiq

MEETING PEOPLE
When answering where you come from, you can simply say the name of your country in English for most nationalities – one of the very few exceptions is France, which is Pyin-thiq.

My name is ….	cănáw/cămá nameh …. (m/f)
Where do you come from?	beh-gá la-dhălèh?
I come from …	…-gá la-ba-deh
I'm here for … weeks	cănaw/cămá di-hma (m/f) … paq ne-meh
Husband/wife	ămyò-thà/ămyò-thămì
Child/children	k'ălè/k'ălè-myà
It's very hot, isn't it?	theiq pu-deh-naw?
Can I take a photograph?	di-hma daq-poun yaiq-c'ìn-ba-deh?
No problem	yá-ba-deh

EMERGENCIES

Help!	keh-ba!
Fire!	mee!
Go away!	thwà-zàn!
Stop!	yaq!
I'm lost	làn pyauq-thwà-bi
I've been robbed	ăk'ò-k'an-yá-deh
Police station	yèh-t'a-ná
I'm ill	ne-măkàun-bù
Call a doctor!	s'ăya-wun-go k'aw-pè-ba!
Hospital	s'è-youn
Pharmacy	s'è-zain

Where is the…?	…beh-hma-lèh?
…toilet?	ein dha…

DIRECTIONS

Where is the…?	…beh-hma-lèh?
How far is it?	beh-lauq wè-dăhlèh?
Left/right	beh-beq/nya-beq
Straight ahead	téh-déh
Near/far	nì-deh/wè-deh
This way	di-beq
Over there	ho-beq-hma

TRANSPORT

Ticket	leq-hmaq
Airport	le-zeiq
Boat (ferry)	thìn-bàw
Bus	baq-săkà
Bus station	kà-geiq
Train station	bu-da
Taxi	teq-si
Car	kà
Bicycle	seq-beìn
When will the … leave?	… beh-ăc'ein t'weq-mălèh?
bus	baq-săkà
plane	le-yin-byan
train	mì-yăt'à

ACCOMMODATION

Hotel	ho-teh
Guesthouse	tèh-k'o-gàn
Can I reserve a room?	ăl'àn ăk'àn co-yu jin-ba-deh?
Do you have any rooms?	ăk'àn à-là?
Double room	hnăyauq-k'àn
Single room	tăyauq-k'àn
Bathroom	ye-c'ò-gàn
How much for …	…beh-lauq-lèh?
…one night?	tăyeq…
…two nights?	hnăyeq…
How much is it?	beh-lauq kyá-dhălèh?

COMMON SIGNS

Open	ဖွင့်သည်	Men	ကျား
Closed	ပိတ်ထားသည်	Ladies	မ
Entrance	အဝင်	Toilets	အိမ်သာ / ရေအိမ်
Exit	အထွက်	No smoking	ဆေးလိပ်မသောက်ရ
No entry	ဝင်ခွင့်မရှိ		

BURMESE NUMBERS

0	၀	thoun-nyá	13	၁၃	s'éh-thoùn
1	၁	tiq	20	၂၀	hnǎs'eh
2	၂	hniq	21	၂၁	hnǎs'eh-tiq
3	၃	thoùn	30	၃၀	thoùn-zeh
4	၄	lè	40	၄၀	lè-zeh
5	၅	ngà	100	၁၀၀	tǎya
6	၆	chauq	200	၂၀၀	hnǎya
7	၇	k'un(-hniq)	300	၃၀၀	thoùn-ya
8	၈	shiq	1000	၁၀၀၀	tǎt'aun
9	၉	kò	2000	၂၀၀၀	hnǎt'aun
10	၁၀	tǎs'eh	10,000	၁၀၀၀၀	tǎthaùn
11	၁၁	s'éh-tiq	100,000	၁၀၀၀၀၀	tǎtheìn
12	၁၂	s'éh-hniq			

Cheap/expensive	zè cho-deh/zè kyì-deh
Passport	paq-sǎpó
Air-conditioning	èh-kun
Fan (electric)	pan-ka

SHOPPING

How much is it?	beh-lauq kyá-dhǎlèh?
Do you have any…?	…shi-là?
lacquerware	yún-deh
silk	pò-deh
silver	ngwe
jade	cauq-seìn
Yes, I have	shí-ba-deh bya
No, I haven't	mǎshí-ba-bù
Cheap/expensive	zè cho-deh/zè kyì-deh
Can you give me a cheaper price?	zè-sháw-ba?
That one	èh-da

FOOD AND DRINK

GENERAL TERMS

Restaurant	sà-thauq-s'ain
Café/teahouse	lǎp'eq-ye-s'ain
Breakfast	mǎneq-sa
Lunch	né-leh-za
Dinner	nyá-za
Knife	dà
Fork	k'ǎyìn
Spoon	zùn
Chopsticks	tu
Plate	bǎgan-byà
Glass	p'an-gweq
Vegetarian (food)	theq-thaq-luq
I don't eat meat or fish	thà-gyì ngà-gyì … shaun-deh
Hot (spicy)	saq-teh
Sweet/sour	c'o-deh/c'in-deh
Cheers!	Chì-yà!

I like that one	èh-da caiq-pa-deh
I'll take it	yu-meh
I'm just looking	cí-youn-ba-bèh

TIMES AND DAYS

Today	di-né
Tomorrow	mǎneq-p'an
Morning	mǎneq
Midday	né-leh
Afternoon	nyá-ne
Night/evening	nyá
Monday	tǎnìn-la-né
Tuesday	in-ga-né
Wednesday	bouq-dǎhù-né
Thursday	ca-dhǎbǎdè-né
Friday	thauq-ca-né
Saturday	sǎne-né
Sunday	tǎnìn-gǎnwe-né

Delicious	kaùn-laiq-ta
What does it come to? (ie the bill)	beh-lauq kyá-dhǎlèh?

RICE AND NOODLES

kya-zan	rice vermicelli
k'auq-s'wèh	noodles
nàn-gyì	thick noodles
t'ǎmìn	rice
t'ǎmìn-gyaw	fried rice

MEAT, FISH AND BASICS

ǎmèh-dhà	beef
bǎzun	prawns
bèh-dhà	duck
kyeq-thà	chicken
ngà	fish
s'eiq-thà	mutton

OLD NAMES OF MYANMAR

Some of Myanmar's old colonial-era names are still in occasional circulation. The main ones you're likely to come across are:

New name	Old name	New name	Old name
Ayeyarwady	Irrawaddy	**Pyay**	Prome
Bagan	Pagan	**Pyin Oo Lwin**	Maymyo
Bago	Pegu	**Rakhine**	Arakan
Dawei	Tavoy	**Sittwe**	Akyab
Mawlamyine	Moulmein	**Tanintharyi**	Tenasserim
Mottama	Martaban	**Thandwe**	Sandoway
Myeik	Mergui	**Thanlyin**	Syriam
Pathein	Bassein	**Yangon**	Rangoon

weq-thà	pork	ceq-mauq-thì	rambutan
chís	cheese	dù-yìn-dhì	durian
hìn	curry	lein-maw-dhì	tangerine
t'ǎmìn hin	curry and rice	ma-lǎka-dhì	guava
ngǎpí	fish paste	mìn-guq-thì	mangosteen
ngǎyouq thì	chilli	na-naq-thì	pineapple
paun-moún	bread	ngǎpyàw-dhì	banana
pèh-byà	tofu	oùn-dhì	coconut
ǎthouq	salad	p'ǎyèh-dhi	watermelon
s'à	salt	pàn-dhì	apple
s'í	oil	peìn-nèh-dhì	jackfruit
t'àw-baq	butter	thǎyeq-thì	mango
thǎgyà	sugar	thìn-bǎw-dhì	papaya

VEGETABLES AND SALAD

hìn-dhì-hìn-yweq	vegetables
ǎthouq	salad
a-lù	potato
bù-dhì	gourd
c'ìn-baun	roselle leaf
céq-thun-byu	garlic
céq-thun-ni	onion
hmo	mushroom
k'ǎyàn-jin-djì	tomato
moun-la-ú-wa	carrot
p'ǎyoun	pumpkin
s'ǎlaq-yweq	lettuce
thǎk'wà-dhi	cucumber

FRUIT

thiq-thì	fruit

DRINKS

thauq-ye	drinking water
ye-thán	purified water
ye-thán-bù	bottle of purified water
ǎè	soft drink
bi-ya	beer
kaw-p'í	coffee (with milk and sugar)
kaw-p'í nwà-nó-néh	coffee with milk
lǎp'eq-ye	black tea
lahpet-ye-gyàn/ ye-nwè-gyàn	green tea
p'yaw-ye	fruit juice
t'àn-ye	toddy
nó mǎt'éh-néh	don't put milk in
thǎgyà mǎt'éh-néh	don't put sugar in
ye-gèh mǎt'éh-néh	don't put ice in

Glossary

Abhaya mudra "Have no fear" Buddhist mudra

Amalaka Lotus-shaped feature found in some stupa designs between the *anda* and spire

Anda The main, bell-shaped section of the stupa, symbolizing the Buddha's upturned alms bowl (*thabeik*)

Andaw Tooth relic

Anyeint Traditional Burmese entertainment combining music, dancing and comedy

Ari Buddhism Early, eclectic form of Burmese Buddhism

ASEAN Association of Southeast Asian Nations

Avalokitesvara The Bodhisattva of universal compassion

Banana bud The slightly bulbous decorative feature immediately below the topmost section of a stupa spire

Betel Popular snack mixing betel nut with other ingredients (see box, p.10)

Bodhi tree Type of fig tree (*Ficus religiosa*) beneath which the Buddha is said to have gained enlightenment; also known as the bo or peepal tree

Bodhisattva A future Buddha who, rather than passing into *nibbana*, has chosen to stay in the world to improve the spiritual welfare of other, unenlightened, beings

BSPP Burma Socialist Programme Party

Burman Colonial-era name for Bamar

Chaung/gyaung Stream or small river

Chinlone Popular Burmese "keepy-uppy" game using a rattan ball

Chinthe Mythical lion-like creature

Dana mudra Traditional Buddhist "offering" mudra; also known as the *varada* mudra

Daw "Mrs" or "aunty"

Deva Divine being or god

Dhamma The Buddha's collected teachings

Dharmachakra mudra Buddhist mudra symbolizing the "Gesture of the Turning of the Wheel of the Law"

Dhyani (samadhi) mudra Traditional mudra showing the Buddha seated in meditation

Ganesh The elephant-headed Hindu god of prosperity

Garuda Mythical bird-like creatures, sacred to both Buddhism and Hinduism

Hamsa Sacred geese (or sometimes swan), and the mount of the Hindu god Brahma. Also known as the *hintha*

Harmika Relic chamber found at the base of the spire in some stupas

Hintha See "hamsa"

Hti The umbrella-like feature placed at the very top of a stupa spire

In Lake

Indra Hindu king of the gods

IWT Inland Water Transport Authority

Jataka Collection of popular folk tales describing the 547 previous lives of the Buddha

Kala Alternative name for *kirthimukha* (see p.391)

Kalasa Decorative "nectar pots", derived from Indian architecture and sometimes found adorning the corners of stupa terraces

Kalpa The current world cycle in Buddhist cosmology

Karaweik Mythical bird; also known as the *karavika*

Kirthimukha Mythical ogre-like creature

KNLA Karen National Liberation Army

Konagamana The second of the five Buddhas of the present world cycle

Kyaik Mon temple

Kyaung Monastery

Kyi/gyi Suffix, meaning "big"

Kyun Island

Lokanat Burmese name for Avalokitesvara (see opposite)

Longyi Sarong-like garment worn by the majority of Burmese

Mahayana The later and more eclectic of the two main schools of Buddhism, centred on the cult of the Bodhisattva

Maitreya The future Buddha Maitreya is predicted to be the fifth and last of the five Buddhas of the current world cycle

Mi-gyaung/kyam Traditional crocodile-shaped, three-string Burmese zither

Mudras A series of canonical poses used in most visual representations of the Buddha (see box, p.392)

Myo Town

Naga Mythical serpent-like creature with divine powers (although can also refer to the Naga people living in northwest Myanmar)

Namaskara mudra Traditional Buddhist mudra showing the Buddha or other figure in the act of praying

Nat Burmese spirits

Nat kadaw *Nat* spirit medium

Nat pwè *Nat* festival

Ngwe Silver

Nibbana Nirvana

Nikaya Monastic order

NLD National League for Democracy

Paccaya Terrace at base of stupa

Pagoda Temple

Pahto Temple (used mainly in Bagan in reference to "hollow" temples)

Pali Extinct Indian language in which most of Buddhism's oldest scriptures were first recorded – the Buddhist equivalent to Hebrew in Christianity or Sanskrit in Hinduism

Palm leaf Used as an alternative to paper thanks to its greater durability in the tropics, with dried leaves bound together into long, narrow books

Parinirvana mudra Traditional mudra showing the reclining Buddha at the moment of entering nirvana

Paya Temple (literally, the Burmese word for "pagoda")

Pwè Festival

Pyatthat Southeast Asian-style multi-tiered roof

Pyigyimun Royal barge

Pyissaya Stupa terraces

Ramayana famous Hindu epic describing the life of Rama, an incarnation of the god Vishnu

Samadhi mudra See *dhyani* mudra

Sangha The worldwide community of Buddhist monks

Saopha A "sky lord" – the hereditary rulers of the Shan peoples

Sariputra One of Buddha's disciples

Sayadaw Abbot

Shikhara Indian-style temple tower

Shinbyu Ceremony marking induction of young boys into the Sangha

Shwe Golden

SLORC State Law and Order Restoration Council

SPDC State Peace and Development Council

Stupa Buddhist monument found in most Burmese temples

Sutra Buddhist (or Hindu) religious text

Taik Library

Tatmadaw The Burmese Armed Forces, comprising army, navy, air force and police

Taung Mountain

Taw/daw Suffix (as in, for instance, Naypyitaw), signifying somewhere sacred or royal

Tazaung Pavilion-style shrine

Temptation of Mara Popular subject of Buddhist art, showing hordes of monsters unleashed by the demon Mara attempting to distract Buddha at the moment of his enlightenment

Thabeik Alms bowl

Thanaka General-purpose Burmese powder/paste used as all-in-one make-up, sunscreen and insect repellent

Thein Ordination hall

Theravada The older of the two main schools of Buddhism and the dominant form of the religion in Myanmar

Thingyan Water festival celebrating the Buddhist New Year

Tripitaka The main collection of Buddhist scriptures

Trishaw Cycle rickshaw (although sometimes used to describe motorized vehicles as well)

U "Mr" or "uncle"

USDP Union Solidarity and Development Party

Varada mudra See *dana* mudra

Viss Burmese unit of weight (equivalent to 1.6kg)

Vitarka mudra "Gesture of Explanation" – one of the traditional Buddhist mudras

Weizza (weikza) Burmese Buddhist cult dedicated to magical practices and beliefs

Yadaya Quasi-magical rituals prescribed by astrologers to ward off misfortune (see box, p.388)

Yama Zatdaw Burmese version of the Ramayana

Yoma Mountain range

Zaungdan Stairway

Zawgyi Alchemist/magician

Zedi Stupa

Zei Market

Small print and index

A ROUGH GUIDE TO ROUGH GUIDES

Published in 1982, the first Rough Guide – to Greece – was a student scheme that became a publishing phenomenon. Mark Ellingham, a recent graduate in English from Bristol University, had been travelling in Greece the previous summer and couldn't find the right guidebook. With a small group of friends he wrote his own guide, combining a contemporary, journalistic style with a thoroughly practical approach to travellers' needs.

The immediate success of the book spawned a series that rapidly covered dozens of destinations. And, in addition to impecunious backpackers, Rough Guides soon acquired a much broader readership that relished the guides' wit and inquisitiveness as much as their enthusiastic, critical approach and value-for-money ethos. These days, Rough Guides include recommendations from budget to luxury and cover more than 120 destinations around the globe, from Amsterdam to Zanzibar, all regularly updated by our team of roaming writers.

Browse all our latest guides, read inspirational features and book your trip at **roughguides.com**.

Rough Guide credits

Editors: Claire Saunders, Georgia Stephens
Layout: Anita Singh
Cartography: Deshpal Dabas, Richard Marchi
Picture editor: Phoebe Lowndes
Proofreader: Jan McCann
Burmese proofreader: John Okell
Managing editor: Andy Turner
Assistant editor: Divya Grace Mathew

Production: Jimmy Lao
Cover photo research: Sarah Stewart-Richardson
Photographer: James Tye
Editorial assistant: Aimee White
Senior DTP coordinator: Dan May
Programme manager: Gareth Lowe
Publishing director: Georgina Dee

Publishing information

This second edition published November 2017 by
Rough Guides Ltd,
80 Strand, London WC2R 0RL
11, Community Centre, Panchsheel Park,
New Delhi 110017, India
Distributed by Penguin Random House
Penguin Books Ltd, 80 Strand, London WC2R 0RL
Penguin Group (USA), 345 Hudson Street, NY 10014, USA
Penguin Group (Australia), 250 Camberwell Road,
Camberwell, Victoria 3124, Australia
Penguin Group (NZ), 67 Apollo Drive, Mairangi Bay,
Auckland 1310, New Zealand
Penguin Group (South Africa), Block D, Rosebank Office
Park, 181 Jan Smuts Avenue, Parktown North, Gauteng,
South Africa 2193
Rough Guides is represented in Canada by DK Canada, 320
Front Street West, Suite 1400, Toronto, Ontario M5V 3B6
Printed in Singapore
© Rough Guides 2017
Maps © Rough Guides

416pp includes index
A catalogue record for this book is available from the
British Library
ISBN: 978-024129-790-2
The publishers and authors have done their best to ensure
the accuracy and currency of all the information in **The
Rough Guide to Myanmar**, however, they can accept
no responsibility for any loss, injury, or inconvenience
sustained by any traveller as a result of information or
advice contained in the guide.
1 3 5 7 9 8 6 4 2

Help us update

We've gone to a lot of effort to ensure that the second
edition of **The Rough Guide to Myanmar** is accurate
and up-to-date. However, things change – places get
"discovered", opening hours are notoriously fickle,
restaurants and rooms raise prices or lower standards. If
you feel we've got it wrong or left something out, we'd like
to know, and if you can remember the address, the price,
the hours, the phone number, so much the better.

Please send your comments with the subject line
"Rough Guide Myanmar Update" to mail@uk
.roughguides.com. We'll credit all contributions and send a
copy of the next edition (or any other Rough Guide if you
prefer) for the very best emails.

ABOUT THE AUTHORS

Stuart Butler is a photographer and writer specializing in the Himalaya, Myanmar and eastern Africa. He first visited Myanmar back in 2001. As soon as he laid eyes on the Shwedagon for the first time he was hooked, and since that first visit he has returned frequently to Myanmar. Originally from southwest England, he today lives with his wife and two young children on the beautiful beaches of southwest France. His website is ⓦstuartbutlerjournalist.com

Tom Deas After being asked politely to leave school at 16, Tom's first job was as a food taster in a pie factory. Soon sacked, his subsequent career moves have seen him drifting from the wine cellars of Cambridge to the mountains of Yunnan, never achieving anything of note until now.

Gavin Thomas has spent most of his life trying to be somewhere else. A regular Rough Guide author for over fifteen years, he has written and contributed to numerous titles including the Rough Guides to Sri Lanka, India, Rajasthan, Cambodia, Dubai and Oman.

Acknowledgements

Stuart Butler In Myanmar I would like to thank William Myatwunna from Good News Travels for his huge help, Marcus Allender from Pegu Travels and ⓦgo-myanmar .com for his help and also Phone Kyaw Moe Myint in Ngwe Saung and the staff at Motherland Inn II in Yangon. Finally, but most importantly, I must thank my wife Heather and children, Jake and Grace, for their endless patience and understanding while I was away from home working on this project.

Tom Deas Thanks to Jo, Joy and Wybe Rood.

Gavin Thomas In Myanmar, thanks to Peter Richards, Sai Pan Pha, Martino and everyone at Loikaw, and to Nan Nan at Oriental Ballooning, and James Mundy at Inside Asia for valuable on-the-ground assistance. At Rough Guides, thanks to my fellow authors Stuart Butler and Tom Deas, to Andy Turner and Edward Aves for setting the ball rolling, to Georgia Stephens for overseeing the whole project so efficiently and to Claire Saunders for a marvellously meticulous old-school edit. And of course to Allison, Laura, Jamie and Rosie for keeping the home fires burning, yet again.

Readers' updates

Thanks to all the readers who have taken the time to write in with comments and suggestions (and apologies if we've inadvertently omitted or misspelt anyone's name):

Russ Austin, Sandra De Bastos, Pippa Behr, Mike Burnett, Sarah Harris, Els Leyssens, Julia MacKenzie, Siegfried Olbrich, Mila Rodriguez, Lee Seldon, Verstuurd Vanaf, Leo Verhoeff, Dennis Vervlossen, Wade and Sarah.

Photo credits

All photos © Rough Guides, except the following:
(Key: t-top; c-centre; b-bottom; l-left; r-right)

1 Picfair.com: Saravut Whanset
2 SuperStock: age fotostock/ José Fuste Raga
4 Corbis: Jon Hicks (tl); Blend Images / Jeremy Woodhouse (tr)
7 Getty Images: Gallo Images
9 Corbis: Christophe Boisvieux (b). **Getty Images**: Felix Hug (t); Peter Stuckings (c)
10 AWL Images: Nigel Pavitt
11 Alamy Stock Photo: Bo Jansson
12 Corbis: Jochen Schlenker
13 Alamy Stock Photo: Sean Pavone (b). **AWL Images**: John Warburton-Lee Photography Ltd / Christian Kober (t). **Glowimages**: Karl Johaentges (c)
14 Corbis: Robert Harding World Imagery / Tuul (b). **Michael Sheldon** (t)
15 Alamy Stock Photo: Petr Svarc (b). **Getty Images**: LightRocket / Thierry Falise (t)
16 Alamy Stock Photo: blickwinkel (b); LOOK Die Bildagentur der Fotografen GmbH (t); Simon Reddy (c)
17 4Corners: Tom Bourdon (tr); Günter Gräfenhain (b); Richard Taylor (tl)
18 Michael Sheldon (t). **Robert Harding Picture Library**: Lee Frost (b)
19 Corbis: Marc Dozier (tl). **Robert Harding Picture Library**: Luca Tettoni (b). **SuperStock**: robertharding / Tuul (tr)
20 AWL Images: Travel Pix Collection (tl). **Robert Harding Picture Library**: Joao Almeida (tr)
22 Corbis: Martin Puddy
54–55 4Corners: Stefano Brozzi
57 Alamy Stock Photo: Peter Sumner

79 AWL Images: Katie Garrod (b). **Corbis**: Tibor Bognár (t)
98–99 Alamy Stock Photo: Arco Images GmbH
101 Alamy Stock Photo: Matthew Williams-Ellis
117 Alamy Stock Photo: Hemis (b). **Michael Sheldon** (t)
138–139 Robert Harding Picture Library: Tuul
141 4Corners: Günter Gräfenhain
157 4Corners: Günter Gräfenhain (b). **AWL Images**: John Warburton-Lee Photography Ltd / Amar Grover (t)
178–179 Alamy Stock Photo: hemis.fr / LEMAIRE Stephane
181 Alamy Stock Photo: Robert Wyatt
198–199 Getty Images: Stefano Politi Markovina
215 Alamy Stock Photo: Gnomeandi (b). **AWL Images**: Peter Adams (t)
234–235 AWL Images: Hemis
257 Corbis: Rober t Harding World Imagery / Stuart Black (b). **Michael Sheldon** (t)
276–277 Dreamstime.com: Dinhhang
279 Photoshot: Tibor Bognar
293 Corbis: Stefano Politi (t). **Alamy Stock Photo**: Nick Fox (b)
310–311 Alamy Stock Photo: Maurice Joseph
313 Alamy Stock Photo: blickwinkel
339 Alamy Stock Photo: Tibor Bognar (b); National Geographic Image Collection (t). **Robert Harding Picture Library**: Still Pictures (c)
356 AWL Images: Gavin Hellier

Cover image: *Temples of Bagan, Myanmar* **AWL Images**: Michele Falzone

Index

Maps are marked in grey

Map symbols

The symbols below are used on maps throughout the book

Main road	⊙	Statue	⚲	Paya/pagoda/monastery	P	Parking
Minor road	⬥	National park/reserve		Buddha statue		Boat/ferry
Highway	⬥	Point of interest		Tower		Vineyard
Pedestrianized road	@	Internet access	🏛	Monument		Hot spring
Steps	🛉	Garden	⌂	Cave		Swimming pool
Unpaved road		Golf course		Escarpment/ridge		Church/cathedral
Railway	⌣	Bridge	▲	Mountain peak		Building
Path	∴	Ruin		Mountain range	□	Market
Wall	♦	Border crossing	☀	Viewpoint	◯	Stadium
Post office		Chinese temple		Petrol station	□	Park/forest
MTT office	✡	Synagogue	✈	International airport	□	Beach
Hospital		Mosque	✕	Domestic airport		Cemetery
Embassy		Hindu temple/gurdwara	★	Bus/taxi/pick-up		Swamp/Marsh
Gate/entrance						

Listings key

■ Accommodation

● Eating

■ Drinking/nightlife

● Shopping